CAMDEN MARKET 4

Lehrerfassung zum Schülerband

Erarbeitet von
Ruth Barker, Michael Biermann, Otfried Börner, Simone Collenberg, Hannelore Debus, Pamela Hanus, Phil Mothershaw-Rogalla, Ingrid Preedy, Sylvia Redlich, Tanja Ripke, Kathleen Unterspann und Jürgen Wrobel

unter Mitwirkung der Redaktion
Dr. Anne Grimm, Demet Kömür, Dr. Verena Nungesser, André Schmitt und Henriette Vahle

Herausgeber der bisherigen Reihe
und Berater der Programmleitung:
Otfried Börner, StD a.D.,
Dr. phil. h.c. Christoph Edelhoff, StD a.D.,
Vorsitzender THE ENGLISH ACADEMY

Fachliche Beratung
Sigrid Boinski, Bianka Gehler, Julia Grossmann, Petra Günther, Kathrin Hough, Holger Nürnberg, Alexander Schülting und Gisela Vogt

Diesterweg
westermann

CAMDEN MARKET 4

Materialien für Schülerinnen und Schüler

- Textbook 4 (ISBN 978-3-425-**73804**-8)
- Workbook 4 mit Lernsoftware und Audio-CD
  (ISBN 978-3-425-**73834**-5)
- Workbook 4 mit Audio-CD
  (ISBN 978-3-425-**73824**-6)
- Lernsoftware 4
  – Einzelplatzlizenz (ISBN 978-3-425-**73884**-0)
  – Schullizenz (ISBN 978-3-425-**73894**-9)
- Arbeitsheft Inklusion 4 mit Audio-CD
  (ISBN 978-3-425-**73784**-3)
- Kit 4 (ISBN 978-3-425-**73844**-4)
- Vocab-App 4 – kostenfreier Download unter
  https://play.google.com/store, Stichwort:
  „Diesterweg"
- Zoom-App 4 – Link zum Download unter
  www.zoom-app.de
- Digitales Schulbuch 4 – Online-Jahres-
  Einzellizenz (ISBN WEB-425-**73798**)

Materialien für Lehrkräfte

- Workbook 4 mit Lösungen und Audio-CD
  (ISBN 978-3-425-**73814**-7)
- Teacher's Manual mit Lösungen 4 (ISBN 978-3-425-**73864**-2)
- Vorschläge für Lernerfolgskontrollen 4
  (ISBN 978-3-425-**73914**-4)
- Audio-CD + DVD 4 für Lehrkräfte (ISBN 978-3-425-**73854**-3)
- Interaktive Whiteboard-Software 4
  – Einzelplatzlizenz (ISBN 978-3-425-**73934**-2)
  – Schullizenz (ISBN 978-3-425-**73994**-6)
- Folien 4 (ISBN 978-3-425-**73924**-3)
- Differenzierende Kopiervorlagen 4 (ISBN 978-3-425-**73874**-1)
- Differenzierende Kopiervorlagen für offenen Unterricht 4
  (ISBN 978-3-425-**73954**-0)
- BiBox – die Bildungsbox für Lehrer und Schüler 4
  – Einzellizenz auf DVD-ROM (ISBN 978-3-425-**73968**-7)
  – Einzellizenz (ISBN WEB-425-**73974**)
  – Kollegiumslizenz (ISBN WEB-425-**73980**)

Fördert individuell – passt zum Schulbuch

Optimal für den Einsatz im Unterricht mit
Camden Market! Den Kompetenzstand
feststellen, Stärken erkennen und Defizite durch individuelle Förder-
materialien ausgleichen. Direkt und online auf Basis der aktuellen
Bildungsstandards und Lehrplananforderungen.

Online-Diagnose

www.diesterweg.de/diagnose

westermann GRUPPE

© 2017 Bildungshaus Schulbuchverlage
Westermann Schroedel Diesterweg Schöningh Winklers GmbH, Braunschweig
www.diesterweg.de

Druck A[1] / Jahr 2017
Alle Drucke der Serie A sind im Unterricht parallel verwendbar.

Redaktion: Caroline Byrt, Dr. Anne Grimm, Demet Kömür, Dr. Verena Nungesser, André Schmitt und Henriette Vahle
Vokabelanhang: Lea Gonsior
Layout: Visuelle Lebensfreude, Hannover
Illustrationen: Ulf Marckwort, Kassel
Umschlaggestaltung: blum design und kommunikation, Hamburg
Druck: westermann druck GmbH, Braunschweig

ISBN 978-3-425-**73984**-7

Herzlich willkommen in der Lehrerfassung zu Camden Market 4!

Worin unterscheidet sich die vorliegende Lehrerfassung vom Schülerband (ISBN 978-3-425-73804-8)?

In der Lehrerfassung sind die Seiten 3 bis 160 des Schülerbandes mit blauen Symbolen, Zusatzinformationen und z. T. Lösungen versehen, die Ihnen die Unterrichtsvorbereitung und die Arbeit im Unterricht erleichtern sollen. (Die Seiten 161 bis 312 des Schülerbandes sind unverändert übernommen.)
Vorne zwischen Impressum und Seite 3 und hinten nach Seite 312 sind zusätzliche, blau unterlegte Seiten eingefügt, so wie diese, die Sie vor sich sehen. Diese Seiten folgen einer vom Schülerband abgekoppelten Seitenzählung: LF1–80 (LF für „Lehrerfassung").
Auf den Seiten LF4–13 finden Sie mehrere Doppelseiten zur Konzeption von **Camden Market**, insbesondere zum Differenzierungskonzept.
Im hinteren Teil, ab Seite LF15, finden Sie den Lösungsanhang: die Lösungen, die sich aus Platzgründen nicht auf den Schülerband-Seiten eintragen ließen.

Inhaltsverzeichnis der blau unterlegten LF-Seiten

In der Lehrerfassung verwendete Abkürzungen

TB Textbook, d. h. der Schülerband (ISBN 978-3-425-**73804**-8)
TM Teacher's Manual (ISBN 978-3-425-**73864**-2)
KVs Differenzierende Kopiervorlagen (ISBN 978-3-425-**73874**-1)
IWS Interaktive Whiteboard-Software (ISBN 978-3-425-**73934**-2)
LSW Lernsoftware (ISBN 978-3-425-**73884**-0)
LF Lehrerfassung

Wegweiser durch die Lehrerfassung

TM: Seitenverweis auf die Unterrichtsempfehlungen im **Teacher's Manual** (ISBN 978-3-425-**73864**-2).

W plus Seitenzahl: Verweis auf die chronologischen Wortlisten hinten im TB – zur schnelleren Orientierung.

BASIS Acting green   W p. 221   TM, p. 43

11 Lots of questions

a) **Look at number 10 again and answer the questions.**
1. Who is Joel Miller?
2. Where in the USA is Evans High School?
3. What have they done at Evans High to go green?
4. How much money did the school get for the project?
5. What is Margaret Hall's job and what did she do for the project?
6. What is Margaret Hall proud of?

b) **Bus stop: Work with a partner and compare your answers.**

c) **Which changes at Evans High do you think are best? Give reasons.**

// dieselben Arbeitsaufträge a) bis c) wie hier, aber bezogen auf den deutlich anspruchsvolleren Text in M5

M6 // M p. 34

Bei jeder **Parallelaufgabe** (→ LF4) im **Basis**-Teil: knappe Informationen zur Pendant-Aufgabe im **More**-Teil.

15 p. 205 Possessiv-pronomen

Bei den **LiF-Verweisen in der Randspalte** ist im Gegensatz zum Schülerband nicht nur die Nummer, z. B. „15", genannt, sondern auch **das eigentliche Pensum.**

12 Cleaning up

a) **During the project at Evans High School the students also cleaned up their lockers. Listen to Joel and Gary. What things did they find?**

b) **Now read the dialogue. Which words do the boys use for these expressions?**

your baseball magazines • my baseball magazines • his job • my jacket • her jacket

Joel: Look, here are some old baseball magazines in my locker. Aren't they yours? You are the baseball freak.

Gary: Let me see ... Yes, they are mine. Throw them away, please. There's a trash bin in the corner.

5 Joel: Listen, this is our environmental project. So the old magazines go into the paper container outside.

Gary: Oh sorry, I forgot. Now, what shall I do with the empty milk bottles? Isn't it

10 Don's job to collect them?

Joel: Correct, it's his. He'll take the bottles to the cafeteria this afternoon.

Gary: Look at this! There's a jacket on my locker ... and it's definitely not mine.

15 Joel: Hmm, let's see. ... I'm pretty sure it's a girl's jacket.

Gary: A girl's jacket on my locker?

Joel: Yeah, Katie has a crush on you, Gary. I'll bet the jacket is hers. Maybe there's a

20 message for you in one of the pockets.

Gary   Joel

Belegstellen für ein **Grammatik-pensum,** das neu ist oder an dieser Stelle gezielt wiederholt wird, sind blau unterstrichen.

Auszeichnung von neuem Vokabular:
– ein dunkleres Blau für aktiven Wortschatz (in den Wortlisten hinten im TB fett gedruckt)
– ein helleres Blau für passiven Wortschatz.

your baseball magazines: yours
my baseball magazines: ...
his job: ...
my jacket: ...
her jacket: ...

Beschriftung von Lehrwerksfiguren. (In Band 4 gibt es zunehmend weniger wiederkehrende Figuren. Der Band löst sich von den Figuren der ersten Bände, stattdessen stehen Gillians Freundin Cheryl und andere US-Jugendliche im Mittelpunkt. Eine konstante Figurenkonstellation ist in Klasse 8 nicht so wichtig wie in Klasse 5 oder auch Klasse 7.)

14 Minimalweg und Vertiefungsmöglichkeiten
Während im Schülerband alle Aufgaben mit weißer Ziffer gestaltet sind, markieren in der Lehrerfassung **blaue Ziffern** die Aufgaben, die Vertiefungsmöglichkeiten bieten (und ggf. ausgelassen werden können), also nicht Bestandteil des für die Progression notwendigen Minimalweges sind.

Verweis auf die **Folien** (ISBN 978-3-425-**73924**-3).

Verweis auf die **Differenzierenden Kopiervorlagen** (ISBN 978-3-425-**73874**-1), unter Nennung der übergeordneten Nummerierung: So gibt es z. B. viermal eine Kopiervorlage mit der übergeordneten Nummerierung 1.7, dann weiter „nummeriert" auf vier Niveaus: , ▁▃▅, ▁▃▅, ▁▃▅ und ☀.

BASIS Acting gre

13 Take action! 👁 👁 📄 Folie 3 📄 KVs 1.7

a) Watch the clip. What can you understand?
b) Watch the clip again. Then look at the pictograms. Which of these things are suggested in the clip? B, E, F

 ➡ p. LF17

c) Watch the clip a third time. What are the English words for "Erdbeben", "Dürre", "Hochwasser" and "Klimawandel"?
earthquake, drought, flood, climate change

Wo immer möglich, sind die **Lösungen an Ort und Stelle** eingetragen. Alle weiteren Lösungen finden Sie auf den blau unterlegten **Seiten LF15–80** am Ende der Lehrerfassung. Eine entsprechende Seitenangabe – z. B. ➡ p. LF17 – hilft beim Auffinden.

14 Choose an activity ✏ 👁 📖 p. 21/14

Verweise, inkl. Seitenzahl und Übungsnummer, wo sich ein Ausweichen auf das **Camden Market Arbeitsheft Inklusion** (ISBN 978-3-425-**73784**-3) anbietet, das die sechs *Themes* auf leichterem Niveau bereithält.

You can ...
- draw or design new pictograms that tell people how to protect the environment. You can look at number 13 for ideas. Show the pictograms to your class and put them up in your classroom or school.
- make a wall dictionary. Collect words and phrases which have to do with the environment. Add the German meaning, too. Then illustrate your dictionary.
- make a "How green are you?" questionnaire for your classmates. Think of questions like:
  – Do you turn off the lights when ... ?
  – Do you close ... ?
  Think of possible answers and decide how many points they will get. Write (funny) results for your questionnaire.
- write an email to an English-speaking school and tell them what you do at school to protect the environment. 🖱 IWS 🖱 LSW 110

LSW: Verweis auf die **Lernsoftware** (ISBN 978-3-425-**73884**-0); die dreistellige Ziffer gibt den Code an, mit dem man zu einer bestimmten Übung der Software gelangt.

IWS: Verweis auf die **Interaktive Whiteboard-Software** (ISBN 978-3-425-**73934**-2).

Differenzieren mit Basis und More

(am Beispiel von Seite 42 und 53)

Camden Market ermöglicht die **Differenzierung mit einem Band.** Der **Basis**-Teil deckt die Grundanforderungen ab. Der **More**-Teil bietet Zusatzangebote für das mittlere und höhere Niveau.

2 **BASIS** American food

8 **Customer interviews**

L 1.11 S 5

How to ...
listen
p. 178

a) Cheryl also spoke to some customers at Super Burger. Listen to three of her interviews. How many men and how many women did she talk to?

In jedem *Theme* gibt es sog. **Parallelaufgaben:** die eine im **Basis**-Teil, das Pendant im **More**-Teil.

customer 1:
– eats at Super Burger four times a week
– likes the price of the food

customer 2:
– eats at Super Burger twice a month
– likes French fries

customer 3:
– three kids
– eats at Super Burger once or twice a week
– son Sam likes Super Hamburger with salad

M3 //M
p. 53

b) Listen again and check her notes. What did Cheryl get wrong? Copy her notes and correct them.
c) Compare your notes with a partner.

8 Eine orange-grüne Aufgabennummer im **Basis**-Teil zeigt an: Hierzu gibt es eine parallel einsetzbare Aufgabe im **More**-Teil. Entsprechend in der Randspalte der Verweis auf die **More**-Aufgabe.

9 **A restaurant review**

a) Test a fast food restaurant in YOUR area. Look at the example for help and find the information for your restaurant.

Name: *Döner Express*
Address: *Venloer Straße, Köln*
Food: *döner, shawarma, falafel, baklava*
My favourite meal: *chicken shawarma (4€)*
Takeaway: ☑ *yes*   ☐ *no*
Delivery: ☐ *yes* ☑ *no*
Music: *pop/Top 40/Arabic*
Service: ☑ *friendly* ☐ *average* ☐ *unfriendly*
Your opinion:
☑ *a must* ☐ *pretty cool* ☐ *worth a visit*
☐ *only if you are really hungry* ☐ *forget it*

Diese parallel (und in den meisten Fällen auch additiv) einsetzbaren Aufgaben erleichtern die Arbeit mit **heterogenen Lerngruppen:** Während leistungsschwächere S die **Basis**-Aufgabe bearbeiten, wenden sich leistungsstärkere S der entsprechenden Aufgabe im **More**-Teil zu. In der Phase der Ergebnissicherung ist dann ein Zusammenführen von **Basis**- und **More**-Niveau nicht nur denkbar, sondern wünschenswert. Die Parallelaufgaben wurden genau im Hinblick darauf konzipiert.

b) Put up all your information in the classroom and talk about it.

The name of the restaurant I tested is ... It's in ...

c) Now write about your fast food restaurant.

The name of the restaurant I tested is ... • It's in ... • You can get ... there. • They (don't) bring food. • They play ... music. • The service is ... • I think it's ...

forty-two

Alle Kompetenzen werden im **Basis**-Teil integriert auf einfachem Niveau angeboten. Stärkere Lerner finden im **More**-Teil passende anspruchsvollere Materialien und Aufgaben. So tragen alle S gemeinsam zum Klassendiskurs bei.

MORE American food   **2**

b) **Find words in the article that match these expressions:**

| a small metal container | the taste that food or drink has |

| sweet with bubbles | not natural | make something stronger |

c) **Four reasons are mentioned why fast food is so popular with kids. What are they? Tell your class about them.**

M3 **Customer interviews**

a) **Cheryl also spoke to some customers at Super Burger. Listen to three of her interviews. How many men and how many women did she talk to?**
b) **Listen again. Find out and take notes:**
   – What do customers 1, 2 and 3 like about fast food?
   – How often do they eat at places like Super Burger?
   – What do they like best?
c) **Compare your notes with a partner.**

M3 Grün-orange Aufgabennummern im **More**-Teil zeigen an:
Hierzu gibt es eine parallel einsetzbare Aufgabe im **Basis**-Teil.
Entsprechend in der Randspalte der Rückverweis auf die **Basis**-Aufgabe.
(Die parallel einsetzbaren Aufgaben haben im **Basis**- und im **More**-Teil dieselbe Überschrift.)

B 8
p. 42

M4 **Fast food: good or bad?**

a) **Some people think fast food is bad, others think it is good. Work with a partner and collect arguments for and against fast food in a grid.**

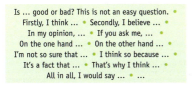

good	bad
- you can eat it quickly	- can be unhealthy
- ...	- ...

b) **Find another pair. One pair is for, the other one is against fast food. Have a discussion. You can look at page 182 for help.**
c) ☀ **Think about all the arguments you talked about. Write a text and give YOUR opinion. Use the phrases below. You can look at page 186 for help.**

Is ... good or bad? This is not an easy question. •
Firstly, I think ... • Secondly, I believe ... •
In my opinion, ... • If you ask me, ... •
On the one hand ... • On the other hand ... •
I'm not so sure that ... • I think so because ... •
It's a fact that ... • That's why I think ... •
All in all, I would say ... • ...

How to ...
discuss
p. 182

How to ...
write your
opinion
p. 186

WB   **M3**
p. 35

Die **Parallelaufgaben** sind die direktesten, aber nicht die einzigen Querverbindungen zwischen **Basis**- und **More**-Teil.
Weitere Informationen: → LF8f.

Weiter differenzieren mit Sonne und Mond
(am Beispiel von Seite 40 und 35)

---

2 **BASIS** American food

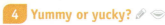

4 **Yummy or yucky?**

wordbank
Food and drink
p. 164

5
WB
p. 24

a) Look at the dishes on pages 38–39 again.
Do you think they are delicious, OK or disgusting?
Sort them in a grid.
b) Which dishes would/wouldn't you like to try?
Talk to a partner and give reasons.

delicious	OK	disgusting
...	...	...

5 ☾ **Fast food**

19R
p. 208

Read the statements. What is fast food for YOU? Talk to a partner.

Fast food? That's unhealthy, cheap food, like hamburgers and French fries. It's for people who can't cook well.

Fast food is fast because you can get it quickly and eat it fast if you need to.

For me fast food is food that ...
... you can prepare easily.
... people sell in the street.
... you don't eat in a restaurant.
... you can eat quickly.
...

I (don't) agree.
For me ...

LAND & LEUTE

Essen in den USA

Essen in den USA – das heißt nicht nur Hamburger, Pizza und Fastfood. Im Allgemeinen versteht man unter amerikanischer Küche traditionelle Gerichte wie Brathähnchen (*fried chicken*), Mais (*corn*), warmen Apfelkuchen (*apple pie*), Käse-Makkaroni (*macaroni and cheese*), Hackbraten (*meat loaf*) und Pfannkuchen (*pancakes*) mit Ahornsirup (*maple syrup*). An wichtigen Feiertagen wie *Thanksgiving* oder Weihnachten gibt es in vielen Familien Truthahnbraten (*roast turkey*).

Die meisten Gerichte sind von den ersten europäischen Einwanderern mitgebracht worden. In jedem Staat der USA wird jedoch etwas anders gekocht. Das hängt nicht nur von den regionalen Zutaten ab, sondern auch davon, woher die dort lebenden Menschen stammen.

So ist in den Südstaaten der afrikanische Einfluss sehr groß. In der Umgebung von New Orleans findet man eine interessante Mischung aus spanischen, französischen und afrikanischen Gerichten, *Cajun* genannt.

Die kalifornische Küche verwendet viel frisches Obst und Gemüse, das auf asiatische, mexikanische und spanische Weise zubereitet wird.

Was meinst du: Welche Lieblingsgerichte haben die Menschen in Deutschland? Sind diese typisch deutsch?

forty

☾ Das **Mond**-Symbol kennzeichnet besonders leichte Aufgaben im **Basis**-Teil.

Darüber hinaus bietet das Workbook **parallel einsetzbare Varianten** von TB-Aufgaben: Randspaltenverweise im TB verweisen auf parallel einsetzbare **Mond**- und **Sonnen**-Aufgaben im WB.

Die parallel einsetzbaren **Mond**- und **Sonnen**-Aufgaben im Workbook ermöglichen **Binnendifferenzierung:** So kann das mittlere Niveau mit dem TB arbeiten, das untere **(Mond)** bzw. obere **(Sonne)** mit dem WB. Oft führen beide Wege zum selben Ergebnis, sodass die **Ergebnissicherung für alle gemeinsam** im Plenum stattfinden kann.

Weitere Möglichkeiten bieten die **Differenzierenden Kopiervorlagen** (ISBN 978-3-425-**73874**-1), die sich an den Aufgaben/Kompetenzen des **Basis**-Teils orientieren. Für jedes *Theme* stehen 22 Kopiervorlagen zur Verfügung. Eine **Lernlandkarte** zu Beginn jedes *Theme* nennt die Kompetenzen: sieben pro *Theme*. Pro Kompetenz sind drei oder vier Symbole abgebildet, stellvertretend für die Niveaus: , und ☀.

Das **Sonnen**-Symbol kennzeichnet anspruchsvolle Texte und Aufgaben im **More**-Teil. Dies ermöglicht Differenzierung bis hin zum **gymnasialen Niveau.**

Auch **More**-Aufgaben werden mit Workbook-Übungen unterstützt: Randspaltenverweise mit **Sonne** im TB verweisen auf **anspruchsvollere, parallel einsetzbare Varianten** im Workbook.

MORE Acting green

5. What is Margaret Hall's job and what did she do for the project?
6. Why does Ms Hall like the greenhouse?
7. What is she proud of?
8. Who is Fred Myers?
b) **Bus stop: Work with a partner and compare your answers.**
c) **Which changes at Evans High do you think are best? Give reasons.**

B ⟍⟍ 11
p. 26

M7 A living wall

a) **Listen to Fred Myers. Who is he talking to?**
b) **Right or wrong? Listen again and correct what's wrong.**
   1. Living walls can be found in cities, buildings and people's homes.
   2. Living walls are also called wild walls.
   3. A living wall is always inside a building.
   4. Living walls act as natural air filters. They remove toxins from the air.
   5. A living wall can make a room a more peaceful place by reducing noise levels.
   6. Especially in summer an outside living wall can reduce energy costs. It acts as insulation.
c) **Tell your class what you learned about a living wall.**

WB ☀ M6

M7 → WB 6
Zu der Hörverstehensaufgabe M7 gibt es eine anspruchsvollere, parallel einsetzbare **Sonnen**-Variante im Workbook: Sicherung des Hörverstehens in Form von *filling in the gaps.*

M8 ☀ Earth Day

Find out about Earth Day on the Internet:
– When is it?
– When did it start?
– Who started it?
– Why was it started?
– What sort of things do people do on Earth Day?
– Where did you find the information?
– ...
Present your information to the class.

www

WB M7
p. 21

M9 An environment cartoon

Look at the cartoon. What can you see? What is its message? Find a title for the cartoon and write about it. Here is some help:

In the cartoon you can see ... •
On the left/right there is/are ... •
... are pushing ... •
There is a rope around ... •
... is pulling ... •
I think the cartoonist wants to say ...

How to ...
talk about pictures
p. 183

thirty-five 35

Aufgaben mit **Sonnen**-Symbol finden sich auf jeder **More**-Doppelseite.

Zusammenspiel von Basis und More

(am Beispiel von Seite 82 und 95)

Die **Basis**-Teile erkennen Sie an den **orangen** Elementen und dem Schriftzug BASIS, weiß auf orangem Grund, oben auf jeder Seite.

4 BASIS Going to America

2 All kinds of people 👄

Look at the statistics and talk about them. What do you find surprising?

3 WB
p. 57

wordbank
Statistics
p. 168

P5 **P**
p. 91

M3 **M**
p. 95

Population of the United States according to ethnic groups (2012)

- 1.1%
- 0.9%
- 5%
- 13%
- 80%

White Americans (including Hispanics or Latinos)

Black and African Americans

Asian Americans

Native Americans

Others

1343W

13 per cent of the population in the US are Black and African Americans.

In the US there are more/fewer … than …

…

3 Leaving home 👄 ✏

a) Work with a partner. Look at the photos and describe them to each other. What can you see? What are the people doing? How do you think they feel?

…eir home country
…y? Work in groups of
…lacemat.
…e on the three most
…n the middle of the placemat.
…results.

go and live with a partner •
war in home country • …

Enge Verzahnung von **Basis** und **More** über Randspaltenverweise im **Basis**-Teil: **Grüne, mit M gekennzeichnete Randspaltenverweise** zeigen an, welche **More**-Aufgaben zu einer Aufgabe passen.
So veranschaulicht das Tortendiagramm *(pie chart)* hier in **Basis 2**, aus welchen ethnischen Gruppen sich die Bevölkerung der USA zusammensetzt. In **M3** gibt es ein weiteres Tortendiagramm: zu *ancestry of US population*.

→ **Beispiel aus Theme 5**
In **Basis 2**, Seite 100, lernen die S den Tagesablauf der US-Jugendlichen Lisa, Josh und Tom kennen (bildgesteuert). In **M1**, Seite 114, lesen sie Toms Onlinechat und Stacys Tagebucheintrag zum verunglückten Rendezvous der beiden; *picture 10* in **Basis 2** zeigt die beiden bei ihrem Rendezvous im mexikanischen Restaurant.
In **M2–M4** dient die Storyline um Tom und Stacy zur Einführung und Festigung der *reported speech (What did they say?)* und der Bedingungssätze, Typ III *(If things had gone differently, …)*.
Zusammenführen der Niveaus: Die **More**-S informieren ihre **Basis**-MitS nach **M4,** was sie über Tom erfahren haben.

Grün ist die Farbe des **More**-Teils: **grüne** Elemente und der Schriftzug MORE, weiß auf grünem Grund, oben auf jeder Seite.
Pro *Theme* gibt es zwei **More**-Doppelseiten, passgenaue zusätzliche Aufgaben für stärkere Lerner.

→ **WB**
Selbstverständlich werden auch **More**-S mit zusätzlichen Übungen im WB gefordert.

MORE Going to America

4

M2 Changes

a) Look at M1 again. Then match the sentence parts and write them down.

1	Before Annie went to America,	**A**	after Annie had died.
2	When Annie arrived in America,	**B**	she had lived in Ireland for 15 years.
3	A statue was built on Ellis Island	**C**	Annie and her family went home.
4	After they had greeted each other,	**D**	Annie could meet her parents.
5	After she had received the $10 gold piece,	**E**	her parents had already lived there for two years.

b) In your exercise book underline the part of each sentence that tells you what happened first. The tense used here is called the *past perfect*.

c) Find examples of the *past perfect* in M1. Copy the sentences and underline the *past perfect* (<u>had gone</u>, ...).

M3 Ancestors

Look at the pie chart. What information does it give you? Talk about the figures with your partner.

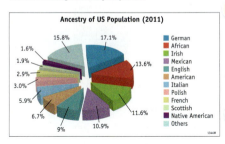

Ancestry of US Population (2011)

- German 17.1%
- African 13.6%
- Irish 11.6%
- Mexican 10.9%
- English 9%
- American 6.7%
- Italian 5.9%
- Polish 3.0%
- French 2.9%
- Scottish 1.9%
- Native American 1.6%
- Others 15.8%

This pie chart shows ...

... per cent of the population in the US have German/... ancestors.

In the US there are more people with Mexican/... ancestors than ...

The biggest group are ...

...

M4 Learning English

a) Listen to Mohamed, Kim and Sergio from number 5. What are they talking about? Write down their names in the order you hear them talk.

b) Listen again. Take notes to answer the questions.
1. Why does Sergio still have problems learning English?
2. Why was it easy for Mohamed to learn English?
3. What other language can Mohamed speak?
4. How did Kim learn English?

B 5
p. 84
L 1.26

Einsatzmöglichkeiten des More-Teils im Unterricht
- gemeinsame Erarbeitung, sofern die Lerngruppe leistungsstark ist,
- in leistungsheterogenen Klassen in Einzel- und Partnerarbeit, z. B. in Freiarbeitsphasen oder im Rahmen des Wochenplans; L sollte den S die Selbstkontrolle ihrer Ergebnisse ermöglichen, z. B. indem er/sie ihnen Lösungsblätter zur Verfügung stellt (die TB-Lösungen liegen dem **TM** gebündelt bei).
- **Pupils as tutors:** More-S sollten die Möglichkeit haben, ihren MitS, die ausschließlich den **Basis**-Teil erarbeiten, ihre Ergebnisse sowie mögliche neue Storyline-Inhalte mitzuteilen. Am Ende von arbeitsteiligen Phasen (leistungsstark vs. leistungsschwächer) sollte immer eine Zusammenführung der Niveaus stehen.

→ **Beispiel aus Theme 6**
In **Basis 4**, Seite 122, lesen die S einen Zeitungsartikel über Waldbrände in Kalifornien.
In **M3**, Seite 135, hören sie (Hör-/Leseverstehen) einen Anruf bei der Notrufzentrale 911, und leistungsstärkere S sind aufgefordert, in einem Rollenspiel (Sprachproduktion) einen eigenen *emergency call* zu gestalten.
Zusammenführen der Niveaus: Die More-S spielen ihre Telefonate den **Basis**-MitS vor. Zuhören und dem Telefonat folgen können auch Basis-S; die rezeptiven Fähigkeiten sind meist besser ausgebildet als die produktiven.

In jedem *Theme* gibt es darüber hinaus sog. **Parallelaufgaben:** die eine im **Basis**-Teil, das Pendant im **More**-Teil. → LF4f.

Differenzierung und individuelle Förderung
(am Beispiel von Seite 58 und 71)

Folgende Methoden des kooperativen Lernens sind in **Camden Market** verankert und werden auf *How to work with others,* Seite 188f., erklärt:
– Think – pair – share (= Grundprinzip des kooperativen Lernens)
– Buzz groups
– Bus stop
– Milling around
– Double circle
– Give and take
– Jigsaw
– Placemat
– Dramatic reading und
– Gallery walk.
Die **Individualisierung des Lernens durch Einzelarbeitsphasen** ist ein wesentlicher Bestandteil von **kooperativen** Lernformen.

Jede Lerngruppe ist heterogen und Lernen ist ein individueller Prozess. Dies muss bei der Unterrichtsgestaltung berücksichtigt werden. Individualisierung bedeutet jedoch nicht, jeder/m S ein eigenes Lernangebot zu machen. Individualisierung, individuelle Förderung und Differenzierung werden im Alltag eher durch ein **Bündel von Prinzipien** realisiert, die bei der Planung und Durchführung von Lernarrangements berücksichtigt werden.

BASIS New York

1 New York City 🖉 👄

a) **Give and take:** Think of New York. Write down two or three facts that you know. Then walk around the classroom and ask your classmates about their facts. Give one of your facts to each classmate you talk to and take one from everyone you talk to.
b) Go through all the facts, then get together in small groups and talk about them. Present your results to the class.

In New York
> there is/are ...
> there must be ...
> you can see/
>   visit/go to ...
>   ...

2 Things to see in New York 👓 👄

Look at the photos and read the information.
– Which sights would you like to see?
– Where would you like to go? Say why.

> I would like to see ... because it sounds interesting/...

> I would like to go to ... because I like ...

1 The Empire State Building
– is easy to find in the skyline
– has 102 floors
– is 443 m high
– has 1,860 steps to the top

2 Central Park
– is one of the largest parks in NYC
– is 4 km long
– has a large zoo

3 The Statue of Liberty
– was given to the people of America by the French in 1886
– is a symbol of freedom
– was the first thing many immigrants saw when they arrived in the US

4 Ellis Island
– was the main immigration station in the USA from 1892 to 1954
– over 12 million immigrants arrived there
– is now a museum about immigration to

→ **Choose-an-activity**-Aufgaben (→ LF12), ein oder zwei pro **Basis**-Teil, sind *task*-orientierte, offene Aufgaben mit Wahlmöglichkeit, bei denen sich die S je nach Neigung, Lerntyp oder bevorzugter Sozialform/Methode für einen Arbeitsauftrag entscheiden.

→ **Camden Market Arbeitsheft Inklusion**
  (ISBN 978-3-425-**73784**-3)
Falls manche Aufgaben zu komplex für einzelne S sind, kann L auf das **Camden Market Arbeitsheft Inklusion** ausweichen. Dort gibt es die *Themes* auf leichterem Niveau. Gleiche Inhalte, aber
– reduziertes Layout,
– vereinfachte Hörtexte,
– kleinschrittigere Aufgabenführung,
– reduzierte und vereinfachte Inhalte.

Camden Market bietet zahlreiche Möglichkeiten zur **Differenzierung und Individualisierung** sowie ein umfassendes und systematisches Übungsangebot. Dabei werden gleichermaßen Angebote für leistungsstärkere S bereitgestellt, lernschwächere S gefördert sowie unterschiedliche Lernertypen einbezogen.

Practice, jeweils zwischen **Basis**- und **More**-Teil, jeweils vier Seiten: Hier werden die **sprachlichen Mittel gefestigt und schriftlich gesichert,** die im **Basis**-Teil vorrangig mündlich behandelt werden. Durch entsprechende Randverweise im **Basis**-Teil ist die Verzahnung gewährleistet. Es empfiehlt sich, die Übungen an passender Stelle **binnendifferenzierend** in den Unterricht „einzuflechten", zum Üben und als Zusatzaufgaben, wenn L Defizite feststellt (bei der Klasse oder bei einzelnen S). L weist die Übungen den S zu, die Defizite aufzuarbeiten haben. Lernschwächeren S hilft L, ein Minimum zu bewältigen, während anderen zusätzliche Aufgaben gestellt werden. Auch können die S ihren individuellen Interessen folgend an den Übungen arbeiten.

PRACTICE New York

P5 Facts about yourself

a) Write down at least five statements about yourself.
Use the correct *past participle* forms of the verbs.

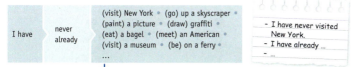

| I have | never already | (visit) New York • (go) up a skyscraper • (paint) a picture • (draw) graffiti • (eat) a bagel • (meet) an American • (visit) a museum • (be) on a ferry • ... |

- I have never visited New York.
- I have already ...
- ...

b) Interview a partner. Take turns.
What have you got in common?

Have you ever ...?   Yes, I have./ No, I haven't.

P6 Definitions

Explain these words from the statements in number 8:

a park • a shop • a mother • a doctor • a stadium • an aunt

Here is some help: ... is a person who ...   ... is a place where ...

Da die **Practice**-Übungen **nicht Teil des für die Progression notwendigen Minimalweges** sind, sind die Übungsziffern in der Lehrerfassung blau eingefärbt (→ LF2).

P7 "Oh no, it's all in German ..."

You are on a class trip to Berlin. You are doing a tour of the city. An American tourist doesn't understand German. Tell him five important things that the tour guide says at the beginning of the tour.

Hallo, meine Damen und Herren! Schön, dass Sie an unserer Stadtführung teilnehmen wollen. Mein Name ist Kai Müller. Ich werde Ihnen heute unsere schöne Stadt zeigen. Die Führung wird etwa zweieinhalb Stunden dauern – das heißt, dass Sie pünktlich um 13 Uhr zu Mittag essen können. Vorher zeige ich Ihnen verschiedene wichtige Sehenswürdigkeiten Berlins. Ich werde Ihnen jeweils kurz etwas über die Geschichte der Orte erzählen. Fragen Sie einfach nach, wenn Sie mehr wissen möchten. OK, dann lassen Sie uns losgehen ...

The tour/tour guide will ...   We can ...   ...

Auslassungspunkte ... findet man oft in **Camden Market.** Die S sollen die Punkte nicht ignorieren, sondern als Aufforderung verstehen, eine Aufgabe um eigene Ideen zu erweitern. L: *Not only does it mean you CAN add your own ideas. In fact, it means you SHOULD add ideas of your own.*

seventy-one 71

→ **WB Test yourself** und **WB Extra practice**
Mithilfe von **Test yourself** stellen die S gezielt fest, was sie schon beherrschen und was sie noch üben müssen. Im Anschluss hält **Extra practice** Aufgaben zur Differenzierung bereit. Wer bei **Test yourself** Schwierigkeiten mit einer bestimmten Aufgabe/Fertigkeit hat, bearbeitet als Nächstes die entsprechende Aufgabe in **Extra practice.**

→ **Optional Jobs** (ab Seite 139): In Klasse 8 werden Fragen der Berufswahl zunehmend wichtig. Klasse 8 ist zudem häufig die Zeit der ersten Berufspraktika der S.
→ Der fakultative **Reading-is-fun**-Anhang (ab Seite 145) bietet auf die *Themes* abgestimmte Lesetexte.

Schülerorientierung und Handlungsorientierung

(am Beispiel von Seite 27 und 65)

Choose an activity ist ein wiederkehrendes **Target-task**-Aufgabenformat im **Basis**-Teil, ein oder zwei pro *Thema*. Die S wenden **Gelerntes in neuen Zusammenhängen** an und stellen ihre kommunikative Kompetenz unter Beweis. Visuelle, auditive und haptisch orientierte Lerner gleichermaßen werden angesprochen und motiviert.

Eine **Target task** ist ein Produkt, das eine Unterrichtseinheit abschließt und in den vorausgehenden Aufgaben und Texten sprachlich, inhaltlich und methodisch vorbereitet wurde.

Choose-an-activity-Vorschläge sind als eben das zu verstehen: Vorschläge. Die S sollten immer auch eine andere, z. B. eine eigene *activity* wählen können. Grundsätzlich gilt: **Choose an activity** *and present it,* d. h. der Präsentation gebührt ebenso viel Zeit und Aufmerksamkeit wie der Produktion.

Zwar sind die Ergebnisse bei diesen kreativen Aufgaben oft recht fehlerhaft, aber die **Korrektheit steht nicht im Vordergrund,** sondern der möglichst unbefangene Umgang mit der Fremdsprache. Nicht selten haben gerade leistungsschwächere S tolle Ideen und sind motiviert, freie Texte zu schreiben. Die Erfahrung, ihren leistungsstärkeren MitS zumindest ebenbürtig zu sein, sollte L ihnen unbedingt ermöglichen.

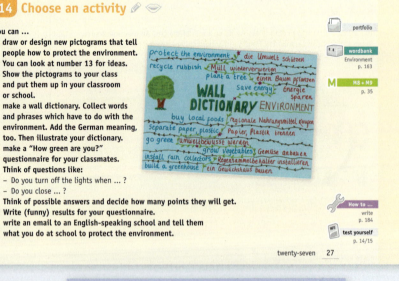

Vorsicht sollte L bei der **Fehlerkorrektur** in selbstständig erarbeiteten sprachlichen Produkten walten lassen. **Die Produkte zeigen den aktuellen Lernstand.** Bitte Fehler nicht rot im Produkt anstreichen. Der Einsatz von ablösbaren Klebezetteln *(sticky notes)* stellt eine bewährte Alternative dar.

Theme 3 wartet auf Seite 65 mit einem **Projektvorschlag** auf. So werden Inhalte, Wortschatz und Strukturen des *Theme* umgewälzt, und die S wenden ihr Wissen in einer Transferleistung, also in einem neuen Kontext, an.

Die S haben bei **Projektaufgaben** viele Freiheiten:
– ob sie allein, zu zweit oder in der Gruppe arbeiten,
– welchen Aspekt des Themas sie wählen,
– wie sie ihre Ergebnisse präsentieren.
Manche S fühlen sich von diesen Freiheiten überfordert. Entsprechend sammelt L mit den S Ideen (um die Fantasie bei weniger kreativ veranlagten S in Gang zu bringen, aber auch um die Vor- und Nachteile bestimmter Vorgehensweisen zu beleuchten), bevor die S sich auf ein Thema/einen Arbeitsablauf festlegen.

BASIS New York

11 A project – YOUR favourite New York sight

PLAN IT
* Work in groups. Choose a New York sight that you would like to know more about:
  the Rockefeller Center, Ellis Island, Central Park, the Yankee Stadium, ...
* Make notes on what you already know about the sight.
* Find more information on the Internet. Try to find photos, too.

DO IT
* Look at everything you have found. Find the most important information in the texts:
  – What do the pictures and headlines tell you?
  – Highlight the most important facts in each paragraph.
  – Try to find a headline for each paragraph.
  – Decide which information you want to present.
* Think about how to present your information:
  – brochure
  – computer presentation
  – ...
* Write down the information. Try to use your own words.
* Choose pictures, maps, ...
* Make a handout with three quiz questions for your classmates.
* Prepare your presentation.

CHECK IT
* Is the English OK?
* Is it interesting? Add details.
* Show it to other classmates or your teacher.
* Edit it. Use a dictionary.
* Practise what you want to say.

PRESENT IT
* Put up your brochure and talk about it *or* show your computer presentation *or* ...
* Swap quiz questions with the other teams. Read and listen carefully to answer the questions.

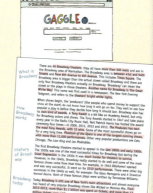

Broadway

What is Broadway?
The Broadway area of Manhattan is between 41st and 54th Streets, and 6th Avenue to 9th Avenue. A Broadway theatre has to be in the Broadway area and it also has to have more than 500 seats. Broadway is also a name of a major street in this area, but there are only four Broadway theatres on that street.

The history of Broadway
In the late 1800s and early 1900s the first Broadway theatres started to appear. The theatres were very popular and successful in the 1920s. In the 1940s Broadway started to do well again and many very famous shows come from this time, for example *Oklahoma!*.

How Broadway works
Broadway has its own awards that are as important as Academy Awards: the Tony Awards. The awards started in 1947. The show with the most Tony Awards (12) is *The Producers*.

The other way to know if a show has been successful is to see how long it has lasted. For example, *The Phantom of the Opera*, with more than 11,000 performances, is one of the longest-running shows.

Broadway today
Broadway is still one of New York's major attractions. Almost everyone knows very popular shows like *Cats, Les Misérables* or *Wicked*. From 2012-2013 more than $1.1 billion was spent on tickets and more than 12 million tickets were sold.

Other information
If you want to buy tickets to see a show, then you can go buy them at the theatre or at little shops in Times Square or at the Lower Manhattan Theater Center.

Abschließend **Besprechen der Projektarbeit:** Wie seid ihr zurechtgekommen? Wie klappte die Zusammenarbeit? War die Zeit ausreichend? Was ist euch gut gelungen? Was habt ihr gelernt? Was würdet ihr beim nächsten Mal anders machen? Rückmeldung möglich als **Daumenfeedback**/Handzeichen im Plenum:
Thumbs up if you enjoyed the project./ Thumbs down if you didn't enjoy it./ Thumbs sideways if you're not sure.

Zwei weitere **Target tasks** in Form von *two-minute talks* (monologisches Sprechen):
– **Theme 1:** *School life in the USA*
– **Theme 4:** *Native Americans*

Leitfragen für die **Check-it**-Phase (Partnerkorrektur):
– *Find three things you like about the text.*
– *Make a list of three questions you have about the text.*
– *Make a list of three "Maybe you could ..." statements.*
Redemittel für die Rückmeldungen in der **Present-it**-Phase:
I really like your brochure/... It's cool/very interesting/clever/entertaining/...
Your text makes/doesn't really make me want to visit the New York sight.
The New York sight sounds fun/exciting/very busy/full of history/...

Welcome to the USA!

Liebe Schülerinnen und Schüler,

Camden Market 4 lädt euch in diesem Schuljahr ein, die Vereinigten Staaten von Amerika kennenzulernen. Ihr werdet eine Menge über die Menschen, die Sprache und die Kultur erfahren. Daher wird euch in den Hör- und Lesetexten *American English* begegnen. Außerdem lernt ihr amerikanische Städte und Sehenswürdigkeiten, die Landschaft und vieles mehr kennen.

In diesem Buch findet ihr viele Hinweise und Materialien, die euch beim Lernen helfen, wie z. B. das *Dictionary*, die *Wordbanks*, die *How to*-Seiten und den Grammatikteil.

Viel Spaß auf eurer Entdeckungsreise durch die USA!

This book is about the USA. What do you already know about the country? Try to answer the questions. The correct letters make a sentence.

1

In the USA there are ...

- **W** 50 states.
- **A** 51 states.
- **B** 52 states.

2

The capital of the USA is ...

- **P** New York City.
- **A** Boston.
- **E** Washington D.C.

3

The first president of the USA was ...

- **L** Abraham Lincoln.
- **A** George Washington.
- **N** John F. Kennedy.

4

A ranger works ...

- **I** on a farm.
- **R** in a national park.
- **Q** in Hollywood.

5

The most important American film award is ...

- **J** the Golden Globe.
- **T** the Grammy.
- **E** the Oscar.

6

An important American holiday in November is ...

- **G** Thanksgiving.
- **B** Independence Day.
- **M** Halloween.

7

The Statue of Liberty is in ...

- **O** New York City.
- **U** Los Angeles.
- **E** New Orleans.

8

The very first settlers to America came from ...

- **S** Africa.
- **I** Asia.
- **C** Europe.

9

Martin Luther King ...

- **W** was a US president.
- **N** won the Nobel Peace Prize.
- **R** was the first African American who won an Oscar.

KNOW ABOUT THE USA?

 pp. 4f.

10 In New York City there are ...

F 2 million people.

I 5 million people.

G more than 8 million people.

11 The colours of the US flag are ...

T red, white and blue.

E red, white and black.

H red, black and yellow.

12 In the 1850s the first jeans in America were made by ...

A John Wrangler.

D Max Lee.

O Levi Strauss.

13 'Moccasins', 'anorak' and 'kayak' are words from ...

T Native American languages.

L African American languages.

R European languages.

14 The letter 'B' in 'NBA' stands for ...

P badminton.

O baseball.

H basketball.

15 Cheerleaders ...

E shout, dance and do stunts at games.

O play American football at school.

N are only popular in the USA.

16 The first hamburger was sold in ...

V 1865.

U 1885.

J 1905.

17 'NYPD' is short for ...

D New York Peace Dealer.

S New York City Police Department.

Z New York Popular Disco.

18 The Super Bowl can be won in ...

A American football.

G soccer.

K basketball.

Your sentence:
W E   A R E   G O I N G   T O   T H E   U S A
1 2   3 4 5   6 7 8 9 10   11 12   13 14 15   16 17 18

HOW IT

How to play the game
Number of players: 2 – 4
You will need: one dice and 2 – 4 counters

1. Throw the dice. The player with the highest number starts.
2. Now throw the dice again and move your counter. Look at the box and read the sentences out loud. You can look up words you don't know in your dictionary.
3. If there is a ladder in your box, move up the ladder to the next box. If there is a snake, move down the snake.
4. The first person to finish is the winner.

30 FINISH
In the last 100 years millions of immigrants have become Americans.

29
Move on to no. 30 if you know the answer to this question: How many states are there in the USA today?

21
The 'Wild West' is often shown in westerns.

22 *Miss a turn.*

20
The army helped the settlers against the Native Americans. A lot of Native Americans were killed.
Go down the snake.

19
More and more settlers moved to the west. The Native Americans didn't like that because the settlers took a lot of their land.
Go up the ladder.

11
The Native Americans helped the settlers. They helped them to farm the land and to plant cotton and corn. They gave them bread and fish.

12
In 1621 the settlers and the Native Americans celebrated the first Thanksgiving together.

10
But life in America was different, so the settlers needed help.

9
The first immigrants from England, the 'settlers', arrived at the east coast of America in 1607.
Go up the ladder.

1 START
Thousands of years ago the first people came to America from Siberia.
Throw again.

2
500 years ago there were about one million people in North America. They lived in hundreds of tribes.

28 The 24 Northern states fought against eleven Southern states. The North won the war in 1865, and the slaves were free. There were now 35 states in the USA.

27 The Northern states were against slavery. A war began in 1861.

Go down the snake.

26 At the same time two million slaves worked on cotton farms in the Southern states.

Throw again.

23 About 1850 the settlers found gold on the Native Americans' land.

Move on two spaces.

24 That's why Native Americans had to leave their land and live on reservations.

Go back to no. 15.

25 By 1850 there were only 340 000 Native Americans left in North America.

Miss a turn.

18 In 1789 George Washington became the first American president.

17 America was born. There were 13 states. On the first flag, there was one star and one stripe for each state.

16 The Americans wanted to be free from England. From 1775 to 1783 they fought against the English and won the war.

Move on two spaces.

13 The settlers moved to the west to start cattle farms. Cowboys looked after the cows.

14 The settlers took land from the Native Americans.

Go down the snake.

15 The settlers needed people to work on their farms, so the first slaves were brought from Africa in 1619.

8 A lot of people in Europe had no work. They hoped to find good farm land and religious freedom in America.

Move on three spaces.

7 In 1492 Christopher Columbus arrived in America.

6 The Pueblo were farmers and lived in houses.

3 Some of these tribes were the Mohawk, the Lakota, the Cherokee and the Pueblo.

Move on to no. 6.

4 The Native Americans were farmers, fishermen and hunters.

Go up the ladder.

5 The Lakota, for example, hunted buffaloes.

Die Struktur von CAMDEN MARKET

Aufbau der *Themes* 1–6

BASIS (Grundanforderungen)

- Erfüllt die **Grundanforderungen** für Klasse 8
- Umfasst zwei Themenkreise zu einem Oberthema
- Ist eng verzahnt mit dem **Practice-Teil**: `P2` **P** *p. 28*
  und dem **More-Teil**: `M4` **M** *p. 33*
- Besonders einfache Texte und Aufgaben sind gekennzeichnet: 🌙
- Jeder Themenkreis schließt mit einer farbig hinterlegten Zielaufgabe *(target task)*,
  wie z. B. **Choose an activity** oder **Project**.

PRACTICE (Übungsteil zum Trainieren und Wiederholen)

- **Übungsteil** zu beiden Themenkreisen des **Basis-Teils**
- Mit Übungen zu Wortschatz, Aussprache und Strukturen sowie Sprachmittlung

MORE (Differenzierung für mittleres und höheres Niveau)

- Bietet **Zusatzmaterial** zur Differenzierung für **mittleres** und **höheres Niveau**
- Ist inhaltlich mit den beiden Themenkreisen des **Basis-Teils** verknüpft
- Mit zusätzlichen und alternativ und/oder parallel zum **Basis-Teil** einsetzbaren Aufgaben
- Parallel einsetzbare Aufgaben `M3` können zeitgleich zu einer Aufgabe im **Basis-Teil** bearbeitet werden. Im Anschluss werden die Ergebnisse von **Basis-** und **More-**Aufgabe zusammengeführt.
- Besonders anspruchsvolle Texte und Aufgaben sind gekennzeichnet: ☀

CAMDEN CHRONICLE (Magazinseite)

- Magazinseite mit Fragen zum *Theme*, interkulturellen Hinweisen und authentischen Texten

Anhang

Reading is Fun 📖	Optionaler Lesestoff zu den *Themes*
Wordbanks 🗃	Thematische Wortschatzsammlungen
How to ... 🔧	Lern- und Arbeitstechniken
Language in Focus 🔍	Grammatikanhang zum Nachschlagen
Words W	Chronologisches Wörterverzeichnis
Dictionary D	Alphabetisches Wörterverzeichnis

Theme 1: Hi to high school!

Die Angebote in *Camden Market* sind nicht linear abzuarbeiten. Die Auswahl der Übungen und Übungsteile richtet sich nach den Schwerpunkten des schulinternen Curriculums.

R = *revision* (Wiederholung)

I

Theme 3: New places, new faces

Die Angebote in *Camden Market* sind nicht linear abzuarbeiten. Die Auswahl der Übungen und Übungsteile richtet sich nach den Schwerpunkten des schulinternen Curriculums.

R = *revision* (Wiederholung)

Theme 5: What's up?

Seite	Themen	Kompetenzen	Target task

BASIS

99 — Free time activities

👄 Über einen typischen Tag von amerikanischen Teenagern sprechen • Ein Verkaufsgespräch vorführen • Eine Bildergeschichte nachspielen

👓 Eine Bildergeschichte verstehen

🎧 Ein Verkaufsgespräch verstehen • Ein Telefongespräch verstehen

✏️ Ein eigenes Einkaufszentrum kreieren • Eine Geschichte zu Ende schreiben • Eine E-Mail verfassen

YOUR free time statistics:
- Über eine Statistik zu Freizeitaktivitäten sprechen
- Die Ergebnisse einer eigenen Umfrage präsentieren

105 — American sports

👄 Über Sportarten sprechen

👓 Einem Artikel über *Cheerleading* Informationen entnehmen • Die Regeln von *American Football* verstehen

🎧 Einen Podcast verstehen

✏️ Die Ereignisse in einer Bildergeschichte aufschreiben

👁 Einem Interview mit einem Eishockey-Spieler Informationen entnehmen

Choose an activity:
- Kleidung und Ausrüstung eines Sportlers/einer Sportlerin beschriften und erklären, was er/sie macht
- Über den Lieblingssport schreiben
- Ein Worträtsel erstellen
- Ein Quiz erstellen

PRACTICE

110 — Free time activities

🗃 Aussprache • Wortschatz: Wortpaare

🔍 Strukturen: R: *Gerund* • R: *Linking words*

🇬🇧 Sprachmittlung: Informationen aus einem Telefonat vermitteln

112 — American sports

🗃 Aussprache • Wortschatz: Sport

🔍 Strukturen: *Reflexive pronouns* • R: *Quantifiers (how much/how many)*

🇬🇧 Sprachmittlung: Informationen zu Stadionführungen vermitteln

MORE

114 — Free time activities

👓 Einen Tagebucheintrag/Chat verstehen

🎧 Einem Radiobericht Informationen entnehmen

✏️ Einen weiteren Chat/Tagebucheintrag schreiben • Eine E-Mail verfassen

🔍 Strukturen: *Reported speech* • *Conditional clauses, type III*

116 — American sports

👓 Einen Online-Artikel und einen Kommentar verstehen • Einen Erfahrungsbericht verstehen

🎧 Einem Nachrichtenbericht Informationen entnehmen

✏️ Eine Meinungsäußerung schreiben

🔍 Strukturen: R: *Questions with question words*

118 — CAMDEN CHRONICLE

- *Did you get it all?:* Fragen zum *Theme*
- *Good to know:* interkulturelle Hinweise
- authentische Texte: *Chants*, Kennenlernsprüche

Die Angebote in *Camden Market* sind nicht linear abzuarbeiten. Die Auswahl der Übungen und Übungsteile richtet sich nach den Schwerpunkten des schulinternen Curriculums.

R = *revision* (Wiederholung)

I

Theme 6: California

ANHANG

Symbole und Verweise

Übungs-/Differenzierungsangebot

P6 (p. 29) **P**	Verweis auf Übungen im Practice-Teil.
M1 (p. 32) **M**	Verweis auf Aufgaben im More-Teil.
6	Hierzu gibt es eine parallel einsetzbare Aufgabe im More-Teil.
M3 // **M** (p. 33)	Verweis auf die parallel einsetzbare Aufgabe im More-Teil.
M3	Hierzu gibt es eine parallel einsetzbare Aufgabe im Basis-Teil.
4 // **B** (p. 22)	Rückverweis auf die parallel einsetzbare Aufgabe im Basis-Teil.

12 (p. 27) WB	Hierzu gibt es im Workbook weitere Übungen.
🌙	Der Mond kennzeichnet im Basis-Teil besonders einfache Aufgaben.
8 (p. 77) WB	Von dieser Aufgabe gibt es eine einfachere, parallel einsetzbare Variante im Workbook.
☀	Die Sonne kennzeichnet schwierige Texte und Aufgaben im More-Teil.
M7 (p. 72) WB	Von dieser Aufgabe gibt es eine anspruchsvollere, parallel einsetzbare Variante im Workbook.
portfolio	Das Ergebnis kann im Portfolio-Ordner abgeheftet werden.

Referenzteil

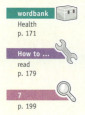

wordbank Health p. 171	In den Wordbanks befinden sich die wichtigsten Wörter zu einem Thema.
How to ... read p. 179	Die Techniken auf den How to ...-Seiten helfen beim Englischlernen.
7 p. 199	Hierzu gibt es eine Erklärung im Grammatik-Teil Language in Focus.

Medien

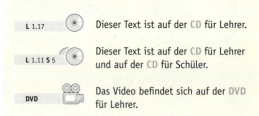

L 1.17	Dieser Text ist auf der CD für Lehrer.
L 1.11 S 5	Dieser Text ist auf der CD für Lehrer und auf der CD für Schüler.
DVD	Das Video befindet sich auf der DVD für Lehrer.

Kompetenzbereiche

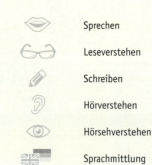

👄	Sprechen
👓	Leseverstehen
✏	Schreiben
👂	Hörverstehen
👁	Hörsehverstehen
🏴	Sprachmittlung

HI TO
HIGH SCHOOL!

In diesem *Theme* ...

» beschäftigst du dich mit amerikanischen Schulen und ihren Besonderheiten.
» lernst du Unterschiede zwischen britischem und amerikanischem Englisch kennen.
» hältst du ein Kurzreferat über amerikanische Schulen.
» sprichst du darüber, was du in der Schule für die Umwelt tun kannst.
» erfährst du, wie eine amerikanische Schule zum Umweltschutz beiträgt.

 W p. 218   TM, p. 23

➡ p. LF15

1 American school life   Folie 1 IWS 📖 pp. 10–12

How to ...
work with others
p. 188

wordbank
At school
p. 161

1
p. 7

a) **Think – pair – share:** What do you know about American schools?

b) Look at the photos from some American schools. What is new/ interesting/**surprising** to you?

> I didn't know that ...

> I think it's surprising that ...

> It's interesting that ...

c) Work with a partner. Choose a picture. Describe it to your partner and let him/her guess which one it is. Take turns.

school bus • flag • lockers •
hat • diploma •
uniform • instruments •
crown • cheerleaders •
American football • …

> In the photo there is a girl with long brown hair. She is standing in front of a locker. There are many photos on the door.

> Oh, I know it! It's photo C.

P3
p. 28

3R
p. 194

How to …
talk about pictures
p. 183

Present progressive

2 ☾ Sounds like school 🎧 📖 p. 11/3

➡ p. LF15

L 1.1 S 1

WB
2
p. 7

Look at the photos on both pages again and listen. What can you hear? Match the right photo with what you hear.

track	photo
1	…
…	…

> I think track 1 goes with photo …

3 Gillian's first day at Lake Park High School

→ p. LF15

L 1.2

3
p. 8

a) Look at the pictures on these two pages. What do you think Gillian is doing?
b) Now listen and read along. Were you right in a)?

A *Last year Cheryl and her parents went to England and stayed with Gillian's family. Now Gillian is spending her summer holiday with the Hills in Illinois. Today is Cheryl's first day of school after her summer break. Gillian goes with her. She is excited but also very nervous. What will a day at an American high school be like?*

Gillian: So what's your timetable for today?
Cheryl: My timetable? Oh, you mean my class schedule. Well, I have six periods: English, math, science and then geography. After lunch I have American history and my last period is web design – my elective.
Gillian: Your what?
Cheryl: My elective. You can choose different electives. I have web design this semester. I'd like to learn how to make a cool website.
Gillian: Wow, that sounds great!
Cheryl: Yeah, I'm really looking forward to it! Unfortunately, it's the last period every day.
Gillian: Oh! That means you've got the same lessons every day?
Cheryl: Sure. Is it different at your school?
Gillian: Yeah. We've got a different timetable for each day.
Cheryl: I don't think I'd be able to remember that.

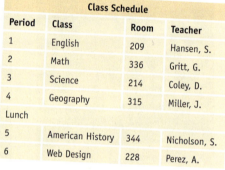

Class Schedule			
Period	Class	Room	Teacher
1	English	209	Hansen, S.
2	Math	336	Gritt, G.
3	Science	214	Coley, D.
4	Geography	315	Miller, J.
Lunch			
5	American History	344	Nicholson, S.
6	Web Design	228	Perez, A.

Folie 2

Cheryl   Gillian

B *7:40 am: Students aren't allowed to take their bags or food into the classrooms. So the girls have to put their things into Cheryl's locker. They also take out the books they need for the first two classes.*

Cheryl: Too late, I'll have to wait to go to the bathroom.
Gillian: Bathroom? Ah, the toilets. Why can't you go now?
Cheryl: 'Cause class is starting now and you need a pass to go to the bathroom.
Gillian: So now you have to wait until break? Poor you!

C *In homeroom a teacher calls out all the names of the students. Then everyone stands up and puts their hand on their heart. Gillian is confused and she stands up, too, but she puts her left hand on her heart. Then everyone turns to the American flag in the corner and says the Pledge of Allegiance. Gillian looks at Cheryl. Oh no – the wrong hand! She is very embarrassed.*

D   *11:30 am: Cheryl and Gillian have their lunch break in the school cafeteria.*   KVs 1.6

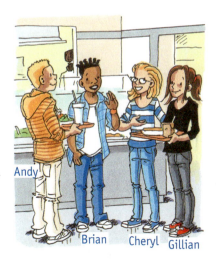

Andy

Brian   Cheryl   Gillian

Cheryl:	So what do you think – do you like it here?
Gillian:	Yes, it's really exciting. I can't believe how different your school is from <u>ours</u>.
Cheryl:	Oh, look! It's Andy and Brian, good friends of <u>mine</u>! Hey guys, this is my friend Gillian. She's staying with me while she's on summer vacation.
Gillian:	Hi. <u>Nice to meet you</u>. So who's who?
Andy:	I'm Andy and this is Brian. Nice to meet you, too. I really love your accent. Where are you from?
Gillian:	I'm from England.
Andy:	Thought so. Man, I wish I had an accent like <u>yours</u>. Welcome to the States, Gillian! I hope you'll like it here.
Cheryl:	<u>Come on</u>, guys. Let's go and have lunch.

E   *2:40 pm: The last period is over.*

Gillian:	Where's the bus?
Cheryl:	Should be here in a minute. Look! It's Andy and Brian again! Hi guys! Are you coming with us?
Andy:	No, sorry. We're taking the late bus because we have basketball practice this afternoon.
Gillian:	Ah, is basketball an elective?
Brian:	No, it's a school club. There are more than 40 clubs at Lake Park!
Cheryl:	Speaking of clubs, do you want to come with me to dance club tomorrow? It's the big homecoming dance in two weeks.
Gillian:	Homecoming? That's when the whole school celebrates, isn't it?
Cheryl:	Exactly! Too bad you won't be here for it.

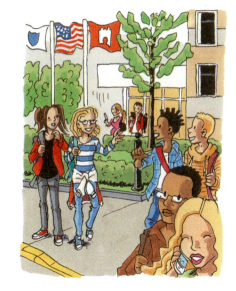

c) **Find the American English words in the texts that mean the same as the British English words.**

📖 p. 14/6   🖱 LSW 102

British English 🇬🇧	American English 🇺🇸
holiday	vacation
timetable	... schedule
maths	math
lesson	period
toilet	bathroom

d) **Read the texts again and match the keywords with parts A – E. Write one sentence for each keyword.**

schedule • cafeteria • clubs • lockers • Pledge of Allegiance

part A: schedule: American students have the same lessons every day.

part B: ...

WB 🌙 **4**
p. 8

P P1 + P2 + P6
p. 28/29

M M1 + M2
p. 32

➡ p. LF15

➡ p.LF15

Modalverben
10R
p. 201

P4 P
p. 29

M3 /// M
p. 33

5 WB
p. 9

// M3: derselbe
Arbeitsauftrag,
ebenfalls *sentence
switchboard,* aber
deutlich mehr
Modalverben

➡ p.LF15

4 School facts ✏ IWS LSW 103

Look at number 3 again. What do you learn about the people and the school?

Gillian The students	is/isn't allowed to are/aren't allowed to has/have to can/can't	spend a day at Cheryl's school. choose an elective. put their bags into lockers. take food into the classroom. wait to go to the toilet. stand up during the Pledge of Allegiance. eat lunch at school. go to the homecoming dance.

5 Electives 👓 👄 KVs 1.1 📖 p. 15/7 🖱 LSW 101

a) Here are some of the electives the students at Lake Park High School
can choose from. Which elective would YOU choose? Say why.

> I would choose ... because
> I like/I'm good at ...

Home economics	Find out all about food and how to prepare it.
Office skills	Learn how to run an office efficiently.
Child development	All you need to know about working with children.
Driver's education	Learn how to drive a car and get your driver's license.
Wood/metal working class	Use tools to make products from wood or metal.
Spanish	Learn to speak this important language.
Drama	Improve your acting skills.
Video game design	Learn how to program video games.

P5 P
p. 29

wordbank 📦
Jobs
p. 162

11R 🔍
p. 203

6 + 7 WB
p. 9/10

Bedingungssätze,
Typ I

b) Look at the list of electives again. What do you think? Talk to a partner. LSW 104

If you want to work as a/an	cook • secretary • actor/actress • ...	
If you are interested in	working with children • building a table/... • learning ... • ...	you can choose ...

c) What electives or clubs are there at YOUR school?
What electives or clubs would you like to have?

🇺🇸 **LAND & LEUTE**

Schulen in den USA

Der Kindergarten in den USA wird als Teil der Schule angesehen und beginnt im Alter von fünf Jahren. Vom Kindergarten bis zur 12. Klasse besteht für jedes Kind Schulpflicht. Nach dem Kindergarten besuchen amerikanische Schüler im Alter von ungefähr 6 bis 11 Jahren die *Elementary School*, dann die *Junior High School* (von ungefähr 11 bis 14 Jahren) und danach die *High School* (von ungefähr 14 bis 18 Jahren). Zum Schulabschluss *(high school diploma)* gibt es eine Feier *(graduation)*, bei der die Schüler besondere Kleidung und Hüte tragen. Am Ende der Abschlussfeier werfen die Schüler ihre Hüte als Zeichen der Freude in die Luft.

Zwischen deutschen und amerikanischen Schulen gibt es ein paar interessante Unterschiede: Zu Beginn des Schultages wird die *Pledge of Allegiance* gesprochen, um die Verbundenheit mit dem amerikanischen Staat und seinen Werten zu bekunden. Der Stundenplan sieht Pflichtfächer und ein Kursangebot mit Wahlfächern *(electives)* vor. Noten werden von A – D vergeben, und wer einen Kurs nicht besteht, bekommt ein F *(fail)*. Die Lehrer haben ihre eigenen Klassenräume, nicht die Schüler. Außerdem besitzt jeder Schüler einen Schulausweis mit Foto, den er immer bei sich tragen muss. Jedes Jahr im Herbst wird ein großes Schulfest *(homecoming)* gefeiert, zu dem auch viele ehemalige Schüler kommen.

Finde heraus, wie der Wortlaut der *Pledge of Allegiance* ist.
Was weißt du über unser Schulsystem?

➡ p. LF16

M | **M4**
p. 33

---

6 **What to do?** 👂 ✏️   KVs 1.4, 1.5  p. 15/7b) LSW 105

➡ p. LF16

a) Guidance counsellors help students and give them advice. Listen to Andy and the guidance counsellor. What is Andy's problem?

b) Listen again and answer the questions. Take notes.
   1. Which electives is Andy interested in?
   2. What can Andy do if he doesn't like his elective?
   3. Why does Andy want to take a language?

c) Is there a person like a guidance counsellor at YOUR school? Who would you talk to if you were in Andy's situation?

Andy

Mr Samuel

WB | **8**
p. 10

◉ L 1.3 S 2

🔧 **How to …**
listen
p. 178

---

7 **YOUR talk – School life in the USA** ✏️ 👄  pp. 16f.

➡ p. LF16

a) Prepare a two-minute talk about school life in the USA. First choose a topic: school day electives schedules …

b) Then go through the Theme again and collect important information about your topic. You can use the Internet, too. Also think about: What is different at YOUR school? What is the same? Take notes.

c) Practise your talk before you present it to a partner or to the class.

📦 **wordbank**
At school
p. 161

WWW

🔧 **How to …**
give a talk
p. 180

 _{p. 220}   TM, p. 43

➡ p. LF17

How to ...
work with others
p. 188

P7 + P9 **P**
p. 30

wordbank
Environment
p. 163

Gerundium
14R
p. 204

9
p. 11

8 **Acting green** at school   Folie 3   p. 18/10 LSW 106

a) **Buzz groups:** **Look at the picture. How can this**
school become greener? Talk about these ideas:

> Go to school by bike or on foot. •
> Ask the cafeteria staff to buy local foods. •
> Recycle rubbish. •
> Separate paper, plastic, ... •
> Plant a school garden. •
> Close windows and doors to save energy. •
> Turn off lights when ... • ...

The students
and teachers
could/should ...

Going .../Asking .../...
is a good/bad idea.

It would be
good to ...

...

b) **What does YOUR school do to protect the environment?**

9 ☾ Things you can do 👂 ✏️   KVs 1.3   p. 19/11   LSW 107

L 1.4

**Listen to an American radio show. What do these teenagers
from San Francisco do for the environment?**

P8
p. 30

1 Carlos (14)	E		A	turns off lights when he/she leaves a room.
2 Akina (15)	C		B	only prints out things he/she really needs.
3 Jake (16)	D		C	just takes a short shower.
4 Mark (17)	B		D	buys milk and juice in bottles that can be recycled.
5 Sheena (14)	F		E	goes to school by bike.
6 Caleb (17)	A		F	doesn't do much.

WB
10
p. 11

10 A school project 👓   KVs 1.1   LSW 108

\\ M5: derselbe
Arbeitsauftrag bei
deutlich anspruchs-
vollerem Text

**Read the interview in a magazine. Can you guess the meaning of new words?
Look up words you can't guess in your dictionary.**

M — M5
p. 34

🔧 How to …
read
p. 179

🔧 How to …
work with a
dictionary
p. 176

➡️ p. LF17

EVANS HIGH GOES GREEN

**Evans High School in Detroit, Michigan, has
made some major environmental changes.
Reporter Jane Graves interviewed two people
who are taking part in the project.**

5 *Joel Miller, you are a student at Evans High.
How do you like the project so far?*
Joel: Well, I think it's great. We as students
can make a real difference. We're changing our
school for the better. It's the place where we
10 spend most of our time.
What has your school done to go green?
Joel: Lots of things. We all had different jobs.
Mine was to help build the living wall. It's a
big green wall of plants that filters air. It's
15 amazing! The air in our school building is much
fresher now. We also planted trees and installed
rain collectors. Plus we built a greenhouse
where we can use that rain water to grow our
own vegetables. They will be on the lunch menu
20 in our cafeteria soon. Come back and try them!

And what has Evans High done to save energy?
Joel: We now have solar panels that power 20
classrooms. And our new school bus is all-
electric – it's one of the first in the country!
Margaret Hall, you are a biology teacher at Evans 25
*High and you helped to get funding for the
project. Was it difficult to find sponsors?*
Ms Hall: Yes, it was hard work. But we were
able to get a $185,000 grant. That helped a lot.
What is your favorite part of the project? 30
Ms Hall: My students and I are very proud of
the app we have developed. It helps you to
check your everyday activities and shows you
where you can save energy.

1 BASIS Acting green

W p.221

➡ p.LF17

11
p. 12

// M6: dieselben
Arbeitsaufträge
a) bis c) wie hier,
aber bezogen
auf den deutlich
anspruchsvolleren
Text in M5

M6 // M
p. 34

M7 M
p. 35

11 Lots of questions

a) Look at number 10 again and answer the questions.
1. Who is Joel Miller?
2. Where in the USA is Evans High School?
3. What have they done at Evans High to go green?
4. How much money did the school get for the project?
5. What is Margaret Hall's job and what did she do for the project?
6. What is Margaret Hall proud of?

b) Bus stop: Work with a partner and **compare** your answers.
c) Which changes at Evans High do you think are best? **Give reasons.**

➡ p.LF17

L 1.5
Possessiv-
pronomen
15
p. 205

How to ...
work with
grammar
p. 190

P10 P
p. 31

12 Cleaning up 🎧 👓 📄 KVs 1.2 📖 p.20/12 und 13 🖱 LSW 109

a) During the project at Evans High School the students also cleaned up their lockers. Listen to Joel and Gary. What things did they find?

b) Now read the dialogue. Which words do the boys use for these expressions?

your baseball magazines • my baseball magazines • his job • my jacket • her jacket

Joel: Look, here are some old baseball magazines in my locker.
Aren't they yours? You are the baseball freak.

Gary: Let me see ... Yes, they are mine. Throw them away, please.
There's a trash bin in the corner.

5 Joel: Listen, this is our environmental project.
So the old magazines go into the paper
container outside.

Gary: Oh sorry, I forgot. Now, what shall I do
with the empty milk bottles? Isn't it

10 Don's job to collect them?

Joel: Correct, it's his. He'll take the bottles to
the cafeteria this afternoon.

Gary: Look at this! There's a jacket on my
locker ... and it's definitely not mine.

15 Joel: Hmm, let's see. ... I'm pretty sure it's a
girl's jacket.

Gary: A girl's jacket on my locker?

Joel: Yeah, Katie has a crush on you, Gary. I'll
bet the jacket is hers. Maybe there's a

20 message for you in one of the pockets.

12 – 14
p. 12/13

your baseball magazines:	yours
my baseball magazines:	... mine
his job:	... his
my jacket:	... mine
her jacket:	... hers

26   twenty-six

13 Take action!   KVs 1.7 IWS p. 21/14 LSW 110 ➡ p. LF17

 DVD

P11
p. 31

a) Watch the clip. What can you understand?

b) Watch the clip again. Then look at the **pictograms**.
   Which of these things are **suggested** in the clip? B, E, F

c) Watch the clip a third time. What are the English words for
   "Erdbeben", "Dürre", "Hochwasser" and "Klimawandel"?
   earthquake, drought, flood, climate change

14 Choose an activity p. 21/14

You can ...

- draw or **design** new pictograms that tell
  people **how to** protect the environment.
  You can look at number 13 for ideas.
  Show the pictograms to your class
  and put them up in your classroom
  or school.
- make a wall dictionary. Collect words
  and phrases which have to do with the
  environment. **Add** the German meaning,
  too. Then **illustrate** your dictionary.
- make a "How green are you?"
  questionnaire for your classmates.
  Think of questions like:
  – Do you turn off the lights when ... ?
  – Do you close ... ?
  Think of **possible** answers and decide how many **points** they will get.
  Write (funny) results for your questionnaire.
- write an email to an **English-speaking** school and tell them
  what you do at school to protect the environment.

portfolio

wordbank
Environment
p. 163

M8 + M9
p. 35

How to ...
write
p. 184

test yourself
p. 14/15

 W p.222   TM, p.57

➡ p.LF18

P1 School words 👓 ✏   🖱 LSW 111

a) What are these words from number 3? Add the **missing vowels** (a, e, i, o, u).

clss • schdl • tmtbl • lctv • smstr • lckr • pss • flg • cftr • hmcmng

b) Make more school words with missing vowels and **test** your partner.

P2 Sound check 👂 👄   🖱 LSW 112

L 1.6

Listen to part D in number 3 again. Stop the **recording** after each sentence.
Say the sentence **yourself**. Try to sound like Cheryl and her friends.

➡ p.LF18

P3 During the break ✏ 👄   🖱 LSW 113

How to ...
talk about
pictures
p. 183

3R
p. 194
Present
progressive

a) Look at picture A and describe it. What can you see?
   What are the people doing?

In the middle/On the left/right there is/are ... • At the top/bottom I can see ... •
The teacher/boy/girl with ... is eating ... /sitting ... / ...

b) Work with a partner and compare both pictures.
   Find the ten things that are different.

In picture A
there is/are ...

In picture B
there is/are ...

In picture A the teacher/
boy/girl with ... is ...

In picture B
he/she is ...

P4 Lake Park rules ✎

➡ p. LF18

🔍 Modalverben
10R
p. 201

a) What are the rules at Lake Park High School?

are allowed to • aren't allowed to • have to • don't have to

1. Students ➕ wear jeans to school.

2. They 🙂 wear a school uniform.

3. They ‼️ do their homework every day.

4. They ✖️ eat during class.

5. They ‼️ put their bags into their lockers.

6. They ‼️ carry their ID card at all times.

7. They ✖️ use their cellphones during class.

8. But they ➕ use them in the cafeteria.

b) Which words in a) can you use for *can* and *can't*?

c) Which rules in a) are different at YOUR school?

P5 Special interests? 👓 ✎

➡ p. LF18

🔍 **11R**
p. 203
Bedingungssätze, Typ I

If you have special interests, you can do many different things at school. Match the sentence parts and fill in the right words:

can • should • will • won't

1 If you are interested in books, D

2 If you like to invent things, A

3 If you are under 16, F

4 If you join the basketball club, E

5 You XX be good at writing B

6 You XX learn how to draw C

A you XX join the science club.

B if you want to work for the school newspaper.

C if you join the art club.

D you XX go to the school library.

E you XX learn how to dribble well.

F you XX be allowed to join the driving club.

P6 A school club 🇬🇧

➡ p. LF19

🔧 **How to ...**
help out
p. 190

Read about the marching band at Lake Park High School. What do you learn about it? Tell a classmate in German.

Der Spielmannszug nimmt an ... teil.

Man kann ...

...

Lake Park Marching Band
From sports games to state competitions, the Lake Park Marching Band takes part in many exciting events. If you can't play an instrument, join the Color Team and show your school spirit using flags and even swords! The band practices all year during Monday lunchtimes and on Thursday afternoons.

 W p. 222   TM, p. 59

→ p. LF19

P7 A "green" word snake ✎

Find the "green" words and phrases in the snake. Write them down.

recycleelectiverubbishsaveenergycheerleadersturnofflightspledgeofallegianceseparatepaper

P8 Sound check ✎ ♪

a) What are these words? Write them down.

1. /ˈʃaʊə/   2. /ˈenədʒi/   3. /plɑːnt/   4. /ˈsepəreɪt/   5. /riːˈsaɪkl/   6. /laɪt/

L 1.7
 b) Listen and check.   1. shower 2. energy 3. plant 4. separate 5. recycle 6. light

→ p. LF19
Imperativ
16R
p. 205

P9 Useful tips ✎ 🖱 LSW 114

You want the man in the picture to act green.
Write down tips for him. You can use these words:

recycle • close • turn off • use • leave ... on • separate • ...	window • computer • water • fridge • paper • TV • rubbish • lights • heating • glass • ...

– Don't leave the computer on.
– Turn off ...
– ...

P10 Whose is it? LSW 115

➡ p. LF19

🔍 15
p. 205
Possessivpronomen

a) Complete the sentences with a **possessive pronoun** from the box.

mine • yours • his • hers • ours • theirs

1. At school Joel has got a locker, it's **XX**.
2. Katie has got a jacket, it's **XX**.
3. Our school has got a greenhouse, it's **XX**.
4. They have got rain collectors, they're **XX**.
5. You have got a job to do, it's **XX**.
6. I've got a new bike, it's **XX**.

b) Look at the sentences in a) again. What are they in German? Tell a partner.

c) What are Cheryl and her parents saying? Complete their questions and answers with a possessive pronoun.

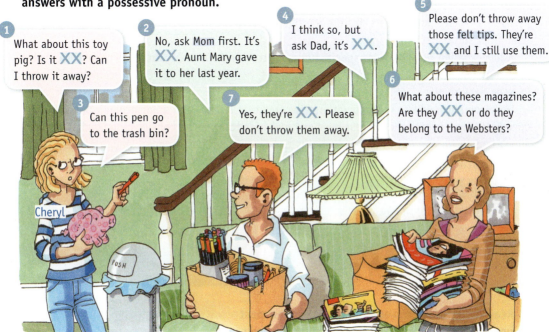

1. What about this toy pig? Is it **XX**? Can I throw it away?
2. No, ask Mom first. It's **XX**. Aunt Mary gave it to her last year.
3. Can this pen go to the trash bin?
4. I think so, but ask Dad, it's **XX**.
5. Please don't throw away those felt tips. They're **XX** and I still use them.
6. What about these magazines? Are they **XX** or do they belong to the Websters?
7. Yes, they're **XX**. Please don't throw them away.

P11 An advert LSW 116

➡ p. LF19

🔧 **How to …**
help out
p. 190

Look at the advert. What do you learn about recycling mobile phones?
Tell a classmate in German.

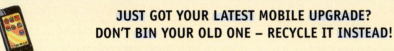

**JUST GOT YOUR LATEST MOBILE UPGRADE?
DON'T BIN YOUR OLD ONE – RECYCLE IT INSTEAD!**

Got a shiny new phone? What do you do with the old one? You could:

- Give it to a friend so that it can be used again.
- Give it to a charity.
- Perhaps you can sell your old mobile phone.
- Your mobile phone company may be able to recycle mobile phones. Find out more online.

Don't forget to remove your SIM card and all your data before you recycle your phone!

W p.223   TM, p.62

M1
p. 18

How to …
read
p. 179

➡ p. LF20

M1   Homecoming week   LSW 117

tug-of-war: 1
homecoming dance: 2
Pajama Day: 3
pie-eating contest: 4

a) Read about homecoming. Which activities are mentioned in the article? Match them with the pictures.

Homecoming is normally every fall, in the last week of September or the first week of October. It is a week of special events for the students and for the graduates who come back to their old high schools.

There are all kinds of activities like karaoke, the homecoming dance, the homecoming parade with the school's marching band, the tug-of-war and the pie-eating contest where students have to eat a pie as fast as possible without using their hands.

There are also sports events like the football game where the school team plays against a team from another school.

A homecoming week includes special fun days, too: On Pajama Day students come to school in their pajamas, on Hat Day everybody wears a hat, and on Class Color Day students wear clothes in their class colors.

Homecoming would be nothing without the tradition of choosing a homecoming king and queen. All the students choose four boys and four girls to form the homecoming court. Then they all vote again for one of these boys and girls to become their homecoming king and queen.

b) Read the article again and take notes of the most important points. Then tell somebody who hasn't read the article about homecoming.

I've read an article about …
I found out that …

➡ p. LF20

L 1.8 S 3

M2
p. 19

M2   A homecoming week to remember   LSW 118

a) First read the beginning of the newspaper article. Then listen to the report about the homecoming week at Spencer High School. Put the events in the right order.

What a homecoming week! This year everything went wrong at Spencer High School's homecoming. On Monday the school was preparing for the big football game when it started to rain. Then, on Tuesday,

homecoming dance • karaoke • tug-of-war • decorating the school • football game

b) Say what happened at Spencer High School. Then finish the newspaper article. LSW 119

5R

p. 197

Past progressive

1. the players – prepare for the football game *when* start to rain
2. the teams – have a tug-of-war *when* a dog – eat all the pies for the pie-eating contest
3. the seniors – sing karaoke *when* the lights – go out
4. the teachers – decorate the school for the homecoming dance *when* Mrs Cook – fall and break her foot
5. the students and teachers – dance at the homecoming dance *when* someone – steal the equipment

1. The players were preparing for the football game when it started to rain.
2. The teams ...

M3 School facts 🖉

➡ p. LF20

Look at number 3 again. What do you learn about the people and the school?

Gillian The students Cheryl	can/can't is/are (not) able to is/are (not) allowed to must has/have to doesn't/don't have to mustn't	spend a day at Cheryl's school. choose an elective. remember a new schedule every day. put their bags into lockers. take food into the classroom. wait to go to the toilet. stand up during the Pledge of Allegiance. eat lunch at school. go to the homecoming dance.

B 4

p. 22

 Modalverben

10R

p. 201

 M3

p. 19

M4 ☀ What's different, what's the same? 🖉 👄

 LSW 220 ➡ p. LF20

a) Compare American high schools to YOUR school. Make a grid.
Go through the Theme again to collect information.

American high school students ...	Students at our school ...
... have the same lessons every day.	... have different lessons every day.
... put their jackets and bags into ...	...
...	...

b) Work with a partner and compare your grids. Then talk about the advantages and disadvantages of the different schools.

I (don't) think it's good/better/
easier/... to have ... because ...

I (don't) agree with you.

I think we should
have ..., too.

→ p. LF21

M5 A school project IWS   LSW 121, 122

10 // B
p. 25

**Read the newspaper report. Can you guess the meaning of new words?
Look up words you can't guess in your dictionary.**

How to ...
read
p. 179

How to ...
work with a
dictionary
p. 176

M4 + M5 WB
p. 20

EVANS HIGH GOES GREEN

**Evans High School, Detroit, Michigan, to
make major environmental changes**
By student Edgar Simsion,
reporting for The Detroit Times

5   With its solar panels and its own all-electric
bus, our school, Evans High, is going green.
   On Friday students planted trees and
installed rain collectors. We opened
our doors to the public, showing our
10 environmental projects for the first time. The
campus now has its own greenhouse, solar
panels that power 20 classrooms and a living
wall – a vertical row of plants that filters the
air. These major environmental changes have
15 been funded by a $185,000 grant.
   Some of our science club students have
already been using our new zero-emission
all-electric school bus. It is one of the first
in the country that is not hybrid-electric,
20 but runs completely on electricity. Joel
Miller, 16, said: "You can really see how the
things we're doing are making our school a
better place."
   The project was organized by Earth Day
25 activist Fred Myers. He said that the students
at Evans High School understand about the
problems for the environment. "We tell the
students to start on their own doorstep and
show them what they can do."

The Detroit Times talked to biology   30
teacher Margaret Hall. She helped to get
funding for the project and is thrilled with
her new greenhouse. She plans to teach
classes in the greenhouse and plant a
vegetable garden.   35
   "I've been trying to teach gardening in
my classes from a textbook," she said on
Friday, looking at the new greenhouse. "Now
– this is the real deal! The students may not
remember what they read in the textbook,   40
but they'll remember this."
   Ms Hall also proudly demonstrated the
"Bloom" app, which was developed by
the school's computer science course. She
explained: "With our app you can keep an   45
eye on your energy usage and get advice on
how to be more environmentally friendly."

→ p. LF21

M6 Lots of questions

a) Look at M5 again and answer the questions.
   1. Who is Joel Miller?
   2. Where in the USA is Evans High School?
   3. What have they done at Evans High to go green?
   4. How much money did the school get for the project?

5. What is Margaret Hall's job and what did she do for the project?
6. Why does Ms Hall like the greenhouse?
7. What is she proud of?
8. Who is Fred Myers?

b) **Bus stop: Work with a partner and compare your answers.**

c) **Which changes at Evans High do you think are best? Give reasons.**

B \\\ 11
p. 26

M7 A living wall 👂 ✏️ LSW 123

a) **Listen to Fred Myers. Who is he talking to?** students at Evans High School

b) **Right or wrong? Listen again and correct what's wrong.**
   1. Living walls can be found in cities, buildings and people's homes. ✓
   2. Living walls are also called wild walls. wrong
   3. A living wall is always inside a building. wrong
   4. Living walls act as natural air filters. They remove toxins from the air. ✓
   5. A living wall can make a room a more peaceful place by reducing noise levels. ✓
   6. Especially in summer an outside living wall can reduce energy costs. It acts as insulation. wrong

c) **Tell your class what you learned about a living wall.**

WB M6
p. 21

L 1.9 S 4

How to ...
listen
p. 178

➡ p. LF21

M8 ☀ Earth Day 👓 👄 LSW 124

Find out about Earth Day on the Internet:
– When is it?
– When did it start?
– Who started it?
– Why was it started?
– What sort of things do people do on Earth Day?
– Where did you find the information?
– ...

Present your information to the class.

➡ p. LF22

WWW

WB M7
p. 21

M9 An environment cartoon ✏️

➡ p. LF22

How to ...
talk about
pictures
p. 183

Look at the cartoon. What can you see? What is its message? Find a title for the cartoon and write about it. Here is some help:

In the cartoon you can see ... •
On the left/right there is/are ... •
... are pushing ... •
There is a rope around ... •
... is pulling ... •
I think the cartoonist wants to say ...

CAMDEN CHRONICLE
LEARN ENGLISH THE CAMDEN WAY

DID YOU GET IT ALL? ➡ p. LF22

» What do students in the USA do and wear when they get their diploma?
» What is an elective?
» Where does Gillian first meet Brian and Andy?
» Why did Andy think of choosing the video game design course?
» What does a green wall do?
» What will the cafeteria at Evans High School offer soon?
» What subject does Ms Hall teach?
» What sport does Gary like?

GOOD TO KNOW ...

Zwischen *British English (BE)* und *American English (AE)* gibt es ein paar Unterschiede, und zwar in der Schreibweise von Wörtern (z. B. *favourite (BE)* – *favorite (AE)*), in der Aussprache (z. B. dance /dɑːns/ *(BE)* – dance /dæns/ *(AE)*) und auch im Wortschatz. Wenn du z. B. bei einer amerikanischen Gastfamilie die Toilette benutzen möchtest, fragst du nicht nach der *toilet*, sondern du sagst: *Where's the bathroom, please?*

You think that recycling is important but boring? Try upcycling – it's fun!

Take waste materials and create something new and useful out of it: for example a cool storage pocket for pencils, scissors, memos etc. made from an old pair of jeans. Simply cut out the pockets and nail them to the wall. Doing your homework will be more fun now, won't it?

LET'S GRAB SOME FOOD

In diesem *Theme* ...

» erfährst du einiges über Essgewohnheiten in den USA.
» beschäftigst du dich mit Fastfood.
» verfasst du eine Restaurantkritik.
» lernst du verschiedene Feste und Bräuche in den USA kennen.
» schreibst du über ein eigenes Fest mit seinen Bräuchen und typischen Gerichten.

p. 225   TM, p. 73

1 Are you hungry?

pp. 24f./1–3

➡ p. LF23

How to ...
work with others
p. 188

wordbank
Food and drink
p. 164

 1
p. 22

a) What would you like for lunch today (**starter**, **main dish**, dessert)? Make notes.
b) **Form** a **double circle** in class and tell **each other** about your lunches.

> First I'd like **tomato** soup, then ... and for dessert ... What about you?

> We eat a lot of fish like salmon in Alaska. It's very healthy!

> First I put **peanut** butter on bread and then I carefully add some **jelly**. My lunch! I just call it my PB&J sandwich!

➡ p. LF23

2 Typical American food?

2
p. 22

P1 + P2
p. 48

3
p. 23

What do different Americans say about food in the USA?
Read and finish the sentences.

1. People in Alaska eat ...
2. A PB&J sandwich is made with ...
3. Typical American fast food is ...
4. The lady with the sunglasses doesn't think ...
5. In Maryland ...
6. Some people in New York like ...
7. Typical **Southern** food is ...
8. People in Texas ...
9. The lady with the grey hair thinks that ...
10. The **Asian American** girl is a ...
11. Tex-Mex is ...
12. **Loco moco** is ...

 KVs 2.2   IWS    p. 26/4

> Well, I don't eat "American" food. I'm vegetarian and I prefer Chinese food. **Chop suey** with tofu is my favorite.

> I love loco moco. It's a **Hawaiian** dish: white **rice** with a hamburger, a **fried egg** and sauce on top. YUMMY!

> I don't know if there are any typical American dishes. We **normally** eat Tex-Mex, that's **Mexican**-style food. You know, chili con carne, fajitas and **stuff** like that.

LSW 201, 202

I think a burger is typical American food. A burger and French fries. Yeah, that's American, American fast food.

I don't think there is one typical American dish. People from so many different countries live here. My family is from Italy and Ireland. A typical meal for us – and one that you can make easily – is pasta with some kind of sauce.

I love to put sauerkraut on my hot dog! A lot of people in Maryland like it this way. But sauerkraut is German, isn't it?

I guess apple pie is America's favorite dessert. It's great with ice cream on top. We sometimes say something is "as American as apple pie"!

I normally have a New York bagel for lunch. It's Jewish, I think. For me this is typical New York food!

A good steak. That is typical American food. In Texas we eat a lot of meat and love to barbecue!

I love typical Southern food. We eat fried chicken, green vegetables and mashed potatoes. And in the summer a lot of watermelon.

---

3 **Have you ever tried … ?**   p. 28/5a)   LSW 203 → p. LF23

6R
p. 198
Present perfect

4
p. 23

Look at the different kinds of food again. Have you ever tried chili con carne, peanut butter, … ? What was it like? Talk to a partner.

Have you ever tried peanut butter/…?

Yes, I have. It was OK/delicious/disgusting/…

No, I haven't because I've never seen it before.

Yes, I have. I didn't like it very much.

No, I haven't but I'd like to try it.

➡ p. LF23

wordbank
Food and drink
p. 164

5
p. 24

4 Yummy or yucky?   p. 28/5b)

a) Look at the dishes on pages 38 – 39 again.
   Do you think they are delicious, OK or disgusting?
   Sort them in a **grid**.

b) Which dishes would/wouldn't you like to try?
   Talk to a partner and give reasons.

delicious	OK	disgusting
...	...	...

➡ p. LF23

19R
p. 208

Adverbs
of manner

5 ☾ Fast food   ⌕ IWS

Read the statements. What is fast food for YOU? Talk to a partner.

Fast food? That's unhealthy, cheap food, like hamburgers and French fries. It's for people who can't cook well.

Fast food is fast because you can get it quickly and eat it fast if you need to.

I (don't) agree. For me ...

For me fast food is food that ...
... you can prepare easily.
... people sell in the street.
... you don't eat in a restaurant.
... you can eat quickly.
...

LAND & LEUTE

Essen in den USA

Essen in den USA – das heißt nicht nur Hamburger, Pizza und Fastfood. Im Allgemeinen versteht man unter amerikanischer Küche traditionelle Gerichte wie Brathähnchen (*fried chicken*), Mais (*corn*), warmen Apfelkuchen (*apple pie*), Käse-Makkaroni (*macaroni and cheese*), Hackbraten (*meat loaf*) und Pfannkuchen (*pancakes*) mit Ahornsirup (*maple syrup*). An wichtigen Feiertagen wie *Thanksgiving* oder Weihnachten gibt es in vielen Familien Truthahnbraten (*roast turkey*).

Die meisten Gerichte sind von den ersten europäischen Einwanderern mitgebracht worden. In jedem Staat der USA wird jedoch etwas anders gekocht. Das hängt nicht nur von den regionalen Zutaten ab, sondern auch davon, woher die dort lebenden Menschen stammen.

So ist in den Südstaaten der afrikanische Einfluss sehr groß. In der Umgebung von New Orleans findet man eine interessante Mischung aus spanischen, französischen und afrikanischen Gerichten, *Cajun* genannt.

Die kalifornische Küche verwendet viel frisches Obst und Gemüse, das auf asiatische, mexikanische und spanische Weise zubereitet wird.

Was meinst du: Welche Lieblingsgerichte haben die Menschen in Deutschland?
Sind diese typisch deutsch?

 KVs 2.4

6 Super Burger   p. 29/6 LSW 204

→ p. LF23

 L 1.10

Cheryl is working on a report on fast food for her school magazine.
She is interviewing Kathy Watts, the manager of Super Burger in Roselle.

a) Listen and find out:
- How many hamburgers are sold most Saturdays? over seven thousand
- Which one is the most popular? the Roselle Special

b) Now read the interview. Would YOU allow your kids to eat at a fast food restaurant every day? Say why.

P P3 - P5
p. 48/49

M M1 + M2
p. 52

Cheryl:	Here I am at Super Burger. And with me is Kathy, who is the manager here. Kathy, Super Burger is open 24 hours a day. Is that right?
Kathy:	Yeah, that's right.
Cheryl:	And are there many customers at night?
Kathy:	Oh, sure! People come in all the time. You can sit more comfortably here than in the other burger places.
Cheryl:	That's nice. Could you tell me how many hamburgers you sell a day?

Kathy

Cheryl

Kathy:	Some days are busier than others. Saturday is our busiest day. We sell over seven thousand hamburgers most Saturdays.

Cheryl:	Awesome! Which one is the most popular?

Kathy:	Well, I'd say it's the Roselle Special. It's pretty hot. Here, please try one.

Cheryl:	Wow! That tastes good. Now Kathy, I know all this fast food is very popular – but is it also healthy?

Kathy:	Sure! We only use the best meat in our burgers. And our salads are really nice and fresh.

Cheryl:	OK ... Would you allow your kids to eat here every day?

Kathy:	Well, not every day. But when I don't have much time to cook, why not?

 6
p. 24

7 Cheryl's thoughts   KVs 2.1 LSW 205

Read the interview in number 6 again. What do you think are Cheryl's thoughts? Write them down.

P P6
p. 49

20
p. 209
Comparison
of adverbs

> quickly • comfortably • healthily • slowly • deliciously

1. You really can sit more XX here than in other burger places. comfortably
2. The customers eat more XX than the guests in normal restaurants. quickly
3. It's better to eat more XX and take your time. slowly
4. You can eat more XX in normal restaurants. healthily
5. I guess my mom can cook more XX than Super Burger. deliciously

p. 226

➡ p. LF24

L 1.11 S 5

How to ...
listen
p. 178

7
p. 25

8 Customer interviews

a) Cheryl also spoke to some customers at Super Burger.
Listen to three of her interviews. How many men
and how many women did she talk to? one man, two women

customer 1:
- eats at Super Burger
  (four) times a week
- likes the price of the
  food

customer 2:
- eats at Super Burger
  twice a month
- likes (French fries)

customer 3:
- (three) kids
- eats at Super Burger
  once or twice a week
- son Sam likes Super
  Hamburger with (salad)

// Auswertung
des Hörtextes auf
höherem Niveau:
a) und c) iden-
tisch, in b) drei
What/How-Fragen

M3
p. 53

b) Listen again and check her **notes**. What did Cheryl
get wrong? **Copy** her notes and **correct** them.

c) Compare your notes with a partner.

➡ p. LF24

8
p. 25

9 A restaurant review   KVs 2.6 pp. 30f./7 und 8 LSW 206

a) Test a fast food restaurant in YOUR area. Look at the **example**
for help and find the information for your restaurant.

Name: *Döner Express*
Address: *Venloer Straße, Köln*
Food: *döner, shawarma, falafel, baklava*
My favourite meal: *chicken shawarma (4€)*
Takeaway: ☑ *yes*   ☐ *no*
Delivery: ☐ *yes*   ☑ *no*
Music: *pop/Top 40/Arabic*
Service: ☑ *friendly*   ☐ *average*   ☐ *unfriendly*
Your opinion:
☑ *a must*   ☐ *pretty cool*   ☐ *worth a visit*
☐ *only if you are really hungry*   ☐ *forget it*

b) Put up all your information in
the classroom and talk about it.

> The name of the
> restaurant I tested is ...
> It's in ...

P7 P
p. 49

How to ...
write
p. 184

c) Now write about your fast food
restaurant.

The name of the restaurant I tested is ... • It's in ... • You can get ... there. •
They (don't) bring food. • They play ... music. • The service is ... • I think it's ...

➡ p. LF24

10 A food poem 👓 👄

a) 🌙 **Listen to the poem and read along.**

L 1.12

Like a pizza with no topping
like baked beans with no toast
like fish without fingers
like Sunday without roast

Like a burger with no ketchup
like milk that's had no shake
like steak pie without the kidney
it's more than I can take

Like Popeye without spinach
like kraut that isn't sauer
like bread without butter
like a cauli with no flower

Like trifle without sherry
like lamb with no mint sauce
like gin without tonic
like a meal with no first course

Like Mac without Donald
like chips without the fish
like ham that's lost its burger
or a wishbone without a wish

What is cheese without biscuits?
What are strawberries with no cream?
Won't you share my chicken nuggets
and be my burger queen?

b) **What food is mentioned? What is the message of the poem?**

c) **Practise reading the poem. You can work with a partner or in
a group. Here are some ideas for what you can do:**
- Clap your hands to give the poem a rhythm.
- Work in a group and read the poem aloud.
- Choose a different speaker for each line or verse.
- Rap the poem.
- ...

Present the poem to the class.

9 + 10
p. 26

11 Choose an activity ✏ 👄

➡ p. LF24

portfolio

You can ...
- **write your own food poem. Look at the
example for help.**
- **imagine you are going to open an
American restaurant. Design a menu with
starters, main dishes, desserts, drinks
and a special dish. Then present your
menu to the class.**
- **design an advert for your favourite/
dream fast food restaurant. Look at P4
again for ideas.**

wordbank
Food and drink
p. 164

M M4
p. 53

p. 227   TM, p. 91

→ p. LF25

11
p. 27

Folie 4

12 Time to celebrate

a) 🌙 **Look at the photos of some special days that are celebrated in the USA.**
- Which of these festivals do YOU celebrate?
- Which ones are new to you?   p. 32/9

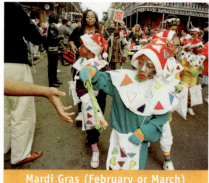

Mardi Gras (February or March)

Thanksgiving (4th Thursday in November)

Halloween (31st October)

Christmas (25th December)

 LSW 207

Eid (at the end of Ramadan)

St Patrick's Day
(17th March)

Diwali (October or November)

Independence Day (4th July)

Cinco de Mayo (5th May)

b) What happens on these special days? Match the sentence parts. IWS

1. On Thanksgiving *E*
2. During Eid *D*
3. On Cinco de Mayo *H*
4. During Diwali *A*
5. On Mardi Gras *B*
6. On Independence Day *C*
7. On St Patrick's Day *F*
8. For Halloween *G*

A Hindus celebrate the victory of light over darkness.

B people wear costumes and dance in the streets.

C there are big parades and lots of people wear red, white and blue clothes.

D Muslims celebrate the end of Ramadan.

E people give thanks for what they have.

F people celebrate Irish culture and usually wear green.

G people decorate pumpkins and wear scary costumes.

H Mexicans in the USA celebrate their culture.

c) When is a special day for YOU and YOUR family?
   Think about it and make notes:
   – When and how do you celebrate it?
   – Whom do you invite?
   Milling around: Tell each other about your special days.

> A special day for me is the 19th July/... That's my birthday. I usually ...

> For my family ... is a special day because we celebrate ...

13 Sounds like celebrating  KVs 2.3 LSW 208

a) Look at the photos again and listen to five dialogues.
   Match them with the correct special day.
b) Listen again. What else did you hear?
   Write down words or phrases that you understood.

dialogue	special day	words/phrases
1	...	...
...	...	...

 wordbank
Celebrations
p. 165

 wordbank
Time
p. 172

 How to ...
work with others
p. 188

 P9 + P13
p. 50/51

 WB 12
p. 27

 ➜ p. LF25

 L 1.13

 How to ...
listen
p. 178

W p. 227

➡ p. LF25

14 Festivals in the USA   KVs 2.5 p. 33/10a LSW 210

M5
p. 54

13
p. 28

How to …
read
p. 179

// M5: weiterer
Blogeintrag;
ähnliche Auswer-
tung wie hier,
aber auf alle drei
Blogeinträge be-
zogen, plus eine
Teilaufgabe d)

a) Read the blog entries about two different festivals. Collect words and information in a grid like this:

festival	food	activities
…	dumplings	…
…	…	…

Chinese New Year

Thanksgiving

News (230) ▼

MY FAVORITE FOOD ON A SPECIAL DAY

Posted by Lee-Lee, San Francisco, 05/06

The most important festival for me is Chinese New Year. The day changes each year because of the lunar calendar.
On this day most Chinese people get together and have dinner with their family and friends.
My cousin and I always play on my computer after the meal.
My favorite food? Jiaozi dumplings! Every Chinese New Year we have them, and they are soooo yummy! You're only allowed to eat them just after midnight. And there's a coin in one of the dumplings. If you find it, they say you'll have a lot of money in your life. But eat carefully – you don't want to break a tooth!

Posted by S@mmy, NY, 05/07

My favorite food is our traditional Thanksgiving dinner, which is – of course – turkey with YUMMY mashed potatoes, cranberry sauce, corn on the cob and apple pie. I really love it!
So every year, on the fourth Thursday of November, my whole family gets together. This year even my uncle from England will be here – I hope it'll be fun for him.
I love Thanksgiving but the best thing is the next day – Black Friday!!! Mom and Dad don't go to work and we go shopping. That's the best part! I love going to the mall ;-)))

lunar calendar, midnight, coin, corn on the cob

b) Find the English words for "Mondkalender", "Mitternacht", "Münze" and "Maiskolben" in the blog entries. Don't use your dictionary.

14
p. 29

P8 + P10 + P11
p. 50

M6
p. 55

c) Complete the sentences.
1. After dinner Lee-Lee and his cousin … always play on Lee-Lee's computer.
2. If you find a coin in your dumpling, you … will have a lot of money in your life.
3. This year's Thanksgiving Sammy's … uncle from England will be there.
4. On Black Friday … Sammy and his parents go shopping.

 IWS

15 The first Thanksgiving   Folie 5 KVs 2.7 IWS LSW 209

a) Watch the **animated slide show** about the history of the first Thanksgiving. What can you understand?

DVD

➡ p. LF26

b) Watch the slide show again. Then put the sentences in the right **order**. What word do you get? PEOPLE

P12
p. 51

15
p. 29

E In October 1621 the Pilgrims invited the Native Americans in the area to celebrate their first harvest.

O Many of the Pilgrims died from cold and disease because they didn't know how to hunt or what plants to eat.

P Over time explorers from all over Europe came to the new world and settled in different parts of North America.

P Samoset and Squanto, two Native Americans who lived in the area, decided to help the new settlers.

E In 1620 the Pilgrims, a religious group from England, landed at Plymouth Bay in Massachusetts.

L The Native Americans taught the settlers how to hunt and build houses. They also showed them new animals and plants.

16 YOUR blog entry – A special day ✏ 👄 📖 p. 33/10c)

a) Write a blog entry about a special day. Think about:
– when the special day is
– what is celebrated on this special day
– what you usually eat
– which food you like **best**
– other things you do on this day
– why you like this day very much
– ...

b) Work with a partner and check your texts. Give your partner feedback on:
– what you like about his/her text
– what you would change to make the text better

c) **Rewrite your blog entry.** Then collect all the texts in class and **hang them up** in your classroom.

A special day for me is Easter. Easter ~~finds~~ **takes** place in spring, usually in March or in April. I really like Easter. **because** The day ~~start~~ **starts** with chocolate! I **always** get up early

and look for Easter eggs that my mother hides in our flat. ~~Then~~ **After breakfast** I help my mum to bake a ~~spezial~~ **special** cake for the

afternoon. For ~~the~~ dinner we ~~are having~~ **have** often **∨** roast lamb. I like

wordbank
Celebrations
p. 165

How to ...
write
p. 184

16
p. 29

How to ...
give feedback
p. 181

M7
p. 55

test yourself
p. 30/31

p. 228   TM, p. 103

P1 Words, words, words LSW 214

a) Look at these words. Write them with your finger on the desk or on your partner's back. Can he/she guess the words?

> jelly • sauce • typical • vegetables • French fries • watermelon • dessert • barbecue • fried egg • apple pie

b) Now spell the words for your partner. Can he/she write them down correctly? Spell other words from pages 38 – 39, too.

 p. LF26

 L 1.14

P2 Sound check LSW 211

a) Listen to the words and **repeat** them.
b) Make three lists. Write the words in the correct list.

> peanut • bread • add • jelly • sandwich • meat • cheap • healthy • hamburger • Mexican • café • watermelon • menu • people • Chinese

/e/	/iː/	/æ/
bread	peanut	add
...	...	...

➡ p. LF26

Relativsätze
17R
p. 206

P3 The girl who ... LSW 212

a) Complete the sentences with *who* or *which*.

1. Cheryl is the girl XX wants to write a report on fast food for the school magazine. who
2. Kathy, XX works at Super Burger in Roselle, has been the manager for two years. who
3. Her restaurant, XX is open 24 hours a day, has thousands of customers every day. which
4. A lot of people XX go to Super Burger order the Roselle Special. who
5. Hamburger and chicken nuggets are dishes XX are very **popular** with kids. which
6. Fresh salads are one kind of fast food XX is healthy. which
7. The people XX work at Super Burger have to wear special uniforms. who
8. The uniforms, XX are red and yellow, look really nice. which

How to ...
work with
grammar
p. 190

b) Work with a partner and compare your sentences.
   When do you use *who*? When do you use *which*? who = people, which = things

P4 The best food in town

→ p. LF27

18R
p. 206
Comparison of adjectives

a) Look at these adjectives from number 6:

> busy • popular • hot • good •
> healthy • nice • fresh

Write them down like this:
busy, busier, (the) busiest
popular, more ..., (the) most ...
...

b) Choose the right form of the adjective and complete the advert for Super Burger. You can also use other adjectives.

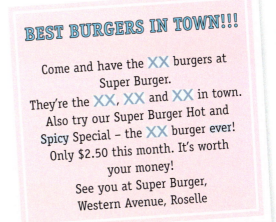

BEST BURGERS IN TOWN!!!

Come and have the XX burgers at Super Burger.
They're the XX, XX and XX in town.
Also try our Super Burger Hot and Spicy Special – the XX burger ever!
Only $2.50 this month. It's worth your money!
See you at Super Burger,
Western Avenue, Roselle

P5 Family dinner LSW 213

→ p. LF27

19R
p. 208
Adverbs of manner

Complete the sentences with the right form: adjective or adverb.

My busy/busily mum works all day, so my dad has to cook for the family. That's great because he's a brilliant/brilliantly cook. He cooks his meals as good/well as the famous cooks on TV! I often have to do the shopping for the family. After school I quick/quickly run to the supermarket. Then I sometimes help my dad in the kitchen. Our kitchen is a very noisy/noisily place because my dad loves to sing loud/loudly. It's horrible, believe me ... My sister is often late/lately for dinner, so my dad looks at her angry/angrily.

P6 Think more carefully

→ p. LF27

20
p. 209
Comparison of adverbs

Complete the sentences with an adverb form.

> more often • faster • better • more quickly • more healthily • more beautifully

1. On Sundays we decorate the breakfast table XX than on other days.
2. I use salt XX than my brother.
3. My mum can cook XX than my grandma.
4. I think we eat XX than my friend's family.
5. I can cut a cucumber XX than my mum.
6. My sister can eat pizza XX than I can.

P7 Food signs

→ p. LF27

How to ...
help out
p. 190

Look at the signs. Tell a friend who doesn't speak English what they mean.

p. 228   TM, p. 105

➡ p. LF27

P8 Word groups

a) Find titles for these word groups.

1. cousin – uncle – mom – dad
2. turkey – corn on the cob – dumplings – apple pie
3. Christmas – Eid – Independence Day – Diwali
4. Friday – year – calendar – midnight
5. green – red – white – blue
6. Muslims – Chinese – Mexicans – Hindus

 time   people   family   ...

b) Now find words for these titles:

clothes   places   sports   jobs

P9 Sound check

L 1.15

a) Copy the words. Then listen: Which letters can't you hear? Underline them.

Chris<u>t</u>mas • <u>k</u>nife • li<u>gh</u>t • lam<u>b</u> • ha<u>l</u>f • <u>h</u>our • midni<u>gh</u>t

b) Listen again and say the words.

➡ p. LF27

Fragen mit
Fragewörtern

21R
p. 209

Satzstellung
22R
p. 210

P10 On special days

a) Look at number 14 again. Then write down the questions in the correct order.

1. does – after – Lee-Lee – do – What – the meal – ?
2. Lee-Lee's favourite food – the family – When – eat – does – ?
3. one of the dumplings – inside – is – What – ?
4. is – favourite food – What – Sammy's – ?
5. is visiting – uncle – Whose – this year – from England – ?
6. Sammy – does – Why – best – Black Friday – like – ?

b) Work with a partner. Ask and answer the questions in a).

➡ p. LF28

Satzstellung
22R
p. 210

P11 I never eat tomatoes

**Think about different food and dishes.
What do YOU *often*/*sometimes*/
never/*always* eat?**

I often eat bananas, apples and bread.
I sometimes ... ...

P12 Gillian likes celebrating LSW 215

Read what Gillian thinks about different festivals and special days.
Pick the right word to connect the sentence parts.

23R
p. 211
Konjunktionen

1. I like Christmas, especially but/when we put up a Christmas tree and decorate it. when
2. We always write Christmas cards and/but send them to friends and family. and
3. I also enjoy Halloween so/because I love wearing costumes. because
4. There is a great St Patrick's Day Parade in London so/but I've never taken part in it. but
5. I'm sure that Rajiv's favourite festival is Diwali because/when he really enjoys the lights and fireworks. because
6. What I love most is my birthday and/when friends and family come and give me presents. when
7. I don't know much about American festivals so/and I should ask Cheryl about them. so

P13 Cinco de Mayo  LSW 216

➡ p. LF28

You find this information on the Internet. Some of your classmates
need help understanding it. Answer their questions.

How to ...
help out
p. 190

> Was wird denn über das Essen gesagt?

> „Decorations" heißt Dekoration, richtig? Was wird dazu geschrieben?

> Und wie soll man sich kleiden?

> Was ist denn eine „piñata"?

> Dort steht „maracas". Was soll das sein?

News (230)▼ Favourites▼

How to celebrate Cinco de Mayo
- Don't eat Mexican-style fast food but enjoy a real Mexican meal with home-made salsa and guacamole.
- Put up Mexican-style decorations like paper flowers or balloons and use the colors of the Mexican flag (green, white, red) on your accessories.
- Put on traditional Mexican clothes. Women can choose brightly colored long skirts. Men can wear a sombrero and a white shirt or a poncho.
- Make a piñata – a decorated box filled with candy and toys. Hang it from the ceiling. Then everyone takes turns at hitting it with a stick so that it opens up. But your eyes are covered so you can't see.
- Put on some Mexican music, for example tejano, banda and cumbia. Buy or make maracas and shake them along to the music. Then invite family, friends or neighbors and have fun.

W p.229   TM, p.107

 ➡ p.LF28

How to ...
read
p. 179

 M1
p. 34

M1 Interviewing Kathy  LSW 217, 220

a) Read the last part of Cheryl's interview with Kathy. What are they talking about?

Cheryl: Some of my friends say they don't come to Super Burger because you have to wait too long for the food. Do you think they are right?

Kathy: Well, if the food takes long, it's because it's freshly prepared. We are a very popular restaurant and that means it takes longer sometimes. But you should tell your friends that they can order food from us an hour before they want it. Then you can pick it up at a fixed time without having to wait.

Cheryl: That sounds great! Another thing I wanted to ask you about was special offers. There are a lot of fast food restaurants in town. How do you make sure people want to come to Super Burger?

Kathy: Well, we spend a lot of time thinking about special offers. If you order enough food, then we deliver it for free to your door. That is always popular with families. There are also a lot of elderly people in Roselle, and we do special meals for them. They can order smaller dishes that are much cheaper.

Cheryl: I'm surprised to hear that. I thought most of your customers were young people.

Kathy: Well, they definitely are! We try to encourage teenagers to come with their friends, so sometimes we have offers like "buy five burgers, get one free", or sometimes they can get free French fries or free drinks.

Cheryl: That's cool! And do you also have special offers for kids? ... Oh, sorry, can you wait a minute, please? Something is wrong with the equipment.

How to ...
write
p. 184

b) Work with a partner. Think about special offers Super Burger has or could have for kids. Continue the dialogue between Kathy and Cheryl.

c) Present your dialogue in class.

➡ p.LF29

 M2
p. 34/35

M2 Why is fast food so popular?

a) Read the magazine article. Which information is most interesting to you?

So why is fast food so popular?

Sugar is the main ingredient that fast food companies use to get kids hooked on their products. One can of fizzy drink contains up to 10 teaspoons of sugar. The average American teenager eats about 44 kilos of sugar in a year – kids want it sweet and tasty! So flavour experts strengthen the flavour artificially and also give their products an attractive artificial colour. A lot of strawberry milkshakes, for example, have probably never even been near a strawberry.

It is not only the sugar and the artificial flavourings that hook children on fast food – it is also advertising on TV and especially on the Internet.

Another way to attract kids is to give away toys with the meals. That way children eat there two or three times more often.

b) Find words in the article that match these expressions:

a small metal container   *can*   the taste that food or drink has   *flavour*

sweet with bubbles   not natural   make something stronger   *strengthen*

fizzy   *artificial*

c) Four reasons are mentioned why fast food is so popular with kids. What are they? Tell your class about them.

M3 Customer interviews LSW 218

➡ p. LF29

L 1.11 S 5

a) Cheryl also spoke to some customers at Super Burger. Listen to three of her interviews. How many men and how many women did she talk to? one man, two women

b) Listen again. Find out and take notes:
– What do customers 1, 2 and 3 like about fast food?
– How often do they eat at places like Super Burger?
– What do they like best?

c) Compare your notes with a partner.

Cheryl

B 8
p. 42

M4 Fast food: good or bad? IWS LSW 219

➡ p. LF29

a) Some people think fast food is bad, others think it is good. Work with a partner and collect arguments for and against fast food in a grid.

good	bad
- you can eat it quickly	- can be unhealthy
- …	- …

b) Find another pair. One pair is for, the other one is against fast food. Have a discussion. You can look at page 182 for help.

c) ☀ **Think about all the arguments you talked about. Write a text and give YOUR opinion. Use the phrases below. You can look at page 186 for help.**

How to …
discuss
p. 182

How to …
write your
opinion
p. 186

WB

M3
p. 35

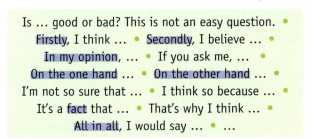
Is … good or bad? This is not an easy question. •
Firstly, I think … • Secondly, I believe … •
In my opinion, … • If you ask me, … •
On the one hand … • On the other hand … •
I'm not so sure that … • I think so because … •
It's a fact that … • That's why I think … •
All in all, I would say … • …

W p. 230   TM, p. 114

→ p. LF30

14 // B
p. 46

How to …
read
p. 179

M4
p. 36

M5 **Festivals in the USA** 👓 ✏️ 🖱 LSW 221

a) Read the blog entries about different festivals on page 46 and the one below. Collect words and information in a grid like this:

festival	food	activities
…	dumplings	…
…	…	…

MY FAVORITE FOOD ON A SPECIAL DAY

https://www.busy-bellies.com

News (230) ▼

Kwanzaa

Posted by Angel, Detroit, 05/09
For our Kwanzaa dinner we have all my favorite food (sweet potatoes, peas and chicken) and – best of all – a seafood soup called gumbo. For those who don't know what it is: Kwanzaa is celebrated from 26th December until New Year's Day. "Kwanzaa" means "first fruits of the harvest" in an African language. There are many African traditions during Kwanzaa. We decorate the home mainly in black, red and green because these are the colors of Kwanzaa.

We also wear traditional African clothes. The women and girls usually wear a colorful dress called kaftan. The men and boys normally wear a colorful shirt and a hat. Last year I wore my mom's kaftan. I felt so pretty and so proud!

Seven is an important number in Kwanzaa. The holiday is seven days long and there is an extra 'a' in the word "Kwanzaa" so that it has seven letters. There are seven candles in a candle holder called kinara – three green candles on the right, three red candles on the left and one black candle in the middle. A candle is lit on each day, the black one is lit first. On the last day we give each other presents that we've made.

lunar calendar, midnight, coin, corn on the cob, seafood, hat

b) Find the English words for "Mondkalender", "Mitternacht", "Münze", "Maiskolben", "Meeresfrüchte" and "Mütze" in the three blog entries. Don't use your dictionary.

c) Complete the sentences.
1. After dinner Lee-Lee and his cousin … always play on Lee-Lee's computer.
2. If you find a coin in your dumpling, you … will have a lot of money in your life.
3. This year's Thanksgiving Sammy's … uncle from England will be there.
4. On Black Friday … Sammy and his parents go shopping.
5. People celebrate Kwanzaa … from 26th December until New Year's Day.
6. A kinara is … a candle holder.

d) Tell someone who hasn't read Angel's blog entry about Kwanzaa. Use your grid from a).

M6 American English or British English? 🎧 ✏️

➡ p. LF30

🔘 **L 1.16**

WB **M5 + M6**
p. 36/37

a) Sammy's uncle Harry from England is helping Sammy's mother with the shopping for their Thanksgiving dinner. Listen to them. What two words does Harry mix up?

b) Look at the **shopping list**. Then listen again. Find words that are different in British and American English. Complete your list from Theme 1.

British English 🇬🇧	American English 🇺🇸
sweets	…
biscuits	…
…	…

Shopping list:
- eggs (12)
- butter
- onions (6/7)
- potatoes
- chips
- turkey
- candy (for the kids)
- cookies
- bread
- French fries

M7 ☀️ Different Thanksgiving dinners 👄 ✏️ Folie 6

➡ p. LF31

🖱 LSW 222–224

a) Work in a small group. Look at the **scenes** from different families' Thanksgiving dinners. What could the people be saying or thinking? Talk about your ideas.

b) Choose one scene. **Think of** a dialogue and make notes. Then **act it out** in class.

WB ☀️ **M7**
p. 37

CAMDEN CHRONICLE
LEARN ENGLISH THE CAMDEN WAY

DID YOU GET IT ALL? → p. LF31

» What is a PB&J sandwich?
» Where does Loco Moco come from?
» What is the busiest day in Super Burger?
» Why do Sam and his mother sometimes eat at Super Burger?
» What do Americans celebrate on 4th July?
» When can you buy green bagels?
» What do Americans eat on Thanksgiving?
» When was the first Thanksgiving?

GOOD TO KNOW ...

In einem Restaurant in den USA darf man sich in der Regel nicht einfach an irgendeinen freien Tisch setzen. Stattdessen muss man am Eingang warten, bis die Bedienung einen zu einem freien Tisch führt. Im Eingangsbereich findet sich ein entsprechendes Schild mit dem Hinweis *Please wait to be seated*. Dies ist in Großbritannien übrigens vielfach auch so.

AMERICAN FOOD INVENTIONS

Popsicle

This was invented by Frank Epperson in 1905, and he was only eleven years old! One night he put his fruit drink outside and left it to freeze. The next morning it was a delicious "popsicle". Frank also invented the "twin-popsicle" (for two people to eat) and the "creamsicle". Guess what is in it.

Chewing gum

The first chewing gum was invented by Frank Henry Fleer in 1906. It was called "Blibber-Blubber" and wasn't very popular. The name was funny but the gum was too sticky to chew. In 1928 Walter E. Diemer made chewing gum with better ingredients. Since then chewing gum has been a big hit.

Cotton candy

This was invented by William Morrison in 1897. Cotton candy is soft, sweet and usually pink. It is made with hot sugar and looks like a cotton ball. It is really delicious to eat, especially at funfairs! Have you ever tried it?

NEW PLACES, NEW FACES

In diesem *Theme* ...

» erfährst du Interessantes über Sehenswürdigkeiten in New York.
» lernst du verschiedene Stadtteile New Yorks und einige ihrer Bewohner kennen.
» arbeitest du an einem Projekt über New York.
» beschäftigst du dich mit dem Alltag von Jugendlichen in anderen Teilen der Welt.
» liest du über *Fairtrade*.

p.231   TM, p. 119

➡ p. LF32

1 New York City 🖉 👄 📖 p. 36/1

How to ...
work with
others
p. 188

a) **Give and take:** Think of New York. Write down two
or three facts that you know. Then walk around the
classroom and ask your classmates about their facts.
Give one of your facts to each classmate you talk to
and take one from everyone you talk to.

b) Go through all the facts, then get together in small
groups and talk about them. Present your **results** to
the class.

In New York ⟩ there is/are ...
there must be ...
you can see/
visit/go to ...
...

➡ p. LF32

2 Things to see in New York 👓 👄 🖱 IWS 📖 p. 37/2

1 + 2
p. 38

Look at the photos and read the information.
– Which sights would you like to see?
– Where would you like to go? Say why.

 LSW 301–304

I would like to see ... because
it sounds interesting/...

I would like to go to ...
because I like ...

**1 The Empire
State Building**
– is easy to find in
the skyline
– has 102 floors
– is 443 m high
– has 1,860 **steps**
to the top

2 Central Park
– is one of the
largest parks in
NYC
– is 4 km long
– has a large zoo

3 The Statue of Liberty
– was given to the people of America by the
French in 1886
– is a **symbol** of **freedom**
– was the first thing many **immigrants** saw
when they arrived in the USA

4 Ellis Island
– was the **main immigration** station in the
USA from 1892 to 1954
– over 12 million immigrants arrived there
– is now a museum about immigration to
the USA

6 Fifth Avenue
– is an important
  shopping street
– has lots of great
  shops
– is one of the most
  expensive streets in
  the world to live on

5 Broadway
– is the longest street in NYC (> 20 km)
– is home to many theaters
– has shown many popular musicals
  such as *Cats* and *The Lion King*

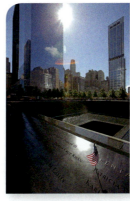

8 Ground Zero is the place where
– the World Trade Center stood
– thousands of people died on
  9/11/2001 when the Twin Towers
  were destroyed (this day is now
  called "nine eleven")
– the new One World Trade Center
  (tallest skyscraper in NYC at
  541 m) and the 9/11 Memorial
  Museum were opened in 2014

7 The MoMA
– is the famous
  Museum of
  Modern Art
– first opened
  in 1929
– is free
  on Friday
  afternoons
  and evenings

9 Times Square
– is a famous square in the heart of Manhattan
– is known for its many large ads (some as tall
  as buildings!) and bright lights
– has shops and restaurants that are open until
  midnight or even 24 hours a day

wordbank
Time
p. 172

M M1 + M2
p. 74/75

---

3 ## What you can do 👄 ✏️

➡ p. LF32

**Look at the sights on both pages again. Then give advice to someone
who wants to spend some time in New York.**

🔍 **11R**
Bedingungs- p. 203
sätze, Typ I

WB **3**
p. 39

If you want to	see visit climb go (to)	animals, shopping at 11 pm, some modern paintings, 1,860 steps, a symbol of freedom, a very expensive street, …	you can go to	…

p. 232

➡ p. LF32

L 1.17

How to …
listen
p. 178

4 A song about New York

a) Listen to the song 'New York City' by They Might Be Giants. What can you understand?
b) Listen again. Is the singer happy or unhappy? Does he like New York? Say why.
c) Look at the sights on pages 58 – 61. Then listen a third time. Which of these sights does the singer mention?

➡ p. LF32

DVD

4
p. 39

5 Sights in the city   IWS p. 38/3

Watch the clip. Describe what you have just seen.
Which of the sights do you know? What are their names?

High Line Park

Grand Central Terminal

View of the One World Trade Center and Lower Manhattan

The Empire State Building at night on St Patrick's Day

Chinatown

Flatiron Building

Brooklyn Bridge

Staten Island Ferry and the Statue of Liberty

Coney Island

The Rockefeller Center Christmas Tree and Ice-Skating Rink

p. 232

➡ p. LF32

L 1.18 S 6

5
p. 40

P1 + P2 + P7   P
p. 70/71

6 Tourists in New York

a) You are going to listen to three interviews with some tourists. First copy the grid.
Then listen and take notes on:
– where they are from
– what they think of first when asked about New York

 pp. 42–43/6 und 7

	Pierre	Lindsay	Steffen
where from?	…	…	…
first things that come to mind	…		

b) Listen again. What information does the reporter give
to the tourists? Add the information to the grid.

c) Work with a partner and compare your notes.

➡ p. LF33

6
p. 41

M3   M
p. 75

wordbank
Travelling
p. 166

7 Visiting New York

a) Make a list of your top three
New York sights.

b) Why did you choose them?
Try to **convince** your classmates
why they should visit them.
Look at pages 58 – 61 for ideas.
Then write it down.

> My favourite New York sight is … •
> a 'must-see' because … •
> the biggest/best/most exciting/… •
> a perfect place to relax /… •
> the ideal place to watch/… • …

c) Put up all the texts in the classroom.
Then look at your classmates' texts.
Put a smiley (☺) on the text
you like most.

 IWS    pp. 40–41/4 und 5

> My top three New York sights
> My favourite sight in New York City is …
> You should go there because …
> …

3

8 From Manhattan to the Bronx   KVs 3.3 pp. 42f./6+7 ➡ p. LF33

a) **Listen to five New Yorkers. In which New York borough do they live?**

 LSW 306 **L 1.19**

I'm from the Middle East but I've lived in New York for eight years. My apartment is in the north of Manhattan, in the part called Harlem. I have a hot dog stall. It's hard work because I work six days a week. But I like New York: There's so much going on here.

the Bronx

Manhattan

Queens

Brooklyn

Bilal Hinawy, 26

Staten Island

You know, a lot of people are scared of the Bronx. And yeah, we had problems here, but it's better now. Man, this is where hip hop started in the 1970s. And we got the Yankee Stadium. I sometimes go and watch games. I live here with my mom and aunt in a small apartment. At home we only speak Spanish 'cause my mom comes from Puerto Rico.

Joshua Rodriguez, 16

I've lived in Queens for eight years and I'm proud of it. People from all over the world live here, not just immigrants from the Caribbean. You can hear all kinds of languages and eat all kinds of food. People here learn how to be cool with each other, or just leave each other in peace.

I live on Staten Island and have done so all my life but I work in Manhattan. I'm a doctor. Every day I take the Staten Island Ferry to work, past the Statue of Liberty. When I see it, I think of my grandparents. They came from Italy in 1912 and 'Lady Liberty' was the first thing they saw when they arrived at Ellis Island.

Paul Beliard, 17

Brooklyn is the best. I grew up here in an old house. I go to high school in Manhattan but I'm glad to get back here in the evening. It's not so loud and busy and there are lots of trees and parks. Brooklyn also has many cool little shops with clothes and shoes.

Marian Jones, 15

Antonia Siempre, 45

\\ M4: Auswertung wie hier in b), aber ohne *sentence switchboard*

b) Now read the statements and say what the people have done or been.  LSW 305

Bilal		lived there for eight years.
Antonia		already watched games in the Yankee Stadium.
Joshua		always been proud to live in Queens.
Marian	has	been to many shops for clothes and shoes.
Paul	have	been a doctor for many years.
... and ...		never visited his family in Puerto Rico.
..., ... and ...		lived in New York all her life/their lives.

P P3 – P5
p. 70/71

M M4
p. 75

M M5
p. 75

6R
p. 198

WB 7 + 8
p. 41/42
Present perfect

W p. 232

9 Talking about neighbourhoods KVs 3.1

P6 P
p. 71

17R
p. 206
Relativsätze

Read these definitions. What is it? Find the words in the statements on page 63.
1. a person who comes to live in a new country immigrant
2. a group of islands which is between North and South America the Caribbean
3. a neighbourhood that some people are scared of the Bronx
4. a word that means the same as flat apartment
5. a neighbourhood which is part of Manhattan Harlem

10 Quiz time p. 44/8

➡ p. LF33

9
p. 42

21R
p. 209

Fragen mit
Fragewörtern

a) Look at number 8 again and make up five questions about the people and their neighbourhoods.

Who? • What? • Where?
When? • Why?

b) Then test your partner. Take turns.

> Who speaks Spanish at home?

> Joshua, right? OK, my turn. Where can you find lots of little shops?

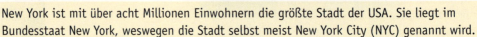

LAND & LEUTE

The Big Apple

New York ist mit über acht Millionen Einwohnern die größte Stadt der USA. Sie liegt im Bundesstaat New York, weswegen die Stadt selbst meist New York City (NYC) genannt wird.

Es gibt verschiedene Legenden, warum New York den Spitznamen *The Big Apple* bekommen hat. Am wahrscheinlichsten ist es, dass Jazzmusiker in den 1930er Jahren den Begriff prägten. New York galt für sie als die beste Stadt für Auftritte, eben als „der große Apfel" unter den vielen Äpfeln an einem Baum.

Die Menschen, die hier leben, kommen aus der ganzen Welt. Es gibt u.a. eine große afro-amerikanische Bevölkerungsgruppe und eine der größten jüdischen Gemeinden der Welt.

New York hat fünf Stadtteile (*boroughs*): Manhattan, Brooklyn, die Bronx, Staten Island und Queens. Sieh dir dazu auch die Karten von New York hinten im Buch an. Manhattan mit seinen Wolkenkratzern ist der berühmteste, aber auch der kleinste Stadtteil New Yorks. Hier leben rund 1,6 Millionen Menschen, und etwa zwei Millionen pendeln täglich zur Arbeit hierher. Der bevölkerungsreichste Stadtteil ist Brooklyn mit 2,5 Millionen Einwohnern. Er ist vor allem für seine kulturelle Vielfalt bekannt. In der Bronx gibt es sehr arme Gegenden, in denen die Verbrechensrate hoch ist. Die Bronx ist aber auch berühmt für ihren Zoo. Staten Island ist der ländlichste Teil New Yorks mit vielen Wäldern und Seen und wurde ursprünglich Richmond genannt. Queens ist New Yorks Stadtteil mit der größten Fläche. Entlang der zentralen *Roosevelt Avenue* sollen Menschen aus über 125 verschiedenen Ländern leben.

Gibt es dort, wo du wohnst, auch verschiedene Viertel? Wie würdest du sie beschreiben?

11 A project – YOUR favourite New York sight ✎ 👄

📁 portfolio

WWW

KVs 3.5, 3.6

📖 p. 44/8

PLAN IT

- **Work in groups. Choose a New York sight that you would like to know more about:**
  the Rockefeller Center, Ellis Island,
  Central Park, the Yankee Stadium, ...
- **Make notes on what you already know about the sight.**
- **Find more information on the Internet. Try to find photos, too.**

DO IT

- **Look at everything you have found. Find the most important information in the texts:**
  - What do the pictures and headlines tell you?
  - Highlight the most important facts in each paragraph.
  - Try to find a headline for each paragraph.
  - Decide which information you want to present.
- **Think about how to present your information:**
  - brochure
  - computer presentation
  - ...
- **Write down the information. Try to use your own words.**
- **Choose pictures, maps, ...**
- **Make a handout with three quiz questions for your classmates.**
- **Prepare your presentation.**

CHECK IT

- **Is the English OK?**
- **Is it interesting? Add details.**
- **Show it to other classmates or your teacher.**
- **Edit it. Use a dictionary.**
- **Practise what you want to say.**

PRESENT IT

- **Put up your brochure and talk about it or show your computer presentation or ...**
- **Swap quiz questions with the other teams. Read and listen carefully to answer the questions.**

What is Broadway	There are 40 Broadway theaters; they all have more than 500 seats and are in the Broadway area of Manhattan. The Broadway area is between 41st and 54th Streets and from 6th Avenue to 9th Avenue. This includes Times Square. The Broadway area is bigger than the actual street called Broadway and there are only four Broadway theaters actually on Broadway. 'Broadway' can mean the street or the plays in those theaters. Another name for Broadway is 'the Great White Way'. This name was first used in a newspaper, *The New York Evening Telegram*, and refers to the theaters' bright white lights.
How Broadway works	When shows begin, the 'producers' (the people who spend money to support the show at the start) do not know how long it will go on for. They wait to see how popular a play is before they decide how long it should last. Broadway also has its own kind of awards. A Tony Award is a bit like an Academy Award, but only for Broadway actors and shows. The Tony Awards started in 1947 and take place every year in the Radio City Music Hall. Neil Patrick Harris has hosted the award ceremony four times—in 2009, 2011, 2012 and 2013. *The Producers* has won the most Tony Awards, with 12 wins. Some of the most successful shows go on for a very long time. *Phantom of the Opera* is one of the longest-running shows, with more than 11,000 performances. Other very popular productions are *Cats, Chicago, The Lion King* and *Les Misérables*.
History of Broadway	The first Broadway theaters started to appear in the late 1800s and early 1900s. The 1920s was one of the most successful times for Broadway but during the Great Depression in the 1930s it was much harder for theaters to survive. However, in the 1940s, Broadway really started to do well and some of the most famous shows come from that time. For example, in 1943 *Oklahoma!* opened and was very successful. It went on for 2212 performances. There were other big successes in the 1940s as well, for example: *The Glass Menagerie* and *A Streetcar Named Desire*. Both of these famous plays were written by Tennessee Williams.
Broadway today	Today Broadway is still one of New York's main attractions and almost everyone has heard of very popular Broadway shows like *Wicked* or *Mamma Mia*. From 2012-2013, more than $1.1 billion was spent on tickets, and more than 12 million tickets were sold.
Other information	If you want to buy Broadway tickets, you can either go to the theaters and buy them at the box office, or you can go to special little shops in Times Square or at the Lower Manhattan Theater Center, where you can buy them more cheaply. The disadvantage is that there is less choice and you have to buy the tickets the same day as the performance.

Broadway

What is Broadway?
The Broadway area of Manhattan is between 41st and 54th Streets, and 6th Avenue to 9th Avenue. A Broadway theatre has to be in the Broadway area and it also has to have more than 500 seats. Broadway is also a name of a major street in this area, but there are only four Broadway theatres on that street.

The history of Broadway
In the late 1800s and early 1900s the first Broadway theatres started to appear. The theatres were very popular and successful in the 1920s. In the 1940s Broadway started to do very well again and many very famous shows come from this time, for example *Oklahoma!*.

How Broadway works
Broadway has its own awards that are as important as Academy Awards: the Tony Awards. The awards started in 1947. The show with the most Tony Awards (12) is *The Producers*.

The other way to know if a show has been successful is to see how long it has lasted. For example, *The Phantom of the Opera*, with more than 11,000 performances, is one of the longest-running shows.

Broadway today
Broadway is still one of New York's major attractions. Almost everyone knows very popular shows like *Cats, Les Misérables* or *Wicked*. From 2012-2013 more than $1.1 billion was spent on tickets and more than 12 million tickets were sold.

Other information
If you want to buy tickets to see a show, then you can buy them at the theatre or at little shops in Times Square or at the Lower Manhattan Theater Center.

🔧 How to ... write p. 184

🔧 How to ... give a talk p. 180

🔧 How to ... give feedback p. 181

p.233   TM, p.139

→ p.LF34

12 YOUR life   KVs 3.4

How to ...
work with others
p. 188

10
p. 43

Buzz groups: What is your life like? Describe it.
– Where do you live? Who do you live with?
– When do you get up, have breakfast and leave the house?
– What do you do in your free time?
– Do you have to do any jobs at home? What jobs?
– Do you have a room of your own?
– Do you have your own TV, computer or mobile phone?

> I live in ... with ...

> I get up at ... I (don't) have breakfast ...

> In my free time I ...

> ...

→ p.LF34

13 Different lives   KVs 3.2   p.45/9   LSW 307

M6
p. 76

M7
p. 77

11 + 12
p. 43/44

How to ...
read
p. 179

wordbank
People
p. 167

// M6: Text über
weitere Jugend-
liche; Auswertung
ähnlich wie hier,
aber auf alle drei
Texte bezogen:
a) identisch,
b) why-Fragen,
c) identisch.

a) Read what two children from different parts of the world say about their lives. What is similar?

Allimar

We live in a village near Kandy in Sri Lanka. I have a sister who is nine years old and two brothers. The little one is five and the other is seven years old. I'm the oldest, I'm ten.

My father is a farmer. He doesn't earn enough money to feed all of us. So my mother went to Saudi Arabia with other women from our village. They found work there.

Now I have to do a lot of my mother's work in the house. I get up early, about half past five every day. First I collect water and make a fire for tea. Then I make bread for everyone and wake my brothers and sister. School starts at nine o'clock and finishes at two o'clock. When we are home again, I make lunch. After lunch I wash the dishes in the river. Later I collect wood for the fire. Then it is time to make the evening meal. It's only a small one with rice and vegetables.

After the meal I do my homework. We don't have any electricity so I use an oil lamp when it gets dark. I go to bed at about half past nine. Sometimes I listen to the radio that our mother sent us.

Raúl

I'm thirteen years old and I'm a shoeshine boy in Mexico City. I live with my two brothers and three sisters in a small house outside the city centre. Our parents died in an accident four years ago.

I get up at six every morning and wake up my sisters. They have to go to the market place and collect water for us. I don't have any breakfast. I leave the house and try to get on a bus to town. I don't have any money so I hang on to the back of the bus.

In the city I jump off the bus and go to the business centre. I clean shoes all morning, mostly expensive ones from business people. Sometimes I earn about 100 pesos but that is not much money to buy food for six people.

At lunchtime I go home and have something to eat. Then I go to school for three hours.

I do my homework in the evening. We have no electricity so when it's too dark to read, I just go to bed. My sisters share a bed – it's the one that belonged to our parents. My brothers and I sleep on the floor.

b) **Right or wrong? Correct what's wrong.**

1. There are six people in Allimar's family. *right*
2. Allimar's father works in Saudi Arabia. *wrong*
3. Allimar washes the dishes in the sea. *wrong*
4. She doesn't have a radio. *wrong*
5. Raúl's sisters collect water at the market. *right*
6. Raúl walks to town because he has no money. *wrong*
7. He has a TV at home. *wrong*
8. He earns a lot of money. *wrong*

c) **Find the sentences with "one" or "ones" in the texts. Write them in your exercise book. What can you write instead of "one" or "ones" in these sentences? Compare your results with a partner.**

P8 – P10
p. 72

→ p. LF34

Stützwörter
one/ones

P11 + P12
p. 72/73

How to …
work with
grammar
p. 190

26
p. 212

WB 13
p. 44

→ p. LF34

14 Sebastian's life 🎧 ✏️ 🖱️ IWS

a) **Look at the photo of Sebastian.
What do you think: Where is he from?**
b) **What could his life be like?
Make some notes on your ideas.**
c) **Now listen to Sebastian and find out:**
   – Where does he live?
   – Who earns the money for the family?
   – What does Sebastian do to earn some money?
   – What else can you understand?
d) **If you could give Sebastian a present, what would it be?**

L 1.20 S 7

WB 14 + 15
p. 45

15 A letter ✏️ 🖱️ LSW 308

Write a letter from Allimar to her mother. Tell her about what has happened in the last month. Use the text in number 13 for help or use your imagination.
Use ...
– time words *(in the morning, after that, then, ...)*,
– linking words *(and, because, but, ...)*,
– adjectives to make the letter interesting and to show how Allimar feels
  (sad, happy, proud, tired, ...).
You can start like this:

Dear Mum,
How are you? We all miss you so much.
Let me tell you what has happened in the last four
weeks. ...

→ p. LF35

How to …
write a letter
p. 185

wordbank
People
p. 167

W p. 233

➡ p. LF35

M9
p. 77

How to …
read
p. 179

16 Fairtrade 👄 👓 📖 p. 46/10

a) Look at the logo on the website. Have you seen it **before**?
What do you know about it?

b) Now read the website. What is it about?

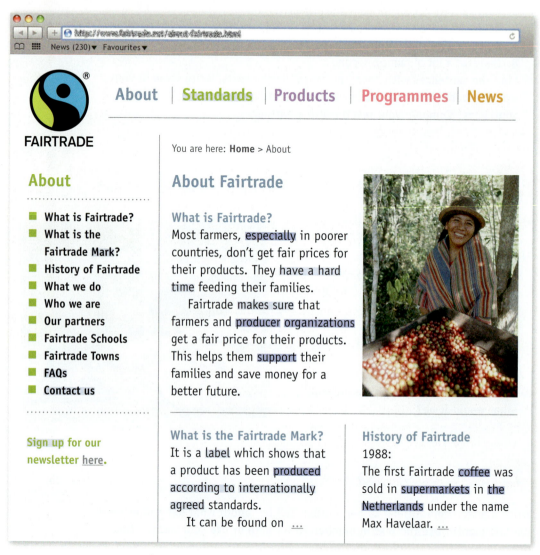

FAIRTRADE

About | Standards | Products | Programmes | News

You are here: **Home** > About

About

- **What is Fairtrade?**
- **What is the Fairtrade Mark?**
- **History of Fairtrade**
- **What we do**
- **Who we are**
- **Our partners**
- **Fairtrade Schools**
- **Fairtrade Towns**
- **FAQs**
- **Contact us**

Sign up for our newsletter here.

About Fairtrade

What is Fairtrade?
Most farmers, especially in poorer countries, don't get fair prices for their products. They have a hard time feeding their families.

Fairtrade makes sure that farmers and producer organizations get a fair price for their products. This helps them support their families and save money for a better future.

What is the Fairtrade Mark?
It is a label which shows that a product has been produced according to internationally agreed standards.

It can be found on …

History of Fairtrade
1988:
The first Fairtrade coffee was sold in supermarkets in the Netherlands under the name Max Havelaar. …

c) Read the website again and find out:
– What does Fairtrade want to do?
– What is the "Fairtrade Mark" (logo) good for?

www

d) Work in groups and find out more about Fairtrade, for example on the Internet. Here are some ideas:
– What is a "Fairtrade School"? How can a school become one?
– What is a "Fairtrade Town"? Are there any in Germany?
– What can we do to support Fairtrade?
Present your information to the class.

16
p. 46/47

17 Helping small farmers LSW 309, 310

➡ p. LF35

a) Read about banana farmers in the Windward Islands. What has changed for them since they started selling their products to Fairtrade organizations?

How to …
read
p. 179

A BETTER LIFE FOR BANANA FARMERS

In the last 20 years life has become very hard for small banana farmers. Big companies can grow bananas much more cheaply than small farmers can and the price of bananas has fallen all over the world.

In the Windward Islands in the Caribbean bananas are grown on small family farms. In the 1990s the island farmers were no longer able to sell enough bananas to make a living. A lot of them had to give up growing bananas.

But some continued on their farms. The farmers joined Fairtrade organizations because for them this was the only way to survive. The banana farmers now get a fair price for their work and their products. So they have at least enough money for themselves and their families. They also get some extra money, which they can use for special projects, such as building better roads. Another good thing is that the farmers now use fewer chemicals. Today about 85% of the banana farmers in the Windward Islands are Fairtrade producers.

So next time you go to a supermarket, why not buy Fairtrade bananas? They cost a bit more than other bananas but you can be sure that you are supporting the people who grew them.

b) ☾ Read the article again and complete the sentences.
1. Fairtrade organizations give banana farmers in the Windward Islands a XX price. fair
2. Now the farmers have enough XX for themselves and their XX. families
3. They also get extra XX for special XX. money – projects
4. Now the farmers also use XX chemicals. fewer
5. Today XX of the banana farmers in the Windward Islands are Fairtrade XX. 85% – producers

P | P13
p. 73

M | M10
p. 77

18 Choose an activity

M | M8
p. 77

portfolio

You can …
- write about a typical day in your life.
  Look at numbers 12 and 13 for help.
- choose one of the countries in numbers 13 and 14: Sri Lanka, Mexico or Brazil. Find a map and pictures. Find out more about this country and about the people who live there. Then present your information to the class.
- find supermarkets in your area which sell Fairtrade products. What kind of products do they offer? Make a list and compare the prices with those of "regular" products. Present your results in class.

A day in my life
I live in Hofgeismar with my mum and my dad.
I usually get up at 6.45 am and have breakfast. I leave the house at 7.30 am. Then I walk to school with my friend Ivo. School usually finishes at …

 test yourself
p. 48/49

p. 234   TM, p. 151

 ➡ p. LF36

P1 City life ✏ LSW 311

a) Write down what comes to your mind when you think of a city.

cars, lots to see, …

b) What is **positive** and **negative** about city life? Make a grid.

positive	negative
lots to see	expensive flats
…	…

P2 Tongue twisters 👂 👄

 L 1.21

Listen to the **tongue twisters.** Then say them yourself.

Red lorry, yellow lorry,
red lorry, yellow lorry.

You know New York.
You need New York.
You know you need unique New York.

P3 Article or no article? ✏ LSW 312

Nomen mit/
ohne Artikel

24
p. 211

Are the names of these places used with or without *the*? Add *the* if **necessary.**
Look at pages 58 – 59 and 63 for help.
1. XX Ellis Island –
2. XX Empire State Building *the*
3. XX Brooklyn –
4. XX Statue of Liberty *the*
5. XX Fifth Avenue –
6. XX Central Park –
7. XX Bronx *the*
8. XX Broadway –

➡ p. LF36

P4 Working with a map 👓 ✏

Look at the maps at the back of your book and complete these sentences.
1. Times Square is on …
2. Brooklyn Bridge goes across the …
3. Chinatown is part of …
4. Coney Island is part of …
5. The Rockefeller Center is on …
6. Manhattan is between …

P5 Facts about yourself ✏️ 👄

➡️ p. LF36

🔍 6R
p. 198
Present perfect

a) Write down at least five statements about yourself.
Use the correct *past participle* forms of the verbs.

| I have | never already | (visit) New York • (go) up a skyscraper • (paint) a picture • (draw) graffiti • (eat) a bagel • (meet) an American • (visit) a museum • (be) on a ferry • ... |

– I have never visited New York.
– I have already ...
– ...

b) Interview a partner. Take turns.
What **have** you got **in common**?

Have you ever ...?

Yes, I have./ No, I haven't.

P6 Definitions ✏️

➡️ p. LF36

🔍 17R
p. 206
Relativsätze

Explain these words from the statements in number 8:

a park • a shop • a mother • a doctor • a stadium • an aunt

Here is some help: ... is a person who ...   ... is a place where ...

P7 "Oh no, it's all in German ..."   KVs 3.7 🖱️ LSW 313

➡️ p. LF36

🔧 How to ...
help out
p. 190

You are on a **class trip** to Berlin. You are doing a tour of the city. An American tourist doesn't understand German. Tell him five important things that the **tour guide** says at the **beginning** of the tour.

Hallo, meine Damen und Herren! Schön, dass Sie an unserer Stadtführung teilnehmen wollen. Mein Name ist Kai Müller. Ich werde Ihnen heute unsere schöne Stadt zeigen. Die Führung wird etwa zweieinhalb Stunden dauern – das heißt, dass Sie pünktlich um 13 Uhr zu Mittag essen können. Vorher zeige ich Ihnen verschiedene wichtige Sehenswürdigkeiten Berlins. Ich werde Ihnen jeweils kurz etwas über die Geschichte der Orte erzählen. Fragen Sie einfach nach, wenn Sie mehr wissen möchten. OK, dann lassen Sie uns losgehen ...

The tour/tour guide will ...

We can ...

...

p.234 TM, p. 153

→ p. LF37

P8 Odd one out ✎

a) Find the odd one out.

1. farmer • teacher • nurse • brother
2. boat • bus • village • car
3. Saudi Arabia • Mexico City • England • Germany

4. TV • oil lamp • computer • radio
5. shoeshine boy • father • sister • mother
6. morning • lunchtime • meal • evening

b) Why is it the odd one out?

1. "Brother" is the odd one out because it is not a job.
2. ... is the odd one out because you can't ...
...

c) Write a new 'odd one out' for your partner.

→ p. LF37

L 1.22

P9 Sound check 👓 👂 🖱 LSW 314

a) What can you read here? Write it down.

1. /ˈælɪmaː həz‿ə ˈsɪstər‿ən tu ˈbrʌðəz/
2. /hə ˈfaːðə ˌdʌznt‿ˈɜːn‿ˌɪˌnʌf ˈmʌni/
3. /raʊˈuːl ˌkliːnz‿ˈʃuːz‿ɪn ˌmeksɪkəʊ ˈsɪti/

b) Listen and check.

→ p. LF37

27R
p. 212
Mengenangaben

P10 Raúl from Mexico City 👓 ✎ 🖱 LSW 315

Complete the sentences with *some* or *any*.

In the morning Raúl's sisters go to the market place and collect **XX** water for the family. Raúl doesn't have **XX** breakfast. He leaves the house and gets on a bus to town. He doesn't have **XX** money so he hangs on to the back of the bus. In the city Raúl earns **XX** money because he cleans shoes all morning. Before he goes to school, he has **XX** rice and beans at home. They don't have **XX** electricity in their house so when it's too dark to read, Raúl goes to bed.

Stützwörter
one/ones
26
p. 212

P11 Don't repeat it, please 👓 ✎

Replace the marked word in each sentence with *one* or *ones*.

1. Have you seen my sneakers? They are the red sneakers with the white label. *ones*
2. This bus is more comfortable than the bus we usually take. *one*
3. Most students at my school take the bus from the city centre. The others take the bus from the station. *one*
4. Our new kitchen is bigger than the kitchen in our old house – and I have to clean it! *one*
5. Our flat has three bedrooms and my sister and I sleep in the two smallest bedrooms. *ones*
6. This computer is much faster than the computer we use at school. *one*

P12 Which ones? LSW 316

 26
p. 212
Stützwörter
one/ones

a) Copy the sentences and complete them with *one* or *ones*.
1. Every morning Allimar makes a fire. It's only a small XX to heat the water. **one**
2. The country where Allimar's mother lives is much bigger than the XX where her children live. **one**
3. Allimar wants to become a teacher. She loves children, especially the little XX. **ones**
4. Every morning Raúl gets on a bus. It's the XX that goes to the city centre. **one**
5. The shoes Raúl cleans are much more expensive than the XX his parents owned. **ones**
6. Raúl loves books, especially exciting XX. **ones**

b) Mark the words *one* or *ones* and the words they stand for in your sentences. Draw a line between the words.

➡ p. LF37

1. Every morning Allimar makes a fire. It's only a small **one** to heat the water.
2. ...

P13 A bake sale party

➡ p. LF38

a) Read the poster. What do you learn about the bake sale party at Haverstock School? Tell a classmate in German.

How to ...
help out
p. 190

Die Klasse 10E veranstaltet ...   Es gibt ...   ... findet statt am ...   ...

b) Listen to a student and a customer at the bake sale party at Haverstock School. What did the students do to organise the party? Where does the money go to? What does the customer buy? Tell a partner in German.

 L 1.23

W p. 234    TM, p. 155

➡ p. LF38

M1 A graffiti artist 👓 👄   📄 Folie 7   🖱 LSW 317, 318

M1
WB
p. 52

How to …
read
p. 179

a) **Are there graffiti paintings in your area? What do you think about graffiti? Talk to a partner.**

b) **Read the article and find out more about graffiti and the artist Keith Haring.**

FROM GRAFFITI TO ART

Graffiti artist Keith Haring

There have always been wall paintings. But modern graffiti **only** started in 1968 when a teenager in New York used felt tips to write his name on lots of walls. Why did he do it? He said he wanted to become famous. Not too long after that more signatures or "graffiti" started to **appear** on the walls of **public** buildings or in the New York **subway**. Many people thought this was **vandalism**. It was also costing the people of New York thousands of dollars to **remove**.

Keith Haring, born in Reading, Pennsylvania, in 1958, was one of the first graffiti artists in New York. But he didn't **spray** his pictures, he used **chalk** instead. Later he made posters which he put up in subway stations.

Very often people watched him drawing his pictures. When Haring had finished a piece (as a graffiti painting is called), people **asked him questions** like: "But what does it mean?" Usually he would **give them an answer** like: "That's **up to you** – I only make the **drawing**." In his pictures you can find **crawling** babies, dancing people, barking dogs, TVs, UFOs and big fish. Later his works became famous and were sold to museums all over the world.

Thanks to Keith Haring some people started to change their opinions on graffiti, and New York **authorities gave graffiti artists more and more space** to spray **legally**. They also offered graffiti workshops, and graffiti art **galleries** opened. Keith Haring died of AIDS in 1990 at the age of 31. He is remembered by many people as a great artist and friend.

*Keith Haring art **exhibition***

c) **Find a good heading for each of the four paragraphs. Compare your ideas with a partner.**

M2
WB
p. 53

d) 🔆 **Take notes on Keith Haring, his life and his work. Then tell somebody who hasn't read the article about Keith Haring.**

M2 Graffiti in New York LSW 319

→ p. LF38

a) Write down the sentences in the correct order. Look at M1 for help.

1. Keith Haring – People – questions about his graffiti – asked
2. would usually give – an answer like "That's up to you." – them – Haring
3. thousands of dollars – was costing – the people of New York – Graffiti vandalism
4. started to give – After a **while** – graffiti artists – more space – the city authorities
5. They – artists – special graffiti workshops – also offered
6. lots of money – Haring – paid – for his paintings – Museums

b) Look at your sentences. They all have two objects.
Underline the verb and mark the two objects in different colours.

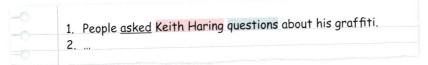

1. People asked Keith Haring questions about his graffiti.
2. ...

Verben mit
zwei Objekten

25
p. 211

How to ...
work with
grammar
p. 190

M3
p. 53

M3 A visit to New York   LSW 320

→ p. LF39

You have just spent two days in New York. Write an email to an English-speaking
friend. Tell him/her:
– where you went/what you visited and why
– how you got there (by bus/on foot/...)
– what you liked/didn't like and why
– what you ate
– what else happened
– ...
Look at pages 58 – 61 and at the maps at the back of your book for ideas.
Then write about it.

wordbank
Travelling
p. 166

How to ...
write a letter
p. 185

M4 From Manhattan to the Bronx   LSW 321

→ p. LF39

Read the statements in number 8a). Say what Bilal, Joshua
and the other three people have done or been.

Bilal and Paul have
lived there for ...

live there for eight years • already watch games in the ... •
be a doctor for many years • always be proud to live in Queens •
never visit his family in Puerto Rico • ...

B **8b**
p. 63

6R
p. 198

Present perfect

M5 The princess of Queens

→ p. LF39

L 1.24

a) Who is the "princess of Queens"? Listen to Helen Petrakis (16) and find out.
b) Listen again and complete the sentences.

1. Helen's whole family is from ...
2. Queens is famous because ...
3. Most guests come from ...
4. Helen really enjoys ...
5. Her parents love ...
6. **Although** Queens is **such** a big place, ...

➡ p. LF39

M6 **Different lives** 👓 ✏ 🖱 LSW 322

13 // B
p. 66

How to ...
read
p. 179

a) Read about Allimar and Raúl on page 66 and about Miriam on this page.
What is similar in their lives?

Miriam

I love going to school. My older sister is 15 now and she has to stay at home. She does all the cooking and looks after my younger brothers and sisters. I feel very lucky that I don't have to stay at home, but I always have to collect water in the mornings. It is fair though because everyone in my family works. My mother and my aunts work in our peanut fields and my father goes to the market in the next village and sells our vegetables and peanuts.

We live about 65 miles from Kumasi, in Ghana. The village we live in is a very small one without a market or a school. My friends and I walk to school together every day and it takes an hour. My parents have said that I can only go to school for another two years. Then I will be 14 and they say I will be old enough to look after the house and my brothers and sisters.

When I think about the future, I feel quite sad and angry. Farm work is very hard and I want to have a different job, one that would make me happy. Of course, I like living in my village: Everyone knows everyone and all my friends and family are from here. But when I'm older, I would like to live in a city, and maybe even abroad! I think I want to be a nurse, but I don't know if I can stay at school long enough. Even now I can't go to school all the time. When we harvest our peanuts, I have to work in the fields all day.

The problem is that we only make enough money to live. If there is a problem with the farm, or if someone gets ill, then sometimes my parents can't pay for us to go to school, or for our uniforms and books. Sometimes we can't buy enough food. I see how hard it is for my parents but there is nothing they can do. I want things to be different when I'm older.

b) Write the answers to these questions in your exercise book.
Why ...
1. ... did Allimar's mother go to Saudi Arabia?
2. ... does Allimar have to work so much in the house?
3. ... does Raúl have to hang on to the back of the bus?
4. ... does Raúl try to earn more than 100 pesos a day?
5. ... has Miriam only got two more years of school?
6. ... does Miriam want to go to school for longer?

Stützwörter
one/ones

How to ...
work with
grammar
p. 190

26
p. 212

c) Find the sentences with "one" or "ones" in the three texts.
Write them in your exercise book.
What can you write instead of "one" or "ones" in these
sentences? Compare your results with a partner.

M7 Think about it!   IWS LSW 323

→ p. LF40

12
p. 203

wordbank
People
p. 167

M4 + M5
p. 54

Bedingungssätze,
Typ II

a) How would YOU feel if you lived like Allimar, Raúl or Miriam?

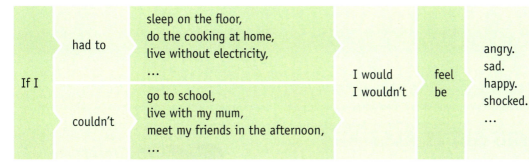

If I	had to	sleep on the floor, do the cooking at home, live without electricity, ...	I would I wouldn't	feel be	angry. sad. happy. shocked. ...
	couldn't	go to school, live with my mum, meet my friends in the afternoon, ...			

b) Imagine: What would happen if ... ?
Write at least three sentences.

> If I lived in a developing country, ...
> If there was no Internet, ...
> If dogs ruled the world, ...
> ...

M8 A diary entry

→ p. LF40

wordbank
People
p. 167

How to ...
write
p. 184

M6
p. 55

Choose Allimar, Raúl, Miriam or Sebastian. Write a diary entry for the person in which
he or she describes his or her feelings after a day of hard work. You can start like this:

> Tuesday, 16th October
> It's nine o'clock now and I'm really tired. It was a long day again
> with lots of work. In the morning ...

M9 The Fairtrade Mark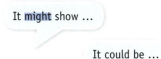

→ p. LF41

M7
p. 55

Look at the logo again. What do you think does it show?

> It might show ...

> The blue field could symbolize ...

> It could be ...

> ...

M10 Raising money   LSW 324

→ p. LF41

L 1.25

a) Listen to a class at Haverstock School. What are they talking about?
b) Listen again and take notes on these questions:
   – What ideas have the students got?
   – What is Oliver's problem?
   – What is the answer to Oliver's problem?
   – What else can you understand?
c) Compare your notes with a partner.

CAMDEN CHRONICLE
LEARN ENGLISH THE CAMDEN WAY

DID YOU GET IT ALL? → p. LF41

» What is the tallest skyscraper in NYC?
» Where can you find a zoo in Manhattan?
» What does the Empire State Building look like on St Patrick's Day?
» How can you get to Staten Island?
» What is Bilal's job?
» What does Raúl do to earn money?
» Why does Allimar miss her mother?
» Where do Sebastian and his brother sometimes watch football matches?

GOOD TO KNOW ...

Die Schreibweise des amerikanischen Datums ist besonders, denn der Monat wird dem Tag vorangestellt. Wenn dich amerikanische Freunde zu einer Party am 02/04/20.. einladen, erscheine nicht am 2. April, denn dann ist die Party schon lange vorbei. Gehe zur Freude der Gastgeber am 4. Februar hin.

Can a football be Fairtrade?

Yes, it can! The best footballs in the world are sewn by hand. Sometimes Asian children make them. They get paid very little and they don't have time to go to school. Fairtrade footballs are sewn by adults who earn enough money to support their families. And their kids don't have to work but can go to school!

You know you're a New Yorker when ...

... you think Central Park is "nature".

... you have never been to the Statue of Liberty or the Empire State Building.

... you don't own an "I ♥ New York" T-shirt.

... your door has more than three locks.

... you order your dinner and have it delivered from the place across the street.

... you are away from home and you miss "real" pizza and "real" bagels.

... you live in a building with a larger population than most American towns.

THEME 4 TM, p. 169

FINDING YOUR PLACE

In diesem *Theme* ...

» informierst du dich über Einwanderer in Amerika.
» sprichst du anhand eines Diagramms über die Bevölkerung der USA.
» lernst du die Familiengeschichte amerikanischer Teenager kennen.
» erfährst du Interessantes über die Ureinwohner Amerikas.
» hältst du ein Kurzreferat über *Native Americans*.

➡ p. LF42

1 Many people, one nation 👓 👄 📖 pp. 50–51/1 und 2

1
p. 56

a) **What do you think or know: What kind of people live in the US?**
b) **Look at the pictures and read the information. What do you find most interesting?**

A
In the last 100 years millions of immigrants have become American citizens.

B
One of the largest groups of Chinese immigrants lives in San Francisco. A lot of Chinese immigrants came to the country during the 1880s to work on the railroad.

C
There are as many as 12 million illegal immigrants living in America. Most of them came because they wanted a better life for themselves and their children. They are usually from Mexico or other parts of Central or South America.

D
People came to America from Siberia thousands of years ago. Until the Europeans came about 500 years ago, the Native Americans lived in harmony with the land. Today there are about 2.5 million Native Americans. Most of them live on reservations.

E
Today it is not so easy to immigrate to the US. One way is to win the 'green card' in a lottery. With a green card you are allowed to live and work in America.

F

The first settlers to America came mainly from England. Then more and more people came to the US from Ireland, Italy, Germany and other countries.

G

The total population of the United States is about 318 million.

H

Immigrants from Mexico, South and Central America are called Hispanics or Latinos. Spanish is often their first language. In some areas of the US more than one third of the population only speaks Spanish so many signs are in English and Spanish.

Gates C101 - C115
Puertas C101 - C115

Gates C70 - C99
Puertas C70 - C99

I

In 1863 there were four million black slaves in the US. After the American Civil War (1861-1865) the slaves were free but still didn't have the same rights as white Americans. During the 1960s people like Martin Luther King and Malcolm X fought for the rights of both African Americans and other black Americans. Today about 40 million blacks live in the US.

➡ p. LF42

c) Find the answers to these questions.

1. What do you need a green card for?
2. How many people live in the US?
3. Where do most illegal immigrants in the US come from?
4. Who fought for the rights of blacks in the 1960s?
5. Why did many Chinese people come to the US in the 1880s?
6. Where did most of the first settlers come from?
7. Why do you find signs in English and Spanish in the US?
8. How many Native Americans live in the US today?

P P1 – P4 + P7
p. 90/91

M M1 + M2
p. 94/95

WB 2
p. 56

➡ p. LF42

3
p. 57

wordbank
Statistics
p. 168

P5 P
p. 91

M3 M
p. 95

2 All kinds of people Folie 8 IWS p. 53/4 und p. 56/6

Look at the **statistics** and talk about them. What do you find surprising? LSW 401, 402

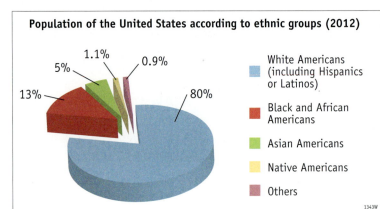

Population of the United States according to ethnic groups (2012)

1.1%
5%
0.9%
13%
80%

White Americans (including Hispanics or Latinos)

Black and African Americans

Asian Americans

Native Americans

Others

1343W

13 per cent of the population in the US are Black and African Americans.

In the US there are more/fewer ... than ...

...

➡ p. LF42

How to ...
talk about pictures
p. 183

wordbank
People
p. 167

4
p. 58

3 Leaving home   Folie 9 p. 52/3 LSW 404

a) Work with a partner. Look at the photos and describe them to each other. What can you see? What are the people doing? How do you think they feel?

How to ...
work with others
p. 188

b) **Placemat:** Why do people leave their home country and go and live in **another** country? Work in groups of four and collect your ideas on a placemat.

go and live with a partner •
war in home country • ...

c) Talk about your ideas. Then decide on the three most important ideas and write them in the middle of the placemat.

d) Tell the class about your placemat results.

4 Family histories   KVs 4.5 IWS 📖 p. 54/5 🖱 LSW 403 ➡ p. LF43

a) These American high school students talk about their families and their **experiences** in the US.

Jigsaw: Sit together in groups of three and choose one of the students. Copy the grid and complete it on your own. Then compare your notes with the rest of your group.

How to ...
work with others
p. 188

How to ...
read
p. 179

WB
5
p. 58

name	family from	why they left	experiences
Mohamed	...	...	...
Kim	...	...	
Sergio	...		

Hi, I'm Mohamed. I'm 16 years old. My family and I came to America when I was little. We left Somalia because of the civil war. I'm glad that my sisters, parents and I are safe but I'm sad when I think of Somalia. We **used to** have our own farm with lots of animals. Now we live in a small apartment in the city and my dad has to work 14 hours a day to earn enough money for all of us. My parents hope that my sisters and I will get a good **education** and will later have an easier life. I sometimes miss life **in the country** but at least we're safe here.

Hi, I'm Kim and I'm from Vietnam. My parents and I have been in the USA for three years. I was twelve when we came here. I couldn't speak English **at all**, so I had a lot of problems at school. But the teachers and the students were very nice to me and helped me a lot. When my parents first told me that they wanted to go to the USA, I was very sad. My parents both had jobs in Vietnam and were **well-paid**, but our **relatives** in the USA **persuaded** them to come and **join** the family. At first I missed my friends from Vietnam a lot. But now I have made some good friends here, too.

Hi, I'm Sergio and I'm 14 years old. I **only** moved to America last year. I live with my father who has been here for five years. He is a doctor but he couldn't find a job in Chile so he decided to come to the USA for a better life. We live in San Francisco – a great place to be. When I arrived, I was very **shy** because I didn't speak a lot of English. But Alek helped me a lot. He's from Russia and my best friend. My parents are **divorced**. My mother still lives in Chile. I often miss her. I hope to go to **college** and earn a lot of money later so that I can visit my mom in Chile and she can visit me in San Francisco. Perhaps I'll be a pilot when I grow up.

b) Now **mix up** the groups so that each group has at least one person for each high school student. Use your grid and **present** the students to each other. Listen and **note down** information about the other two students in your grid.

c) Look at the **reasons** for immigrating in your grid again. Are they similar to your ideas in number 3?

P
P6
p. 91

M4 //■M
p. 95

L 1.26

// Auswertung
auf höherem
Niveau: a) nahezu
identisch (ergänzt
um *What are they
talking about?*),
b) *answering
questions*

6 ■WB
p. 59

5 Learning English

a) All three teenagers had to learn English when they got to the US. Listen to Mohamed, Kim and Sergio and write down their names in the order you hear them talk. K – S – M

b) Listen again. Which statement best describes which teenager?

A still has some difficulty with English   Sergio

B speaks a different language at home   Mohamed

C learned English at school and by watching TV   Kim

➡ p. LF43

6 A new beginning   p. 57/7

Imagine YOU had to start a new life in another country. What would it be like? Talk to a partner.

| I think I would | miss
have to learn
have to find
have to get used to | a new language.
my old friends.
a new home.
life in a different country.
the customs.
… |

➡ p. LF43

7 ■WB
p. 59

7 What are they like?   Folie 10

a) Look at the pictures.
What stereotypes about the Americans are shown in them?

What other stereotypes about the Americans do you know? Talk to a partner.

b) Can you think of stereotypes about the Germans? Talk about your ideas with a partner. Look at the pictures for help.

c) What do you think about the stereotypes in a) and b)?

I don't believe all Americans/Germans … because …

I think it's right/wrong that …

I think so because …

8 Do as the Americans do ...    ➡ p. LF44

16R
p. 205
Imperativ

a) New Americans also have to learn what they should and shouldn't do in the US. Look at the list. What do you find surprising? Give reasons.

DOs	DON'Ts
Smile! 🙂 Americans are usually very friendly. But friendliness doesn't always mean friendship.	Don't stare at people or things that you may not like or think are strange. Always try to keep an open mind.
Do say "I'm sorry" if someone bumps into you or if you bump into someone. In America both people usually apologize after an accident.	Don't copy from books or other students' homework. In the US it is important to show that you have done your own work.

b) Work with a partner and make a list of DOs and DON'Ts for Germany.

9 This land is your land ➡ p. LF44

L 1.27

a) Listen to the song 'This land is your land' by Woody Guthrie. What can you understand?
b) Listen again and read or sing along. Then talk about the song.

> I think the song is about ...

> The music is fast/slow.

> I (don't) like the melody/rhythm/lyrics.

> The music sounds happy/sad/...

This land is your land, this land is my land
From California to the New York Island
From the Redwood Forest to the Gulf Stream waters
This land was made for you and me.

As I was walking that ribbon of highway
I saw above me that endless skyway
I saw below me that golden valley
This land was made for you and me.

I roamed and I rambled and I followed my footsteps
To the sparkling sands of her diamond deserts
While all around me a voice was sounding
This land was made for you and me.

When the sun came shining, and I was strolling
And the wheat fields waving and the dust clouds rolling
A voice was chanting, as the fog was lifting,
This land was made for you and me.

c) Look at the lyrics again. How is the USA described? What places are mentioned?

 8 + 9
p. 60

10 Choose an activity   KVs 4.4 p. 57/7 ➡ p. LF44

portfolio

wordbank
Statistics
p. 168

You can ...
- **imagine you are going to live in another country. What would you take with you? Make a list. Show it to your partner and explain why you would take these things.**
- **make a chart that shows where the people in your class or in your home town or in Germany come from. Look at number 2 for help. Present your chart in class.**
- **look at the pictures in number 3 again. Choose one of the people and tell his or her family history. Use your imagination and number 4 for help.**

➡ p. LF45

How to ...
work with others
p. 188

11 Native Americans ✏ 👄

Think – pair – share: What comes to your mind when you think of Native Americans? Organise your **findings** in a **word web**.

🖱 IWS   📖 p. 58/8

➡ p. LF45

10 – 13
p. 61/62

12 Then and now 👓 ✏   🖱 IWS   📖 p. 59/9   🖱 LSW 406

a) Match the pictures with the texts.   1-E   2-G   3-F   4-H   5-A   6-B   7-C   8-D

A

Some tribes built totem poles to remember legends or celebrate important events.

B

Blowing smoke into another person's face is a sign of respect.

C

Native Americans adapted to the regions they lived in. In cold regions they hunted seals.

D

A pow-wow is a modern event where Native Americans come together for dancing, singing and meeting friends. It is a time to remember and share traditions.

E

The Grand Canyon Skywalk opened in 2007. It is a glass bridge and it looks like a horseshoe. Many tourists visit it every year. The Hualapai are glad because it has brought money and jobs to their area.

F

Many Native Americans still live on reservations. They have their own small community with a police station and a school.

G

People often think that all Native Americans wear headdresses with feathers. But only some tribes, like the Lakota, wear them.

H

When they went hunting, Native Americans lived in tepees. In the north the Inuit made igloos out of snow and ice.

Relativsätze
17R
p. 206

P **P8 + P12**
p. 92/93

WB **14 + 15**
p. 63

b) What can you find out about Native Americans?
Make sentences but don't use 'that' more than twice.

Native Americans		are made of feathers.
Some tribes built totem poles		lived in cold regions hunted seals.
The Grand Canyon Skywalk is a bridge	who	Native Americans built when they went hunting.
The Lakota wear headdresses	that	showed pictures and told stories.
Pow-wows are festivals	which	live in the north are Inuit.
A tepee is a house		are celebrated by Native Americans today.
Many Native Americans		you can see through.

13 **A bus trip to …**

KVs 4.3

→ p. LF45

L 1.28

How to …
listen
p. 178

WB **16**
p. 64

a) Listen to the tour guide.
Which of the pictures on both
pages is she talking about? no. 1
b) Copy the grid. Then listen and
take notes.
c) Compare your notes with a partner.

name: …
how long to build: …
how many people:
how high:
other information:

W p. 239

LAND & LEUTE

Native American land in the USA today

Salt Lake City • San Francisco • Denver • Phoenix • New York • New Orleans

0   1000 km

Die ersten Amerikaner

Niemand weiß genau, wann die ersten Menschen nach Amerika kamen. Vermutlich war es zwischen 25.000 und 10.000 v. Chr. Die ersten Bewohner Amerikas waren Jäger aus Sibirien.

Lange Zeit bezeichnete man die ersten Bewohner Amerikas als *Indians*. Christoph Kolumbus nannte sie so, weil er bei seiner Landung in Amerika 1492 dachte, er sei in Indien. Die amerikanischen Ureinwohner lebten in vielen verschiedenen Stämmen mit eigener Sprache und Kultur.

Als die weißen Einwanderer ab dem 17. Jahrhundert in großer Zahl das Land der *Native Americans* besiedelten, mussten die Ureinwohner gegen sie kämpfen, um ihr Land und ihre Lebensweise zu verteidigen. Viele von ihnen wurden gezwungen, ihr Land zu verlassen und in Gebieten zu leben, die ihnen von den Weißen zugewiesen wurden, den sogenannten Reservaten.

Auch heute wohnen die meisten *Native Americans* in Reservaten und viele sind sehr arm. Sie kämpfen mit Arbeitslosigkeit und Alkoholismus. Die Stämme versuchen, in den Reservaten bessere Lebensbedingungen zu schaffen. Viele pflegen ihre Traditionen – nicht nur, um damit Touristen anzulocken und Geld zu verdienen, sondern vor allem, um sie für ihre Nachfahren zu erhalten.

Finde mit dem Atlas heraus, wo Sibirien liegt. Auf welche Weise sind die ersten Bewohner vermutlich nach Amerika gelangt? (zu Fuß über die Beringstraße) ➡ p. LF45

P14
P
p. 93

➡ p. LF45

DVD

17
p. 64

14 The history of the Native Americans 👁 👄

a) Read the German text above. Then watch the clip about the history of the Native Americans. What can you understand?

b) Watch the clip again. Then read the statements. Are they right or wrong? Correct what's wrong.

1. The first people in America were hunters from Europe. wrong
2. Some Native American tribes hunted buffaloes, some sailed the ocean and fished. ✓
3. The white settlers brought diseases with them that killed large numbers of Native Americans. ✓
4. In the late 1900s the US government forced Native Americans to live on reservations. wrong
5. Today there are more than 350 tribes in the US. wrong
6. Native Americans are trying to improve life on the reservations and keep up their traditions. ✓

c) Watch the clip a third time and check your answers.

LSW 407–409

15 A Native American KVs 4.1, 4.2, 4.6 pp. 60–61/10 und 11

a) Read Tawny's blog entry. What tribe is she from? Navajo

 LSW 410

How to …
read
p. 179

About me

My name is Tawny Hale, I'm 16 and I live in Pico Rivera, California, with my sister Leya, my dad Ben and my grandparents. During the week I'm just like all the other girls at school: I go to Salazar High School, where my favorite subjects are math, English, health and US history. Sometimes after school I go to the mall with my friends. I like alternative rock and hip hop. I guess I'm not typical because I'm from the Navajo tribe. My cousin and I are the only Native Americans at our school. Most of the students are Mexican Americans.

My sister and I began learning traditional dances almost as soon as we could walk. My grandma taught us. I like taking part in the traditions and ceremonies. We make our own outfits, which takes a lot of time. The feathers and accessories are passed on to us and are quite old. We wear them with pride.

I want to go to college after high school but I'm not sure what I want to study. There is one thing I know for sure: I want to become a spokesperson for our people.

b) Choose a good heading for each of the three paragraphs.

➡ p. LF46

> Tawny's hopes and dreams for the future • School life •
> Keeping up traditions • Meet Tawny • Life on the reservation

\\ M5: weiterer Blogeintrag; Auswertung nahezu identisch, aber auf unterschiedlich anspruchsvolle Texte bezogen

c) Make a fact file about Tawny's life. Think about:
name, age, family, …

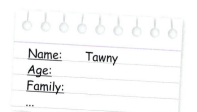

Name: Tawny
Age:
Family:
…

d) Report on a friend or classmate. Use the categories from your fact file for help.

Marc is 13 years old. He lives in Kassel and goes to …

M \\ **M5**
p. 96

P **P9 – P11 + P13**
p. 92/93

M **M6 – M8**
p. 97

16 YOUR talk – Native Americans IWS

➡ p. LF46

How to …
give a talk
p. 180

a) Prepare a two-minute talk about Native Americans. First choose a topic:

pow-wows   the Navajo   totem poles   reservations   …

b) Then go through the Theme and collect important information about your topic. You can use the Internet, too. Take notes.

c) Practise your talk before you present it to a partner or to the class.

 WWW

 WB **test yourself**
p. 66/67

➡ p. LF46

How to ...
work with a
dictionary
p. 176/177

P1 Opposites ✏ 🖱 LSW 411

a) What are the opposites of these adjectives?
You can use a dictionary for help.

legal – ...   difficult – ...   interesting – ...   large – ...

poor – ...   unimportant – ...   friendly – ...   fast – ...

safe – ...   cheap – ...   modern – ...   quiet – ...

How to ...
work with words
p. 175

b) Use ten adjectives with nouns.
illegal immigrants, ...

➡ p. LF47

P2 A word game ✏

a) How many English words can you make out of
the letters in "illegal immigrants"?
b) Compare your words with a partner.
Who found more words?

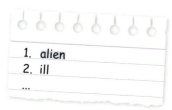

1. alien
2. ill
...

➡ p. LF47

P3 Rhyming pairs 👂 ✏

a) Find the rhyming pairs.

year • came • win •
four • free • fought •
two • find • they •
land • read • group

year – here
came – ...
...

three • here • taught •
stand • same • shoe •
need • bin • pay •
door • soup • kind

L 1.29   **b) Listen and check your pairs.**

➡ p. LF47

How to ...
work with words
p. 175

P4 Nouns from verbs ✏

a) Look at the verbs. Find the nouns for them. They all
end with -tion. You can use a dictionary for help.

immigrate • inform • invent •
organise • invite • decorate •
present • produce • celebrate

verbs	nouns
immigrate	immigration
inform	...
...	

b) Look at the nouns you have found. What happens
to the "e" at the end of some of the verbs?

P5 Statistics

18R
p. 206
Comparison
of adjectives

**Look at the statistics in number 2 again. Use the words
in the box to complete the sentences.**

> smallest • largest • biggest • Native Americans •
> White Americans • Black and African Americans • fewer • more

1. The white population is the XX group. biggest
2. The 2nd XX group are the XX. largest – Black and African Americans
3. The Native American population is the XX group. smallest
4. There are XX Asian Americans than XX. more – Native Americans
5. There are XX Black and African Americans than XX. fewer – White Americans

P6 Hopes and dreams LSW 412

➡ p. LF47

8R
p. 200
Zukunft mit *will*

**What do you think your future will be like?
Write about your hopes and dreams.**

Perhaps/Maybe	I will	live in ...
I hope	I won't	have ...
I'm sure		be ...
I think		work as a/an ...
		travel to ...
		...

P7 Special signs LSW 413

➡ p. LF47

How to ...
help out
p. 190

**Look at the signs. Tell a friend who doesn't
speak English or Spanish what they mean.**

 W p. 240   TM, p. 199

➡ p. LF47

P8 Letter detective

**a) Look through the texts in number 12 again.
Find words with these letters:**

-ea	-ee	-oo
seals	...	...
...		

**b) What other words with these letters do you know?
Add them to your grid.**

**c) Write five sentences or a short text with words
from your grid.**

P9 Finding words

**Look at number 15 again. Find words in the
blog entry that match these expressions:**

1. classes at school subjects
2. things which you add to your clothes accessories
3. a kind of university college
4. a large building with many shops inside mall
5. something which lots of people do and have done for a long time tradition
6. someone who speaks for a group of people spokesperson

➡ p. LF48

P10 Different spelling ✏ LSW 414

What's the British spelling of these American English words?

math • favorite • color • theater •
neighbor • program • center • mom

➡ p. LF48

P11 Sound check   LSW 415

L 1.30

a) Listen to these words and make two lists.

another • together • math • feather • their • with • birthday • that • think • north • they • both • brother • thing		$/\theta/$	$/\eth/$
		math	another
		...	...

b) Listen again and say the words.

P12 Some facts   IWS 🖱 LSW 416

Simple past
4R
p. 195

Complete the sentences with the correct *simple past* forms of the verbs in the box.

> hunt • live • travel • be • open • make • tell • marry • build

1. Native Americans XX in tepees when they went hunting. lived
2. Some tribes XX totem poles which showed pictures and XX stories. made – told
3. The Inuit XX igloos out of snow and ice and they XX seals. built – hunted
4. The Grand Canyon Skywalk XX in 2007. opened
5. Before they had horses, Native Americans XX on foot. travelled/traveled
6. Pocahontas XX the daughter of a Native American chief. She XX an English settler. was – married

P13 Interviewing Tawny ✏️ 👄

➡ p. LF48

21R + 22R
p. 209/210

21R: Fragen mit Fragewörtern
22R: Satzstellung

a) Write down the interview questions in the correct order.

1. name – what's – your – ?
2. you – old – are – how – ?
3. where – live – you – do – ?
4. live – do – you – with – who – ?
5. are – at school – what – favourite subjects – your – ?
6. what – free time – do – in – your – you – do – ?
7. your – are – for – the future – plans – what – ?

> May I ask you some questions?
>
> Yes, sure.

b) Take Tawny's role and answer the questions in a). Take notes.
c) Work with a partner and practise the interview. You can present it to the class.

P14 Native American reservations

➡ p. LF49

How to ...
help out
p. 190

You find this information on Native American reservations on the Internet.
Your friend looks at it and doesn't understand much. Tell your friend in German.

Today there are about four million Native Americans in the US and Canada. Most of them live on reservations, of which there are over 300. The largest reservation belongs to the Navajo tribe and is almost twice as big as Belgium or Maryland.

Some reservations are very popular with tourists who like to hunt buffaloes, elks or turkeys. Other tribes earn money by breeding and selling horses, or they exploit their mineral resources such as oil and gold. But many tribes earn most of their money with gambling. In nearly every second reservation today there is a casino where you can play bingo and poker.

_{p. 240}   TM, p. 202

➡ p. LF49

M1 **Annie Moore's story** IWS

a) **Read Annie's story. Why is Annie a special person?**

Loving and leaving Ireland

It was December 1891. Annie Moore stood in line with her two younger brothers, Philip and Anthony. They were waiting to board the SS Nevada, a ship that would take them from Cobh in Ireland to New York. Annie's red hair blew in the breeze and tears fell

5   from her eyes. She could not believe they were leaving their Irish homeland.

Annie wondered if she would ever return to the "Emerald Isle". She cried when she thought that she might never see the beautiful green valleys again. Would she be able to eat Irish stew

10 in America? Would they continue to celebrate St Patrick's Day? Could she go to the Catholic Church in New York? There were many questions going through her head.

Annie's statue

Yet she knew she had to get on the ship. Although she was sad, she was also excited about seeing her parents again. They had gone to America two years earlier with her older brother.

15 It would be wonderful to have the whole family together. Her parents had jobs in New York. Life was better than it had been in Ireland. In 1845 there was a great potato famine in Ireland. Ireland depended on the potato and when the crop was destroyed, one million Irish people died from starvation. This caused many Irish people to emigrate.

Annie and her brothers were on the ship for 12 days. They were in a large room with many

20 other people. The ship was crowded and the food was poor. It was very cold on the ship. Many people got seasick.

On January 1st, 1892, the ship reached New York. The Statue of Liberty welcomed them as they sailed into the harbour. It was a beautiful sight and everyone cheered and cried. Annie was very happy that the trip was almost over. Then the captain announced that the ship would

25 dock at Ellis Island.

Annie was the first person to leave the ship. She was very surprised when an official gave her a $10 gold piece. She had never seen so much money and did not know why he had given it to her. He explained that Ellis Island was new and the $10 were a gift to the first person who left the ship. It was Annie's 15th birthday!

30 And so it happened that Annie became the first immigrant to land on the newly opened Ellis Island. Today, over 120 years later, a statue of Annie stands on Ellis Island, which is now a museum.

M1
p. 69

b) **Read Annie's story again and make a timeline with dates and events. Show the timeline to your class and talk about Annie.**

c) ☀ **Write a summary of Annie's story. Take notes on place, time, people and action first and use your timeline from b). Then give the most important information. Look at page 187 for help. You can start like this:**

> The story is about Annie Moore. In 1891 she and her two brothers board a ship ...

M2 Changes LSW 418

➡ p. LF49

a) Look at M1 again. Then match the sentence parts and write them down.

1 Before Annie went to America, **B**

2 When Annie arrived in America, **E**

3 A statue was built on Ellis Island **A**

4 After they had greeted each other, **C**

5 After she had received the $10 gold piece, **D**

A after Annie had died.

B she had lived in Ireland for 15 years.

C Annie and her family went home.

D Annie could meet her parents.

E her parents had already lived there for two years.

b) In your exercise book underline the part of each sentence that tells you what happened first. The tense used here is called the *past perfect*.

c) Find examples of the *past perfect* in M1. Copy the sentences and underline the *past perfect* (had gone, …).

Past perfect

WB **M2**
p. 69

7
p. 199

How to …
work with grammar
p. 190

M3 Ancestors Folie 8 LSW 417, 419

➡ p. LF49

Look at the pie chart. What information does it give you?
Talk about the figures with your partner.

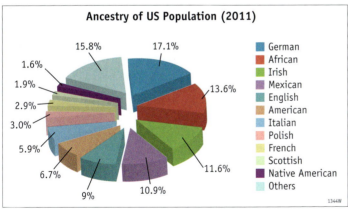

Ancestry of US Population (2011)

German
African
Irish
Mexican
English
American
Italian
Polish
French
Scottish
Native American
Others

15.8%   17.1%
1.6%
1.9%   13.6%
2.9%
3.0%
5.9%   11.6%
6.7%
9%   10.9%

1344W

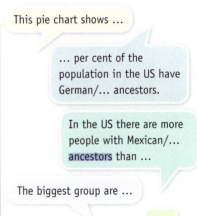

This pie chart shows …

… per cent of the population in the US have German/… ancestors.

In the US there are more people with Mexican/… ancestors than …

The biggest group are …

…

wordbank
Statistics
p. 168

WB **M3**
p. 70

M4 Learning English

➡ p. LF50

a) Listen to Mohamed, Kim and Sergio from number 5. What are they talking about? Write down their names in the order you hear them talk. Kim – Sergio – Mohamed

b) Listen again. Take notes to answer the questions.
1. Why does Sergio still have problems learning English?
2. Why was it easy for Mohamed to learn English?
3. What other language can Mohamed speak?
4. How did Kim learn English?

B 5
p. 84

L 1.26

WB **M4**
p. 70

4

MORE Native Americans

 p.241   TM, p.207

M5 **A Native American** 👓 ✏️ 🖱️ LSW 420, 421

How to ...
read
p. 179

a) Read Lenno's blog entry. What tribe is he from? Ute

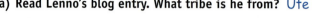

A UTE IN UTAH

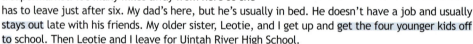

About me

My name is Lenno and I'm 16. I live on a reservation in Utah. I love early mornings on our reservation when it's very quiet and you can see the beautiful mountains miles away across the desert. This is one of the times when I'm glad I live on a reservation. The air is clean and you know it hasn't been polluted by thousands of cars and factories.

But as soon as I'm up, it's a little stressful around the house. I'm from a big family and my mom works in a supermarket. It's many miles away from here so she has to leave just after six. My dad's here, but he's usually in bed. He doesn't have a job and usually stays out late with his friends. My older sister, Leotie, and I get up and get the four younger kids off to school. Then Leotie and I leave for Uintah River High School.

Our school is great. We learn the Ute language and we have classes in beadwork, drumming and dancing. I like history, too, because we always learn something about Native Americans and our own Ute tribe. I study hard to get a good job later – I don't want to end up like my dad.

Things have really changed. When my mom and dad were young, they had to live at a boarding school where they weren't allowed to speak Ute. The teachers tried to make them more like white people. It was terrible.

After school I usually do something with my friends. I think most people my age wouldn't want to be Native American. Many white people still think of us as wild Indians from old movies or people who have no jobs, ride around in old cars and live in tepees. When I go shopping in the nearby town, I can almost hear people thinking 'dirty, stupid Indians'. But that's just prejudice. Although life is sometimes hard on the 'rez', it's home and I'm proud to be Ute. Maybe, one day, all people will understand my favorite Ute saying:

Don't walk behind me; I may not lead.
Don't walk in front of me; I may not follow.
Walk beside me that we may be as one.

M5
p. 71

➡️ p. LF50

b) Choose a good heading for each of the five paragraphs.

c) Make a fact file about Lenno's life. Think about:
name, age, family, ...

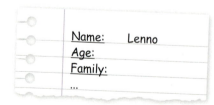

Name: Lenno
Age:
Family:
...

15 // B
p. 89

d) Report on a friend or classmate. Use the categories from your fact file for help.

Marc is 13 years old. He lives in Kassel and goes to ...

M6 What if … ? ✏ 🖱 LSW 422

➡ p. LF50

🔍 **12**
p. 203

Bedingungssätze,
Typ II

a) Look at these sentences and finish them.

> If I lived on a reservation, I would …

> If I went to a boarding school, …

> If I were Native American, …

> If I had classes in drumming and dancing, …

> If I weren't allowed to speak my own language, …

🔧 **How to …**
work with
grammar
p. 190

b) 🔆 **Look at your sentences from a). How do you form if-clauses that are
not likely or can never happen? Write down the rule.**

WB **M6**
p. 72

M7 Native American teenagers 👂 ✏ 🖱 LSW 423

a) Listen to two young Native Americans. What tribe are they from?

> Navajo • Ute • Lakota • Cherokee

Jessie: Lakota
DJ: Navajo

💿 **L 1.31 S 8**

🔧 **How to …**
listen
p. 178

**b) Copy the grid. Then listen again. What are the teenagers' likes,
dislikes, hopes and worries? Take notes.**

WB 🔆 **M7**
p. 72

➡ p. LF51

	Jessie	DJ
age	…	…
likes	…	
dislikes		
hopes		
worries		

**c) Listen a third time and collect phrases that the teenagers use to talk
about their feelings.**
d) What are YOUR likes, dislikes, hopes and worries? Write about them.

M8 An interview ✏ 👄 🖱 LSW 424

➡ p. LF51

🔍 **21R**
p. 209

Fragen mit
Fragewörtern

**Work with a partner and prepare an interview with a Native American teenager.
Think of at least ten questions you would like to ask him or her.**

Where? What? Why? Who? When? How? … ?

**One of you takes the teenager's role and gives the answers.
Present your interview to the class.**

CAMDEN CHRONICLE
LEARN ENGLISH THE CAMDEN WAY

DID YOU GET IT ALL? ➡ p. LF52

» Where did the immigrants after the first settlers come from?
» What are people called who came to the USA from Mexico and Central or South America?
» When were the black slaves freed?
» What percentage of the American population is Native American?
» What do Native Americans do at a pow-wow?
» Who wears headdresses with feathers?
» Where does the glass used for the Grand Canyon Skywalk come from?
» Who wants to become a spokesperson for Native Americans?

GOOD TO KNOW ...

Lange Zeit wurden die Ureinwohner Amerikas als Indianer bzw. *Indians* bezeichnet. Der Name geht auf Christoph Kolumbus zurück. Heutzutage spricht man von *Native Americans*. Dieser Name wird von den Ureinwohnern Amerikas sehr begrüßt und ist auch viel angemessener, denn er drückt aus, dass sie bereits lange vor den europäischen Entdeckern und Siedlern dort lebten.

The turtle plays an important role in Native American culture. It is a symbol of long life, good health and protection. The Iroquois and other tribes believed that the earth was formed on the back of a giant turtle. That's why they called North America "Turtle Island".

The Kids in School with Me

When I studied my A-B-C's
And learned arithmetic,
I also learned in public school
What makes America tick:
The kid in front
And the kid behind
And the kid across the aisle,

The Italian kid
And the Polish kid
And the girl with the Irish smile,
The colored kid
And the Spanish kid
And the Russian kid my size,
The Jewish kid
And the Grecian kid
And the girl with the Chinese eyes –

We were a regular Noah's ark,
Every race beneath the sun,
But our motto for graduation was:
One for All and All for One!
The kid in front
And the kid behind
And the kid across from me –
Just American kids together
The kids in school with me.

©Langston Hughes (*1902 – †1967)

WHAT'S UP?

In diesem *Theme* ...

» erfährst du, was amerikanische Jugendliche in ihrer Freizeit machen.

» erstellst du ein Einkaufsgespräch.

» führst du eine Umfrage zum Freizeitverhalten durch.

» lernst du Wissenswertes über amerikanische Sportarten.

» interviewst du jemanden zum Thema Sport.

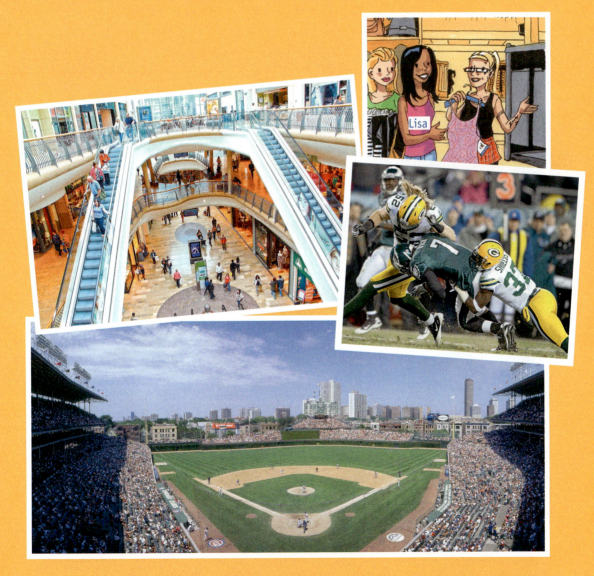

 p. 242   TM, p. 213

➡ p. LF53

How to ...
work with others
p. 188

wordbank
Free time
p. 168

1 + 2
p. 73

1 When school's out ✏ 👄 📖 p. 64/1 🖱 LSW 501

a) **Think:** How many free time activities can you write down in one minute?

b) **Pair:** Work with a partner. Who has got more activities? Compare your results and add new activities to your list.

c) **Share:** Sit together with another pair and put your free time activities in groups (sports, ...).

➡ p. LF53

M1 – M4
p. 114/115

2 A typical day 👄 ✏ 📄 Folie 11 🖱 IWS 📖 p. 65/2 🖱 LSW 502

a) Look at the pictures. What do these American teenagers do on a typical day?

> On a typical day Lisa ...

> After school she ...

go to school by bus/car • do sports •
meet friends at the mall • surf the Internet •
do homework • go shopping • phone friends • ...

Lisa, 14	**Josh, 14**	**Tom, 16**

b) What **might** the people in the pictures be saying or thinking?
   Choose a picture and write a **speech bubble** or a **thought bubble**.
   Can your partner guess which picture or person you chose?

c) What do YOU do on a typical day? Write about it. p. 66/3

> In the morning ... • After school ... •
> In the afternoon ... • In the evening ... • ...

You can draw a picture story, too.

WB **3** p. 74

3 **Shop till you drop**   KVs 5.4 IWS   LSW 503   ➡ p. LF53

a) 🌙 **Read the sentences. What does the customer say?**
   What does the shop assistant say? Make two lists.

wordbank
Shopping
p. 170

WB **4** p. 75

Let me show you to the fitting rooms.

How much is it?

customer:

You're welcome.

Is it on sale?

shop assistant:

How would you like to pay for that? By card or with cash?

Can I help you with anything?

Yes, please, I'm looking for ...

Where can I try it on?

That's $..., please.

How do you think it looks?

I'll get you the dress in a smaller size.

I'll put your receipt in the bag.

It's too big. Does it come in a smaller size?

b) **Bus stop: When you have finished a), go
   to the bus stop in your classroom.
   Find a partner and compare your lists.**

c) **Listen to Lisa shopping in a clothes shop
   and look at your lists.
   Underline the phrases you hear
   in your lists.**

d) **Work with a partner. Think of other words
   or phrases you can use when you go
   shopping. Add them to your lists.
   Then make up a dialogue.
   Act out your shopping scene to the class.**

How to ...
work with others
p. 188

L 1.32

Lisa

p. 243

➡ p. LF54

4 **A mall**   📖 p. 67/4 🖱 LSW 504, 505

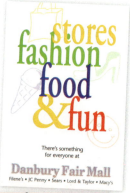

a) Look at the **cover** of the brochure. What is a mall? Explain in one sentence.

Gerundium
14R
p. 204

b) Is there a mall in YOUR area? What kind of shops are there? What can you do there? What do you think about going to the mall?

P1 + P3 + P4 P
p. 110/111

> I (don't) like/love/hate/ enjoy going to the mall.

> Looking at clothes/Having a drink/... is great/boring/...

M5 M
p. 115

c) Design your own mall. Decide what shops, cafés, restaurants and fun activities you would like to put in it. **Label** your mall plan. 📖 p. 68/5

➡ p. LF54

5 **Lisa and Amy** 👓 ✏

5 🌙
p. 75

Read the beginning of the story.

> One day, when Lisa and her friend Amy were at the mall, they felt really bored.
> "We always **hang out** at this mall. I know all the shops already," said Amy.
> "Yeah, you're right. It's the same stuff every day," answered Lisa.
> "Hey, let's do something exciting for a change," suggested Amy.
> "What do you think we should do?", asked Lisa.
> ...

How to ...
write
p. 184

What happens **next**? Finish the story with about ten sentences. Find a title for your story, too.

➡ p. LF54

6 **On the phone** 👂 ✏ KVs 5.3

L 1.33 ◎

a) Listen to the phone call. What are Josh and Alex going to do this afternoon?

How to ...
listen
p. 178

> go shopping • watch a film •
> meet at a café • (hang out at the mall)

b) Listen again. Take notes on these questions:
1. What time are the boys going to meet?
2. How are they going to get there?
3. Why does Alex call Josh a second time?
4. Where exactly are the boys going to meet?

6 + 7 📝
p. 76

P6 + P7 P
p. 111

c) **Compare** your notes with a partner.

7 **A picture story** 👓 👄 📄 Folie 12 🖱 IWS

Hero for one day
An exciting time at the mall
A real Crusher fan!

a) **Read the picture story and find a title for it.**

📖 p. 69/6

b) **In groups practise reading the story. Think about how your character feels. Is he/she happy, angry or bored? Then try to learn your role by heart and act out the scenes in class.**

🔧 **How to ...** work with others p. 188

p. 243

8 A day at the mall   KVs 5.6

P2 + P5 P
p. 110/111

Look at number 7 again and match the sentence parts.
Then write down the sentences to get a summary of the story.

1. Josh and Ben are at the mall B
2. When Alex arrives at 3:15 pm, E
3. They hear that the singer Crusher G
4. When a girl suddenly faints, C
5. Crusher notices D
6. One of his bodyguards tells him A
7. The singer thanks Josh for his help F

A. that a girl has fainted and that Josh helped her.
B. and they are waiting for Alex.
C. Josh catches her and gets the paramedics.
D. that something is wrong.
E. the friends join a crowd of girls.
F. and gives him a ticket to his next concert.
G. is presenting his new album.

// M6: Nach-
erzählen der
Geschichte aus
der Sicht des
Mädchens, das in
Ohnmacht gefal-
len ist, Textsorte
ebenfalls E-Mail.
In **Basis** Vorbe-
reitung mit TB 8,
in **More** ohne
Hilfestellung

M6 // M
p. 115

8
p. 77

How to …
write
p. 184

➡ p. LF55

9 You won't believe it!

The next day Josh is writing an email to a friend to tell him what happened at the mall.
Write Josh's email. Use your summary from number 8 for help. You can start like this:

> Hi Derek,
> You won't believe what happened to me yesterday! I was at the mall with my friends
> Alex and Ben. There was a crowd of girls in the mall and we found out that …

➡ p. LF55

10 YOUR free time statistics   KVs 5.1   p.70/7   LSW 506

wordbank
Statistics
p. 168

14R
p. 204
Gerundium

9
p. 77

a) Look at the statistics and talk about how American teenagers spend their free time.

> American teenagers watch TV for about 132 minutes on an average day.

> They spend … minutes on reading/…

> The most/least popular activity is …

Free time activities of American teenagers (on an average day, ages 15 – 19)

watching TV	~ 132 min
using computers, playing computer games	~ 54 min
meeting friends, talking/writing to them	~ 48 min
doing sports	~ 48 min
reading	~ 6 min
relaxing and thinking	~ 6 min

SOURCE: Bureau of Labor Statistics, American Time Use Survey, 2013

wordbank
Free time
p. 168

b) Do a class survey on free time activities.

> How long do you watch TV for on an average day?

> Reading isn't very popular. … is more popular than … Our class spends … minutes on …

Then present your results.

11 American sports   IWS p.71/8 LSW 507

a) 🌙 **Match each picture with the right sport.**

baseball • volleyball • soccer • boxing • gymnastics •
basketball • cheerleading • American football • ice hockey

1. basketball
2. soccer
3. ice hockey
4. cheerleading
5. American football
6. baseball

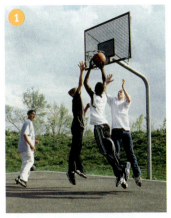  

➡ p. LF55

b) **Which words go with which sports in a)?**

goalkeeper • puck • throw • net • foul • pompom •
half time • linesman • penalty • jump • basket •
helmet • kick • pass • kickoff • dribble • hit

What other words do you know that go with these sports?

c) **Watch the interview with Nicholas Angell, a professional ice hockey player from the US.**
Find out:
– What pieces of equipment does he need?
– How did he become interested in ice hockey?
– What has been his worst injury?
What else can you understand? LSW 508

 wordbank
Free time
p. 168

M M7
p. 116

 10 + 11
p. 78

 DVD

p.243

→ p. LF56

How to ...
read
p. 179

12 Come and join us! 👓 ✏️ 📖 p.72/9

a) Read Ashley's article about cheerleading. Find the sentences
that tell you what cheerleading is and take notes.

Hi! Let me introduce myself. My name is Ashley Miller and I'm a member of our school's cheerleading team, the Pirates. We go to all the football games and cheer our school teams on. But we are not just football fans – we support all of our school teams, whether they win or lose!

Cheerleading is a sport just like football or soccer and teams can take part in competitions all over the world. You have to be in really good shape for it.

We write our own chants. We also practice singing and dancing and really enjoy ourselves. Every time the teams leave the field or take time out to discuss strategies, we put on our own show.

I started cheerleading six years ago. The coach asked me to join because she saw I was good at gymnastics.

My favorite stunt is pyramid-building and I love climbing to the top. But you have to be careful because you can hurt yourself or another person.

I have to watch my weight. Actually everybody on the team has to stay slim but sometimes we treat ourselves to a big pizza after a hard practice. We practice two or three times a week – right now we are practicing for the state championships. The team really believes in itself and we all want to win!

Some of our stunts are a little bit dangerous but I always say "No risk, no fun". Come and join us!

P8
p. 112

b) What does it take to be a good cheerleader?
Read the article again and find out what Ashley
has to do and what she has to be good at.

> Ashley has to ...
> She has to be good at ...

13 Cheerleaders hurray! 👓 ✏️ 📄 KVs 5.2 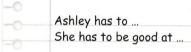 🖱️ LSW 509

Reflexiv-
pronomen

🔍
29
p. 214

Look at number 12 again and complete the sentences.

P11 + P12
p. 112/113

yourself • herself • itself • themselves *(2x)*

12
p. 79

1. Ashley Miller introduces **XX** to the readers. *herself*
2. She and her cheerleading team really enjoy **XX**. *themselves*
3. You have to be careful on top of the pyramid because you can hurt **XX**. *yourself*
4. Sometimes the cheerleaders treat **XX** to a big pizza after a hard practice. *themselves*
5. The team wants to win the state championships and really believes in **XX**. *itself*

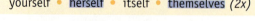

IWS

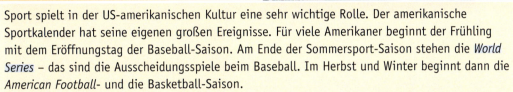

🇺🇸 LAND & LEUTE

Sport zu jeder Jahreszeit

Sport spielt in der US-amerikanischen Kultur eine sehr wichtige Rolle. Der amerikanische Sportkalender hat seine eigenen großen Ereignisse. Für viele Amerikaner beginnt der Frühling mit dem Eröffnungstag der Baseball-Saison. Am Ende der Sommersport-Saison stehen die *World Series* – das sind die Ausscheidungsspiele beim Baseball. Im Herbst und Winter beginnt dann die *American Football*- und die Basketball-Saison.

Manche Sportevents sind nationale Ereignisse, z. B. der *Opening Day* (Baseball) oder der *Super Bowl* (*American Football*). Andere Feiertage sind ebenfalls berühmt für ihre sportlichen Höhepunkte wie die *American Football*-Spiele der Colleges an Neujahr und *Thanksgiving*.

Jede Mannschaft hat ihre eigenen *Cheerleaders* – junge Leute (meistens Mädchen), die mit Schlachtrufen, Tanzen, Springen und Händeklatschen die Zuschauer zum Anfeuern animieren. *American Football*, Leichtathletik, Basketball und Baseball sind für Jungen zu einem sehr wichtigen Teil ihres Schullebens geworden. Bei den Mädchen sind die beliebtesten Sportarten Leichtathletik, Basketball, Volleyball und Fußball. Für viele Schüler ist es genauso wichtig, im Sport erfolgreich zu sein wie in Mathe, Englisch oder den Naturwissenschaften.

Welche Sportarten, Mannschaften und Sportler sind in Deutschland am beliebtesten?

14 At the game with Dad 🎧 ✏️ 📄 Folie 13 ➡ p. LF56

WB **13** p. 79

a) Look at the pictures.
   What do you think happened to Aaron, a boy from New York?

took the ... to ... • watched ... • felt ... • bought ... • met ... • ...

b) Now listen to Aaron's story and find the pictures that *don't* fit. 1 and 6

 L 1.34 S 9

W p. 244

How to ...
read
p. 179

15 All about American football   KVs 5.5 ⬜ p. 74/11

a) Read about the rules of American football.

News (230) ▼ Favourites ▼

So you want to play American football? It's a cool sport but you have to learn the rules first.

In American football players have to get the ball across the opponents' goal line or kick it through the goalposts.

You need a field (120 yards long and 53.33 yards wide) and two teams with eleven players each. There are a few extra players, too.

The game is played in four quarters. In high school games the quarters are twelve minutes each, but in the national games quarters are fifteen minutes long.

Each team has offensive and defensive players. The defensive players can tackle the ball carrier and keep other players out of the way. The offensive players can block the other team's players so that they can't get to the player carrying the ball.

Scoring is easy:
1. A team gets six points for a touchdown. This is when they get the ball over their opponents' goal line.
2. If they get across the goal line, they can also try to kick the ball through the goalposts. They get one extra point if they make it.
3. And if they carry the ball across the goal line again, they get another two points.
4. A team can get three points for a field goal. This is when a player has kicked the ball through the goalposts, from the field, without a touchdown first.

➡ p. LF56

How to ...
work with a
dictionary
p. 176

b) Look at these words from the text. Sort them from A – Z. Then look them up in a dictionary. Decide: Which meaning fits best?

> opponent • goal line • goalposts •
> offensive • defensive • tackle • quarter

c) Find the words in the text for:
1. a player who doesn't play from the beginning but can join later extra player
2. getting points in a game scoring
3. the place where people play American football field
4. stopping a player from the other team tackling/blocking

P9 + P10 P
p. 112

14
p. 80

d) Explain these words in English:

> team • quarter • high school • opponent

16 American football rules LSW 510

Look at number 15 again and complete the rules.

In American football you need XX teams. Each team has XX players. *two – eleven*
The teams score points when they get the XX over the opponents' goal line. *ball*
Players can also XX the ball through the goalposts. There are XX quarters in *kick – four*
a high school game. Each XX is XX minutes long. *quarter – twelve*

\\ *right/wrong-Sicherung*

M \\ M8
p. 116

WB 15 + 16
p. 80

17 Sports, sports, sports   p. 73/10

a) **Think about these questions:**
   – What sports are you good at?   – What sports do you do in your free time?
   – What sports are you terrible at?   – What sports do you watch on TV?
   – What sports do you do at school?   – What sports would you like to try?
b) **Pair:** Work with a partner. Ask and answer the questions
   in a). Take notes.
c) **Share:** Sit together with another pair and tell them
   about your partner.

> Gülay is good at basketball but she isn't good at gymnastics. At school she plays …

➡ p. LF56

How to …
work with others
p. 188

WB 17 + 18
p. 81

P P13 + P14
p. 113

18 Choose an activity p. 75/12

You can …
- draw a sportsperson of your **choice**
  or find a picture in a magazine.
  **Label the clothes and equipment
  and explain what he/she does.**
- write about your favourite sport.
  Before you start, make notes on:
  – name of the sport
  – where you play it
  – number of players
  – equipment
  – basic rules
  – …
- make a **wordsearch** with American
  football words for your partner.
- make a quiz for your class about
  the rules of American football or
  about a sport you know well.

➡ p. LF57

portfolio

wordbank
Free time
p. 168

How to …
write
p. 184

M M9 + M10
p. 116/117

WB 19
p. 82

Roller Soccer

What is it?
Roller soccer is football on inline skates. It was invented in 1995 by Zack Phillips in San Francisco.

What equipment do you need?
You need a standard football, inline skates, a helmet, wrist guards and pads for your knees and elbows.

Where can you play it?
You can play it in a sports hall or on asphalt.

How do you play it?
You need five players in each team. You play two halves of 25 minutes. The players may not touch the ball with their arms or hands and the goalkeeper should not touch the ball with his/her hands. The aim is to score more goals than the other team.

Roller soccer is very fast and exciting – like ice hockey. Just try it!

WB test yourself
p. 83/84

➡ p. LF57

P1 Pairs ✏ 🖱 LSW 511

**Find the missing words and
write down the pairs.**

TV – watch
sports – ???

meet – friends
surf – ???

morning – breakfast
evening – ???

mall – shops
house – ???

games – play
homework – ???

customer – buy
shop assistant – ???

➡ p. LF57

P2 Sound check 👓 👂

a) Who or what is it?
1. Lots of students go to school XX.
2. Another word for shopping centre is XX.
3. A person who sells things in a shop is a XX.
4. When you buy something, you usually get a XX.
5. Someone who guards famous people is a XX.
6. A large number of people in the same place is a XX.

/rɪˈsiːt/   /ˈʃɒp_ə‚sɪst(ə)nt/

/ˈbɒdi‚gɑːd/   /mɔːl/

/‚baɪ ˈbʌs/   /kraʊd/

L 1.35
b) Listen and check.

➡ p. LF57

Gerundium
14R
p. 204

P3 What they like and don't like doing ✏ 🖱 LSW 512

**a) Look at the pictures. Write down what the teenagers like ➕ , love ➕ ➕ ,
don't like ➖ or hate ➖ ➖ doing.**

Lisa ➕

Josh ➕ ➕

Alex ➖

Tom ➖ ➖

b) What do YOU like/love/hate/... doing? Write about it.

P4 Tom

Read about Tom. Use the right word to connect the sentence parts.

1. Tom is 16 years old and/because is allowed to drive a car. and
2. He usually goes to school by car but/because he doesn't like the school bus. because
3. Tom enjoys listening to music so/when he comes home from school. when
4. Homework is something he can't stand but/and he has to do it. but
5. Tom loves eating tacos when/so he often goes to fast food restaurants. so
6. Yesterday he had a date with Stacy but/because she didn't enjoy it. but

23R
p. 211
Konjunktionen

P5 Pictures

There are a lot of pictures in the first part of Theme 5 (pages 100 – 104). Choose your favourite one and describe it to a partner.
What can you see? What are the people doing?
Can your partner find the picture?

In my favourite picture you can see ...
There is/are ...

➡ p. LF57

How to ...
talk about pictures
p. 183

P6 Say it in English LSW 513

**a) What can you say on the phone when you want to meet up with a friend?
Match the sentences.**

How to ...
help out
p. 190

1 Wie beginnst du das Telefonat? **E**

2 Wie sagst du, was du gerade machst? **F**

3 Wie machst du einen Vorschlag? **D**

4 Wie sagst du, dass du (nicht) einverstanden bist? **G**

5 Wie fragst du, wann ihr euch treffen wollt? **A**

6 Wie sagst du, dass du mit der Uhrzeit einverstanden bist? **C**

7 Wie verabschiedest du dich? **B**

A When do you want to meet? At 3.30?

B OK, see you./See you, bye.

C 3.30 sounds good.

D Do you feel like going to the mall/... ?

E Hi Lea! It's Casey. What's up?

F Not much. Just chilling/watching a film/...

G Sure, why not./Hm, what about ... ?

b) Work with a partner. Use the sentences from a) for a dialogue.

➡ p. LF58

P7 A phone call KVs 5.7

➡ p. LF58

 L 1.36

**Listen to two American teenagers, Mark and Rick.
Tell a partner in German about Rick's plans for this afternoon.**

How to ...
help out
p. 190

➡ p. LF58

P8 Missing letters ✎

a) What are these words from number 12?

1. c ▪▪▪h
2. s ▪▪▪▪r
3. r ▪▪k
4. h ▪▪t
5. s▪▪▪t
6. i▪▪▪▪▪▪e

b) **Take other words from number 12. Turn them into words
with missing letters and test your partner.**

➡ p. LF58

P9 Finding words ✎

Look at number 15 again and find more words for the list.

people	things they do	things they need
players	play	rules
…	…	…

➡ p. LF58

L 1.37

P10 Sound check 👂 👄   🖱 LSW 514

a) **Listen to the words and repeat them.**
b) **Which words are spoken like** *national* **(Ooo)?
Which words are spoken like** *gymnastics* **(oOo)?
Make two lists.**

pyramid • championships • equipment • strategies •
defensive • dangerous • opponent • offensive

Ooo	oOo
national	gymnastics
…	…

c) **Listen again and check your lists.**

➡ p. LF59

29
p. 214
Reflexivpronomen

P11 Different **pronouns** ✎

**Copy the grid and complete it with
all the personal pronouns.
Then fill in the reflexive pronouns.**

ourselves • itself • myself • themselves •
herself • yourself • himself • yourselves

personal pronouns	reflexive pronouns
I	myself
you	…
…	…

P12 You can do it by yourself! 👓 ✏️ 🖱️ LSW 515

29
p. 214
Reflexivpronomen

Use your grid from P11 and complete the sentences.
1. Before the match Kenan looked at XX in the mirror. himself
2. Yesterday I introduced XX to the new coach. myself
3. Our coach says we just need to believe in XX. ourselves
4. They have to prepare XX for an important competition. themselves
5. You play better if you all enjoy XX at training. yourselves
6. Sonya hurt XX badly when she fell off her bike. herself
7. My friend's dog taught XX how to ride a skateboard. itself
8. Remember Johnny, you can treat XX to a big meal after the game! yourself

P13 How much? How many? ✏️ 👄 🖱️ LSW 516

27R
p. 212
Mengenangaben

Complete the questions with *much* **or** *many*.
Then ask and answer them with a partner.
1. How XX hours do you spend watching sports programmes on TV? many
2. How XX time do you spend doing sports each week? much
3. How XX money do you spend on sports clothes each month? much
4. How XX different kinds of sports can you name in English? many

P14 At a German football stadium 🇬🇧🇩🇪

➡️ p. LF59

🔧 **How to ...**
help out
p. 190

An American tourist wants to visit the big football stadium in your area.
He found this leaflet in German. Can you help him? Give your answers in English.

Excuse me, how
long are the tours?

Are there tours
every day?

Where do the
tours start?

How much are the
tours for teenagers?

Stadionführungen

Wir bieten allen Interessierten 90-minütige
Stadionführungen.

Zeiten: Di. - Fr. um 14 und 16 Uhr,
Sa. - So. um 13, 15 und 17 Uhr
Keine Stadionführungen an Spieltagen!
Preise: Erwachsene: 5,- Euro;
Kinder, Jugendliche und Rentner: 3,- Euro;
Gruppen (ab 10 Personen): 35,- Euro
Treffpunkt: An der Bushaltestelle vor dem Stadion
Gruppen sollten sich bitte vorher bei uns anmelden
(Tel.: 47 80 33).
Für Einzelbesucher ist keine Anmeldung erforderlich.

➡ p.LF59

How to ...
read
p. 179

28
p. 213
Indirekte Rede

M1 **After Tom and Stacy's date** LSW 517, 518

a) Work with a partner. One of you reads the diary entry, the other reads the Internet chat. Then tell each other what happened during the **date**.

Wednesday, 5th April

OH MY GOODNESS! I had the worst time ever with Tom!!! First, he arrived late. His excuse? He said he had almost forgotten! Things got worse: Tom wanted Mexican food. When I told him I preferred Italian, he said I would like it and took me to a Mexican fast food restaurant! I even had to pay for my own food, but at least it was cheap. Next thing, he met his friend Chad there. They talked about yesterday's baseball game for like half an hour – and Tom ignored me the whole time!!! I felt like walking home. After dinner Tom drove me home and before I got out of the car, he tried to kiss me. I turned away and just got out of the car. I can't believe it! Then he said he would call me later. 😐 And I thought he was a really nice guy! BOYS!!!

Add Subject Call Video More

chr1$: so how did it go with stacy?
tom: great!
chr1$: so gimme details!
tom: I didn't want 2 look 2 excited so I picked her up late
chr1$: lol what were you thinking?
tom: that wasn't OK?
chr1$: i wouldn't do that
tom: anyway we had mexican food – she said she had never eaten it before
chr1$: did she like it?
tom: think so. even saw chad at the restaurant
chr1$: what's he up to?
tom: not much, we only talked for a few minutes
chr1$: so did you kiss her at the end?
tom: no, im making her wait
chr1$: lol so when u gonna call her?
tom: im gonna wait a few days – keep her guessing ;-)

b) What went wrong on Tom and Stacy's date?

c) What do you think happens next?
Write a second chat between Tom and Chris or Stacy's diary entry from a few days later.

> Tom arrived late.

> Stacy didn't like ...

➡ p.LF60

M1 + M2 WB
p. 87

M2 **What did they say?**  IWS LSW 519

a) What did Tom and Stacy **actually** say to each other? Find the sentences in M1 that match these statements. Write down both sentences in your exercise book.

> Sorry, I almost forgot about our date.

> I've never eaten Mexican food before.

> Don't worry. You'll like Mexican food!

> You know, I really prefer Italian food.

Tom   Stacy

How to ...
work with grammar
p. 190

28
p. 213
Indirekte Rede

b) ☀ Look at each pair of sentences you have written down. Say what changes take place when you turn **direct speech** into **reported speech**.

M3 If only they had a second chance ...

Bedingungssätze,
Typ III

13
p. 204

M3
p. 88

Read M1 again. If things had been different, how might the date have gone?
Match the correct sentence parts. What word do you get? dating

1. If Tom had been on time, D

2. If Stacy had said more clearly that she preferred Italian food, A

3. If Tom had taken Stacy to a good Mexican restaurant, T

4. Stacy wouldn't have felt so ignored I

5. If Stacy had walked home, N

6. Maybe the date would have gone better G

I if Tom hadn't talked to Chad for so long.

O if Tom hadn't driven her home.

D Stacy would have been in a better mood.

T she might have found something she liked.

G if Tom had asked Chris for advice before.

A perhaps Tom would have taken her to a different restaurant.

S Chad would have been very happy.

N Tom might have realized Stacy was not having a good time.

M4 If things had gone differently ...   LSW 521

Bedingungssätze,
Typ III

13
p. 204

M4
p. 88

Use the *past perfect* of these verbs
to complete the sentences.

be • take *(2x)* • not go • ignore

1. If Tom XX the bus, he would have arrived on time. had taken
2. If Tom XX Stacy to an Italian restaurant, she would have enjoyed the food. had taken
3. If Tom XX Stacy a little longer while he was talking to Chad, she would have walked home. had ignored
4. If Tom XX more of a gentleman, maybe Stacy would have kissed him. had been
5. If Stacy XX on the date with Tom, she would have watched a film. hadn't gone

M5 A radio report

➡ p. LF60

L 1.38

How to ...
listen
p. 178

How to ...
discuss
p. 182

a) **Listen to the radio report. What is it about?** malls in America
b) **Read the questions. Then listen again and take notes.**
   – Why does each city need its own mall?
   – What is a plaza?
   – What do large malls offer?
   – What do malls have to have?
c) **Compare your results with a partner. Then discuss: What is the same**
   as in Germany? What is different?

M6 You won't believe it!

➡ p. LF61

B 9
p. 104

How to ...
write
p. 184

The next day the girl who fainted is writing an email to a friend
to tell him/her what happened at the mall. Write the girl's email.

 p. 246   TM, p. 259

➡ p. LF61

M7 Where is everyone? LSW 520

L 1.39

a) Look at the photos. What do you think happens once a year in the US?

b) Now listen to the news report. Why are the streets empty in the photo?

M5
p. 89

c) Read the questions. Then listen again and take notes.
- What time does the game start?
- What can you watch before the game?
- Why is the trophy named after Vince Lombardi?

➡ p. LF61

M8 American football rules

16 // B
p. 109

Look at number 15 again. Then read the statements.
Are they right or wrong? Correct what's wrong.

1. In American football you can carry or kick the ball. ✓
2. There are 22 players in each team. wrong
3. The offensive players block the players of the other team. ✓
4. A touchdown is when the team gets the ball across the opponents' goal line. ✓

5. A team gets four points for a touchdown. wrong
6. For a field goal you have to have scored a touchdown first. wrong
7. In high school games the quarters are not as long as in national games. ✓

➡ p. LF61

M9 Sport kills? LSW 522

M6
p. 89

a) Read this article from an online newspaper. Do you agree with the author? Say why.

M7
p. 90

> **Sport kills**
> I often ask myself: Why do people do sport?
> When I go for a walk in the park, I see joggers sweating and moaning. They always look exhausted and don't seem to enjoy themselves. In February a friend of mine went skiing in Austria. He came back with a broken leg and still has problems walking. Then the other day I read about a young surfer in Hawaii who got killed by a shark. So for me it is clear: Sport is exhausting, dangerous and can even kill people. If you want a good and healthy life, relax and

b) Now read a comment on the article above. What arguments does Antonia use? Are they convincing?

> Posted by Antonia 23 • 9 minutes ago   January 12th
> That's simply not true: Sport doesn't kill. It's a fact that doing sport is important for your body and health. People who do sport regularly are fitter and feel better. If you ask me, it's important that you choose the right sport and do it properly. It's definitely not the sport that kills but wrong behaviour. People who don't do sport often eat more and are more likely to smoke. Think about it!

c) **Write a comment on the article in a) or on one of these statements. Collect arguments first, then write down your opinion. You can look at page 186 for help.**

Germans can only play football.

Female football players should earn as much as **male** football players.

How to …
write your opinion
p. 186

wordbank
Health
p. 171

➡ p. LF62

How to …
read
p. 179

M10 Donna's biggest challenge 👓 ✏ 🖱 LSW 523, 524

a) **Look at the picture, the title and the headings.**
   What do you think the report is about?
b) **Now read Donna's report and find out if you were right in a).**

BUTT OUT – I QUIT

Why I started
I started at 13. Some of my friends started smoking and I joined them because I wanted to **fit in**. The kids I smoked with **seemed** cool – I felt some **peer pressure** I guess.

Why I stopped
I felt **stressed** when I couldn't smoke. I quit volleyball training because I had no energy. Even walking made me feel tired. My parents were angry and wanted me to stop. They said I smelled of smoke all the time.

How I did it
I tried **nicotine gum** instead of **cigarettes**, but it didn't work. Then I tried smoking **less** – 20 cigarettes in the first week, then 10 in the next week. Finally I **put out** my last butt – I quit.

The hardest part
The first weeks were the hardest. I wanted a cigarette when I woke up. At first I had **headaches** and even less energy than before. I wanted something in my mouth so I wouldn't smoke. I ate lots and **gained** a few **pounds**. Gaining weight and feeling bad made things very difficult. But after a few weeks I lost weight again and started feeling better. My **skin** and hair look better now that I don't smoke anymore.

My message to you
It's hard but you can do it. **Patches** or nicotine gum work for some people. It's important to find out what works for you, and that people help. My family and friends helped me a lot. Lots of kids think smoking won't hurt them, but it can **ruin** your life. So stop now – while you're still young and healthy.

c) **Read the report again and collect all the words and expressions that have to do with smoking.**

put out, quit,
…

d) **Write down questions that you can answer with information from the report. Then find a partner to answer them.**

When did Donna start smoking?
Why did she … ?
…

WB M8
p. 90

wordbank
Health
p. 171

21R
p. 209
Fragen mit
Fragewörtern

CAMDEN CHRONICLE
LEARN ENGLISH THE CAMDEN WAY

DID YOU GET IT ALL? → p. LF62

» Where can customers try on clothes in a shop?
» What time are Josh, Alex and Ben going to meet at the mall?
» Why are the girls at the mall screaming?
» Why does Josh get a ticket to Crusher's concert?
» What do cheerleaders do?
» What does Ashley's team want to win?
» What is a touchdown in American football?
» How long is an American football field?

> Oh, just awful. I've got a terrible headache and I'm tired and my feet are cold and ...

GOOD TO KNOW ...

Wenn dich jemand fragt *How are you?*, solltest du ihm oder ihr nicht von deinem Kopfweh oder deinen kalten Füßen erzählen. In den USA stellen die Leute dir diese Frage nicht, um herauszufinden, wie du dich fühlst. Sie sind einfach nur höflich. Du kannst eine kurze Antwort geben wie *Great*, *Good* oder *OK*. Viele Leute antworten auch mit *Fine, thanks*.

Chants and cheers

> We're gonna F-I-G-H-T
> We're gonna S-C-O-R-E
> We're gonna fight
> We're gonna score
> We're gonna win tonight!
> WOHOO!

> Are you ready for the challenge?
> Are you ready to be stopped?
> We're the mighty Panthers,
> And we're reaching for the top.
> YES, reaching for the top!

Chat-up lines

It isn't easy to ask someone out on a date. That's why people say something funny or romantic to get someone's attention.

> I've seen your picture before, in the dictionary under "beautiful"!

> Do you have a map? I need one because I keep getting lost in your eyes.

> I lost my phone number, can I borrow yours?

> When they made the alphabet, they should have put U and I together.

> Are you accepting applications for your fan club?

CALIFORNIA

In diesem *Theme* ...

» lernst du Kalifornien kennen, den *Golden State*.
» sprichst du darüber, was man bei bestimmten Berufen können muss.
» beschäftigst du dich mit einem Freizeitpark in Hollywood.
» sprichst du über verschiedene Filmgenres.
» verfasst du eine Filmkritik.

➡ p. LF63

L 1.40

➡ p. LF63

1 California – here we come! 👂 👄 📖 p. 78/1

a) Listen to the song by Katy Perry. What comes to your mind when you think of California?
b) **Brainstorm** with a partner.

2 Lots to see and do in California 👓 ✏ 📖 pp. 79–80/2

wordbank
Weather
p. 172

1 + 2
p. 91

a) Look at the information. **Where** can you go in California? **What** can you do?
What can you see? **Who** can you meet? **What** problems are there? **Fill in** the grid.

| places
you can go to | activities
you can do | people
you can meet | problems
in California |
|---|---|---|---|
| Golden Gate Bridge | go cycling and inline skating in Santa Monica | ... | ... |
| ... | ... | ... | ... |

P1 **P**
p. 130

A California is famous for its many landscapes: desert, forests, mountains, hills and the ocean.

B The Golden Gate Bridge in San Francisco is one of California's most famous sights.

D Los Angeles, the second largest city in the US, has a population of nearly 4 million people.

C Park rangers look after and help visitors in California's nine national parks.

E Cycling and inline skating in Santa Monica – Venice Beach is 4.5 km long.

F Silicon Valley is the area in California that is known for its high tech industry.

G Theme parks like Disneyland and some film studios attract millions of visitors each year.

H LA Lakers: This famous basketball team have been champions 16 times.

I Hot and dry weather in California makes forest fires much worse.

J Hollywood is the centre of the American film industry.

K Stunt performers perform dangerous situations for many of the movies filmed in California.

L 67 people died in the 1989 earthquake in San Francisco.

M Border patrol guards protect the US-Mexican border near San Diego. About 2.6 million illegal immigrants live in California.

N Lifeguards keep the beaches of Los Angeles safe.

b) **Placemat: What would you like to see or do in California?**
Work in groups of four and collect your ideas on a placemat.
In your group, agree on three activities and write them in the middle of the placemat.
Then tell the class about your results.

 LSW 601

How to …
work with others
p. 188

M   M1
p. 134

WB   3 + 4
p. 92

3 ☾ **Working in California** 👂 😮 IWS

1. lifeguard
2. stunt performer   ➡ p. LF63
3. park ranger
4. tour guide

Listen to the four people. Which of these jobs do they do? p. 81/3

⊙   L 1.41

firefighter • pilot • park ranger • actor •
stunt performer • lifeguard • cook • tour guide

Person 1 is a/an …

🔍   24
Nomen mit/ohne Artikel p. 211

P   P2
p. 130

➡ p. LF63

4 A newspaper article   LSW 602

How to ...
read
p. 179

5
p. 93

a) Look at the picture and guess what the article is about.
b) Read the text in one go. Then choose the best headline for the report.

Movie stars die in wildfires

After the wildfires

Mexico helps to put out wildfires

Wildfires make California dangerous place to live

New York City destroyed

November 9, 2007

LOS ANGELES It's finally over. After nearly three weeks the fires in the forests of California were put out. During those three weeks nine people were killed, 85 people were injured and thousands of homes were destroyed.

The wildfires started on October 20. There were 18 fires all over the state and they destroyed an area bigger than New York City. Although the fires came very close, it can only have been good luck that none of the state's national parks were damaged by them.

Across the state hundreds of thousands of people had to leave their homes because it was too dangerous for them to stay. One of the biggest fires was in Malibu, Los Angeles, where many movie stars like Leonardo DiCaprio, Jennifer Aniston and Tom Cruise live. Many people had to stay in schools, churches and sports stadiums where they were given food, drink and medicine.

The real heroes during this difficult time were the firefighters. Around 8,900 men and women worked day and night to put out the fires. Some firefighters even came from across the border in Mexico to help. During the three weeks of fires there were many stories of bravery, for example one young boy was rescued by a firefighter who landed his helicopter in a burning forest.

61 firefighters were injured by the flames. This newspaper would like to thank all the men and women who helped out.

So what now? Well, there are still many questions. How did the fires start? Who is responsible? Who is going to pay for all the damage? What will happen to the people who have lost their homes? Let's all work together so that the people of California can start living normal lives again soon.

6 + 7
p. 93

M2 //M
p. 134

30R
p. 214 Passiv

M3 M
p. 135

P3 P
p. 130

c) **Read the report again and complete the sentences.** KVs 6.1
   1. After three weeks the fires were ...
   2. Nine people were killed, 85 people were injured and ...
   3. Luckily, none of the state's national parks were ...
   4. In schools, churches and sports stadiums people were ...
   5. A young boy was ...
   6. 61 firefighters were ...

5 Jobs in California   IWS p. 81/3

➡ p. LF64

a) Look at the jobs. What is important for each of them?

> If you want to be a firefighter/..., you should ...

 wordbank
Jobs
p. 162

be good with your hands • get along well with other people •
be good at working with computers • be able to work long hours •
be able to do shift work • be very fit • like to work outdoors/indoors •
know martial arts • know how to drive/swim/... • be brave/creative • ...

 LSW 603

24
Nomen mit/ohne Artikel p. 211

8 + 9
p. 94

make-up artist

firefighter

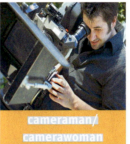
cameraman/
camerawoman

programmer

park ranger

lifeguard

tour guide

stunt performer

b) Work in small groups. Choose one of the jobs above and make a word web like this:

equipment · ... · where · ... · show people around places · TOUR GUIDE · what he or she does · ... · working hours · ... · should · ... · be friendly

c) Put up your word webs in your classroom.
Present them to your classmates in a gallery walk.

 How to ...
work with others
p. 188

6 A job for YOU? KVs 6.4, 6.6

 p. 82/4

What job wouldn't you like to do?
What would be a good job for you?
Look at number 5 for ideas and use
your word web from 5b) to describe the job.
Say why you think this job would be right or
wrong for you.

> I wouldn't like to be a park ranger because they usually work outdoors. Park rangers also have to be brave and help people in national parks where there are wild animals. I would like to be a make-up artist. I think that would be the right job for me. I am creative and good with my hands. I get along well with other people, too.

➡ p. LF64

 wordbank
Jobs
p. 162

p.249

➡ p. LF64

P4 P
p. 131

10 WB
p. 95

7 California's national parks p. 83/5, p. 84/7

a) Look at the map of California.
There are nine national parks.
Where are they? Talk to your partner.

> ... National Park is in the north/south/east/west/ north-west/south-east of ...

b) Now read about four of the nine national parks.
Which ones would you like to visit? Say why. LSW 604

Redwood National Park
Size: 112,618 acres
Founded: 1968
Attractions: some of the world's tallest trees (some are 2,000 years old and 300 feet tall)
Animals: for example pelicans, eagles, owls, black bears and cougars

National Parks
1 Redwood
2 Lassen Volcanic
3 Yosemite
4 Kings Canyon
5 Sequoia
6 Pinnacles
7 Death Valley
8 Channel Islands
9 Joshua Tree

Death Valley National Park
Size: 3,373,063 acres
Founded: 1933
Attractions: desert scenery, sand dunes and ghost towns, highest point: Telescope Peak (11,049 feet), lowest point: Badwater (282 feet below sea level), wild flowers in spring
Animals: for example lizards, scorpions, coyotes and cougars

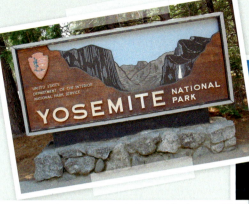

Yosemite National Park

Size: 747,956 acres
Founded: 1890
Attractions: mountains, valleys, cliffs and waterfalls in the Sierra Nevada
Animals: for example black bears, cougars and snakes

Channel Islands National Park

Size: 249,561 acres, half of them are under the ocean
Founded: 1938
Attractions: sea cliffs, caves and beaches, over 2,000 different plants
Animals: for example foxes, sea lions, pelicans and blue whales (the world's largest animals)

P P5 + P6
p. 131

M M4
p. 135

8 **Choose an activity**   KVs 6.5   p. 84/6   ➡ p. LF65

portfolio

You can ...
- **make a collage about California.** Think about sights, people, places, ...
  Put up your collage in the classroom and talk about it.
- **find out about** one of the other five national parks in California and make a fact file.
  Look at number 7 for help. Also give some information on things you can do there and add pictures. Present your fact file in class.
- **plan a two-week trip to California.** Think about where you would like to go and what you would like to see and experience. Present your plan in class.

www

→ p. LF65

M5 //M
p. 136

How to ...
read
p. 179

11 + 12 WB
p. 96

P10 + P12 P
p. 133

// M5: acht
anspruchsvollere
Fragen zum Flyer

9 Visit Hollywood Film Studios! p. 85/8 LSW 605

Work with a partner. Look at the leaflet and find out:

1. Can you visit the studios at Christmas?
2. When do the studios close in November?
3. In what languages do they offer the tours?
4. What is a Front of Line Pass good for?
5. Where can you get information on group tours?
6. How much is a normal day ticket for a mother with two children (2 and 5 years old)?

Hollywood Film Studios

OPENING TIMES Summer: 8:30 am – 10 pm **BOX OFFICE HOURS** Summer: 8 am – 6 pm
Non-summer: 9 am – 7 pm Non-Summer: 8:30 am – 4 pm

PRICES Normal Pass (day ticket) Ages 3+ $84.00
Front of Line Pass (day ticket, no waiting time) Ages 3+ $149.00
VIP Experience Ages 5+ $299.00
Entrance for children under 3 FREE

GROUP INFORMATION For reservations and rates call
(818) 4708351 at any time

GENERAL INFORMATION Open daily except Thanksgiving and Christmas.
Spanish and Chinese-language tours every day.

🇺🇸 LAND & LEUTE

Hollywood

Hollywood (dt.: Stechpalmenwald) ist ein Stadtteil von Los Angeles mit ca. 210.000 Einwohnern. Weltbekannt wurde Hollywood als Zentrum der US-amerikanischen Filmindustrie. Große Hollywood-Studios heute sind z. B. die *Universal Studios* und *Warner Brothers*. In den Hollywood Hills über der Stadt befindet sich das bekannte Hollywood-Schild, das 1923 errichtet wurde, um für den Verkauf von Grundstücken zu werben.
Der *Walk of Fame* ist sicherlich der berühmteste Gehweg der Welt. Er wurde 1958 eingerichtet und erstreckt sich über 18 Häuserblöcke. Mit den Sternen, die in den Gehweg eingelassen sind, werden Prominente geehrt, die eine wichtige Rolle in der Unterhaltungsindustrie hatten oder haben. Aber auch Mickey Mouse oder berühmte Filmtiere wie Lassie sind hier verewigt. Bis jetzt sind schon über 2.500 Sterne vergeben.

Welche Personen fallen dir ein, die mit einem Stern geehrt worden sind?
Finde heraus, wo es auf der Welt noch einen *Walk of Fame* gibt.

→ p. LF66

10 **Take a tour!** KVs 6.3 p. 86/9 LSW 606, 607 ➡ p. LF66

a) 🌙 **Look at the second part of the leaflet. What can you see on these tours?**

TOURS

A Get ready to live the most exciting adventure in 65 million years. Meet scary dinosaurs like the T-Rex in the DINOSAUR JUNGLE.

B Fight and try to survive in the world of ROBOTS ALIVE! Remember that the future of the human race is counting on you.

C What's that noise? Can you feel that? Get ready for the shock of your life. Feel your heart race as an EARTHQUAKE strikes.

D Meet BIG GORILLA. He's as big as a house and as heavy as three elephants. And he's ready to take things into his own hands.

On tour		you can see	
	A		a battle between machines and humans.
	B		a big and heavy monster.
	C		how earthquakes are made in films.
	D		dinosaurs that lived 65 million years ago.

b) **Listen to Alan, Brandon and Meg at the film studios. Find out …**
- in what order they went on the tours. C → A → D → B
- who is really exhausted after the four tours.
  Brandon

c) **Which tour would YOU like to go on? Say why.**

I would like to go on tour … because …

 L 1.42

P7
p. 132

11 **Enjoying a movie**

a) **Look at the cartoon. What can you see? What is happening? Here is some help:**

In the cartoon you can see …
On the screen there is …
The sharks are …
The shark on the left …

b) **Say what is funny about the cartoon.**

 p. 87/10

➡ p. LF66

How to …
talk about pictures
p. 183

P9
p. 132

I JUST LOVE HAPPY ENDINGS

TITANIC

offthemark.com
ATLANTIC FEATURE ©1999 MARK PARISI

BASIS Made in Hollywood

 p. 250

 p. LF66

12 What type of film?   p.87/11 LSW 608

a) Which of these statements best describe the types of film YOU watch?

A My favourite films always **deal with** love, **hate** and friendship.

B I'm a big fan of films with aliens in them.

C There's got to be a great love story in any film I watch!

D I only watch films that make me laugh.

E I love **animated films** – especially **computer-animated** ones!

F I like films that make you scream!

G The films I find the most interesting are films about legends or **myths**.

H I like films that have got a hero in them who fights the bad guys and always wins!

13
p. 97

b) Now match each statement with the right type of film.

A   B   H   C   D   F   E   G

drama • science fiction • action • **romance** • **comedy** • horror • animation • fantasy

How to ... work with others p. 188

c) Think – pair – share: How many film titles can you write down for each type of film?

 p. LF66
How to ... read p. 179

13 A review   IWS p.88/12 LSW 609, 610

14
p. 98

a) Read a review of the film "The Bling Ring". Would you like to see the film? Give reasons.

FILM CLUB // / ////// / // /// / / //// /

United States: 2013
Running time: 90 min.
Cast: Israel Broussard,
    Katie Chang,
    Taissa Farmiga,
    Claire Julien,
    Emma Watson
Director: Sofia Coppola

The film tells the story of five teenagers in Los Angeles, one boy (Marc) and four girls (Rebecca, Nicki, Sam and Chloe). They use the Internet to find out where celebrities such as Paris Hilton, Orlando Bloom and Megan Fox live and if they are out of town. If this is the case, the teenagers **enter** the celebrities' houses in Hollywood. They look at how the stars live and what they own. They steal shoes, bags, clothes, cash and **jewellery**. Afterwards the teenagers wear the stolen clothes. They also sell some of the things and

post photos of them on social media sites.
The police finally identify the group. The teenagers are **arrested** and sent to **prison**.
"The Bling Ring" is an exciting film. I enjoyed it because it shows you the world of the rich and famous – a world you haven't seen before. Critics say that the film is a bit boring because it only shows one burglary after another. Judge for yourself!

b) Find words in the review that match these expressions:

➡ p. LF67

things you wear as decoration, for example rings	a place where criminals are kept

take something that isn't yours	famous people	the actors and actresses in a film

c) Write a review about a film/series YOU have seen. These questions may help you:
- What is the title of the film/series?
- When was it made?
- How long is it?
- Who are the actors and actresses?
- Who is the director?
- What type of film/series is it?
- What is it about?
- Why did/didn't you like the film/series?
- How many stars would you give it?
- ...

Now work with a partner and check your texts. Rewrite your reviews and hang them up in your classroom.

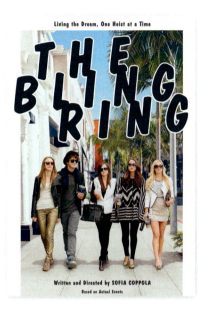

Living the Dream, One Heist at a Time

THE BLING RING

Written and Directed by SOFIA COPPOLA
Based on Actual Events

How to ...
write a review
p. 187

WB **15**
p. 98

P **P8 + P11**
p. 132/133

M **M6 - M8**
p. 136/137

WB **16**
p. 99

---

14 **Choose an activity**  pp. 89–90/13

portfolio

➡ p. LF67

You can ...
- **make a fan poster of your favourite actor/actress or film/series.**
- **make a star with the name of your favourite actor or actress.**
  Prepare a short talk about him or her. In class, put your stars on the floor and take a tour.
- **imagine you had the chance to look around your favourite celebrity's home. Who would it be? What would you see/find there? Make notes and tell your class.**
- **prepare a short talk about your favourite film/series. Think about:**
  - when you saw the film/series
  - the story (what? when? where?)
  - the actors/actresses
  - why you like the film/series
  - ...

EMMA WATSON

Personal Life:
- She lived in Paris until she was 5.
- She studied at Brown University and at Oxford.
- She was born on 15th April 1990.

Famous Films:
- She played Hermione in the Harry Potter films.
- She was also in The Perks of Being a Wallflower and The Bling Ring.

How to ...
give a talk
p. 180

WB **test yourself**
p. 100/101

p. 251 TM, p. 293

➡ p. LF67

P1 Nature words ✎ 🖱 LSW 611

a) Look at number 2 again and collect words and phrases about nature.
   Make a list.
b) Add nature words you already know.

➡ p. LF67

L 1.43

P2 Sound check 👂 ✎ 🖱 LSW 612

a) Copy the grid. Then listen to the eight people.
   Is the speaker American or British? Tick (✓) the right box.

speakers	AE	BE	words that helped to decide
speaker 1		✓	timetable
speaker 2			...
...			...

b) Listen again. Which words helped you to decide in each statement?

Passiv

30R

p. 214

P3 Some facts about California 👓 ✎ KVs 6.1 🖱 IWS

🖱 LSW 613

Complete the sentences with the correct *past participle* forms of
the verbs in the box.

> open • find • make •
> know • produce • invent

1. California is XX by many names such as "The Land of Milk and Honey" and "The Golden State". known
2. In 1973, an 11 kilogram gold nugget was XX by an amateur gold digger in the Yuba River. found
3. Blue jeans and skateboards were XX in California. invented
4. The first cinema in the US was XX in Los Angeles on 2 April 1902. opened
5. Over 64 million litres of wine are XX in California each year. produced
6. The first Californian flag was XX by a group of American settlers. made

P4 Some research

➡ p. LF68

Work with a partner and find out:

1. Which of these US states share a border with California? Oregon, Arizona, Nevada

/ˈteksəs/   /nəˈbræskə/   /ˈɒrɪɡən/   /ˌærɪˈzəʊnə/   /ˌæləˈbæmə/   /nɪˈvɑːdə/

2. What is the name of the largest city, the highest mountain and the longest river in California?
3. What time is it in California at the moment?
4. Every state in the US has got a state animal. What is the state animal of California?

P5 National park quiz 📝 👄 📋 KVs 6.2

➡ p. LF68

21R
p. 209
Fragen mit
Fragewörtern

a) Look at number 7 again and prepare questions. Here is some help:

Where can you find ... ?

How old are some ... ?

When was ... founded?/Which park was founded in ... ?

What is the name of the highest/lowest point in ... ?

What animals live in ... ?

... ?

b) Now quiz your partner. Take turns.

P6 Park rules 🇬🇧 🇩🇪 📋 KVs 6.7

➡ p. LF68

🔧 **How to ...**
help out
p. 190

You are in Yosemite National Park. Another German tourist who doesn't speak much English needs help. Tell him/her the rules in German.

Man darf nicht/ soll nicht ...

Man muss/soll ...

...

Yosemite National Park – PARK RULES

- Always carry enough water with you.
- Be prepared for sudden changes in the weather.
- Do not hike on your own, always make sure another person is with you.
- Stay on trails to protect plant life.
- Be careful when driving: wild animals crossing.
- Do not feed the animals.
- Put trash into the available cans.
- If you see a bear, report it to a ranger.
- Keep your food in the special bear-proof lockers.
- Never approach bears or give them food.
- If a bear approaches you, make as much noise as possible by yelling very loudly to scare it away.

W p. 251   TM, p. 295

→ p. LF68

P7 An acrostic

Look at the example and write YOUR acrostic. You can also use other words from Theme 6 like "California" or "Los Angeles".

H ot
O utside
L OS Angeles
L ots of famous actors
Y eah !
W al k
O f Fame
O pen
D aily

HOLLYWOOD

P8 Sound check

 LSW 614

 L 1.44

Listen carefully. Which words can you hear? Write them down.

1. back – (bag)
2. (sing) – thing
3. (set) – sad
4. wet – (vet)
5. close – (clothes)
6. site – (side)

→ p. LF69

P9 At the cinema

a) Look at the pictures. What can you see? Talk to a partner.

How to …
write
p. 184

b) Work with your partner again and write the story.
You can start like this:
Last Saturday … and … went to the cinema. First … bought tickets. Then …
Suddenly …   In the end …

P10 The studios' opening times 👓 ✏️

Look at number 9 again. Complete the sentences with a word from the box.

in • from • until • to • at • during • on

1. The film studios are open for visitors XX Saturdays and Sundays. on
2. They are also open XX the week. during
3. In summer you can visit the studios XX 8.30 am XX 10 pm. from – to
4. You can buy tickets XX 6 pm because the shop closes XX 6 pm. until – at
5. XX summer there are tours through the studios every two hours. In

P11 Being a star in Hollywood 👓 ✏️  LSW 615 ➡ p. LF69

a) Form adverbs from these adjectives and write them down.

regular • quick • polite • healthy • beautiful

regularly, …

19R
p. 208
Adverbs of manner

b) Use your adverbs from a) to complete the sentences.

Do you sometimes dream of being a Hollywood star? It isn't as much fun as you may think:
A movie star has to travel XX. He or she always has to answer reporters' questions XX.
At home and in a restaurant a movie star has to eat XX. He or she has to learn lines for
film parts really XX. A movie star also has to smile for photos XX.

P12 At a German film studio 🇬🇧 LSW 616 ➡ p. LF69

How to …
help out
p. 190

**You have visitors from the USA who don't speak German. You want
to take them to a German film studio. Tell your visitors in English
what the website says. Give only the most important facts.**

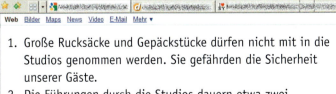

1. Große Rucksäcke und Gepäckstücke dürfen nicht mit in die
   Studios genommen werden. Sie gefährden die Sicherheit
   unserer Gäste.
2. Die Führungen durch die Studios dauern etwa zwei
   Stunden. Für kleine Kinder ist es häufig sehr anstrengend,
   so lange zu stehen. Wir empfehlen deshalb, keine kleinen
   Kinder mit in die Studios zu nehmen.
3. Am Wochenende bilden sich oft lange Warteschlangen vor
   den Studios. Um Wartezeiten zu vermeiden, sollten Gäste
   morgens schon gegen 9 Uhr kommen.

Don't take …, please.

The tours …

You should …

…

→ p. LF69

M1 The Golden State

L 1.45

How to ...
listen
p. 178

M1
p. 104

a) **Listen to the song 'The Golden State' by City and Colour.**
   What is it about?

b) **Listen again and read along. How does the song make you feel?**
   What do you think about the music and the lyrics?

> The song makes me feel ...

> The music sounds ...

> I (don't) like the melody/ rhythm/lyrics because ...

Why's everyone still singing about California?
Haven't we heard enough about the Golden State?
I guess if you like sandy beaches and blue ocean water
There's just something about it, to which I cannot relate
I need to see the leaves change and the snowflakes falling
I need to hear the call, the wind whistling through the winter pines

Why's everyone still singing about California?
Haven't we heard enough about the Golden State?
And people still follow them dreams to sweet California
And from time to time I pass on by, but I will never stay

Sure there are beautiful people, in the city of lost angels
They're living like they're kings and queens, from some royal age
But fortune and fame won't save you, when California
Is wiped out by the ring of fire or a great earthquake

Why's everyone still singing about California?
...

c) **Look at the lyrics again. What does the singer think about California?**
   Does he want to live there? Why/Why not?

d) **Would YOU like to live in California? Give reasons.**

→ p. LF70

M2 A newspaper article

4c // B
p. 122

3OR
p. 214 Passiv

Read the report on page 122 again. What happened to the people and places mentioned in the report? Note down the facts and compare them with a partner.

> – Thousands of homes were destroyed.
> – People had to leave their homes.
> – ...

M3 Calling the emergency services LSW 617–619

➡ p. LF70

In the US you **dial** 911 to reach the **fire department**, the police or an **ambulance**.
In Britain the numbers for the **emergency** services are 999 or 112.

a) **Listen to the emergency call. What has happened?**
b) **Now read the phone dialogue. What questions do you have to answer when you call the emergency services?**

L 2.1

WB M2 p. 104/105

Operator:	911 emergencies.
Caller:	Hi … we need help, please.
Operator:	Which service do you need – ambulance, fire or police?
Caller:	Fire, please.
Operator:	What has happened?
Caller:	Our toaster **caught fire** and now there's a huge fire in the kitchen.
Operator:	OK. What's your name and your phone number, please?
Caller:	Bobby Root. 323 366 5158
Operator:	OK. And where are you? What's your address?
Caller:	We're **right** outside our house. It's 422 Toledo Street, Los Angeles.
Operator:	Is **anybody hurt**?
Caller:	No, everybody is OK.
Operator:	Thank you, Bobby. Now, stay where you are. The firefighters will be there in a few minutes.

c) **Work with a partner and make a phone dialogue for another emergency call. Then present it to the class. Here are some ideas:**

How to …
write
p. 184

WB M3 p. 105

M4 National Park Hotline   LSW 620

➡ p. LF70

a) **Listen to a call to the National Park Hotline. What is the caller planning to do on his visit to a national park?** camp at the park
b) **Listen again and find out:**
   1. Which national park does the caller want to visit? Yosemite
   2. Which website should the caller look at? www.nps.gov
   3. What should the caller do before his visit? plan trip carefully; book camping sites early
   4. What time does the call take place? 6 pm in Germany / 9 am in California
   Take notes. Then compare them with a partner.

L 2.2

How to …
listen
p. 178

p. 252 TM, p. 302

➡ p.LF70

M5 Visit Hollywood Film Studios!   LSW 621

9 // B
p. 126

Work with a partner. Look at the leaflet on page 126 and find out:

1. On what days are the studios closed? Thanksgiving and Christmas
2. When do the studios close in February? at 7 pm
3. What tours are offered to visitors from Madrid or Beijing? tours in Spanish and Chinese
4. What is a Front of Line Pass good for? if you don't want to have to wait
5. What is the most **exclusive** way to visit the studios? VIP Experience ticket ($299)
6. Where and when can you get information on group tours? phone them at (818) 4708351
7. How much is a normal day ticket for a **couple** with three children (2, 5 and 9 years old)? $336
8. You are at the studios. Where can you buy the tickets? at the box office

➡ p.LF71

M6 Jessica goes to Hollywood   LSW 622

8R + 9R
p. 200

M4 + M5
p. 106/107

8R: Zukunft mit *will*
9R: Zukunft mit *going to*

a) Read about Jessica, a girl who wants to go to Hollywood to become a big star. What do you think is going to happen to her when she gets to Hollywood? Talk to a partner.

Jessica ran away from home after she had a terrible **fight** with her mother. She thought Hollywood would be the right place to start a new life. She planned to go to **auditions** and hoped to be discovered. She wanted to be a movie star.

I think she's going to …

Maybe she'll …

If she's lucky, she'll …

L 2.3

b) Now listen to what happens when Jessica gets to Hollywood. Did you guess correctly?

c) Listen again and take notes on these questions:
1. What did Jessica do when she first got to Hollywood?
2. What did Jessica do to earn money?
3. Why was Jessica sometimes late for work?
4. What did Jessica's boss do when she told him why she was sometimes late?
5. Where did Jessica go after she talked to her boss?
6. Why is Jessica so worried?
Compare your notes with a partner.

How to …
write
p. 184

d) ☀ What do you think will happen next? Work with a partner and write a dialogue between Jessica and Samantha. Then act it out in class.

M7 At the audition IWS LSW 623

➡ p. LF71

7
p. 199
Past perfect

Look at the pictures. Write down what happened to Jessica when she went to another audition in Hollywood.

1. After Jessica had learned about the audition, she went to the film studio.
2. After she had gone to the film studio, she …

learn about the audition

go to the film studio

fill in a form

read a text

have lunch

act out the scene

wait for the answer

call her mother

M8 YOU at an audition   LSW 624

➡ p. LF71

WB
M6
p. 107

a) Which audition would you like to go to or would you like to watch? Say why.

| I'd like to | go to a watch a | singing soap opera dancing modelling … | audition because | I'm good at dancing. I like watching soaps. I'd love to … … |

b) How would you prepare for it or how would you advise a friend?
Think about:
– clothes and make-up
– friends or family to go with you
– your "act": speech, song, dance, …
– the information for the judges: about yourself, your plans, your "act"
– …

I would wear …

I'd tell my friend to wear …

CAMDEN CHRONICLE
LEARN ENGLISH THE CAMDEN WAY

DID YOU GET IT ALL? ➡ p. LF72

» What is the job of a park ranger?
» Where can you find California's high tech industry?
» Why did so many people in California have to leave their homes?
» In which national park can you find some of the world's tallest trees?
» When are the Hollywood Film Studios closed?
» On which tour do Alan, Brandon and Meg go first?
» What is the film "The Bling Ring" about?

American licence plates ➡ p. LF72

What do they say?

GOOD TO KNOW ...

In den USA zeigen die Menschen weniger Haut als bei uns. An Stränden und in Schwimmbädern tragen selbst Babys und Kleinkinder Badekleidung und kleine Mädchen Bikinioberteile. Oben ohne und Nacktbaden sind in der Regel gesetzlich verboten und können in vielen Bundesstaaten mit erheblichen Geldbußen bestraft werden.

YOUR YEAR   Folie 14

Your year with Camden Market 4 is over. What was ...

• your favourite Theme?
• your favourite page?
• your favourite picture or photo?
• your favourite story?

Op1 Jobs, jobs, jobs ✏️ 👄

➡️ p. LF73

a) **How many jobs do you know in English? Write them down. You've got three minutes.**

b) **Now work with a partner and compare your lists. Who has got more words?**

Op2 Different jobs 👄 ✏️

➡️ p. LF73

a) **Look at the photos. What do these people do?**

wordbank
Jobs
p. 162

> take care of ill people/animals • work with flowers and plants •
> repair or install electrical equipment • cut and style people's hair •
> protect buildings and shops • make phone calls and prepare letters •
> paint walls, doors or the outside of houses

A painter …

painter

hairdresser

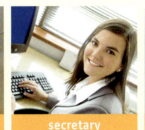
secretary

nurse/male nurse

electrician

vet's assistant

security guard

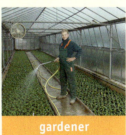
gardener

b) **What do you think about the jobs in a)
and the jobs you collected in Op1?
Make a grid like this.**

Jobs				
interesting	boring	important	dangerous	just OK

c) **Milling around: What would YOU like to be? Interview each other.**

I'd like to be
a/an … because …

How to …
work with others
p. 188

> … it's an interesting/exciting job. •
> … I'll earn enough money to buy a car/a house/nice clothes. •
> … I like working with wood/metal/my hands/children/animals/people/… •
> … I love working indoors/outdoors/in a team/alone. • …

Op OPTIONAL Jobs

→ p. LF73

Op3 A new experience 👓 ✏️

a) **Look at the pictures. Have a guess:**
  – Where are Gillian and Cheryl?
  – Why are they in these places?
  – What are they doing?
  – Do they like it?

How to ...
read
p. 179

b) **Now read the emails.**
  Were you right in a)?

| Send | Chat | Attach | Save draft |

To: gillian.collins@ ▓▓▓▓▓.▓▓▓
Subject: I'm a web designer! :-)
From: cherylhill@ ▓▓▓▓.▓▓▓

Remember the elective I chose for this semester? Web design! It was really boring at first. But now we're learning how to add great colors and backgrounds to our websites. And guess what? Last week I "shadowed" a web designer, Steve, in his office here in town. "Shadowing" is like your work experience, but just for a day. Awesome! Steve showed me how to make really cool websites by also adding sound and videos. Oh, and Steve was so cute! Too bad it was only for one day.

| Send | Chat | Attach | Save draft |

To: cherylhill@ ▓▓▓▓.▓▓▓
Subject: I'm working!
From: gillian.collins@ ▓▓▓▓▓.▓▓▓

Dear Cheryl,
Thanks for your mail. We're doing our work experience now, too. Two weeks without school! I have a job at our local building centre. I know a lot about DIY – my boss was quite surprised. I start at 9 and I've been on time every day so far. The first day was awful. I cleaned shelves, then cleaned more shelves and then – how surprising – cleaned even more shelves. My jeans looked so dirty at the end of the day. Yuck! The next day I counted a lot of different products. Then I had to put the numbers into a portable computer. Then on day 3 I was allowed to help customers. A man came in with a question about a drill. I was a bit nervous at first, but I felt good because I was able to help him. But six hours every day is a long time. My feet! I have to do a lot of writing, too. All kinds of forms and a CV before I started. AND a report at the end. My teacher is coming in tomorrow. Perhaps I can sell him some tools, haha. OK, long day tomorrow – I'm off to bed!
Love, Gillian

c) **Read the emails again and find out who ...**
  1. ... didn't have to go to school for two weeks. Gillian
  2. ... had to choose sound and videos. Cheryl
  3. ... had to clean shelves. Gillian
  4. ... helped a customer with a problem. Gillian
  5. ... liked a web designer. Cheryl
  6. ... found her elective very boring at first. Cheryl
  Write down more sentences and let a partner find out who it was.

Op4 Gillian's interview

➡ p. LF74

a) In Gillian's email you learned about her work experience.
Read the email again, then copy the word web and complete it.

how long
where
...
filled in forms
her jobs
before work experience
...
Gillian's work experience
...
...
working hours
other info
...
...

b) Work with a partner. Use your word web from a) and prepare an interview with Gillian for the school newspaper. One of you is the reporter, the other takes Gillian's role. Present your interview to the class.

How long is your work experience?

I work ...

...

How many hours do you work every day?

Where do you work?

What do you ...?

What are your jobs?

...

Op5 Talking about work experience

➡ p. LF75

 L 2.4

a) What do Gillian's classmates say about their work experience?
Copy the grid. Then listen and take notes.

How to ...
listen
p. 178

name	where	working hours	liked	didn't like	other info
Aidan	garage	7 am – 2 pm	checking cars for problems	...	...
Caroline	...	...	...	...	...
Nick	...	...	...	...	...

b) Now choose one person. Use your notes to talk about him/her.
Include one piece of false information. Can your classmates find it?

OPTIONAL Jobs

➡ p. LF75

Op6 Aidan's CV 👓 ✏️

a) Look at Aidan's CV. What does it tell you about him?

His surname is …
He lives in …
He was born in …
He goes to …
He went to …
He speaks …
…

Aidan Bradley

---

21 Pratt Street, London NW1 0LY
Home: 020 ▓▓▓ – Mobile: 0760 ▓▓▓ – Email: aidb@ ▓▓▓

Date of birth:	3rd March 20▓▓
Place of birth:	Birmingham, UK
Experience:	Summer job with Lucky Motors, Garage Services, London
Education:	2010 – now Haverstock School, London
	2005 – 2010 Fleet Primary School, London
Languages:	English, Spanish
Hobbies:	basketball, music, cars

b) Write your own CV. Then present it in class.

➡ p. LF76

Op7 Aidan's report 👓 👄

**a) After his work experience Aidan wrote about it. At first he didn't like his report.
Then a classmate helped him to edit his text. First read Aidan's text.**

My work experience as a car technician

did my work experience   Brent
I ~~worked~~ at the garage in ~~Bent~~ Street. I worked there for two weeks.
Normally,   strong   My job was to help
I wore blue overalls and ~~I wore~~ shoes. ~~I helped~~ the car technicians.

I had to wash the cars and ~~I had to~~ clean the floors~~.~~, too.
The car technicians
I had a morning break at 9 o'clock and a lunch break at 12 o'clock.
Then I often   I am really interested in   enjoy
I had to make tea for the other technicians. ~~I like~~ cars and working with my hands.
 learned to   even   , but
I ~~can~~ connect a computer to the engine. I can change a tyre~~. But~~ the boss wouldn't
                        because he was
let me do it in the garage. I don't like the boss~~. He is~~ very unfriendly.
        That is why
He didn't show me new things. I didn't really enjoy my work experience.

b) Then look at the checklist. Work with a partner and find examples for each point in Aidan's edited text.

Checklist for texts:

1 Don't begin all your sentences with the same words.

2 Try to use some of these words: **really**, **normally**, **often**, **too**, …

3 Try to connect sentences. Use **and**, **but**, **then**, **because**, **that is why**, …

4 Use interesting adjectives.

5 Check your spelling.

Op8 Choose an activity

 p. LF76

 portfolio

 How to …
write
p. 184

How to …
give feedback
p. 181

 wordbank
Jobs
p. 162

You can …

- write a report about a job or work experience you did. Think about:
  - what kind of job it was
  - when you did it
  - where you did it
  - how long you worked
  - what other information you can give
  - if you liked/didn't like it and why

  Swap your report with a partner.
  Edit his/her report and give each other feedback.

- make a poster or computer presentation about a job you would like to do.
  - Collect pictures or photos.
  - Describe the job and say why you think it is right for you.

  You can look at Op2 for help.

- interview a person you know about his/her job, for example the school secretary, the headteacher or someone in your family or neighbourhood. Find out:
  - What is his/her job?
  - Where does he/she work?
  - When and how long does he/she work?
  - What does and doesn't he/she like about the job?
  - …

  Present your results in class.

Jobs then[1] and now

waiter/waitress

In the past[2] a waiter or waitress wrote down orders[3] on a piece of paper. Today orders are typed[4] into a portable computer.

taxi driver

In the past a taxi driver knew the route by heart or looked it up on a map. Today the route is worked out[5] by a navigation system.

secretary

In the past a secretary wrote letters with a typewriter[6]. Today letters are written with the help of a computer.

assembly line worker

In the past an assembly line worker[7] put the parts of a fridge together by hand. Today the work is done by a robot.

---

[1]then – *damals*; [2]past – *Vergangenheit*; [3]order – *Bestellung*; [4]type – *tippen*; [5]work out – *errechnen, ausrechnen*; [6]typewriter – *Schreibmaschine*; [7]assembly line worker – *Fließbandarbeiter/in*

A School Dance

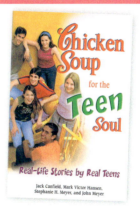

***Chicken Soup for the Teen Soul*[1] is a book written by American teenagers. Read about Adam's feelings before a school dance.**

I had always been an adventurous[2] kind of guy until I encountered[3] the school dance. The dance itself was not a problem; my friends and I hung out, ate pizza, and listened to music.
5 But then strange, unexpected[4] things started happening. A few of the guys began pairing up with girls and dancing to slow songs. I sat wondering how it all worked. How do you know if a girl wants to dance with you? What do you
10 say? Just then one of my friends came back with his head drooping[5].

"I got rejected[6]!" he said quietly. "She turned me down flat[7]."

I sighed[8]. It made me sick to think that I
15 could get rejected, too. How was I ever going to get up enough courage[9] to ask a girl to dance?

In the weeks before the next dance, I started noticing girls in my classes. Some were too tall.
20 Some were too quiet. Some were too loud. But there was one girl I kept thinking about. She seemed just right for me to ask to dance. The thought gave me butterflies[10]. I knew I should ask her to dance at the next dance.

25 Fortunately[11], my friends encouraged[12] me the day of the big dance, each with different advice.

One said, "We'll go with you and stand behind."

30 "It's no big deal," another said. But he had already danced with two girls. *It was easy for him,* I thought.

Then it was time. My hair had recently been cut and was gelled to perfection. I picked out
35 my favorite shirt and jeans. I brushed my teeth with my two-in-one toothpaste with mouthwash

and whitening ingredients[13]. On the way, my dad gave me a pep talk[14]. "Be confident[15]! Look her in the eye, and be friendly." As he waved good-bye, he added, "Go get 'em, son!" 40
I rolled my eyes, thinking, *What does he know?*

Entering the building, I lost my courage. Walking around with my friends, I frantically[16] looked for her. When I finally spotted her, I watched her like an eagle. As the minutes 45
ticked by, my courage returned.

That night, her dark brown hair hung loose on her shoulders. The light shone on the glitter on her cheeks[17], and her lips glistened with lip gloss. Her pink shirt was stamped with the word 50
"Abercrombie" and her bell-bottom jeans were hanging over white tennis shoes.

When the dance was almost over, the DJ announced[18] that there would be one more slow song. As I began to walk toward her, I 55
thought, *Should I really do this?* My feet grew heavier with each step. I could hear the music beginning in the background. The gym smelled like dust[19] mixed with cologne[20]. I saw her talking with her friends. When I finally reached 60
her, I looked into her sparkling brown eyes.

"Will you dance with me?" I asked.
"Yes!" she exclaimed[21].

I placed my hands around her waist while she placed her arms around my neck. We began 65
to sway back and forth[22] to the music. As we danced, every now and then some friends would

→

---

¹soul – *Seele*; ²adventurous – *abenteuerlustig*; ³encounter sth – *auf etw treffen*; ⁴unexpected – *unerwartet*; ⁵drooping – *(herunter)hängend*; ⁶reject – *zurückweisen*; ⁷turn sb down flat – *jdn abblitzen lassen*; ⁸sigh – *seufzen*; ⁹courage – *Mut*; ¹⁰butterfly – *Schmetterling*; ¹¹fortunately – *zum Glück*; ¹²encourage sb – *jdn ermutigen*; ¹³ingredient – *Bestandteil, Wirkstoff*; ¹⁴pep talk – *aufmunternde Worte*; ¹⁵confident – *zuversichtlich, selbstbewusst*; ¹⁶frantically – *wie wild, verzweifelt*; ¹⁷cheek – *Wange*; ¹⁸announce – *verkünden*; ¹⁹dust – *Staub*; ²⁰cologne – *Kölnischwasser (Duftwasser)*; ²¹exclaim – *rufen*; ²²sway back and forth – *sich hin und her wiegen*

give me a wink[23], a nod[24], or a thumbs-up[25]. *This isn't too bad*, I thought. *This is actually* 70 *fun*. When the dance ended, my emotions were running wild as I waved good-bye.

On the drive home, I couldn't stop smiling. Not only had I conquered my fear[26], but dancing with the girl wasn't too bad either[27].

[23]wink – *(Augen)zwinkern*; [24]nod – *Nicken*; [25]thumbs-up – *Daumen hoch*; [26]conquer one's fear – *seine Angst überwinden*; [27]not either – *auch nicht*

→ p. LF77

Choose an activity

- **Which motto fits Adam's story best? Talk to a partner.**

> No risk, no fun! • I get what I want • Boy gets girl • Watch out girls, here I come! • Dancing with girls isn't so easy! • Girls can be really scary sometimes • …

- **What do you think the girl was thinking before Adam asked her? Work with a partner and write down your ideas.**
- **Adam wants to see the girl again. He decides to write an email asking her out on a date. Write his email.**

B The story of the first Thanksgiving ![book icon] p. 92/A

What do you remember about Thanksgiving? 1-B 2-A 3-C 4-B

1 On Thanksgiving …
 A the children thank their parents.
 B everyone gives thanks for the food they have.
 C the white Americans thank the Native Americans.

2 On Thanksgiving people often eat …
 A turkey.   B steaks.   C hamburgers.

3 Thanksgiving is celebrated in …
 A spring.   B summer.   C fall.

4 The first American Thanksgiving was celebrated about …
 A 40 years ago.   B 400 years ago.   C 4000 years ago.

Read the story and see if you remembered correctly.

On 16th September 1620, the Pilgrim Fathers set sail from Plymouth in England towards[1] Virginia, USA. 102 passengers[2] travelled on the ship called the Mayflower. The people on board 5 were leaving to find a new home, far across the ocean in America. There they hoped to be free to practise religion[3] their own way.

The journey[4] was long and stormy. Huge waves crashed across the deck of the Mayflower. The Pilgrims were sick[5] and frightened[6]. But they did 10

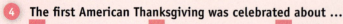

[1]towards – *in Richtung*; [2]passenger – *Passagier/in*; [3]practise religion – *Religion ausüben*; [4]journey – *Reise*; [5]sb is sick – *jdm ist schlecht/übel*; [6]frightened – *Angst haben*

not lose hope. On 21st November they reached[7] land at Cape Cod at the north-east coast of today's state of Massachusetts, which they later named Plymouth Rock. At last the tired Pilgrims
15 had arrived in America.

Winter had begun, and the Pilgrims needed homes. They wanted to begin building. On land they found fields and a dark green forest. They cut down huge trees for wood to build their
20 homes. Then, on Christmas Day, they began to build.
That winter many of the Pilgrims became very sick. Some of them died. Those who could, cared for[8] the others. Then, in March, they had
25 a surprise.
Native Americans came to offer friendship. The Pilgrim leader and the native leader Chief Massasoit met. They feasted[9] and talked. Then they made a promise to help each other. One
30 Native American, who spoke English, decided to stay with the Pilgrims. His name was Squanto.

Spring had come. It was time to plant. The Pilgrims planted peas and barley[10] brought from England, but they knew nothing about growing
35 corn. Squanto showed them. He also told them where to hunt and how to fish in this new land. The forest had many things the Pilgrims needed. It gave them wood for their homes and fires. There were deer[11], nuts[12] and berries[13]. But the
40 forest was also dark and frightening[14]. At night the Pilgrims could hear the howling[15] of the wolves[16].

One summer day, young John Billington went berry picking[17]. He left the forest path[18] and got
45 lost. John walked through the forest for many days. He only had berries and wild plants to eat. At night he slept under the trees. Finally

some Native Americans found him and sent word[19] to Plymouth. Governor[20] Bradford sent a boat to bring John home. The Native Americans 50 sang and danced, and everyone exchanged[21] presents. The Pilgrims were happy that young John had been found.

The green trees of summer turned red and gold. The corn grew tall and became dry and yellow. 55 Huge orange pumpkins covered the fields. Wild geese[22] filled the sky[23] and turkeys gobbled[24] everywhere. The Pilgrims began to gather[25] the corn and pumpkins. It was time to give thanks to God[26] for the good harvest. 60
On a sunny October day in 1621, Governor Bradford declared[27] a time for thanksgiving. The women and children slowly roasted[28] fat[29] geese and wild turkeys over the fires. Pies and corn bread baked in the outdoor ovens[30]. 65
Chief Massasoit and his people came with presents. Then, with songs and prayers[31], the Thanksgiving celebration began. For three days everyone ate, sang, and played games. Together the Pilgrims and Native Americans lived in 70 peace[32] and a friendship grew.

With the Pilgrims' journey began the largest migration[33] of peoples in history. By the end of the 19th century about 11 million people had followed the Pilgrims across the Atlantic. 75

---

[7]reach – *erreichen*; [8]care for sb – *sich um jdn kümmern*; [9]feast – *schlemmen*; [10]barley – *Gerste*; [11]deer – *Hirsch*; [12]nut – *Nuss*; [13]berry – *Beere*; [14]frightening – *beängstigend*; [15]howling – *Heulen*; [16]wolf (*pl* wolves) – *Wolf*; [17]pick – *pflücken*; [18]path – *Weg*; [19]send word – *Mitteilung machen*; [20]governor – *Gouverneur*; [21]exchange – *austauschen*; [22]goose (*pl* geese) – *Gans*; [23]sky – *Himmel*; [24]gobble – *kollern*; [25]gather – *sammeln*; [26]God – *Gott*; [27]declare – *verkünden*; [28]roast – *braten*; [29]fat – *dick, fett*; [30]oven – *(Back)ofen*; [31]prayer – *Gebet*; [32]peace – *Frieden*; [33]migration – *Zu- und Abwanderung*

C Hannah and Zach

Read a story about the first love of two teenagers in New York.

A Hannah and Zach meet for the first time.

I normally hated taking the bus home after school. It took ages and it was always so hot and full. But that one day, I was so happy I was on that bus.

5 That one day, I got on, showed my bus pass, found a seat and then looked up … to see a boy from school staring at[1] me.
He was tall with dark brown, curly[2] hair. That hair framed[3] a face with big, dark eyes and – as
10 he saw me looking at him – the most beautiful smile I had ever seen.
The bus stopped and people got off. It pulled away again. As more and more people got off the bus, it got quite empty, but still he was
15 staring at me. Saying nothing, just staring as if he couldn't stop.
I, in return, couldn't look anywhere but at him, either[4]. I felt like I knew him, like I'd always known him.

At some point we got to my stop. I got up and 20 moved towards the door and so did he. He was getting off, too. The bus stopped suddenly, and I nearly fell – but he caught my arm just in time.

As I stepped off[5] the bus, I found that I was 25 shivering[6], even though[7] it wasn't cold outside. Excitement bubbled up[8] inside me as I said, "Hi, my name's Hannah. Thanks for … you know …" Suddenly shy, I couldn't meet his eye. Not taking his eyes off me once, he said, 30 "Hi, I'm Zach. And you're welcome. See you around … Hannah."
Smiling, he walked away. I just stood there, watching him until he was out of sight …

→ p. LF77

● **Read part A again. Describe Hannah and Zach. Look at the adjectives in the box.**

> friendly • happy • sad • blond • excited • brown • shy • beautiful •
> long • curly • short • tall • small • surprised • proud • tired •
> frightened[9] • bored • slim • cool • young • clever • dark • strong • …

Describe what Zach looks like:

Zach has … hair.
He is …

Describe how Hannah feels:

Hannah is excited/…
because …

---

[1]stare at – *anstarren*; [2]curly – *lockig, gekräuselt*; [3]frame – *umrahmen*; [4]not either – *auch nicht*; [5]step off – *aussteigen*;
[6]shiver – *zittern*; [7]even though – *selbst wenn, wenn auch*; [8]bubble up – *aufsprudeln*; [9]frightened – *verängstigt*

B Zach's brother is worried about him.

"Zach, what's up? You're always alone nowadays[10], and you look so sad. What's going on?" Zach looked at his brother. "Aaron, I don't know what to do. There's this girl. Hannah.
5 She's amazing. She's funny, smart, beautiful ..."
"Doesn't sound like much of a problem, Zach!" laughed Aaron. Zach didn't laugh, though, he just dropped his head lower and said, so quietly that Aaron could barely[11] hear him,
10 "She's white, Aaron. She's white and all my friends ... they think it's weird[12] that I like a white girl. Love a white girl. I think I love her, Aaron."
Aaron put his arm around his brother. "Zach, I've never seen you care about a girl this much. 15 If your friends are really your friends, they will just want to see you happy. And you know what? If they don't, then they're not worth worrying about. Think about it – do you want to lose this girl?" 20

- **What is Zach's problem?**

Zach is ...
He is in love with a ... girl.
He doesn't know ...
His friends ...

- **What could or should he do?**
➡ p. LF77

| Zach | could should | go on a date with Hannah. see Hannah again. stop thinking about Hannah. talk to his friends. ... |

C Hannah and Zach finally go on a date.

I came out of class. Another class that I hadn't really listened to. All I could think about was Zach. At least I hadn't lost my appetite. They say that happens when you're in love. In love.
5 Oh my god, did I just think that? I shook my head as I hurried towards the cafeteria.
I was in such a rush[13] that I almost didn't see him, standing in front of a window in the corridor. As I walked up to him, he turned and
10 saw me. "Hannah ... hey!" he said. He looked around us, then, finally, he looked me in the eye. I felt my world stand still. "It's lunchtime," I said. "I'm hungry. Do you wanna come get some lunch with me?" I usually met my friends
15 for lunch, but they would understand ...
Zach smiled and nodded[14] and we walked towards the cafeteria together. In the queue, two of his friends came up to us.
"Come on, Zach, we're meeting the others for lunch," one of them said. The other stared at 20 me. "Come on, man, what're you hanging around with her for?" he asked Zach. I looked at my feet and felt my cheeks[15] go red.
Zach was quiet. Really quiet. Then he looked at his friends and said to me, "Come on, Hannah. 25 Let's go." Taking my arm he led me away from them. "Let's go to the park. I'm sick of[16] this place. Sick of them," he said.
We walked out of school and headed to[17] Central Park, picking up a burger on the way. 30 We chatted, about school and exams and, finally, he told me about the problem with his friends. As he was talking, almost without noticing[18], he took my hand. The tingling[19] started in my fingers and spread[20] all the way 35 down to my toes[21].

---

[10]nowadays – *hier: in der letzten Zeit*; [11]barely – *kaum*; [12]weird – *seltsam*; [13]in a rush – *in Eile*; [14]nod – *nicken*;
[15]cheek – *Wange*; [16]be sick of sb/sth – *jdn/etw satthaben*; [17]head to – *sich auf den Weg nach ... machen*;
[18]notice – *bemerken*; [19]tingling – *Kribbeln*; [20]spread – *ausbreiten*; [21]toe – *Zeh*

- **Hannah and Zach are on their first date. What happens?**
  Read part C again and put the pictures in the right order.   2 – 4 – 3 – 1

➡ p. LF77

- **The boys stare at Hannah and Zach. Zach feels bad. What would YOU do?**

If I	had a … girlfriend/boyfriend, were with a … girl/boy,	I would	… …

D A few months later, Zach's friends still haven't accepted Hannah.

"Zach, I think we need to work this out[22].
I know you love me, but you miss your
friends – I can see that," I said to him one day.
"I know. But I'm still angry at them.
5 Why can't they see how much you mean to me?
Why does it even matter[23] to them that you're
white?"

I looked at him, torn between[24] his love for me
and keeping friends he had grown up with.
Even if his friends had been like my parents –   10
not exactly enthusiastic but at least accepting –
it would have been OK for him. It would have
been a start.
I loved him so much, and felt so helpless …

- **Write down what Hannah and Zach may think.**

We've seen each
other for …
months.
I want to …
Why … ?

I love him so much.
But I'm afraid[25] his
friends …

- **What do YOU think?**
  What could Hannah and Zach do?
  Talk about it.

Hannah Zach They	should could must	talk to meet ask plan …	…

---

[22]work sth out – *etw lösen*; [23]matter – *von Bedeutung sein*; [24]torn between – *hin- und hergerissen zwischen*;
[25]be afraid – *Angst haben*

D How the raven[1] got its black feathers p. 93/B

What do you think: Why have ravens got black feathers?

L 2.5

At the beginning of time the raven flew high up into the sky[2] to the home of the birds. The birds were all the same colour and shape[3]. The raven wanted to make all of the birds different from one another, so he went to the four Great Spirits[4] in the sky with
5   his idea. He said, "The birds are all the same colour and shape. They look so uninteresting. If you give me the paints[5] and the brushes[6], I will paint all of the birds different colours."

The Spirits agreed and then the raven said, "If I do all of this work for you, I would like you to paint me so that I'm the most
10   beautiful bird in the world." The Spirits agreed again and the raven started painting the birds. When he had finished, each bird was different and their feathers were all the colours of the rainbow: red, orange, yellow, green, blue, indigo[7] and violet.

The raven went to the four Great Spirits and said, "I have kept my promise[8], now you
15   must keep yours." So the first Great Spirit painted the raven with wonderful colours and patterns[9] and made him the most beautiful bird in the world. The raven said, "I don't think you have painted me very well. I'm no different from all the other birds." The raven hoped the Spirit would make him even more beautiful. So each of the other three Great Spirits added even more beautiful colours and patterns to the first Great Spirit's work but the raven still
20   said, "I'm no different from the other birds."

After the fourth Great Spirit had finished painting, the raven said, "You have cheated me[10]. I kept my promise and painted all of the birds. You haven't kept your promise to make me the most beautiful bird in the world." When the Great Spirits heard this, they were very angry with the raven. They poured[11] all of their paint over him so that all the colours and patterns
25   mixed together. The result was a dark, dark black. Then they sent the raven back home.

And that is how the raven got its black feathers.

Choose an activity

➡ p. LF78

- Draw a picture for each paragraph. You can add speech bubbles, too.
- Turn the story into a play. Work in groups and act it out.
- What does the raven say to the other ravens who are unhappy about their black feathers? Write a dialogue.
- Do you know any other stories like this one? Choose one and present it to the class.

---

[1]raven – *Rabe*; [2]sky – *Himmel*; [3]shape – *Form, Art*; [4]spirit – *Geist*; [5]paint – *Farbe*; [6]brush – *Pinsel*; [7]indigo – *indigoblau*; [8]keep a promise – *ein Versprechen halten*; [9]pattern – *Muster*; [10]cheat sb – *jdn täuschen/betrügen*; [11]pour – *gießen, schütten*

E The USA – a land of immigrants

Read about how the USA became a land of immigrants.

For thousands of years the North American continent was inhabited[1] only by Native Americans. The United States that we know today, however[2], is a nation of immigrants. The
5 first immigrants to arrive in North America in the 17th century came mainly from England, Germany and the Netherlands. Like many others, the majority[3] of German immigrants came hoping to practise their religion[4] freely.
10 Twenty per cent of the population was made up of African Americans, mainly slaves, who were taken there from Africa to work.

In the middle of the 19th century immigrants began to arrive from different parts of the
15 world. Many of these immigrants came from China and Japan. They worked for low wages[5] on the transcontinental railroad or for the mining[6] industry.

The second half of the 19th century was also
20 a time of strong German immigration:

- In the early 1850s 1 million Germans immigrated to the United States – many of them were farmers from the south-west of Germany.
- About 723,000 Germans came to the United 25 States in the 1870s, in particular[7] German Jews[8] and Catholics who left because of social and economic[9] discrimination[10].
- The biggest wave of Germans (1,445,000) immigrated to the United States in the 30 1880s. Many of these were industrial[11] workers looking for jobs in factories. They hoped for better living conditions[12] in a democratic America.

Early German immigrants arrived in the port[14] 35 of Philadelphia and many chose to start a new life in Pennsylvania. Later German immigrants mostly decided to settle in Wisconsin, Michigan, Minnesota, North and South Dakota, Nebraska and Iowa – the so called "German belt[15]". Many 40 city names are similar to German city names

---

[1]inhabit – *bewohnen*; [2]however – *jedoch*; [3]majority – *Mehrheit*; [4]practise religion – *Religion ausüben*; [5]wage(s) – *Lohn*;
[6]mining – *Bergbau*; [7]in particular – *insbesondere*; [8]Jew – *Jude/Jüdin*; [9]economic – *wirtschaftlich*; [10]discrimination –
Diskriminierung, Benachteiligung; [11]industrial – *Industrie-*; [12]living conditions – *Lebensbedingungen*; [13]democratic –
demokratisch; [14]port – *Hafen*; [15]belt – *Gürtel*; [16]pass through – *durchlaufen, passieren*; [17]the Isle of Tears – *die Träneninsel*

such as Frankfort, Karlsruhe, Heidelberg or New Ulm. Frankfort is a very popular city name in the USA.

45 On January 1st 1892 the Ellis Island Immigration Station opened in New York. Between 1892 and 1954 more than 12 million immigrants passed through[16] Ellis Island. It became known as "The Isle of Tears[17]".

Immigrants had to prove that they were in 50 good health and that they could financially[18] support themselves. They also had to be able to read and write. Those who could not were sent back home.

Despite[19] these rules and regulations[20], 55 thousands of people continued to immigrate into the United States. In 1924 the US government passed[21] "The Immigration Act[22]". This new system allowed more people to come from the countries of the first immigrants, for 60 example England, Germany and Scandinavia[23] and not so many from the poorer areas of Southern and Eastern Europe. People also had to get a visa[24] before coming to the USA. This was a way of turning away[25] unwanted 65 immigrants even before they had a chance to reach the USA.

Even in the 21st century the USA still continues to be a country which is attractive to immigrants. The number of immigrants 70 (legal and illegal) living in the country hit a new record of 40 million in 2010.

These days people need a Green Card to live and work in the USA. Every year there is a lottery in which you can win a Green Card. 50,000 visas are given to people all around the world each year.

- **Ellis Island was called "The Isle of Tears". Hamburg harbour, from which many left Germany, was called "The Port of Hope". Can you imagine why?**
➡ p. LF78

- **Both Ellis Island and Hamburg BallinStadt have become museums documenting[26] emigration[27] and immigration. There are more museums, for example in Cork (Ireland) or Bremerhaven. Choose one of them, collect information and give a presentation.**

---

[18]financially – *finanziell*; [19]despite – *trotz*; [20]regulation – *Vorschrift*; [21]pass – *verabschieden*; [22]act – *Gesetz*; [23]Scandinavia – *Skandinavien*; [24]visa – *Visum*; [25]turn away – *abweisen*; [26]document – *dokumentieren*; [27]emigration – *Auswanderung*

F The Perks[1] of Being a Wallflower[2]

Read the following[3] extract[4] from Stephen Chbosky's novel[5]
The Perks of Being a Wallflower. It is about a boy called
Charlie who has just started high school. He writes letters
in his diary to someone known only as 'Friend'.

➡ p. LF78

- Note down what you find out about Charlie, Sam and Patrick.

- Say how Sam and Patrick are different from the other
  students Charlie has met at high school so far.

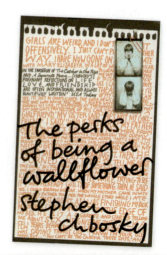

October 6, 1991

Dear friend,

I feel ashamed[6] I went to the high school
football game the other day[7], and I don't know

5   exactly why. In middle school, Michael and I
would go to the games sometimes even though[8]
neither of us[9] were popular enough to go. It
was just a place to go on Fridays when we didn't
want to watch television. [...] But this time, I

10 went alone because Michael is gone, and Susan
hangs around different boys now, and Bridget is
still crazy, and Carl's mom sent him to a Catholic
school, and Dave with the awkward[10] glasses
moved away. I was just kind of watching people,

15 seeing who was in love and who was just
hanging around, and I saw that kid I told you
about. Remember Nothing? Nothing was there
at the football game, and he was one of the few
people who was not an adult that was actually

20 watching the game. I mean really watching the
game. He would yell things out[11].
"C'mon, Brad!" That's the name of our

quarterback[12]. Now, normally I am very shy, but
Nothing seemed like the kind of guy you could
just walk up to at a football game even though   25
you were three years younger and not popular.
"Hey, you're in my shop class[13]." He's a very
friendly person.
"I'm Charlie." I said, not too shy.
"And I'm Patrick. And this is Sam." He pointed   30
to[14] a very pretty girl next to him. And she
waved to me.
"Hey, Charlie." Sam had a very nice smile. They
both told me to have a seat[15], and they both
seemed to mean it, so I took a seat. I listened   35
to Nothing yell at the field. And I listened to
his play-by-play analysis[16]. And I figured out[17]
that this was a kid who knew football very well.
He actually knew football as well as my brother.
Maybe I should call Nothing "Patrick" from now   40
on since[18] that is how he introduced himself,
and that is what Sam calls him. Incidentally[19],
Sam has brown hair and very very pretty green
eyes. The kind of green that doesn't make a
big deal[20] about itself. I would have told you   45
that sooner[21], but under the stadium lights,

---

[1]perk – *Vergünstigung, Vorteil*; [2]wallflower – *Mauerblümchen*; [3]following – *folgende(r, s)*; [4]extract – *Auszug*; [5]novel – *Roman*;
[6]feel ashamed – *sich schämen*; [7]the other day – *neulich, vor einigen Tagen*; [8]even though – *obwohl*; [9]neither of us – *keine(r) von
uns*; [10]awkward – *peinlich*; [11]yell out – *schreien*; [12]quarterback – *Spielmacher im American Football*; [13]shop class – *Werkunterricht*;
[14]point (to) – *zeigen/deuten (auf)*; [15]have a seat – *sich (hin)setzen*; [16]analysis – *Analyse*; [17]figure out – *herausfinden*;
[18]since – *da, weil*; [19]incidentally – *übrigens*; [20]make a big deal – *viel Wind/großes Theater machen*; [21]sooner – *früher*

everything looked kind of washed out. It wasn't until we went to the Big Boy, and Sam and Patrick started to chain-smoke that I got a
50 good look at her. The nice thing about the Big Boy was the fact that Patrick and Sam didn't just throw around inside jokes and make me struggle to keep up[22]. Not at all. They asked me questions.
55 "How old are you, Charlie?"
"Fifteen."
"What do you want to do when you grow up?"
"I don't know just yet."
"What's your favorite band?"
60 "I think maybe the Smiths because I love their song 'Asleep,' but I'm really not sure one way or the other[23] because I don't know any other songs by them too well."
"What's your favorite movie?"
65 "I don't know really. They're all the same to me."
"How about your favorite book?"
"This Side of Paradise by F. Scott Fitzgerald."
"Why?"
70 "Because it was the last one I read."
This made them laugh because they knew I meant it honest, not show-off[24]. Then they told me their favorites and we sat quiet. I ate the pumpkin pie because the lady said it was

in season[25], and Patrick and Sam smoked more   75
cigarettes. I looked at them, and they looked really happy together. A good kind of happy. And then though[26] I thought Sam was very pretty and nice, and she was the first girl I ever wanted to ask on a date someday[27] when I can   80
drive, I did not mind[28] that she had a boyfriend, especially if he was a good guy like Patrick.
"How long have you been 'going out'?" I asked. Then, they started laughing. Really laughing hard.   85
"What's so funny?" I said.
"We're brother and sister," Patrick said, still laughing.
"But you don't look alike[29]," I said.
That's when Sam explained that they were   90
actually stepsister[30] and stepbrother[31] since Patrick's dad married Sam's mom. I was very happy to know that because I would like to ask Sam on a date someday.
[...]   95
It would be very nice to have a friend again. I would like that even more than a date.

Love always,

Charlie

- **Would you like to read the whole book? Why/Why not?**

- **There is a film called *The Perks of Being a Wallflower*. Watch it in class. Do you like the story? Give reasons.**

➡ p. LF79

---

[22]struggle to keep up – *mühsam mithalten können*; [23]one way or the other – *so oder so*; [24]show-off – *angeberisch*; [25]be in season – *Saison haben*; [26]though – *obwohl*; [27]someday – *irgendwann (einmal)*; [28]mind – *etw dagegen haben*; [29]look alike – *sich ähnlich sehen*; [30]stepsister – *Stiefschwester*; [31]stepbrother – *Stiefbruder*

READING IS FUN

G Going west

Read about settlers going west in the 19th century.

After the US government took control[1] of large areas of land on the Pacific Ocean in the 1840s, the fertile[2] land in California and Oregon tempted[3] many Americans to leave the east and
5 its social and economic[4] problems behind, and to go west.

Some of the first people to arrive in the west were Christian missionaries[5]. They wanted to spread[6] their Christian faith[7] among[8] the Native
10 Americans. But it was not as easy as they had expected[9]. The Native Americans kept their traditional beliefs, or were more interested in knowing their new neighbours in order to[10] learn how to farm or use guns[11].

15 Most of the 350,000 people that crossed North America between 1840 and 1870 were normal men, women and children who hoped to build a better life in the west on their own piece of land. Most of them travelled along two routes
20 – the Oregon and California Trails. Both routes began at the Missouri River and took them over the Plains[12] and the Rocky Mountains. Those going to California went south at Fort Hall, and those going to Oregon went north. Settlers had
25 normally been travelling for about six months when they finally arrived at their destination[13].

The first emigrants[14] had problems with their long and heavy wagons[15]. That's why they started to use smaller wagons that were easier
30 to handle and only needed two animals to pull them.

By the 1840s people had been making the 2000-mile journey[16] west for several[17] years, and it became possible to buy guidebooks[18] for the trip. They told emigrants what they had to buy 35 for the trip – tools, food, special clothes, etc. Since[19] these things could be very expensive, people often had to sell a lot of their things to pay for the trip.

Days on the trail were long, often starting 40 at 4 am. Everybody had a job to do. Men, for example, drove the wagons, looked after the animals and hunted buffalo for meat, while women built fires, prepared meals, washed clothes and looked after the children. When the 45 sun went down, the wagons stopped and were arranged[20] in a circle around a central fire so that they had at least some protection from the weather, wild animals or possible attacks.

Although many settlers were afraid of Native 50 American attacks, these were actually quite rare[21]. The greatest dangers were diseases like cholera and accidents such as falling under a moving wagon or drowning[22] in rivers.

---

[1]take control – *die Kontrolle übernehmen*; [2]fertile – *fruchtbar*; [3]tempt sb – *jdn locken*; [4]economic – *wirtschaftlich*; [5]Christian missionaries – *christliche Missionare*; [6]spread – *verbreiten*; [7]faith – *Glaube*; [8]among – *unter*; [9]expect – *erwarten*; [10]in order to – *um zu*; [11]gun – *(Schuss)waffe*; [12]plain – *Ebene, Flachland*; [13]destination – *(Reise)ziel*; [14]emigrant – *Auswanderer/Auswanderin*; [15]wagon – *(Plan)wagen*; [16]journey – *Reise*; [17]several – *einige*; [18]guidebook – *Reiseführer, Ratgeber*; [19]since – *da, weil*; [20]arrange – *anordnen*; [21]rare – *selten*; [22]drown – *ertrinken*

55 In 1849 everybody was talking about the
news: "Gold in California!" A man called James
Marshall had discovered a gold nugget in 1848.
People started spreading the news which led[23]
to the so-called "gold rush[24]": Hundreds of
60 thousands of people made their way across the
country hoping to find gold themselves.

Like sailors[25], farmers and settlers before, gold
miners[26] also needed special clothes that were
strong and did not tear[27] easily. The German
65 immigrant Levi Strauss sold blue jeans to the
mining communities. In the year 1853 he
founded his company in San Francisco. Levi's
jeans are still one of the most famous American
brands[28].

- **Choose the best headline for the text. Give reasons for your choice.** ➡ p. LF79

  1 On the Oregon Trail   **2** Going west: the challenges   **3** Why go west?

- **Find a good heading for each paragraph.**

Trails to Oregon and California

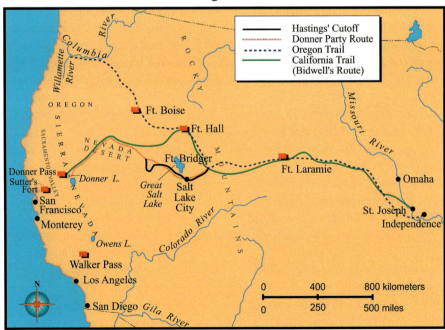

©1996 MAGELLAN Geographix^SM Santa Barbara, CA (800) 929-4MAP

---

[23]lead *(Vergangenheitsform:* led) – *führen;* [24]rush – *Rausch;* [25]sailor – *Matrose;* [26]miner – *Schürfer/in;*
[27]tear – *(zer)reißen;* [28]brand – *Marke*

H Child labour[1]?

→ p. LF79

Look at these pictures of child stars. Which stars do you recognize[2]? What do you know about them?

Ryan Gosling • Kristen Stewart • Jodie Foster •
Leonardo DiCaprio • Scarlett Johansson • Britney Spears •
Christian Bale • Neil Patrick Harris • Miley Cyrus

Read an interview with nine-year-old child actor Adam. How is his life different from yours?

Reporter: Why do you like acting, Adam?

Adam: Well, it's really exciting. The best part is when I get asked to do a second audition, a callback. It means I might get the part.

Reporter: I can imagine! What do you find hardest about acting?

Adam: You know, the directors don't always explain exactly what they want you to do.

Reporter: Do you go to a regular school?

Adam: No, I'm home-schooled. It's perfect for me because it makes it easier to go to auditions. Plus, I can spend lots of time with my parents.

Reporter: How easy is it to talk about acting with your friends?

Adam: They help me a lot! They're always telling me I'll be a great actor ... but we mainly talk about normal stuff[3].

Reporter: So, do you enjoy auditions?

Adam: Yes, I do. But I like callbacks a lot more because my dad gives me ten dollars and I feel proud.

Reporter: You must get a little nervous, too.

Adam: Yes, I get really embarrassed[4] if I say the wrong line on camera. It looks bad.

Reporter: It sounds like you put a lot of pressure[5] on yourself.

Adam: Yes, everyone does, right? If I do something badly, I get annoyed[6] because I know that I can do better.

Reporter: Have you ever thought that you didn't want to act anymore?

Adam: One time, my dad was a bit too strict with me then. But I definitely want to be an actor because I love meeting interesting people and seeing new places.

---

[1]child labour – *Kinderarbeit*; [2]recognize – *(wieder)erkennen*; [3]stuff *(informal)* – *Zeug, Kram*;
[4]embarrassed – *verlegen, peinlich berührt*; [5]pressure – *Druck, Stress*; [6]annoyed – *verärgert*

Read the following extract from the UN[7] Convention[8] on the Rights of a Child. What do you think: Are the rights of a child violated[9] when they are child stars?

➡ p. LF79

Article 32 (Child Labour)

The government should protect children from work that is dangerous or might harm[10] their health or their education. While the Convention protects children from harmful and exploitative[11] work, there is nothing in it that prohibits[12] parents from expecting[13] their children to help at home in ways that are safe and appropriate[14] to their age. (…) Children's work should not jeopardize[15] any of their other rights, including their right to education, or the right to relaxation and play.

Now read the following article. Find out: How do parents and Hollywood treat[16] child stars? What kind of problems do child stars often have? Why?

In later life many child stars end up dead, depressed[17], take drugs[18], have financial problems or trouble with the law[19]. Parents and Hollywood don't realize that these young stars
5   have problems until it's too late.

The early deaths[20] of teenage film stars, for example from suicide[21] or from drug abuse[22], are extreme examples. When parents encourage[23] their children to be stars, they
10   should know about the dangers, too. They often make their children lead extremely unhappy lives because they put them under too much pressure. Although not all child stars die early, they are also likely to have
15   more problems with the law, such as drunken driving or stealing.

There are many theories about why so many child stars have problems in later life. "Normal teenagers" have to go through the problems
20   of puberty[24], such as bad skin. Parents of child stars do not let them experience these normal teenage problems. They pamper[25] and protect them too much in a make-believe[26] world. When that world suddenly ends, the children

have to adjust[27] to the real world. Not all of them can.   25

Some child stars are extremely unhappy during their childhood. Their parents don't see them suffer[28] because they are obsessed[29] with the idea of fame and success. They watch them   30 work for hours without giving them a chance to be children.

Those young actors, singers and models who manage to survive without losing themselves in drugs, criminal activity or depression often   35 have other problems. They may come from broken homes and must listen to their parents fight over them and their money. Sometimes they even have to fight their own parents in order to keep the money they have earned   40 through hard work. Children often let their parents look after their financial affairs[30] but parents are not always the best people to trust[31]. Hollywood and the public[32] have long watched parents exploit[33] their children and   45 take their money. But the state of California has done very little to protect children from these risks. It is time the state acted and changed its laws.

---

[7]UN (= United Nations) – *Vereinte Nationen*; [8]convention – *Abkommen*; [9]violate – *verstoßen (gegen), verletzen*; [10]harm – *schaden*; [11]exploitative – *ausbeuterisch*; [12]prohibit – *verbieten*; [13]expect – *erwarten*; [14]appropriate – *angemessen*; [15]jeopardize – *gefährden*; [16]treat – *behandeln*; [17]depressed – *depressiv*; [18]drug – *Droge*; [19]law – *Gesetz*; [20]death – *Tod*; [21]suicide – *Selbstmord*; [22]abuse – *Missbrauch*; [23]encourage – *ermutigen*; [24]puberty – *Pubertät*; [25]pamper – *verwöhnen*; [26]make-believe – *Fantasie-*; [27]adjust (to) – *anpassen (an)*; [28]suffer – *leiden*; [29]obsessed (with) – *besessen (von)*; [30]affair – *Angelegenheit*; [31]trust – *vertrauen*; [32]the public – *die Öffentlichkeit*; [33]exploit – *ausbeuten*

READING IS FUN

I Silicon Valley

➡ p. LF80

Have you ever heard of the term[1] "Silicon Valley"? Can you guess what it stands for?

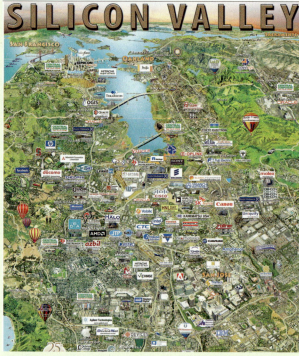

In the 1950s American scientists[2] discovered that silicon[3] could be used for making electronic devices[4]. Silicon is important for making
5 electronic switches[5] which control electrical signals. Because of this discovery[6], scientists were able to make digital watches, calculators, computers and more.

10 The main area where this technology was first developed was in northern California, south-west of San Francisco in the Santa Clara valley. The technology quickly became
15 popular and lots of companies started to create electrical products in this area. As a result, the area became known as Silicon Valley.

Today the term "Silicon Valley" stands
20 for the latest technology developments[7]. Many of the world's largest technology companies such as Microsoft, Apple and Intel started here. Today it's impossible[8] to imagine a (western) classroom, workplace or even house without one product from 25 one of these companies.

More recent[9] companies which are based[10] in the area are Google, Facebook and Netflix.

➡ p. LF80

- **How many of these companies have you heard of? How many products from these companies have you used in the last week?**

Adobe	Hewlett-Packard (HP)
Apple	Mozilla
Cisco	Netflix
eBay	Paypal
Electronic Arts	SanDisk
Evernote	Twitter
Facebook	Yahoo!
Google	

- **Write a fact file about a company in Silicon Valley. Choose one of the companies from the list or another one you know. Think about:**

  – When was the company started?
  – What does the company do?
  – How has the company changed?
  – ...

[1]term – *Begriff*; [2]scientist – *Wissenschaftler/in*; [3]silicon – *Silizium*; [4]device – *Gerät*; [5]switch – *Schalter*;
[6]discovery – *Entdeckung*; [7]development – *Entwicklung*; [8]impossible – *unmöglich*; [9]recent – *neu*; [10]based – *ansässig*

A   At school

In the classroom

door • window • board •
bookcase • desk • chair •
bin • paper • book •
schoolbag • computer •
map • classroom rules •
poster • calendar • ...

Things in a schoolbag

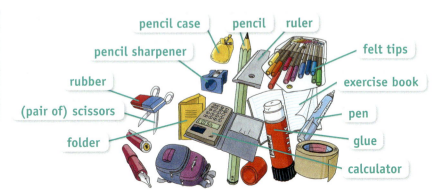

pencil case • pencil • ruler
pencil sharpener
rubber
(pair of) scissors
folder
felt tips
exercise book
pen
glue
calculator

Places at school

classroom • cafeteria • library •
locker • gym • homeroom *(AE)* •
office • sports ground • playground •
toilet *(BE)*/bathroom *(AE)* • ...

People at school

teacher • student • classmate •
headteacher • guidance counsellor •
secretary • ...

Timetables *(BE)*/Schedules *(AE)* and subjects

lesson *(BE)*/period *(AE)* • elective *(AE)* •
art • biology • drama •
English • French • Spanish • German •
geography • maths *(BE)*/math *(AE)* •
PE (physical education) • history •
home economics • science • web
design • wood/metal working class • ...

Class Schedule			
Period	**Class**	**Room**	**Teacher**
1	English	209	Hansen,
2	Math	336	Gritt, G.
3	Science	214	Coley, D
4	Geography	315	Miller, J
Lunch			
5	American History	344	Nicholso
6	Web Design	228	Perez, A.

What you do at school

ask a guidance counsellor for help • be a member of the drama/
basketball/ ... club • have basketball practice • do sports •
break the rules • celebrate homecoming *(AE)* •
choose an elective *(AE)* • check your timetable *(BE)*/
schedule *(AE)* • do a project • do homework •
study for a test • get good marks on a test • pass a test •
put things into your locker • have lunch •
join a club • need a pass to go to the bathroom *(AE)* •
wait until break • take a break • take the bus • ...

B Jobs

I think I will be a nurse because I like helping people.

I'd like to be a technician. I'm good at working with my hands.

jobs	what people with these jobs do
actor/actress	act in films or plays
builder	repair and build houses
cameraman/camerawoman	film the scenes of a film; use the camera
car technician	repair cars
cook	cook/prepare meals in a restaurant
electrician	repair or install electrical equipment
firefighter	fight fires, help people
gardener	work in a park; look after flowers, plants and trees
hairdresser	wash, cut and style people's hair
lifeguard	keep beaches safe; help people in need
make-up artist	put make-up on actors/actresses or models
(male) nurse	look after ill people in a hospital
painter	paint walls, doors or the outside of houses
park ranger	look after parks and wild animals
police officer	catch criminals; keep people and the streets safe
programmer	write computer programs
security guard	protect buildings and shops
shop assistant	work in a shop; help customers; sell things
stunt performer	perform dangerous situations for films
tour guide	show people around new places
waiter/waitress	serve customers in a café or restaurant
...	...

Skills you may need for work

be good with your hands •
have experience in/with ... •
know how to drive/swim/ ... •
be good at working with computers/
languages/ ... • get along well with
other people • be creative/flexible/
brave/fit/friendly/ ... • ...

Jobs can be ...

dangerous • fun • interesting •
hard • creative • easy • boring •
exciting • special • terrible • great • ...

How to get a job

do work experience • write a CV •
fill in an application form •
prepare for a job interview • ...

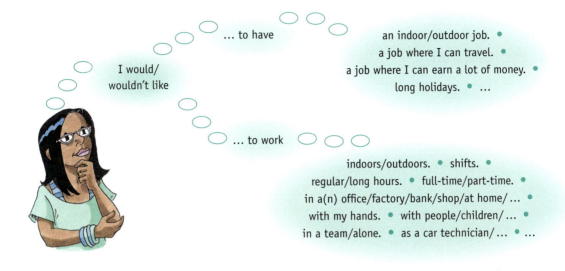

... to have

- an indoor/outdoor job.
- a job where I can travel.
- a job where I can earn a lot of money.
- long holidays. • ...

I would/ wouldn't like

... to work

- indoors/outdoors. • shifts.
- regular/long hours. • full-time/part-time.
- in a(n) office/factory/bank/shop/at home/ ...
- with my hands. • with people/children/ ...
- in a team/alone. • as a car technician/ ... • ...

C Environment

Protecting the environment

act green • buy local foods •
use products that aren't dangerous to the
environment • grow plants • plant trees •
go to school by bike or on foot •
pick up rubbish • recycle paper/rubbish •
separate paper/plastic/ ... •
save water/energy •
only print out things you really need •
close windows and doors to save energy •
turn off lights when they aren't needed •
use less water • take a short shower •
repair things • ...

Let's start to protect our environment today!

Remember: Small changes can make a big difference!

air   earth

animals

water

plants

planet

land   ocean

Using "green" technology

use solar panels • build a living wall •
install rain collectors •
build a greenhouse •
use an all-electric school bus • ...

D Food and drink

At the restaurant

choose try order have	a meal a starter the main dish side orders a drink dessert

Are you ready to order?

Can I have the menu, please?

What would you like to eat?

How much is the fish, please?

Can I get you anything else?

I'd like/I'll have the steak, please.

Anything to drink with that?

That's £18, please.

Could you bring the bill, please?

On the menu

starters and main dishes	desserts	beverages
soup • salad • pumpkin • corn on the cob • baked beans • French fries *(AE)*/chips *(BE)* • mashed potatoes • fried egg • pancake • dumplings • roast beef • roast lamb • steak • pork • turkey • salmon • sushi • fish and chips • tofu • pie • bagel • sandwich • chili con carne • fajitas • nachos • lasagne • pizza • pasta • macaroni and cheese • loco moco • chop suey • curry • burger • hot dog • fried chicken • meat loaf • ...	apple pie • ice cream • watermelon • cookie *(AE)*/ biscuit *(BE)* • candy *(AE)*/ sweets *(BE)* • ...	juice • fizzy drink • lemonade • milk • milkshake • cola • water • coffee • tea • wine • beer • ...

Food can be ...

good • bad • delicious • yummy • yucky • disgusting • terrible • sweet • hot • spicy • healthy • unhealthy • fresh • old • traditional • expensive • tasty • artificial • ...

E Celebrations

Happy birthday!

birthday

New Year's Eve

Happy New Year!

Merry Christmas!

Christmas

Celebrations and festivals

New Year's Eve • Halloween • Eid •
Christmas • Hanukkah • Easter •
Thanksgiving • Mardi Gras • carnival •
Independence Day • Cinco de Mayo •
wedding • Valentine's Day •
birthday • Mother's Day • Diwali •
St Patrick's Day • Chinese New Year • ...

Would you like to
come to my party?

Sure. Thanks for
the invitation.

Special food

(roast) turkey • cranberry sauce •
mashed potatoes • dumplings • corn on
the cob • seafood • roast lamb •
birthday cake • Easter eggs •
candy *(AE)*/sweets *(BE)* • ...

My favourite festival is Easter.
It is in spring. We look for eggs
on Easter Sunday. Afterwards we
always have a big family breakfast.

Activities

go to/have a party • have a big meal •
cook a special meal • make/bake a cake •
go out for dinner • visit friends •
celebrate with family and friends •
get together with family and friends •
give/get presents • write invitations •
send cards • decorate the house •
decorate pumpkins • go to bed late •
have a great time • dance • sing songs •
wait for the midnight countdown •
watch the fireworks • set off fireworks •
make/wear a costume • dress up •
wear special/traditional clothes • give thanks for
what you have • celebrate your culture •
go to church • look for Easter eggs •
play music • play games • watch a parade • ...

F Travelling

Places and buildings

area • city • town • village •
neighbourhood • street • road •
department store • shop • mall •
supermarket • market • restaurant •
snack bar • school • library • hospital •
playground • sports centre •
sports ground • skate park •
swimming pool • football stadium •
adventure centre • cinema •
theatre • museum • gallery •
church • castle • statue • tower •
skyscraper • bridge • zoo •
park • square • farm • factory •
airport • harbour • bus stop •
train/underground station • house •
flat • room • hotel •
holiday apartment • campsite •
river • lake • mountain • forest •
field • beach • the sea • island • ...

Countries

Germany • Spain • France •
Italy • Greece • Turkey •
the Netherlands • Russia • Poland •
Ireland • Great Britain • the USA •
Brazil • Australia • ...

Places can be ...
- beautiful
- famous
- quiet
- noisy
- busy
- packed with people
- interesting
- boring
- expensive
- clean
- dirty
- safe
- dangerous
- ...

Sightseeing and holiday activities

go sightseeing • take photos of famous sights •
visit a museum/castle/ ... • go to the park/beach/ ... •
go to the top of ... • have a picnic/barbecue • eat ice
cream • see a musical • watch a game •
relax in the sun • enjoy the weather •
meet new people • write postcards • buy souvenirs •
go shopping/hiking/swimming/... • ...

Talking about sights

- ... was built in ...
- ... was opened in ...
- ... is the oldest/tallest/
  longest ...
- ... is famous because ...
- You should really see ...
- It's in/near ...

Traffic

take the underground *(BE)*/
subway *(AE)*/ferry/ ... •
go by bus/train/ .../on foot •
travel by car/plane/
ship/ ... • ...

G People

family members
- mother – father (parents)
- daughter – son
- sister – brother
- grandmother – grandfather (grandparents)
- aunt – uncle
- cousin – cousin
- relative
- ancestor

other people
- woman – man
- wife – husband
- girl – boy
- child, teenager
- friend, classmate
- neighbour
- guy
- citizen
- immigrant

> My friend Rajiv is tall and good-looking.

> I like him because he is friendly and funny.

Describing people

positive	neutral	negative
good-looking • beautiful • strong • pretty • brave • polite • active • honest • clever • nice • helpful • hard-working • self-confident • optimistic • charming • friendly • creative • successful • funny • …	small • large • tall • thin • long • short • blond • dark • old • young • strict • rich • poor • careful • slow • fast • quiet • shy • …	angry • strange • unfriendly • ugly • terrible • mean • silly • stupid • crazy • horrible • ill • …

Feelings

positive	negative
happy • good • great • surprised • proud • wonderful • excited • glad • fantastic • safe • …	unhappy • bad • terrible • angry • jealous • lonely • frightened • scared • nervous • confused • bored • sad • surprised • frustrated • shocked • embarrassed • tired • hungry • cold • worried • disappointed • horrible • homesick • …

You can …
- be in love with a boy/girl
- love your parents/pet/…
- laugh about a joke
- be proud of your sister/…
- be angry with your brother/…
- leave someone in peace
- apologize to someone
- miss a friend/…
- cry because you are sad
- feel embarrassed because …
- be scared of spiders/…
- be afraid of big dogs/…
- hate cleaning your room
- be tired of hard work
- be illegal in a country
- survive an injury/war

Different people

American • Asian • Chinese • European • English • French • German • Polish • Native American • Hispanic • African American • Asian American • Mexican American • …

H Statistics

Numbers and statistics

a/one million • a/one thousand •
a/one hundred • per cent •
total • a/one quarter • a/one third •
half • two thirds • population •
people • survey • pie chart • …

What percentage of students play football?

37 per cent.

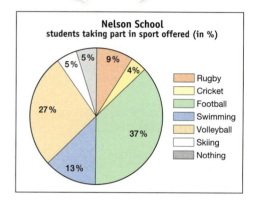

Nelson School
students taking part in sport offered (in %)

- Rugby
- Cricket
- Football
- Swimming
- Volleyball
- Skiing
- Nothing

9% 4% 5% 5% 13% 27% 37%

You write:
12.4%
You say:
twelve point
four per cent

Statistics can be …

surprising • shocking •
interesting • helpful • …

The pie chart shows/
the statistics/the
figures show …

More/Fewer than …
per cent …

There are more/fewer
… than …

… per cent of the
population have
French/… ancestors.

… per cent of the
population are …

The smallest/biggest
group are …

I Free time

Activities

Playing board
games is fun!

meet (my) friends • listen to music • watch TV/a film • play the guitar/piano/… •
play computer games/board games/chess • go to the cinema/zoo/youth club/
a party/concert • dance • relax/chill • visit a museum/castle/… • take photos •
sleep over at a friend's house • phone/call a friend • chat to friends/on the Internet •
read books/magazines • collect stickers/football cards/… • go shopping •
be in/join a club • surf the Internet • have a drink with (my) friends •
hang out at a mall/… • have a good time • …

Sports

You <u>play</u> ...
- table tennis
- football *(BE)/* soccer *(AE)*
- American football
- basketball
- volleyball
- (ice) hockey
- ...

You <u>go</u> ...
- swimming
- dancing
- cycling
- inline skating
- riding
- skiing
- ...

You <u>do</u> ...
- karate
- judo
- gymnastics
- kickboxing
- cheerleading
- ...

I love playing basketball!

things you need (equipment)	where you do it	how you play it (rules)
ball • basket • goal • goalpost • helmet • skateboard • hockey stick • pompom • net • ...	in a park • in a sports hall • at a sports centre • on a sports field • on the street • ...	you need ... players in a team • you play two halves/ ... quarters/ ... minutes/ ... • the aim is to ... • you get a point/ ... when you score a goal/ ... • players must .../may not ... • ...

People in sports

sportsperson • dancer • (defensive/offensive) player • opponent • runner • swimmer • athlete • ball carrier • team • team captain • coach • referee • linesman • goalkeeper • fan • ...

I do judo.

I like it because it keeps me fit.

I started judo training three years ago.

I train twice a week.

Talking about sports

have a (friendly) match • watch a game/ match • cheer on your team • practise new tricks • train once/twice/three times a week • get a point • win/lose a game/match/race • play injured • kick/throw the ball • score a goal • catch the ball • carry the ball • tackle an opponent • block a player • ...

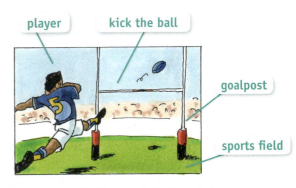

player

kick the ball

goalpost

sports field

The player is kicking the ball through the goalposts to get a point for his team.

J Shopping

Shops

bike shop • market stall •
pet shop • mall •
shopping centre •
snack bar • supermarket •
sweet shop • toy shop • ...

supermarket

mall

buy a poster at a stall

go shopping at the market

look for a T-shirt/...

buy ↔ sell   customer ↔ seller   cheap ↔ expensive

How much is/are ... ?

Hello. I'm looking for .../
Excuse me, have you got ... ?/
I'd like ..., please.

What can I do for you?/
Can I help you?

I'll get you ...
Here you are.

Have you got anything cheaper?

Sorry, I don't have any ... but I have some ...

Is it on sale?

It's .../They are ...

Can I try ... on, please?

It's a special offer.

I think I'll take it/them.

Let me show you to the fitting rooms.

No, thank you.

Thank you. Bye.

Anything else?

Here you are.

Thanks. Bye.
Have a nice day.

Here's your change.
I'll put your receipt in the bag.

That's £ ..., please.

K Health

The body

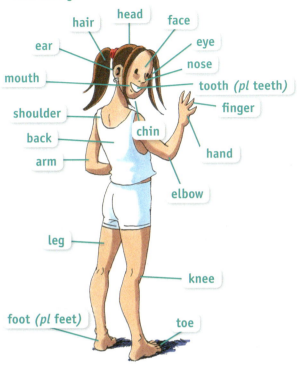

hair · head · face · eye · nose · ear · mouth · tooth *(pl teeth)* · finger · shoulder · chin · back · arm · hand · elbow · leg · knee · foot *(pl feet)* · toe

Keep fit and healthy!
- Eat healthy food.
- Drink lots of water.
- Do sports.
- Get enough sleep.
- Feel good.
- Don't smoke.

Inside the body

muscle • bone •
stomach • ...

Health problems

be	ill/injured
feel	ill
have	a bike accident
have got	an injury a (bad) cold a cut foot a sore eye a broken leg backache toothache stomach ache chickenpox

Doing sports ...

- ... is important for your body and health.
- ... makes you fit and feel better.
- ... is good if you choose the right sport.
- ... is good if you do it properly.
- ... makes you eat less.
- ... makes you less likely to smoke.
- ...

Smoking

feel peer pressure • start smoking •
want to fit in • smoke cigarettes •
ruin your life • feel stressed/tired/
bad/... • have no energy •
smell of smoke • have headaches •
quit smoking • try nicotine gum or
patches • put out a butt • ...

No, thank you.
I don't smoke.

L Time

What time is it, please?

It's six forty-seven./It's thirteen minutes to seven.

You say: the 3rd of April
You write: 3rd April **or** 3 April **or** 3/4/...

3/4/20..: In *BE* this is the **3rd of April**. In *AE* this is the **4th of March**.

days of the week	months	When?	How often?
• Monday	• December ⎤	• on Monday/Tuesday/...	• always
• Tuesday	• January ⎬ winter	• in the morning/ afternoon/evening	• often
• Wednesday	• February ⎦	• in (the year) 2014	• usually
• Thursday	• March ⎤	• at the weekend	• sometimes
• Friday	• April ⎬ spring	• at five o'clock	• never
• Saturday	• May ⎦	• last Monday/week/ year/...	• once/twice/ three times a day/...
• Sunday	• June ⎤	• three days/... ago	
	• July ⎬ summer	• before	
	• August ⎦	• after (that)	
	• September ⎤	• afterwards	
	• October ⎬ autumn	• then	
	• November ⎦	• later	
		• finally	

M Weather

Hot and dry weather in California makes forest fires much worse.

It is ...

What's the weather like?

hot   warm   cold

Wenn man ankommt oder geht

Good morning.	Guten Morgen.
Sorry, I'm late.	Tut mir leid, dass ich zu spät komme.
Sorry, I don't have my exercise book with me.	Tut mir leid, ich habe mein Heft nicht dabei.
Sorry, I don't have my homework with me.	Tut mir leid, ich habe meine Hausaufgaben nicht dabei.
What's for homework?	Was haben wir als Hausaufgabe auf?
See you tomorrow.	Bis morgen.

Wenn es ein Problem gibt

What's the matter with you?	Was ist mit dir los?
I'm fine./I feel sick.	Mir geht's gut./Mir ist schlecht.
I've got a headache.	Ich habe Kopfschmerzen.
Can I open the window, please?	Kann ich bitte das Fenster öffnen?
Can I go to the toilet, please?	Kann ich bitte zur Toilette gehen?

Wenn man Hilfe braucht

Can you help me, please?	Können Sie/Kannst du mir bitte helfen?
I've got a question.	Ich habe eine Frage.
I don't understand this.	Ich verstehe das hier nicht.
How can I do this exercise?	Wie mache ich diese Aufgabe?
What's ... in English/German?	Was heißt ... auf Englisch/Deutsch?
What does ... mean?	Was bedeutet ... ?
Can you write it on the board, please?	Können Sie/Kannst du das bitte an die Tafel schreiben?
Can you say it again, please?	Können Sie/Kannst du das bitte noch einmal sagen?
Sorry, I don't know.	Tut mir leid, das weiß ich nicht.
What page, please?	Auf welcher Seite bitte?

Wenn man zusammen arbeitet oder spielt

Whose turn is it?	Wer ist dran?
I (don't) like this story.	Diese Geschichte gefällt mir (nicht).
I think it's good/interesting/funny.	Ich finde ... gut/interessant/komisch.
I think it's terrible/boring/sad.	Ich finde ... schrecklich/langweilig/traurig.
Do you want to work with me?	Möchtest du mit mir arbeiten?

Wenn man mit dem Computer arbeitet

What's your email address?	Was ist deine E-Mail-Adresse?
You can click on this link.	Du kannst auf diesen Link klicken.
Can I print it out/download it?	Kann ich das ausdrucken/herunterladen?
I saved it.	Ich habe es abgespeichert.
My computer has crashed.	Mein Computer ist abgestürzt.

Was die Lehrerin oder der Lehrer sagt

Open your books at page ...	Öffnet eure Bücher auf Seite ...
Turn to page ...	Blättert zu Seite ...
Look at line ...	Seht euch Zeile ... an.
Read the text on page ...	Lies/Lest den Text auf Seite ...
Work in pairs.	Arbeitet zu zweit.
Work in groups of four/five/...	Arbeitet zu viert/fünft/...
Sit in a circle.	Bildet einen Sitzkreis.
Listen to the CD/MP3/...	Hör/Hört die CD/MP3/... an.
Write about ...	Schreibe/Schreibt über ...
Talk about ...	Sprich/Sprecht über ...
Ask questions about ...	Stelle/Stellt Fragen zu ...
Answer the question, please.	Beantworte/Beantwortet bitte die Frage.
Match the sentences.	Ordne/Ordnet die Sätze zu.
Who wants to read the text?	Wer möchte den Text vorlesen?
Write down the answers.	Schreibe/Schreibt die Antworten auf.
Act out the dialogue.	Spiel/Spielt den Dialog vor.
Change roles.	Tauscht die Rollen.
Make your own dialogue.	Entwirf/Entwerft selbst ein Gespräch.
Take a card.	Nimm/Nehmt eine Karte.
Come to the blackboard, please.	Komm/Kommt bitte zur Tafel.
Collect the exercise books, please.	Sammle/Sammelt bitte die Hefte ein.
Do this exercise at home, please.	Mach/Macht diese Aufgabe bitte zu Hause.
Please be quiet.	Sei/Seid bitte ruhig.
Please sit down.	Setz dich/Setzt euch bitte.
Please speak up.	Sprich/Sprecht bitte lauter.

You can do better.	Du kannst das besser.
Try again.	Versuch es noch einmal.
That's it.	Das ist alles.
Well done.	Gut gemacht.

A ... work with words

Wörter richtig schreiben

- Wenn du merkst, dass du bei der Schreibweise einiger englischer Wörter (wiederholt) Schwierigkeiten hast, kannst du Folgendes tun: Schreibe die Wörter auf kleine Zettel und markiere die Stellen, die dir Probleme bereiten. Hänge die Zettel in deinem Zimmer auf. Du wirst merken, dass du die Wörter bald richtig schreiben kannst.

whole

language

peaceful

Wörter richtig bilden

- Um Wörter zu lernen und zu behalten, ist es manchmal hilfreich zu wissen, wie sie gebildet werden. So lassen sich z. B. Gegenteile bilden, indem eine Vorsilbe (*prefix*) wie *un-*, *im-* oder *dis-* hinzugefügt wird. Oder es lassen sich Nomen bilden, indem an ein Verb eine Nachsilbe (*suffix*) wie *-ion*, *-tion* oder *-er* gehängt wird.

word	opposite
friendly	**un**friendly
polite	**im**polite
likes	**dis**likes
advantage	**dis**advantage
...	...

verb	noun
invent	invent**ion**
produce	produc**tion**
play	play**er**
teach	teach**er**
...	...

Wörter in Zusammenhängen lernen

- Es ist für unser Gehirn einfacher, Wörter in sinnvollen Einheiten zu lernen als einzeln. Wenn du also eine neue Vokabel in deinem Heft, Ordner oder auf einer Karteikarte notierst, dann versuche, ein oder mehrere Wörter hinzuzufügen, die dazu passen.

during ➔ during the holidays, during the lesson

plant ➔ plant a tree

- Du lernst die neuen Vokabeln auch schneller, wenn du Sätze mit ihnen bildest und diese aufschreibst.

during ➔ I had lots of fun during the holidays.

plant ➔ We planted a tree in the garden.

B ... work with an English-German dictionary

Das richtige deutsche Wort finden

Wenn du ein englisches Wort nicht verstehst, kannst du ein Wörterbuch zu Hilfe nehmen.
Hier findest du ein paar Hinweise, wie das geht:

1. Wonach du suchen solltest

- Die meisten Wörter wirst du schnell finden. Manche Wörter stehen jedoch nicht so im Wörterbuch, wie man sie in englischen Texten findet. Wenn du z. B. das Wort *cheers* in dem Satz *Charlie cheers his football team on* nicht verstehst, wirst du *cheers* nicht im Wörterbuch finden. Dort steht nämlich nur die Grundform (Infinitiv) *cheer* – und danach musst du suchen.

2. Orientiere dich an den Leitwörtern

- Beim Nachschlagen im Wörterbuch kannst du dich an den Leitwörtern oben auf den Seiten orientieren. Die Leitwörter sagen dir, welche Wörter auf der jeweiligen Seite zu finden sind.

Leitwörter

| **cheat sheet – checkable** | | 112 | 113 | | **cheekbone – cheer** |

cheat sheet *n US (sl)* Spicker *m*, Spickzettel *m*
check [tʃek] **I.** *n* **1.** *(inspection)* Überprüfung *f*, Kontrolle *f*; *security* ~ Sicherheitskontrolle *f* **2.** *to take a quick* ~ schnell

♦ **check in I.** *v/i (at airport)* einchecken; *(at hotel)* sich *akk* [an der Rezeption] anmelden; *to* ~ *at a hotel in* einem Hotel absteigen; **II.** *v/t to* ~ *sb in (at airport)* jdn abfertigen [= einchecken]

dance ~ *to* ~ Wange an Wange tanzen **2.** *no pl (impertinence)* Frechheit *f*, Unverschämtheit *f*, Dreistigkeit *f*; *to be a* ~ eine Unverschämtheit sein; *to give a* ~ frech zu jmd sein; *to have the* ~ *to do sth* die Stirn haben [o die Dreistigkeit

tigkeit *f*
cheeky [ˈtʃiːki] *adj (impertinent)* frech, dreist; *(lacking respect)*schnippisch, vorlaut; *to be* ~ *to sb* zu jdm frech, [o unverschämt] sein
cheep [tʃiːp] **I.** *n* **1.** *(of bird)* Piepser *m fam; (act)* Piepen

3. Finde die passende Übersetzung

- Hast du *cheer* im Wörterbuch gefunden, wirst du sehen, dass es dort mehrere Einträge gibt.
- Die Abkürzungen geben dir Auskunft über die Wortarten.

  n = *noun*
  v/i oder v/t = *verb*
  adj = *adjective*
  conj = *conjunction*

cheer [tʃɪə, US tʃɪr] **I.** *n* **1.** *(shout)* Hurraruf *m*, Beifallsruf *m*; *(cheering)* Jubel *m*; *three ~ s for the champion!* ein dreifaches Hoch auf den Sieger!; *two ~s* super! **2.** *no pl (joy)* Jubel *m*, Freude *f* **II.** *v/i to* ~ *for sb* jdn anfeuern
♦ **cheer on** *v/t to* ~ *sb on* jdn anfeuern
♦ **cheer up 1.** *v/i* vergnügt[er] werden; *~ up!* lass denn Kopf nicht hängen!, Kopf hoch!; **2.** *v/t to* ~ *sb up* jdn aufheitern

Zu welcher Wortart gehört *cheers* in unserem Satz? Genau, es ist ein Verb.
- Sieh dir nun für das Verb *cheer* alle Übersetzungen an. Hier findest du auch **cheer on** als zusammengesetzten Ausdruck. Das Zeichen (~) ist ein Platzhalter, hier für das Verb.
- Nun kannst du den Satz *Charlie cheers his football team on* übersetzen: Charlie feuert seine Fußballmannschaft an.

C ... work with a German-English dictionary

Das richtige englische Wort finden

Auch wenn du deutsche Wörter oder Sätze ins Englische übersetzen willst,
kann dir ein Wörterbuch dabei helfen.

1. Bevor du zum Wörterbuch greifst

- Überlege, ob du auch ohne Wörterbuch auskommst. Vielleicht kennst du ja ein deutsches
  Wort mit gleicher oder ähnlicher Bedeutung. Wenn du z. B. das englische Wort für
  „verlassen" nicht kennst, kannst du auch *go away* (weggehen) sagen.
- Du kannst auch versuchen, deinen deutschen Satz zu vereinfachen. Anstatt
  „Tom verbringt gerne Zeit im Einkaufszentrum" kannst du einfach sagen
  „Tom mag das Einkaufszentrum". Dafür brauchst du kein Wörterbuch.

2. Wörter nachschlagen

- Nimm nicht gleich die erste Übersetzung, wenn du Wörter im Wörterbuch nachschlägst.
  Für viele deutsche Wörter gibt es verschiedene Übersetzungen. Sieh dir deshalb deinen
  deutschen Satz genau an, bevor du wählst: „Zu Weihnachten gibt es bei uns **Plätzchen**."
  Hier passt die Übersetzung *biscuit* am besten.

> Zusätze wie *Gebäck* verraten,
> in welchem Zusammenhang
> ein Wort gebraucht wird.

> *f*, *m* oder *nt* geben an, ob das
> Wort weiblich (*f*), männlich
> (*m*) oder sächlich (*nt*) ist.

> **Plätzchen** *nt* **1.** spot, little place **2.** *(Gebäck)*
> biscuit *(Brit)*, cookie *(US)*

> US = American English
> Brit = British English

- Wenn du Verben nachschlägst, solltest du
  immer nach der Grundform (Infinitiv) suchen.
  Für den Satz „Meine Tante **reist** drei Tage vor
  Ende des Ramadans **an**" schlägst du also
  „anreisen" nach.

> **anreisen** *v/i sein* **1.** *(ein Ziel anfahren)*
> to travel [here/there]; *reist du mit dem*
> *eigenen Wagen an?* will you be travelling
> [*or* coming] by car? **2.** *(eintreffen)* to arrive

3. Wörter überprüfen

- Wenn du nicht sicher bist, ob das englische Wort wirklich passt, überprüfe es noch
  einmal. Schlage es im englisch-deutschen Teil deines Wörterbuches nach. Dort findest
  du oft weitere Verwendungsbeispiele und auch die Lautschrift, falls du Hilfe bei der
  Aussprache brauchst.

 **... listen**

Ohren auf! Worum geht es überhaupt?

Du kennst ja schon einige Tricks, wie du einen Hörtext besser
verstehen kannst:

1. Vor dem Hören
• Wie lautet die Überschrift des Hörtextes? Welche Hinweise gibt sie dir?
• Gibt es Bilder zum Text? Was ist zu sehen?
• Überlege: Worum könnte es wohl gehen? Was weißt du schon über das Thema?
  Was erwartest du?

2. Beim Hören
• Höre dir das Gespräch oder die Geschichte einmal ganz an. Du musst nicht jedes
  einzelne Wort verstehen. Versuche herauszufinden, worum es geht. Wer ist beteiligt?
  Was passiert?
  Achte auch auf die Geräusche. Sie geben dir oft Hinweise auf den Ort und das
  Geschehen. Wie klingen die Stimmen der Personen? Begeistert? Aufgeregt?
• Lies dir die Höraufgabe im Buch genau durch. Was sollst du herausfinden?
  Höre dir das Gespräch oder die Geschichte ein zweites Mal an. Kannst du die
  Höraufgabe im Buch jetzt lösen? Wenn nicht, dann höre dir den Text noch ein
  weiteres Mal an.
• Wenn es zu einem Hörtext keine Aufgabe gibt, können dir diese Fragen weiterhelfen:

Who?	**Where?**	**When?**	**What?**
(Wer spricht? Um wen geht es?)	(Wo findet das Gespräch/ die Geschichte statt?)	(Wann findet es/ sie statt?)	(Worüber wird ge- sprochen? Was passiert?)

• Mache dir Notizen zu den Fragen, auf die du eine Antwort weißt.

3. Zu guter Letzt
• Vergleiche deine Ergebnisse mit einer Partnerin oder einem Partner. Was habt ihr
  herausgefunden? Haben sich eure Erwartungen bestätigt?

> **TIPP**
>
> **Nutze jede Gelegenheit, um Englisch zu hören!**
> • Mit der *Camden Market*-CD kannst du zu Hause dein Hörverstehen trainieren.
> • Höre dir englische Musik an und achte auf den Text. Was kannst du schon verstehen?
> • Sieh dir einen Film, den du schon kennst, auf Englisch an. Fast alle Filme sind mit
>   englischem Ton (mit oder ohne Untertitel) erhältlich.

... read

Lesen leicht gemacht

1. Vor dem Lesen
- Wie lautet die Überschrift? Welche Hinweise gibt sie dir?
- Gibt es Bilder zum Text? Was ist zu sehen?
- Überlege: Um was für einen Text handelt es sich? Worum könnte es wohl gehen?

2. Verschiedene Lesetechniken
- **Skimming:** Beim *skimming* überfliegst du den Text erst einmal. Versuche herauszufinden, worum es geht. Was passiert? Wer ist beteiligt? Dafür brauchst du nicht jedes Wort zu verstehen.
- **Reading for detail:** Du liest den Text gründlich, um möglichst viele Details herauszufinden. Mit den *wh*-Fragen kannst du die wichtigsten Informationen herausbekommen. Schlüsselwörter *(keywords)* sind wichtige Wörter, die dir helfen, einen Text zu verstehen.
- **Scanning:** Beim *scanning* suchst du gezielt nach bestimmten Informationen, zum Beispiel nach speziellen Fakten.

Who?
Where?
What?
When?
Why?

Washed up whale too sick to save

A whale which washed up on a beach in Suffolk had to be put to sleep by vets. The 10 metre long fin whale was badly injured when it was found in the early hours of Monday.
Vets tried to rescue the animal but it was too ill to make the journey back to sea.
Fin whales are the second largest animal on the planet and are an endangered species.
Specialist divers couldn't save it.
Faye Archell from the British Divers Marine Life Rescue group said: "It would be wrong for us to put a sick animal back into the sea. We are frustrated about it but we can't help it."

3. Einen Text verstehen
- Du brauchst nicht jedes Wort zu verstehen. Häufig kannst du die Bedeutung eines unbekannten Wortes aus dem Satzzusammenhang erschließen. Oft kennst du auch ein deutsches Wort oder ein Wort aus einer anderen dir bekannten Sprache, das ganz ähnlich ist.
- Wenn du einen Text liest und eine Aufgabe dazu bearbeitest, ist es wichtig, sich Notizen zu machen. Lies dir die einzelnen Absätze genau durch und finde heraus, worum es in ihnen geht. Notiere dir für jeden Absatz die wichtigste Information. Oft ist es hilfreich, Informationen in einer Tabelle zu sammeln, z. B. positive und negative Punkte. Informationen, die voneinander abhängen, kannst du auch gut in einem Wortnetz strukturieren.

F ... give a talk

Wenn du etwas vor der Klasse präsentierst

1. Bevor du etwas vorträgst

- Überlege: Was ist dein Thema? Was möchtest du sagen? Wie viel Zeit hast du für deinen Vortrag?
- Sammle deine Gedanken und schreibe sie in Stichpunkten auf, z. B. in einem *word web* oder auf Karteikarten.
- Entscheide, in welcher Reihenfolge du die Dinge sagen und wie du anfangen möchtest.
- Fertige ein Poster oder eine Folie an, um deinen Vortrag anschaulich zu machen. Du kannst aber auch eine *PowerPoint*-Präsentation gestalten.
- Überlege dir kleine Aufgaben für deine Zuhörer, damit sie aufmerksam bleiben. Erstelle z. B. einen Lückentext oder ein Quiz. Du kannst sie auch bitten, einen Feedback-Bogen als Rückmeldung zu deinem Vortrag auszufüllen. So erfährst du, was du demnächst noch besser machen kannst.

TIPP

So sieht ein gelungenes Vortrags-Poster aus:

- ansprechende Überschrift
- interessante Informationen
- verständliche Sätze, aber: nicht zu viel Text
- große Bilder und Schrift: → Jeder im Raum muss sie sehen und lesen können.
- saubere Schrift
- Bilder mit Bildunterschriften

- Übe deinen Vortrag vor dem Spiegel, vor Mitschülern, Freunden oder deiner Familie – oder nimm deinen Vortrag zur Probe auf, z. B. mit einem Handy oder einem Easi-Speak-Mikrofon. Überprüfe, wie lange dein Vortrag dauert. Hast du flüssig gesprochen? Kannst du alle Wörter korrekt aussprechen?

2. Bei deinem Vortrag

- Sprich langsam und deutlich.
- Sieh deine Zuhörer an, wenn du sprichst.
- Versuche, frei zu sprechen. Du kannst die wichtigsten Punkte von deinen Notizen, deinen Karteikarten oder deinem Poster/deiner Folie ablesen.
- Zeige deinen Zuhörern auf deinem Poster oder deiner Folie, worüber du gerade sprichst. So wird dein Vortrag für die Klasse noch interessanter.

3. Nützliche Redewendungen

Zu Beginn deines Vortrags:	*Hello, everybody. My talk is about …/I'd like to talk about …*
	First of all, I'm going to … Then I'll talk about …
	Finally I'll …
Im Hauptteil:	*On my poster you can see …*
	Look at this picture. It shows …
	Another thing I want to tell you about is …
	My first/second/next/last point is …
Wenn du mal den Faden verlierst:	*Just a moment, please./Wait a second.*
Zum Schluss:	*Thank you for listening. Have you got any questions?*

G ... give feedback

Wenn du Rückmeldung/Feedback geben möchtest

- Um im Englischen immer besser und sicherer zu werden, ist es wichtig, dass ihr euch gegenseitig Rückmeldung zu euren Vorträgen, Postern, Geschichten und sonstigen Arbeiten gebt.
- Nenne zuerst immer die Dinge, die dir gut gefallen haben. Dann kannst du Verbesserungsvorschläge machen. Bleibe dabei stets höflich.

Positives Feedback:

> I really liked your ... because ...
> Your story/dialogue/... is very lively/really interesting/... because ...
> The part about ... is exciting/funny/... because ...
> I especially like the part where/when ...
> Your presentation was easy to understand.
> You spoke loudly and clearly.
> Your poster looks attractive.
> The pictures go well with the texts.

Verbesserungsvorschläge:

> You could make your text more interesting/lively/... if you add ...
> Use more adjectives/linking words/... to make your text ...
> Maybe next time you could use more pictures on your poster.
>   I would also add ...
> I would use a different word here. What about ... ?
> Why don't you use ... ? It would make the story/dialogue/... more lively/...

TIPP

Sprich Englisch, sooft du kannst!
- Höre dir die *Camden Market*-CD an und lies die Texte laut mit. Versuche, die Aussprache der Sprecher nachzuahmen. Du kannst auch englische Lieder mitsingen.
- Lies einen Text aus dem Buch laut vor oder sprich Englisch und nimm dich auf. Dann kannst du dich selbst anhören und überprüfen, wie dein Englisch klingt.
- Sprich Englisch mit jemandem, der ebenfalls Englisch sprechen kann.

H ... discuss

Wenn du etwas diskutierst

Diskussionen finden täglich über alle möglichen Themen statt. Oft sind solche Diskussionen spontan und ungeplant. Wenn es um ernsthaftere Themen geht, können dir die folgenden Hinweise nützlich sein.

1. Bevor du diskutierst

- Sieh dir das Thema der Diskussion genau an. Wie stehst du zu dem Thema? Mache dir Gedanken über mögliche Argumente.
- Stichpunkte und Wortnetze sind eine gute Hilfe, um nichts Wichtiges zu vergessen.
- Denke auch an Argumente, die gegen deine Meinung sprechen. Überlege dir Antworten auf diese Argumente.

2. Während du diskutierst

- Höre genau zu, was die anderen Diskussionsteilnehmer sagen. Stelle sicher, dass du ihre Argumente verstehst.
- Wenn du etwas nicht verstehst, frage höflich nach.
- Äußere deine Meinung. Bleibe dabei immer höflich und freundlich.

> **TIPP**
> - Bestimmt einen Diskussionsleiter. Er/Sie sollte darauf achten, dass alle Gesprächsteilnehmer zu Wort kommen können, beim Thema bleiben und die vereinbarte Redezeit einhalten.
> - Bildet eine neutrale Gruppe, die während der Diskussion Notizen macht und nachher Feedback gibt.

3. Nützliche Redewendungen

Wenn du eine Meinung äußern möchtest:

> I think …
> I believe …
> In my opinion, …
> I would say …
> I'm sure …

Wenn du eine Meinung begründen möchtest:

> I think so because …
> Let me give you an example: …
> The reason is …
> Well, it's a fact that …

Wenn du jemandem zustimmen möchtest:

> Yes, that's true.
> I think you're right.
> I agree (with you).
> I think so, too.
> That's a good/important point.

Wenn du jemandem widersprechen möchtest:

> I know, but …
> Sorry, I don't agree with you.
> I don't think so.
> I don't think that's true.

Wenn du nachfragen möchtest:

> Could you say that again, please?
> Do you mean that …?
> I don't quite understand what you mean.
> Can you please explain what you mean?

I ... talk about pictures

Über Bilder sprechen und sie beschreiben

Um ein Bild oder Foto zu beschreiben, gehst du am besten so vor:

1. Fange allgemein an

• Sage erst einmal, was du auf dem Bild oder Foto allgemein siehst.
  In the picture I can see a street with lots of people.

2. Wähle eine bestimmte Reihenfolge

• Sage nun, wen oder was du siehst und wo sich die Personen, Tiere und Gegenstände
  befinden. Dabei macht es Sinn, eine bestimmte Reihenfolge zu wählen: von links nach
  rechts oder von oben nach unten.
  In the middle/On the left/On the right I can see ...
  At the top there is ...
  At the bottom there are ...

3. Werde nun genauer

• Benutze **Präpositionen** wie *in, on, in front of, behind, next to, between, over* oder *under*,
  um genauer zu beschreiben, wo sich eine Person, ein Tier oder ein Gegenstand befindet.
  *There is a girl with a dog **in front of** the black car.*
  *There are two motorbikes **in** the street.*
  *The bird is **next to** the woman with the green dress and the cat.*

4. Beschreibe, was passiert

• Beschreibe, was die abgebildeten Personen oder Tiere tun. Benutze dazu das ***present
  progressive**.*
  *The boy with the pizza in the middle **is crossing** the street.*
  *The man with the pink T-shirt at the top **is taking** a picture.*
  *The woman on the right **is waving** at the girl on the motorbike.*

 **... write**

Tipps und Tricks zum Schreiben

1. Plane deinen Text

- Überlege: Was für einen Text willst du schreiben?
- Sammle Ideen und Wörter zum Thema deines Textes, z. B. in einem *word web* oder einer Liste.
- Bringe deine Ideen und Wörter in eine sinnvolle Reihenfolge.

2. Schreibe den Text

- Schreibe erst einmal kurze, einfache Sätze auf. Oder:
- Sieh dir Texte im Buch an, die sich mit dem Thema beschäftigen. Du kannst nützliche Satzanfänge und Ausdrücke übernehmen.
- Fange deine Sätze unterschiedlich an.
- Verbinde deine Ideen und Sätze mit *linking words* wie *and, or, but, so, because*.
- Benutze *time words*, um zu sagen, wann etwas geschieht, z. B. *in the morning, then, later, after (that), yesterday*.
- Adjektive und Adverbien machen deinen Text interessanter.
  Charlie ran forward and scored a goal.
  ➔ *Charlie ran forward quickly and scored a fantastic goal.*
- Überlege dir eine passende Überschrift.

3. Überarbeite den Text

- Sieh dir deinen Text noch einmal genau an. Hast du alles richtig geschrieben? Schlage schwierige Wörter im Wörterbuch nach.
- Bist du bei der Grammatik unsicher? Schau im LiF-Teil ab Seite 191 nach.
- Tauscht eure Texte untereinander aus. Markiert mit einem Bleistift im fremden Text, was euch gefällt, was unverständlich ist, was noch ergänzt werden könnte und was verbessert werden sollte.
  Diese Symbole kannst du dafür verwenden:

++	*(This is good!)*
??	*(I don't understand this.)*
~~	*(I don't think this English is correct.)*

  Sprecht anschließend darüber. Seht euch dazu auch *How to give feedback* auf Seite 181 an.
- Wenn du deinen Text fertig hast, schreibe ihn ins Reine. Das kannst du handschriftlich oder mithilfe eines Textverarbeitungsprogramms am Computer machen.

4. Präsentiere deinen Text

- Du kannst deinen Text nun präsentieren, indem du ihn z. B. vorliest, aufnimmst, aushängst oder in einem *class book* veröffentlichst. Danach heftest du deinen Text in deiner Portfolio-Mappe ab.

K ... write a letter

Einen Brief schreiben

Die Form eines Briefes hängt davon ab, an wen du schreiben willst. Ein Brief an einen Freund/eine Freundin sieht anders aus als ein Brief an eine dir unbekannte Person oder an eine Organisation. Man spricht von persönlichen und formellen Briefen. E-Mails schreibst du übrigens ganz ähnlich.

1. Ein persönlicher Brief

Fange die erste Zeile mit einem Großbuchstaben an.

Beginne deinen Brief mit *Dear ...,* oder *Hi ...,*

Kranzallee 60
14055 Berlin
Germany

2nd March 20..

Deine Adresse (ohne deinen Namen) gehört in die rechte obere Ecke.

So kannst du deinen Brief beenden: *Best wishes, Love, Lots of love, Yours, All the best, ...*

Dear Helen,
Thanks a lot for your letter. It was great to hear about your school trip to France. Did you get a chance to go to Paris? Yesterday I watched a programme about Australia on TV. I'd really like to go there one day to see Sydney, Ayers Rock, the Great Barrier Reef and lots of other places. The animals there are also fascinating. Did you know that there is an animal called wallaby which looks just like a small kangaroo? Hope to hear from you soon.
Love,
Ella

Das Datum folgt unter der Adresse auf der rechten Seite.

Am Ende deines Briefes kannst du die andere Person bitten, dir zurückzuschreiben.

2. Ein formeller Brief

Schreibe den Namen und die Adresse der Organisation oder der Person auf die linke Seite.

Brentanostraße 2
65187 Wiesbaden
Germany

Greenpeace
Canonbury Villas
London N1 2PN
UK

23rd April 20..

Dear Sir or Madam,
My class is doing a project on the environment and I would like to have some information about recycling for my project group. Have you got any leaflets that you could send me? Would it be possible for you to send me the names and addresses of other organizations that could help me?
Thank you very much for your help. I look forward to hearing from you soon.
Yours faithfully,
Oliver Grimm

Wenn du den Namen des Empfängers nicht kennst, schreibe *Dear Sir or Madam*. Kennst du den Namen, so beginne mit *Dear Mr/Ms/Mrs ...,*

Sei immer höflich.

Erkläre zu Beginn, warum du den Brief schreibst. Fasse dich dabei kurz.

Beende den Brief mit *Yours faithfully* (= Mit freundlichen Grüßen/Hochachtungsvoll). Wenn du den Namen des Empfängers jedoch kennst, schreibst du *Yours sincerely* (= Mit freundlichen/herzlichen Grüßen).

... write your opinion

Eine kurze Meinungsäußerung schreiben

In einer Meinungsäußerung nimmst du Stellung zu einem bestimmten Thema oder einem Problem, das in einem Text dargestellt wird. Dabei vergleichst du Vor- und Nachteile und begründest deine Meinung.

1. Bevor du anfängst zu schreiben

- Notiere die Ideen, die dir zum Thema einfallen. Eine Tabelle mit *pros and cons* oder *examples and reasons* hilft, deine Ideen zu ordnen.
- Mache dir klar, welche Position oder Meinung du vertrittst. Entscheide dich: Bist du dafür? Bist du dagegen? Wenn du dir nicht sicher bist, zähle Beispiele dafür und dagegen auf und wäge sie mit Begründungen gegeneinander ab.

2. Beim Schreiben

So kannst du anfangen: Formuliere einen Satz, der das Interesse der Leser weckt und das Thema einleitet.

Bringe deine Ideen in eine gute Reihenfolge:
Firstly, ...
Secondly, ...
Finally, ...

> Today lots of people want to leave the city and move to a village in the countryside. The question is: Is village life good or bad?
> If you ask me, there are a lot of good and bad things about village life. Let's start with the good things: Firstly, I think it is good for people with children. It's a fact that there are fewer cars and the air is much cleaner so the children can play outside a lot. In my opinion, the countryside looks nicer: There are more trees and fields and normally there is less rubbish. Some people say that cities are better though – there are more shops and the public transport is better. Cities also have a better choice of schools and libraries. All in all, I would say village life is the right thing for me – it's nice to have some peace and quiet!

Drücke deine Meinung klar aus:
I think ...
I believe ...
In my opinion, ...
I'm sure ...
Let me give you an example: ...

Begründe deine Meinung:
I think so because ...
The reason is ...
It's a fact that ...

Wäge deine Argumente gegeneinander ab:
Some people say ..., but I think ...
I'm not so sure that ...
On the one hand ..., but on the other hand ...
Although ...

So kannst du enden:
That's why I think ...
All in all, I would say ...

3. Überarbeite deinen Text

- Hast du in der Einleitung verständlich ausgedrückt, worum es geht?
- Zeigt dein Text klar deine Entscheidung pro oder kontra bzw. dein Bemühen, Argumente gegeneinander abzuwägen?
- Hast du Beispiele mit Begründungen genannt?
- Hast du einen Schluss formuliert, der deine Meinung klar zum Ausdruck bringt?
- Stimmen Satzbau, Grammatik und Rechtschreibung?

M ... write a summary

Eine Zusammenfassung schreiben

Eine Zusammenfassung verkürzt längere Texte, um den Lesern möglichst knapp und klar den wesentlichen Inhalt zu vermitteln.

1. Plane deinen Text
- Lies den ganzen Text mehrmals durch, um dir einen Überblick zu verschaffen: Worum geht es? Kannst du wichtige von unwichtigen Informationen unterscheiden? Wenn du eine Kopie des Textes hast, nimm einen Marker und kennzeichne die Stellen, die du für unverzichtbar hältst.
- In einer Tabelle mit den Überschriften *place, time, people, action* kannst du dir Notizen machen.

2. Schreibe den Text
- Benutze in deiner Zusammenfassung die einfache Gegenwart *(simple present)*.
- Beginne mit einem einleitenden Satz: *The text/story/article/... is about ...*
- Stütze dich auf deine Notizen. Verzichte auf wörtliche Rede und ausschmückende Details.
- Benutze *time words wie first, then, afterwards, while, ...*

3. Überarbeite deinen Text
- Hast du alle wesentlichen Informationen wiedergegeben?
- Sind sie in der richtigen Reihenfolge angeordnet?
- Stimmen Satzbau, Grammatik und Rechtschreibung?

N ... write a review

Eine Kritik verfassen

In einer Kritik drückst du deine Meinung aus, z. B. zu einem Film oder einer Serie. Die Kritik soll den Lesern helfen zu entscheiden, ob sie den Film oder die Serie ansehen möchten.

- Mache dir Notizen, während du dir den Film/die Serie ansiehst *(who, where, what, when, why)*.

Schreibe nun eine Kritik ähnlich der, die du zu *The Bling Ring* in Theme 6 gelesen hast:
- Nenne den Titel des Films/der Serie.
- Gib die technischen Daten an (Erscheinungsort und Jahr, Länge) und erwähne, wer mitspielt *(cast)* und wer Regie geführt hat *(director)*.
- Schreibe, um welche Art von Film/Serie es sich handelt *(comedy, drama, ...)*.
- Sage, worum es in dem Film/der Serie geht, aber verrate nicht zu viel, wie z. B. Überraschungen oder das Ende.
- Bleibe sachlich, wenn du deine Meinung äußerst, damit die Leser sich ihre eigene Meinung bilden können.
- Bewerte den Film/die Serie abschließend mit 1 – 5 Sternen.

HOW TO …

0 … work with others

Zusammen seid ihr stark!

Think – pair – share
Um Ideen zu einem Thema zu sammeln, kannst du in drei Schritten vorgehen:
1. *Think:* Sammle deine Gedanken und Ideen und mache dir Notizen.
2. *Pair:* Tausche dich mit einem Partner/einer Partnerin aus. Ergänze neue Ideen in deiner Liste.
3. *Share:* Teilt dann eure Gedanken und Ideen mit einem anderen Paar.

Buzz groups
Bei dieser Arbeitsform sprecht ihr alle mit leiser Stimme, damit sich die verschiedenen Gruppen nicht gegenseitig stören. *Buzz* heißt summen oder brummen und beschreibt den Geräuschpegel, der dabei im Raum entsteht.
1. Bildet *buzz groups* mit drei bis fünf Gruppenmitgliedern. Sprecht über das vorgegebene Thema. Ein Gruppenmitglied macht Notizen.
2. Wählt einen Sprecher/eine Sprecherin, der/die die Ergebnisse eurer *buzz group* in der Klasse vorstellt.

Bus stop

Bei dieser Arbeitsform tauscht du dich mit einem Mitschüler/einer Mitschülerin über ein Arbeitsergebnis aus.
1. Arbeite alleine an der vorgegebenen Aufgabe.
2. Gehe, wenn du fertig bist, mit deinem Arbeitsergebnis zu einem Treffpunkt im Klassenzimmer. Dieser ist als *bus stop* gekennzeichnet.
3. Warte dort auf einen Mitschüler/eine Mitschülerin, der/die ebenfalls fertig ist, und vergleicht eure Ergebnisse.

Milling around
Mit der Methode *milling around* (auf Deutsch: umherlaufen) kannst du dich mit deinen Klassenkameraden zu einem Thema austauschen.
1. Gehe durch die Klasse, ohne dass du dabei sprichst.
2. Wenn dein Lehrer/deine Lehrerin ein Zeichen gibt oder „Stop!" sagt, sprich mit der Person, vor der du gerade stehst. Tauscht euch über die Aufgabe aus.
3. Notiere deine Ergebnisse und gehe weiter.

Double circle

Auch dies ist eine Arbeitsform, bei der du die Ideen und Gedanken von vielen verschiedenen Leuten in deiner Klasse erfährst.
1. Bildet in der Klasse zwei Kreise: einen Innenkreis und einen Außenkreis.
2. Diejenigen von euch, die sich gegenüberstehen, unterhalten sich über ein vorher bestimmtes Thema.
3. Wenn dein Lehrer/deine Lehrerin ein Zeichen gibt, dreht ihr euch in den beiden Kreisen in entgegengesetzte Richtungen weiter. Nun tauscht ihr euch mit einem neuen Partner/einer neuen Partnerin über das Thema aus.

Give and take

Hierbei handelt es sich um eine gute Methode, um neue Ideen oder Informationen zu sammeln.

1. Jede/r faltet ein leeres Blatt Papier so, dass es aus sechs bis acht gleich großen Feldern besteht. Schreibt zwei bis drei Ideen oder Informationen zu einem Thema in die Felder – eine Idee/Information pro Feld.
2. Anschließend geht ihr im Klassenzimmer umher und befragt eure Klassenkameraden, um neue Ideen oder Informationen zu sammeln. Pro Mitschüler/in dürft ihr eine neue Idee/Information „geben" und eine neue Idee/Information „nehmen", um euer Blatt zu vervollständigen.
3. Seht euch eure Ideen/Informationen in Ruhe an. Bildet dann kleine Gruppen und besprecht euer Material.
4. Eure Ergebnisse könnt ihr abschließend in der Klasse vorstellen.

Jigsaw

Jigsaw (auf Deutsch: Puzzle) ist eine gute Methode, um in kleinen Gruppen an verschiedenen Texten (oder Textteilen) zu arbeiten.

1. Einigt euch in eurer Gruppe auf einen Text (oder Textteil) und lest ihn gründlich. Jede/r von euch macht sich Notizen, die ihr anschließend in der Gruppe vergleicht.
2. Findet euch dann in neuen Gruppen zusammen, sodass in jeder Arbeitsgruppe Vertreter/innen aller Texte (oder Textteile) beisammen sind. Berichtet anhand eurer Notizen über euren Text (oder Textteil). Macht euch Notizen zu den Texten, die ihr nicht selbst gelesen habt.
3. Ihr wisst nun über alle Texte (oder Textteile) Bescheid.

Placemat

Auf einer *placemat* (auf Deutsch: Tischvorlage, Platzdeckchen) sammelst du mit deinen Gruppenmitgliedern zu einem Thema gleichzeitig Ideen.

1. Jede/r von euch macht auf einem Teil eines großen Bogens Papier Notizen.
2. Anschließend dreht ihr die *placemat* so lange, bis jede/r alle Beiträge gelesen hat.
3. Einigt euch dann in der Gruppe auf gemeinsame Gedanken und notiert sie in der Mitte des Blattes.
4. Schließlich stellt ein Gruppenmitglied das Ergebnis in der Klasse vor.

Dramatic reading

Um einen Text mit verschiedenen Rollen lebendig vorzutragen, bietet sich *dramatic reading* an:

1. Lies den Text zu deiner Rolle mit leiser Stimme mehrmals durch.
2. Schaue dir jeden Satz einzeln an und präge ihn dir ein. Sieh dann hoch und sprich den Satz nach. Schaue deine Gruppenmitglieder dabei an. Arbeite den ganzen Text auf diese Weise durch.
3. Überlege, wie sich die Person gerade fühlt, deren Rolle du liest. Ist sie verärgert, fröhlich, ... ? Versuche, die Sätze entsprechend zu lesen und zu betonen.

Gallery walk

Wenn verschiedene Arbeitsgruppen Produkte (z. B. Poster) erstellt haben, könnt ihr einen Rundgang in der Klasse durchführen.

1. Hängt die Poster an verschiedenen Stellen im Klassenzimmer auf.
2. Findet euch dann in neuen Gruppen zusammen, in denen jeweils ein Mitglied der ursprünglichen Arbeitsgruppe vertreten ist.
3. Die Gruppen gehen von Poster zu Poster, und der jeweilige Experte/ die jeweilige Expertin erklärt sein/ihr Poster.

HOW TO ...

P ... work with grammar

Grammatikregeln auf der Spur

Versuche, Grammatikregeln selbst aufzuspüren.
Auf diese Weise kannst du sie nämlich besser behalten.

- Schaue dir dafür englische Texte an. Sammle mehrere Beispiele für eine Grammatikregel, z. B. für die Possessivbegleiter und Possessivpronomen.
- Schreibe die Beispiele untereinander. Was fällt dir auf? Was sieht hier ähnlich aus? Markiere die Stellen.

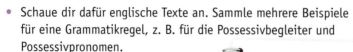

It's not my jacket.   It's not mine.
Aren't they your magazines?   Aren't they yours?
Isn't it his job?   Isn't it his?

- Sieh dir die Beispiele gut an. Was kannst du erkennen? Welche Veränderungen treten auf? Beschreibe und notiere dann deine Regel.
- Schaue nun im LiF-Teil ab Seite 191 nach, ob du richtigliegst. Ändere oder ergänze deine Regel falls nötig.

Q ... help out

So kannst du jemandem sprachlich aushelfen

1. Gib den Sinn wieder

Bei der Sprachmittlung musst du nicht Wort für Wort übersetzen. Wichtiger ist es, den Sinn einer Aussage oder Information wiederzugeben.
Das kannst du auch in deinen eigenen Worten machen.

... yes, I'm often nervous when I sing in front of large crowds. But I really love to sing in London.

Sie ist aufgeregt vor vielen Leuten, aber sie singt gern in London.

2. Umschreibe Wörter

Es kann vorkommen, dass du in deiner Gegend einen englischsprachigen Reisenden triffst, der deine Hilfe benötigt. Da du in solchen Situationen oft kein Wörterbuch zur Hand hast, kannst du wichtige Wörter auch umschreiben. Hab keine Angst vor Fehlern.

Apfelschorle?! What does that mean?

Apfelschorle ist ein Gemisch aus Apfelsaft und Sprudel.

Apfelschorle is apple juice with mineral water.

3. Bilde kurze Sätze

Bilde einfache, kurze Sätze, wenn du den Sinn wiedergibst.

LiF steht für *Language in Focus*. Das ist der Grammatikteil von *Camden Market*, in dem die englische Sprache genauer unter die Lupe genommen wird. Du findest in LiF die grammatischen Regeln. Wenn vorne im Buch z. B. 7 p. 199 🔍 steht, kannst du in LiF unter Nummer 7 auf Seite 199 die passenden Regeln nachschlagen.

Das „R" hinter manchen Nummern steht für *revision* (Wiederholung). So gekennzeichnete Regeln kennst du bereits aus den letzten Jahren.

Auf dieser und der nächsten Seite findest du die grammatischen Begriffe auf Englisch und Deutsch.

Grammatical terms

Englisch	LiF	Deutsch	Beispiel
adjective	18R	Adjektiv	a perfect day, a big house
adverb		Adverb	
adverb of frequency	22R	Häufigkeitsadverb	often, sometimes, never, …
adverb of manner	19R-20	Adverb der Art und Weise	James sings badly.
article	24	Artikel	
definite article		bestimmter Artikel	the
indefinite article		unbestimmter Artikel	a/an
comparison		Vergleich	
comparative	18R, 20	Komparativ (1. Steigerungsform)	André is taller than Anne. The film was more interesting than the book.
superlative	18R, 20	Superlativ (2. Steigerungsform)	Steven is the oldest boy. Sue is the most beautiful girl.
conditional clause I	11R	Bedingungssatz, Typ I	If it rains, I will stay at home.
conditional clause II	12	Bedingungssatz, Typ II	If I were rich, I would fly to NYC.
conditional clause III	13	Bedingungssatz, Typ III	If Tom had left earlier, he wouldn't have missed the bus.
future		Futur (Zukunft)	
going to-future	9R	Futur mit *going to*	She's going to buy a book.
will-future	8R	Futur mit *will*	I'm sure he will be a pop star.
gerund	14R	Gerundium	I like going to parties.
imperative	16R	Imperativ (Befehlsform)	Please sit down! Don't shout!
infinitive		Infinitiv (Grundform)	walk, read, go, …
linking word	23R	Konjunktion	and, because, but, so, …
long form	1R	Langform	I am, he is, they are, …
modal verb	10R	Modalverb	can, must, need, should, …
noun	24	Nomen (Hauptwort, Substantiv)	song, ball, car, dog, …
object	25	Objekt	We've got a car.
passive	30R	Passiv	My watch was made in China.
past participle	6R, 7	Partizip Perfekt	eaten, gone, started, …
past perfect	7	Vorvergangenheit	He didn't bring his homework because the dog had eaten it.
past tense		Vergangenheit	
simple past	4R	einfache Vergangenheit	They played football yesterday.
past progressive	5R	Verlaufsform der Vergangenheit	Emma was reading a book.

personal pronoun		Personalpronomen	
object pronoun		Objektpronomen	me, you, him, her, it, us, them
subject pronoun	15	Subjektpronomen	I, you, he, she, it, we, they
plural		Plural (Mehrzahl)	
regular/irregular		regelmäßig/unregelmäßig	cars, books, .../children, men, ...
possessive determiner	15	Possessivbegleiter	my, your, his, her, its, our, their
possessive pronoun	15	Possessivpronomen	mine, yours, his, hers, ours, theirs
preposition		Präposition	in, on, next to, behind, ...
present perfect	6R	Perfekt	David has cleaned the kitchen.
present tense		Präsens (Gegenwart)	
simple present	2R	einfache Gegenwart	I often walk to school.
present progressive	3R	Verlaufsform der Gegenwart	It's raining.
prop word	26	Stützwort	one, ones
question		Frage	
question word	21R	Fragewort	who, where, what, how, ...
yes/no question	1R-6R	Entscheidungsfrage	Are you from Germany?
reflexive pronoun	29	Reflexivpronomen	myself, yourself, himself, ...
relative clause	17R	Relativsatz	That's the man who helped me.
reported speech	28	Indirekte Rede	She said (that) she liked reading.
short answer	1R-6R	Kurzantwort	Yes, I am./No, I'm not.
short form	1R	Kurzform	I'm, he's, they're, ...
singular		Singular (Einzahl)	dog, friend, house, ...
statement		Aussagesatz	She's from Camden./
positive/negative		bejaht/verneint	I don't like football.
subject		Subjekt	School is great./Jo and I like tea.
verb		Verb	
regular/irregular	4R, 6R,	regelmäßig/unregelmäßig	look, walk, .../meet, see, ...
with two objects	25	mit zwei Objekten	The dog brings Tom his shoes.
word order	22R	Satzstellung	
subject – verb – object		Subjekt – Verb – Objekt	Sarah likes popcorn.

1R Das Verb be (The verb be)

Die Formen des Verbs *be* gibt es als Kurzformen und als Langformen. Die Kurzformen (*short forms*) verwendet man oft beim Sprechen. Beim Schreiben verwendet man die Langformen (*long forms*).

Langform	Kurzform		
I am	I'm	I'm eleven.	*Ich bin ...*
you are	you're	You're my friend.	*Du bist ...*
he is	he's	He's from Manchester.	*Er ist ...*
she is	she's	She's my sister.	*Sie ist ...*
it is	it's	It's late.	*Es ist ...*
we are	we're	We're hungry.	*Wir sind ...*
you are	you're	You're nice.	*Ihr seid ...*
they are	they're	They're in the garden.	*Sie sind ...*

We're good friends.

Die Formen von *be* kannst du ganz einfach verneinen, indem du *not* einfügst:

He is from Camden. ➔ *He is not from Camden./He isn't from Camden.*

They are friends. ➔ *They are not friends./They aren't friends.*

Wenn du eine Entscheidungsfrage mit *be* stellen möchtest, vertauschst du einfach das **Subjekt** und die Form von *be*:

Cheryl is from Illinois.

Is Cheryl from Illinois?

2R Die einfache Gegenwart (The simple present)

a) Bejahte und verneinte Aussagesätze

Das *simple present* verwendest du, ...

* um über Gewohnheiten oder regelmäßige Handlungen zu sprechen:
  *They **play** basketball every Monday.*
* um über aufeinander folgende Handlungen zu sprechen:
  *First Cheryl **gets** up. Then she **has** breakfast. After that she **takes** the bus to school.*
* um über Zustände zu sprechen, die längere Zeit andauern:
  *Cheryl and her family **live** in Illinois.*

He she it – the **-s** must fit.

simple present: **Aussagesätze**		
I often	play	football.
You sometimes	play	tennis.
He never	plays	basketball.
She	plays	the guitar.
It always	plays	with other dogs.
We	play	basketball every Monday.
You always	play	hockey.
They	play	games at the weekend.

! Bei *he, she* und *it* (in der 3. Person Singular) hängst du ein **-s** an.

● Endet das Verb mit *-ss, -sh, -ch* oder *-x*, hängst du bei *he, she, it* ein **-es** an:
*He wash**es** his face in the morning.*   *She often watch**es** TV.*

! Auch bei *do* und *go* fügst du in der 3. Person Singular **-es** an.

● do / duː / –   she does / dʌz /   go / ɡəʊ / –   she goes / ɡəʊz /.

! Bei Verben, die auf *-y* enden (z. B. *tidy up* und *empty*), gilt folgende Regel:

● Kommt ein Konsonant vor dem *-y*, so wird das *-y* zu **-ies**:
*She often tid**ies** up her room.*   *He sometimes empt**ies** the dishwasher.*

➔

simple present: Verneinung

I	don't play	basketball.
You	don't go	to Lake Park High.
He	doesn't work	in New York.
She	doesn't live	in California.
It	doesn't look	like a dog.
We	don't walk	to school.
You	don't know	Andy's sister.
They	don't like	lunch at school.

Gillian *doesn't like* rubbish.

! Bei der Verneinung von Sätzen mit *be, can* oder *have got* brauchst du *don't* oder *doesn't* nicht:
He is not from New York.   *I can't play American football.*   *I haven't got a computer.*

b) Entscheidungsfragen und Kurzantworten

Entscheidungsfragen sind Fragen, auf die man mit „Ja" oder „Nein" antworten kann.

Entscheidungsfragen und Kurzantworten mit *be, can, have got*

Are you thirteen?	Yes, I am.	No, I'm not.
Can you play an instrument?	Yes, I can.	No, I can't.
Has Andy got a sister?	Yes, he has.	No, he hasn't.

Do you like cats?

No, I don't.

Entscheidungsfragen und Kurzantworten mit *do* + Verb

Do you play volleyball?	Yes, I do.	No, I don't.
Does Brian know Gillian?	Yes, he does.	No, he doesn't.

3R Die Verlaufsform der Gegenwart (The present progressive)

a) Bejahte und verneinte Aussagesätze

Das *present progressive* verwendest du, wenn du sagen möchtest, was jemand gerade tut oder was gerade passiert – also für Vorgänge, die gerade ablaufen und noch nicht abgeschlossen sind:

present progressive: Aussagesätze

I am watching TV.	Ich sehe (gerade) fern.
You are writing an email.	Du schreibst (gerade) eine E-Mail.
He is drinking orange juice.	Er trinkt (gerade) Orangensaft.
She is sitting on the sofa.	Sie sitzt (gerade) auf dem Sofa.
Oh no, it is raining again!	Oh nein, es regnet schon wieder.
We are eating pizza.	Wir essen (gerade) Pizza.
You are playing football.	Ihr spielt (gerade) Fußball.
Listen, they are singing a song.	Hör mal, sie singen (gerade) ein Lied.

So bildest du das *present progressive:*
Form von *be (am, is, are)* + Infinitiv des Verbs + Endung *-ing*:
He is drinking orange juice.

! Endet das Verb auf *-e*, dann fällt das *-e* in der Verlaufsform weg.
*writ**e*** ➔ *writing*   *danc**e*** ➔ *dancing*

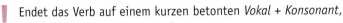

The monster is reading the newspaper.

! Endet das Verb auf einem kurzen betonten *Vokal + Konsonant,*
wird der Konsonant verdoppelt.
sit ➔ *sitting*   *run* ➔ *running*

Für die Verneinung fügst du einfach ein *not* hinter die Form von *be* ein:
Caroline is not writing a letter.   *George isn't reading a book. He's watching TV.*

b) Fragen und Kurzantworten

Auch in der Verlaufsform kannst du Entscheidungsfragen bilden:

Charlie is reading a book.

Is Charlie reading a book?

Is George helping his mum?   – *Yes, he is./No, he isn't.*
Are Caroline and George playing basketball? – *Yes, they are./No, they aren't.*

Bei Fragen mit Fragewort stellst du das Fragewort an den Satzanfang:

What are you doing? Where are you going?

4R Die einfache Vergangenheit (The simple past)

a) Bejahte und verneinte Aussagesätze

Das *simple past* verwendest du, wenn du über etwas sprechen willst, das in der Vergangenheit liegt und abgeschlossen ist – z. B. wenn du berichtest, was du erlebt hast, oder wenn du eine Geschichte erzählst.

Infinitiv + ed

watched   walked

Regelmäßige Verben (Regular verbs)
Das *simple past* der regelmäßigen Verben bildest du, indem du die Endung *-ed* an den Infinitiv anhängst:
watch + ed ➔ *watched*

helped   started

simple past: regelmäßige Formen	
Yesterday I watched a film about elephants.	*Gestern habe ich einen Film über Elefanten gesehen.*
Last Monday Rajiv helped his parents.	*Letzten Montag hat Rajiv seinen Eltern geholfen.*

! Achte auf folgende Besonderheiten in der Schreibung:
● Endet das Verb auf *-e*, dann wird nur *-d* angehängt.
like ➜ *lik**ed***
Endet das Verb auf einem kurzen betonten *Vokal + Konsonant*, wird der Konsonant verdoppelt.
stop ➜ *sto**pp**ed*
Endet das Verb auf *Konsonant + -y*, dann lautet die Endung im *simple past -ied*.
try ➜ *tr**ied***

Unregelmäßige Verben (Irregular verbs)

Bei unregelmäßigen Verben wird das *simple past* nicht mit *-ed* gebildet. Du musst ihre Formen wie neue Vokabeln lernen. Auf den Seiten 310 und 311 findest du eine Liste der unregelmäßigen Verben.

Be hat als einziges englisches Verb zwei Formen im *simple past*, *was* und *were*:
I/he/she/it was – *you/we/they were*

Weitere unregelmäßige Verben findest du in diesen Sätzen:

Infinitiv	simple past	
be	was/were	I was very hungry after school. They were in London last week.
have	had	Sarah had a great holiday.
go	went	She went to Spain with her family.
find	found	She and her sister found many nice postcards.
do	did	They did lots of interesting things together.

I read many books in the holidays.

Wenn du sagen willst, was in der Vergangenheit nicht geschehen ist, verwendest du *not* oder die Kurzform *n't*, die an *was/were* angehängt wird.

simple past: bejahter Satz	simple past: verneinter Satz
I was at school on Monday.	I wasn't at school on Monday.
They were friendly at the hotel.	They weren't friendly at the hotel.

Wenn im Satz kein *was/were* steht, musst du *didn't (did not)* vor das Verb stellen.
Didn't ist die Vergangenheitsform von *don't* und *doesn't*. *Didn't* ist bei allen Personen gleich.
Das Verb selbst bleibt im Infinitiv, weil *didn't* schon die Vergangenheit anzeigt.

simple past: bejahter Satz	simple past: verneinter Satz
Brian talked to Cheryl yesterday.	Brian didn't talk to Cheryl yesterday.
I went to Hamburg last year.	I didn't go to Hamburg last year.

b) Entscheidungsfragen und Kurzantworten

simple past: Entscheidungsfragen und Kurzantworten		
Did you **go** on holiday?	Yes, I did.	No, I didn't.
Did Gillian **visit** Cheryl in Illinois?	Yes, she did.	No, she didn't.

simple past: Entscheidungsfragen und Kurzantworten mit *was/were*		
Were you at the party yesterday?	Yes, I was.	No, I wasn't.
Was it good?	Yes, it was.	No, it wasn't.

Did Rajiv *buy* a new
football yesterday?
– *Yes, he did.*

5R Die Verlaufsform der Vergangenheit
(The past progressive)

a) Bejahte und verneinte Aussagesätze

Das *past progressive* drückt aus, ...
- was jemand gerade tat oder was gerade passierte.
- was gerade vor sich ging, als etwas anderes geschah.

*Emma was reading a
book when her father
came to say good night.*

So bildest du das *past progressive*:
Simple past-Form von *be (was/were)* + **Infinitiv des Verbs** + **Endung -ing**.
*The girl **was wearing** her pajamas.*   Das Mädchen trug ihren Pyjama.

past progressive	simple past
The players **were preparing** for the football game *Die Spieler bereiteten sich auf das American Football-Spiel vor,*	when it **started** to rain. *als es anfing zu regnen.*
While the players **were warming** up, *Während die Spieler sich aufwärmten,*	the coach **arrived**. *kam der Trainer.*

was gerade passierte: *past progressive* → ↑ **neues Ereignis: simple past**

Für die Verneinung fügst du einfach ein *not* hinter die Form von *be* ein:
*The girls were **not** decorating the school.*   *The marching band was**n't** playing all the time.*

b) Fragen und Kurzantworten

Was the homecoming king laughing? – *Yes, he was./No, he wasn't.*
Were the students having a tug-of-war? – *Yes, they were./No, they weren't.*

What was the marching band playing?
Where were they sitting?

LANGUAGE IN FOCUS

6R Das Perfekt (The present perfect)

a) Bejahte und verneinte Aussagesätze

Das *present perfect* verwendest du, ...

- wenn etwas irgendwann, noch nie oder noch nicht geschehen ist:
  *Tracy **has** never **tried** peanut butter.*
  Tracy hat noch nie Erdnussbutter probiert.

*She **has bought** new clothes.*

- wenn ein Vorgang in der Vergangenheit noch Auswirkungen auf die Gegenwart hat:
  *David **has cleaned** the kitchen.*
  David hat die Küche geputzt (sie ist noch sauber).

Das *present perfect* bildest du mit *have/has* + Partizip Perfekt (past participle).
Die Verneinung bildest du mit *haven't/hasn't* + Partizip Perfekt.

present perfect: Aussagesätze und Verneinung			
I	have	cleaned	the kitchen.
He	has	gone	to New York.
We	have	eaten	bagels.
She	hasn't	been	to Texas.
They	haven't	helped	him.

*The boys **have tidied up** their room.*

Das *present perfect* kannst du mit Adverbien der unbestimmten Zeit verwenden, z. B. mit *already, just, ever, never*. Es ist in solchen Sätzen nicht wichtig, wann genau etwas geschehen ist.
Die Adverbien stehen dann direkt vor dem Partizip Perfekt:
*I have **already** done my homework.* – Ich habe meine Hausaufgaben schon gemacht.
*Angela has **just** seen the Queen.* – Angela hat eben/gerade die Queen gesehen.

! Beachte die Ausnahme: *yet* steht am Satzende.
*I haven't been to Berlin **yet**.* – Ich war noch nicht in Berlin.

b) Fragen und Kurzantworten

Entscheidungsfragen im *present perfect* bildest du, indem du das Subjekt und *have/has* vertauschst. Bei Fragen mit Fragewörtern steht das Fragewort am Satzanfang:

present perfect: Fragen und Kurzantworten					
	Have	you	finished	your homework?	Yes, I have./No, I haven't.
	Has	Jill	bought	a new mobile?	Yes, she has./No, she hasn't.
What	have	you	done?		
Why	hasn't	she	come?		

c) Das Partizip Perfekt

Bei regelmäßigen Verben bildest du das Partizip Perfekt *(past participle)* mit dem Infinitiv + *-ed*.

Infinitiv	*simple past*	*past participle*
clean	cleaned	cleaned
help	helped	helped
play	played	played

Unregelmäßige Verben haben unregelmäßige Formen. Diese solltest du wie Vokabeln lernen.

Infinitiv	*simple past*	*past participle*
be	was/were	been
do	did	done
have	had	had
buy	bought	bought

Auf den Seiten 310 und 311 findest du eine Liste der unregelmäßigen Verben.

7 Die Vorvergangenheit (The past perfect)

Das *past perfect* verwendest du, wenn du über eine Handlung sprechen möchtest, die vor einer anderen Handlung in der Vergangenheit stattgefunden hat. Die zweite Handlung steht im *simple past*. Beide Handlungen sind abgeschlossen.

After Annie's parents had gone to America, they found jobs in New York.
Nachdem Annies Eltern nach Amerika gegangen waren, fanden sie Arbeit in New York.

Das *past perfect* bildest du so: Form von *had* + Partizip Perfekt (past participle).

1. Handlung	2. Handlung
past perfect	*simple past*
After Annie **had died**, *Nachdem Annie gestorben war,*	a statue was built on Ellis Island. *wurde auf Ellis Island eine Statue gebaut.*
Annie's family **had lived** in Ireland *Annies Familie hatte in Irland gelebt,*	before they came to the USA. *bevor sie in die USA kamen.*

Die Verneinung bildest du mit *hadn't* + Partizip Perfekt (past participle).

Annie's parents hadn't had any money before they came to New York.
Annies Eltern hatten kein Geld gehabt, bevor sie nach New York kamen.

Wenn du das *past perfect* bildest, musst du auf das Partizip Perfekt achten (➜ LiF 6Rc). Bei regelmäßigen Verben endet es auf *-ed*. Bei unregelmäßigen Verben wird das Partizip Perfekt nicht mit *-ed* gebildet. Du musst ihre Formen wie neue Vokabeln lernen. Auf den Seiten 310 und 311 findest du eine Liste der unregelmäßigen Verben.

8R Die Zukunft mit *will* (The will-future)

Wenn du über die Zukunft sprechen willst, benutzt du das *will-future*. Mit dem *will-future* kannst du Vermutungen aussprechen und Vorhersagen oder Versprechen äußern.

Das *will-future* bildest du mit **will** und dem **Infinitiv des Verbs**.
Auch *will* hat eine Kurzform. Sie lautet *'ll*. *Will* ist in allen Personen gleich.

Zukunft mit *will*: Aussagesätze	
I **will help** you.	*Ich werde dir helfen.*
You**'ll find** new friends.	*Du wirst neue Freunde finden.*
The weather **will be** great tomorrow.	*Das Wetter wird morgen großartig sein.*

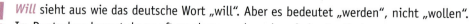

> I**'ll** see you at the station.

> OK, I**'ll** be there at ten.

! *Will* sieht aus wie das deutsche Wort „will". Aber es bedeutet „werden", nicht „wollen".
● Im Deutschen kannst du es oft weglassen, aber niemals im Englischen:

Next time I'll catch you. — Das nächste Mal krieg' ich dich!
Das nächste Mal werde ich dich kriegen!

Die Verneinung bildest du mit **will not** oder der Kurzform **won't**.

Zukunft mit *will*: Verneinung	
I **won't win** the match.	*Ich werde das Spiel nicht gewinnen.*
He **won't get** a dog.	*Er wird keinen Hund bekommen.*
It **won't be** cold on Wednesday.	*Am Mittwoch wird es nicht kalt sein.*

Zukunft mit *will*: Fragen und Antworten	
Will Tom **get** a good job?	Yes, he **will**./No, he **won't**.
Where **will** you **live** in ten years?	I think I will live in Berlin.

9R Die Zukunft mit *going to* (The *going to*-future)

Die Zukunft mit *going to* verwendest du, wenn du sagen willst, was jemand für die Zukunft plant oder vorhat. Im Deutschen gibt es keine Zeitform, die dem *going to* entspricht. Du hast aber verschiedene Möglichkeiten, es wiederzugeben:

We**'re going to** fly to London tomorrow.	*Wir werden morgen nach London fliegen.* *Wir möchten/wollen morgen nach London fliegen.* *Wir planen/haben vor, morgen nach London zu fliegen.*

Du bildest die Zukunft mit *going to* mit
einer **Form von** *be* + *going to* + **Infinitiv des Verbs**.

Zukunft mit *going to*: Aussagesätze			
I'm	going to	fly	to Spain next week.
Rajiv is	going to	help	his parents in their shop.

*He is going to buy
an ice cream.*

Zukunft mit *going to*: Verneinung			
I'm not	going to	call	her tomorrow.
She isn't	going to	go	to the party.
They aren't	going to	visit	Emma's aunt.

*Are you going to
go to the party?*

Zukunft mit *going to*: Fragen und Antworten	
Are you going to watch the film tonight?	Yes, **I am.**/No, **I'm not.**
What are you going to do?	I'm going to call Dan.

10R Modalverben (Modal verbs)

Die meisten Modalverben haben nur Formen für das *simple present*.
Im *simple past* und im *will-future* verwendest du deshalb die Ersatzformen.

a) Fähigkeit: *can/can't – be able to/not be able to*

Mit *can* kannst du sagen, ...
- was jemand tun kann
- was jemand tun darf.

He **can** swim.	*Er kann schwimmen.*
You **can** watch TV.	*Du darfst fernsehen.*

Can steht mit dem Infinitiv und bleibt in allen Personen gleich.

! Die Ersatzform von *can* ist *be able to*. Im *simple past* kannst du aber auch *could* benutzen.

Emma and Charlie **were able to** help Mr Miller.	*Emma und Charlie konnten Herrn Miller helfen.*
Rajiv **couldn't** do his maths homework because it was too difficult.	*Rajiv konnte seine Mathehausaufgaben nicht machen, weil sie zu schwierig waren.*

Could benutzt du auch für höfliche Bitten und Aufforderungen.

| **Could** I take your pencil, please? | *Könnte ich bitte deinen Bleistift nehmen?* |

b) Erlaubnis: *can/can't – be allowed to/not be allowed to – must not*

Can/can't, *be allowed to* und *must not* benutzt du, wenn du …
- um etwas bittest
- um Erlaubnis fragst oder jemandem etwas erlaubst
- etwas verbietest.

You **can** use your mobile phones in the cafeteria but you **are not allowed to** use them during class.	*Ihr könnt eure Handys in der Cafeteria benutzen, aber ihr dürft sie nicht im Unterricht benutzen.*
Cheryl **is allowed to** wear T-shirts to school.	*Cheryl darf in der Schule T-Shirts tragen.*
In Germany cars **mustn't** drive on the left.	*In Deutschland dürfen Autos nicht links fahren.*

! *Must not* oder die Kurzform *mustn't* klingt wie im Deutschen „muss nicht", heißt aber „etwas nicht dürfen".

You **mustn't** talk now.

c) Notwendigkeit: *must/have to – needn't/don't have to*

- *Must* klingt wie das deutsche Wort „muss" und heißt auch *müssen*. In der Regel kannst du *must* auch durch *have to/has to* ersetzen.

Claire **must** tidy up her room. *oder* Claire **has to** tidy up her room.	*Claire muss ihr Zimmer aufräumen.*

- *Must* hat keine eigene Vergangenheitsform. Daher wird die *simple past*-Form von *have to* benutzt.

Before there were lights, people **had to** use candles.	*Bevor es Lampen gab, mussten die Menschen Kerzen benutzen.*

- Wenn du sagen willst, was jemand *nicht* tun muss, benutzt du *don't/doesn't have to*.

I **have to** take out the rubbish but I **don't have to** clean the kitchen.

- Auch mit *need not* oder *needn't* kannst du ausdrücken, dass etwas nicht notwendig ist.

You **needn't** do your homework now. You can do it later.	*Du brauchst deine Hausaufgaben nicht jetzt zu machen. Du kannst sie später machen.*

11R Bedingungssätze, Typ I (Conditional clauses, type I)

Ein Bedingungssatz besteht aus einem *if*-Satz *(if-clause)* und einem Hauptsatz *(main clause)*:

- Der *if*-Satz nennt eine Bedingung. Der Hauptsatz drückt aus, was passiert, wenn die Bedingung erfüllt ist.
- Im *if*-Satz steht das *simple present*, im Hauptsatz das *will-future*.

if-Satz: simple present	Hauptsatz: will-future	
If you **miss** the bus,	you **will be** late.	*Wenn du den Bus verpasst, kommst du zu spät.*
If it **rains**,	they **won't go** outside.	*Wenn es regnet, werden sie nicht rausgehen.*

Bedingungssätze können entweder mit dem *if*-Satz oder mit dem Hauptsatz beginnen.
Wenn sie mit dem *if*-Satz beginnen, werden sie mit einem Komma getrennt.
If you go to the cinema, I'll come with you.
I'll come with you if you go to the cinema.

They **won't** go to the beach **if** it rains.

Im Hauptsatz kannst du auch Modalverben (z. B. *can*, *must*) oder den Imperativ verwenden:

*If it snows, we **can go** inside.*	–	Wenn es schneit, können wir reingehen.
*If you like her, you **must call** her.*	–	Wenn du sie magst, musst du sie anrufen.
*If you need help, **ask** Lisa.*	–	Wenn du Hilfe brauchst, frag Lisa.

12 Bedingungssätze, Typ II (Conditional clauses, type II)

- Mit dem Bedingungssatz, Typ II, drückst du aus, was unter einer nur gedachten Bedingung passieren würde oder könnte. Dabei geht es um Ereignisse, die <u>unwahrscheinlich</u> oder <u>unmöglich</u> sind.

- Der *if*-Satz *(if-clause)* steht im *simple past*.
  Im Hauptsatz *(main clause)* steht **would** oder **could** vor dem Infinitiv:

if-Satz: simple past	Hauptsatz mit *would/* **could** + Infinitiv	
If Allimar's father **earned** enough money,	her mother **could live** with them.	*Wenn Allimars Vater genug Geld verdiente, könnte ihre Mutter mit ihnen zusammen leben.*
If Allimar **had** electricity,	she **wouldn't use** an oil lamp when it gets dark.	*Wenn Allimar Elektrizität hätte, würde sie keine Öllampe benutzen, wenn es dunkel wird.*
If I **went** to a reservation,	I **could talk** to Native Americans.	*Wenn ich in ein Reservat ginge, könnte ich mit amerikanischen Ureinwohnern sprechen.*

- Bei *if*-Sätzen heißt es üblicherweise *"If I were ...",* aber du kannst auch *"If I was ..."* sagen. Beide Formen sind hier richtig.
  If I **were** really good at football, I would play for Arsenal.
  Wenn ich im Fußball richtig gut wäre, würde ich für Arsenal spielen.

  If I **was** rich, I would be happy.
  Wenn ich reich wäre, wäre ich glücklich.

13 Bedingungssätze, Typ III (Conditional clauses, type III)

- Mit dem Bedingungssatz, Typ III, drückst du aus, was in der Vergangenheit hätte passieren können, aber nicht passiert ist. Die Bedingung im *if*-Satz ist nicht mehr erfüllbar.

- Der *if*-Satz *(if-clause)* steht im *past perfect*.
  Im Hauptsatz *(main clause)* steht **would** oder **could** + **have** + **Partizip Perfekt (past participle)**:

if-Satz: *past perfect*	Hauptsatz mit *would/ could* + *have* + Partizip	
If Tom **had been** nicer to Stacy,	she **would have dated** him again.	*Wenn Tom netter zu Stacy gewesen wäre, hätte sie ihn noch einmal getroffen.*
If they **had gone** to an Italian restaurant,	Stacy **could have eaten** pizza.	*Wenn sie in ein italienisches Restaurant gegangen wären, hätte Stacy Pizza essen können.*

14R Das Gerundium (The gerund)

Wird ein Verb wie ein Nomen verwendet, nennt man das Gerundium *(gerund).*
Im Englischen hängst du dafür ein *-ing* an den Infinitiv des Verbs:

Going to school by bike can be fun.
Mit dem Fahrrad zur Schule fahren kann Spaß machen.

- Das Gerundium kann Subjekt eines Satzes sein:
  Separating paper is good for the environment. – Die Trennung von Papier ist gut für die Umwelt.

- Das Gerundium folgt oft nach bestimmten Verben wie *like, love, enjoy, hate, start* und *stop*:
  He *likes saving* energy. – Er mag es, Energie zu sparen.

- Du benutzt das Gerundium auch nach bestimmten Ausdrücken wie *can't stand, good at* oder *bad at*:
  I'm *good at playing* basketball. – Ich kann gut Basketball spielen.
  She *can't stand swimming*. – Sie kann Schwimmen nicht ausstehen.

15 Possessivpronomen (Possessive pronouns)

Du kennst bereits die **Possessivbegleiter (my, your, …)**. Sie zeigen an, wem etwas gehört.
Possessivpronomen benutzt du, wenn du ein Nomen mit Possessivbegleiter, das bereits
genannt wurde, nicht wiederholen möchtest.

Is this your jacket? It's not *mine.* –
Ist das deine Jacke? Sie gehört nicht mir./Es ist nicht **meine**.

Are you going to take your smartphone, Gillian?
– Yes, are you taking *yours, too?*
Nimmst du dein Smartphone mit, Gillian?
– Ja, nimmst du **deins** auch mit?

Personalpronomen	Possessivbegleiter	Possessivpronomen
I	my	mine
you	your	yours
he	his	his
she	her	hers
it	its	–
we	our	ours
you	your	yours
they	their	theirs

! Zu **it/its** gibt es kein Possessivpronomen.

16R Imperativ (The imperative)

> Don't talk in class, please.

Mit dem Imperativ (der Befehlsform) kannst du
Bitten, Befehle oder Anweisungen ausdrücken:
Please *open* *the window, Lisa.*

Im Englischen hat der Imperativ dieselbe Form
wie der Infinitiv und bleibt im Singular und Plural gleich.
Help me, please. – Bitte **hilf** mir./Bitte **helft** mir.

Wenn jemand etwas nicht tun soll, stellst du einfach *do not* oder *don't* vor das Verb.
Don't forget *your keys.*

! Wenn du nur den Imperativ verwendest, kann das im Englischen sehr
unhöflich klingen. Höflicher ist es, wenn du **please** hinzufügst.

17R Relativsätze (Relative clauses)

Mit Relativsätzen kannst du eine Person oder eine Sache genauer beschreiben.
Ein Relativsatz beginnt meist mit einem Relativpronomen: *who*, *which* oder *that*.
Dabei verwendest du *who* für Personen und *which* für Dinge.

	Relativsatz	
Someone	**who** eats healthily must be fit.	*Jemand, der sich gesund ernährt, muss fit sein.*
There are many people	**who** like fast food.	*Es gibt viele Menschen, die Fastfood mögen.*
Kathy works at the Super Burger	**which** is in Roselle.	*Kathy arbeitet in dem Super Burger, der in Roselle ist.*
Cheryl wrote a report on fast food	**which** was really good.	*Cheryl schrieb einen Bericht über Fastfood, der richtig gut war.*

Das Relativpronomen *that* kannst du sowohl für Dinge als auch für Personen benutzen.
*Ice hockey is a sport **that** can be dangerous.*   –   Eishockey ist ein Sport, der gefährlich sein kann.
*There are lots of people **that** dance to the music.*   –   Es gibt viele Leute, die zu der Musik tanzen.

18R Steigerung und Vergleich von Adjektiven (Comparison of adjectives)

Wenn du Personen oder Sachen miteinander vergleichen möchtest, kannst du ein Adjektiv steigern.
Die Steigerungsformen heißen **comparative** (Komparativ) und **superlative** (Superlativ).

a) Steigerung von Adjektiven mit *-er* und *-est*

Einsilbige Adjektive (z. B. *cheap, old, young*) werden durch das Anhängen von *-er* und *-est* gesteigert.

Adjektiv	Komparativ	Superlativ
cheap	cheap**er**	(the) cheap**est**
old	old**er**	(the) old**est**
few	few**er**	(the) few**est**

Bei zweisilbigen Adjektiven, die auf *-y* enden, wird aus dem *-y* ein *-i*.

Adjektiv	Komparativ	Superlativ
pretty	prett**ier**	(the) prett**iest**
easy	eas**ier**	(the) eas**iest**
friendly	friendl**ier**	(the) friendl**iest**

! Bei manchen Adjektiven ändert
sich die Schreibweise.

Adjektiv	Komparativ	Superlativ
nice	nic**er**	(the) nic**est**
hot	hot**ter**	(the) hot**test**
big	big**ger**	(the) big**gest**

Einige Adjektive haben unregelmäßige
Steigerungsformen. Diese Formen musst
du wie Vokabeln lernen.

Adjektiv	Komparativ	Superlativ
good	**better**	(the) **best**
bad	**worse**	(the) **worst**
much/many	**more**	(the) **most**

b) Steigerung von Adjektiven mit *more* und *most*

Mehrsilbige Adjektive werden mit *more* und *most* gesteigert.
Du stellst dabei *more* oder *most* vor das Adjektiv. Das Adjektiv bleibt unverändert.

Adjektiv	Komparativ	Superlativ
interesting	**more** interesting	(the) **most** interesting
beautiful	**more** beautiful	(the) **most** beautiful

c) Vergleichssätze

Willst du ungleiche Dinge miteinander vergleichen, benutzt du
den Komparativ mit *than*.

Vergleichssätze	
Burgers at Super Burger are **better than** any other burgers.	*Burger bei Super Burger sind besser als andere Burger.*
Fast food is **more popular than** traditional food.	*Fastfood ist beliebter als traditionelles Essen.*

Sind die Eigenschaften von zwei Dingen oder Personen gleich, benutzt du *as ... as*.

Vergleichssätze	
The cucumber is **as fresh as** the tomatoes.	*Die Gurke ist genauso frisch wie die Tomaten.*
The seats are **as comfortable as** my sofa at home.	*Die Sitze sind genauso bequem wie mein Sofa zu Hause.*

19R Adverbien der Art und Weise (Adverbs of manner)

Wenn du beschreiben möchtest, wie jemand etwas tut oder wie etwas geschieht, benutzt du ein Adverb der Art und Weise. Adverbien der Art und Weise bildest du, indem du an das Adjektiv die Endung *-ly* anhängst:

Adjektiv	Adverb	
loud	loud**ly**	The boys speak very **loudly**.
bad	bad**ly**	Susan cooks **badly**.
slow	slow**ly**	Tom always eats **slowly**.

Bei manchen Adverbien ändert sich die Schreibweise, wenn *-ly* angehängt wird. *-y* wird zu *-ily*; *-le* wird zu *-ly*; *-l* wird zu *-lly*.

Adjektiv	Adverb	
happy	happ**ily**	Caroline laughed **happily**.
easy	eas**ily**	You can prepare hot dogs **easily**.
terrible	terrib**ly**	Simon dances **terribly**.
beautiful	beautiful**ly**	Mona smiles **beautifully**.

*He sings **badly**.*

! Einige Adverbien haben Sonderformen, die du wie Vokabeln lernen musst.
Manche Adjektive und Adverbien sind gleich:

Adjektiv	Adverb	
good	**well**	Rajiv is a good guitar player. He plays the guitar **well**.
fast	**fast**	Jack is a fast runner. He runs **fast**.
hard	**hard**	Gillian is a hard worker. She works **hard**.

Adverbien der Art und Weise stehen nach dem Verb.
In Sätzen mit Objekt stehen sie nach dem Objekt.

Subjekt	Verb	Objekt	Adverb
Gillian	works		**hard**.
Rajiv	plays	the guitar	**well**.

*Rajiv dances very **well**.*

20 Steigerung von Adverbien (Comparison of adverbs)

Du weißt bereits, wie Adjektive gesteigert werden (➔ LiF 18R).
Für die Steigerung von Adverbien gelten die gleichen Regeln.

Amy cooks more deliciously than Jason.
Amy kocht leckerer als Jason.

Kathy works harder at Super Burger than other managers.
Kathy arbeitet härter bei Super Burger als andere Manager.

*Sam eats more healthily
than he would like to eat.*

Einsilbige Adverbien werden durch das
Anhängen von *-er* und *-est* gesteigert.

Adverb	Komparativ	Superlativ
fast	fast**er**	(the) fast**est**
hard	hard**er**	(the) hard**est**

Mehrsilbige Adverbien,
die auf *-ly* enden, steigerst du
mit *more* und *most*.

Adverb	Komparativ	Superlativ
slowly	**more** slowly	(the) **most** slowly
quickly	**more** quickly	(the) **most** quickly
deliciously	**more** deliciously	(the) **most** deliciously

Es gibt auch unregelmäßige Steigerungsformen, die du wie Vokabeln lernen musst:

Adverb	Komparativ	Superlativ
well	**better**	(the) **best**
badly	**worse**	(the) **worst**
much	**more**	(the) **most**

21R Fragen mit Fragewörtern (Questions with question words)

Fragen mit Fragewörtern mit *be, can, have got*

Where is George?	*Wo ist George?*
What was the weather like?	*Wie war das Wetter?*
When can I call you?	*Wann kann ich dich anrufen?*
Who has got an idea?	*Wer hat eine Idee?*

Who?	*Wer?*
What?	*Was?*
When?	*Wann?*
Where?	*Wo?*
Why?	*Warum?*
How?	*Wie?*

! Mit *who* fragst du nach Personen, mit *where* nach Orten.
● Ein Merkspruch: *Who, who, who* – **wer** bist du?
    Where, where, where – **wo** kommst du her?

Auch bei Fragen mit *do* stellst du das Fragewort an den Satzanfang:

Fragen mit Fragewörtern mit *do* + Verb	
Why does Lee-Lee **like** the dumplings?	*Warum mag Lee-Lee die Knödel?*
Where do you **celebrate** St Patrick's Day?	*Wo feierst du St Patrick's Day?*
What did you **do** on Halloween?	*Was habt ihr an Halloween gemacht?*
How long did you **stay** out?	*Wie lange warst du draußen?*

Bei Fragen mit *who* braucht man kein *do* oder *does*, wenn *who* Subjekt ist:
Who celebrates Diwali?

22R Die Satzstellung (Word order)

Im englischen Aussagesatz ist die Satzstellung meist: Subjekt – Verb – Objekt (S – V – O):

Subjekt *(subject)*	Verb *(verb)*	Objekt *(object)*	
I	like	ice cream.	
Charlie and his friends	play	football.	

Im Englischen stehen Häufigkeitsadverbien *(adverbs of frequency)*
meist zwischen Subjekt und Verb:

Subjekt	Häufigkeitsadverb	Verb		
I	**sometimes**	help	at home.	*Ich helfe manchmal zu Hause.*
Leon	**never**	walks	to school.	*Leon läuft nie zur Schule.*

! Häufigkeitsadverbien stehen hinter den Formen von *can* und *be*:
We can **sometimes** get up late on Saturdays.
She's **always** late.

> Like nine before ten, it's **where** before **when**.

Orts- und Zeitangaben stehen in der Regel am Ende eines Satzes. Wenn
sie zusammen in einem Satz vorkommen, steht immer „Ort" vor „Zeit".

	Ortsangabe	Zeitangabe
My aunt lived	in Australia	from 2001 to 2013.
But she came	home	for Christmas every year.

Um eine Zeitangabe stärker zu betonen, kannst du sie auch an den Satzanfang stellen.

Zeitangabe		Ortsangabe
On Thanksgiving	the whole family gets together	at my grandparents' house.

23R Konjunktionen (Linking words)

Linking words sind Wörter, mit denen du Sätze verbinden kannst.

> What did you say? Sorry, I can't hear you very well **because** my dad is hoovering the floor.

Konjunktionen	
Kathy is fourteen **and** Stacy is 15 years old.	… *und* …
Carol likes ice cream **but** she doesn't like chocolate.	… *aber* …
Charlie is happy **because** he can play football.	… *weil* …
Ben went into the house **when** it started to rain.	… *als* …
We have enough food **so** we don't need to go shopping.	… *also* …

24 Nomen mit und ohne Artikel
(Nouns with and without articles)

- Wie im Deutschen gibt es auch im Englischen einen bestimmten Artikel *(the)* und einen unbestimmten Artikel *(a/an)*. Die meisten Nomen werden immer mit einem (bestimmten oder unbestimmten) Artikel benutzt.
  a bottle – the two bottles on the table
  an accident – the accident on 2nd Street

- Nur Namen für Kontinente, Länder, Städte, Straßen und Seen werden nicht mit einem Artikel benutzt – es sei denn, der Name enthält schon selbst einen Artikel, wie z. B. *the USA* und *the Statue of Liberty*.

- Wenn du über Berufe von Personen sprechen willst, fällt der Artikel im Deutschen weg.
  Im Englischen benutzt du immer den unbestimmten Artikel *(a/an)*.
  Linda has an interesting job. She is **an** *actress.*
  Linda hat einen interessanten Beruf. Sie ist Schauspielerin.

25 Verben mit zwei Objekten (Verbs with two objects)

Wie im Deutschen gibt es auch im Englischen viele Verben, die zwei Objekte haben können, z. B. *give, offer, show.*

Man unterscheidet direkte und indirekte Objekte.
Das indirekte Objekt steht meistens für eine Person, das direkte Objekt für eine Sache.

	indirektes Objekt	direktes Objekt
Please get	Grandma	a cup of coffee.
I'll show	Sarah	my new painting.
Did they ask	you	a lot of questions?

26 Stützwörter: *one/ones* (Prop words)

Du benutzt *one*, um ein Nomen nicht zu wiederholen:
I have two brothers. The little one is five and the other is seven years old.
Ich habe zwei Brüder. Der kleine ist fünf und der andere ist sieben Jahre alt.

Wenn das Bezugswort im Plural steht, musst du *ones* benutzen:
Raúl cleans shoes, mostly expensive ones from business people.
Raúl putzt Schuhe, meistens teure von Geschäftsleuten.

! Im Deutschen kannst du das Nomen einfach weglassen, wenn du es nicht wiederholen möchtest.
Im Englischen ist das nicht möglich. Du musst die Stützwörter *one* oder *ones* benutzen.
Which T-shirt should I take? The yellow one or the blue one?
Welches T-Shirt soll ich nehmen? Das gelbe oder das blaue?

27R Mengenangaben (Quantifiers)

Mit *some* und *any* werden Mengen wie z. B. „etwas" oder „einige" bezeichnet.
Die Mengenangabe *not ... any* bedeutet „kein" oder „keine".
Some und *any* werden aber oft nicht übersetzt.
In bejahten Aussagesätzen verwendest du *some*, in verneinten Aussagesätzen und in Fragen *any*.

Bejahte Aussagesätze mit *some*	Fragen und verneinte Aussagesätze mit *any*	
There are **some** apples in the kitchen. *In der Küche sind (ein paar) Äpfel.*	Are there **any** apples? *Gibt es Äpfel?*	We have**n't** got **any** apples. *Wir haben keine Äpfel.*
I need **some** milk for my cornflakes. *Ich brauche (etwas) Milch für meine Cornflakes.*	Have you got **any** milk? *Hast du (etwas) Milch?*	There is**n't** any milk. *Es gibt keine Milch.*

! Wenn du jemanden höflich um etwas bittest oder ihm etwas anbietest,
benutzt du *some* auch in Fragen:
Can I have some milk, please?   *Would you like some tea?*

Nach denselben Regeln wie *some* und *any* benutzt du auch ihre
Zusammensetzungen *something* und *(not) anything*.
*I'm sure they'll have **something** you like.   There is**n't anything** in the fridge.*

Mit *how much* fragst du nach unbestimmten, nicht zählbaren Mengen
(z. B. *water, milk, time, money, chocolate, ...*):
How much money do you spend on clothes each month? – I spend $20.

Mit *how many* fragst du nach der Anzahl von Dingen:
How many players are there in an American football team? – There are eleven players.

28 Indirekte Rede (Reported speech)

● Wenn du berichten willst, was jemand gesagt hat, verwendest du die indirekte Rede (reported speech).

Direkte Rede	**Indirekte Rede**	
	Begleitsatz	Wiedergegebene Aussage
Stacy: "I'm sixteen."	➜ Stacy says (that)	she is sixteen.

● Die indirekte Rede besteht aus einem Begleitsatz und der wiedergegebenen Aussage. Beide Satzteile können durch *that* verbunden werden, man kann es aber auch weglassen.

● Wenn du etwas berichten willst, das du gerade gehört hast und das jetzt noch stimmt oder allgemeingültig ist, benutzt du im Begleitsatz und in der wiedergegebenen Aussage die Zeitform der Gegenwart.

Ashley: "You **have to be** really fit to be a cheerleader." ➜ Ashley **thinks** (that) you **have to be** really fit to be a cheerleader.

● Im Allgemeinen stehen die Verben im Begleitsatz und in der wiedergegebenen Aussage in der Vergangenheit. Die Zeitform der wiedergegebenen Rede rückt dann sozusagen eine Stufe weiter in die Vergangenheit als die direkte Rede (Zeitverschiebung = *backshift of tenses*). Aus dieser Tabelle kannst du ablesen, wie sich die Zeiten verändern.

direct speech		*reported speech*
simple present	➜	simple past
simple past	➜	past perfect
present perfect	➜	past perfect
will	➜	would
can	➜	could
should	➜	should

And then Tom said that I would like Mexican food. But I didn't! So I said …

Stacy: "Tom, you **are** late!" ➜ Stacy told Tom (that) he **was** late.
Tom: "I **saw** Chad at the restaurant." ➜ Tom said (that) he **had seen** Chad at the restaurant.

Stacy to Tom: "I **haven't eaten** that before." ➜ Stacy told Tom (that) she **hadn't eaten** that before.

● Meistens musst du Teile der indirekten Rede anpassen oder ergänzen, damit dein Gesprächspartner versteht, was du meinst. Das betrifft zum Beispiel die Pronomen und die Verbform, aber auch Angaben zu Ort und Zeit.

Stacy: "**I** have a date with Tom **today**." ➜ Stacy explained (that) **she** had a date with Tom **that day**.

29 Reflexivpronomen (Reflexive pronouns)

- Du verwendest Reflexivpronomen, wenn das Subjekt und das Objekt in einem Satz dieselbe Person bezeichnen.
Don't cut yourself!
We made ourselves comfortable.

Gillian is looking at herself.

Personalpronomen	Reflexivpronomen
I	myself
you	yourself
he	himself
she	herself
it	itself
we	ourselves
you	yourselves
they	themselves

!
- Bei manchen Sätzen musst du im Englischen ein Reflexivpronomen benutzen, im Deutschen aber nicht.
Help yourself. – Bediene dich. (statt: Bediene dich *selbst*.)

- Im Englischen werden Reflexivpronomen auch benutzt, um ein Nomen oder Pronomen besonders zu betonen. Sie bedeuten dann im Deutschen *selbst* oder *selber*.
I can't repair this myself. – Ich kann das nicht **selber** reparieren.
You said that yourself. – Du hast das **selbst** gesagt.

30R Das Passiv (The passive)

Aktivsätze sagen uns, wer oder was handelt. Wenn es aber nicht wichtig oder klar ist, wer etwas tut oder getan hat, kannst du das Passiv verwenden.

Das Passiv bildest du so: Form von *be* + **Partizip Perfekt (past participle)**

English **is spoken** all over the world.	*Englisch wird überall auf der Welt gesprochen.*
Matches **are used** to make fire.	*Streichhölzer werden zum Feuer machen benutzt.*
My computer **was made** in China.	*Mein Computer wurde in China hergestellt.*
These books **were written** in Germany.	*Diese Bücher wurden in Deutschland geschrieben.*

Wenn du in einem Passivsatz doch einmal die handelnde Person oder die Ursache für etwas nennen willst, hängst du sie mit *by* („von", „durch") an den Satz an:
The first car was invented by Karl Benz.
The house was destroyed by fire.

These dragons **were made** in China.

So funktionieren die Wortlisten

Es gibt alphabetische Wortlisten *(Dictionaries)* und Wortlisten nach *Themes*.

Alphabetische Wortlisten *(Dictionaries)*

Camden Market hat zwei *Dictionaries:* Im *English-German dictionary* ab Seite 253 kannst du nach-schlagen, wenn du die Bedeutung von einem englischen Wort aus dem Buch wissen möchtest. Im *German-English dictionary* ab Seite 286 kannst du nachschlagen, wenn dir mal ein englisches Wort nicht einfällt.

Wortlisten nach *Themes*

In den Wortlisten nach *Themes* ab Seite 218 findest du alle neuen Wörter in der Reihenfolge, in der sie in den *Themes* vorkommen. Hier siehst du, wie du die Wortlisten benutzen kannst:

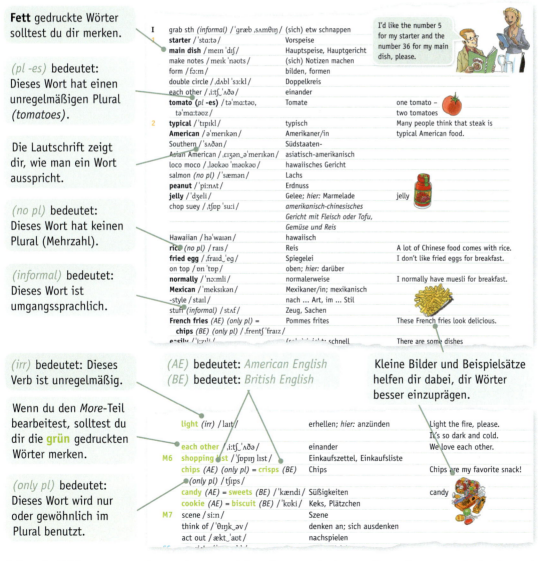

Fett gedruckte Wörter solltest du dir merken.

(pl -es) bedeutet: Dieses Wort hat einen unregelmäßigen Plural *(tomatoes)*.

Die Lautschrift zeigt dir, wie man ein Wort ausspricht.

(no pl) bedeutet: Dieses Wort hat keinen Plural (Mehrzahl).

(informal) bedeutet: Dieses Wort ist umgangssprachlich.

(irr) bedeutet: Dieses Verb ist unregelmäßig.

Wenn du den *More*-Teil bearbeitest, solltest du dir die **grün** gedruckten Wörter merken.

(only pl) bedeutet: Dieses Wort wird nur oder gewöhnlich im Plural benutzt.

(AE) bedeutet: *American English*
(BE) bedeutet: *British English*

Kleine Bilder und Beispielsätze helfen dir dabei, dir Wörter besser einzuprägen.

I	grab sth *(informal)* /ˈɡræb ˌsʌθɪŋ/	(sich) etw schnappen
1	**starter** /ˈstɑːtə/	Vorspeise
	main dish /meɪn ˈdɪʃ/	Hauptspeise, Hauptgericht
	make notes /meɪk ˈnəʊts/	(sich) Notizen machen
	form /fɔːm/	bilden, formen
	double circle /ˌdʌbl ˈsɜːkl/	Doppelkreis
	each other /ˌiːtʃ ˈʌðə/	einander
	tomato *(pl -es)* /təˈmɑːtəʊ, təˈmɑːtəʊz/	Tomate
2	**typical** /ˈtɪpɪkl/	typisch
	American /əˈmerɪkən/	Amerikaner/in
	Southern /ˈsʌðən/	Südstaaten-
	Asian American /ˌeɪʒən_əˈmerɪkən/	asiatisch-amerikanisch
	loco moco /ˌləʊkəʊ ˈməʊkəʊ/	hawaiisches Gericht
	salmon *(no pl)* /ˈsæmən/	Lachs
	peanut /ˈpiːnʌt/	Erdnuss
	jelly /ˈdʒeli/	Gelee; *hier:* Marmelade
	chop suey /ˌtʃɒp ˈsuːi/	amerikanisch-chinesisches Gericht mit Fleisch oder Tofu, Gemüse und Reis
	Hawaiian /həˈwaɪən/	hawaiisch
	rice *(no pl)* /raɪs/	Reis
	fried egg /ˌfraɪd ˈeɡ/	Spiegelei
	on top /ɒn ˈtɒp/	oben; *hier:* darüber
	normally /ˈnɔːmli/	normalerweise
	Mexican /ˈmeksɪkən/	Mexikaner/in; mexikanisch
	-style /staɪl/	nach ... Art, im ... Stil
	stuff *(informal)* /stʌf/	Zeug, Sachen
	French fries *(AE) (only pl)* = chips *(BE) (only pl)* /frentʃ ˈfraɪz/	Pommes frites
	easily /ˈiːzɪli/	schnell

one tomato – two tomatoes

Many people think that steak is typical American food.

jelly

A lot of Chinese food comes with rice.
I don't like fried eggs for breakfast.

I normally have muesli for breakfast.

These French fries look delicious.

There are some dishes

I'd like the number 5 for my starter and the number 36 for my main dish, please.

	light *(irr)* /laɪt/	erhellen; *hier:* anzünden
	each other /ˌiːtʃ ˈʌðə/	einander
M6	**shopping list** /ˈʃɒpɪŋ lɪst/	Einkaufszettel, Einkaufsliste
	chips *(AE) (only pl)* = crisps *(BE)* /tʃɪps/	Chips
	candy *(AE)* = sweets *(BE)* /ˈkændi/	Süßigkeiten
	cookie *(AE)* = biscuit *(BE)* /ˈkʊki/	Keks, Plätzchen
M7	scene /siːn/	Szene
	think of /ˈθɪŋk_əv/	denken an; sich ausdenken
	act out /ækt_ˈaʊt/	nachspielen

Light the fire, please. It's so dark and cold.
We love each other.

Chips are my favorite snack!

candy

Folgende Abkürzungen werden noch verwendet: *sb = somebody*   *etw = etwas*   *jmd = jemand*
sth = something   *jdm/jdn = jemandem/jemanden*

English sounds

Im Englischen spricht man Wörter oft anders aus, als man sie schreibt.
Deshalb ist die Lautschrift sehr nützlich: Sie gibt an, wie ein Wort ausgesprochen wird.
Hier ist eine Liste mit Lautschriftzeichen zusammen mit Beispielwörtern, in denen der
entsprechende Laut vorkommt.

Vokale

/ɑ:/	arm
/ʌ/	but
/e/	desk
/ə/	a, an
/ɜ:/	girl, bird
/æ/	apple
/ɪ/	in, it
/i/	every
/i:/	easy, eat
/ɒ/	orange
/ɔ:/	all, story
/ʊ/	look
/u/	February
/u:/	food

Doppellaute

/aɪ/	eye, buy
/aʊ/	our
/eə/	there
/eɪ/	take, they
/ɪə/	here
/ɔɪ/	boy
/əʊ/	go, old
/ʊə/	you're

Konsonanten

/b/	bag, club
/d/	duck, card
/f/	fish, laugh
/g/	get, dog
/h/	hot
/j/	you
/k/	can, duck
/l/	lot, small
/m/	more, mum
/n/	now, sun
/ŋ/	song, long
/p/	present, top
/r/	red, right
/s/	sister, class (scharfes **s**)
/t/	time, cat
/z/	nose, dogs (weiches **s**)
/ʒ/	television
/dʒ/	orange
/ʃ/	sure, English
/tʃ/	child, cheese
/ð/	these, mother (weicher Laut)
/θ/	mouth, think (harter Laut)
/v/	very, have
/w/	what, word

Betonungszeichen für die folgende Silbe

/'/	Hauptbetonung
/ˌ/	Nebenbetonung

The English alphabet

a	/eɪ/	**h**	/eɪtʃ/	**o**	/əʊ/	**v**	/vi:/
b	/bi:/	**i**	/aɪ/	**p**	/pi:/	**w**	/'dʌblju:/
c	/si:/	**j**	/dʒeɪ/	**q**	/kju:/	**x**	/eks/
d	/di:/	**k**	/keɪ/	**r**	/a:/	**y**	/waɪ/
e	/i:/	**l**	/el/	**s**	/es/	**z**	/zed/
f	/ef/	**m**	/em/	**t**	/ti:/		
g	/dʒi:/	**n**	/en/	**u**	/ju:/		

Ähnliche Wörter im Deutschen und Englischen

Es gibt viele Wörter, die im Englischen und im Deutschen gleich sind. Sie unterscheiden sich oft nur dadurch, dass die meisten von ihnen im Deutschen groß geschrieben werden. Viele dieser Wörter sprechen wir gleich aus.

Diese Wörter stehen nicht in den Wortlisten, weil sie dir ja nicht neu sind. Bei denen, die ein bisschen anders ausgesprochen werden als im Deutschen, ist die Lautschrift farbig hervorgehoben.

action / ˈækʃn /
adjective / ˈædʒɪktɪv /
adverb / ˈædvɜːb /
AIDS / eɪdz /
American football
  / əˌmerɪkən ˈfʊtˌbɔːl /
animation / ˌænɪˈmeɪʃn /
anorak / ˈænəˌræk /
app / æp /
asphalt / ˈæsfælt /
baby / ˈbeɪbi /
badminton
  / ˈbædmɪntən /
bagel / ˈbeɪgl /
ball / bɔːl /
band / bænd /
baseball / ˈbeɪsˌbɔːl /
basketball
  / ˈbɑːskɪtˌbɔːl /
blog / blɒg /
bodyguard / ˈbɒdiˌgɑːd /
box / bɒks /
burger / ˈbɜːgə /
café / ˈkæfeɪ /
cafeteria / ˌkæfəˈtɪəriə /
camping / ˈkæmpɪŋ /
cartoon / kɑːˈtuːn /
champion / ˈtʃæmpiən /
chat / tʃæt /
cheerleader / ˈtʃɪəˌliːdə /
chicken nugget
  / ˈtʃɪkɪn ˌnʌgɪt /
clip / klɪp /
collage / ˈkɒlɑːʒ /
computer
  / kəmˈpjuːtə /
container / kənˈteɪnə /
cool / kuːl /
cowboy / ˈkaʊˌbɔɪ /
design / dɪˈzaɪn /

disco / ˈdɪskəʊ /
DJ / ˈdiːˌdʒeɪ /
dollar / ˈdɒlə /
DVD / ˌdiː viː ˈdiː /
email / ˈiːmeɪl /
event / ɪˈvent /
fair / feə /
falafel / fəˈlɑːfl /
fan / fæn /
fast food / ˌfɑːst ˈfuːd /
feedback / ˈfiːdbæk /
film / fɪlm /
fit / fɪt /
form / fɔːm /
foul / faʊl /
gold / gəʊld /
golden / ˈgəʊldn /
gorilla / gəˈrɪlə /
graffiti / grəˈfiːti /
guacamole
  / ˌgwɑːkəˈməʊli /
hamburger
  / ˈhæmˌbɜːgə /
hey / heɪ /
high tech / haɪtek /
hip hop / ˈhɪp hɒp /
horror / ˈhɒrə /
hot dog / ˌhɒt ˈdɒg /
hotel / həʊˈtel /
hotline / ˈhɒtˌlaɪn /
hybrid / ˈhaɪbrɪd /
ideal / aɪˈdɪəl /
inline skate
  / ˈɪnlaɪn ˌskeɪt /
Internet / ˈɪntənet /
interview / ˈɪntəˌvjuː /
jeans / dʒiːnz /
jogger / ˈdʒɒgə /
karaoke / ˌkæriˈəʊki /
ketchup / ˈketʃəp /

kid / kɪd /
kilo / ˈkiːləʊ /
Latino/Latina
  / læˈtiːnəʊ, læˈtiːnə /
live / laɪv /
make-up / ˈmeɪkˌʌp /
mayonnaise
  / ˌmeɪəˈneɪz /
million / ˈmɪljən /
modern / ˈmɒdən /
monster / ˈmɒnstə /
motto / ˈmɒtəʊ /
muffin / ˈmʌfɪn /
museum / mjuːˈziːəm /
musical / ˈmjuːzɪkl /
national / ˈnæʃnəl /
newsletter / ˈnjuːzˌletə /
normal / ˈnɔːml /
OK / ˌəʊˈkeɪ /
online / ˈɒnlaɪn /
outfit / ˈaʊtfɪt /
panther / ˈpænθə /
partner / ˈpɑːtnə /
party / ˈpɑːti /
pass / pɑːs /
piñata / pinˈjɑːtə /
poker / ˈpəʊkə /
pop (music)
  / (ˈ)pɒp (ˌmjuːzɪk) /
poster / ˈpəʊstə /
quiz / kwɪz /
rap / ræp /
recycling / riːˈsaɪklɪŋ /
region / ˈriːdʒn /
sandwich / ˈsænwɪdʒ /
sauerkraut
  / ˈsaʊəˌkraʊt /
science fiction
  / ˌsaɪəns ˈfɪkʃn /
shopping / ˈʃɒpɪŋ /

show / ʃəʊ /
skateboard
  / ˈskeɪtˌbɔːd /
smiley / ˈsmaɪli /
snack / snæk /
sofa / ˈsəʊfə /
soft drink
  / ˌsɒft ˈdrɪŋk /
sound check
  / ˈsaʊnd tʃek /
sponsor / ˈspɒnsə /
standard / ˈstændəd /
star / stɑː /
steak / steɪk /
studio / ˈstjuːdiəʊ /
super / ˈsuːpə /
surfer / ˈsɜːfə /
taco / ˈtækəʊ /
taxi / ˈtæksi /
team / tiːm /
teenager / ˈtiːnˌeɪdʒə /
tennis / ˈtenɪs /
text / tekst /
ticket / ˈtɪkɪt /
toast / təʊst /
toaster / ˈtəʊstə /
touchdown
  / ˈtʌtʃˌdaʊn /
tourist / ˈtʊərɪst /
tradition / trəˈdɪʃn /
training / ˈtreɪnɪŋ /
UFO / ˈjuːefəʊ /
upcycling / ˈʌpˌsaɪklɪŋ /
verb / vɜːb /
video / ˈvɪdiəʊ /
web design
  / ˈweb dɪˌzaɪn /
website / ˈwebˌsaɪt /
western / ˈwestən /
wild / waɪld /

Die Vokabeln der *Intro*-Seiten 4-7 kannst du im *English-German dictionary* ab Seite 253 nachschlagen.

Theme 1 – Hi to high school!

I	**high school** / ˈhaɪ ˌskuːl /	weiterführende Schule in den USA (Klasse 9-12)	Cheryl goes to high school in Illinois.
	theme / θiːm /	Thema; Lektion, Kapitel	
1	**American** / əˈmerɪkən /	amerikanisch	Cheryl is an American girl.
	share / ʃeə /	teilen	
	surprising / səˈpraɪzɪŋ /	überraschend	It's surprising that the first Americans came from Asia.
	that / ðæt /	dass	
	describe / dɪˈskraɪb /	beschreiben	
	take turns / ˌteɪk ˈtɜːnz /	sich abwechseln	
	locker / ˈlɒkə /	Schließfach, Spind	Cheryl puts her bag in her locker.
	diploma / dɪˈpləʊmə /	Diplom; *hier:* Abschlusszeugnis	
	crown / kraʊn /	Krone	Kings and queens wear crowns.
2	match (with) / mætʃ /	zuordnen	
	track / træk /	Weg, Pfad; *hier:* Nummer	
	go with / ˈgəʊ wɪð /	gehören zu, passen zu	Which shoes go best with this dress?
3	read along / ˌriːd_əˈlɒŋ /	mitlesen	
	nervous / ˈnɜːvəs /	nervös; aufgeregt	Are you nervous before a test?
	(class) schedule *(AE)* = timetable *(BE)* / ˈʃedjuːl /	Stundenplan	
	well / wel /	nun (ja), tja	
	period *(AE)* = lesson *(BE)* / ˈpɪəriəd /	Stunde	
	math *(AE)* = maths *(BE)* / mæθ /	Mathe	
	elective *(AE)* / ɪˈlektɪv /	Wahlfach, Wahlkurs	
	semester *(AE)* / səˈmestə /	Semester; *hier:* (Schul)halbjahr	
	look forward to sth / ˌlʊk ˈfɔːwəd_tə ˌsʌmθɪŋ /	sich auf etw freuen	I'm looking forward to my birthday.
	yeah *(informal)* / jeə /	ja	
	be allowed to do sth / bi_əˌlaʊd tə ˈduː ˌsʌmθɪŋ /	etwas tun dürfen	Are you allowed to go out at the weekend?
	take out / ˌteɪk_ˈaʊt /	hinausbringen; *hier:* herausnehmen	take out ↔ put in
	class *(AE)* = lesson *(BE)* / klɑːs /	(Unterrichts)stunde	
	bathroom *(AE)*; *here:* toilet *(BE)* / ˈbɑːθˌruːm /	Bad(ezimmer); *hier:* Toilette	
	'cause (= because) *(informal)* / kʌz /	weil, da	
	pass / pɑːs /	Pass; *hier:* Erlaubnisschein	
	poor you / pɔː ˈjuː /	du Arme(r)	
	homeroom *(AE)* / ˈhəʊmˌruːm /	Klassenzimmer, in dem sich die Schüler am Anfang des Schultages versammeln	
	call out / ˌkɔːl_ˈaʊt /	aufrufen	
	stand up / ˌstænd_ˈʌp /	aufstehen	stand up ↔ sit down
	confused / kənˈfjuːzd /	verwirrt, durcheinander	I just don't understand this. I'm so confused.
	Pledge of Allegiance / ˌpledʒ_əv_əˈliːdʒ(ə)ns /	Treueschwur *(gegenüber dem Staat und der Fahne der USA)*	
	ours / ˈaʊəz /	unsere(r, s)	It's our car. → It's ours.
	mine / maɪn /	meine(r, s); *hier:* mir	Leo is a friend of mine.

Well, Gillian, would you like some pancakes?

Oh, poor you!

guys *(only pl) (informal)* / gaɪz /	Leute	
vacation *(AE)* = holiday *(BE)* / vəˈkeɪʃn /	Ferien, Urlaub	
Nice to meet you. / ˌnaɪs tə ˈmiːt jə /	Es freut mich, Sie/dich kennen zu lernen.	Hello, nice to meet you.
accent / ˈæksnt /	Akzent	
man *(informal)* / mæn /	Mensch, Mann	
yours / jɔːz /	deine(r, s); eure(r, s); Ihre(r, s)	It's your skateboard. → It's yours.
the States *(informal)* / ðə ˈsteɪts /	die Staaten	
Come on! / ˌkʌmˈɒn /	Auf geht's!, Na los!	
practice / ˈpræktɪs /	Übung; Training	
speaking of … / ˈspiːkɪŋ‿əv /	da/wo wir gerade von … sprechen	Come on, you can do it!
homecoming *(AE)* / ˈhəʊmˌkʌmɪŋ /	*amerikanisches Schulfest mit Ehemaligentreffen*	
dance / dɑːns /	Tanz; *hier:* Ball	
whole / həʊl /	ganz, gesamt	I can't eat the whole cake.
exactly / ɪɡˈzæktli /	genau	
keyword / ˈkiːˌwɜːd /	Schlüsselwort	Remember, no talking during the test!
part / pɑːt /	Teil	
fact / fækt /	Fakt	
during / ˈdjʊərɪŋ /	während	
home economics *(only pl)* / ˌhəʊm‿iːkəˈnɒmɪks /	Hauswirtschaft(slehre)	
find out / faɪndˈaʊt /	herausfinden	
prepare / prɪˈpeə /	(sich) vorbereiten; zubereiten	How do you prepare for a test?
office / ˈɒfɪs /	Büro	He is working in his office.
skill / skɪl /	Geschick; *hier:* Fähigkeit, Fertigkeit	
run *(irr)* / rʌn /	laufen, rennen; *hier:* betreiben, führen	
efficient / ɪˈfɪʃnt /	effizient	
development / dɪˈveləpmənt /	Entwicklung	
driver's education *(no pl)* / ˈdraɪvəz‿edjʊˌkeɪʃn /	Fahrunterricht	
driver's license *(AE)* = driving licence *(BE)* / ˈdraɪvəz ˌlaɪsns, ˈdraɪvɪŋ ˌlaɪsns /	Führerschein	
wood/metal working class / ˈwʊd, ˈmetl ˌwɜːkɪŋ klɑːs /	Werkunterricht, Werken	
wood / wʊd /	Holz	The cupboard is made of wood.
metal / ˈmetl /	Metall	
tool / tuːl /	Werkzeug	tools
product / ˈprɒdʌkt /	Produkt, Erzeugnis	
language / ˈlæŋgwɪdʒ /	Sprache	I can speak two languages: English and German.
drama / ˈdrɑːmə /	Schauspielerei; *hier:* Theater	
improve / ɪmˈpruːv /	verbessern	
acting *(no pl)* / ˈæktɪŋ /	Schauspielerei, Schauspiel-	
program / ˈprəʊɡræm /	programmieren	He programs something different every day.
secretary / ˈsekrətri /	Sekretär/in	

LL	elementary school (AE) = primary school (BE) / elɪˈmentri ˌskuːl, ˈpraɪməri ˌskuːl /	Grundschule
	junior high school / ˌdʒuːniə ˈhaɪ ˌskuːl /	*Mittelstufenschule in den USA*
	high school diploma / ˈhaɪ ˌskuːl dɪˌpləʊmə /	*Abschlusszeugnis der Highschool*
	graduation (no pl) / ˌgrædʒuˈeɪʃn /	Schulabschluss; Abschlussfeier
	fail / feɪl /	ungenügend *(Schulnote)*
6	guidance counsellor / ˈgaɪdns ˌkaʊnslə /	*Beratungslehrer, Vertrauenslehrer*
	advice (no pl) / ədˈvaɪs /	Rat(schlag)
	take notes / teɪk ˈnəʊts /	(sich) Notizen machen
	situation / ˌsɪtʃuˈeɪʃn /	Situation, Lage
7	talk / tɔːk /	Gespräch; Unterhaltung; *hier:* Vortrag
	two-minute / tuːˈmɪnɪt /	zweiminütig
	topic / ˈtɒpɪk /	Thema
	present / prɪˈzent /	präsentieren
8	act / ækt /	handeln, sich verhalten
	green / griːn /	grün; *hier:* umweltfreundlich, ökologisch
	buzz group / ˈbʌz gruːp /	Form der Gruppenarbeit
	staff (no pl) / stɑːf /	Mitarbeiter, Personal
	local / ˈləʊkl /	örtlich; *hier:* regional, aus der Umgebung
	food / fuːd /	Nahrungsmittel
	recycle / riːˈsaɪkl /	wiederverwerten, recyceln
	separate / ˈsepəreɪt /	trennen
	plant / plɑːnt /	pflanzen
	save / seɪv /	retten; *hier:* sparen
	protect / prəˈtekt /	(be)schützen
	environment / ɪnˈvaɪrənmənt /	Umgebung; *hier:* Umwelt
9	**print (out)** / prɪnt /	(aus)drucken
	take a shower / teɪk ə ˈʃaʊə /	duschen
	shower / ˈʃaʊə /	Dusche
	recycled / riːˈsaɪkld /	wiederverwertet, recycelt
10	**project** / ˈprɒdʒekt /	Projekt
	meaning / ˈmiːnɪŋ /	Bedeutung
	look up / lʊkˈʌp /	nachschlagen
	dictionary / ˈdɪkʃənri /	Wörterbuch
	go green / ˌgəʊ ˈgriːn /	umweltbewusst werden
	major / ˈmeɪdʒə /	bedeutend, wichtig, groß
	environmental / ɪnˌvaɪrənˈmentl /	ökologisch, die Umwelt betreffend
	interview / ˈɪntəˌvjuː /	befragen; *hier:* interviewen
	so far / ˌsəʊ ˈfɑː /	bisher, bis jetzt
	make a difference / ˌmeɪk ə ˈdɪfrəns /	einen Unterschied machen; *hier:* etw verändern, etw bewirken
	change / tʃeɪndʒ /	(sich) (ver)ändern

recycle ⟷ throw away
You have to separate your rubbish.

He is saving money to buy a new bike.

He takes a shower every morning.

If you don't know a word, you can look it up in a dictionary.

You can change your school, too.

TIPP

Probier's mal mit Gemütlichkeit
Nicht nur für das Vokabellernen gilt: Du solltest dich an dem Ort, an dem du arbeitest, wohlfühlen und durch nichts abgelenkt sein! Eine gewisse Ordnung erleichtert das Arbeiten. Mache regelmäßig Pausen, in denen du z. B. das Fenster öffnest, etwas trinkst und dich bewegst. So kannst du dich besser konzentrieren.

for the better / fə ðə ˈbetə /	zum Besseren, zum Guten	
mine / maɪn /	meine(r, s)	It's my mobile. → It's mine.
living / ˈlɪvɪŋ /	lebend	
filter / ˈfɪltə /	filtern	
air (no pl) / eə /	Luft	Balloons are full of air.
install / ɪnˈstɔːl /	installieren	
rain collector / ˈreɪn kəˌlektə /	Regensammelbehälter	
plus (informal) / plʌs /	außerdem	
greenhouse / ˈgriːnˌhaʊs /	Gewächshaus, Treibhaus	
grow (irr) / grəʊ /	wachsen; hier: anbauen	This is what you need to grow plants.
solar panel / ˌsəʊlə ˈpænəl /	Sonnenkollektor	
power / ˈpaʊə /	antreiben; hier: versorgen	
all- / ɔːl /	ausschließlich, ganz	
electric / ɪˈlektrɪk /	elektrisch	
Ms / məz /	Frau (Anrede für verheiratete und unverheiratete Frauen)	Ms Hancock is my favourite teacher.
biology (no pl) / baɪˈɒlədʒi /	Biologie	Do you like biology?
funding (no pl) / ˈfʌndɪŋ /	Finanzierung	
grant / grɑːnt /	Zuschuss, Fördermittel	
favorite (AE) = favourite (BE) / ˈfeɪvrət /	Lieblings-	
develop / dɪˈveləp /	(sich) entwickeln	Amy has an interesting hobby: She develops games and apps.
everyday / ˈevrideɪ /	alltäglich, Alltags-	
compare / kəmˈpeə /	vergleichen	
give reasons / gɪv ˈriːznz /	begründen, Gründe angeben	
clean up / kliːn ˈʌp /	sauber machen, reinigen	
dialogue / ˈdaɪəlɒg /	Gespräch, Dialog	
expression / ɪkˈspreʃn /	Ausdruck	
freak / friːk /	Fanatiker/in	
trash (AE) = rubbish (BE) / træʃ /	Müll, Abfall	
shall / ʃæl /	sollen	Shall I help you with your homework?
empty / ˈempti /	leer	empty ↔ full
definitely / ˈdefnətli /	eindeutig, definitiv	
pretty (informal) / ˈprɪti /	ziemlich	
have a crush on sb / ˌhævə ˈkrʌʃ ɒn ˌsʌmbədi /	in jdn verknallt sein	
bet (irr) / bet /	wetten	
hers / hɜːz /	ihre(r, s)	It's her jacket. → It's hers.
take action / teɪk ˈækʃn /	handeln, etw unternehmen	
pictogram / ˈpɪktəgræm /	Piktogramm	
suggest / səˈdʒest /	vorschlagen	
design / dɪˈzaɪn /	entwerfen	
how to / haʊ tə /	wie man	
add / æd /	hinzufügen	
illustrate / ˈɪləˌstreɪt /	illustrieren, bebildern	
questionnaire / ˌkwestʃəˈneə /	Fragebogen	
possible / ˈpɒsəbəl /	möglich	
point / pɔɪnt /	Punkt	
English-speaking / ˈɪŋglɪʃˌspiːkɪŋ /	englischsprachig	

The numbers in the left margin: 11, 12, 13, 14

WORDS THEME 1

P1	missing /ˈmɪsɪŋ/	fehlend
	vowel /ˈvaʊəl/	Vokal
P2	recording /rɪˈkɔːdɪŋ/	Aufnahme
	yourself (pl yourselves)	dich, dir; selbst/ihr,
	/jəˈself, jəˈselvz/	euch; selbst
P4	carry /ˈkæri/	tragen
	ID card (= identity card)	(Personal)ausweis
	/ˌaɪˈdiː kɑːd, aɪˈdentɪti kɑːd/	
	at all times /ətˌɔːl ˈtaɪmz/	immer, jederzeit
	cellphone (AE) = mobile phone (BE)	Mobiltelefon, Handy
	/ˈselˌfəʊn/	
P5	interest /ˈɪntrəst/	Interesse
	fill in /fɪlˈɪn/	ausfüllen; hier: einsetzen
	dribble /ˈdrɪbl/	dribbeln
P6	marching band /ˈmɑːtʃɪŋ ˌbænd/	Spielmannszug, Blaskapelle
	state /steɪt/	staatlich; hier: auf
		bundesstaatlicher Ebene
	color team (AE) /ˈkʌləˌtiːm/	Fahnenschwinger im
		Spielmannszug
	spirit (no pl) /ˈspɪrɪt/	(Team)geist
	even /ˈiːvn/	selbst; sogar
	sword /sɔːd/	Schwert
	practice (AE) = practise (BE)	üben, trainieren
	/ˈpræktɪs/	
P7	phrase /freɪz/	Satz; Ausdruck, (Rede)wendung
	write down /raɪt ˈdaʊn/	aufschreiben
P9	useful /ˈjuːsfl/	nützlich, hilfreich
	heating (no pl) /ˈhiːtɪŋ/	Heizung
P10	whose is/are ... /ˈhuːzˌɪz/ɑː/	wem gehört/gehören ...
	complete /kəmˈpliːt/	vervollständigen
	possessive pronoun	Possessivpronomen
	/pəˌzesɪv ˈprəʊnaʊn/	
	theirs /ðeəz/	ihre(r,s)
	mom (AE) = mum (BE) (informal)	Mama, Mutti
	/mɒm/	
	felt tip /ˈfeltˌtɪp/	Filzstift
P11	advert (= advertisement)	Anzeige, Inserat; hier: Werbung
	/ˈædvɜːt, ədˈvɜːtɪsmənt/	
	just /dʒʌst/	gleich; hier: gerade
	latest /ˈleɪtɪst/	jüngste(r, s); hier: neueste(r, s)
	upgrade /ʌpˈgreɪd/	Aufrüsten; hier: neueste Version
	bin /bɪn/	wegwerfen
	instead (of) /ɪnˈsted (ˌəv)/	stattdessen; (an)statt
	shiny /ˈʃaɪni/	glänzend
	charity /ˈtʃærəti/	Wohltätigkeitsorganisation
	company /ˈkʌmpni/	Firma
	remove /rɪˈmuːv/	entfernen
	SIM card /ˈsɪm ˌkɑːd/	SIM-Karte
	data /ˈdeɪtə/	Daten, (persönliche) Angaben
M1	mention /ˈmenʃn/	erwähnen

TIPP

British English und American English
In diesem Buch lernst du Unterschiede zwischen *British English (BE)* und *American English (AE)* kennen. Es gibt Unterschiede in der Schreibweise und Aussprache. Manchmal gibt es ganz unterschiedliche Wörter für dieselbe Sache.
Hier sind ein paar Beispiele:

Schreibweise:

(BE) 🇬🇧	(AE) 🇺🇸
colour	color
practise	practice
favourite	favorite
theatre	theater
programme	program
...	...

Wortschatz:

(BE) 🇬🇧	(AE) 🇺🇸
holiday	vacation
timetable	schedule
trainer	sneaker
film	movie
...	...

Aussprache:

(BE) 🇬🇧	(AE) 🇺🇸
dance /dɑːns/	dance /dæns/
can't /kɑːnt/	can't /kænt/
water /ˈwɔːtə/	water /ˈwɔːtər/
...	...

TIPP
Lege dir selbst eine Wortliste zu *American* und *British English* an. Ergänze sie um Wörter, die dir im Laufe des Buches begegnen.

222 two hundred and twenty-two

article /ˈɑːtɪkl/	Artikel	
fall *(AE)* = autumn *(BE)* /fɔːl/	Herbst	
graduate /ˈɡrædʒuət/	Schulabgänger/in; Absolvent/in	A graduate is someone who has finished high school.
tug-of-war /ˌtʌɡ‿əv ˈwɔː/	Tauziehen	
pie-eating contest /ˌpaɪ‿iːtɪŋ ˈkɒntest/	Kuchenwettessen	
pie /paɪ/	Pastete; *hier:* Kuchen	
possible /ˈpɒsəbəl/	möglich	
include /ɪnˈkluːd/	beinhalten, einschließen	
pajamas *(AE)* = pyjamas *(BE)* /pəˈdʒɑːməz/	Schlafanzug, Pyjama	
class /klɑːs/	(Schul)klasse; *hier:* Jahrgang	
color *(AE)* = colour *(BE)* /ˈkʌlə/	Farbe	
form /fɔːm/	bilden, formen	We formed a girls' football team.
court /kɔːt/	Gericht; *hier:* Hofstaat, Gefolge	
vote (for sb) /vəʊt/	(jdn) wählen, (für jdn) abstimmen	I'll vote for Kenan.

I made you a birthday pie!

M2
order /ˈɔːdə/	Ordnung, Reihenfolge	
go wrong /ɡəʊ ˈrɒŋ/	schief gehen	Our plan has gone wrong.
football /ˈfʊtbɔːl/	Fußball; *hier:* (American) Football	
senior *(AE)* /ˈsiːniə/	*Schüler/in einer Highschool- oder Collegeabgangsklasse*	
equipment *(no pl)* /ɪˈkwɪpmənt/	Ausrüstung, Ausstattung	Here is some sports equipment.

M4
grid /ɡrɪd/	Gitter; *hier:* Tabelle	
advantage /ədˈvɑːntɪdʒ/	Vorteil	
disadvantage /ˌdɪsədˈvɑːntɪdʒ/	Nachteil	

M5
major /ˈmeɪdʒə/	bedeutend, wichtig, groß	major = important
environmental /ɪnˌvaɪrənˈmentl/	ökologisch, die Umwelt betreffend	My dad is a member of an environmental group.
report /rɪˈpɔːt/	berichten	
electric /ɪˈlektrɪk/	elektrisch	
the public /ðə ˈpʌblɪk/	die Öffentlichkeit, die Allgemeinheit	
campus /ˈkæmpəs/	Universität; *hier:* Schulgelände, Campus	
greenhouse /ˈɡriːnˌhaʊs/	Gewächshaus, Treibhaus	
living /ˈlɪvɪŋ/	lebend	
vertical /ˈvɜːtɪkl/	senkrecht, vertikal	vertical ↔ horizontal
row /rəʊ/	Reihe	We were in the front row at the concert.
fund /fʌnd/	finanzieren	
zero-emission /ˌzɪərəʊ‿ɪˈmɪʃn/	abgasfrei, Nullemissions-	
run on sth /ˈrʌn‿ɒn ˌsʌmθɪŋ/	mit etw betrieben werden	
organize *(AE)* = **organise** *(BE)* /ˈɔːɡənaɪz/	organisieren	
the earth /ðiː‿ˈɜːθ/	die Erde	the earth
activist /ˈæktɪvɪst/	Aktivist/in	
environment /ɪnˈvaɪrənmənt/	Umgebung; *hier:* Umwelt	Recycle rubbish to protect the environment.
on one's own doorstep /ɒn wʌnz‿ˌəʊn ˈdɔːˌstep/	vor der eigenen Haustür	

be thrilled / bi: ˈθrɪld /	außer sich vor Freude sein, sich wahnsinnig darüber freuen	
gardening *(no pl)* / ˈgɑːdnɪŋ /	Gartenarbeit, Gärtnern	
textbook / ˈtekstˌbʊk /	Lehrbuch, Schulbuch	Don't forget your textbook!
the real deal *(informal)* / ðə ˌrɪəl ˈdiːl /	das einzig Wahre	
may not / meɪ ˈnɒt /	nicht dürfen; *hier:* vielleicht nicht	
demonstrate / ˈdemənˌstreɪt /	zeigen, vorführen	I'll demonstrate how this machine works.
bloom / bluːm /	blühen	
computer science *(no pl)* / kəmˈpjuːtə ˌsaɪəns /	Informatik	This is the computer science classroom.
keep an eye on sth/sb *(informal)* / ˌkiːp ən ˈaɪ ɒn ˌsʌmθɪŋ / ˌsʌmbədi /	ein (wachsames) Auge auf etw/jdn haben, etw/jdn im Auge behalten	
usage *(no pl)* / ˈjuːsɪdʒ /	Verbrauch	Everyone can reduce their electricity usage.
advice *(no pl)* / ədˈvaɪs /	Rat(schlag)	Gillian phoned a friend to ask for advice.
environmentally friendly / ɪnˌvaɪrənˌmentli ˈfrendli /	umweltfreundlich	

M7	correct / kəˈrekt /	korrigieren	
	inside / ɪnˈsaɪd /	drinnen; innen; *hier:* im Inneren	inside ⟷ outside
	act as sth / ˈækt ˌæz ˌsʌmθɪŋ /	als etw dienen	
	natural / ˈnætʃrəl /	natürlich	It's natural for cats to hunt mice.
	toxin / ˈtɒksɪn /	Gift	
	peaceful / ˈpiːsfl /	friedlich; *hier:* ruhig	They have a peaceful life.
	reduce / rɪˈdjuːs /	verringern, reduzieren, verkleinern	
	noise level / ˈnɔɪz levl /	Geräuschpegel, Lärmpegel	
	especially / ɪˈspeʃli /	besonders	I love vegetables, especially carrots.
	cost / kɒst /	Kosten, Preis	
	insulation / ˌɪnsjʊˈleɪʃn /	Isolierung, Dämmung	
M8	find out about / faɪnd ˈaʊt əˌbaʊt /	sich informieren über	
M9	message / ˈmesɪdʒ /	Nachricht; *hier:* Botschaft, Message	
	push / pʊʃ /	drücken; *hier:* schieben	Karla doesn't need anyone to push her wheelchair.

	cartoonist / kɑːˈtuːnɪst /	Karikaturist/in	
CC	the ... way / ðə ˈweɪ /	auf die ... Art	
	get *(irr)* / get /	erhalten, bekommen; *hier:* verstehen	
	course / kɔːs /	Kurs	
	waste material / ˈweɪst məˌtɪəriəl /	Abfall	
	create / kriˈeɪt /	erschaffen; gestalten	
	storage *(no pl)* / ˈstɔːrɪdʒ /	Lagerung; *hier:* Aufbewahrung	
	memo / ˈmeməʊ /	Notiz; Merkzettel	
	simply / ˈsɪmpli /	einfach	
	nail / neɪl /	nageln	

Theme 2 – Let's grab some food

I'd like the number 5 for my starter and the number 36 for my main dish, please.

I	grab sth *(informal)* /ˈɡræb ˌsʌmθɪŋ/	(sich) etw schnappen	
1	**starter** /ˈstɑːtə/	Vorspeise	
	main dish /meɪn ˈdɪʃ/	Hauptspeise, Hauptgericht	
	make notes /meɪk ˈnəʊts/	(sich) Notizen machen	
	form /fɔːm/	bilden, formen	
	double circle /ˌdʌbl ˈsɜːkl/	Doppelkreis	
	each other /ˌiːtʃ ˈʌðə/	einander	
	tomato *(pl -es)* /təˈmɑːtəʊ, təˈmɑːtəʊz/	Tomate	one tomato – two tomatoes
2	**typical** /ˈtɪpɪkl/	typisch	Many people think that steak is typical American food.
	American /əˈmerɪkən/	Amerikaner/in	
	Southern /ˈsʌðən/	Südstaaten-	
	Asian American /ˌeɪʒən əˈmerɪkən/	asiatisch-amerikanisch	
	loco moco /ˌləʊkəʊ ˈməʊkəʊ/	hawaiisches Gericht	
	salmon *(no pl)* /ˈsæmən/	Lachs	
	peanut /ˈpiːnʌt/	Erdnuss	
	jelly /ˈdʒeli/	Gelee; *hier:* Marmelade	jelly
	chop suey /ˌtʃɒp ˈsuːi/	*amerikanisch-chinesisches Gericht mit Fleisch oder Tofu, Gemüse und Reis*	
	Hawaiian /həˈwaɪən/	hawaiisch	
	rice *(no pl)* /raɪs/	Reis	A lot of Chinese food comes with rice.
	fried egg /ˌfraɪd ˈeg/	Spiegelei	I don't like fried eggs for breakfast.
	on top /ɒn ˈtɒp/	oben; *hier:* darüber	
	normally /ˈnɔːmli/	normalerweise	I normally have muesli for breakfast.
	Mexican /ˈmeksɪkən/	Mexikaner/in; mexikanisch	
	-style /staɪl/	nach ... Art, im ... Stil	
	stuff *(informal)* /stʌf/	Zeug, Sachen	
	French fries *(AE) (only pl)* = chips *(BE) (only pl)* /ˌfrentʃ ˈfraɪz/	Pommes frites	These French fries look delicious.
	easily /ˈiːzɪli/	(sehr) leicht; schnell	There are some dishes I can make easily.
	this way /ˈðɪs weɪ/	so, auf diese Art und Weise	
	apple pie /ˈæpl ˌpaɪ/	gedeckter Apfelkuchen	an apple pie
	Jewish /ˈdʒuːɪʃ/	jüdisch	
	barbecue /ˈbɑːbɪˌkjuː/	grillen	
	fried chicken /ˌfraɪd ˈtʃɪkɪn/	Brathähnchen	
	mashed potatoes /ˌmæʃt pəˈteɪtəʊz/	Kartoffelbrei	Tom likes mashed potatoes more than normal potatoes.
	watermelon /ˈwɔːtəˌmelən/	Wassermelone	
3	**before** /bɪˈfɔː/	zuvor, vorher	before ↔ after
4	yucky *(informal)* /ˈjʌki/	eklig, widerlich	
	sort /sɔːt/	sortieren	
	grid /ɡrɪd/	Gitter; *hier:* Tabelle	
5	statement /ˈsteɪtmənt/	Aussage; Äußerung	
	need to /ˈniːd tə/	müssen	
LL	corn *(no pl)* /kɔːn/	Getreide, Korn; *hier:* Mais	
	macaroni and cheese /ˌmækəˌrəʊni ən ˈtʃiːz/	Käse-Makkaroni	
	meat loaf /ˌmiːt ˈləʊf/	Hackbraten	

Why did the man in the restaurant order alphabet soup?
/bɪkɒz hi wɒntɪd tə ˈriːd sʌmθɪŋ waɪl hi wəz ˌiːtɪŋ/

	pancake /ˈpæŋkeɪk/	Pfannkuchen	
	maple syrup /ˌmeɪpəl ˈsɪrəp/	Ahornsirup	
	roast turkey /ˌrəʊst ˈtɜːki/	Truthahnbraten	
6	report /rɪˈpɔːt/	Bericht	
	manager /ˈmænɪdʒə/	Geschäftsführer/in	
	which one /ˈwɪtʃ wʌn/	welche(r, s)	
	popular /ˈpɒpjʊlə/	beliebt	Football is a very popular sport.
	allow /əˈlaʊ/	erlauben	
	at night /æt ˈnaɪt/	nachts	Ghosts only come out at night.
	all the time /ˌɔːl ðə ˈtaɪm/	dauernd, ständig	
	busy /ˈbɪzi/	beschäftigt; *hier:* arbeitsreich, stark besucht	The café is always busy when it's sunny.
	thousand /ˈθaʊznd/	Tausend	
	awesome *(informal)* /ˈɔːsm/	super, spitze	
7	thought /θɔːt/	Gedanke	
	take one's time /teɪk wʌnz ˈtaɪm/	sich Zeit lassen	
8	note /nəʊt/	Notiz	
	get sth wrong /get ˌsʌmθɪŋ ˈrɒŋ/	etw falsch verstehen	
	copy /ˈkɒpi/	abschreiben	
	correct /kəˈrekt/	korrigieren	
9	review /rɪˈvjuː/	Kritik, Rezension	
	example /ɪgˈzɑːmpl/	Beispiel	
	takeaway (food) /ˈteɪkəˌweɪ/	Essen zum Mitnehmen	
	delivery /dɪˈlɪvri/	Lieferung	
	Arabic /ˈærəbɪk/	Arabisch; arabisch	
	service /ˈsɜːvɪs/	Service; Bedienung	This restaurant has excellent service.
	average /ˈævrɪdʒ/	durchschnittlich	
	must *(no pl)* /mʌst/	Muss	
	be worth sth /biː ˈwɜːθ ˌsʌmθɪŋ/	etw wert sein	
	visit /ˈvɪzɪt/	Besuch	
10	**poem** /ˈpəʊɪm/	Gedicht	William Shakespeare wrote many poems.
	topping /ˈtɒpɪŋ/	Belag; Garnierung	
	baked beans *(only pl)* /ˌbeɪkt ˈbiːnz/	Bohnen in Tomatensauce	
	fish finger /ˌfɪʃ ˈfɪŋgə/	Fischstäbchen	
	Sunday roast /ˈsʌndeɪ rəʊst/	Sonntagsbraten	
	shake /ʃeɪk/	Schütteln	
	steak and kidney pie /ˌsteɪk‿ən ˌkɪdni ˈpaɪ/	Rindfleisch-Nieren-Pastete	
	spinach *(no pl)* /ˈspɪnɪdʒ/	Spinat	
	cauliflower /ˈkɒliˌflaʊə/	Blumenkohl	
	wishbone /ˈwɪʃˌbəʊn/	Gabelbein *(zusammengewachsene Schlüsselbeinknochen der Vögel)*	
	wish /wɪʃ/	Wunsch	Make a wish and then blow out the birthday candles.
	trifle /ˈtraɪfl/	Trifle *(englisches Schicht-Dessert)*	
	mint *(no pl)* /mɪnt/	Minze	
	course /kɔːs/	Kurs; *hier:* Gang	
	biscuit /ˈbɪskɪt/	Keks	
	mention /ˈmenʃn/	erwähnen	
	message /ˈmesɪdʒ/	Nachricht; *hier:* Botschaft, Message	

Yes, I'll give her your message.

clap one's hands /ˌklæp wʌnz ˈhændz/	in die Hände klatschen	
rhythm /ˈrɪðəm/	Rhythmus, Takt	
aloud /əˈlaʊd/	laut	
speaker /ˈspiːkə/	Redner/in	
line /laɪn/	Linie; *hier:* Zeile	
verse /vɜːs/	Strophe	
rap /ræp/	rappen	
11 imagine /ɪˈmædʒɪn/	sich vorstellen	
open /ˈəʊpən/	(sich) öffnen; *hier:* eröffnen	
advert (= advertisement) /ˈædvɜːt, ədˈvɜːtɪsmənt/	Anzeige, Inserat	

12 **festival** /ˈfestɪvl/	Fest; Festival	What is your favourite festival?
Thanksgiving /ˈθæŋksˌgɪvɪŋ/	Thanksgiving *(amerikanisches Erntedankfest)*	
Eid /iːd/	*islamisches Fest zum Abschluss des Fastenmonats Ramadan*	In den USA wird *Thanksgiving* am vierten Donnerstag im November gefeiert, in Kanada am zweiten Montag im Oktober.
Diwali /dɪˈwɑːli/	*hinduistisches Lichterfest*	
Independence Day /ɪndɪˈpendəns ˌdeɪ/	*amerikanischer Unabhängigkeitstag*	
Cinco de Mayo /ˌsɪŋkəʊ də ˈmeɪə/	*mexikanischer Feiertag*	
Hindu /ˌhɪnˈduː/	Hindu; hinduistisch	
victory /ˈvɪktri/	Sieg	We won! Victory is ours!
darkness *(no pl)* /ˈdɑːknəs/	Dunkelheit, Finsternis	You could only see their eyes in the darkness.
Muslim /ˈmʊzləm/	Muslim/in; muslimisch	
give thanks /gɪv ˈθæŋks/	danken, sich bedanken	On Thanksgiving people give thanks for what they have.
culture /ˈkʌltʃə/	Kultur	
pumpkin /ˈpʌmpkɪn/	Kürbis	Do you decorate pumpkins for Halloween?
think about (sb/sth) /ˈθɪŋk əˌbaʊt/	an (jdn/etw) denken; sich (etw) überlegen	
whom /huːm/	wen; wem	
mill around /mɪl əˈraʊnd/	umherlaufen	
13 what else /wɒt ˈels/	was noch, was sonst	
14 entry /ˈentri/	Eintrag	
like this /laɪk ˈðɪs/	so; solche(r, s)	
dumpling /ˈdʌmplɪŋ/	Knödel, Kloß; Teigtasche	The soup has dumplings in it.
post sth /ˈpəʊst ˌsʌmθɪŋ/	etw schicken; *hier:* etw ins Internet stellen, etw posten	
lunar calendar /ˌluːnə ˈkælɪndə/	Mondkalender	
get together /ˌget təˈgeðə/	sich treffen	After school they get together by the river.
Jiaozi dumpling /dʒɪəˈɒzi ˌdʌmplɪŋ/	*chinesisches Teigtaschengericht*	
midnight *(no pl)* /ˈmɪdˌnaɪt/	Mitternacht	midnight = twelve o'clock at night
coin /kɔɪn/	Münze, Geldstück	Gillian collects 50p coins.
traditional /trəˈdɪʃnəl/	traditionell	Lots of families have a traditional
turkey /ˈtɜːki/	Truthahn/-henne, Pute/r	Thanksgiving dinner with turkey.

cranberry /ˈkrænbəri/	Cranberry, Moosbeere	
corn on the cob /ˌkɔːn‿ɒn ðə ˈkɒb/	Maiskolben	
Black Friday *(AE)* /ˌblæk ˈfraɪdeɪ/	*Freitag nach Thanksgiving, an dem viel eingekauft wird*	
mall /mɔːl/	Einkaufszentrum	mall = shopping centre
15 animated /ˈænɪˌmeɪtɪd/	animiert	
slide show /ˈslaɪd ʃəʊ/	Diashow	
order /ˈɔːdə/	Ordnung, Reihenfolge	
the Pilgrims /ðə ˈpɪlgrɪms/	die Pilger(väter)	
Native American /ˌneɪtɪv‿əˈmerɪkən/	*amerikanischer Ureinwohner/ amerikanische Ureinwohnerin; indianisch*	The Native Americans were the first people living in America.
harvest /ˈhɑːvɪst/	Ernte	They will help the farmer with the harvest.
cold /kəʊld/	Kälte	
disease /dɪˈziːz/	Krankheit	
hunt /hʌnt/	jagen	Cats usually hunt mice.
over time /ˌəʊvə ˈtaɪm/	im Lauf der Zeit, mit der Zeit	
explorer /ɪkˈsplɔːrə/	Forscher/in, Entdecker/in	
all over /ˈɔːl‿ˌəʊvə/	überall in	
Europe /ˈjʊərəp/	Europa	People from Europe settled in different parts of North America.
settle /ˈsetl/	sich niederlassen	
North America /ˌnɔːθ‿əˈmerɪkə/	Nordamerika	
settler /ˈsetlə/	Siedler/in	The settlers had to learn how to hunt and build houses.
religious /rəˈlɪdʒəs/	religiöse(r, s), Religions-	
16 best /best/	am meisten/liebsten/besten	
rewrite /ˌriːˈraɪt/	neu schreiben; umschreiben	
hang up sth /ˈhæŋ‿ʌp ˌsʌmθɪŋ/	etw aufhängen	
take place /teɪk ˈpleɪs/	stattfinden	
roast lamb /ˌrəʊst ˈlæm/	Lammbraten	
P2 repeat /rɪˈpiːt/	wiederholen	
P3 popular (with) /ˈpɒpjʊlə/	beliebt (bei)	
P4 in town /ɪn ˈtaʊn/	in der Stadt	
like this /laɪk ˈðɪs/	so	
spicy /ˈspaɪsi/	würzig; scharf	
ever /ˈevə/	jemals; *hier:* überhaupt	
P5 brilliant *(informal)* /ˈbrɪljənt/	toll, hervorragend	
supermarket /ˈsuːpəˌmɑːkɪt/	Supermarkt	
P7 serve /sɜːv/	servieren	
daily /ˈdeɪli/	täglich	
air-conditioned /ˈeə kənˌdɪʃnd/	klimatisiert, mit Klimaanlage	
P9 underline /ˌʌndəˈlaɪn/	unterstreichen	
P10 inside /ɪnˈsaɪd/	drinnen; innen; *hier:* im Inneren	
whose /huːz/	wessen	
P12 pick /pɪk/	aussuchen, auswählen	
connect /kəˈnekt/	verbinden	
especially /ɪˈspeʃli/	besonders	
put up /pʊt‿ˈʌp/	aufhängen; *hier:* aufstellen	
fireworks *(only pl)* /ˈfaɪəˌwɜːks/	Feuerwerk	

Teamwork
Zu zweit macht das Vokabellernen mehr Spaß. Fragt euch gegenseitig ab. Tauscht euch auch darüber aus, wie ihr am besten Wörter lernt. Wenn ihr Lust habt, könnt ihr selbst Lückentexte, Kreuzwort- oder Buchstabenrätsel für den Partner/die Partnerin erstellen.

TIPP

	most / məʊst /	am meisten
P13	decoration / ˌdekəˈreɪʃn /	Dekoration, Schmuck
	maracas / məˈrækəz /	*Rumba-Rasseln*
	home-made / ˌhəʊm ˈmeɪd /	hausgemacht, selbst gemacht
	salsa *(no pl)* / ˈsælsə /	Salsasoße
	color *(AE)* = colour *(BE)* / ˈkʌlə /	Farbe
	accessory / əkˈsesəri /	Accessoire; Zubehör
	brightly / ˈbraɪtli /	hell, leuchtend
	colored *(AE)* = coloured *(BE)* / ˈkʌləd /	bunt, farbig
	decorated / ˈdekəreɪtɪd /	geschmückt, verziert
	filled / fɪld /	gefüllt
	candy *(AE)* = sweets *(BE)* / ˈkændi /	Süßigkeiten
	hang *(irr)* / hæŋ /	(auf)hängen
	ceiling / ˈsiːlɪŋ /	(Zimmer)decke
	stick / stɪk /	Stock
	open up / ˈəʊpən ʌp /	(sich) öffnen
	covered / ˈkʌvəd /	zugedeckt, bedeckt, verhüllt
	put on / pʊt ˈɒn /	anziehen; *hier:* auflegen
	shake *(irr)* / ʃeɪk /	schütteln
	along / əˈlɒŋ /	(zusammen) mit
	neighbor *(AE)* = neighbour *(BE)* / ˈneɪbə /	Nachbar/in

What did the mayonnaise say to the fridge?

/ kləʊz ðə ˌdɔː aɪm ˌdresɪŋ /

TIPP

Mache sie zu deinen Wörtern!
Am besten kannst du dir Wörter merken, die du selbst verwendet hast. Darum: Bilde Sätze mit den Wörtern, die du dir merken willst. Sie können auch lustig sein oder sich reimen.

M1	take *(irr)* / teɪk /	(mit)nehmen; *hier:* brauchen, dauern	It takes three hours to get from Hamburg to Berlin by car.
	pick up / ˌpɪk ˈʌp /	aufheben; *hier:* abholen	Her mother picked her up from the airport.
	fixed / fɪkst /	fest(gesetzt), verabredet	
	make sure / ˌmeɪk ˈʃɔː /	sich versichern, darauf achten; *hier:* dafür sorgen	
	deliver / dɪˈlɪvə /	liefern	The postman delivers the mail every day.
	elderly / ˈeldəli /	ältere(r, s)	My mum helps elderly people in the neighbourhood.
	encourage sb / ɪnˈkʌrɪdʒ ˌsʌmbədi /	jdn ermutigen; *hier:* jdn ermuntern	
	continue / kənˈtɪnjuː /	fortfahren, fortführen	
M2	main / meɪn /	Haupt-	We eat our main meal of the day in the evening.
	ingredient / ɪnˈgriːdiənt /	Zutat	Use fresh ingredients in your food.
	company / ˈkʌmpni /	Firma	
	be hooked (on sth) / bi ˈhʊkt /	total verrückt nach etw sein; von etw abhängig sein	
	can / kæn /	Dose	a can of baked beans
	fizzy drink / ˌfɪzi ˈdrɪŋk /	süßes, kohlensäurehaltiges Getränk	a fizzy drink
	contain / kənˈteɪn /	enthalten	Ketchup contains a lot of sugar.
	teaspoon / ˈtiːˌspuːn /	Teelöffel	
	tasty / ˈteɪsti /	schmackhaft, lecker	tasty = yummy
	flavour / ˈfleɪvə /	Geschmack; Aroma	This drink has a bitter flavour.
	expert / ˈekspɜːt /	Experte/Expertin	

	strengthen /ˈstreŋθn/	verstärken, intensivieren	
	artificial /ˌɑːtɪˈfɪʃl/	künstlich	artificial ⟷ natural
	attractive /əˈtræktɪv/	attraktiv, verlockend	David finds Lily attractive.
	never even /ˌnevərˈiːvn/	(noch) nicht (ein)mal	
	flavouring /ˈfleɪvərɪŋ/	Aroma, Geschmacksstoff	
	hook sb /ˈhʊk ˌsʌmbədi/	jdn abhängig machen	
	advertising (no pl) /ˈædvəˌtaɪzɪŋ/	Werbung, Reklame	
	attract /əˈtrækt/	anziehen	
	give away /gɪv ə̮ˈweɪ/	verschenken	
	that way /ˈðæt weɪ/	so, auf diese Weise	
	match /mætʃ/	passen zu	
	taste (no pl) /teɪst/	Geschmack	I love the taste of chocolate.
	bubble /ˈbʌbl/	Blase	
	reason /ˈriːzn/	Grund	
M4	**argument** /ˈɑːgjʊmənt/	Auseinandersetzung, Streit; _hier:_ Argument	
	discussion /dɪˈskʌʃn/	Diskussion	They are having an angry discussion.
	think about (sb/sth) /ˈθɪŋk ə̮ˌbaʊt/	an (jdn/etw) denken; über (jdn/etw) nachdenken	
	give one's opinion (on sth) /gɪv wʌnz ə̮ˈpɪnjən/	seine Meinung (zu etw) äußern, (zu etw) Stellung nehmen	
	below /bɪˈləʊ/	unten; unter(halb)	
	firstly /ˈfɜːstli/	erstens	
	secondly /ˈsekəndli/	zweitens	
	in my opinion /ɪn ˈmaɪ ə̮ˌpɪnjən/	meiner Meinung/Ansicht nach	Well, in my opinion every child should have a pet.
	on the one hand /ɒn ðə ˈwʌn ˌhænd/	einerseits	On the one hand lots of people love pets because they are cute,
	on the other hand /ɒn ðiˌˈʌðə ˌhænd/	andererseits	but on the other hand it's expensive to keep a pet.
	fact /fækt/	Fakt	
	all in all /ˌɔːl ɪn ˌˈɔːl/	alles in allem	All in all, I would say that a cat is the right pet for me.
M5	Kwanzaa /ˈkwɑːnz ə/	_von Amerikanern afrikanischer Herkunft gefeiertes nicht-religiöses Fest_	
	sweet potato /ˌswiːt pəˈteɪtəʊ/	Süßkartoffel	
	seafood (no pl) /ˈsiːˌfuːd/	Meeresfrüchte	
	gumbo (no pl) /ˈgʌmbəʊ/	_Suppe mit Meeresfrüchten_	
	African /ˈæfrɪkən/	Afrikaner/in; afrikanisch	
	mainly /ˈmeɪnli/	hauptsächlich, in erster Linie	Bennet's friends are mainly boys from his class.
	colorful (AE) = colourful (BE) /ˈkʌləfl/	farbenfroh, farbenprächtig, farbenfreudig; bunt, farbig	
	kaftan /ˈkæftæn/	_weites Kleid_	
	extra /ˈekstrə/	zusätzlich	
	candle holder /ˈkændlˌhəʊldə/	Kerzenständer	
	kinara /kɪˈnɑːrə/	_siebenarmiger Kwanzaa-Kerzenständer_	

Give me one good reason why you are not in bed!

Sometimes I like to prepare traditional African food.

	light *(irr)* / laɪt /	erhellen; *hier:* anzünden	Light the fire, please. It's so dark and cold.
	each other / ˌiːtʃ ˈʌðə /	einander	We love each other.
M6	**shopping list** / ˈʃɒpɪŋ lɪst /	Einkaufszettel, Einkaufsliste	
	chips *(AE) (only pl)* = **crisps** *(BE) (only pl)* / tʃɪps /	Chips	Chips are my favorite snack!
	candy *(AE)* = **sweets** *(BE)* / ˈkændi /	Süßigkeiten	candy
	cookie *(AE)* = **biscuit** *(BE)* / ˈkʊki /	Keks, Plätzchen	
M7	scene / siːn /	Szene	
	think of / ˈθɪŋk‿əv /	denken an; sich ausdenken	
	act out / ækt‿ˈaʊt /	nachspielen	
CC	popsicle / ˈpɒpsɪkl /	Eis am Stiel	
	freeze / friːz /	gefrieren, einfrieren, zufrieren	
	creamsicle / ˈkriːmsɪkl /	*Sahneeis am Stiel*	
	sticky / ˈstɪki /	klebrig	
	ingredient / ɪnˈgriːdiənt /	Zutat	
	since then / sɪns ˈðen /	seitdem, seit damals	
	cotton candy *(no pl)* / ˌkɒtn ˈkændi /	Zuckerwatte	
	cotton ball / ˈkɒtn ˌbɔːl /	Wattebällchen	
	funfair / ˈfʌnˌfeə /	Vergnügungspark; Jahrmarkt	
	be seated / bi ˈsiːtɪd /	einen Sitzplatz/Tisch zugewiesen bekommen	

A tongue twister
Double bubble gum, bubbles double.

Theme 3 – New places, new faces

1	result / rɪˈzʌlt /	Ergebnis; Folge	
2	skyline / ˈskaɪˌlaɪn /	Skyline; Horizont	
	step / step /	Stufe	The cat is on the top step.
	the Statue of Liberty / ðə ˌstætʃuː‿əv ˈlɪbəti /	die Freiheitsstatue	
	people / ˈpiːpl /	Volk	
	the French / ðə ˈfrentʃ /	die Franzosen	
	symbol / ˈsɪmbl /	Symbol, Zeichen	The Statue of Liberty is a symbol of freedom.
	freedom *(no pl)* / ˈfriːdəm /	Freiheit	
	immigrant / ˈɪmɪgrənt /	Einwanderer/in	
	main / meɪn /	Haupt-	The main street in our city is full of cars.
	immigration *(no pl)* / ˌɪmɪˈgreɪʃn /	Einwanderung, Immigration	immigrant – immigration
	be home to sth/sb / bi ˈhəʊm tə ˌsʌmθɪŋ/ˌsʌmbədi /	etw/jdn beheimaten	
	theater *(AE)* = **theatre** *(BE)* / ˈθɪətə /	Theater	
	such as / sʌtʃ æz /	wie (zum Beispiel)	NYC has many famous sights such as Central Park and Fifth Avenue.
	free / friː /	frei; *hier:* gratis, umsonst	
	destroy / dɪˈstrɔɪ /	zerstören	A fire has destroyed my aunt's house.
	trade / treɪd /	Handel	

	skyscraper /ˈskaɪˌskreɪpə/	Wolkenkratzer	There are lots of skyscrapers in NYC.
	memorial /məˈmɔːrɪəl/	Denkmal	
	square /skweə/	Quadrat; *hier:* Platz	A famous square in London is Trafalgar Square.
	ad (= advertisement) /æd, ədˈvɜːtɪsmənt/	Anzeige; *hier:* Werbung	
	bright /braɪt/	hell	It was a lovely bright winter's day.
	even /ˈiːvn/	selbst; sogar	
3	**painting** /ˈpeɪntɪŋ/	Bild, Gemälde	
5	view /vjuː/	Sicht; (Aus)blick, Aussicht	
	ferry /ˈferi/	Fähre	
	ice-skating rink /ˈaɪsskeɪtɪŋ rɪŋk/	Schlittschuhbahn	
6	come to sb's mind /kʌm tə ˌsʌmbədiz ˈmaɪnd/	jdm einfallen	
7	convince /kənˈvɪns/	überzeugen	
	must-see /ˌmʌstˈsiː/	*etw, das man gesehen haben muss*	
8	New Yorker /njuːˈjɔːkə/	New Yorker/in	
	borough /ˈbʌrə/	Stadtteil, Bezirk	
	the Middle East /ðə ˌmɪdl ˈiːst/	der Nahe Osten	the Middle East: countries such as Israel, Lebanon, Turkey and Iran
	for /fɔː/	für; *hier:* seit	I've lived in Wiesbaden for ten years.
	part /pɑːt/	Teil	Let's watch the second part of the film tomorrow.
	ferry /ˈferi/	Fähre	a ferry
	the Caribbean /ðə ˌkærɪˈbiːən/	die Karibik; die Karibischen Inseln	
	be cool with sb/sth /bi ˈkuːl wɪð ˌsʌmbədi/ˌsʌmθɪŋ/	kein Problem mit jdm/etw haben	
	each other /ˌiːtʃˈʌðə/	einander	They love each other.
	leave sb in peace /ˌliːv ˌsʌmbədi ɪn ˈpiːs/	jdn in Frieden/Ruhe lassen	Stop it! Leave your brother in peace!
	grow up /grəʊˈʌp/	erwachsen werden; *hier:* aufwachsen	
	busy /ˈbɪzi/	beschäftigt; *hier:* belebt, verkehrsreich	The station is always very busy at the weekends.
9	**neighbourhood** /ˈneɪbəˌhʊd/	Viertel; Nachbarschaft	
	definition /ˌdefəˈnɪʃn/	Definition, Erklärung	
	South America /ˌsaʊθˈəˈmerɪkə/	Südamerika	South America is south of North America.
10	make up sth /ˌmeɪkˈʌp ˌsʌmθɪŋ/	(sich) etw ausdenken, etw erfinden	
11	plan /plæn/	planen	
	headline /ˈhedˌlaɪn/	Schlagzeile	
	highlight sth /ˈhaɪlaɪt ˌsʌmθɪŋ/	etw hervorheben/unterstreichen	
	paragraph /ˈpærəˌgrɑːf/	Absatz, Abschnitt	
	brochure /ˈbrəʊʃə/	Broschüre	
	presentation /ˌpreznˈteɪʃn/	Präsentation	
	detail /ˈdiːteɪl/	Detail, Einzelheit	
	edit /ˈedɪt/	bearbeiten, redigieren	
	swap /swɒp/	tauschen	

Do you have to text now? Even at dinner?

TIPP

Nur 10 Minuten!
Übe Vokabeln immer nur ca. 10 Minuten, aber dafür regelmäßig! Das bringt mehr als mal eine ganze Stunde oder nur zweimal im Monat.

12	of one's own /əv wʌnz ˌˈəʊn/	eigene(r, s)	
13	similar /ˈsɪmɪlə/	ähnlich	
	earn /ɜːn/	verdienen	He earns enough to feed his family.
	feed (irr) /fiːd/	füttern, zu Essen geben; hier: ernähren	feed – fed – fed
	Saudi Arabia /ˌsaʊdi əˈreɪbiə/	Saudi-Arabien	
	collect /kəˈlekt/	sammeln; hier: holen	
	wash the dishes /wɒʃ ðə ˈdɪʃɪz/	abspülen, Geschirr spülen	Do you wash the dishes at home?
	lamp /læmp/	Lampe	
	about /əˈbaʊt/	ungefähr	She goes to bed at about 9.30 pm.
	shoeshine /ˈʃuːʃaɪn/	Schuhputz-	
	outside /ˌaʊtˈsaɪd/	im Freien, draußen; hier: außerhalb	
	wake up /weɪk ˌˈʌp/	aufwecken; aufwachen	When do you wake up in the morning?
	town /taʊn/	Stadt	There is no cinema in our town.
	hang on to sth /hæŋ ˌˈɒn tʊ ˌsʌmθɪŋ/	sich an etw festhalten, sich an etw klammern	
	jump off /dʒʌmp ˌˈɒf/	herunterspringen	She jumped off the bridge.
	business /ˈbɪznəs/	Handel, Gewerbe	
	peso /ˈpeɪsəʊ/	Peso (Währung)	
	share /ʃeə/	teilen	He doesn't like to share his food.
15	imagination /ɪˌmædʒɪˈneɪʃn/	Fantasie, Vorstellungskraft; Einbildung	
	linking word /ˈlɪŋkɪŋ wɜːd/	Bindewort	
16	before /bɪˈfɔː/	zuvor, vorher; hier: schon (einmal)	
	standard /ˈstændəd/	Standard; Richtlinie; Wertvorstellung	
	mark /mɑːk/	(Schul)note; hier: Siegel, Kennzeichnung	
	FAQ (= Frequently Asked Question) /ˌef eɪ ˈkjuː/	FAQ, häufig gestellte Frage	
	contact sb /ˈkɒntækt ˌsʌmbədi/	jdn kontaktieren, sich mit jdm in Verbindung setzen	
	sign up /ˌsaɪn ˌˈʌp/	sich anmelden	
	especially /ɪˈspeʃli/	besonders	Gillian loves sweets, especially chocolate.
	have a hard time doing sth /hæv ə hɑːd ˌtaɪm ˈduːɪŋ ˌsʌmθɪŋ/	es schwer haben, etw zu tun	
	make sure /ˌmeɪk ˈʃɔː/	sich versichern, darauf achten	
	producer /prəˈdjuːsə/	Produzent/in; Hersteller, Erzeuger	California is a large producer of fruit and vegetables.
	organization /ˌɔːɡənaɪˈzeɪʃn/	Organisation	
	support /səˈpɔːt/	(unter)stützen	Charlie and Rajiv support each other.
	label /ˈleɪbl/	Etikett, Label; Marke	
	produce /prəˈdjuːs/	herstellen, erzeugen, produzieren	produce – producer
	according to /əˈkɔːdɪŋ tʊ/	laut, nach, gemäß	
	internationally /ˌɪntəˈnæʃnəli/	international	
	agreed /əˈɡriːd/	vereinbart; akzeptiert	

coffee / ˈkɒfi /	Kaffee	Would you like tea or coffee?
supermarket / ˈsuːpəˌmɑːkɪt /	Supermarkt	
the Netherlands / ðə ˈneðlənz /	die Niederlande	
17 all over the world / ˌɔːlˌəʊvə ðə ˈwɜːld /	auf der ganzen Welt	Some companies have shops all over the world.
make a living / ˌmeɪk ə ˈlɪvɪŋ /	seinen Lebensunterhalt verdienen	
continue / kənˈtɪnjuː /	fortfahren, fortführen	
survive / səˈvaɪv /	überleben	Only four people survived the plane crash.
at least / ət ˈliːst /	mindestens, wenigstens	At least 20 people were killed in the road accident.
themselves / ðemˈselvz /	sich (selbst); selbst	
extra / ˈekstrə /	zusätzlich	He paid for an extra bag.
another / əˈnʌðə /	noch ein(e, r, s)	Could I have another cup of tea, please?
few / fjuː /	wenige	Why are there so few people at the party?
chemical / ˈkemɪkl /	Chemikalie	
article / ˈɑːtɪkl /	Artikel	
18 Brazil / brəˈzɪl /	Brasilien	
regular / ˈregjʊlə /	regelmäßig; *hier:* normal	
P1 positive / ˈpɒzətɪv /	positiv	
negative / ˈnegətɪv /	negativ	
P2 tongue twister / ˈtʌŋ ˌtwɪstə /	Zungenbrecher	
lorry / ˈlɒri /	Lkw, Last(kraft)wagen	
unique / juːˈniːk /	einzigartig	
P3 necessary / ˈnesəsri /	nötig, notwendig, erforderlich	
P5 past participle / ˌpɑːst ˈpɑːtɪsɪpl /	Partizip Perfekt	
have sth in common / hæv ˌsʌmθɪŋˌɪn ˈkɒmən /	etwas gemein haben	
P7 class trip / ˈklɑːs trɪp /	Klassenfahrt	
tour guide / ˈtʊə gaɪd /	Reiseführer/in, Reiseleiter/in	
beginning / bɪˈgɪnɪŋ /	Anfang	
P8 be the odd one out / biː ðiˌɒd wʌnˌˈaʊt /	aus der Reihe fallen, nicht dazugehören	
P11 replace / rɪˈpleɪs /	ersetzen	
mark / mɑːk /	markieren, kennzeichnen	
sneaker *(AE)* = trainer *(BE)* / ˈsniːkə /	Turnschuh	
P12 own / əʊn /	besitzen	
line / laɪn /	Linie	
P13 bake sale / ˈbeɪk seɪl /	Kuchenbasar, Verkauf selbst gebackenen Kuchens	
year / jɪə /	Jahr; *hier:* Jahrgang(sstufe)	
come along / ˌkʌmˌəˈlɒŋ /	mitgehen, mitkommen; *hier:* vorbeikommen	
cookie *(AE)* = biscuit *(BE)* / ˈkʊki /	Keks, Plätzchen	
raise money / reɪz ˈmʌni /	Geld aufbringen/auftreiben	
organise / ˈɔːgənaɪz /	organisieren	
M1 artist / ˈɑːtɪst /	Künstler/in	He is a wonderful artist.
only / ˈəʊnli /	nur; *hier:* erst	My sister Zoe is only three years old.

TIPP

Gegensätze
Neue Vokabeln musst du nicht immer in Listen schreiben. Du kannst sie auch anders sortieren, zum Beispiel indem du Gegensätze zusammenstellst. Wie viele Wörter kennst du schon, die sich so zusammenstellen lassen?
stand up ↔ sit down
few ↔ many

TIPP

Spell check
Buchstabiere ein Wort für eine/n Partner/in. Wechselt euch ab und kontrolliert anschließend gegenseitig, ob alles richtig geschrieben ist. Für jedes richtige Wort gibt es einen Punkt. Wer ist der *spelling king* oder die *spelling queen*?

	appear / əˈpɪə /	erscheinen	The ghost appeared suddenly.
	public / ˈpʌblɪk /	öffentlich	I hate using public toilets.
	subway *(AE)* = underground *(BE)*	U-Bahn	
	/ ˈsʌbˌweɪ /		
	vandalism *(no pl)* / ˈvændəˌlɪzm /	Vandalismus, Sachbeschädigung	
	remove / rɪˈmuːv /	entfernen	Last week we removed chewing gum from our school desks.
	spray / spreɪ /	(be)sprühen	
	chalk *(no pl)* / tʃɔːk /	Kreide	
	be up to sb / biˌʌp tʊ ˈsʌmbədi /	von jdm abhängen	
	drawing / ˈdrɔːɪŋ /	Zeichnung	You can make cool drawings with chalk.
	crawl / krɔːl /	krabbeln; kriechen	The baby crawled up to its cake.
	thanks to / ˈθæŋks tə /	dank, wegen	
	authority / ɔːˈθɒrəti /	Behörde	
	space / speɪs /	Platz, Raum	
	legal / ˈliːɡl /	legal, gesetzlich zulässig	legal ↔ illegal
	gallery / ˈɡæləri /	Galerie	
	exhibition / ˌeksɪˈbɪʃn /	Ausstellung	There are lots of exhibitions in NYC.
	heading / ˈhedɪŋ /	Überschrift, Titel	
M2	**while** *(no pl)* / waɪl /	Weile	This morning I had to wait a while for the bus.
	object / ˈɒbdʒekt /	Objekt	
M5	**princess** / ˌprɪnˈses /	Prinzessin	
	although / ɔːlˈðəʊ /	obwohl, obgleich	Although my mum has a mobile phone, she never uses it.
	such / sʌtʃ /	solche(r,s)	
M6	though / ðəʊ /	(je)doch	
	field / fiːld /	Wiese, Weide, Feld	
	abroad / əˈbrɔːd /	im Ausland	He wants to visit his uncle abroad.
	harvest / ˈhɑːvɪst /	ernten	
M7	**developing country**	Entwicklungsland	Children in developing countries are usually poor and don't go to school.
	/ dɪˈveləpɪŋ ˌkʌntri /		
	rule / ruːl /	regieren	
M9	**might** / maɪt /	könnte	Rajiv might tidy up his room.
	field / fiːld /	Wiese, Weide, Feld; *hier:* Bereich	
	symbolize / ˈsɪmbəlaɪz /	symbolisieren	Romeo and Juliet symbolize true love.
CC	sew *(irr)* / səʊ /	nähen	
	Asian / ˈeɪʃn /	asiatisch	
	adult / ˈædʌlt /	Erwachsene/r	
	lock / lɒk /	Schloss	
	deliver / dɪˈlɪvə /	liefern	
	across the street / əˌkrɒs ðə ˈstriːt /	gegenüber(liegend)	
	population / ˌpɒpjʊˈleɪʃn /	Bevölkerung	

Theme 4 – Finding your place

1	nation / ˈneɪʃn /	Nation, Land	USA = United States of America
	the US (= United States)	die Vereinigten Staaten	US = United States
	/ ðə ˌjuː ˈes, ðə juːˌnaɪtɪd ˈsteɪts /		
	citizen / ˈsɪtɪzn /	(Staats)bürger/in	
	railroad *(AE)* = **railway** *(BE)*	Gleise, Schienen;	
	/ ˈreɪlˌrəʊd /	*hier:* (Eisen)bahn	
	illegal / ɪˈliːgl /	illegal	illegal ↔ legal
	Central America / ˌsentrəl̮ əˈmerɪkə /	Mittelamerika	
	Siberia / saɪˈbɪəriə /	Sibirien	
	European / juərəˈpiːən /	Europäer/in; europäisch	France and Italy are European countries.
	harmony *(no pl)* / ˈhɑːməni /	Harmonie; Eintracht	
	reservation / ˌrezəˈveɪʃn /	Reservierung; *hier:* Reservat (= *ein den Indianern vorbehaltenes Gebiet*)	Many Native Americans still live on reservations today.
	immigrate / ˈɪmɪˌgreɪt /	einwandern	In the 1880s 1.5 million Germans immigrated to the US.
	green card *(AE)* / ˌgriːn ˈkɑːd /	Aufenthaltserlaubnis mit Arbeitsgenehmigung, Greencard	
	lottery / ˈlɒtəri /	Lotterie	
	America / əˈmerɪkə /	Amerika	
	mainly / ˈmeɪnli /	hauptsächlich, in erster Linie	I mainly love Britain because I can eat fish and chips there.
	total / ˈtəʊtl /	Gesamt-	
	population / ˌpɒpjʊˈleɪʃn /	Bevölkerung	
	Hispanic / hɪˈspænɪk /	Hispano-Amerikaner/in; hispanisch	
	first language / ˌfɜːst ˈlæŋgwɪdʒ /	Muttersprache	Is your first language German?
	third / θɜːd /	Drittel	
	slave / sleɪv /	Sklave/Sklavin	There were many slaves in the southern US states.
	civil war / ˌsɪvl ˈwɔː /	Bürgerkrieg	
	right / raɪt /	Recht	You have no right to take away my mobile phone.
	both ... and ... / ˈbəʊθ ˌənd /	sowohl ... als auch ...	
	African American / ˌæfrɪkən̮ əˈmerɪkən /	Afroamerikaner/in; afroamerikanisch	Martin Luther King was a famous African American.
2	statistics / stəˈtɪstɪks /	Statistik	
	ethnic / ˈeθnɪk /	ethnisch, Volks-	
	including / ɪnˈkluːdɪŋ /	einschließlich	
	Asian American / ˌeɪʒən̮ əˈmerɪkən /	Amerikaner/in asiatischer Herkunft; asiatisch-amerikanisch	His friend is Asian American.
	per cent / pəˈsent /	Prozent	
3	placemat / ˈpleɪsˌmæt /	Set, Platzdeckchen	
	another / əˈnʌðə /	noch ein(e, r, s); *hier:* ein anderer/anderes, eine andere	
	war / wɔː /	Krieg	war ↔ peace
4	**experience** / ɪkˈspɪəriəns /	Erfahrung, Erlebnis	I had a terrible experience when I was on holiday.
	jigsaw / ˈdʒɪgsɔː /	Puzzle	

used to do sth /ˌjuːstˌtu ˈduː ˌsʌmθɪŋ/	früher etw getan haben	
education *(no pl)* /ˌedjʊˈkeɪʃn/	(Aus)bildung	You go to school to get a good education.
in the country /ɪn ðə ˈkʌntri/	auf dem Land	
not at all /ˌnɒtˌətˌˈɔːl/	überhaupt nicht	Are you tired? – No, not at all!
well-paid /ˌwelˈpeɪd/	gut bezahlt	
relative /ˈrelətɪv/	Verwandte(r), Angehörige(r)	relatives = aunts, uncles, …
persuade /pəˈsweɪd/	überreden, überzeugen	
join /dʒɔɪn/	mitmachen bei; beitreten; *hier:* zusammenfügen; sich anschließen	Let's join the others.
only /ˈəʊnli/	nur; *hier:* erst	My sister Zoe is only three years old.
shy /ʃaɪ/	schüchtern	
divorced /dɪˈvɔːst/	geschieden	Gillian's parents are divorced.
college /ˈkɒlɪdʒ/	*Bildungseinrichtung; hier:* Universität, Hochschule	He is studying hard so that he can go to a good college.
mix up /mɪksˌˈʌp/	verwechseln; *hier:* vermischen	
present /ˈpreznt/	Geschenk	
note down /nəʊt ˈdaʊn/	(sich) notieren	
reason /ˈriːzn/	Grund	
5 difficulty /ˈdɪfɪklti/	Schwierigkeit, Problem	
6 **get used to sth** /get ˈjuːstˌtu ˌsʌmθɪŋ/	sich an etw gewöhnen	He has got used to the rain.
custom /ˈkʌstəm/	Brauch, Sitte	
7 stereotype /ˈsteriəˌtaɪp/	Stereotyp, Klischee	
8 as /əz/	als; *hier:* wie	
dos and don'ts /ˌduːzˌən ˈdəʊnts/	was man tun und was man nicht tun sollte	
smile /smaɪl/	lächeln	Smile and be happy!
friendliness *(no pl)* /ˈfrendlɪnɪs/	Freundlichkeit	
friendship /ˈfrendʃɪp/	Freundschaft	
bump into sth/sb /ˌbʌmpˌˈɪntə ˌsʌmθɪŋ, ˌsʌmbədi/	mit etw/jdm zusammenstoßen	
apologize /əˈpɒləˌdʒaɪz/	sich entschuldigen	I'm so sorry. I want to apologize for the stupid things I said.
stare at sb/sth /ˈsteəˌət ˌsʌmbədi, ˌsʌmθɪŋ/	jdn/etw anstarren	
may not /meɪ ˈnɒt/	nicht dürfen; *hier:* vielleicht nicht	
keep an open mind /ˌkiːpˌənˌˈəʊpən ˌmaɪnd/	aufgeschlossen bleiben	
copy /ˈkɒpi/	abschreiben	Please copy the sentences from the board.
9 sing along /ˌsɪŋˌəˈlɒŋ/	mitsingen	
melody /ˈmelədi/	Melodie	
rhythm /ˈrɪðəm/	Rhythmus, Takt	
lyrics *(only pl)* /ˈlɪrɪks/	(Lied)text	Do you know the lyrics of your favourite song?
California /ˌkæləˈfɔːniə/	Kalifornien	
gulf stream /ˈgʌlf striːm/	Golfstrom	

water /ˈwɔːtə/	Gewässer	
ribbon /ˈrɪbən/	Band, Streifen	
highway /ˈhaɪˌweɪ/	Bundesstraße, Highway	A highway is a wide road for travelling fast between towns and cities.
above /əˈbʌv/	über	
endless /ˈendləs/	endlos, unendlich	
skyway /ˈskaɪˌweɪ/	*hier:* Himmel	
below /bɪˈləʊ/	unten; unter(halb)	
roam /rəʊm/	umherstreifen, umherziehen	
ramble /ˈræmbl/	wandern	
footstep /ˈfʊtˌstep/	Schritt	Everyone could hear her footsteps as she went up the stairs.
sparkling /ˈspɑːklɪŋ/	funkelnd, glitzernd	
sand /sænd/	Sand(strand)	
diamond /ˈdaɪəmənd/	Diamant	
desert /ˈdezət/	Wüste	It is always very hot in the desert.
voice /vɔɪs/	Stimme	Rajiv can sing very well. He has a wonderful voice.
shine *(irr)* /ʃaɪn/	scheinen (Sonne)	shine – shone – shone
stroll /strəʊl/	schlendern, bummeln	
wheat *(no pl)* /wiːt/	Weizen	
field /fiːld/	Wiese, Weide, Feld	He works all day in the fields.
wave /weɪv/	winken; *hier:* wogen	
dust *(no pl)* /dʌst/	Staub	
cloud /klaʊd/	Wolke	There are a lot of dark clouds in the sky.
chant /tʃɑːnt/	singen	
lift /lɪft/	(hoch)heben; *hier:* sich auflösen	
10 chart /tʃɑːt/	Diagramm, Schaubild, Grafik	
home town /ˌhəʊm ˈtaʊn/	Heimatort	
11 finding /ˈfaɪndɪŋ/	Entdeckung; Ergebnis	
word web /ˈwɜːd web/	Wortnetz	
12 then /ðen/	dann; *hier:* damals	
tribe /traɪb/	Stamm	The tribes had their own rules and traditions.
totem pole /ˈtəʊtəm ˌpəʊl/	Totempfahl	
legend /ˈledʒnd/	Sage, Legende	
blow *(irr)* /bləʊ/	blasen, wehen	blow – blew – blown
smoke *(no pl)* /sməʊk/	Rauch	Don't blow your smoke at me!
another /əˈnʌðə/	noch ein(e, r, s); *hier:* ein anderer/anderes, eine andere	Another word for "clever" is "intelligent".
adapt (to) /əˈdæpt/	sich anpassen	
seal /siːl/	Seehund, Robbe	A seal is a large sea animal that eats fish.
pow-wow /ˈpaʊˌwaʊ/	Powwow *(indianische Versammlung)*	
horseshoe /ˈhɔːsˌʃuː/	Hufeisen	
Hualapai /ˈhwæləpeɪ/	Hualapai(indianer)	

	community /kəˈmjuːnəti/	Gemeinde; Gemeinschaft	
	police station /pəˈliːsˌsteɪʃn/	Polizeirevier, Polizeiwache	police station = the building where the local police work
	headdress /ˈhedˌdres/	Kopfschmuck	
	feather /ˈfeðə/	Feder	The bird has brightly coloured feathers.
	Lakota /ləˈkəʊtə/	Lakota(indianer)	
	tepee /ˈtiːpiː/	Indianerzelt	
	igloo /ˈɪgluː/	Iglu	
	ice *(no pl)* /aɪs/	Eis	Penguins live on the ice.
LL	Indian /ˈɪndiən/	Inder/in; *hier: veraltete Bezeichnung für amerikanische Ureinwohner*	
14	above /əˈbʌv/	oben	
	hunter /ˈhʌntə/	Jäger/in	All cats are hunters.
	buffalo *(pl - or -es)* /ˈbʌfələʊ, ˈbʌfələʊz/	Büffel	Some Native American tribes hunted buffaloes.
	ocean /ˈəʊʃn/	Meer; Ozean	The island is in the middle of the ocean.
	government /ˈgʌvənmənt/	Regierung	
	force sb (to do sth) /ˈfɔːsˌsʌmbədi/	jdn zwingen (etw zu tun)	
	keep up sth /ˌkiːpˈʌpˌsʌmθɪŋ/	etw fortführen, etw weiterhin tun	
15	just /dʒʌst/	gleich; *hier: genau*	
	Navajo /ˈnævəhəʊ/	Navajo(indianer)	
	Mexican American /ˌmeksɪkənˈəˈmerɪkən/	Amerikaner/in mexikanischer Herkunft; mexikanisch-amerikanisch	
	as soon as /əzˈsuːnˌəz/	sobald	I'll come as soon as I've finished my homework.
	ceremony /ˈserəməni/	Zeremonie, Feier	
	pass on (sth) /pɑːsˈɒn/	(etw) weitergeben	
	pride *(no pl)* /praɪd/	Stolz	pride (noun) – proud (adjective)
	spokesperson *(pl -people)* /ˈspəʊksˌpɜːsn/	Sprecher/in	
	heading /ˈhedɪŋ/	Überschrift, Titel	
	hope /həʊp/	Hoffnung	
	fact file /ˈfækt ˌfaɪl/	Steckbrief	
	report (on sb/sth) /rɪˈpɔːt/	(über jdn/etw) berichten	
	category /ˈkætəgri/	Kategorie	
P1	opposite /ˈɒpəzɪt/	Gegenteil	
	legal /ˈliːgl/	legal, gesetzlich zulässig	
	unimportant /ˌʌnɪmˈpɔːtnt/	unwichtig	
	noun /naʊn/	Substantiv	
P2	alien /ˈeɪliən/	Außerirdische(r), Alien	
P3	rhyming pair /ˈraɪmɪŋ peə/	Reimpaar	
P4	end /end/	enden	
	inform /ɪnˈfɔːm/	informieren	
P7	leash /liːʃ/	Leine	
	due to sth /ˌdjuː tʊ ˈsʌmθɪŋ/	wegen/aufgrund einer Sache	
	emergency /ɪˈmɜːdʒnsi/	Notfall	

Kim's game

Schreibe zehn Wörter auf ein Blatt Papier. Nimm dir drei Minuten Zeit, um sie dir einzuprägen. Dann drehe das Blatt um. Versuche nun, alle Wörter auswendig auf die Rückseite zu schreiben. Wie viele hast du dir gemerkt?

TIPP

	shuttle bus /ˈʃʌtl bʌs/	Zubringerbus, Shuttlebus	
	thin /θɪn/	dünn	
P9	match /mætʃ/	passen (zu)	
	university /ˌjuːnɪˈvɜːsəti/	Universität	
P10	spelling /ˈspelɪŋ/	Rechtschreibung	
	program (AE) = programme (BE) /ˈprəʊɡræm/	Programm	
	center (AE) = centre (BE) /ˈsentə/	Zentrum, Center	
P12	simple past /ˌsɪmpl ˈpɑːst/	einfache Vergangenheit	
	chief /tʃiːf/	Leiter/in; hier: Häuptling	
P13	role /rəʊl/	Rolle	
P14	Canada /ˈkænədə/	Kanada	
	Belgium /ˈbeldʒəm/	Belgien	
	elk /elk/	Elch	
	breed (irr) /briːd/	züchten	
	exploit /ɪkˈsplɔɪt/	ausbeuten, ausschöpfen	
	mineral resources (only pl) /ˈmɪnrəl rɪˌzɔːsɪz/	Bodenschätze	
	gambling (no pl) /ˈɡæmblɪŋ/	Glücksspiel	
	casino /kəˈsiːnəʊ/	(Spiel)kasino	
M1	stand in line /ˌstænd ɪn ˈlaɪn/	anstehen	
	board (a ship) /bɔːd/	(ein Schiff) besteigen	They boarded the ship last night.
	breeze /briːz/	Brise	
	homeland /ˈhəʊmˌlænd/	Heimat(land)	
	wonder /ˈwʌndə/	sich fragen	They are wondering what to do.
	the Emerald Isle /ðiˈemrəldˌaɪl/	die Grüne Insel	
	Irish stew /ˌaɪrɪʃ ˈstjuː/	gekochtes Hammelfleisch mit Weißkraut und Kartoffeln	
	continue to do sth /kənˌtɪnjuː tʊ ˈduː ˌsʌmθɪŋ/	weiter(hin) etw tun	
	Catholic /ˈkæθlɪk/	Katholik/in; katholisch	Is that a Catholic church?
	yet /jet/	schon; bis jetzt; hier: trotzdem	
	famine /ˈfæmɪn/	Hungersnot	We are lucky to live in a country where there is no famine.
	depend on sth /dɪˈpend ɒn ˌsʌmθɪŋ/	von etw abhängen	
	crop /krɒp/	Ernte	Last year the farmers had a good crop.
	starvation (no pl) /stɑːˈveɪʃn/	Unterernährung, Mangelernährung	
	cause sb to do sth /ˌkɔːz ˌsʌmbədi tʊ ˈduː ˌsʌmθɪŋ/	jdn veranlassen, etw zu tun	
	emigrate /ˈemɪɡreɪt/	auswandern, emigrieren	emigrate ⟷ immigrate
	crowded /ˈkraʊdɪd/	überfüllt	The bus stop was quite crowded.
	poor /pɔː/	arm; hier: unzureichend, mangelhaft	
	seasick /ˈsiːˌsɪk/	seekrank	Many people on the ship got seasick during the storm.
	welcome /ˈwelkəm/	willkommen heißen, begrüßen	
	harbour /ˈhɑːbə/	Hafen	The ship sailed into the harbour.
	sight /saɪt/	Sehenswürdigkeit; hier: Anblick	

Reimwörter

Damit du dir besser merken kannst, wie bestimmte Wörter ausgesprochen werden, suche Reimwörter für sie. Dir wird auffallen, dass die Reimwörter nicht immer dieselbe Schreibweise haben.

war – door

feather – together

TIPP

	announce /əˈnaʊns/	bekannt geben, verkünden	They've just announced that our train will arrive five minutes later.
	dock /dɒk/	anlegen, andocken	
	official /əˈfɪʃl/	Beamte(r)/Beamtin	
	gift /ɡɪft/	Geschenk	gifts = presents
	statue /ˈstætʃuː/	Statue, Standbild	
	timeline /ˈtaɪmˌlaɪn/	Zeitstrahl	
	summary /ˈsʌməri/	Zusammenfassung; Inhaltsangabe	
	action /ˈækʃn/	Handlung; Aktion	
M2	greet /ɡriːt/	(be)grüßen	She opened the door and greeted the guests.
	receive /rɪˈsiːv/	empfangen, erhalten	I received an email from my uncle yesterday.
	tense /tens/	Zeitform, Tempus	
	past perfect /ˌpɑːst ˈpɜːfɪkt/	Plusquamperfekt	
M3	ancestor /ˈænsestə/	Vorfahr(e)/Vorfahrin	Our ancestors had red hair, too!
	pie chart /ˈpaɪ tʃɑːt/	Tortendiagramm	
	figures (only pl) /ˈfɪɡəz/	Zahlen(material)	
	ancestry /ˈænsestri/	Abstammung	
	Polish /ˈpəʊlɪʃ/	polnisch	Polish = from Poland
M5	Ute /juːt/	Ute-Indianer/in; Ute-; Ute (Sprache)	
	pollute /pəˈluːt/	verschmutzen	Don't pollute the air! Take the bus!
	stressful /ˈstresfl/	stressig, anstrengend	My mum has a really stressful job.
	stay out /steɪ ˈaʊt/	ausbleiben, wegbleiben	
	get sb off to somewhere /ɡet ˌsʌmbədi ˌɒf tʊ ˈsʌmweə/	jdn wohin bringen	
	beadwork (no pl) /ˈbiːdwɜːk/	Perlenstickerei	
	drumming (no pl) /ˈdrʌmɪŋ/	Trommeln	
	hard /hɑːd/	hart; schwer; hier: fleißig	
	end up /ˌend ˈʌp/	enden	He wanted to be a famous actor but he ended up as a waiter.
	boarding school /ˈbɔːdɪŋ ˌskuːl/	Internat	
	nearby /ˌnɪəˈbaɪ/	nahe/in der Nähe gelegen, benachbart	I bought my shirt in a nearby shop.
	prejudice (no pl) /ˈpredʒʊdɪs/	Vorurteil, Voreingenommenheit	There is a lot of prejudice against other ethnic groups.
	rez (= reservation) (informal) /rez/	Reservat (= ein den Indianern vorbehaltenes Gebiet)	
	saying /ˈseɪɪŋ/	Sprichwort	One English saying is, "No man is an island."
	lead (irr) /liːd/	(an)führen, leiten	lead – led – led
	beside /bɪˈsaɪd/	neben	
	be as one /bi ˌəz ˈwʌn/	eins sein	
M6	what if /wɒt ˌɪf/	was ist/wäre, wenn	
	clause /klɔːz/	Satz(teil)	
	likely /ˈlaɪkli/	wahrscheinlich	
M7	Cherokee /ˈtʃerəkiː/	Cherokee(indianer)	

	likes *(only pl)* / laɪks /	Vorlieben
	dislikes *(only pl)* / dɪsˈlaɪks /	Abneigungen
	hope / həʊp /	Hoffnung
	worry / ˈwʌri /	Sorge
CC	free / friː /	befreien, freilassen
	percentage / pəˈsentɪdʒ /	Prozentsatz, Anteil
	protection / prəˈtekʃn /	Schutz
	Iroquois / ˈɪrəkwɔɪ /	Irokese
	the earth / ðiˌ ˈɜːθ /	die Erde
	giant / ˈdʒaɪənt /	riesig
	the A-B-C's *(AE) (informal)* / ðiˌ ˌeɪbiːˈsiːz /	das ABC; das Einmaleins
	arithmetic *(no pl)* / əˈrɪθmətɪk /	Rechnen
	public school *(AE)* / ˌpʌblɪk ˈskuːl /	staatliche/öffentliche Schule
	what makes sb tick / ˌmeɪks sʌmbədi ˈtɪk /	wie jmd tickt, was jdn bewegt
	aisle / aɪl /	Gang
	Polish / ˈpəʊlɪʃ /	polnisch
	smile / smaɪl /	Lächeln
	colored *(AE)* = coloured *(BE)* / ˈkʌləd /	bunt, farbig; *hier: veraltete Bezeichnung für Afroamerikaner*
	Grecian / ˈgriːʃn /	griechisch
	regular / ˈregjʊlə /	regelmäßig; *hier:* regelrechte(r, s), richtige(r, s)
	Noah's ark / ˌnəʊəz ˈɑːk /	die Arche Noah
	race / reɪs /	Rennen; *hier:* Rasse
	beneath / bɪˈniːθ /	unter

likes and dislikes = things you like and don't like

verb	–	noun
hope	–	hope
worry	–	worry
kiss	–	kiss
dance	–	dance
cost	–	cost
...	–	...

TIPP

Verknüpfungen herstellen
Bei Wörtern, die überhaupt nicht in deinen Kopf wollen, kannst du:
- dir das Wort bildlich vorstellen,
- ein kleines Bild dazu zeichnen,
- an ein Ereignis denken, das du selbst erlebt hast,
- einen Satz auswendig lernen, in dem das Wort vorkommt,
- dir eine Eselsbrücke (z. B. einen Reim) ausdenken.

Theme 5 – What's up?

I	What's up? *(informal)* / wɒtsˌ ˈʌp /	Wie gehts?; Was geht?; Was gibts?
1	out / aʊt /	draußen; *hier:* aus
2	surf the Internet / ˌsɜːf ðiˌ ˈɪntənet /	im Internet surfen
	might / maɪt /	könnte
	speech bubble / ˈspiːtʃ ˌbʌbl /	Sprechblase
	thought bubble / ˈθɔːt ˌbʌbl /	Denkblase, Gedankenblase
3	shop till you drop / ˈʃɒp tɪl jə ˌdrɒp /	Einkaufen bis zum Umfallen
	fitting room / ˈfɪtɪŋ ˌruːm /	Umkleide, Anprobe
	be on sale / biːˌ ɒn ˈseɪl /	zum Verkauf stehen; *hier:* im Angebot sein, reduziert sein
	cash *(no pl)* / kæʃ /	Bargeld
	try on / traɪˌ ˈɒn /	anprobieren
	receipt / rɪˈsiːt /	Beleg; Kassenbon
	shop / ʃɒp /	einkaufen
	think of / ˈθɪŋkˌ əv /	denken an; sich ausdenken
	act out / æktˌ ˈaʊt /	nachspielen
	scene / siːn /	Szene

Rajiv loves surfing the Internet.

You can try on the clothes in the fitting room over there.

All shorts are on sale today.

Can I pay in cash?

This is the receipt. We bought quite a lot.

4	cover / ˈkʌvə /	Titelseite, Cover	
	have a drink /ˌhæv‿ə ˈdrɪŋk/	etwas trinken gehen	They had a drink in the café.
	label / ˈleɪbl /	beschriften	
5	**hang out** *(informal)* /hæŋ‿ˈaʊt/	sich aufhalten, abhängen	They always hang out together after school.
	for a change / fər‿ə ˈtʃeɪndʒ /	zur Abwechslung	
	next / nekst /	dann, als Nächstes	
7	hang around /ˌhæŋ‿əˈraʊnd/	herumhängen	
	scream / skriːm /	schreien; kreischen	Gillian screamed at her parents.
	crazy / ˈkreɪzi /	verrückt	
	check out sth /ˌtʃek‿ˈaʊt ˌsʌmθɪŋ/	etw untersuchen/überprüfen; *hier:* sich etw ansehen	
	album / ˈælbəm /	(Musik)album	What's your favourite album?
	yuck *(informal)* /jʌk/	igitt	
	guy *(informal)* / gaɪ /	Kerl, Typ	Charlie is a really nice guy.
	faint / feɪnt /	ohnmächtig werden	Karla doesn't remember what happened after she fainted.
	paramedic /ˌpærəˈmedɪk/	Rettungssanitäter/in	
	character / ˈkærɪktə /	Charakter; Figur	
	by heart / baɪ ˈhɑːt /	auswendig	
8	summary / ˈsʌməri /	Zusammenfassung; Inhaltsangabe	
	thank / θæŋk /	danken	She thanked him for his help.
	be wrong / bi ˈrɒŋ /	nicht stimmen	That's wrong. ↔ That's right.
	crowd / kraʊd /	(Menschen)menge, Zuschauermenge	
10	**least** / liːst /	am wenigsten	They went to the least expensive restaurant in town.
	source / sɔːs /	Quelle	
	use / juːs /	Verwendung, Gebrauch	
	survey / ˈsɜːveɪ /	Untersuchung, Umfrage	
11	**soccer** *(AE)* = **football** *(BE) (no pl)* / ˈsɒkə /	Fußball	She loves playing soccer.
	boxing *(no pl)* / ˈbɒksɪŋ /	Boxen	
	gymnastics *(only pl)* / dʒɪmˈnæstɪks /	Turnen	I do gymnastics every Tuesday.
	ice hockey *(no pl)* / ˈaɪs ˌhɒki /	Eishockey	
	net / net /	Netz	
	pompom / ˈpɒmpɒm /	Pompom, Puschel, Bommel	
	half time /ˌhɑːf ˈtaɪm/	Halbzeit	Haverstock were leading 3-0 at half time.
	linesman / ˈlaɪnzmən /	Linienrichter/in	
	penalty / ˈpenlti /	Strafe; Strafstoß, Elfmeter	
	kick / kɪk /	treten, schießen, kicken	He kicked the ball as hard as he could.
	kickoff / ˈkɪkˌɒf /	Anpfiff, Anstoß	
	professional / prəˈfeʃnəl /	Profi	
	equipment *(no pl)* / ɪˈkwɪpmənt /	Ausrüstung, Ausstattung	Here is some sports equipment.
	worst / wɜːst /	schlechteste(r, s), schlimmste(r, s)	worst ↔ best
	injury / ˈɪndʒəri /	Verletzung	Last year Charlie had a knee injury.
12	**introduce** /ˌɪntrəˈdjuːs/	vorstellen	Yesterday I introduced myself to the new teacher.
	myself / maɪˈself /	mich, mir; selbst	

cheer on / tʃɪərˌˈɒn /	anfeuern	
whether / ˈweðə /	ob	He asked me whether I was from Germany.
be in good shape / bi_ɪn ˌgʊd ˈʃeɪp /	in guter (körperlicher) Verfassung sein, in Form sein	
chant / tʃɑːnt /	Sprechgesang, Sprechchor	
enjoy oneself / ɪnˈdʒɔɪ wʌnˌself /	sich amüsieren; *hier:* sich vergnügen, Spaß haben	They are enjoying themselves.
ourselves / aʊəˈselvz /	uns; selbst	Let's buy ourselves lots of popcorn.
take time out / ˌteɪk ˌtaɪmˌˈaʊt /	eine Pause machen	
discuss / dɪˈskʌs /	besprechen; diskutieren	We should discuss what to do now.
strategy / ˈstrætədʒi /	Strategie, Taktik	
put on / pʊtˌˈɒn /	anziehen; *hier:* aufführen	
coach / kəʊtʃ /	Trainer(in)	Samira is a great tennis coach.
stunt / stʌnt /	Stunt; *hier:* Figur	
pyramid / ˈpɪrəmɪd /	Pyramide	
yourself (*pl* **yourselves**) / jəˈself, jəˈselvz /	dich, dir; selbst/ihr, euch; selbst	Look at yourself, Dad. You look fantastic!
watch sth / ˈwɒtʃ ˌsʌmθɪŋ /	etw beobachten; *hier:* auf etw achten	
weight / weɪt /	Gewicht	My uncle needs to lose some weight.
actually / ˈæktʃuəli /	eigentlich	The sweets were actually for Sam, not for you.
treat oneself to sth / ˈtriːt wʌnself tə ˌsʌmθɪŋ /	sich etw gönnen	
right now / raɪt ˈnaʊ /	gerade, jetzt, im Augenblick	I'm doing my homework right now.
championship / ˈtʃæmpiənʃɪp /	Meisterschaft	
itself / ɪtˈself /	sich (selbst); selbst	
risk / rɪsk /	Risiko, Gefahr	
take (*irr*) / teɪk /	(mit)nehmen; *hier:* brauchen	
hurray / hʊˈreɪ /	hurra	
herself / həˈself /	sich (selbst); selbst	
themselves / ðemˈselvz /	sich (selbst); selbst	
reader / ˈriːdə /	Leser/in	He has always been a big reader.

13

> **reflexive pronouns**
> myself, yourself,
> himself, herself,
> itself, ourselves,
> yourselves, themselves

World Series / ˌwɜːld ˈsɪəriːz /	*Ausscheidungsspiele/Finale der US-amerikanischen Baseball-Profiligen*	
Opening Day / ˌəʊpnɪŋ ˈdeɪ /	*erster Spieltag in US-amerika-nischen Baseball-Ligen*	
Super Bowl / ˈsuːpə ˌbəʊl /	*Meisterschaftsspiel im US-amerikanischen Profi-Football*	
fit (*irr*) / fɪt /	passen (zu)	
opponent / əˈpəʊnənt /	Gegner/in; Gegenspieler/in	
goal line / ˈgəʊlˌlaɪn /	Torlinie	
goalpost / ˈgəʊlˌpəʊst /	Torpfosten	
yard / jɑːd /	Yard (= 0,91 Meter)	
wide / waɪd /	breit	The streets are wide enough for large cars.
each / iːtʃ /	jeweils	
offensive / əˈfensɪv /	Angriffs-	
defensive / dɪˈfensɪv /	Verteidigungs-	

LL

14
15

	tackle sb /ˈtækl ˌsʌmbədi/	jdn angreifen	You have to tackle someone to get the ball.
	ball carrier /ˈbɔːl ˌkæriə/	Ballträger/in, Ballführer/in	
	block /blɒk/	blockieren, den Weg versperren	They didn't block the girl who was carrying the ball, so she scored.
	carry /ˈkæri/	tragen	
	score /skɔː/	einen Punkt machen, punkten	
	point /pɔɪnt/	Punkt	
18	choice /tʃɔɪs/	Wahl	
	basic /ˈbeɪsɪk/	grundlegend, wesentlich; Grund-	
	wordsearch /ˈwɜːdsɜːtʃ/	Wortsuchrätsel	
	roller soccer (no pl) /ˈrəʊlə ˌsɒkə/	Fußball auf Rollschuhen	
	wrist guard /ˈrɪst gɑːd/	Handgelenkschoner/-schützer	
	pad /pæd/	Polster; hier: Schoner, Schützer	
	elbow /ˈelbəʊ/	Ellbogen	
	aim /eɪm/	Ziel, Absicht	
P1	surf /sɜːf/	surfen	
P2	guard /gɑːd/	bewachen	
P4	date /deɪt/	Datum; hier: Verabredung, Date	
P6	meet up (irr) /ˌmiːtˈʌp/	jdn treffen	
	see you /ˈsiː juː/	bis dann, bis bald	
	feel like doing sth /ˌfiːl ˌlaɪk ˈduːɪŋ ˌsʌmθɪŋ/	Lust haben, etw zu tun	
	chill (informal) /tʃɪl/	chillen, relaxen	
P8	turn into /ˌtɜːnˈɪntʊ/	umwandeln in, verändern in	
P11	pronoun /ˈprəʊnaʊn/	Pronomen	
	personal pronoun /ˌpɜːsnəl ˈprəʊnaʊn/	Personalpronomen	
	reflexive pronoun /rɪˌfleksɪv ˈprəʊnaʊn/	Reflexivpronomen	
	himself /hɪmˈself/	sich (selbst); selbst	
P12	mirror /ˈmɪrə/	Spiegel	
	fall off /fɔːlˈɒf/	herunterfallen	
P13	name /neɪm/	(be)nennen	
P14	leaflet /ˈliːflət/	Prospekt, Broschüre	
M1	date /deɪt/	Datum; hier: Verabredung, Date	Their first date was to a restaurant.
	Oh my goodness! /əʊ maɪ ˈgʊdnes/	Ach du meine Güte!	
	like (informal) /laɪk/	ungefähr, bestimmt	
	ignore /ɪgˈnɔː/	ignorieren	Don't listen to him! Just ignore him!
	gimme (= give me) (informal) /ˈgɪmi/	gib mir	
	detail /ˈdiːteɪl/	Detail, Einzelheit	Please listen to every detail of his talk.
	lol (= laugh(ing) out loud) /ˌelˌəʊˈel/	Abkürzung für: laut lachen(d)	
	anyway /ˈeniˌweɪ/	jedenfalls, sowieso	I didn't go to the party. I don't like dancing and I didn't get an invitation anyway.
	be up to sth /bi ˌʌp tə ˌsʌmθɪŋ/	etw machen; etw vorhaben	
	gonna (= going to) (informal) /ˈgɒnə/	werden	

TIPP

Falsche Freunde

Im Englischen gibt es viele Wörter, die deutschen Wörtern zwar sehr ähnlich sehen, aber eine ganz andere Bedeutung haben. Man nennt sie deshalb *false friends* (falsche Freunde). Für diese Wörter kannst du dir ein Merkblatt „Vorsicht Falle" anlegen.

artist = Künstler/in (NICHT: Artist/in)

desert = Wüste (NICHT: Dessert, Nachtisch)

receipt = Beleg; Kassenbon (NICHT: Rezept)

gift = Geschenk (NICHT: Gift)

capital = Hauptstadt (NICHT: Kapital)

	keep sb guessing /ˌkiːp ˈsʌmbədi ˈgesɪŋ/	jdn auf die Folter spannen	
M2	actually /ˈæktʃuəli/	eigentlich; *hier:* wirklich, tatsächlich	
	direct speech /dɪˌrekt ˈspiːtʃ/	direkte Rede	
	reported speech /rɪˌpɔːtɪd ˈspiːtʃ/	indirekte Rede	
M3	**on time** /ɒn ˈtaɪm/	pünktlich; rechtzeitig	He is never on time in the mornings.
	clear /klɪə/	klar, eindeutig	
	mood /muːd/	Laune, Stimmung	Karla is in a very bad mood.
	realize sth /ˈrɪəlaɪz/	sich einer Sache bewusst werden, etw merken	
	have a good time /ˌhæv ə ˌɡʊd ˈtaɪm/	sich amüsieren, Spaß haben	Did you have a good time in Spain?
M4	**gentleman** /ˈdʒentlmən/	Gentleman, (vornehmer) Herr	My uncle is a real gentleman.
M5	plaza /ˈplɑːzə/	Marktplatz; *hier: Essbereich in einem Einkaufszentrum*	
M7	trophy /ˈtrəʊfi/	Trophäe, Preis	
M9	**sweat** /swet/	schwitzen	It's so hot, I'm sweating!
	moan /məʊn/	stöhnen	Stop moaning, please!
	exhausted /ɪɡˈzɔːstɪd/	erschöpft	He is always exhausted after work.
	skiing /ˈskiːɪŋ/	Skifahren, Skilaufen	
	Austria /ˈɒstriə/	Österreich	I love skiing in Austria.
	the other day /ðiˌʌðə ˈdeɪ/	neulich, vor einigen Tagen	I met Boris the other day.
	shark /ʃɑːk/	Hai(fisch)	
	convincing /kənˈvɪnsɪŋ/	überzeugend	
	regular /ˈreɡjʊlə/	regelmäßig; gleichmäßig	She goes jogging regularly.
	proper /ˈprɒpə/	korrekt, richtig	He is the proper person for the job.
	behaviour *(no pl)* /bɪˈheɪvjə/	Verhalten, Benehmen	
	be more likely to do sth /bi mɔː ˌlaɪkli tə ˈduː ˌsʌmθɪŋ/	eher/wahrscheinlicher etw tun	
	smoke /sməʊk/	rauchen	Stop smoking, please!
	female /ˈfiːmeɪl/	weiblich	
	male /meɪl/	männlich	male ↔ female
M10	**challenge** /ˈtʃælɪndʒ/	Herausforderung	Maths has always been a challenge for him.
	butt *(informal)* /bʌt/	Glimmstängel, Kippe	
	quit *(irr)* /kwɪt/	aufhören (mit)	
	fit in /fɪt ˈɪn/	sich einfügen, dazupassen	
	seem /siːm/	scheinen	
	peer pressure *(no pl)* /ˈpɪə ˌpreʃə/	Druck durch Gleichaltrige, sozialer Druck	
	stressed /strest/	gestresst	What's wrong with you? Are you stressed?
	nicotine gum *(no pl)* /ˈnɪkətiːn ɡʌm/	Nikotinkaugummi	
	cigarette /ˌsɪɡəˈret/	Zigarette	
	less /les/	weniger	The doctor told her to eat less sugar.
	put out sth /pʊt ˈaʊt ˌsʌmθɪŋ/	etw ausmachen; etw löschen	put out ↔ put on
	headache /ˈhedeɪk/	Kopfschmerzen, Kopfweh	I have a terrible headache.

gain / geɪn /	erwerben; *hier:* zunehmen		
pound / paʊnd /	Pfund		
skin / skɪn /	Haut	Her skin has gone red.	
patch / pætʃ /	Pflaster		
ruin / ˈruːɪn /	ruinieren, zerstören	First the cat ruined the sofa, then the carpet.	

CC	cheer / tʃɪə /	Jubel
	gonna (= going to) *(informal)* / ˈɡɒnə /	werden
	challenge / ˈtʃælɪndʒ /	Herausforderung
	mighty / ˈmaɪti /	gewaltig, mächtig, stark
	reach (for) / riːtʃ /	greifen (nach)
	chat-up line / ˈtʃætʌp ˌlaɪn /	Anmachspruch
	ask sb out / ˌɑːsk sʌmbədiˈaʊt /	sich mit jdm verabreden
	romantic / rəʊˈmæntɪk /	romantisch
	attention *(no pl)* / əˈtenʃn /	Achtung, Aufmerksamkeit
	keep doing sth / kiːp ˈduːɪŋ ˌsʌmθɪŋ /	etw weiter tun; *hier:* etw wiederholt/immer wieder tun
	get lost / get ˈlɒst /	sich verirren, sich verlaufen
	borrow / ˈbɒrəʊ /	leihen
	accept / əkˈsept /	aufnehmen, zulassen; akzeptieren
	application / ˌæplɪˈkeɪʃn /	Bewerbung

TIPP

Vokabeln umschreiben
Wenn du dir ein Wort einfach nicht merken kannst, versuche es zu umschreiben. Überlege dir, was das Wort bedeutet, und schreibe dir einen kurzen englischen Satz dazu auf, zum Beispiel:

vegetarian = someone who doesn't eat meat
receipt = it shows you what you bought and how much it cost

Theme 6 – California

1	brainstorm / ˈbreɪnˌstɔːm /	ein Brainstorming machen	
2	lots (= a lot) *(informal)* / lɒts /	viel, jede Menge	
	fill in / fɪlˈɪn /	ausfüllen	
	landscape / ˈlændˌskeɪp /	Landschaft	
	hill / hɪl /	Hügel	A hill is smaller than a mountain.
	visitor / ˈvɪzɪtə /	Besucher/in	visit – visitor
	national park / ˌnæʃnl ˈpɑːk /	Nationalpark	
	nearly / ˈnɪəli /	fast, beinahe	nearly = almost
	industry / ˈɪndəstri /	Branche, Gewerbe; Industrie	
	theme park / ˈθiːm ˌpɑːk /	Themenpark; Freizeitpark	
	attract / əˈtrækt /	anziehen	
	dry / draɪ /	trocken	dry ⟷ wet
	forest fire / ˈfɒrɪst ˌfaɪə /	Waldbrand	
	stunt performer / ˈstʌnt pəˌfɔːmə /	Stuntman, Stuntgirl	
	perform / pəˈfɔːm /	vorführen; aufführen; *hier:* durchführen	
	movie *(AE)* = film *(BE)* / ˈmuːvi /	(Kino-, Spiel)film	They are watching a movie.
	film / fɪlm /	filmen, drehen	
	earthquake / ˈɜːθˌkweɪk /	Erdbeben	Earthquakes can be very dangerous.
	border patrol guard / ˌbɔːdə pəˈtrəʊl ɡɑːd /	Grenzposten, Grenzbeamter/beamtin	
	protect / prəˈtekt /	(be)schützen	A helmet protects your head.

border / ˈbɔːdə /	Grenze	There is a border between the US and Mexico.
lifeguard / ˈlaɪfˌgɑːd /	Rettungsschwimmer/in; Bademeister/in	
agree on / əˈgriː‿ɒn /	einer Meinung sein über; *hier:* sich einigen auf	
4 be about / bi‿əˈbaʊt /	handeln von	
in one go / ˌɪn wʌn ˈgəʊ /	in einem Durchgang, auf einmal	
wildfire / ˈwaɪldˌfaɪə /	Lauffeuer, nicht zu kontrollie- render (Großflächen)brand	
put out sth / pʊt‿ˈaʊt ˌsʌmθɪŋ /	etw ausmachen; etw löschen	We have to put out the fire before we leave.
home / həʊm /	Zuhause, Heim; *hier:* Haus	
although / ɔːlˈðəʊ /	obwohl, obgleich	Although she has a mobile phone, she never uses it.
close / kləʊs /	nah(e)	
luck *(no pl)* / lʌk /	Glück	Oh, what luck!
none / nʌn /	keine(r, s)	
damage / ˈdæmɪdʒ /	schaden; (be)schädigen	Last month's storm damaged lots of trees.
across / əˈkrɒs /	über; *hier:* im ganzen	
hundreds of thousands *(only pl)* / ˌhʌndrədz‿əv ˈθaʊzndz /	Hunderttausende	
around / əˈraʊnd /	um; *hier:* ungefähr	
bravery *(no pl)* / ˈbreɪvəri /	Tapferkeit, Mut	
helicopter / ˈheliˌkɒptə /	Hubschrauber	
burn *(irr)* / bɜːn /	(ver)brennen	burn – burnt/burned – burnt/burned
flame / fleɪm /	Flamme	He sat by the fire and looked at the flames.
help out / ˌhelp‿ˈaʊt /	(aus)helfen, unterstützen	
responsible / rɪˈspɒnsəbl /	verantwortlich	
damage *(no pl)* / ˈdæmɪdʒ /	Schaden; (Be)schädigung	damage (verb) – damage (noun)
luckily / ˈlʌkɪli /	glücklicherweise	
5 **get along (with sb)** / get‿əˈlɒŋ /	sich (mit jdm) verstehen	Gillian and Cheryl get along really well.
work long hours / wɜːk ˌlɒŋ‿ˈaʊəz /	lange arbeiten; Überstunden machen	
shift work *(no pl)* / ˈʃɪft ˌwɜːk /	Schichtarbeit, Schichtdienst	My mum does shift work in a hospital.
outdoors / ˌaʊtˈdɔːz /	im Freien, draußen	
indoors / ɪnˈdɔːz /	drinnen	indoors ↔ outdoors
martial art / ˌmɑːʃl‿ˈɑːt /	Kampfsport(art)	
make-up artist / ˌmeɪkʌp‿ˈɑːtɪst /	Maskenbildner/in, Visagist/in	
cameraman/-woman / ˈkæmrəˌmæn, ˈkæmrəˌwʊmən /	Kameramann/-frau	
programmer / ˈprəʊˌgræmə /	Programmierer/in	A programmer writes computer programs.
working hours *(only pl)* / ˈwɜːkɪŋ‿ˌaʊəz /	Arbeitszeit	Doctors often have long working hours.
show sb around / ˌʃəʊ sʌmbədi‿əˈraʊnd /	jdn herumführen	
gallery walk / ˈgæləri wɔːk /	Galerierundgang	

7	north-west / ˌnɔːθˈwest /	Nordwesten	It will be cold in the north-west of
	south-east / ˌsaʊθˈiːst /	Südosten	Scotland, but warm in the
			south-east of England.
	acre / ˈeɪkə /	Angelsächsisches Flächenmaß,	
		entspricht etwa 4047 m²	
	found / faʊnd /	gründen	
	attraction / əˈtrækʃn /	Attraktion	
	pelican / ˈpelɪkən /	Pelikan	
	eagle / ˈiːgl /	Adler	Look! There is a black eagle!
	owl / aʊl /	Eule	Owls only fly at night.
	black bear / ˈblæk beə /	Schwarzbär	
	cougar / ˈkuːgə /	Puma	
	scenery (no pl) / ˈsiːnəri /	Landschaft	
	dune / djuːn /	Düne	
	ghost town / ˈgəʊst taʊn /	Geisterstadt	
	low / ləʊ /	niedrig	low ⟷ high
	sea level (no pl) / ˈsiː ˌlevl /	Meeresspiegel	
	lizard / ˈlɪzəd /	Eidechse, Echse	Lizards usually live in hot places.
	scorpion / ˈskɔːpiən /	Skorpion	
	coyote / kɔɪˈəʊti /	Kojote	
	cliff / klɪf /	Klippe, Kliff	
	waterfall / ˈwɔːtəˌfɔːl /	Wasserfall	The waterfall is really loud.
	cave / keɪv /	Höhle	Caves are dark and scary.
	fox / fɒks /	Fuchs	There are a lot of foxes in big cities.
	sea lion / ˈsiː ˌlaɪən /	Seelöwe	
	blue whale / ˈbluː ˌweɪl /	Blauwal	
8	find out about / faɪnd ˈaʊt əˌbaʊt /	sich informieren über	
	two-week / tuː ˈwiːk /	zweiwöchig	
	experience / ɪkˈspɪəriəns /	erleben, erfahren	
9	Front of Line Pass	Ticket ohne Wartezeit	
	/ ˌfrʌnt əv ˈlaɪn ˌpɑːs /		
	day ticket / ˈdeɪ ˌtɪkɪt /	Tageskarte, Tagesticket	
	opening times (only pl)	Öffnungszeiten	
	/ ˈəʊpnɪŋ ˌtaɪmz /		
	non- / nɒn /	nicht-	
	box office / ˈbɒks ˌɒfɪs /	Kasse (im Kino/Theater)	
	hours (only pl) / ˈaʊəz /	(Öffnungs)zeiten	
	pass / pɑːs /	Pass; hier: Eintrittskarte, Ticket	
	VIP (= very important person)	VIP, Promi	
	/ ˌviː aɪ ˈpiː /		
	entrance / ˈentrəns /	Eingang; hier: Eintritt(sgebühr)	
	reservation / ˌrezəˈveɪʃn /	Reservierung	
	rate / reɪt /	Rate, Quote; hier: Preis, Kosten	
	at any time / æt ˈeni taɪm /	jederzeit, zu jeder Zeit	
	general / ˈdʒenrəl /	allgemein, generell	
	except / ɪkˈsept /	außer, bis auf	
10	take a tour / ˌteɪk ə ˈtʊə /	an einer Führung/Tour teilnehmen,	
		eine Tour/Führung machen	
	get ready (for sth) / get ˈredi /	sich (für etw) bereit machen	
	dinosaur / ˈdaɪnəˌsɔː /	Dinosaurier	Dinosaurs lived a very long time ago.

I just wanted to phone to ask about your opening times.

Can I make a reservation for 8 pm, please?

	jungle /ˈdʒʌŋgl/	Dschungel, Urwald	Tarzan grew up in the jungle.
	alive /əˈlaɪv/	lebendig	
	human /ˈhjuːmən/	menschlich	
	count on sb /kaʊnt ɒn ˈsʌmbədi/	auf jdn zählen	
	shock /ʃɒk/	Schock	He got a shock when he looked in the mirror.
	race /reɪs/	rennen; *hier:* heftig schlagen, rasen	
	strike *(irr)* /straɪk/	(zu)schlagen	
	take sth into one's own hands /teɪk ˌsʌmθɪŋ ˌɪntə wʌnz ˌˈəʊn hændz/	etw selbst in die Hand nehmen	
	battle /ˈbætl/	Kampf, Schlacht	Lots of people died in the battle.
	human /ˈhjuːmən/	Mensch	
	exhausted /ɪgˈzɔːstɪd/	erschöpft	
11	screen /skriːn/	Leinwand; Bildschirm	
	shark /ʃɑːk/	Hai(fisch)	Sharks are intelligent animals.
	happy ending /ˌhæpiˈendɪŋ/	Happyend, gutes Ende	
12	type /taɪp/	Art; Typ, Sorte	
	deal with /ˈdiːl wɪð/	sich befassen mit; *hier:* handeln von	
	hate *(no pl)* /heɪt/	Hass	hate ⟷ love
	any /ˈeni/	irgendwelche, irgendein(e); *hier:* jede(r, s)	
	animated film /ˌænɪmeɪtɪd ˈfɪlm/	(Zeichen)trickfilm, Animationsfilm	
	computer-animated /kəmˌpjuːtəˈæniˌmeɪtɪd/	computeranimiert	
	myth /mɪθ/	Mythos	
	drama /ˈdrɑːmə/	Schauspielerei; *hier:* Drama, Tragödie	"Romeo and Juliet" is a drama.
	romance /rəʊˈmæns/	Romanze; *hier:* Liebesfilm	
	comedy /ˈkɒmədi/	Komödie	Comedies are great. They make me laugh.
	fantasy /ˈfæntəsi/	Fantasie; *hier:* Fantasy	
13	**(the) United States** /juːˌnaɪtɪd ˈsteɪts/	Vereinigte Staaten	the United States = the US
	running time /ˈrʌnɪŋ ˌtaɪm/	Laufzeit	
	cast /kɑːst/	Besetzung, Ensemble	
	director /dəˈrektə/	Direktor/in, Leiter/in; *hier:* Regisseur/in	
	celebrity /səˈlebrəti/	berühmte Persönlichkeit, Star	
	case /keɪs/	Fall	
	enter /ˈentə/	betreten	enter = go or come into a place
	jewellery *(no pl)* /ˈdʒuːəlri/	Schmuck	She loves jewellery, especially rings.
	post sth /ˈpəʊst ˌsʌmθɪŋ/	etw schicken; *hier:* etw ins Internet stellen, etw posten	
	social media /ˌsəʊʃl ˈmiːdiə/	soziale Medien, Social Media	
	site *(informal)* /saɪt/	Website	
	identify sb /aɪˈdentɪfaɪ ˌsʌmbədi/	jdn identifizieren	
	arrest sb /əˈrest ˌsʌmbədi/	jdn verhaften	The police arrested the criminals.
	prison /ˈprɪzn/	Gefängnis	Time for you to go to prison!

	the rich *(no pl)* / ðə ˈrɪtʃ /	die Reichen
	the famous *(no pl)* / ðə ˈfeɪməs /	die Berühmten
	critic / ˈkrɪtɪk /	Kritiker/in, Rezensent/in
	burglary / ˈbɜːɡləri /	Einbruch, Einbruchdiebstahl
	judge / dʒʌdʒ /	urteilen, entscheiden
	criminal / ˈkrɪmɪnl /	Verbrecher/in, Kriminelle/r
	series *(only pl)* / ˈsɪəriːz /	Serie, Reihe
14	look around / ˌlʊk_əˈraʊnd /	sich umsehen/umschauen (in)
	personal / ˈpɜːsnəl /	persönlich; privat
P2	tick / tɪk /	abhaken, ankreuzen
P3	kilogram / ˈkɪləˌɡræm /	Kilo(gramm)
	nugget / ˈnʌɡɪt /	Klumpen, Nugget
	amateur / ˈæmətə /	Amateur/in, Hobby-
	digger / ˈdɪɡə /	Bagger; *hier:* Gräber/in
	litre / ˈliːtə /	Liter
	wine / waɪn /	Wein
	Californian / ˌkæləˈfɔːniən /	kalifornisch
P4	research *(no pl)* / riˈsɜːtʃ /	Forschung; Recherche
	at the moment / æt ðə ˈməʊmənt /	im Moment
P5	quiz sb / ˈkwɪz_ˌsʌmbədi /	jdn befragen/prüfen
P6	sudden / ˈsʌdn /	plötzlich
	hike / haɪk /	wandern
	trail / treɪl /	Weg, Pfad
	available / əˈveɪləbl /	verfügbar
	can / kæn /	Dose; *hier:* Mülleimer
	bear / beə /	Bär
	report / rɪˈpɔːt /	berichten, melden
	bear-proof / ˈbeəˌpruːf /	sicher vor Bären; bärensicher
	approach / əˈprəʊtʃ /	sich nähern, zukommen auf
	yell / jel /	laut schreien
	scare away / ˌskeər_əˈweɪ /	verscheuchen, abschrecken
P7	acrostic / əˈkrɒstɪk /	Akrostichon *(Text, bei dem bestimmte Buchstaben jeder Zeile von oben nach unten gelesen ein Wort ergeben)*
P8	set *(irr)* / set /	(ein)stellen; (fest)setzen
P9	in the end / ˌɪn ðiˌˈend /	am Ende, zum Schluss
P11	regular / ˈreɡjʊlə /	regelmäßig; gleichmäßig
	may / meɪ /	können; *hier:* vielleicht
	lines *(only pl)* / laɪnz /	Text
	part / pɑːt /	Teil; *hier:* Rolle
M1	**sandy** / ˈsændi /	sandig
	relate to sth / rɪˈleɪt tə ˌsʌmθɪŋ /	Zugang zu etw finden
	need to / ˈniːd tə /	müssen
	snowflake / ˈsnəʊˌfleɪk /	Schneeflocke
	call / kɔːl /	(Telefon)anruf; *hier:* Ruf
	whistle / wɪsl /	pfeifen
	pine / paɪn /	Kiefer, Pinie
	them (= these) *(informal)* / ðem /	diese

TIPP

Wortbedeutungen erschließen
Bevor du zum Wörterbuch greifst, um die Bedeutung eines englischen Wortes nachzuschlagen, solltest du dir das Wort genau ansehen. Vielleicht ist es ein Wort, das aus zwei Einzelwörtern besteht. Die Bedeutung kannst du erschließen, wenn dir ein Bestandteil schon bekannt ist, zum Beispiel:
forest fire
shift work
fitting room
mashed potatoes

TIPP

Neue Wörter verstehen
Manche Adjektive verändern mit einer Vorsilbe wie zum Beispiel *un-* ihre Bedeutung. Die Vorsilbe *un-* weist auf das Gegenteil hin:

healthy ↔ unhealthy
friendly ↔ unfriendly
important ↔ unimportant
... ↔ ...

They went to a lovely sandy beach.

If it gets worse, I'll need to go to the doctor's.

Can you whistle with your fingers?

	pass on by / ˌpɑːs ˌɒn ˈbaɪ /	vorbeifahren	
	lost / lɒst /	verloren	His wallet is lost. Will he find it again?
	angel / ˈeɪndʒl /	Engel	angel ↔ devil
	royal / ˈrɔɪəl /	königlich	The British royal family live in Buckingham Palace.
	age / eɪdʒ /	Alter; *hier:* Zeitalter, Ära	
	fortune / ˈfɔːtʃən /	Vermögen, Reichtum	The castle cost a fortune.
	fame *(no pl)* / feɪm /	Ruhm	Not all actors enjoy fame.
	wipe out / ˌwaɪp ˈaʊt /	auswischen; *hier:* auslöschen	
	the Ring of Fire / ˌrɪŋ ˌəv ˈfaɪə /	der (pazifische) Feuergürtel/ Feuerring (*Vulkanreihe im Pazifischen Ozean*)	
M3	emergency / ɪˈmɜːdʒnsi /	Notfall	If it's not an emergency, then you have to wait to see the doctor.
	service / ˈsɜːvɪs /	Service; Bedienung; *hier:* Dienst, Hilfe	
	dial / ˈdaɪəl /	wählen	Sorry, I think I dialled the wrong number.
	fire department *(AE)* =	Feuerwehr	
	fire brigade *(BE)* / ˈfaɪə dɪˌpɑːtmənt, ˈfaɪə brɪˌɡeɪd /		There goes the fire brigade!
	ambulance / ˈæmbjʊləns /	Krankenwagen, Rettungswagen	An ambulance takes people to hospital.
	operator / ˈɒpəˌreɪtə /	Telefonist/in, Vermittlung	
	caller / ˈkɔːlə /	Anrufer/in	caller – call
	catch fire / ˌkætʃ ˈfaɪə /	in Brand geraten, Feuer fangen	The car caught fire.
	right / raɪt /	richtig; *hier:* genau, direkt	
	anybody / ˈeniˌbɒdi /	(irgend)jemand	Did anybody see what happened?
	hurt / hɜːt /	verletzt, verwundet	Her hand is badly hurt.
M5	exclusive / ɪkˈskluːsɪv /	exklusiv	
	couple / ˈkʌpl /	Paar	They are a nice couple.
M6	fight / faɪt /	Kampf, Streit	
	audition / ɔːˈdɪʃn /	Vorsprechen; Vorsingen; Vortanzen; Vorspielen	She went to an audition and got a job in a musical show.
M7	learn about / ˌlɜːn əˈbaʊt /	erfahren von/über	
	fill in / fɪl ˈɪn /	ausfüllen	Charlie was able to fill in the form online.
	form / fɔːm /	Form; *hier:* Formular	
	act out / ˌækt ˈaʊt /	nachspielen; *hier:* spielen	
	scene / siːn /	Szene	
M8	modelling *(no pl)* / ˈmɒdlɪŋ /	Modeln; Model-	
	advise / ədˈvaɪz /	(be)raten	
	act / ækt /	Handlung; *hier:* Nummer, Darstellung	
	speech / spiːtʃ /	Rede	
	judge / dʒʌdʒ /	Richter/in; *hier:* Jurymitglied	
CC	licence plate *(AE)* / ˈlaɪsns ˌpleɪt /	Nummernschild	
	republic / rɪˈpʌblɪk /	Republik	

In den USA lassen sich viele Leute besondere Nummernschilder für ihre Autos anfertigen. Die Buchstaben- und Ziffernabfolge ergibt ausgesprochen z. B. einen kurzen Satz, einen Slogan oder den Namen des Autobesitzers oder der Autobesitzerin. Sie heißen deshalb auch *vanity plates*, also Eitelkeits-Schilder.

Die Vokabeln aus dem *Optional – Jobs* kannst du im *English-German dictionary* ab Seite 253 nachschlagen.

Hier findest du die Wörter, die in deinem Buch vorkommen.

- Die **fett gedruckten** Wörter solltest du dir merken.
- Wenn du den *More*-Teil bearbeitest, solltest du dir auch die grün gedruckten Wörter merken.
- 1/1 bedeutet: Dieses Wort kommt in *Theme* 1, Aufgabe 1 vor.
- I bedeutet: Dieses Wort kommt in Band I (5. Klasse) vor. Entsprechend steht II für Band 2 (6. Klasse) und III für Band 3 (7. Klasse).
- Folgende Abkürzungen werden noch verwendet:

  Intro = S. 4 – 7   LL = *Land & Leute*   P = *Practice*
  M = *More*   CC = *Camden Chronicle*   Op = *Optional – Jobs*

A

a/an /ə, ən/ ein(e) I
a bit /ə ˈbɪt/ ein bisschen II
a box of chocolates /ə bɒks ˌəv ˈtʃɒkləts/ eine Schachtel Pralinen II
a day /ə ˈdeɪ/ pro/am Tag III
a few /ə ˈfjuː/ einige III
a little /ə ˈlɪtl/ ein bisschen II
a lot (of) /ə ˈlɒt/ sehr; viel(e) I
a week /ə ˈwiːk/ pro/in der Woche III
a year /ə ˈjɪə/ pro/im Jahr II
the A-B-C's *(AE) (informal)* /ði ˌeɪbiːˈsiːz/ das ABC; das Einmaleins 4/CC
be able to do sth /bi ˌeɪbl tə ˈduː ˌsʌmθɪŋ/ etw tun können II
about /əˈbaʊt/ über I; ungefähr 3/13
be about /bi əˈbaʊt/ handeln von 6/4
above /əˈbʌv/ über 4/9; oben 4/14
abroad /əˈbrɔːd/ im Ausland 3/M6
accent /ˈæksnt/ Akzent 1/3
accept /əkˈsept/ aufnehmen, zulassen; akzeptieren 5/CC
accessory /əkˈsesəri/ Accessoire; Zubehör 2/P13
accident /ˈæksɪdnt/ Unfall III
according to /əˈkɔːdɪŋ tʊ/ laut, nach, gemäß 3/16
acre /ˈeɪkə/ *Angelsächsisches Flächenmaß, entspricht etwa 4047 m² 6/7*
across /əˈkrɒs/ über III
across /əˈkrɒs/ im ganzen 6/4
across the street /əˌkrɒs ðə ˈstriːt/ gegenüber(liegend) 3/CC
acrostic /əˈkrɒstɪk/ Akrostichon *(Text, bei dem bestimmte Buchstaben jeder Zeile von oben nach unten gelesen ein Wort ergeben)* 6/P7
act /ækt/ Handlung; Nummer, Darstellung 6/M8
act /ækt/ handeln, sich verhalten 1/8
act as sth /ˈækt ˌæz ˌsʌmθɪŋ/ als etw dienen 1/M7
act out /ˌækt ˈaʊt/ spielen 6/M7
act out /ˌækt ˈaʊt/ nachspielen 2/M7
acting *(no pl)* /ˈæktɪŋ/ Schauspielerei, Schauspiel- 1/5
action /ˈækʃn/ Handlung; Aktion 4/M1
take action /ˌteɪk ˈækʃn/ handeln, etw unternehmen 1/13
active /ˈæktɪv/ aktiv II
activist /ˈæktɪvɪst/ Aktivist/in 1/M5
activity /ækˈtɪvəti/ Aktivität I
actor/actress /ˈæktə, ˈæktrəs/ Schauspieler/in I
actually /ˈæktʃuəli/ eigentlich 5/12
actually /ˈæktʃuəli/ wirklich, tatsächlich 5/M2
ad (= advertisement) /æd, ədˈvɜːtɪsmənt/ Anzeige; Werbung 3/2
adapt (to) /əˈdæpt/ sich anpassen 4/12
add /æd/ hinzufügen III
address /əˈdres/ Adresse III
adult /ˈædʌlt/ Erwachsene/r 3/CC
advantage /ədˈvɑːntɪdʒ/ Vorteil 1/M4
adventure /ədˈventʃə/ Abenteuer, Erlebnis II
advert (= advertisement) /ˈædvɜːt, ədˈvɜːtɪsmənt/ Anzeige, Inserat; Werbung III
advertising *(no pl)* /ˈædvəˌtaɪzɪŋ/ Werbung, Reklame 2/M2
advice *(no pl)* /ədˈvaɪs/ Rat(schlag) 1/M5
advise /ədˈvaɪz/ (be)raten 6/M8
be afraid (of sth/sb) /ˌbi əˈfreɪd/ (vor etw/jdm) Angst haben II
Africa /ˈæfrɪkə/ Afrika III
African /ˈæfrɪkən/ Afrikaner/in 2/M5; afrikanisch 2/M5
African American /ˌæfrɪkən əˈmerɪkən/ Afroamerikaner/in; afroamerikanisch 4/1
after /ˈɑːftə/ nach I
after /ˈɑːftə/ nachdem II
after that /ˌɑːftə ˈðæt/ anschließend, danach I
afternoon /ˌɑːftəˈnuːn/ Nachmittag I
in the afternoon /ˌɪn ðiˈɑːftənuːn/ am Nachmittag, nachmittags I
this afternoon /ˌðɪs ˌɑːftəˈnuːn/ heute Nachmittag II
afterwards /ˈɑːftəwədz/ danach, anschließend; später II
again /əˈgen/ wieder, noch (ein)mal I
against /əˈgenst/ gegen II
age /eɪdʒ/ Alter II
age /eɪdʒ/ Zeitalter, Ära 6/M1
(three days) ago /əˈgəʊ/ vor (drei Tagen) II
agree (with sb) /əˈgriː/ (jdm)

zustimmen II

agree on /əˈgriː‿ɒn/ einer Meinung sein über; sich einigen auf 6/2

agreed /əˈgriːd/ vereinbart; akzeptiert 3/16

aim /eɪm/ Ziel, Absicht 5/18

air *(no pl)* /eə/ Luft 1/10

air-conditioned /ˈeə kənˌdɪʃnd/ klimatisiert, mit Klimaanlage 2/P7

airport /ˈeəˌpɔːt/ Flughafen II

aisle /aɪl/ Gang 4/CC

alarm clock /əˈlɑːm ˌklɒk/ Wecker II

album /ˈælbəm/ (Musik)album 5/7

alien /ˈeɪliən/ Außerirdische(r), Alien II

alive /əˈlaɪv/ lebendig 6/10

all /ɔːl/ alle(s) I

all- /ɔːl/ ausschließlich, ganz 1/10

all in all /ˌɔːl‿ɪn‿ˈɔːl/ alles in allem 2/M4

all over /ˈɔːl‿ˌəʊvə/ überall in 2/15

all over the world /ˈɔːl‿ˌəʊvə ðə ˈwɜːld/ auf der ganzen Welt 3/17

all the time /ˌɔːl ðə ˈtaɪm/ dauernd, ständig 2/6

allow /əˈlaʊ/ erlauben 2/6

allowed /əˈlaʊd/ erlaubt III

be allowed to do sth /bi‿əˌlaʊd tə ˈduː ˌsʌmθɪŋ/ etw tun dürfen 1/3

almost /ˈɔːlməʊst/ fast, beinahe III

alone /əˈləʊn/ allein II

along /əˈlɒŋ/ (zusammen) mit 2/P13

get along (with sb) /get‿əˈlɒŋ/ sich (mit jdm) verstehen 6/5

aloud /əˈlaʊd/ laut 2/10

already /ɔːlˈredi/ schon II

also /ˈɔːlsəʊ/ auch I

although /ɔːlˈðəʊ/ obwohl, obgleich 6/4

altogether /ˌɔːltəˈgeðə/ völlig, ganz; insgesamt III

always /ˈɔːlweɪz/ immer I

am (= ante meridiem) /ˈeɪˈem, ˌænti məˈrɪdiəm/ morgens,

vormittags *(nur hinter Uhrzeit zwischen Mitternacht und 12 Uhr mittags)* III

amateur /ˈæmətə/ Amateur/in, Hobby- 6/P3

amazing *(informal)* /əˈmeɪzɪŋ/ toll, unglaublich II

ambulance /ˈæmbjʊləns/ Krankenwagen, Rettungswagen 6/M3

America /əˈmerɪkə/ Amerika 4/1

American /əˈmerɪkən/ Amerikaner/in 2/2; amerikanisch 1/1

ancestor /ˈænsestə/ Vorfahr(e)/ Vorfahrin 4/M3

ancestry /ˈænsestri/ Abstammung 4/M3

and /ænd/ und I

angel /ˈeɪndʒl/ Engel 6/M1

angry /ˈæŋgri/ verärgert; zornig; wütend II

animal /ˈænɪml/ Tier I

animated /ˈænɪˌmeɪtɪd/ animiert 2/15

animated film /ˈænɪmeɪtɪd ˈfɪlm/ (Zeichen)trickfilm, Animationsfilm 6/12

announce /əˈnaʊns/ bekannt geben, verkünden 4/M1

another /əˈnʌðə/ noch ein(e, r, s) 3/17; ein anderer/anderes, eine andere 4/12

answer /ˈɑːnsə/ Antwort I

answer /ˈɑːnsə/ (be)antworten III

any /ˈeni/ irgendwelche, irgendein(e); etwas II

any /ˈeni/ jede(r, s) 6/12

not any /nɒt‿ˈeni/ kein(e) II

at any time /æt‿ˈeni taɪm/ jederzeit, zu jeder Zeit 6/9

anybody /ˈeniˌbɒdi/ (irgend) jemand 6/M3

not anymore /ˌnɒt eniˈmɔː/ nicht mehr II

anything /ˈeniˌθɪŋ/ (irgend)(et)was II

not anything /nɒt‿ˈeniˌθɪŋ/ nichts II

Anything else? /ˌeniθɪŋ‿ˈels/ Darf es noch etwas sein? I

anyway /ˈeniˌweɪ/ jedenfalls, sowieso 5/M1

apartment /əˈpɑːtmənt/ Wohnung II

apologize /əˈpɒləˌdʒaɪz/ sich entschuldigen 4/8

appear /əˈpɪə/ erscheinen 3/M1

apple /ˈæpl/ Apfel II

apple pie /ˈæpl ˌpaɪ/ gedeckter Apfelkuchen 2/2

application /ˌæplɪˈkeɪʃn/ Bewerbung 5/CC

approach /əˈprəʊtʃ/ sich nähern, zukommen auf 6/P6

April /ˈeɪprəl/ April I

Arabic /ˈærəbɪk/ Arabisch; arabisch 2/9

area /ˈeəriə/ Gebiet, Region; Viertel, Gegend III

argument /ˈɑːgjʊmənt/ Auseinandersetzung, Streit; Argument 2/M4

arithmetic *(no pl)* /əˈrɪθmətɪk/ Rechnen 4/CC

Noah's ark /ˌnəʊəz ˈɑːk/ die Arche Noah 4/CC

armchair /ˈɑːmˌtʃeə/ Sessel, Lehnstuhl I

army /ˈɑːmi/ Armee, Heer Intro

around /əˈraʊnd/ um III

around /əˈraʊnd/ herum, umher II

around /əˈraʊnd/ ungefähr 6/4

arrest sb /əˈrest ˌsʌmbədi/ jdn verhaften 6/13

arrive /əˈraɪv/ ankommen I

art /ɑːt/ Kunst I

article /ˈɑːtɪkl/ Artikel 1/M1

artificial /ˌɑːtɪˈfɪʃl/ künstlich 2/M2

artist /ˈɑːtɪst/ Künstler/in 3/M1

as /əz/ als II

as /əz/ wie 4/8

as … as /əz əz/ (genau)so … wie … II

as soon as /əz‿ˈsuːn‿əz/ sobald 4/15

Asia /ˈeɪʒə/ Asien Intro

Asian /ˈeɪʃn/ asiatisch 3/CC

Asian American /ˌeɪʒən‿əˈmerɪkən/ Amerikaner/in asiatischer Herkunft; asiatisch-amerikanisch 4/2

ask /ɑːsk/ fragen; bitten I

ask for directions /ˌɑːsk fə dɪˈrekʃnz/ nach dem Weg fragen III

ask sb out /ˌɑːsk sʌmbədɪˈaʊt/ sich mit jdm verabreden 5/CC

vet's assistant /ˈvets_əˌsɪstnt/ Tierarzthelfer/in Op2

astronaut /ˈæstrəˌnɔːt/ Astronaut/in I

at /æt/ auf, an, in, bei; um I

at all times /ətˌɔːl ˈtaɪmz/ immer, jederzeit 1/P4

at first /ət ˈfɜːst/ anfangs, zuerst II

at least /ət ˈliːst/ mindestens, wenigstens 3/17

ate /eɪt/ *Vergangenheitsform von „eat"*

athlete /ˈæθliːt/ Athlet/in III

the Atlantic (Ocean) /ðiˌətˌlæntɪk(ˌˈəʊʃn)/ der Atlantische Ozean III

attack /əˈtæk/ angreifen I

attention (no pl) /əˈtenʃn/ Achtung, Aufmerksamkeit 5/CC

attract /əˈtrækt/ anziehen 2/M2

attraction /əˈtrækʃn/ Attraktion 6/7

attractive /əˈtræktɪv/ attraktiv, verlockend 2/M2

audition /ɔːˈdɪʃn/ Vorsprechen; Vorsingen; Vortanzen; Vorspielen 6/M6

August /ˈɔːɡəst/ August I

aunt /ɑːnt/ Tante I

Australia /ɒˈstreɪliə/ Australien II

Austria /ˈɒstriə/ Österreich 5/M9

author /ˈɔːθə/ Schriftsteller/in, Autor/in II

authority /ɔːˈθɒrəti/ Behörde 3/M1

autograph /ˈɔːtəˌɡrɑːf/ Autogramm II

autumn /ˈɔːtəm/ Herbst I

available /əˈveɪləbl/ verfügbar 6/P6

average /ˈævrɪdʒ/ durchschnittlich 2/9

award /əˈwɔːd/ Auszeichnung, Preis Intro

away /əˈweɪ/ weg II

give away /ɡɪvˌəˈweɪ/ verschenken 2/M2

awesome (informal) /ˈɔːsm/ super, spitze 2/6

awful /ˈɔːfl/ furchtbar, schrecklich Op3

B

back /bæk/ Rücken; Rückseite I

back /bæk/ zurück II

backache /ˈbækeɪk/ Rückenschmerzen III

background /ˈbækˌɡraʊnd/ Hintergrund Op3

bad /bæd/ schlecht I; schlimm, stark III

too bad /ˌtuː ˈbæd/ wirklich schade III

bag /bæɡ/ Tasche I

bake /beɪk/ backen II

bake sale /ˈbeɪk seɪl/ Kuchenbasar, Verkauf selbst gebackenen Kuchens 3/P13

baked beans (only pl) /ˌbeɪkt ˈbiːnz/ Bohnen in Tomatensauce 2/10

ball carrier /ˈbɔːl ˌkæriə/ Ballträger/in, Ballführer/in 5/15

balloon /bəˈluːn/ Ballon I

banana /bəˈnɑːnə/ Banane I

marching band /ˈmɑːtʃɪŋ ˌbænd/ Spielmannszug, Blaskapelle 1/P6

bandage /ˈbændɪdʒ/ Verband III

barbecue /ˈbɑːbɪˌkjuː/ grillen 2/2

have a barbecue /ˌhævˌə ˈbɑːbɪˌkjuː/ grillen, eine Grillparty feiern II

bark /bɑːk/ bellen II

barn /bɑːn/ Scheune, (Vieh)stall I

basic /ˈbeɪsɪk/ grundlegend, wesentlich; Grund- 5/18

basket /ˈbɑːskɪt/ Korb I

bathroom /ˈbɑːθˌruːm/ Bad(ezimmer) I

bathroom (AE); here: toilet (BE) /ˈbɑːθˌruːm/ Toilette 1/3

battle /ˈbætl/ Kampf, Schlacht 6/10

be (irr) /biː/ sein I

be as one /biˌəz ˈwʌn/ eins sein 4/M5

be up to sth /biˌˈʌp tə ˌsʌmθɪŋ/ etw machen; etw vorhaben 5/M1

be wrong /bi ˈrɒŋ/ nicht stimmen 5/8

beach /biːtʃ/ Strand II

beadwork (no pl) /ˈbiːdwɜːk/ Perlenstickerei 4/M5

bean /biːn/ Bohne III

baked beans (only pl) /ˌbeɪkt ˈbiːnz/ Bohnen in Tomatensauce 2/10

bear /beə/ Bär 6/P6

black bear /ˈblæk beə/ Schwarzbär 6/7

bear-proof /ˈbeəˌpruːf/ sicher vor Bären; bärensicher 6/P6

beard /bɪəd/ Bart II

beautiful /ˈbjuːtəfl/ schön I

became /bɪˈkeɪm/ *Vergangenheitsform von „become"*

because /bɪˈkɒz/ weil I

become (irr) /bɪˈkʌm/ werden I

bed /bed/ Bett I

bedroom /ˈbedruːm/ Schlafzimmer I

been /biːn/ *siehe „be"*

before /bɪˈfɔː/ vor I; bevor II; zuvor, vorher 2/3

before /bɪˈfɔː/ schon (einmal) 3/16

begin (irr) /bɪˈɡɪn/ anfangen, beginnen III

beginning /bɪˈɡɪnɪŋ/ Anfang III

in the beginning /ɪn ðə bɪˈɡɪnɪŋ/ am Anfang, zu Beginn II

behaviour (no pl) /bɪˈheɪvjə/ Verhalten, Benehmen 5/M9

behind /bɪˈhaɪnd/ hinter I

Belgium /ˈbeldʒəm/ Belgien 4/P14

believe (in) /bɪˈliːv/ glauben (an) II

belong to sb/sth /bɪˈlɒŋ tə ˌsʌmbədi/ˌsʌmθɪŋ/ jdm/zu etw gehören II

below /bɪˈləʊ/ unten; unter(halb) 2/M4

beneath /bɪˈniːθ/ unter 4/CC

beside /bɪˈsaɪd/ neben 4/M5

best /best/ beste(r, s) I

best /best/ am meisten/ liebsten/besten I

best wishes /ˌbest ˈwɪʃɪz/ viele Grüße II

bet *(irr)* /bet/ wetten 1/12

better /ˈbetə/ besser; lieber, mehr II

for the better /fə ðə ˈbetə/ zum Besseren, zum Guten 1/10

between /bɪˈtwiːn/ zwischen I

big /bɪg/ groß I

bike /baɪk/ (Fahr)rad I

ride a bike /ˌraɪd ə ˈbaɪk/ (Fahr)rad fahren I

bill /bɪl/ Rechnung III

bin /bɪn/ Mülleimer, Mülltonne I

bin /bɪn/ wegwerfen 1/P11

biology *(no pl)* /baɪˈɒlədʒi/ Biologie 1/10

bird /bɜːd/ Vogel II

date of birth /ˈdeɪt əv ˈbɜːθ/ Geburtsdatum III

place of birth /ˈpleɪs əv ˈbɜːθ/ Geburtsort Op6

birthday /ˈbɜːθdeɪ/ Geburtstag I

Happy birthday! /ˌhæpi ˈbɜːθdeɪ/ Alles Gute zum Geburtstag! I

biscuit /ˈbɪskɪt/ Keks 2/10

a bit /ə ˈbɪt/ ein bisschen II

bite *(irr)* /baɪt/ beißen I

black /blæk/ schwarz I

black bear /ˈblæk beə/ Schwarzbär 6/7

Black Friday *(AE)* /ˌblæk ˈfraɪdeɪ/ *Freitag nach Thanksgiving, an dem viel eingekauft wird* 2/14

blew /bluː/ *Vergangenheitsform von „blow"*

block /blɒk/ blockieren, den Weg versperren 5/15

bloom /bluːm/ blühen 1/M5

blow *(irr)* /bləʊ/ blasen, wehen 4/12

blue /bluː/ blau I

blue whale /ˈbluː ˌweɪl/ Blauwal 6/7

board /bɔːd/ Brett; Tafel II

board (a ship) /bɔːd/ (ein Schiff) besteigen 4/M1

board game /ˈbɔːd geɪm/ Brettspiel I

boarding school /ˈbɔːdɪŋ ˌskuːl/ Internat 4/M5

boat /bəʊt/ Boot; Schiff II

body /ˈbɒdi/ Körper I

bone /bəʊn/ Knochen III

book /bʊk/ Buch I

bookcase /ˈbʊkˌkeɪs/ Bücherregal, Bücherschrank I

border /ˈbɔːdə/ Grenze 6/2

border patrol guard /ˌbɔːdə pəˈtrəʊl gɑːd/ Grenzposten, Grenzbeamter/beamtin 6/2

bored /bɔːd/ gelangweilt II

boring /ˈbɔːrɪŋ/ langweilig I

born /bɔːn/ geboren II

borough /ˈbʌrə/ Stadtteil, Bezirk 3/8

borrow /ˈbɒrəʊ/ leihen 5/CC

boss /bɒs/ Chef/in II

both /bəʊθ/ beide(s) III

both ... and ... /ˈbəʊθ ˌənd/ sowohl ... als auch ... 4/1

bottle /ˈbɒtl/ Flasche II

at the bottom (of) /æt ðə ˈbɒtəm/ unten, am unteren Ende (von) III

bought /bɔːt/ *Vergangenheitsform von „buy"*

box office /ˈbɒksˌɒfɪs/ Kasse (im Kino/Theater) 6/9

boxing *(no pl)* /ˈbɒksɪŋ/ Boxen 5/11

boy /bɔɪ/ Junge I

boyfriend /ˈbɔɪfrend/ (fester) Freund I

brainstorm /ˈbreɪnˌstɔːm/ ein Brainstorming machen 6/1

brave /breɪv/ mutig, unerschrocken II

bravery *(no pl)* /ˈbreɪvəri/ Tapferkeit, Mut 6/4

Brazil /brəˈzɪl/ Brasilien 3/18

bread *(no pl)* /bred/ Brot III

bread roll /ˈbred rəʊl/ Brötchen I

break /breɪk/ Pause I

break *(irr)* /breɪk/ (zer)brechen III

lunch break /ˈlʌntʃ ˌbreɪk/ Mittagspause Op7

breakfast /ˈbrekfəst/ Frühstück I

breed *(irr)* /briːd/ züchten 4/P14

breeze /briːz/ Brise 4/M1

bridge /brɪdʒ/ Brücke II

bright /braɪt/ hell 3/2

brightly /ˈbraɪtli/ hell,

leuchtend 2/P13

brilliant *(informal)* /ˈbrɪljənt/ toll, hervorragend III

bring *(irr)* /brɪŋ/ (mit)bringen I

Britain /ˈbrɪtn/ Großbritannien II

British /ˈbrɪtɪʃ/ britische(r, s) III

the British *(only pl)* /ðə ˈbrɪtɪʃ/ die Briten III

brochure /ˈbrəʊʃə/ Broschüre 3/11

broken /ˈbrəʊkən/ zerbrochen, kaputt; gebrochen III

broken /ˈbrəʊkən/ *siehe „break"*

bronze /brɒnz/ Bronze, Bronze- II

brother /ˈbrʌðə/ Bruder I

brothers and sisters /ˌbrʌðəz ænd ˈsɪstəz/ Geschwister II

brought /brɔːt/ *Vergangenheitsform von „bring"*

brown /braʊn/ braun I

brush /brʌʃ/ bürsten; putzen I

bubble /ˈbʌbl/ Blase 2/M2

budgie (= budgerigar) /ˈbʌdʒi, ˈbʌdʒəriˌgɑː/ Wellensittich I

buffalo *(pl - or -es)* /ˈbʌfələʊ, ˈbʌfələʊz/ Büffel 4/14

build *(irr)* /bɪld/ bauen II

builder /ˈbɪldə/ Bauarbeiter/in II

building /ˈbɪldɪŋ/ Gebäude II

building centre /ˈbɪldɪŋ ˌsentə/ Baumarkt Op3

built /bɪlt/ *Vergangenheitsform von „build"*

bully /ˈbʊli/ Rüpel; Rabauke; jemand, der andere drangsaliert II

bully /ˈbʊli/ tyrannisieren, drangsalieren, mobben II

bullying *(no pl)* /ˈbʊliɪŋ/ Mobbing II

bump into sth/sb /ˌbʌmpˈɪntə ˌsʌmθɪŋ, ˌsʌmbədi/ mit etw/jdm zusammenstoßen 4/8

burglary /ˈbɜːgləri/ Einbruch, Einbruchdiebstahl 6/13

burn *(irr)* /bɜːn/ (ver)brennen 6/4

bus stop /ˈbʌs ˌstɒp/ Bushaltestelle II

business /ˈbɪznəs/ Handel,

Gewerbe 3/13

busy /ˈbɪzi/ beschäftigt II;
stark besucht 2/6; belebt,
verkehrsreich 3/8

busy /ˈbɪzi/ arbeitsreich II

but /bʌt/ aber I

butt (informal) /bʌt/
Glimmstängel, Kippe 5/M10

buy (irr) /baɪ/ kaufen I

buzz group /ˈbʌz gruːp/ Form der
Gruppenarbeit 1/8

by /baɪ/ bei, in der Nähe; mit,
durch; von II

by (eight o'clock) /baɪ/
(spätestens) bis (acht Uhr) II

bye (informal) /baɪ/ tschüss I

bye for now /ˈbaɪ fə naʊ/ bis
bald II

C

cage /keɪdʒ/ Käfig I

cake /keɪk/ Kuchen I

calculator /ˈkælkjʊˌleɪtə/
(Taschen)rechner I

calendar /ˈkælɪndə/ Kalender I

lunar calendar /ˌluːnə ˈkælɪndə/
Mondkalender 2/14

California /ˌkæləˈfɔːniə/
Kalifornien 4/9

Californian /ˌkæləˈfɔːniən/
kalifornisch 6/P3

(phone) call /(ˈfəʊn) kɔːl/
(Telefon)anruf II

call /kɔːl/ Ruf 6/M1

call /kɔːl/ anrufen II

call /kɔːl/ nennen III

call out /ˌkɔːlˈaʊt/ aufrufen 1/3

be called /bi: ˈkɔːld/ heißen I

caller /ˈkɔːlə/ Anrufer/in 6/M3

came /keɪm/ Vergangenheitsform
von „come"

cameraman/-woman
/ˈkæmrəˌmæn, ˈkæmrəˌwʊmən/
Kameramann/-frau 6/5

campsite /ˈkæmpˌsaɪt/
Campingplatz, Zeltplatz II

campus /ˈkæmpəs/ Universität;
Schulgelände, Campus 1/M5

can /kæn/ Dose 2/M2

can /kæn/ Mülleimer 6/P6

can /kæn/ können I

Canada /ˈkænədə/ Kanada 4/P14

candle /ˈkændl/ Kerze II

candle holder /ˈkændlˌhəʊldə/
Kerzenständer 2/M5

candy (AE) = sweets (BE)
/ˈkændi/ Süßigkeiten 2/M6

cap /kæp/ Kappe I

capital /ˈkæpɪtl/ Hauptstadt Intro

captain /ˈkæptɪn/ Kapitän/in III

car /kɑː/ Auto I

caravan /ˈkærəvæn/
Wohnwagen II

card /kɑːd/ Pappe, Karton;
Karte I

get well card /get ˈwel kɑːd/
Genesungskarte II

take care of /teɪk ˈkeər əv/ sich
kümmern um, versorgen II

career /kəˈrɪə/ Beruf; Karriere III

careful /ˈkeəfl/ vorsichtig;
sorgfältig II

the Caribbean /ðə ˌkærɪˈbiːən/
die Karibik; die Karibischen
Inseln 3/8

carnival /ˈkɑːnɪvl/ Karneval III

carpet /ˈkɑːpɪt/ Teppich I

ball carrier /ˈbɔːl ˌkæriə/
Ballträger/in, Ballführer/in 5/15

carrot /ˈkærət/ Möhre, Karotte,
Mohrrübe II

carry /ˈkæri/ tragen 5/15

cartoon /kɑːˈtuːn/ Cartoon,
Karikatur; Zeichentrickfilm II

cartoonist /kɑːˈtuːnɪst/
Karikaturist/in 1/M9

case /keɪs/ Fall 6/13

cash (no pl) /kæʃ/ Bargeld 5/3

cash machine /ˈkæʃ məˌʃiːn/
Geldautomat III

casino /kəˈsiːnəʊ/
(Spiel)kasino 4/P14

cast /kɑːst/ Besetzung,
Ensemble 6/13

castle /ˈkɑːsl/ Burg; Schloss II

cat /kæt/ Katze I

catch (irr) /kætʃ/ fangen I;
festnehmen II

catch fire /kætʃ ˈfaɪə/ in Brand
geraten, Feuer fangen 6/M3

category /ˈkætəgri/
Kategorie 4/15

Catholic /ˈkæθlɪk/
Katholik/in; katholisch 4/M1

cattle (no pl) /ˈkætl/ Vieh;
Rinder Intro

caught /kɔːt/
Vergangenheitsform von „catch"

cauliflower /ˈkɒliˌflaʊə/
Blumenkohl 2/10

'cause (= because) (informal)
/kʌz/ weil, da 1/3

cause sb to do sth
/ˌkɔːz ˌsʌmbədi tʊ ˈduː; ˌsʌmθɪŋ/
jdn veranlassen, etw zu
tun 4/M1

cave /keɪv/ Höhle 6/7

ceiling /ˈsiːlɪŋ/ (Zimmer)decke I

celebrate /ˈseləˌbreɪt/ feiern II

celebration /ˌseləˈbreɪʃn/ Feier,
Fest II

celebrity /səˈlebrəti/ berühmte
Persönlichkeit, Star 6/13

cellphone (AE) = mobile phone
(BE) /ˈselˌfəʊn/ Mobiltelefon,
Handy 1/P4

center (AE) = centre (BE)
/ˈsentə/ Zentrum, Center 4/P10

Central America
/ˌsentrəl əˈmerɪkə/
Mittelamerika 4/1

centre /ˈsentə/ Zentrum,
Center I

century /ˈsentʃəri/
Jahrhundert II

ceremony /ˈserəməni/ Zeremonie,
Feier 4/15

chair /tʃeə/ Stuhl I

chalk (no pl) /tʃɔːk/ Kreide 3/M1

challenge /ˈtʃælɪndʒ/
Herausforderung 5/M10

championship /ˈtʃæmpiənʃɪp/
Meisterschaft 5/12

change /tʃeɪndʒ/ (Ver)ände-
rung; Wechselgeld III

change /tʃeɪndʒ/ (sich)
(ver)ändern 1/10

change /tʃeɪndʒ/ wechseln II

for a change /fər ə ˈtʃeɪndʒ/ zur
Abwechslung 5/5

chant /tʃɑːnt/ Sprechgesang,
Sprechchor 5/12

chant /tʃɑːnt/ singen 4/9

character /ˈkærɪktə/ Charakter;
Figur 5/7

charity /ˈtʃærəti/

Wohltätigkeitsorganisation III

charming /ˈtʃɑːmɪŋ/ bezaubernd, charmant II

chart /tʃɑːt/ Diagramm, Schaubild, Grafik 4/10

chat /tʃæt/ chatten, sich unterhalten II

chat-up line /ˈtʃætʌp ˌlaɪn/ Anmachspruch 5/CC

cheap /tʃiːp/ billig, preiswert II

check /tʃek/ überprüfen, kontrollieren I

check out sth /ˌtʃekˈaʊt ˌsʌmθɪŋ/ etw untersuchen/überprüfen; sich etw ansehen 5/7

checklist /ˈtʃekˌlɪst/ Checkliste, Kontrollliste 0p7

cheer /tʃɪə/ Jubel 5/CC

cheer /tʃɪə/ jubeln III

cheer on /tʃɪərˈɒn/ anfeuern 5/12

Cheer up! /tʃɪərˈʌp/ Lass (doch) den Kopf nicht hängen!, Kopf hoch! III

cheese (no pl) /tʃiːz/ Käse III

chemical /ˈkemɪkl/ Chemikalie 3/17

chemistry /ˈkemɪstri/ Chemie I

Cherokee /ˈtʃerəkiː/ Cherokee(indianer) Intro

chess (no pl) /tʃes/ Schach(spiel) II

chew /tʃuː/ kauen II

(chewing) gum (no pl) /(ˈtʃuːɪŋ) gʌm/ Kaugummi II

chicken /ˈtʃɪkɪn/ Huhn; Hähnchen I

fried chicken /ˌfraɪdˈtʃɪkɪn/ Brathähnchen 2/2

chickenpox (no pl) /ˈtʃɪkɪnˌpɒks/ Windpocken II

chief /tʃiːf/ Leiter/in; Häuptling 4/P12

child (pl **children**) /tʃaɪld, ˈtʃɪldrən/ Kind I

chill (informal) /tʃɪl/ chillen, relaxen 5/P6

chimney /ˈtʃɪmni/ Kamin; Schornstein II

chin /tʃɪn/ Kinn II

Chinese /ˌtʃaɪˈniːz/ Chinesisch II

Chinese /ˌtʃaɪˈniːz/ chinesisch II

chips (AE) (only pl) = **crisps** (BE) (only pl) /tʃɪps/ Chips 2/M6

chips (only pl) (BE) /tʃɪps/ Pommes frites II

chocolate (no pl) /ˈtʃɒklət/ Schokolade I

a box of chocolates /ə bɒks_əv ˈtʃɒkləts/ eine Schachtel Pralinen II

choice /tʃɔɪs/ Wahl 5/18

choose (irr) /tʃuːz/ auswählen I

chop suey /ˌtʃɒp ˈsuːi/ amerikanisch-chinesisches Gericht mit Fleisch oder Tofu, Gemüse und Reis 2/2

chose /ʃəʊz/ Vergangenheitsform von „choose"

Christmas /ˈkrɪsməs/ Weihnachten II

Christmas Day /ˌkrɪsməs ˈdeɪ/ erster Weihnachtsfeiertag II

Christmas Eve /ˌkrɪsməsˈiːv/ Heiligabend II

church /tʃɜːtʃ/ Kirche II

cigarette /ˌsɪgəˈret/ Zigarette 5/M10

Cinco de Mayo /ˌsɪŋkəʊ də ˈmeɪə/ mexikanischer Feiertag 2/12

cinema /ˈsɪnəmə/ Kino I

circle /ˈsɜːkl/ Kreis II

citizen /ˈsɪtɪzn/ (Staats)bürger/in 4/1

city /ˈsɪti/ (Groß)stadt I

civil war /ˌsɪvl ˈwɔː/ Bürgerkrieg 4/1

clap one's hands /ˌklæp wʌnz ˈhændz/ in die Hände klatschen 2/10

class /klɑːs/ (Schul)klasse I

class /klɑːs/ Jahrgang 1/M1

class (AE) = lesson (BE) /klɑːs/ (Unterrichts)stunde 1/3

class trip /ˈklɑːs trɪp/ Klassenfahrt 3/P7

classmate /ˈklɑːsˌmeɪt/ Klassenkamerad/in, Mitschüler/in I

classroom /ˈklɑːsˌruːm/ Klassenzimmer I

clause /klɔːz/ Satz(teil) 4/M6

clean /kliːn/ sauber machen, reinigen, putzen I

clean /kliːn/ sauber I

clean up /kliːnˈʌp/ sauber machen, reinigen 1/12

clear /klɪə/ klar, eindeutig 5/M3

clever /ˈklevə/ klug, gescheit, schlau II

click /klɪk/ (an)klicken, drücken III

cliff /klɪf/ Klippe, Kliff 6/7

climb /klaɪm/ (hinauf)klettern; (hinauf)steigen II

climbing /ˈklaɪmɪŋ/ Klettern, Bergsteigen; Kletter- III

clock /klɒk/ Uhr I

close /kləʊz/ schließen, zumachen I

close /kləʊs/ nah(e) 6/4

clothes (only pl) /kləʊðz/ Kleider, Kleidung I

cloud /klaʊd/ Wolke 4/9

cloudy /ˈklaʊdi/ bewölkt, bedeckt I

club /klʌb/ Klub, Verein I

coach /kəʊtʃ/ Trainer(in) 5/12

coast /kəʊst/ Küste I

coffee /ˈkɒfi/ Kaffee 3/16

coffin /ˈkɒfɪn/ Sarg II

coin /kɔɪn/ Münze, Geldstück 2/14

cold /kəʊld/ Erkältung, Schnupfen III; Kälte 2/15

cold /kəʊld/ kalt I

colleague /ˈkɒliːg/ Kollege/ Kollegin; Mitarbeiter/in III

collect /kəˈlekt/ sammeln I; holen 3/13

rain collector /ˈreɪn kəˌlektə/ Regensammelbehälter 1/10

college /ˈkɒlɪdʒ/ Bildungs- einrichtung; Universität, Hochschule 4/4

color (AE) = colour (BE) /ˈkʌlə/ Farbe 1/M1

color team (AE) /ˈkʌlə ˌtiːm/ Fahnenschwinger im Spielmannszug 1/P6

colored (AE) = coloured (BE) /ˈkʌləd/ bunt, farbig 2/P13; veraltete Bezeichnung für Afroamerikaner 4/CC

colorful (AE) = colourful

(BE) /ˈkʌləfl/ farbenfroh, farbenprächtig, farbenfreudig; bunt, farbig 2/M5

colour /ˈkʌlə/ Farbe I

colourful /ˈkʌləfl/ farbenfroh, farbenprächtig II

come *(irr)* /kʌm/ kommen I

come along /ˌkʌm_əˈlɒŋ/ mitgehen, mitkommen; vorbeikommen 3/P13

come in /kʌm_ˈɪn/ hereinkommen I

Come on! /ˌkʌm_ˈɒn/ Auf geht's!, Na los! 1/3

come to sb's mind /kʌm tə ˌsʌmbədiz ˈmaɪnd/ jdm einfallen 3/6

comedy /ˈkɒmədi/ Komödie 6/12

comfortable /ˈkʌmftəbl/ bequem I

comment /ˈkɒment/ Kommentar, Bemerkung III

have sth in common /hæv ˌsʌmθɪŋ_ɪn ˈkɒmən/ etwas gemein haben 3/P5

community /kəˈmjuːnəti/ Gemeinde; Gemeinschaft 4/12

company /ˈkʌmpni/ Firma 2/M2

compare /kəmˈpeə/ vergleichen 1/11

competition /ˌkɒmpəˈtɪʃn/ Wettbewerb II

complete /kəmˈpliːt/ vervollständigen 1/P10

completely /kəmˈpliːtli/ völlig, ganz I

comprehensive school /ˌkɒmprɪˈhensɪv ˌskuːl/ Gesamtschule II

computer science *(no pl)* /kəmˈpjuːtə ˌsaɪəns/ Informatik 1/M5

computer-animated /kəmˌpjuːtərˈˈænɪˌmeɪtɪd/ computeranimiert 6/12

concentrate /ˈkɒnsnˌtreɪt/ sich konzentrieren II

concert /ˈkɒnsət/ Konzert II

confused /kənˈfjuːzd/ verwirrt, durcheinander 1/3

connect /kəˈnekt/ verbinden 2/P12

contact sb /ˈkɒntækt ˌsʌmbədi/ jdn kontaktieren, sich mit jdm in Verbindung setzen 3/16

contain /kənˈteɪn/ enthalten 2/M2

pie-eating contest /ˌpaɪ_iːtɪŋ ˈkɒntest/ Kuchenwettessen 1/M1

continue /kənˈtɪnjuː/ fortfahren, fortführen 2/M1

continue to do sth /kənˌtɪnjuː tʊ ˈduː ˌsʌmθɪŋ/ weiter(hin) etw tun 4/M1

convince /kənˈvɪns/ überzeugen 3/7

convincing /kənˈvɪnsɪŋ/ überzeugend 5/M9

cook /kʊk/ Koch/Köchin II

cook /kʊk/ kochen II

cookie *(AE)* = biscuit *(BE)* /ˈkʊki/ Keks, Plätzchen 2/M6

do the cooking /ˌduː ðə ˈkʊkɪŋ/ kochen I

cool down /ˌkuːl ˈdaʊn/ sich beruhigen II

be cool with sb/sth /bi ˈkuːl wɪð ˌsʌmbədi/ˌsʌmθɪŋ/ kein Problem mit jdm/etw haben 3/8

copy /ˈkɒpi/ abschreiben 4/8

corn *(no pl)* /kɔːn/ Getreide, Korn Intro; Mais 2/LL

corn on the cob /ˌkɔːn_ɒn ðə ˈkɒb/ Maiskolben 2/14

corner /ˈkɔːnə/ Ecke II

correct /kəˈrekt/ korrigieren 1/M7

correct /kəˈrekt/ richtig, korrekt II

cost /kɒst/ Kosten, Preis 1/M7

cost *(irr)* /kɒst/ kosten III

costume /ˈkɒstjuːm/ Tracht, Kostüm II

cotton /ˈkɒtn/ Baumwolle Intro

cotton ball /ˈkɒtn ˌbɔːl/ Wattebällchen 2/CC

cotton candy *(no pl)* /ˌkɒtn ˈkændi/ Zuckerwatte 2/CC

couch /kaʊtʃ/ Couch, Sofa II

cougar /ˈkuːgə/ Puma 6/7

could /kʊd/ könnte(st, n, t) I

guidance counsellor /ˈgaɪdns ˌkaʊnslə/ Beratungslehrer, Vertrauenslehrer 1/6

count /kaʊnt/ zählen Op3

count on sb /kaʊnt ɒn ˈsʌmbədi/ auf jdn zählen 6/10

counter /ˈkaʊntə/ Spielfigur Intro

country /ˈkʌntri/ Land III

developing country /dɪˈveləpɪŋ ˌkʌntri/ Entwicklungsland 3/M7

in the country /ɪn ðə ˈkʌntri/ auf dem Land 4/4

couple /ˈkʌpl/ Paar 6/M5

course /kɔːs/ Kurs I

course /kɔːs/ Gang 2/10

court /kɔːt/ Gericht; Hofstaat, Gefolge 1/M1

cousin /ˈkʌzn/ Cousin/e I

cover /ˈkʌvə/ Titelseite, Cover 5/4

covered /ˈkʌvəd/ zugedeckt, bedeckt, verhüllt 2/P13

cow /kaʊ/ Kuh I

coyote /kɔɪˈəʊti/ Kojote 6/7

cranberry /ˈkrænbəri/ Cranberry, Moosbeere 2/14

crash /kræʃ/ stürzen III

crawl /krɔːl/ krabbeln; kriechen 3/M1

crazy /ˈkreɪzi/ verrückt 5/7

go crazy *(informal)* /gəʊ ˈkreɪzi/ durchdrehen, ausflippen I

cream /kriːm/ Sahne II; Creme, Salbe III

creamsicle /ˈkriːmsɪkl/ *Sahneeis am Stiel* 2/CC

create /kriˈeɪt/ erschaffen; gestalten II

creative /kriˈeɪtɪv/ kreativ II

criminal /ˈkrɪmɪnl/ Verbrecher/in, Kriminelle/r II

crisps *(only pl)* *(BE)* /krɪsps/ Chips I

critic /ˈkrɪtɪk/ Kritiker/in, Rezensent/in 6/13

crocodile /ˈkrɒkədaɪl/ Krokodil III

crop /krɒp/ Ernte 4/M1

cross /krɒs/ durchqueren; überqueren II

crowd /kraʊd/ (Menschen)menge, Zuschauermenge 5/8

crowded /ˈkraʊdɪd/ überfüllt 4/M1

crown /kraʊn/ Krone 1/1

have a crush on sb /ˌhæv_ə ˈkrʌʃ ɒn ˌsʌmbədi/ in jdn verknallt sein 1/12

cry /kraɪ/ weinen; schreien II
cucumber /ˈkjuː͵kʌmbə/ (Salat)gurke III
culture /ˈkʌltʃə/ Kultur 2/12
cup /kʌp/ Tasse I
cupboard /ˈkʌbəd/ Schrank II
curry /ˈkʌri/ Curry(gericht) III
curtain /ˈkɜːtn/ Vorhang II
cushion /ˈkʊʃn/ Kissen I
custom /ˈkʌstəm/ Brauch, Sitte 4/6
customer /ˈkʌstəmə/ Kunde/ Kundin II
cut (irr) /kʌt/ schneiden II
cute /kjuːt/ süß, niedlich I
CV (= curriculum vitae) /͵siːˈviː (= kə͵rɪkjʊləm ˈviːtaɪ)/ Lebenslauf Op3
cycle /ˈsaɪkl/ Rad fahren II
cycling /ˈsaɪklɪŋ/ Radfahren, Radeln III
cyclist /ˈsaɪklɪst/ Radfahrer/in III

D

dad (informal) /dæd/ Papa, Vati I
daily /ˈdeɪli/ täglich 2/P7
damage (no pl) /ˈdæmɪdʒ/ Schaden; (Be)schädigung 6/4
damage /ˈdæmɪdʒ/ schaden; (be)schädigen 6/4
dance /dɑːns/ Tanz II; Ball 1/3
dance /dɑːns/ tanzen I
dancer /ˈdɑːnsə/ Tänzer/in III
dancing (no pl) /ˈdɑːnsɪŋ/ Tanzen I
danger /ˈdeɪndʒə/ Gefahr III
dangerous /ˈdeɪndʒərəs/ gefährlich I
dark /dɑːk/ dunkel I
darkness (no pl) /ˈdɑːknəs/ Dunkelheit, Finsternis 2/12
data /ˈdeɪtə/ Daten, (persön-liche) Angaben 1/P11
date /deɪt/ Datum I
date /deɪt/ Verabredung, Date 5/M1
date of birth /ˈdeɪt͵əv ͵bɜːθ/ Geburtsdatum III
daughter /ˈdɔːtə/ Tochter I
day /deɪ/ Tag I
a day /ə ˈdeɪ/ pro/am Tag III
one day /ˈwʌn deɪ/ eines

Tages II
the other day /ði͵ʌðə ˈdeɪ/ neulich, vor einigen Tagen 5/M9
day ticket /ˈdeɪ ͵tɪkɪt/ Tageskarte, Tagesticket 6/9
dead /ded/ tot II
the real deal (informal) /ðə ͵riːəl ˈdiːl/ das einzig Wahre 1/M5
deal with /ˈdiːl wɪð/ sich be-fassen mit; handeln von 6/12
dealer /diːlə/ Händler/in; Dealer/in Intro
dear /dɪə/ liebe(r) (Anrede) I
December /dɪˈsembə/ Dezember I
decide /dɪˈsaɪd/ (sich) entscheiden; beschließen II
decorate /ˈdekə͵reɪt/ schmücken, dekorieren II
decorated /ˈdekəreɪtɪd/ geschmückt, verziert 2/P13
decoration /͵dekəˈreɪʃn/ Dekoration, Schmuck 2/P13
defensive /dɪˈfensɪv/ Verteidigungs- 5/15
definitely /ˈdefnətli/ eindeutig, definitiv 1/12
definition /͵defəˈnɪʃn/ Definition, Erklärung 3/9
delicious /dɪˈlɪʃəs/ köstlich, lecker II
deliver /dɪˈlɪvə/ liefern 2/M1
delivery /dɪˈlɪvri/ Lieferung 2/9
demonstrate /ˈdemən͵streɪt/ zeigen, vorführen 1/M5
department store /dɪˈpɑːtmənt ͵stɔː/ Kaufhaus II
depend on sth /diˈpend ͵ɒn ͵sʌmθɪŋ/ von etw abhängen 4/M1
depressed /dɪˈprest/ deprimiert I
describe /dɪˈskraɪb/ beschreiben 1/1
desert /ˈdezət/ Wüste 4/9
design /dɪˈzaɪn/ entwerfen 1/14
web designer /ˈweb dɪ͵zaɪnə/ Webdesigner/in Op3
desk /desk/ Schreibtisch I
dessert /dɪˈzɜːt/ Nachtisch, Dessert III
destroy /dɪˈstrɔɪ/ zerstören 3/2
detail /ˈdiːteɪl/ Detail, Einzelheit 5/M1

detective /dɪˈtektɪv/ (Privat)detektiv/in II
develop /dɪˈveləp/ (sich) entwickeln 1/10
developing country /dɪˈveləpɪŋ ͵kʌntri/ Entwicklungsland 3/M7
development /dɪˈveləpmənt/ Entwicklung 1/5
devil /ˈdevl/ Teufel II
dial /ˈdaɪəl/ wählen 6/M3
dialogue /ˈdaɪəlɒg/ Gespräch, Dialog 1/12
diamond /ˈdaɪəmənd/ Diamant 4/9
diary /ˈdaɪəri/ Tagebuch II
dice (pl -) /daɪs/ Würfel Intro
dictionary /ˈdɪkʃənri/ Wörterbuch 1/10
did /dɪd/ Vergangenheitsform von „do"
die /daɪ/ sterben II
difference /ˈdɪfrəns/ Unterschied II
make a difference /͵meɪk͵ə ˈdɪfrəns/ einen Unterschied machen; etw verändern, etw bewirken 1/10
different /ˈdɪfrənt/ anders, andere(r, s); verschieden, unterschiedlich II
difficult /ˈdɪfɪklt/ schwierig, schwer I
difficulty /ˈdɪfɪklti/ Schwierigkeit, Problem 4/5
digger /ˈdɪgə/ Bagger; Gräber/in 6/P3
dinner /ˈdɪnə/ Abendessen; Mittagessen II
dinosaur /ˈdaɪnə͵sɔː/ Dinosaurier 6/10
diploma /dɪˈpləʊmə/ Diplom; Abschlusszeugnis 1/1
high school diploma /ˈhaɪ ͵skuːl dɪ͵pləʊmə/ Abschlusszeugnis der Highschool 1/LL
direct speech /dɪ͵rekt ˈspiːtʃ/ direkte Rede 5/M2
direction /dɪˈrekʃn/ Richtung II
ask for directions /͵ɑːsk fə dɪˈrekʃnz/ nach dem Weg fragen III
give directions /͵gɪv dɪˈrekʃnz/ den Weg beschreiben III

director /dəˈrektə/ Direktor/in, Leiter/in II

director /dəˈrektə/ Regisseur/in 6/13

dirty /ˈdɜːti/ dreckig, schmutzig I

disabled /dɪsˈeɪbld/ behindert III

disadvantage /ˌdɪsədˈvɑːntɪdʒ/ Nachteil 1/M4

disappointed /ˌdɪsəˈpɔɪntɪd/ enttäuscht III

discover /dɪˈskʌvə/ entdecken II

discuss /dɪˈskʌs/ besprechen; diskutieren 5/12

discussion /dɪˈskʌʃn/ Diskussion 2/M4

disease /dɪˈziːz/ Krankheit 2/15

disgusting /dɪsˈɡʌstɪŋ/ widerlich III

dish (pl -es) /dɪʃ/ Gericht II

main dish /meɪn ˈdɪʃ/ Hauptspeise, Hauptgericht 2/1

wash the dishes /wɒʃ ðə ˈdɪʃɪz/ abspülen, Geschirr spülen 3/13

dishwasher /ˈdɪʃˌwɒʃə/ Geschirrspülmaschine I

dislikes (only pl) /dɪsˈlaɪks/ Abneigungen 4/M7

divorced /dɪˈvɔːst/ geschieden 4/4

Diwali /dɪˈwɑːli/ hinduistisches Lichterfest 2/12

DIY (= Do It Yourself) /ˌdiː aɪ ˈwaɪ/ Heimwerken Op3

do (irr) /duː/ machen, tun I

dock /dɒk/ anlegen, andocken 4/M1

doctor /ˈdɒktə/ Arzt/Ärztin II

dog /dɒɡ/ Hund I

done /dʌn/ siehe „do" I

door /dɔː/ Tür I

doorbell /ˈdɔːˌbel/ Türklingel III

on one's own doorstep /ɒn wʌnzˌəʊn ˈdɔːˌstep/ vor der eigenen Haustür 1/M5

dos and don'ts /ˌduːz ən ˈdəʊnts/ was man tun und was man nicht tun sollte 4/8

double circle /ˌdʌbl ˈsɜːkl/ Doppelkreis 2/1

down /daʊn/ (nach) unten; hinunter, hinab III

download /ˌdaʊnˈləʊd/ herunterladen, downloaden III

dragon /ˈdræɡən/ Drache I

drama /ˈdrɑːmə/ Schauspielerei; Theater 1/5; Drama, Tragödie 6/12

draw (irr) /drɔː/ zeichnen I

drawing /ˈdrɔːɪŋ/ Zeichnung 3/M1

dream /driːm/ Traum I

dress /dres/ Kleid I

dress up (as) /dres ˈʌp/ sich verkleiden (als)

dribble /ˈdrɪbl/ dribbeln 1/P5

drill /drɪl/ Bohrer, Bohrmaschine Op3

drink /drɪŋk/ Getränk I

drink (irr) /drɪŋk/ trinken I

have a drink /ˌhæv ə ˈdrɪŋk/ etwas trinken gehen 5/4

drive (irr) /draɪv/ fahren II

driven /drɪvn/ siehe „drive" II

driver /ˈdraɪvə/ Fahrer/in II

driver's education (no pl) /ˈdraɪvəzˌedjʊˌkeɪʃn/ Fahrunterricht 1/5

driver's license (AE) = driving licence (BE) /ˈdraɪvəz ˌlaɪsns, ˈdraɪvɪŋ ˌlaɪsns/ Führerschein 1/5

drop /drɒp/ fallen lassen II

shop till you drop /ˈʃɒp tɪl jə ˌdrɒp/ Einkaufen bis zum Umfallen 5/3

drove /drəʊv/ Vergangenheitsform von „drive"

drum /drʌm/ Trommel III

drumming (no pl) /ˈdrʌmɪŋ/ Trommeln 4/M5

dry /draɪ/ trocken 6/2

duck /dʌk/ Ente I

due to sth /ˌdjuː tʊ ˈsʌmθɪŋ/ wegen/aufgrund einer Sache 4/P7

dumpling /ˈdʌmplɪŋ/ Knödel, Kloß; Teigtasche 2/14

dune /djuːn/ Düne 6/7

during /ˈdjʊərɪŋ/ während 1/4

dust (no pl) /dʌst/ Staub 4/9

E

each /iːtʃ/ jede(r, s) III

each /iːtʃ/ jeweils 5/15

each other /ˌiːtʃ ˈʌðə/ einander 3/8

eagle /ˈiːɡl/ Adler 6/7

ear /ɪə/ Ohr I

early /ˈɜːli/ früh, zeitig II

earn /ɜːn/ verdienen 3/13

earring /ˈɪərɪŋ/ Ohrring II

the earth /ðiˈɜːθ/ die Erde 1/M5

earthquake /ˈɜːθˌkweɪk/ Erdbeben 6/2

easily /ˈiːzɪli/ (sehr) leicht; schnell 2/2

east /iːst/ Osten III

Easter /ˈiːstə/ Ostern, Osterfest II

easy /ˈiːzi/ einfach; leicht I

eat (irr) /iːt/ essen I

eaten /ˈiːtn/ siehe „eat"

edit /ˈedɪt/ bearbeiten, redigieren 3/11

education (no pl) /ˌedjʊˈkeɪʃn/ (Aus)bildung 4/4

driver's education (no pl) /ˈdraɪvəzˌedjʊˌkeɪʃn/ Fahrunterricht 1/5

efficient /ɪˈfɪʃnt/ effizient 1/5

egg /eɡ/ Ei I

fried egg /ˌfraɪd ˈeɡ/ Spiegelei 2/2

Eid /iːd/ islamisches Fest zum Abschluss des Fastenmonats Ramadan 2/12

elbow /ˈelbəʊ/ Ellbogen II

elderly /ˈeldəli/ ältere(r, s) 2/M1

elective (AE) /ɪˈlektɪv/ Wahlfach, Wahlkurs 1/3

electric /ɪˈlektrɪk/ elektrisch 1/M5

electrical equipment /ɪˌlektrɪklˌɪˈkwɪpmənt/ elektrische Geräte, Elektrogeräte Op2

electrician /ɪˌlekˈtrɪʃn/ Elektriker/in Op2

electricity (no pl) /ɪˌlekˈtrɪsəti/ Elektrizität, Strom III

elementary school (AE) = primary school (BE) /elɪˈmentri ˌskuːl, ˈpraɪməri ˌskuːl/ Grundschule 1/LL

elephant /ˈelɪfənt/ Elefant I

elk /elk/ Elch 4/P14

what else /wɒt ˈels/ was noch, was sonst 3/14

embarrassed /ɪmˈbærəst/
verlegen, peinlich berührt II

the Emerald Isle /ðiˌˈemrəldˌˌaɪl/
die Grüne Insel 4/M1

emergency /ɪˈmɜːdʒnsi/
Notfall 6/M3

emigrate /ˈemɪgreɪt/
auswandern, emigrieren 4/M1

empty /ˈempti/ ausräumen,
(ent)leeren I

empty /ˈempti/ leer 1/12

encourage sb /ɪnˈkʌrɪdʒ ˌsʌmbədi/
jdn ermutigen; jdn
ermuntern 2/M1

end /end/ Ende II

end /end/ enden II

in the end /ˌɪn ðiˈend/
am Ende, zum Schluss 6/P9

end up /ˌendˈˌʌp/ enden 4/M5

endless /ˈendləs/ endlos,
unendlich 4/9

energy /ˈenədʒi/ Energie, Kraft II

engine /ˈendʒɪn/ Motor,
Maschine 0p7

English /ˈɪŋglɪʃ/ Englisch;
englisch I

in English /ˌɪnˈˌɪŋglɪʃ/ auf
Englisch I

English-speaking /ˈɪŋglɪʃˌspiːkɪŋ/
englischsprachig 1/14

enjoy /ɪnˈdʒɔɪ/ mögen;
genießen I

enjoy oneself /ɪnˈdʒɔɪ
wʌnˌself/ sich amüsieren; sich
vergnügen, Spaß haben 5/12

enough /ɪˈnʌf/ genügend,
ausreichend, genug II

enter /ˈentə/ betreten 6/13

entrance /ˈentrəns/ Eingang;
Eintritt(sgebühr) 6/9

entry /ˈentri/ Eintrag 2/14

envelope /ˈenvələʊp/
Briefumschlag, Kuvert II

environment /ɪnˈvaɪrənmənt/
Umgebung; Umwelt 1/M5

environmental /ɪnˌvaɪrənˈmentl/
ökologisch, die Umwelt
betreffend 1/M5

environmentally friendly
/ɪnˌvaɪrənˌmentli ˈfrendli/
umweltfreundlich 1/M5

equipment (no pl) /ɪˈkwɪpmənt/
Ausrüstung, Ausstattung 5/11

escalator /ˈeskəˌleɪtə/
Rolltreppe III

escape /ɪˈskeɪp/ Flucht II

escape /ɪˈskeɪp/ (ent)fliehen,
ausbrechen; entkommen II

especially /ɪˈspeʃli/
besonders 3/16

ethnic /ˈeθnɪk/ ethnisch,
Volks- 4/2

Europe /ˈjʊərəp/ Europa 2/15

European /ˌjʊərəˈpiːən/
Europäer/in; europäisch 4/1

even /ˈiːvn/ selbst; sogar 3/2

even /ˈiːvn/ noch 0p3

never even /ˌnevərˈˌiːvn/
(noch) nicht (ein)mal 2/M2

evening /ˈiːvnɪŋ/ Abend II

in the evening /ˌɪn ðiˈiːvnɪŋ/
am Abend, abends I

ever /ˈevə/ jemals II

ever /ˈevə/ überhaupt 2/P4

every /ˈevri/ jede(r, s) I

everybody /ˈevriˌbɒdi/ jede(r);
alle III

everyday /ˈevrideɪ/ alltäglich,
Alltags- 1/10

everyone /ˈevriwʌn/ jede(r);
alle I

everything /ˈevriθɪŋ/ alles II

everywhere /ˈevriweə/ überall III

exactly /ɪgˈzæktli/ genau 1/3

example /ɪgˈzɑːmpl/ Beispiel I

for example /fərˌɪgˈzɑːmpl/
zum Beispiel I

except /ɪkˈsept/ außer, bis
auf 6/9

excited /ɪkˈsaɪtɪd/ aufgeregt II;
begeistert III

exciting /ɪkˈsaɪtɪŋ/ aufregend;
spannend I

exclusive /ɪkˈskluːsɪv/
exklusiv 6/M5

excuse /ɪkˈskjuːs/
Entschuldigung; Ausrede I

Excuse me! /ɪkˈskjuːz ˌmi/
Entschuldigen Sie bitte!,
Entschuldigung! I

exercise /ˈeksəsaɪz/ Übung;
Bewegung III

exercise book /ˈeksəsaɪz ˌbʊk/
Heft I

exhausted /ɪgˈzɔːstɪd/
erschöpft 5/M9

exhibition /ˌeksɪˈbɪʃn/
Ausstellung 3/M1

exit /ˈeksɪt/ Ausgang III

expensive /ɪkˈspensɪv/ teuer II

experience /ɪkˈspɪəriəns/
Erfahrung, Erlebnis 4/4

experience /ɪkˈspɪəriəns/
erleben, erfahren 6/8

work experience (no pl)
/ˈwɜːk ɪkˌspɪəriəns/ Praktikum;
Berufserfahrung 0p3

expert /ˈekspɜːt/ Experte/
Expertin 2/M2

explain /ɪkˈspleɪn/ erklären II

exploit /ɪkˈsplɔɪt/ ausbeuten,
ausschöpfen 4/P14

explore /ɪkˈsplɔː/ erforschen,
untersuchen II

explorer /ɪkˈsplɔːrə/ Forscher/in,
Entdecker/in 2/15

expression /ɪkˈspreʃn/
Ausdruck 1/12

extra /ˈekstrə/ zusätzlich 3/17

extreme /ɪkˈstriːm/ extrem I

eye /aɪ/ Auge I

keep an eye on sth/sb
(informal) /ˌkiːpˌənˌˈaɪˌɒn
ˌsʌmθɪŋ/ˌsʌmbədi/ ein
(wachsames) Auge auf etw/
jdn haben, etw/jdn im Auge
behalten 1/M5

F

face /feɪs/ Gesicht I

fact /fækt/ Fakt 2/M4

fact file /ˈfækt ˌfaɪl/
Steckbrief 4/15

factory /ˈfæktri/ Fabrik; Werk II

fail /feɪl/ ungenügend
(Schulnote) 1/LL

faint /feɪnt/ ohnmächtig
werden 5/7

fall (AE) = autumn (BE) /fɔːl/
Herbst 1/M1

fall (irr) /fɔːl/ fallen III

fall down /fɔːl ˌdaʊn/ hinfallen I

fall off /fɔːlˌˈɒf/
herunterfallen 5/P12

fallen /ˈfɔːlən/ siehe „fall"

false /fɔːls/ falsch 0p5

fame *(no pl)* /feɪm/ Ruhm 6/M1

family /ˈfæmli/ Familie I

famine /ˈfæmɪn/ Hungersnot 4/M1

the **famous** *(no pl)* /ðə ˈfeɪməs/ die Berühmten 6/13

famous /ˈfeɪməs/ berühmt I

fantastic *(informal)* /fænˈtæstɪk/ fantastisch, wunderbar I

fantasy /ˈfæntəsi/ Fantasie; Fantasy 6/12

FAQ (= Frequently Asked Question) /ˌef eɪ ˈkjuː/ FAQ, häufig gestellte Frage 3/16

far /fɑː/ weit II

so **far** /ˌsəʊ ˈfɑː/ bisher, bis jetzt 1/10

farm /fɑːm/ Bauernhof I

farm (land) /fɑːm/ (Land) bebauen Intro

farmer /ˈfɑːmə/ Bauer/Bäuerin I

fast /fɑːst/ schnell I

father /ˈfɑːðə/ Vater I

Father Christmas /ˌfɑːðə ˈkrɪsməs/ Weihnachtsmann II

fault /fɔːlt/ Schuld; Fehler II

favorite *(AE)* = **favourite** *(BE)* /ˈfeɪvrət/ Lieblings- 1/10

favourite /ˈfeɪvrət/ Lieblings- I

feather /ˈfeðə/ Feder 4/12

February /ˈfebruəri/ Februar I

feed *(irr)* /fiːd/ füttern, zu Essen geben I; ernähren 3/13

feel *(irr)* /fiːl/ (sich) fühlen II

feel like doing sth /ˌfiːl ˌlaɪk ˈduːɪŋ ˌsʌmθɪŋ/ Lust haben, etw zu tun 5/P6

feel sorry for sb /ˌfiːl ˈsɒri fə ˌsʌmbədi/ Mitleid mit jdm haben III

feeling /ˈfiːlɪŋ/ Gefühl III

fell /fel/ *Vergangenheitsform von „fall"*

felt /felt/ *Vergangenheitsform von „feel"*

felt tip /ˈfelt ˌtɪp/ Filzstift I

female /ˈfiːmeɪl/ weiblich 5/M9

ferry /ˈferi/ Fähre 3/8

festival /ˈfestɪvl/ Fest; Festival II

few /fjuː/ wenige 3/17

a **few** /ə ˈfjuː/ einige III

field /fiːld/ Wiese, Weide, Feld 4/9

field /fiːld/ Bereich 3/M9

fight /faɪt/ Kampf, Streit 6/M6

fight *(irr)* /faɪt/ (be)kämpfen II

fighter /ˈfaɪtə/ Kämpfer(in) III

figures *(only pl)* /ˈfɪɡəz/ Zahlen(material) 4/M3

fill in /fɪlˈɪn/ ausfüllen 6/M7

fill in /fɪlˈɪn/ einsetzen 1/P5

filled /fɪld/ gefüllt 2/P13

animated film /ˌænɪmeɪtɪd ˈfɪlm/ (Zeichen)trickfilm, Animationsfilm 6/12

film /fɪlm/ filmen, drehen 6/2

filter /ˈfɪltə/ filtern 1/10

finally /ˈfaɪnli/ schließlich, endlich; zum Schluss II

find *(irr)* /faɪnd/ finden I

find out /faɪndˈaʊt/ herausfinden 1/5

find out about /faɪndˈaʊtˌəˌbaʊt/ sich informieren über 1/M8

finding /ˈfaɪndɪŋ/ Entdeckung; Ergebnis 4/11

fine /faɪn/ in Ordnung, gut II

I'm fine. /aɪm ˈfaɪn/ Es geht mir gut. I

finish /ˈfɪnɪʃ/ beenden, aufhören I

fire /faɪə/ Feuer I

forest fire /ˈfɒrɪst ˌfaɪə/ Waldbrand 6/2

catch fire /ˌkætʃ ˈfaɪə/ in Brand geraten, Feuer fangen 6/M3

fire department *(AE)* = **fire brigade** *(BE)* /ˈfaɪə dɪˌpɑːtmənt, ˈfaɪə brɪˌɡeɪd/ Feuerwehr 6/M3

firefighter /ˈfaɪəˌfaɪtə/ Feuerwehrmann/-frau II

fireworks *(only pl)* /ˈfaɪəˌwɜːks/ Feuerwerk 2/P12

first /fɜːst/ erste(r, s) I; zuerst, als Erstes II

at first /ət ˈfɜːst/ anfangs, zuerst II

first language /ˌfɜːst ˈlæŋɡwɪdʒ/ Muttersprache 4/1

first name /ˈfɜːst ˌneɪm/ Vorname III

first of all /ˌfɜːst ˌəvˌˈɔːl/ erstens, als erstes II

firstly /ˈfɜːstli/ erstens 2/M4

fish *(pl - or -es)* /fɪʃ, fɪʃ, ˈfɪʃɪz/ Fisch I

fish /fɪʃ/ fischen, angeln III

fish finger /ˌfɪʃ ˈfɪŋɡə/ Fischstäbchen 2/10

fish tank /ˈfɪʃ tæŋk/ Aquarium I

fisherman /ˈfɪʃəmən/ Fischer Intro

fit *(irr)* /fɪt/ passen (zu) 5/14

fit in /fɪtˈɪn/ sich einfügen, dazupassen 5/M10

fitting room /ˈfɪtɪŋ ˌruːm/ Umkleide, Anprobe 5/3

fixed /fɪkst/ fest(gesetzt), verabredet 2/M1

fizzy drink /ˈfɪzi ˌdrɪŋk/ süßes, kohlensäurehaltiges Getränk 2/M2

flag /flæɡ/ Fahne; Flagge II

flame /fleɪm/ Flamme 6/4

flat /flæt/ Wohnung III

flat /flæt/ flach; platt II

flavour /ˈfleɪvə/ Geschmack; Aroma 2/M2

flavouring /ˈfleɪvərɪŋ/ Aroma, Geschmacksstoff 2/M2

floor /flɔː/ Boden I; Stockwerk III

flour *(no pl)* /ˈflaʊə/ Mehl II

flower /ˈflaʊə/ Blume II

fly *(irr)* /flaɪ/ fliegen I

fog /fɒɡ/ Nebel II

foggy /ˈfɒɡi/ neblig II

folder /ˈfəʊldə/ Mappe, Schnellhefter I

follow /ˈfɒləʊ/ folgen II

food /fuːd/ Nahrungsmittel 1/8

food *(no pl)* /fuːd/ Essen I

foot *(pl feet)* /fʊt, fiːt/ Fuß I

on foot /ɒn ˈfʊt/ zu Fuß II

football /ˈfʊtbɔːl/ Fußball I

football /ˈfʊtbɔːl/ (American) Football 1/M2

footstep /ˈfʊtˌstep/ Schritt 4/9

for /fɔː/ für I; seit 3/8

for example /fərˌɪɡˈzɑːmpl/ zum Beispiel I

for free /fɔː ˈfriː/ gratis, umsonst I

for the better /fə ðə ˈbetə/ zum Besseren, zum Guten 1/10

force sb (to do sth)

/ˈfɔːs ˌsʌmbədi/ jdn zwingen
(etw zu tun) 4/14

forest /ˈfɒrɪst/ Wald II

forest fire /ˈfɒrɪst ˌfaɪə/
Waldbrand 6/2

forget *(irr)* /fəˈget/ vergessen I

forgot /fəˈgɒt/ *Vergangenheitsform von „forget"*

forgotten /fəˈgɒtn/ *siehe
„forget"*

fork /fɔːk/ Gabel I

form /fɔːm/ Form; Formular 6/M7

form /fɔːm/ bilden, formen 1/M1

fortune /ˈfɔːtʃən/ Vermögen,
Reichtum 6/M1

look forward to sth /ˌlʊk
ˈfɔːwəd tə ˌsʌmθɪŋ/ sich auf
etw freuen 1/3

fought /fɔːt/ *Vergangenheitsform
von „fight"*

found /faʊnd/ gründen 6/7

found /faʊnd/ *Vergangenheitsform von „find"*

fox /fɒks/ Fuchs 6/7

France /frɑːnts/ Frankreich I

freak /friːk/ Fanatiker/in 1/12

free /friː/ befreien,
freilassen 4/CC

free /friː/ frei I; gratis,
umsonst 3/2

for free /fɔː ˈfriː/ gratis,
umsonst I

freedom *(no pl)* /ˈfriːdəm/
Freiheit 3/2

freeze /friːz/ gefrieren,
einfrieren, zufrieren 2/CC

French /frentʃ/ Französisch;
französisch II

the French /ðə ˈfrentʃ/ die
Franzosen 3/2

French fries *(AE) (only pl)* =
chips *(BE) (only pl)* /ˌfrentʃ
ˈfraɪz/ Pommes frites 2/2

fresh /freʃ/ frisch II

Friday /ˈfraɪdeɪ/ Freitag I

fridge *(informal)* /frɪdʒ/
Kühlschrank II

fried chicken /ˌfraɪd ˈtʃɪkɪn/
Brathähnchen 2/2

fried egg /ˌfraɪd ˈeg/
Spiegelei 2/2

friend /frend/ Freund/in I

friendliness *(no pl)* /ˈfrendlɪnɪs/
Freundlichkeit 4/8

friendly /ˈfrendli/ freundlich I

friendship /ˈfrendʃɪp/
Freundschaft 4/8

be frightened (of) /bi: ˈfraɪtnd/
Angst haben, sich fürchten
(vor) II

from /frəm/ von, aus I

in front of /ɪn ˈfrʌntˌəv/ vor I

Front of Line Pass /ˌfrʌntˌəv ˈlaɪn
ˌpɑːs/ *Ticket ohne Wartezeit* 6/9

fruit /fruːt/ Frucht; Obst I

frustrated /frʌˈstreɪtɪd/
frustriert; enttäuscht III

full /fʊl/ voll II

fun *(no pl)* /fʌn/ Spaß I

fun /fʌn/ lustig, witzig,
spaßig I

be (great) fun /bi: (ˌgreɪt) ˈfʌn/
(viel) Spaß machen III

make fun of sb /meɪk ˈfʌnˌəv
ˌsʌmbədi/ sich über jdn lustig
machen I

fund /fʌnd/ finanzieren 1/M5

funding *(no pl)* /ˈfʌndɪŋ/
Finanzierung 1/10

funfair /ˈfʌnˌfeə/ Vergnügungs-
park; Jahrmarkt 2/CC

funny /ˈfʌni/ lustig, witzig,
komisch I

fur /fɜː/ Fell; Pelz II

future /ˈfjuːtʃə/ Zukunft II

G

gain /geɪn/ erwerben;
zunehmen 5/M10

gallery /ˈgæləri/ Galerie 3/M1

gallery walk /ˈgæləri wɔːk/
Galerierundgang 6/5

gambling *(no pl)* /ˈgæmblɪŋ/
Glücksspiel 4/P14

game /geɪm/ Spiel I

garage /ˈgærɑːʒ/ Garage;
(Kfz-)Werkstatt Op5

garden /ˈgɑːdn/ Garten I

gardener /ˈgɑːdnə/ Gärtner/in II

gardening *(no pl)* /ˈgɑːdnɪŋ/
Gartenarbeit, Gärtnern 1/M5

gave /geɪv/ *Vergangenheitsform
von „give"*

general /ˈdʒenrəl/ allgemein,

generell 6/9

gentleman /ˈdʒentlmən/
Gentleman, (vornehmer)
Herr 5/M4

geography /dʒiˈɒgrəfi/
Erdkunde, Geografie I

German /ˈdʒɜːmən/ Deutsch;
deutsch I

in German /ɪn ˈdʒɜːmən/ auf
Deutsch I

Germany /ˈdʒɜːməni/
Deutschland I

get *(irr)* /get/ erhalten,
bekommen; holen I; werden II

get *(irr)* /get/ steigen II

get *(irr)* /get/ verstehen 1/CC

get along (with sb) /getˌəˈlɒŋ/
sich (mit jdm) verstehen 6/5

get lost /get ˈlɒst/ sich verirren,
sich verlaufen 5/CC

get married /get ˈmærɪd/
heiraten II

get ready (for sth) /get ˈredi/
sich (für etw) bereit
machen 6/10

get sb off to somewhere /get
ˌsʌmbədiˌɒf tʊ ˈsʌmweə/ jdn
wohin bringen 4/M5

get sth wrong /get ˌsʌmθɪŋ ˈrɒŋ/
etw falsch verstehen 2/8

get together /ˌgetˌtəˈgeðə/ sich
treffen 2/14

get up /getˌˈʌp/ aufstehen I

get used to sth /get ˈjuːstˌtu
ˌsʌmθɪŋ/ sich an etw
gewöhnen 4/6

get well /get ˈwel/ gesund
werden II

get well card /get ˈwel kɑːd/
Genesungskarte II

Get well soon. /get wel ˈsuːn/
Gute Besserung! II

ghost /gəʊst/ Geist, Gespenst II

ghost town /ˈgəʊst taʊn/
Geisterstadt 6/7

giant /ˈdʒaɪənt/ Riese III

giant /ˈdʒaɪənt/ riesig 4/CC

gift /gɪft/ Geschenk 4/M1

gimme (= give me) *(informal)*
/ˈgɪmi/ gib mir 5/M1

girl /gɜːl/ Mädchen I

girlfriend /ˈgɜːlˌfrend/ (feste)

Freundin III

give (irr) /gɪv/ geben I

give a talk /ˌgɪv_ə 'tɔ:k/ einen Vortrag halten 1/7

give away /gɪv_ə'weɪ/ verschenken 2/M2

give directions /ˌgɪv dɪ'rekʃnz/ den Weg beschreiben III

give one's opinion (on sth) /gɪv wʌnz_ə'pɪnjən/ seine Meinung (zu etw) äußern, (zu etw) Stellung nehmen 2/M4

give reasons /gɪv 'ri:znz/ begründen, Gründe angeben 1/11

give thanks /gɪv 'θæŋks/ danken, sich bedanken 2/12

give up /ˌgɪv_'ʌp/ aufgeben III

given /gɪvn/ siehe „give"

glad /glæd/ glücklich, froh I

glass /glɑ:s/ Glas II

glasses (only pl) /'glɑ:sɪz/ Brille I

glove /glʌv/ Handschuh I

go (irr) /gəʊ/ gehen I; fahren II

in one go /ˌɪn wʌn 'gəʊ/ in einem Durchgang, auf einmal 6/4

go crazy (informal) /gəʊ 'kreɪzi/ durchdrehen, ausflippen I

go for a walk /ˌgəʊ fər_ə 'wɔ:k/ spazieren gehen I

go green /ˌgəʊ 'gri:n/ umweltbewusst werden 1/10

go out /gəʊ_'aʊt/ (hinaus) gehen; ausgehen III

go shopping /gəʊ 'ʃɒpɪŋ/ einkaufen gehen I

go with /'gəʊ wɪð/ gehören zu, passen zu 1/2

go wrong /gəʊ 'rɒŋ/ schief gehen 1/M2

goal /gəʊl/ Tor III

score a goal /skɔ:r_ə 'gəʊl/ ein Tor schießen III

goal line /'gəʊl_ˌlaɪn/ Torlinie 5/15

goalkeeper /'gəʊl_ˌki:pə/ Tormann/Torfrau III

goalpost /'gəʊl_ˌpəʊst/ Torpfosten 5/15

goat /gəʊt/ Ziege I

god /gɒd/ Gott II

going to /'gəʊɪŋ tə/ werden II

goldfish (pl -) /'gəʊld_ˌfɪʃ/ Goldfisch I

gone /gɒn/ siehe „go"

gonna (= going to) (informal) /'gɒnə/ werden 5/M1

good /gʊd/ gut I

be good at sth /bi 'gʊd_ˌæt ˌsʌmθɪŋ/ gut in etw sein; etw gut können I

Good luck! /gʊd 'lʌk/ Viel Glück! III

good-looking /ˌgʊd'lʊkɪŋ/ gut aussehend I

Oh my goodness! /əʊ maɪ 'gʊdnes/ Ach du meine Güte! 5/M1

got /gɒt/ Vergangenheitsform von „get"

government /'gʌvənmənt/ Regierung 4/14

grab sth (informal) /'græb ˌsʌmθɪŋ/ (sich) etw schnappen 2/I

graduate /'grædʒuət/ Schulabgänger/in; Absolvent/in 1/M1

graduation (no pl) /ˌgrædʒu'eɪʃn/ Schulabschluss; Abschlussfeier 1/LL

grammar /'græmə/ Grammatik 4/M6

grandfather /'græn_ˌfɑ:ðə/ Großvater I

grandma (informal) /'græn_ˌmɑ:/ Oma, Omi I

grandmother /'græn_ˌmʌðə/ Großmutter I

grandparents (only pl) /'græn_ˌpeərənts/ Großeltern I

grant /grɑ:nt/ Zuschuss, Fördermittel 1/10

grass (no pl) /grɑ:s/ Gras; Wiese, Rasen II

great /greɪt/ groß, riesig; großartig, wunderbar I

Great Britain /ˌgreɪt 'brɪtn/ Großbritannien II

Grecian /'gri:ʃn/ griechisch 4/CC

Greece /gri:s/ Griechenland II

green /gri:n/ grün I

green /gri:n/ umweltfreundlich,

ökologisch 1/8

go green /ˌgəʊ 'gri:n/ umweltbewusst werden 1/10

green card (AE) /ˌgri:n 'kɑ:d/ Aufenthaltserlaubnis mit Arbeitsgenehmigung, Greencard 4/1

greenhouse /'gri:n_ˌhaʊs/ Gewächshaus, Treibhaus 1/M5

greet /gri:t/ (be)grüßen 4/M2

grew /gru:/ Vergangenheitsform von „grow"

grey /greɪ/ grau I

grid /grɪd/ Gitter; Tabelle 1/M4

group /gru:p/ Gruppe I

buzz group /'bʌz gru:p/ Form der Gruppenarbeit 1/8

grow (irr) /grəʊ/ wachsen; anbauen 1/10

grow up /grəʊ_'ʌp/ erwachsen werden II; aufwachsen 3/8

grown /grəʊn/ siehe „grow"

guard /gɑ:d/ bewachen 5/P2

border patrol guard /ˌbɔ:də pə'trəʊl gɑ:d/ Grenzposten, Grenzbeamter/beamtin 6/2

security guard /sɪ'kjʊərəti ˌgɑ:d/ Sicherheitsbedienstete/r, Wachmann/-frau Op2

guess /ges/ (er)raten; vermuten, schätzen II

have a guess /ˌhæv_ə 'ges/ raten, schätzen Op3

keep sb guessing /ˌki:p sʌmbədi 'gesɪŋ/ jdn auf die Folter spannen 5/M1

guest /gest/ Gast III

guidance counsellor /'gaɪdns ˌkaʊnslə/ Beratungslehrer, Vertrauenslehrer 1/6

guinea pig /'gɪni ˌpɪg/ Meerschweinchen I

guitar /gɪ'tɑ:/ Gitarre I

gulf stream /'gʌlf stri:m/ Golfstrom 4/9

nicotine gum (no pl) /'nɪkəti:n gʌm/ Nikotinkaugummi 5/M10

gumbo (no pl) /'gʌmbəʊ/ Suppe mit Meeresfrüchten 2/M5

guy (informal) /gaɪ/ Kerl, Typ 5/7

guys (only pl) (informal) /gaɪz/

Leute 1/3

gym (= gymnasium) /dʒɪm, dʒɪmˈneɪziəm/ Turnhalle II

gymnastics *(only pl)* /dʒɪmˈnæstɪks/ Turnen 5/11

H

had /hæd/ *Vergangenheitsform von „have"*

hair *(no pl)* /heə/ Haar(e) I

hairdresser /ˈheəˌdresə/ Friseur/in II

half *(pl* **halves***)* /haːf, haːvz/ Hälfte III

half /haːf/ halb III

half past (eight) /ˈhaːf ˌpaːst/ halb (neun) I

half time /ˌhaːf ˈtaɪm/ Halbzeit 5/11

hall /hɔːl/ Flur III

hall /hɔːl/ Halle; Saal II

ham *(no pl)* /hæm/ Schinken III

on the one hand /ɒn ðə ˈwʌn ˌhænd/ einerseits 2/M4

on the other hand /ɒn ðiˈ ʌðə ˌhænd/ andererseits 2/M4

clap one's hands /ˌklæp wʌnz ˈhændz/ in die Hände klatschen 2/10

take sth into one's own hands /teɪk ˌsʌmθɪŋˌɪntə wʌnzˈ əʊn hændz/ etw selbst in die Hand nehmen 6/10

hang *(irr)* /hæŋ/ (auf)hängen I

hang around /ˌhæŋˌəˈraʊnd/ herumhängen 5/7

hang on to sth /hæŋˈɒn tʊ ˌsʌmθɪŋ/ sich an etw festhalten, sich an etw klammern 3/13

hang out *(informal)* /hæŋˈaʊt/ sich aufhalten, abhängen 5/5

hang up sth /ˈhæŋˌʌp ˌsʌmθɪŋ/ etw aufhängen 2/16

happen /ˈhæpən/ geschehen, passieren I

happy /ˈhæpi/ glücklich; zufrieden; fröhlich II

Happy birthday! /ˌhæpi ˈbɜːθdeɪ/ Alles Gute zum Geburtstag! I

happy ending /ˌhæpiˈ endɪŋ/ Happyend, gutes Ende 6/11

harbour /ˈhaːbə/ Hafen 4/M1

hard /haːd/ hart; schwer II

hard /haːd/ fleißig 4/M5

try hard to do sth /ˌtraɪ ˈhaːd ˌtə du: sʌmθɪŋ/ sich sehr bemühen, etw zu tun II

have a hard time doing sth /hævˌə haːd ˌtaɪm ˈduːɪŋ ˌsʌmθɪŋ/ es schwer haben, etw zu tun 3/16

hard-working /ˌhaːdˈwɜːkɪŋ/ fleißig II

harmony *(no pl)* /ˈhaːməni/ Harmonie; Eintracht 4/1

harvest /ˈhaːvɪst/ Ernte 2/15

harvest /ˈhaːvɪst/ ernten 3/M6

hat /hæt/ Hut; Mütze I

hate *(no pl)* /heɪt/ Hass 6/12

hate /heɪt/ hassen, nicht ausstehen können I

have *(irr)* /hæv/ haben I; essen I

have a drink /ˌhævˌə ˈdrɪŋk/ etwas trinken gehen 5/4

have a good time /ˌhævˌə ˌɡʊd ˈtaɪm/ sich amüsieren, Spaß haben 5/M3

have a guess /ˌhəvˌə ˈɡes/ raten, schätzen 0p3

have got /hæv ˈɡɒt/ haben I

have to /ˈhæv tə/ müssen I

Hawaiian /həˈwaɪən/ hawaiisch 2/2

he /hi/ er I

head /hed/ Kopf I

headache /ˈhedeɪk/ Kopfschmerzen, Kopfweh 5/M10

headdress /ˈhedˌdres/ Kopfschmuck 4/12

heading /ˈhedɪŋ/ Überschrift, Titel 3/M1

headline /ˈhedˌlaɪn/ Schlagzeile 3/11

headteacher /ˌhedˈtiːtʃə/ Schulleiter/in, Rektor/in II

health *(no pl)* /helθ/ Gesundheit III

healthy /ˈhelθi/ gesund II

hear *(irr)* /hɪə/ hören I

heart /haːt/ Herz III

by heart /baɪ ˈhaːt/ auswendig 5/7

heat /hiːt/ erhitzen III

heating *(no pl)* /ˈhiːtɪŋ/ Heizung 1/P9

heavy /ˈhevi/ schwer III

helicopter /ˈheliˌkɒptə/ Hubschrauber 6/4

hello /həˈləʊ/ hallo I

helmet /ˈhelmɪt/ Helm III

help /help/ Hilfe I

help /help/ helfen I

help out /ˌhelpˌˈaʊt/ (aus) helfen, unterstützen 1/P6

helpful /ˈhelpfl/ hilfsbereit; hilfreich, nützlich III

her /hɜː/ sie; ihr(e, n) I

here /hɪə/ hier(her) I

Here you are. /ˌhɪə juˌˈaː/ Hier, bitte!, Bitte schön! I

hero *(pl* **-es***)* /ˈhɪərəʊ, ˈhɪərəʊz/ Held/in II

hers /hɜːz/ ihre(r, s) 1/12

herself /həˈself/ sich (selbst); selbst 5/13

hi /haɪ/ hallo, hi I

hide *(irr)* /haɪd/ (sich) verstecken II

high /haɪ/ hoch II

high school /ˈhaɪ ˌskuːl/ *weiterführende Schule in den USA (Klasse 9-12)* 1/I

high school diploma /ˈhaɪ ˌskuːl dɪˌpləʊmə/ *Abschlusszeugnis der Highschool* 1/LL

highlight /ˈhaɪˌlaɪt/ Höhepunkt, Highlight II

highlight sth /ˈhaɪlaɪt ˌsʌmθɪŋ/ etw hervorheben/ unterstreichen 3/11

highway /ˈhaɪˌweɪ/ Bundesstraße, Highway 4/9

hike /haɪk/ wandern 6/P6

hiking *(no pl)* /ˈhaɪkɪŋ/ Wandern II

hill /hɪl/ Hügel 6/2

him /hɪm/ ihm, ihn I

himself /hɪmˈself/ sich (selbst); selbst 5/P11

Hindu /ˌhɪnˈduː/ Hindu; hinduistisch 2/12

hippo (= hippopotamus) /ˈhɪpəʊ, ˌhɪpəˈpɒtəməs/ Nilpferd II

his / hɪz / sein(e, r) I

Hispanic / hɪˈspænɪk / Hispano-Amerikaner/in; hispanisch 4/1

history / ˈhɪstri / Geschichte I

hit *(irr)* / hɪt / schlagen; treffen; stoßen (gegen) III

hold *(irr)* / həʊld / halten III

hole / həʊl / Loch II

holiday / ˈhɒlɪdeɪ / Urlaub, Ferien I

holiday / ˈhɒlɪdeɪ / Feiertag Intro

go on holiday / ˌgəʊ ˌɒn ˈhɒlɪdeɪ / Urlaub machen, in den Urlaub fahren II

home / həʊm / Zuhause, Heim I; Haus 6/4

home / həʊm / zu Hause, nach Hause II

at home / ət ˈhəʊm / zu Hause I

home economics *(only pl)* / ˌhəʊm ˌiːkəˈnɒmɪks / Hauswirtschaft(slehre) 1/5

be home to sth/sb / bi ˈhəʊm tə ˌsʌmθɪŋ/ˌsʌmbədi / etw/jdn beheimaten 3/2

home town / ˌhəʊm ˈtaʊn / Heimatort II

home-made / ˌhəʊm ˈmeɪd / hausgemacht, selbst gemacht 2/P13

homecoming *(AE)* / ˈhəʊmˌkʌmɪŋ / *amerikanisches Schulfest mit Ehemaligentreffen* 1/3

homeland / ˈhəʊmˌlænd / Heimat(land) 4/M1

homeroom *(AE)* / ˈhəʊmˌruːm / *Klassenzimmer, in dem sich die Schüler am Anfang des Schultages versammeln* 1/3

homework *(no pl)* / ˈhəʊmˌwɜːk / Hausaufgaben I

honest / ˈɒnɪst / ehrlich II

honey *(no pl)* / ˈhʌni / Honig I

hook sb / ˈhʊk ˌsʌmbədi / jdn abhängig machen 2/M2

be hooked (on sth) / bi ˈhʊkt / total verrückt nach etw sein; von etw abhängig sein 2/M2

hoover / ˈhuːvə / staubsaugen I

hope / həʊp / Hoffnung 4/M7

hope / həʊp / hoffen I

horoscope / ˈhɒrəˌskəʊp / Horoskop II

horrible / ˈhɒrəbl / schrecklich III

horse / hɔːs / Pferd I

horseshoe / ˈhɔːsˌʃuː / Hufeisen 4/12

hospital / ˈhɒspɪtl / Krankenhaus III

hot / hɒt / heiß I; scharf III

hour / ˈaʊə / Stunde I

hours *(only pl)* / ˈaʊəz / (Öffnungs)zeiten 6/9

work long hours / wɜːk ˌlɒŋ ˈaʊəz / lange arbeiten; Überstunden machen 6/5

house / haʊs / Haus I

how / haʊ / wie I

How are you? / haʊ ˈɑː ju / Wie geht es dir/Ihnen/euch? I

How much is/are ... ? / ˌhaʊ ˈmʌtʃ ɪz/ɑː / Was kostet/kosten ...? I

How old are you? / haʊ ˈəʊld ə jʊ / Wie alt bist du/seid ihr? I

how to / haʊ tə / wie man 1/1

Hualapai / ˈhwæləpeɪ / Hualapai(indianer) 4/12

huge / hjuːdʒ / riesig, riesengroß II

human / ˈhjuːmən / Mensch 6/10

human / ˈhjuːmən / menschlich 6/10

hundreds of thousands *(only pl)* / ˌhʌndrədz əv ˈθaʊzndz / Hunderttausende 6/4

hungry / ˈhʌŋgri / hungrig I

hunt / hʌnt / jagen 2/15

hunter / ˈhʌntə / Jäger/in 4/14

hurray / hʊˈreɪ / hurra 5/13

hurry / ˈhʌri / sich beeilen III

hurry up / ˌhʌri ˈʌp / sich beeilen I

hurt *(irr)* / hɜːt / wehtun, schmerzen III

hurt sb / ˈhɜːt ˌsʌmbədi / jdn verletzen, jdm wehtun I

hurt / hɜːt / verletzt, verwundet 6/M3

husband / ˈhʌzbənd / Ehemann I

I

I / aɪ / ich I

I'm fine. / aɪm ˈfaɪn /

Es geht mir gut. II

ice *(no pl)* / aɪs / Eis 4/12

ice cream / ˈaɪsˌkriːm / Eiskrem I

ice hockey *(no pl)* / ˈaɪs ˌhɒki / Eishockey 5/11

ice-skating rink / ˈaɪsskeɪtɪŋ rɪŋk / Schlittschuhbahn 3/5

ICT (= information and communication technology) / ˌaɪ siː ˈtiː, ˌɪnfəˌmeɪʃn ən kəˌmjuːnɪˌkeɪʃn tekˈnɒlədʒi / Informatik I

ID card (= identity card) / ˌaɪˈdiː kɑːd, aɪˈdentɪti kɑːd / (Personal)ausweis 1/P4

idea / aɪˈdɪə / Idee I

identify sb / aɪˈdentɪfaɪ ˌsʌmbədi / jdn identifizieren 6/13

if / ɪf / wenn, falls III

what if / wɒt ˈɪf / was ist/wäre, wenn 4/M6

igloo / ˈɪglu / Iglu 4/12

ignore / ɪgˈnɔː / ignorieren 5/M1

ill / ɪl / krank II

illegal / ɪˈliːgl / illegal 4/1

illustrate / ˈɪləˌstreɪt / illustrieren, bebildern 1/14

imagination / ɪˌmædʒɪˈneɪʃn / Fantasie, Vorstellungskraft; Einbildung 3/15

imagine / ɪˈmædʒɪn / sich vorstellen 2/11

immigrant / ˈɪmɪgrənt / Einwanderer/in 3/2

immigrate / ˈɪmɪˌgreɪt / einwandern 4/1

immigration *(no pl)* / ˌɪmɪˈgreɪʃn / Einwanderung, Immigration 3/2

important / ɪmˈpɔːtnt / wichtig I

improve / ɪmˈpruːv / verbessern 1/5

in / ɪn / in I

in a minute / ɪnˌə ˈmɪnɪt / gleich, sofort I

in front of / ɪn ˈfrʌntˌəv / vor I

in one go / ˌɪn wʌn ˈgəʊ / in einem Durchgang, auf einmal 6/4

in the end / ˌɪn ðiˌˈend / am Ende, zum Schluss 6/P9

include / ɪnˈkluːd / beinhalten, einschließen 1/M1

including / ɪnˈkluːdɪŋ /

einschließlich 4/2

incredible /ɪnˈkredəbl/ unglaublich II

Independence Day /ˌɪndɪˈpendəns ˌdeɪ/ *amerikanischer Unabhängigkeitstag* Intro

India /ˈɪndiə/ Indien II

Indian /ˈɪndiən/ Inder/in; *veraltete Bezeichnung für amerikanische Ureinwohner* 4/LL

Indian /ˈɪndiən/ indisch; indianisch II

indoors /ɪnˈdɔːz/ drinnen 6/5

industry /ˈɪndəstri/ Branche, Gewerbe; Industrie 6/2

inform /ɪnˈfɔːm/ informieren 4/P4

information *(no pl)* /ˌɪnfəˈmeɪʃn/ Information I

piece of information /ˌpiːs_əv_ˌɪnfəˈmeɪʃn/ Information 0p5

ingredient /ɪnˈgriːdiənt/ Zutat 2/M2

injured /ˈɪndʒəd/ verletzt III

injury /ˈɪndʒəri/ Verletzung 5/11

insect /ˈɪnsekt/ Insekt II

inside /ɪnˈsaɪd/ drinnen; innen III

inside /ɪnˈsaɪd/ im Inneren 1/M7

install /ɪnˈstɔːl/ installieren 1/10

instead (of) /ɪnˈsted (_əv)/ stattdessen; (an)statt II

insulation /ˌɪnsjʊˈleɪʃn/ Isolierung, Dämmung 1/M7

interest /ˈɪntrəst/ Interesse 1/P5

interested (in sth) /ˈɪntrəstɪd/ interessiert (an etw) II

interesting /ˈɪntrəstɪŋ/ interessant I

internationally /ˌɪntəˈnæʃnəli/ international 3/16

surf the Internet /ˌsɜːf ðiˈɪntənet/ im Internet surfen 5/2

interview /ˈɪntəˌvjuː/ befragen; interviewen 1/10

into /ˈɪntʊ/ in III

introduce /ˌɪntrəˈdjuːs/ vorstellen 5/12

invent /ɪnˈvent/ erfinden III

invention /ɪnˈvenʃn/ Erfindung III

invitation /ˌɪnvɪˈteɪʃn/ Einladung I

invite /ɪnˈvaɪt/ einladen I

Ireland /ˈaɪələnd/ Irland II

Irish /ˈaɪrɪʃ/ Irisch; irisch II

Irish stew /ˌaɪrɪʃ ˈstjuː/ *gekochtes Hammelfleisch mit Weißkraut und Kartoffeln* 4/M1

iron /ˈaɪən/ bügeln I

Iroquois /ˈɪrəkwɔɪ/ Irokese 4/CC

island /ˈaɪlənd/ Insel III

it /ɪt/ es I

(it's) your turn /ˈjɔː ˌtɜːn/ du bist dran I

Italian /ɪˈtæliən/ Italienisch; italienisch II

Italy /ˈɪtəli/ Italien II

its /ɪts/ sein(e), ihr(e) II

itself /ɪtˈself/ sich (selbst); selbst 5/12

J

jacket /ˈdʒækɪt/ Jacke I

jam /dʒæm/ Marmelade I

January /ˈdʒænjuəri/ Januar I

jealous /ˈdʒeləs/ eifersüchtig III

jelly /ˈdʒeli/ Gelee; Marmelade 2/2

jewellery *(no pl)* /ˈdʒuːəlri/ Schmuck 6/13

Jewish /ˈdʒuːɪʃ/ jüdisch 2/2

Jiaozi dumpling /dʒɪəˈɒzi ˌdʌmplɪŋ/ *chinesisches Teigtaschengericht* 2/14

jigsaw /ˈdʒɪgsɔː/ Puzzle 4/4

join /dʒɔɪn/ mitmachen bei; beitreten I; zusammenfügen; sich anschließen 4/4

judge /dʒʌdʒ/ Richter/in, Jurymitglied 6/M8

judge /dʒʌdʒ/ urteilen, entscheiden 6/13

juggler /ˈdʒʌglə/ Jongleur/in II

juice /dʒuːs/ Saft I

July /dʒʊˈlaɪ/ Juli I

jump /dʒʌmp/ springen I

jump off /dʒʌmp_ˈɒf/ herunterspringen 3/13

June /dʒuːn/ Juni I

jungle /ˈdʒʌŋgl/ Dschungel, Urwald 6/10

junior high school /ˌdʒuːniə ˈhaɪ ˌskuːl/ *Mittelstufenschule in den USA* 1/LL

just /dʒʌst/ gleich; einfach II; nur III

just /dʒʌst/ gerade III

just /dʒʌst/ genau 4/15

just a minute /ˌdʒʌst_ə ˈmɪnɪt/ einen Moment/Augenblick bitte III

K

kaftan /ˈkæftæn/ *weites Kleid* 2/M5

kangaroo /ˌkæŋgəˈruː/ Känguru I

kayak /ˈkaɪæk/ Kajak Intro

keep *(irr)* /kiːp/ (be)halten; aufbewahren I

keep an eye on sth/sb *(informal)* /ˌkiːp_ən_ˈaɪ_ɒn ˌsʌmθɪŋ/ˌsʌmbədi/ ein (wachsames) Auge auf etw/jdn haben, etw/jdn im Auge behalten 1/M5

keep an open mind /ˌkiːp_ən_ˈəʊpən ˌmaɪnd/ aufgeschlossen bleiben 4/8

keep doing sth /kiːp ˈduːɪŋ ˌsʌmθɪŋ/ etw weiter tun; etw wiederholt/immer wieder tun 5/CC

keep sb guessing /ˌkiːp sʌmbədi ˈgesɪŋ/ jdn auf die Folter spannen 5/M1

keep up sth /ˌkiːp_ˈʌp sʌmθɪŋ/ etw fortführen, etw weiterhin tun 4/14

keeper /ˈkiːpə/ Tierpfleger/in II

kettle /ketl/ Wasserkocher III

key /kiː/ Schlüssel I

keyword /ˈkiːˌwɜːd/ Schlüsselwort 1/3

kick /kɪk/ treten, schießen, kicken 5/11

kickoff /ˈkɪkˌɒf/ Anpfiff, Anstoß 5/11

kill /kɪl/ töten III

kilogram /ˈkɪləˌgræm/ Kilo(gramm) 6/P3

kilometre /ˈkɪləˌmiːtə/ Kilometer III

kinara /kɪˈnɑːrə/ *siebenarmiger Kwanzaa-Kerzenständer* 2/M5

kind /kaɪnd/ Art, Sorte II
king /kɪŋ/ König II
kiss /kɪs/ Kuss II
kiss /kɪs/ küssen II
kitchen /ˈkɪtʃən/ Küche I
knee /niː/ Knie II
knew /njuː/ *Vergangenheitsform von „know"*
knife *(pl **knives**)* /naɪf, naɪvz/ Messer I
knock sb /ˈnɒk ˌsʌmbədi/ jdn stoßen III
know *(irr)* /nəʊ/ wissen; kennen I
known /nəʊn/ *siehe „know"*
Kwanzaa /ˈkwɑːnz ə/ *von Amerikanern afrikanischer Herkunft gefeiertes nicht- religiöses Fest* 2/M5

L

label /ˈleɪbl/ Etikett, Label; Marke 3/16
label /ˈleɪbl/ beschriften 5/4
ladder /ˈlædə/ Leiter Intro
lady /ˈleɪdi/ Frau; Dame II
lake /leɪk/ See II
Lakota /ləˈkəʊtə/ Lakota(indianer) Intro
lamb /læm/ Lamm I
lamp /læmp/ Lampe 3/13
land /lænd/ (Fest)land III
land /lænd/ landen III
landscape /ˈlændˌskeɪp/ Landschaft 6/2
language /ˈlæŋgwɪdʒ/ Sprache 1/5
first language /ˌfɜːst ˈlæŋgwɪdʒ/ Muttersprache 4/1
large /lɑːdʒ/ groß I
last /lɑːst/ letzte(r, s) I
late /leɪt/ (zu) spät I
be late /bi ˈleɪt/ (zu) spät kommen, sich verspäten I
later /ˈleɪtə/ später II
latest /ˈleɪtɪst/ jüngste(r, s); neueste(r, s) 1/P11
laugh /lɑːf/ lachen I
lawn /lɔːn/ Rasen III
lead *(irr)* /liːd/ (an)führen, leiten 4/M5
leaf *(pl **leaves**)* /liːf, liːvz/

Blatt II
leaflet /ˈliːflət/ Prospekt, Broschüre 5/P14
learn *(irr)* /lɜːn/ lernen I
learn about /ˌlɜːn ə'baʊt/ erfahren von/über 6/M7
leash /liːʃ/ Leine 4/P7
least /liːst/ am wenigsten 5/10
leave *(irr)* /liːv/ verlassen II; lassen III; abfahren III
leave sb in peace /ˌliːv ˌsʌmbədi ˌɪn ˈpiːs/ jdn in Frieden/Ruhe lassen 3/8
left /left/ (nach) links II; übrig III
left /left/ *Vergangenheitsform von „leave"*
on the/your left /ˌɒn ðə/jɔː ˈleft/ links, auf der linken Seite II
leg /leg/ Bein I
legal /ˈliːgl/ legal, gesetzlich zulässig 3/M1
legend /ˈledʒnd/ Sage, Legende 4/12
lemonade /ˌleməˈneɪd/ Limonade I
less /les/ weniger 5/M10
lesson /ˈlesn/ Stunde I
let *(irr)* /let/ lassen II
let's (= let us) /lets, ˈletˌəs/ lass(t) uns I
Let's go! /lets ˈgəʊ/ Los!, Auf geht's! II
letter /ˈletə/ Brief; Buchstabe III
library /ˈlaɪbrəri/ Bibliothek, Bücherei I
licence plate *(AE)* /ˈlaɪsns ˌpleɪt/ Nummernschild 6/CC
life *(pl **lives**)* /laɪf, laɪvz/ Leben II
lifeguard /ˈlaɪfˌgɑːd/ Rettungsschwimmer/in; Bademeister/in 6/2
lift /lɪft/ Aufzug, Lift III
lift /lɪft/ (hoch)heben; sich auflösen 4/9
light /laɪt/ Licht I
light *(irr)* /laɪt/ erhellen; anzünden 2/M5
light bulb /ˈlaɪt ˌbʌlb/ Glühbirne III
like /laɪk/ mögen I

like /laɪk/ wie II
like *(informal)* /laɪk/ ungefähr, bestimmt 5/M1
like this /laɪk ˈðɪs/ so 2/P4; solche(r, s) 2/14
What's ... like? /wɒts ˈlaɪk/ Wie ist ...? II
likely /ˈlaɪkli/ wahrscheinlich 4/M6
be more likely to do sth /bi mɔː ˌlaɪkli tə ˈduː ˌsʌmθɪŋ/ eher/ wahrscheinlicher etw tun 5/M9
likes *(only pl)* /laɪks/ Vorlieben 4/M7
line /laɪn/ Linie; Zeile 2/10
goal line /ˈgəʊlˌlaɪn/ Torlinie 5/15
stand in line /ˌstænd ˌɪn ˈlaɪn/ anstehen 4/M1
lines *(only pl)* /laɪnz/ Text 6/P11
linesman /ˈlaɪnzmən/ Linienrichter/in 5/11
linking word /ˈlɪŋkɪŋ wɜːd/ Bindewort 3/15
lion /ˈlaɪən/ Löwe I
list /lɪst/ Liste I
listen (to) /ˈlɪsn (tuː)/ (zu)hören I
litre /ˈliːtə/ Liter 6/P3
little /ˈlɪtl/ klein I
a little /ə ˈlɪtl/ ein bisschen II
live /lɪv/ leben, wohnen I
living /ˈlɪvɪŋ/ lebend 1/M5
make a living /ˌmeɪk ə ˈlɪvɪŋ/ seinen Lebensunterhalt verdienen 3/17
living room /ˈlɪvɪŋ ˌruːm/ Wohnzimmer I
lizard /ˈlɪzəd/ Eidechse, Echse 6/7
meat loaf /ˌmiːt ˈləʊf/ Hackbraten 2/LL
local /ˈləʊkl/ örtlich Op3; regional, aus der Umgebung 1/8
lock /lɒk/ Schloss 3/CC
locker /ˈlɒkə/ Schließfach, Spind 1/1
loco moco /ˌləʊkəʊ ˈməʊkəʊ/ hawaiisches Gericht 2/2
logo /ˈləʊgəʊ/ Abzeichen, Logo II
lol (= laugh(ing) out loud) /ˌelˌəʊˈel/ *Abkürzung für:*

laut lachen(d) 5/M1

lonely /ˈləʊnli/ einsam II

long /lɒŋ/ lang I

look /lʊk/ sehen, schauen I; aussehen II

look after /ˌlʊkˈɑːftə/ sich kümmern um I

look around /ˌlʊkəˈraʊnd/ sich umsehen/umschauen (in) 6/14

look at /ˈlʊkˌət/ betrachten, sehen, anschauen I

look for /ˈlʊk fɔː/ suchen (nach) I

look forward to sth /ˌlʊk ˈfɔːwəd tə ˌsʌmθɪŋ/ sich auf etw freuen 1/3

look up /ˈlʊkˌʌp/ nachschlagen Intro

lorry /ˈlɒri/ Lkw, Last(kraft)wagen 3/P2

lose (irr) /luːz/ verlieren II

lost /lɒst/ verloren 6/M1

lost /lɒst/ Vergangenheitsform von „lose"

get lost /get ˈlɒst/ sich verirren, sich verlaufen 5/CC

a lot (of) /ə ˈlɒt/ sehr; viel(e) I

lots (= a lot) (informal) /lɒts/ viel, jede Menge 6/2

lots of /ˈlɒtsˌəv/ viel, jede Menge I

lottery /ˈlɒtəri/ Lotterie 4/1

loud /laʊd/ laut II

love /lʌv/ Liebe I

love /lʌv/ herzliche Grüße, alles Liebe II

love /lʌv/ lieben; sehr gern mögen I

sb would love (to) /ˌsʌmbədi wʊd ˈlʌv/ jmd möchte sehr gern III

lovely /ˈlʌvli/ schön, hübsch I

low /ləʊ/ niedrig 6/7

luck (no pl) /lʌk/ Glück 6/4

Good luck! /gʊd ˈlʌk/ Viel Glück! III

luckily /ˈlʌkɪli/ glücklicherweise 6/4

lucky /ˈlʌki/ glücklich, glücksbringend, Glücks- II

be lucky /biː ˈlʌki/ Glück haben I

lunar calendar /ˌluːnə ˈkælɪndə/ Mondkalender 2/14

lunch /lʌntʃ/ Mittagessen I

lunch break /ˈlʌntʃˌbreɪk/ Mittagspause 0p7

lunchtime /ˈlʌntʃˌtaɪm/ Mittagszeit; Mittagspause II

lyrics (only pl) /ˈlɪrɪks/ (Lied)text 4/9

M

macaroni and cheese /ˌmækəˌrəʊniˌən ˈtʃiːz/ Käse-Makkaroni 2/LL

machine /məˈʃiːn/ Maschine I

made /meɪd/ Vergangenheitsform von „make"

magazine /ˌmægəˈziːn/ Zeitschrift, Magazin I

magic (no pl) /ˈmædʒɪk/ Magie, Zauber III

magician /məˈdʒɪʃn/ Zauberer/Zauberin III

mail (no pl) /meɪl/ Post 0p3

main /meɪn/ Haupt- 3/2

main dish /meɪn ˈdɪʃ/ Hauptspeise, Hauptgericht 2/1

mainly /ˈmeɪnli/ hauptsächlich, in erster Linie 4/1

major /ˈmeɪdʒə/ bedeutend, wichtig, groß 1/M5

make (irr) /meɪk/ machen I

make a difference /ˌmeɪkˌə ˈdɪfrəns/ einen Unterschied machen; etw verändern, etw bewirken 1/10

make a living /ˌmeɪkˌə ˈlɪvɪŋ/ seinen Lebensunterhalt verdienen 3/17

make fun of sb /meɪk ˈfʌnˌəv ˌsʌmbədi/ sich über jdn lustig machen I

make money /meɪk ˈmʌni/ Geld verdienen II

make notes /meɪk ˈnəʊts/ (sich) Notizen machen 2/1

make sure /ˌmeɪk ˈʃɔː/ sich versichern, darauf achten 3/16; dafür sorgen 2/M1

make up sth /ˌmeɪkˌʌp ˌsʌmθɪŋ/ (sich) etw ausdenken, etw erfinden 3/10

put on make-up /pʊtˌɒn ˈmeɪkˌʌp/ sich schminken II

make-up artist /ˌmeɪkʌpˌˈɑːtɪst/ Maskenbildner/in, Visagist/in 6/5

what makes sb tick /ˌmeɪks sʌmbədi ˈtɪk/ wie jmd tickt, was jdn bewegt 4/CC

male /meɪl/ männlich 5/M9

mall /mɔːl/ Einkaufszentrum 2/14

man (pl men) /mæn, men/ Mann I

man (informal) /mæn/ Mensch, Mann 1/3

manage /ˈmænɪdʒ/ es schaffen III

manager /ˈmænɪdʒə/ Geschäftsführer/in 2/6

many /ˈmeni/ viele I

map /mæp/ (Land)karte I

maple syrup /ˌmeɪpəl ˈsɪrəp/ Ahornsirup 2/LL

maracas /məˈrækəz/ Rumba-Rasseln 2/P13

March /mɑːtʃ/ März I

marching band /ˈmɑːtʃɪŋ ˌbænd/ Spielmannszug, Blaskapelle 1/P6

mark /mɑːk/ (Schul)note II

mark /mɑːk/ Siegel, Kennzeichnung 3/16

mark /mɑːk/ markieren, kennzeichnen 3/P11

market /ˈmɑːkɪt/ Markt I

get married /get ˈmærɪd/ heiraten II

marry /ˈmæri/ heiraten II

martial art /ˌmɑːʃlˌˈɑːt/ Kampfsport(art) 6/5

mashed potatoes /ˌmæʃt pəˈteɪtəʊz/ Kartoffelbrei 2/2

match /mætʃ/ Spiel I; Streichholz, Zündholz III

match /mætʃ/ passen (zu) 4/P9

match (with) /mætʃ/ zuordnen 1/2

math (AE) = maths (BE) /mæθ/ Mathe 1/3

maths /mæθs/ Mathe I

What's the matter? /ˌwɒts ðə ˈmætə/ Was ist (denn) los? II

May /meɪ/ Mai I

may /meɪ/ können; dürfen II

may /meɪ/ vielleicht 6/P11

may not /meɪ ˈnɒt/ nicht dürfen II

may not /meɪ ˈnɒt/ vielleicht

nicht 1/M5

maybe /ˈmeɪbi/ vielleicht, möglicherweise I

me /miː/ mir, mich I

meal /miːl/ Mahlzeit, Essen II

mean *(irr)* /miːn/ bedeuten; meinen III

mean /miːn/ gemein, fies II

meaning /ˈmiːnɪŋ/ Bedeutung 1/10

meat *(no pl)* /miːt/ Fleisch I

meat loaf /ˌmiːt ˈləʊf/ Hackbraten 2/LL

medal /ˈmedl/ Medaille II

medicine *(no pl)* /ˈmedsn/ Medizin, Medikament(e) III

meet *(irr)* /miːt/ (sich) treffen; kennenlernen I

Nice to meet you. /ˌnaɪs tə ˈmiːt jə/ Es freut mich, Sie/dich kennen zu lernen. 1/3

meet up *(irr)* /ˌmiːt ˈʌp/ jdn treffen 5/P6

melody /ˈmelədi/ Melodie 4/9

member /ˈmembə/ Mitglied I

memo /ˈmeməʊ/ Notiz; Merkzettel 1/CC

memorial /məˈmɔːriəl/ Denkmal 3/2

mention /ˈmenʃn/ erwähnen 1/M1

menu /ˈmenjuː/ Speisekarte III

message /ˈmesɪdʒ/ Nachricht II; Botschaft, Message 2/10

met /met/ *Vergangenheitsform von „meet"*

metal /ˈmetl/ Metall III

wood/metal working class /ˈwʊd, ˈmetl ˈwɜːkɪŋ klɑːs/ Werkunterricht, Werken 1/5

metre /ˈmiːtə/ Meter II

Mexican /ˈmeksɪkən/ Mexikaner/in; mexikanisch 2/2

Mexican American /ˌmeksɪkənˈəˈmerɪkən/ Amerikaner/in mexikanischer Herkunft; mexikanisch-amerikanisch 4/15

microwave /ˈmaɪkrəˌweɪv/ Mikrowelle(nherd) III

middle /ˈmɪdl/ Mitte III

in the middle /ˌɪn ðə ˈmɪdl/ in der Mitte; mitten in/auf II

the Middle East /ðə ˌmɪdl ˈiːst/ der Nahe Osten 3/8

midnight *(no pl)* /ˈmɪdˌnaɪt/ Mitternacht 2/14

might /maɪt/ könnte 3/M9

mighty /ˈmaɪti/ gewaltig, mächtig, stark 5/CC

mile /maɪl/ Meile III

milk *(no pl)* /mɪlk/ Milch I

milkshake /ˈmɪlkʃeɪk/ Milchshake II

mill around /mɪl_əˈraʊnd/ umherlaufen 2/12

come to sb's mind /kʌm tə ˌsʌmbədiz ˈmaɪnd/ jdm einfallen 3/6

keep an open mind /ˌkiːp_ənˈəʊpən ˌmaɪnd/ aufgeschlossen bleiben 4/8

mine /maɪn/ mir 1/3; meine(r, s) 1/10

mineral resources *(only pl)* /ˈmɪnrəl rɪˌzɔːsɪz/ Bodenschätze 4/P14

miniskirt /ˈminiˌskɜːt/ Minirock II

mint *(no pl)* /mɪnt/ Minze 2/10

minute /ˈmɪnɪt/ Minute I

in a minute /ˌɪn_əˈmɪnɪt/ gleich, sofort I

just a minute /ˌdʒʌst_əˈmɪnɪt/ einen Moment/Augenblick bitte III

mirror /ˈmɪrə/ Spiegel III

miss /mɪs/ verpassen; vermissen I

miss a turn /ˈmɪs_ə ˌtɜːn/ eine Runde aussetzen Intro

missing /ˈmɪsɪŋ/ fehlend 1/P1

mix /mɪks/ (ver)mischen, anrühren III

mix up /mɪksˈʌp/ verwechseln III

mix up /mɪksˈʌp/ vermischen 4/4

moan /məʊn/ stöhnen 5/M9

mobile (= mobile phone) /ˈməʊbaɪl, ˌməʊbaɪl ˈfəʊn/ Mobiltelefon, Handy I

moccasin /ˈmɒkəsɪn/ Mokassin Intro

modelling *(no pl)* /ˈmɒdlɪŋ/ Modeln; Model- 6/M8

Mohawk /ˈməʊˌhɔːk/ Mohawk(indianer) Intro

mom *(AE)* = mum *(BE)* *(informal)* /mɒm/ Mama, Mutti 1/P10

moment /ˈməʊmənt/ Moment, Augenblick II

at the moment /æt ðə ˈməʊmənt/ im Moment II

Monday /ˈmʌndeɪ/ Montag I

money *(no pl)* /ˈmʌni/ Geld I

make money /meɪk ˈmʌni/ Geld verdienen II

raise money /reɪz ˈmʌni/ Geld aufbringen/auftreiben 3/P13

monkey /ˈmʌŋki/ Affe I

month /mʌnθ/ Monat I

mood /muːd/ Laune, Stimmung 5/M3

moon /muːn/ Mond II

moonlight /ˈmuːnˌlaɪt/ Mondlicht II

more /mɔː/ (noch) mehr I

morning /ˈmɔːnɪŋ/ Morgen I

in the morning /ˌɪn ðə ˈmɔːnɪŋ/ morgens, am Morgen, vormittags I

this morning /ðɪs ˈmɔːnɪŋ/ heute Morgen III

morning break /ˈmɔːnɪŋ ˌbreɪk/ Frühstückspause II

most /məʊst/ die meisten II

most /məʊst/ am meisten III

most (of) /məʊst/ das meiste (von), ein Großteil 3/4

mother /ˈmʌðə/ Mutter I

motorbike /ˈməʊtəˌbaɪk/ Motorrad II

mountain /ˈmaʊntɪn/ Berg II

mouse *(pl mice)* /maʊs, maɪs/ Maus I

mouth /maʊθ/ Mund I

move /muːv/ sich bewegen; umziehen II

movie *(AE)* = **film** *(BE)* /ˈmuːvi/ (Kino-, Spiel)film 6/2

mow *(irr)* /məʊ/ mähen III

Mr /ˈmɪstə/ Herr *(Anrede)* I

Mrs /ˈmɪsɪz/ Frau *(Anrede)* I

Ms /məz/ Frau *(Anrede für verheiratete und unverheiratete*

Frauen) 1/10

much /mʌtʃ/ viel; sehr I

muesli *(no pl)* /ˈmjuːzli/ Müsli I

mum *(informal)* /mʌm/ Mama, Mutti I

Munich /ˈmjuːnɪk/ München II

muscle /ˈmʌsl/ Muskel III

mushroom /ˈmʌʃruːm/ Pilz III

music *(no pl)* /ˈmjuːzɪk/ Musik I

Muslim /ˈmʊzləm/ Muslim/in; muslimisch 2/12

must *(no pl)* /mʌst/ Muss 2/9

must /mʌst/ müssen II

must not /mʌst ˈnɒt/ nicht dürfen II

must-see /ˌmʌstˈsiː/ etw, das man gesehen haben muss 3/7

my /maɪ/ mein(e) I

my name is /maɪ ˈneɪmˏɪz/ ich heiße I

myself /maɪˈself/ mich, mir; selbst 5/12

myth /mɪθ/ Mythos 6/12

N

nail /neɪl/ nageln 1/CC

name /neɪm/ Name I

name /neɪm/ (be)nennen 5/P13

my name is /maɪ ˈneɪmˏɪz/ ich heiße I

What's your name? /ˌwɒts jə ˈneɪm/ Wie heißt du?, Wie heißen Sie? I

narrow /ˈnærəʊ/ eng, schmal II

nation /ˈneɪʃn/ Nation, Land 4/1

national park /ˌnæʃnl ˈpɑːk/ Nationalpark 6/2

Native American /ˌneɪtɪvˏəˈmerɪkən/ amerikanischer Ureinwohner/ amerikanische Ureinwohnerin; indianisch 2/15

natural /ˈnætʃrəl/ natürlich 1/M7

nature *(no pl)* /ˈneɪtʃə/ Natur II

naughty /ˈnɔːti/ ungezogen, frech II

Navajo /ˈnævəhəʊ/ Navajo(indianer) 4/15

near /nɪə/ nah(e) I

nearby /ˌnɪəˈbaɪ/ nahe/in der Nähe gelegen, benachbart 4/M5

nearly /ˈnɪəli/ fast, beinahe 6/2

necessary /ˈnesəsri/ nötig, notwendig, erforderlich 3/P3

need /niːd/ brauchen I

need to /ˈniːd tə/ müssen 6/M1

negative /ˈnegətɪv/ negativ III

neighbor *(AE)* = neighbour *(BE)* /ˈneɪbə/ Nachbar/in 2/P13

neighbour /ˈneɪbə/ Nachbar/in I

neighbourhood /ˈneɪbəˌhʊd/ Viertel; Nachbarschaft 3/9

nervous /ˈnɜːvəs/ nervös; aufgeregt 1/3

net /net/ Netz 5/11

the Netherlands /ðə ˈneðlənz/ die Niederlande 3/16

never /ˈnevə/ nie(mals) I

never even /ˌnevərˈiːvn/ (noch) nicht (ein)mal 2/M2

new /njuː/ neu I

New Year /ˌnjuːˈjɪə/ Neujahr II

New Year's Eve /ˌnjuː jɪəzˏˈiːv/ Silvester II

New Yorker /njuː ˈjɔːkə/ New Yorker/in 3/8

New Zealand /njuː ˈziːlənd/ Neuseeland III

news *(no pl)* /njuːz/ Neuigkeit; Nachrichten II

newspaper /ˈnjuːzˌpeɪpə/ Zeitung III

next /nekst/ nächste(r, s) I

next /nekst/ dann, als Nächstes 5/5

next to /ˈnekstˏtə/ neben I

nice /naɪs/ schön, angenehm; nett, freundlich I

Nice to meet you. /ˌnaɪs tə ˈmiːt jə/ Es freut mich, Sie/dich kennen zu lernen. 1/3

nicotine gum *(no pl)* /ˈnɪkətiːn gʌm/ Nikotinkaugummi 5/M10

night /naɪt/ Nacht I

night /naɪt/ Abend III

at night /æt ˈnaɪt/ nachts 2/6

no /nəʊ/ nein; kein(e) I

no one /ˈnəʊ wʌn/ keiner, niemand II

Noah's ark /ˌnəʊəz ˈɑːk/ die Arche Noah 4/CC

the Nobel Peace Prize /ðə nəʊˌbel ˈpiːs ˌpraɪz/ Friedensnobelpreis Intro

noise /nɔɪz/ Lärm, Krach; Geräusch II

noise level /ˈnɔɪz levl/ Geräuschpegel, Lärmpegel 1/M7

noisy /ˈnɔɪzi/ laut III

non- /nɒn/ nicht- 6/9

none /nʌn/ keine(r, s) 6/4

normally /ˈnɔːmli/ normalerweise 2/2

north /nɔːθ/ Norden III

north /nɔːθ/ nördlich, Nord- III

North America /ˌnɔːθˏəˈmerɪkə/ Nordamerika 2/15

north-west /ˌnɔːθˈwest/ Nordwesten 6/7

northern /ˈnɔːðən/ nördlich, Nord- Intro

Northern Ireland /ˌnɔːðnˏˈaɪələnd/ Nordirland III

nose /nəʊz/ Nase I

not /nɒt/ nicht I

not any /nɒtˏˈeni/ kein(e) II

not anymore /ˌnɒt eniˈmɔː/ nicht mehr II

not at all /nɒtˏətˏˈɔːl/ überhaupt nicht 4/4

not yet /nɒt ˈjet/ noch nicht II

note /nəʊt/ Notiz 2/8

note down /nəʊt ˈdaʊn/ (sich) notieren 4/4

make notes /meɪk ˈnəʊts/ (sich) Notizen machen 2/1

take notes /teɪk ˈnəʊts/ (sich) Notizen machen II

take notes /teɪk ˈnəʊts/ (sich) Notizen machen 1/6

nothing /ˈnʌθɪŋ/ nichts II

notice /ˈnəʊtɪs/ bemerken I

noun /naʊn/ Substantiv 4/P1

November /nəʊˈvembə/ November I

now /naʊ/ jetzt I

right now /raɪt ˈnaʊ/ gerade, jetzt, im Augenblick 5/12

nugget /ˈnʌgɪt/ Klumpen, Nugget 6/P3

number /ˈnʌmbə/ Zahl; Ziffer, Nummer I

nurse /nɜːs/ (Kranken)schwester, (Kranken)pfleger II

O

(seven) o'clock /ə'klɒk/ (sieben) Uhr I

object /'ɒbdʒekt/ Objekt 3/M2

ocean /'əʊʃn/ Meer; Ozean 4/14

October /ɒk'təʊbə/ Oktober I

be the odd one out /bi: ði‿'ɒd wʌn‿'aʊt/ aus der Reihe fallen, nicht dazugehören 3/P8

of /əv/ von I

of course /əv 'kɔːs/ natürlich I

off /ɒf/ weg 0p3

get sb off to somewhere /get ˌsʌmbədi‿ˌɒf tʊ 'sʌmweə/ jdn wohin bringen 4/M5

offensive /ə'fensɪv/ Angriffs- 5/15

offer /'ɒfə/ Angebot III

offer /'ɒfə/ (an)bieten II

office /'ɒfɪs/ Büro 1/5

official /ə'fɪʃl/ Beamte(r)/ Beamtin 4/M1

often /'ɒfn/ oft, häufig I

Oh my goodness! /əʊ maɪ 'ɡʊdnəs/ Ach du meine Güte! 5/M1

oil /ɔɪl/ Öl III

old /əʊld/ alt I

How old are you? /haʊ‿'əʊld‿ə jʊ/ Wie alt bist du/seid ihr? I

Olympic Games /ə'lɪmpɪk 'ɡeɪmz/ Olympische Spiele II

on /ɒn/ auf, an; in; am; im I

on one's own /ɒn wʌnz‿'əʊn/ allein(e) III

on time /ɒn 'taɪm/ pünktlich; rechtzeitig 5/M3

on top /ɒn 'tɒp/ oben; darüber 2/2

once /wʌns/ einmal II

one /wʌn/ eins; ein(e) I

be as one /bi‿əz 'wʌn/ eins sein 4/M5

one day /'wʌn deɪ/ eines Tages II

on the one hand /ɒn ðə 'wʌn ˌhænd/ einerseits 2/M4

one hundred /ˌwʌn 'hʌndrəd/ einhundert I

onion /'ʌnjən/ Zwiebel III

only /'əʊnli/ nur I; erst 4/4

only /'əʊnli/ einzige(r, s) III

open /'əʊpən/ (sich) öffnen I

open /'əʊpən/ eröffnen 2/11

open /'əʊpən/ offen, geöffnet I

open up /'əʊpən ʌp/ (sich) öffnen 2/P13

Opening Day /ˌəʊpnɪŋ 'deɪ/ *erster Spieltag in US-amerikanischen Baseball-Ligen* 5/LL

opening times *(only pl)* /'əʊpnɪŋ ˌtaɪmz/ Öffnungszeiten 6/9

operator /'ɒpəˌreɪtə/ Telefonist/in, Vermittlung 6/M3

opinion /ə'pɪnjən/ Meinung, Ansicht II

in my opinion /ɪn 'maɪ‿ə‿pɪnjən/ meiner Meinung/Ansicht nach 2/M4

give one's opinion (on sth) /ɡɪv wʌnz‿ə'pɪnjən/ seine Meinung (zu etw) äußern, (zu etw) Stellung nehmen 2/M4

opponent /ə'pəʊnənt/ Gegner/in; Gegenspieler/in 5/15

opposite /'ɒpəzɪt/ Gegenteil 4/P1

opposite /'ɒpəzɪt/ gegenüber(liegend) III

optimistic /ˌɒptɪ'mɪstɪk/ optimistisch, zuversichtlich II

or /ɔː/ oder I

orange /'ɒrɪndʒ/ Orange, Apfelsine I

orange /'ɒrɪndʒ/ orange(farben) I

order /'ɔːdə/ Ordnung, Reihenfolge 1/M2

order /'ɔːdə/ bestellen III

organise /'ɔːɡənaɪz/ organisieren 3/P13

organization /ˌɔːɡənaɪ'zeɪʃn/ Organisation 3/16

organize *(AE)* = organise *(BE)* /'ɔːɡənaɪz/ organisieren 1/M5

other /'ʌðər/ andere(r, s) I

the other day /ði‿ˌʌðə 'deɪ/ neulich, vor einigen Tagen 5/M9

on the other hand /ɒn ði‿'ʌðə ˌhænd/ andererseits 2/M4

our /aʊə/ unser(e) I

ours /'aʊəz/ unsere(r, s) 1/3

ourselves /aʊə'selvz/ uns; selbst 5/12

out /aʊt/ draußen; aus 5/1

out of /'aʊt‿əv/ (her)aus II

out of work /aʊt‿əv 'wɜːk/ arbeitslos III

outdoors /ˌaʊt'dɔːz/ im Freien, draußen 6/5

outside /ˌaʊt'saɪd/ im Freien, draußen I; außerhalb 3/13

outside /ˌaʊt'saɪd/ nach draußen, raus II

outside /ˌaʊt'saɪd/ Außenseite 0p2

over /'əʊvə/ über I; hinüber; vorbei III

over there /ˌəʊvə 'ðeə/ dort (drüben) I

over time /ˌəʊvə 'taɪm/ im Lauf der Zeit, mit der Zeit 2/15

overalls *(only pl)* /'əʊvərˌɔːlz/ Overall, Arbeitsanzug 0p7

owl /aʊl/ Eule 6/7

own /əʊn/ eigene(r, s) II

own /əʊn/ besitzen 3/P12

on one's own /ɒn wʌnz‿'əʊn/ allein(e) III

on one's own doorstep /ɒn wʌnz‿ˌəʊn 'dɔːˌstep/ vor der eigenen Haustür 1/M5

P

p (= penny, pence) /piː, 'penni, pens/ Penny, Centstück II

the Pacific (Ocean) /ðə pə‿sɪfɪk(‿'əʊʃn)/ der Pazifische Ozean III

pack /pæk/ packen I

package /'pækɪdʒ/ Paket III

packed /pækt/ voll III

pad /pæd/ Polster; Schoner, Schützer 5/18

page /peɪdʒ/ Seite III

paid /peɪd/ *Vergangenheitsform von „pay"*

paint /peɪnt/ (an)malen II

painter /'peɪntə/ Maler/in; Anstreicher/in; Lackierer/in 0p2

painting /'peɪntɪŋ/ Bild, Gemälde 3/3

pair /peə/ Paar III

pajamas *(AE)* = pyjamas *(BE)* /pə'dʒɑːməz/ Schlafanzug, Pyjama 1/M1

palace /'pæləs/ Palast II

pancake /ˈpæŋkeɪk/ Pfannkuchen 2/LL

solar panel /ˌsəʊlə ˈpænəl/ Sonnenkollektor 1/10

panic /ˈpænɪk/ Panik III

paper (no pl) /ˈpeɪpə/ Papier I

parade /pəˈreɪd/ Parade, Umzug III

paragraph /ˈpærəˌɡrɑːf/ Absatz, Abschnitt 3/11

paramedic /ˌpærəˈmedɪk/ Rettungssanitäter/in 5/7

parents (only pl) /ˈpeərənts/ Eltern I

national park /ˌnæʃnl ˈpɑːk/ Nationalpark 6/2

theme park /ˈθiːm ˌpɑːk/ Themenpark; Freizeitpark 6/2

parrot /ˈpærət/ Papagei I

part /pɑːt/ Teil 3/8

part /pɑːt/ Rolle 6/P11

pass /pɑːs/ Pass; Erlaubnisschein 1/3; Eintrittskarte, Ticket 6/9

Front of Line Pass /ˌfrʌnt‿əv ˈlaɪn ˌpɑːs/ Ticket ohne Wartezeit 6/9

pass by /ˌpɑːs baɪ/ vorbeifahren, vorbeigehen III

pass on by /ˌpɑːs‿ɒn ˈbaɪ/ vorbeifahren 6/M1

pass on (sth) /ˌpɑːs‿ɒn/ (etw) weitergeben 4/15

past /pɑːst/ vorbei/vorüber an II

past participle /ˌpɑːst ˈpɑːtɪsɪpl/ Partizip Perfekt 3/P5

past perfect /ˌpɑːst ˈpɜːfɪkt/ Plusquamperfekt 4/M2

pasta (no pl) /ˈpæstə/ Nudeln III

patch /pætʃ/ Pflaster 5/M10

patient /ˈpeɪʃnt/ Patient/in III

paw /pɔː/ Pfote, Tatze II

pay (irr) /peɪ/ (be)zahlen I

PE (= physical education) /ˌpiːˈiː, ˌfɪzɪklˌedjʊˈkeɪʃn/ Sport(unterricht) I

pea /piː/ Erbse III

peace /piːs/ Frieden Intro

leave sb in peace /ˌliːv ˌsʌmbədiˌɪn ˈpiːs/ jdn in Frieden/Ruhe lassen 3/8

peaceful /ˈpiːsfl/ friedlich; ruhig 1/M7

peanut /ˈpiːnʌt/ Erdnuss 2/2

peer pressure (no pl) /ˈpɪə ˌpreʃə/ Druck durch Gleichaltrige, sozialer Druck 5/M10

pelican /ˈpelɪkən/ Pelikan 6/7

pen /pen/ Stift I

penalty /ˈpenlti/ Strafe; Strafstoß, Elfmeter 5/11

pencil /ˈpensl/ Bleistift I

pencil case /ˈpensl ˌkeɪs/ (Feder)mäppchen I

pencil sharpener /ˈpensl ˌʃɑːpnə/ (Bleistift)spitzer I

penguin /ˈpeŋgwɪn/ Pinguin I

people /ˈpiːpl/ Volk 3/2

people (no pl) /ˈpiːpl/ Leute, Menschen I

pepper (no pl) /ˈpepə/ Pfeffer III

per cent /pəˈsent/ Prozent 4/2

percentage /pəˈsentɪdʒ/ Prozentsatz, Anteil 4/CC

perfect /ˈpɜːfɪkt/ perfekt II

perform /pəˈfɔːm/ vorführen; aufführen; durchführen 6/2

perfume /ˈpɜːfjuːm/ Parfüm II

perhaps /pəˈhæps/ vielleicht II

period (AE) = lesson (BE) /ˈpɪəriəd/ Stunde 1/3

person /ˈpɜːsn/ Person, Mensch II

personal /ˈpɜːsnəl/ persönlich; privat 6/14

personal pronoun /ˌpɜːsnəl ˈprəʊnaʊn/ Personalpronomen 5/P11

persuade /pəˈsweɪd/ überreden, überzeugen 4/4

peso /ˈpeɪsəʊ/ Peso (Währung) 3/13

pet /pet/ Haustier I

pet /pet/ streicheln I

phone /fəʊn/ anrufen I

(phone) call /(ˈfəʊn) kɔːl/ (Telefon)anruf II

(tele)phone /fəʊn/ Telefon I

photo /ˈfəʊtəʊ/ Foto I

take photos /ˌteɪk ˈfəʊtəʊz/ Bilder machen, fotografieren II

phrase /freɪz/ Satz; Ausdruck, (Rede)wendung 1/P7

piano /piˈænəʊ/ Klavier II

pick /pɪk/ aussuchen, auswählen 2/P12

pick up /ˌpɪk‿ˈʌp/ aufheben; abholen 2/M1

pickpocket /ˈpɪkˌpɒkɪt/ Taschendieb/in III

pictogram /ˈpɪktəɡræm/ Piktogramm 1/13

picture /ˈpɪktʃə/ Bild, Foto I

pie /paɪ/ Pastete; Kuchen 1/M1

steak and kidney pie /ˌsteɪk‿ən ˌkɪdni ˈpaɪ/ Rindfleisch-Nieren-Pastete 2/10

pie chart /ˈpaɪ tʃɑːt/ Tortendiagramm 4/M3

pie-eating contest /ˈpaɪ‿iːtɪŋ ˌkɒntest/ Kuchenwettessen 1/M1

piece /piːs/ Stück III

piece of information /ˌpiːs‿əv ˌɪnfəˈmeɪʃn/ Information 0p5

pig /pɪɡ/ Schwein I

the Pilgrims /ðə ˈpɪlɡrɪms/ die Pilger(väter) 2/15

pilot /ˈpaɪlət/ Pilot/in II

pine /paɪn/ Kiefer, Pinie 6/M1

pink /pɪŋk/ rosa, pink I

pirate /ˈpaɪrət/ Pirat, Seeräuber I

place /pleɪs/ Ort; Platz I

take place /teɪk ˈpleɪs/ stattfinden III

place of birth /ˌpleɪs‿əv ˈbɜːθ/ Geburtsort 0p6

placemat /ˈpleɪsˌmæt/ Set, Platzdeckchen 4/3

plan /plæn/ planen 3/11

plane /pleɪn/ Flugzeug II

plant /plɑːnt/ Pflanze II

plant /plɑːnt/ pflanzen 1/8

plastic /ˈplæstɪk/ Plastik, Kunststoff III

plate /pleɪt/ Teller I

platform /ˈplætˌfɔːm/ Plattform; Bahnsteig, Gleis III

play /pleɪ/ Spiel; (Theater)stück I

play /pleɪ/ spielen I

player /ˈpleɪə/ Spieler/in I

playground /ˈpleɪˌɡraʊnd/ Spielplatz I

plaza /ˈplɑːzə/ Marktplatz;

Essbereich in einem Einkaufszentrum 5/M5

please /pli:z/ bitte I

Pledge of Allegiance /ˌpledʒ‿əv‿əˈli:dʒ(ə)ns/ *Treue-schwur (gegenüber dem Staat und der Fahne der USA)* 1/3

plus *(informal)* /plʌs/ außerdem 1/10

pm (= post meridiem) /ˌpi:ˈem, ˌpəʊst məˈrɪdiəm/ nachmittags, abends *(nur hinter Uhrzeit zwischen 12 Uhr mittags und Mitternacht)* III

pocket /ˈpɒkɪt/ Tasche III

pocket money *(no pl)* /ˈpɒkɪt ˌmʌni/ Taschengeld III

poem /ˈpəʊɪm/ Gedicht 2/10

point /pɔɪnt/ Punkt 5/15

Poland /ˈpəʊlənd/ Polen II

police *(no pl)* /pəˈli:s/ Polizei II

police department /pəˈli:s dɪˌpɑ:tmənt/ Polizeidienststelle Intro

police officer /pəˈli:s ˌɒfɪsə/ Polizeibeamter/-beamtin II

police station /pəˈli:s‿ˌsteɪʃn/ Polizeirevier, Polizeiwache 4/12

Polish /ˈpəʊlɪʃ/ polnisch 4/M3

polite /pəˈlaɪt/ höflich II

pollute /pəˈlu:t/ verschmutzen 4/M5

pompom /ˈpɒmpɒm/ Pompom, Puschel, Bommel 5/11

poor /pɔ:/ arm I

poor /pɔ:/ unzureichend, mangelhaft 4/M1

poor you /pɔ: ˈju:/ du Arme(r) 1/3

popsicle /ˈpɒpsɪkl/ *Eis am Stiel* 2/CC

popular /ˈpɒpjʊlə/ beliebt 2/6

population /ˌpɒpjʊˈleɪʃn/ Bevölkerung 4/1

portable /ˈpɔ:təbl/ tragbar Op3

portfolio /pɔ:ˈfəʊliəʊ/ (Akten)mappe 1/14

positive /ˈpɒzətɪv/ positiv 3/P1

possessive pronoun /pəˌzesɪv ˈprəʊnaʊn/ Possessivpronomen 1/P10

possible /ˈpɒsəbəl/ möglich 1/M1

post sth /ˈpəʊst ˌsʌmθɪŋ/ etw schicken; etw ins Internet stellen, etw posten 6/13

postcard /ˈpəʊstˌkɑ:d/ Postkarte II

potato *(pl -es)* /pəˈteɪtəʊ, pəˈteɪtəʊz/ Kartoffel II

sweet potato /ˌswi:t pəˈteɪtəʊ/ Süßkartoffel 2/M5

mashed potatoes /ˌmæʃt pəˈteɪtəʊz/ Kartoffelbrei 2/2

pound /paʊnd/ Pfund *(brit. Währung)* II

pound /paʊnd/ Pfund 5/M10

pow-wow /ˈpaʊˌwaʊ/ Powwow *(indianische Versammlung)* 4/12

power /ˈpaʊə/ antreiben; versorgen 1/10

powerful /ˈpaʊəfl/ mächtig III

powerful /ˈpaʊəfl/ stark, heftig III

practice /ˈpræktɪs/ Übung; Training 1/3

practice *(AE)* = practise *(BE)* /ˈpræktɪs/ üben, trainieren 1/P6

practise /ˈpræktɪs/ üben III

prefer /prɪˈfɜ:/ vorziehen, bevorzugen, lieber mögen III

pregnant /ˈpregnənt/ schwanger III

prejudice *(no pl)* /ˈpredʒʊdɪs/ Vorurteil, Voreingenommenheit 4/M5

prepare /prɪˈpeə/ (sich) vorbereiten; zubereiten 1/5

present /ˈpreznt/ Geschenk I

present /prɪˈzent/ präsentieren 1/7

presentation /ˌprezn̩ˈteɪʃn/ Präsentation 3/11

president /ˈprezɪdənt/ Präsident/in Intro

peer pressure *(no pl)* /ˈpɪə ˌpreʃə/ Druck durch Gleichaltrige, sozialer Druck 5/M10

pretty /ˈprɪti/ hübsch II

pretty *(informal)* /ˈprɪti/ ziemlich 1/12

price /praɪs/ Preis I

pride *(no pl)* /praɪd/ Stolz 4/15

primary school /ˈpraɪməri ˌsku:l/ Grundschule II

princess /ˌprɪnˈses/ Prinzessin 3/M5

print (out) /prɪnt/ (aus)drucken 1/9

prison /ˈprɪzn/ Gefängnis 6/13

prisoner /ˈprɪznə/ Gefangene/r III

prize /praɪz/ Preis, Gewinn II

probably /ˈprɒbəbli/ wahrscheinlich II

produce /prəˈdju:s/ herstellen, erzeugen, produzieren 3/16

producer /prəˈdju:sə/ Produzent/in; Hersteller, Erzeuger 3/16

product /ˈprɒdʌkt/ Produkt, Erzeugnis 1/5

professional /prəˈfeʃnəl/ Profi 5/11

program /ˈprəʊɡræm/ programmieren 1/5

program *(AE)* = programme *(BE)* /ˈprəʊɡræm/ Programm 4/P10

programme /ˈprəʊɡræm/ Sendung; Programm II

programmer /ˈprəʊˌɡræmə/ Programmierer/in 6/5

project /ˈprɒdʒekt/ Projekt 1/10

promise /ˈprɒmɪs/ versprechen II

possessive pronoun /pəˌzesɪv ˈprəʊnaʊn/ Possessivpronomen 1/P10

pronoun /ˈprəʊnaʊn/ Pronomen 5/P11

proper /ˈprɒpə/ korrekt, richtig 5/M9

protect /prəˈtekt/ (be)schützen 6/2

protection /prəˈtekʃn/ Schutz 4/CC

proud (of sb) /praʊd/ stolz (auf jmd) II

prove /pru:v/ beweisen III

pub /pʌb/ Kneipe, Gaststätte III

the public /ðə ˈpʌblɪk/ die Öffentlichkeit, die Allgemeinheit 1/M5

public /ˈpʌblɪk/ öffentlich 3/M1

public school *(AE)* /ˌpʌblɪk ˈsku:l/ staatliche/öffentliche Schule 4/CC

Pueblo /ˈpwebləʊ/ Pueblo(indianer) Intro

pull /pʊl/ ziehen III
pumpkin /ˈpʌmpkɪn/ Kürbis 2/12
purple /ˈpɜːpl/ violett,
lila(farben) I
push /pʊʃ/ drücken;
schieben 1/M9
put (irr) /pʊt/ setzen, legen,
stellen I
put into /ˈpʊt ˌɪntə/ eingeben Op3
put on /pʊt ˈɒn/ anziehen;
auftragen III
put on /pʊt ˈɒn/ auflegen 2/P13;
aufführen 5/12
put on make-up /pʊt ˌɒn
ˈmeɪkˌʌp/ sich schminken II
put out sth /pʊt ˈaʊt ˌsʌmθɪŋ/
etw ausmachen; etw
löschen 6/4
put up /pʊt ˈʌp/ aufhängen III
put up /pʊt ˈʌp/ aufstellen 2/P12
pyramid /ˈpɪrəmɪd/ Pyramide 5/12

Q

quality /ˈkwɒləti/ Qualität III
quarter (to/past) /ˈkwɔːtə/
Viertel (vor/nach) I
queen /kwiːn/ Königin II
question /ˈkwestʃn/ Frage I
question sb /ˈkwestʃn ˌsʌmbədi/
jdn befragen III
questionnaire /ˌkwestʃəˈneə/
Fragebogen 1/14
queue /kjuː/ Schlange, Reihe II
quick /kwɪk/ schnell II
quiet /ˈkwaɪət/ leise, ruhig I
quit (irr) /kwɪt/ aufhören
(mit) 5/M10
quite /kwaɪt/ ziemlich III
quiz sb /ˈkwɪz ˌsʌmbədi/ jdn
befragen/prüfen 6/P5

R

rabbit /ˈræbɪt/ Kaninchen I
race /reɪs/ Rennen III
race /reɪs/ Rasse 4/CC
race /reɪs/ rennen; heftig
schlagen, rasen 6/10
radio station /ˈreɪdiəʊ ˌsteɪʃn/
Radiosender II
railroad (AE) = **railway** (BE)
/ˈreɪlˌrəʊd/ Gleise, Schienen;
(Eisen)bahn 4/1

rain /reɪn/ Regen III
rain /reɪn/ regnen II
rain collector /ˈreɪn kəˌlektə/
Regensammelbehälter 1/10
rainbow /ˈreɪnˌbəʊ/
Regenbogen II
rainforest /ˈreɪnˌfɒrɪst/
Regenwald II
rainy /ˈreɪni/ regnerisch I
raise money /reɪz ˈmʌni/ Geld
aufbringen/auftreiben 3/P13
ramble /ˈræmbl/ wandern 4/9
ran /ræn/ Vergangenheitsform
von „run"
ranger /ˈreɪndʒə/ Aufseher/in,
Ranger/in Intro
rap /ræp/ rappen 2/10
rat /ræt/ Ratte II
rate /reɪt/ Rate, Quote; Preis,
Kosten 6/9
RE (= religious education)
/ˌɑː(r) ˈiː, rəˌlɪdʒəs ˌedjʊˈkeɪʃn/
Religion(sunterricht) I
reach /riːtʃ/ erreichen III
reach (for) /riːtʃ/ greifen
(nach) 5/CC
read (irr) /riːd/ lesen I
read along /ˌriːd əˈlɒŋ/
mitlesen 1/3
read out loud /ˌriːd ˌaʊt ˈlaʊd/
laut vorlesen Intro
reader /ˈriːdə/ Leser/in 5/13
ready /ˈredi/ fertig, bereit I
get ready (for sth) /get ˈredi/
sich (für etw) bereit
machen 6/10
real /rɪəl/ wirklich; echt II
the real deal (informal) /ðə ˌrɪəl
ˈdiːl/ das einzig Wahre 1/M5
realize sth /ˈrɪəlaɪz/ sich einer
Sache bewusst werden,
etw merken 5/M3
really /ˈrɪəli/ wirklich I
reason /ˈriːzn/ Grund 2/M2
give reasons /gɪv ˈriːznz/
begründen, Gründe
angeben 1/11
receipt /rɪˈsiːt/ Beleg;
Kassenbon 5/3
receive /rɪˈsiːv/ empfangen,
erhalten 4/M2
recipe /ˈresəpi/ Rezept III

recording /rɪˈkɔːdɪŋ/
Aufnahme 1/P2
recycle /riːˈsaɪkl/
wiederverwerten, recyceln 1/8
recycled /riːˈsaɪkld/
wiederverwertet, recycelt 1/9
red /red/ rot I
reduce /rɪˈdjuːs/ verringern,
reduzieren, verkleinern 1/M7
referee /ˌrefəˈriː/
Schiedsrichter/in III
reflexive pronoun
/rɪˌfleksɪv ˈprəʊnaʊn/
Reflexivpronomen 5/P11
regular /ˈregjʊlə/ regelmäßig;
gleichmäßig 5/M9
regular /ˈregjʊlə/ normal 3/18;
regelrechte(r, s),
richtige(r, s) 4/CC
relate to sth /rɪˈleɪt tə ˌsʌmθɪŋ/
Zugang zu etw finden 6/M1
relative /ˈrelətɪv/ Verwandte(r),
Angehörige(r) 4/4
relax /rɪˈlæks/
sich entspannen II
relaxed /rɪˈlækst/ entspannt;
locker, gelassen II
religious /rəˈlɪdʒəs/ religiöse(r,
s), Religions- Intro
remember /rɪˈmembə/
(an etw) denken II
remember /rɪˈmembə/ sich
erinnern (an) I
remove /rɪˈmuːv/ entfernen 3/M1
repair /rɪˈpeə/ reparieren II
repeat /rɪˈpiːt/ wiederholen II
replace /rɪˈpleɪs/ ersetzen 3/P11
report /rɪˈpɔːt/ Bericht I
report /rɪˈpɔːt/ berichten 1/M5
report /rɪˈpɔːt/ berichten,
melden 6/P6
report (on sb/sth) /rɪˈpɔːt/ (über
jdn/etw) berichten 4/15
reported speech /rɪˌpɔːtɪd ˈspiːtʃ/
indirekte Rede 5/M2
republic /rɪˈpʌblɪk/ Republik 6/CC
rescue /ˈreskjuː/ retten III
research (no pl) /rɪˈsɜːtʃ/
Forschung; Recherche 6/P4
reservation /ˌrezəˈveɪʃn/
Reservierung 6/9; Reservat
(= ein den Indianern

vorbehaltenes Gebiet) 4/1

respect *(no pl)* /rɪˈspekt/ Respekt, Achtung II

responsible /rɪˈspɒnsəbl/ verantwortlich 6/4

result /rɪˈzʌlt/ Ergebnis; Folge III

return (ticket) /rɪˈtɜːn/ Hin- und Rückfahrkarte III

return /rɪˈtɜːn/ zurückkehren III

review /rɪˈvjuː/ Kritik, Rezension 2/9

rewrite /ˌriːˈraɪt/ neu schreiben; umschreiben 2/16

rez (= reservation) *(informal)* /rez/ Reservat (= *ein den Indianern vorbehaltenes Gebiet)* 4/M5

rhyming pair /ˈraɪmɪŋ peə/ Reimpaar 4/P3

rhythm /ˈrɪðəm/ Rhythmus, Takt 4/9

ribbon /ˈrɪbən/ Band, Streifen 4/9

rice *(no pl)* /raɪs/ Reis 2/2

the rich *(no pl)* /ðə ˈrɪtʃ/ die Reichen 6/13

rich /rɪtʃ/ reich II

ride *(irr)* /raɪd/ fahren; reiten I

ride a bike /ˌraɪd ə ˈbaɪk/ (Fahr)rad fahren I

riding *(no pl)* /ˈraɪdɪŋ/ Reiten I

right /raɪt/ Recht 4/1

right /raɪt/ richtig I; (nach) rechts II

right /raɪt/ genau, direkt 6/M3

be right /bi: ˈraɪt/ Recht haben I

on the/your right /ˌɒn ðə/jɔː ˈraɪt/ rechts, auf der rechten Seite II

right now /raɪt ˈnaʊ/ gerade, jetzt, im Augenblick 5/12

ring *(irr)* /rɪŋ/ klingeln, läuten III

the Ring of Fire /ˌrɪŋ əv ˈfaɪə/ der (pazifische) Feuergürtel/ Feuerring *(Vulkanreihe im Pazifischen Ozean)* 6/M1

risk /rɪsk/ Risiko, Gefahr 5/12

river /ˈrɪvə/ Fluss I

road /rəʊd/ Straße III

roam /rəʊm/ umherstreifen,

umherziehen 4/9

roar /rɔː/ brüllen II

roast lamb /ˌrəʊst ˈlæm/ Lammbraten 2/16

roast turkey /ˌrəʊst ˈtɜːki/ Truthahnbraten 2/LL

Sunday roast /ˈsʌndeɪ rəʊst/ Sonntagsbraten 2/10

robot /ˈrəʊbɒt/ Roboter II

rock /rɒk/ Stein, Fels(en) III

role /rəʊl/ Rolle 4/P13

roll /rəʊl/ rollen III

roller soccer *(no pl)* /ˈrəʊlə ˌsɒkə/ *Fußball auf Rollschuhen* 5/18

romance /rəʊˈmæns/ Romanze; Liebesfilm 6/12

romantic /rəʊˈmæntɪk/ romantisch 5/CC

room /ruːm/ Zimmer I

rope /rəʊp/ Seil III

row /rəʊ/ Reihe 1/M5

royal /ˈrɔɪəl/ königlich 6/M1

rubber *(BE)* /ˈrʌbə/ Radiergummi I

rubbish *(no pl)* /ˈrʌbɪʃ/ Müll I

ruin /ˈruːɪn/ ruinieren, zerstören 5/M10

rule /ruːl/ Regel II

rule /ruːl/ regieren 3/M7

ruler /ˈruːlə/ Lineal I

run *(irr)* /rʌn/ laufen, rennen I

run *(irr)* /rʌn/ betreiben, führen 1/5

run on sth /ˈrʌn ɒn ˌsʌmθɪŋ/ mit etw betrieben werden 1/M5

runner /ˈrʌnə/ Läufer/in I

running /ˈrʌnɪŋ/ Laufen, Rennen III

running time /ˈrʌnɪŋ ˌtaɪm/ Laufzeit 6/13

Russia /ˈrʌʃə/ Russland I

Russian /ˈrʌʃn/ Russisch; russisch II

S

sad /sæd/ traurig II

safe /seɪf/ sicher II

said /sed/ *Vergangenheitsform von „say"*

sail /seɪl/ Segel III

sail /seɪl/ segeln III

salad /ˈsæləd/ Salat II

be on sale /bi: ɒn ˈseɪl/ zum Verkauf stehen; im Angebot sein, reduziert sein 5/3

salmon *(no pl)* /ˈsæmən/ Lachs 2/2

salsa *(no pl)* /ˈsælsə/ Salsasoße 2/P13

salt *(no pl)* /sɔːlt/ Salz III

the same /ðə ˈseɪm/ der-/die-/dasselbe II

sand /sænd/ Sand(strand) 4/9

sandy /ˈsændi/ sandig 6/M1

Saturday /ˈsætədeɪ/ Samstag I

sauce /sɔːs/ Soße II

Saudi Arabia /ˌsaʊdi əˈreɪbiə/ Saudi-Arabien 3/13

sausage /ˈsɒsɪdʒ/ Wurst, Würstchen I

save /seɪv/ retten III; speichern, sichern III; sparen 1/8

saw /sɔː/ *Vergangenheitsform von „see"*

say *(irr)* /seɪ/ sagen I

saying /ˈseɪɪŋ/ Sprichwort 4/M5

scare /skeə/ Angst machen, erschrecken III

scare away /ˌskeər əˈweɪ/ verscheuchen, abschrecken 6/P6

be scared (of sth) /bi: ˈskeəd/ (vor etw) Angst haben II

scarf *(pl **-s** or **scarves**)* /skɑːf, skɑːvz/ Schal I

scary /ˈskeəri/ Furcht erregend; unheimlich II

scene /siːn/ Szene 6/M7

scenery *(no pl)* /ˈsiːnəri/ Landschaft 6/7

(class) schedule *(AE)* = timetable *(BE)* /ˈʃedjuːl/ Stundenplan 1/3

school /skuːl/ Schule I

boarding school /ˈbɔːdɪŋ ˌskuːl/ Internat 4/M5

elementary school *(AE)* = primary school *(BE)* /elɪˈmentri ˌskuːl, ˈpraɪməri ˌskuːl/ Grundschule 1/LL

high school /ˈhaɪ ˌskuːl/ *weiterführende Schule in den USA (Klasse 9-12)* 1/I

junior high school /ˌdʒuːniə ˈhaɪ

ˌskuːl / *Mittelstufenschule in den USA* 1/LL

public school *(AE)* / ˌpʌblɪk 'skuːl / staatliche/öffentliche Schule 4/CC

schoolbag / 'skuːlbæg / Schultasche I

science / 'saɪəns / (Natur) wissenschaft I

(pair of) scissors *(only pl)* / 'sɪzəz / Schere I

score / skɔː / einen Punkt machen, punkten 5/15

score a goal / skɔːr_ə 'gəʊl / ein Tor schießen III

scorpion / 'skɔːpiən / Skorpion 6/7

Scotland / 'skɒtlənd / Schottland II

Scottish / 'skɒtɪʃ / schottisch III

scream / skriːm / schreien; kreischen 5/7

screen / skriːn / Leinwand; Bildschirm 6/11

the sea *(no pl)* / ðə 'siː / das Meer, die See II

sea level *(no pl)* / 'siː ˌlevl / Meeresspiegel 6/7

sea lion / 'siː ˌlaɪən / Seelöwe 6/7

seafood *(no pl)* / 'siːˌfuːd / Meeresfrüchte 2/M5

seal / siːl / Seehund, Robbe 4/12

search / sɜːtʃ / (durch)suchen III

seasick / 'siːˌsɪk / seekrank 4/M1

be seated / bi 'siːtɪd / einen Sitzplatz/Tisch zugewiesen bekommen 2/CC

second / 'sekənd / Sekunde III

second / 'sekənd / zweite(r, s) I

secondly / 'sekəndli / zweitens 2/M4

secret / 'siːkrət / geheim III

secretary / 'sekrətri / Sekretär/in 1/5

security guard / sɪ'kjʊərəti ˌgɑːd / Sicherheitsbedienstete/r, Wachmann/-frau 0p2

see *(irr)* / siː / sehen I

see you / 'siː ju / bis dann, bis bald II

seem / siːm / scheinen 5/M10

seen / siːn / *siehe „see"*

self-confident / ˌself'kɒnfɪdnt /

selbstbewusst, selbstsicher II

sell *(irr)* / sel / verkaufen I

seller / 'selə / Verkäufer/in II

semester *(AE)* / sə'mestə / Semester; (Schul)halbjahr 1/3

send *(irr)* / send / (zu)schicken II

senior *(AE)* / 'siːniə / *Schüler/in einer Highschool- oder Collegeabgangsklasse* 1/M2

sent / sent / *Vergangenheitsform von „send"*

sentence / 'sentəns / Satz I

separate / 'sepəreɪt / trennen 1/8

September / sep'tembə / September I

series *(only pl)* / 'sɪəriːz / Serie, Reihe 6/13

serve / sɜːv / servieren 2/P7

service / 'sɜːvɪs / Service; Bedienung 2/9

service / 'sɜːvɪs / Dienst, Hilfe 6/M3

set *(irr)* / set / (ein)stellen; (fest)setzen 6/P8

set the table / ˌset ðə 'teɪbl / den Tisch decken II

settle / 'setl / sich niederlassen 2/15

settler / 'setlə / Siedler/in 2/15

sew *(irr)* / səʊ / nähen 3/CC

sewn / səʊn / *siehe „sew"*

shadow / 'ʃædəʊ / Schatten II

shadow sb / 'ʃædəʊ ˌsʌmbədi / jdn beschatten; jdm bei der Arbeit zusehen 0p3

shake / ʃeɪk / Schütteln 2/10

shake *(irr)* / ʃeɪk / schütteln 2/P13

shall / ʃæl / sollen 1/12

be in good shape / bi_ɪn ˌgʊd 'ʃeɪp / in guter (körperlicher) Verfassung sein, in Form sein 5/12

share / ʃeə / teilen 3/13

shark / ʃɑːk / Hai(fisch) 6/11

she / ʃiː / sie I

sheep *(pl -)* / ʃiːp / Schaf I

shelf *(pl shelves)* / ʃelf, ʃelvz / Regal I

shift work *(no pl)* / 'ʃɪft ˌwɜːk / Schichtarbeit, Schichtdienst 6/5

shine *(irr)* / ʃaɪn / scheinen (Sonne) 4/9

shiny / 'ʃaɪni / glänzend 1/P11

ship / ʃɪp / Schiff I

shirt / ʃɜːt / Hemd; Bluse I

shock / ʃɒk / Schock 6/10

shocked / ʃɒkt / schockiert, entsetzt III

shoe / ʃuː / Schuh I

shoeshine / 'ʃuːʃaɪn / Schuhputz- 3/13

shop / ʃɒp / Geschäft, Laden I

shop / ʃɒp / einkaufen 5/3

shop assistant / 'ʃɒp_əˌsɪstənt / Verkäufer/in II

shop till you drop / 'ʃɒp tɪl jə ˌdrɒp / Einkaufen bis zum Umfallen 5/3

do the shopping / ˌduː ðə 'ʃɒpɪŋ / einkaufen (gehen) I

go shopping / gəʊ 'ʃɒpɪŋ / einkaufen gehen I

shopping list / 'ʃɒpɪŋ lɪst / Einkaufszettel, Einkaufsliste 2/M6

short / ʃɔːt / kurz III

should / ʃʊd / sollte/müsste I

shoulder / 'ʃəʊldə / Schulter III

shout / ʃaʊt / schreien, rufen I

show *(irr)* / ʃəʊ / zeigen II

show sb around / ʃəʊ sʌmbədi_ə'raʊnd / jdn herumführen 6/5

shower / 'ʃaʊə / Dusche 1/9

take a shower / teɪk_ə 'ʃaʊə / duschen 1/9

shown / ʃəʊn / *siehe „show"*

shuttle bus / 'ʃʌtl bʌs / Zubringerbus, Shuttlebus 4/P7

shy / ʃaɪ / schüchtern 4/4

Siberia / saɪ'bɪəriə / Sibirien Intro

side / saɪd / Seite II

sight / saɪt / Sehenswürdigkeit II

sight / saɪt / Anblick 4/M1

sign / saɪn / Zeichen; (Straßen-/ Verkehrs)schild II

sign up / ˌsaɪnˌ'ʌp / sich anmelden 3/16

signature / 'sɪgnətʃə / Unterschrift III

silly / 'sɪli / dumm; albern III

silver / 'sɪlvə / silbern II

SIM card / 'sɪm ˌkɑːd / SIM-Karte 1/P11

similar / 'sɪmɪlə / ähnlich 3/13

simple past /ˌsɪmpl ˈpɑːst/ einfache Vergangenheit 4/P12

simply /ˈsɪmpli/ einfach 1/CC

since /sɪns/ seit III

since then /sɪns ˈðen/ seitdem, seit damals 2/CC

sing (irr) /sɪŋ/ singen I

sing along /ˌsɪŋ ə'lɒŋ/ mitsingen 4/9

singer /ˈsɪŋə/ Sänger/in II

single (ticket) /ˈsɪŋɡl/ Einzelfahrkarte III

sister /ˈsɪstə/ Schwester I

brothers and sisters /ˌbrʌðəz ænd ˈsɪstəz/ Geschwister II

sit (irr) /sɪt/ sitzen I

site (informal) /saɪt/ Website 6/13

situation /ˌsɪtʃuˈeɪʃn/ Situation, Lage 1/6

size /saɪz/ Größe III

skiing /ˈskiːɪŋ/ Skifahren, Skilaufen 5/M9

skill /skɪl/ Geschick; Fähigkeit, Fertigkeit 1/5

skin /skɪn/ Haut 5/M10

skirt /skɜːt/ Rock I

skyline /ˈskaɪˌlaɪn/ Skyline; Horizont 3/2

skyscraper /ˈskaɪˌskreɪpə/ Wolkenkratzer 3/2

skyway /ˈskaɪˌweɪ/ Himmel 4/9

slave /sleɪv/ Sklave/Sklavin 4/1

slavery (no pl) /ˈsleɪvəri/ Sklaverei Intro

sleep (irr) /sliːp/ schlafen I

sleep over /sliːp ˌˈəʊvə/ übernachten, über Nacht bleiben II

slide show /ˈslaɪd ʃəʊ/ Diashow 2/15

slim /slɪm/ schlank, schmal, dünn III

slow /sləʊ/ langsam II

small /smɔːl/ klein I

smell /smel/ Geruch; Duft; Gestank I

smell (of) /smel/ riechen (nach) II

smile /smaɪl/ lächeln 4/8

smile /smaɪl/ Lächeln 4/CC

smoke (no pl) /sməʊk/ Rauch 4/12

smoke /sməʊk/ rauchen 5/M9

snake /sneɪk/ Schlange I

sneaker (AE) = trainer (BE) /ˈsniːkə/ Turnschuh 3/P11

snow (no pl) /snəʊ/ Schnee II

snowflake /ˈsnəʊˌfleɪk/ Schneeflocke 6/M1

snowy /ˈsnəʊi/ schneereich; verschneit I

so /səʊ/ so I; deshalb; also II

so far /ˌsəʊ ˈfɑː/ bisher, bis jetzt 1/10

soap (no pl) /səʊp/ Seife III

soap (opera) /ˈsəʊp (ˌˈɒprə)/ Seifenoper, Soap II

soccer (AE) = football (BE) (no pl) /ˈsɒkə/ Fußball 5/11

social media /ˌsəʊʃl ˈmiːdiə/ soziale Medien, Social Media 6/13

sock /sɒk/ Socke I

soft /sɒft/ weich III

solar panel /ˌsəʊlə ˈpænəl/ Sonnenkollektor 1/10

sold /səʊld/ Vergangenheitsform von „sell"

some /sʌm/ einige; etwas I

somebody /ˈsʌmbədi/ jemand II

someone /ˈsʌmwʌn/ jemand II

something /ˈsʌmθɪŋ/ etwas I

sometimes /ˈsʌmtaɪmz/ manchmal I

somewhere /ˈsʌmweə/ irgendwo II

son /sʌn/ Sohn I

soon /suːn/ bald I

sore /sɔː/ wund, entzündet III

sorry /ˈsɒri/ Verzeihung!, Entschuldigung!; Wie bitte? I

(I'm) sorry. /ˈsɒri/ Entschuldigung, das tut mir leid. II

feel sorry for sb /ˌfiːl ˈsɒri fə sʌmbədi/ Mitleid mit jdm haben III

sort /sɔːt/ Art, Sorte I

sort /sɔːt/ sortieren 2/4

sound /saʊnd/ Geräusch, Klang; Ton II

sound /saʊnd/ klingen, sich anhören I

soup /suːp/ Suppe III

source /sɔːs/ Quelle 5/10

south /saʊθ/ Süden III

South Africa /saʊθ ˈæfrɪkə/ Südafrika II

South America /ˌsaʊθ əˈmerɪkə/ Südamerika 3/9

south-east /ˌsaʊθ'iːst/ Südosten 6/7

Southern /ˈsʌðən/ Südstaaten- 2/2

southern /ˈsʌðən/ südlich, Süd- Intro

space /speɪs/ Platz, Raum 3/M1

space /speɪs/ Feld Intro

spaceship /ˈspeɪsˌʃɪp/ Raumschiff II

Spain /speɪn/ Spanien I

Spanish /ˈspænɪʃ/ Spanisch; spanisch I

sparkling /ˈspɑːklɪŋ/ funkelnd, glitzernd 4/9

speak (irr) /spiːk/ sprechen, reden II

speaker /ˈspiːkə/ Redner/in 2/10

speaking of ... /ˈspiːkɪŋ ˌəv/ da/wo wir gerade von ... sprechen 1/3

special /ˈspeʃl/ besondere(r, s), speziell I

special offer /ˌspeʃl ˈɒfə/ Sonderangebot III

speech /spiːtʃ/ Rede 6/M8

direct speech /dɪˌrekt ˈspiːtʃ/ direkte Rede 5/M2

reported speech /rɪˌpɔːtɪd ˈspiːtʃ/ indirekte Rede 5/M2

speech bubble /ˈspiːtʃ ˌbʌbl/ Sprechblase 5/2

spell (irr) /spel/ buchstabieren I

spelling /ˈspelɪŋ/ Rechtschreibung 4/P10

spend (irr) /spend/ ausgeben (Geld); verbringen (Zeit) II

spice /spaɪs/ Gewürz III

spicy /ˈspaɪsi/ würzig; scharf 2/P4

spider /ˈspaɪdə/ Spinne II

spinach (no pl) /ˈspɪnɪdʒ/ Spinat 2/10

spirit (no pl) /ˈspɪrɪt/ (Team)geist 1/P6

spit (irr) /spɪt/ spucken I

split up /splɪt ˌˈʌp/ sich teilen; sich trennen III

spokesperson (pl -people) /ˈspəʊksˌpɜːsn/ Sprecher/in 4/15

spooky (informal) /ˈspuːki/ unheimlich; schaurig II

spoon /spuːn/ Löffel I

sports (only pl) /spɔːts/ Sport; Sportart I

sports field /ˈspɔːts fiːld/ Sportplatz, Spielfeld III

sports ground /ˈspɔːts ˌɡraʊnd/ Sportplatz I

sports hall /ˈspɔːts hɔːl/ Sporthalle III

sportsperson /ˈspɔːtsˌpɜːsn/ Sportler/in III

spray /spreɪ/ (be)sprühen 3/M1

spring /sprɪŋ/ Frühling I

square /skweə/ Quadrat; Platz 3/2

stadium /ˈsteɪdiəm/ Stadion II

staff (no pl) /stɑːf/ Mitarbeiter, Personal 1/8

stage /steɪdʒ/ Bühne II

stairs (only pl) /steəz/ Treppe III

stall /stɔːl/ (Verkaufs)stand II

stamp /stæmp/ Briefmarke I

stand (irr) /stænd/ stehen; ertragen, ausstehen, aushalten I

stand in line /ˌstænd ɪn ˈlaɪn/ anstehen 4/M1

stand up /ˌstændˈʌp/ aufstehen 1/3

standard /ˈstændəd/ Standard; Richtlinie; Wertvorstellung 3/16

star /stɑː/ Stern II

star sign /ˈstɑː saɪn/ Sternzeichen II

stare at sb/sth /ˈsteə ət ˌsʌmbədi, ˌsʌmθɪŋ/ jdn/etw anstarren 4/8

start /stɑːt/ anfangen, beginnen I

starter /ˈstɑːtə/ Vorspeise 2/1

starvation (no pl) /stɑːˈveɪʃn/ Unterernährung, Mangelernährung 4/M1

state /steɪt/ (Bundes)staat Intro

state /steɪt/ staatlich; auf bundesstaatlicher Ebene 1/P6

statement /ˈsteɪtmənt/ Aussage; Äußerung 2/5

the States (informal) /ðə ˈsteɪts/ die Staaten 1/3

station /ˈsteɪʃn/ Bahnhof; Station II

radio station /ˈreɪdiəʊ ˌsteɪʃn/ Radiosender II

statistics /stəˈtɪstɪks/ Statistik 4/2

statue /ˈstætʃuː/ Statue, Standbild 4/M1

the Statue of Liberty /ðə ˌstætʃuː əv ˈlɪbəti/ die Freiheitsstatue 3/2

stay /steɪ/ bleiben I; untergebracht sein, wohnen II

stay out /ˌsteɪˈaʊt/ ausbleiben, wegbleiben 4/M5

stay up /ˌsteɪˈʌp/ aufbleiben, wach bleiben I

steak and kidney pie /ˌsteɪk ən ˌkɪdni ˈpaɪ/ Rindfleisch-Nieren-Pastete 2/10

steal (irr) /stiːl/ stehlen, klauen II

step /step/ Stufe 3/2

stereo /ˈsteriəʊ/ (Stereo)anlage II

stereotype /ˈsteriəˌtaɪp/ Stereotyp, Klischee 4/7

stick /stɪk/ Stock I

sticky /ˈstɪki/ klebrig 2/CC

still /stɪl/ (immer) noch, noch immer III

stomach ache /ˈstʌməkˌeɪk/ Magenschmerzen, Bauchschmerzen III

stone /stəʊn/ Stein III

stood /stʊd/ Vergangenheitsform von „stand"

stop /stɒp/ aufhören; beenden; anhalten I

stop /stɒp/ aufhalten III

storage (no pl) /ˈstɔːrɪdʒ/ Lagerung; Aufbewahrung 1/CC

storm /stɔːm/ Sturm III

story /ˈstɔːri/ Geschichte, Erzählung I

straight (on) /streɪt/ gerade(aus) II

strange /streɪndʒ/ sonderbar, komisch II

strategy /ˈstrætədʒi/ Strategie, Taktik 5/12

strawberry /ˈstrɔːbri/ Erdbeere III

street /striːt/ Straße I

strengthen /ˈstreŋθn/ verstärken, intensivieren 2/M2

stressed /ˈstrest/ gestresst 5/M10

stressful /ˈstresfl/ stressig, anstrengend 4/M5

strict /strɪkt/ streng II

strike (irr) /straɪk/ (zu)schlagen 6/10

stripe /straɪp/ Streifen Intro

stroll /strəʊl/ schlendern, bummeln 4/9

strong /strɒŋ/ stark I

strong /strɒŋ/ robust, stabil Op7

student /ˈstjuːdnt/ Student/in, Studierende/r; Schüler/in I

study /ˈstʌdi/ studieren; lernen II

stuff (informal) /stʌf/ Zeug, Sachen 2/2

stunt /stʌnt/ Stunt; Figur Intro

stunt performer /ˈstʌnt pəˌfɔːmə/ Stuntman, Stuntgirl 6/2

stupid /ˈstjuːpɪd/ dumm, blöd I

style /staɪl/ frisieren II

-style /staɪl/ nach ... Art, im ... Stil 2/2

subject /ˈsʌbdʒɪkt/ Thema; (Schul)fach I

subway (AE) = underground (BE) /ˈsʌbˌweɪ/ U-Bahn 3/M1

success (no pl) /səkˈses/ Erfolg III

successful /səkˈsesfl/ erfolgreich III

such /sʌtʃ/ solche(r,s) 3/M5

such as /sʌtʃ æz/ wie (zum Beispiel) 3/2

sudden /ˈsʌdn/ plötzlich 6/P6

suddenly /ˈsʌdnli/ plötzlich, auf einmal I

sugar (no pl) /ˈʃʊɡə/ Zucker II

suggest /səˈdʒest/ vorschlagen 1/13

suitcase /ˈsuːtˌkeɪs/ Koffer II

summary /ˈsʌməri/ Zusammenfassung; Inhaltsangabe 4/M1

summer /ˈsʌmə/ Sommer I

summer camp /ˈsʌmə ˌkæmp/ Ferienlager III

sun /sʌn/ Sonne II

Sunday /ˈsʌndeɪ/ Sonntag I

Sunday roast /ˈsʌndeɪ rəʊst / Sonntagsbraten 2/10

sunglasses *(only pl)* /ˈsʌnˌglɑːsɪz/ Sonnenbrille I

sunny /ˈsʌni/ sonnig I

sunrise /ˈsʌnˌraɪz/ Sonnenaufgang II

sunshine *(no pl)* /ˈsʌnʃaɪn/ Sonnenschein III

Super Bowl /ˈsuːpə ˌbəʊl/ *Meisterschaftsspiel im US-amerikanischen Profi-Football* Intro

supermarket /ˈsuːpəˌmɑːkɪt/ Supermarkt 3/16

support /səˈpɔːt/ (unter)stützen 3/16

sure /ʃɔː/ sicher I

make sure /ˌmeɪk ˈʃɔː/ sich versichern, darauf achten 3/16; dafür sorgen 2/M1

surf /sɜːf/ surfen 5/P1

surf the Internet /ˌsɜːf ðiˌˈɪntənet/ im Internet surfen 5/2

surname /ˈsɜːˌneɪm/ Familienname, Nachname III

surprise /səˈpraɪz/ Überraschung II

surprised /səˈpraɪzd/ überrascht II

surprising /səˈpraɪzɪŋ/ überraschend 1/1

survey /ˈsɜːveɪ/ Untersuchung, Umfrage 5/10

survive /səˈvaɪv/ überleben 3/17

swap /swɒp/ tauschen 3/11

sweat /swet/ schwitzen 5/M9

sweet /swiːt/ Süßigkeit I

sweet /swiːt/ süß I

sweet potato /ˌswiːt pəˈteɪtəʊ/ Süßkartoffel 2/M5

swim *(irr)* /swɪm/ schwimmen I

swimmer /ˈswɪmə/ Schwimmer/in III

swimming /ˈswɪmɪŋ/ Schwimmen I

swimming pool /ˈswɪmɪŋ puːl/ Schwimmbecken, -bad I

sword /sɔːd/ Schwert 1/P6

symbol /ˈsɪmbl/ Symbol, Zeichen 3/2

symbolize /ˈsɪmbəlaɪz/ symbolisieren 3/M9

T

table /ˈteɪbl/ Tisch I

set the table /ˌset ðə ˈteɪbl/ den Tisch decken II

table tennis *(no pl)* /ˈteɪbl ˌtenɪs/ Tischtennis I

tackle sb /ˈtækl ˌsʌmbədi/ jdn angreifen 5/15

tail /teɪl/ Schwanz II

take *(irr)* /teɪk/ (mit)nehmen; bringen I

take *(irr)* /teɪk/ brauchen, dauern 5/12

take a shower /ˌteɪk_ə ˈʃaʊə/ duschen 1/9

take a tour /ˌteɪk_ə ˈtʊə/ an einer Führung/Tour teilnehmen, eine Tour/Führung machen 6/10

take action /ˌteɪk_ˈækʃn/ handeln, etw unternehmen 1/13

take care of /ˌteɪk ˈkeər_əv/ sich kümmern um, versorgen II

take notes /ˌteɪk ˈnəʊts/ (sich) Notizen machen II

take one's time /ˌteɪk wʌnz ˈtaɪm/ sich Zeit lassen 2/7

take out /ˌteɪk_ˈaʊt/ hinausbringen I; herausnehmen 1/3

take part (in) /ˌteɪk ˈpɑːt/ teilnehmen (an) II

take photos /ˌteɪk ˈfəʊtəʊz/ Bilder machen, fotografieren II

take place /ˌteɪk ˈpleɪs/ stattfinden III

take sth into one's own hands /ˌteɪk ˌsʌmθɪŋ_ˌɪntə wʌnz_ˈəʊn hændz/ etw selbst in die Hand nehmen 6/10

take time out /ˌteɪk ˌtaɪm_ˈaʊt/ eine Pause machen 5/12

take turns /ˌteɪk ˈtɜːnz/ sich abwechseln 1/1

takeaway (food) /ˈteɪkəˌweɪ/ Essen zum Mitnehmen 2/9

taken /ˈteɪkən/ *siehe „take"*

talented /ˈtæləntɪd/ talentiert, begabt III

talk /tɔːk/ Gespräch; Unterhaltung; Vortrag 1/7

talk (to) /tɔːk/ sprechen/reden/

sich unterhalten (mit) I

give a talk /ˌgɪv_ə ˈtɔːk/ einen Vortrag halten 1/7

tall /tɔːl/ hoch; groß I

tap /tæp/ Wasserhahn III

taste *(no pl)* /teɪst/ Geschmack 2/M2

taste /teɪst/ schmecken III

tasty /ˈteɪsti/ schmackhaft, lecker 2/M2

taught /tɔːt/ *Vergangenheitsform von „teach"*

tea /tiː/ Tee I

teach *(irr)* /tiːtʃ/ unterrichten I; beibringen III

teacher /ˈtiːtʃə/ Lehrer/in I

tear /tɪə/ Träne I

teaspoon /ˈtiːˌspuːn/ Teelöffel 2/M2

technician /tekˈnɪʃn/ Techniker/in II

(tele)phone /fəʊn/ Telefon I

telephone box /ˈtelɪfəʊn bɒks/ Telefonzelle III

tell *(irr)* /tel/ erzählen; sagen I

temple /ˈtempl/ Tempel II

tense /tens/ Zeitform, Tempus 4/M2

tepee /ˈtiːpiː/ Indianerzelt 4/12

terrible /ˈterəbl/ schrecklich, furchtbar II

test /test/ Prüfung, Test; Klassenarbeit II

test /test/ prüfen, testen III

text message /ˈtekst ˌmesɪdʒ/ SMS, Kurznachricht III

textbook /ˈtekstˌbʊk/ Lehrbuch, Schulbuch 1/M5

the (River) Thames /ðə ˈtemz/ die Themse II

than /ðæn/ als II

thank /θæŋk/ danken 5/8

thank you /ˈθæŋk juː/ danke I

thanks /θæŋks/ danke I

give thanks /ˌgɪv ˈθæŋks/ danken, sich bedanken 2/12

thanks a lot /ˌθæŋks_ə ˈlɒt/ vielen Dank II

thanks to /ˈθæŋks tə/ dank, wegen 3/M1

Thanksgiving /ˈθæŋksˌgɪvɪŋ/ Thanksgiving *(amerikanisches Erntedankfest)* 2/12 that /ðæt/ das; der/die/das I; dass 1/1

that way /ˈðæt weɪ/ so, auf diese Weise 2/M2

that's why /ˈðæts waɪ/ deshalb; das ist der Grund, warum I

the /ðə/ der/die/das I

the ... way /ðə ˈweɪ/ auf die ... Art 1/CC

theater (AE) = theatre (BE) /ˈθɪətə/ Theater 3/2

their /ðeə/ ihr(e) I

theirs /ðeəz/ ihre(r,s) 1/P10

them /ðem/ sie, ihnen I

them (= these) (informal) /ðem/ diese 6/M1

theme /θiːm/ Thema; Lektion, Kapitel 1/I

theme park /ˈθiːm ˌpɑːk/ Themenpark; Freizeitpark 6/2

themselves /ðemˈselvz/ sich (selbst); selbst 5/13

then /ðen/ dann, danach I

then /ðen/ damals 4/12

there /ðeə/ dort, da I

over there /ˌəʊvə ˈðeə/ dort (drüben) I

there are /ðeərˈɑː/ es gibt, da sind I

there is /ðeərˈɪz/ es gibt, da ist I

these (pl of this) /ðiːz/ diese I

they /ðeɪ/ sie I

thin /θɪn/ dünn II

thing /θɪŋ/ Ding, Gegenstand, Sache I

think (irr) /θɪŋk/ denken, glauben, meinen I

think about (sb/sth) /ˈθɪŋk_əˌbaʊt/ an (jdn/etw) denken; sich (etw) überlegen 2/12; über (jdn/etw) nachdenken 2/M4

think of /ˈθɪŋk_əv/ denken an; sich ausdenken 2/M7

this /ðɪs/ diese(r, s); das I

this morning /ðɪs ˈmɔːnɪŋ/ heute Morgen III

this way /ˈðɪs weɪ/ so, auf diese Art und Weise 2/2

those (pl of that) /ðəʊz/ diese; jene I

though /ðəʊ/ (je)doch 3/M6

thought /θɔːt/ Gedanke 2/7

thought /θɔːt/ Vergangenheitsform

von „think"

thought bubble /ˈθɔːt ˌbʌbl/ Denkblase, Gedankenblase 5/2

hundreds of thousands (only pl) /ˌhʌndrədz_əv ˈθaʊzndz/ Hunderttausende 6/4

be thrilled /bi: ˈθrɪld/ außer sich vor Freude sein, sich wahnsinnig darüber freuen 1/M5

thriller /ˈθrɪlə/ Krimi, Thriller I

through /θruː/ durch II

throw (irr) /θrəʊ/ werfen III

Thursday /ˈθɜːzdeɪ/ Donnerstag I

tick /tɪk/ abhaken, ankreuzen 6/P2

what makes sb tick /ˌmeɪks sʌmbədi ˈtɪk/ wie jmd tickt, was jdn bewegt 4/CC

day ticket /ˈdeɪ ˌtɪkɪt/ Tageskarte, Tagesticket 6/9

ticket counter /ˈtɪkɪt ˌkaʊntə/ Fahrkartenschalter III

tidy up /ˌtaɪdi ˈʌp/ aufräumen I

tie /taɪ/ Krawatte II

time /taɪm/ (Uhr)zeit I; Mal II

all the time /ˌɔːl ðə ˈtaɪm/ dauernd, ständig 2/6

have a good time /ˌhæv_ə ˌgʊd ˈtaɪm/ sich amüsieren, Spaß haben 5/M3

on time /ɒn ˈtaɪm/ pünktlich; rechtzeitig 5/M3

at any time /æt_ˈeni taɪm/ jederzeit, zu jeder Zeit 6/9

have a hard time doing sth /hæv_ə hɑːd ˌtaɪm ˈduːɪŋ ˌsʌmθɪŋ/ es schwer haben, etw zu tun 3/16

over time /ˌəʊvə ˈtaɪm/ im Lauf der Zeit, mit der Zeit 2/15

running time /ˈrʌnɪŋ ˌtaɪm/ Laufzeit 6/13

take one's time /teɪk wʌnz ˈtaɪm/ sich Zeit lassen 2/7

take time out /ˌteɪk ˌtaɪm_ˈaʊt/ eine Pause machen 5/12

What time is it? /wɒt_ˈtaɪm ˌɪz_ɪt/ Wie spät/Wie viel Uhr ist es? I

timeline /ˈtaɪmˌlaɪn/ Zeitstrahl 4/M1

at all times /ət_ˈɔːl ˈtaɪmz/ immer, jederzeit 1/P4

timetable /ˈtaɪmteɪbl/ Stundenplan I; Fahrplan III

tip /tɪp/ Tipp II

tired /ˈtaɪəd/ müde I

title /ˈtaɪtl/ Titel III

to /tə/ in, nach, zu, an; vor; bis I

today /təˈdeɪ/ heute I

together /təˈgeðə/ zusammen, gemeinsam I

get together /ˌget_təˈgeðə/ sich treffen 2/14

toilet /ˈtɔɪlət/ Toilette, Klo III

told /təʊld/ Vergangenheitsform von „tell"

tomato (pl -es) /təˈmɑːtəʊ, təˈmɑːtəʊz/ Tomate 2/1

tomorrow /təˈmɒrəʊ/ morgen I

tongue twister /ˈtʌŋ ˌtwɪstə/ Zungenbrecher 3/P2

tonight /təˈnaɪt/ heute Abend III

tonight /təˈnaɪt/ heute Nacht III

too /tuː/ zu; auch I

too bad /ˌtuː ˈbæd/ wirklich schade III

took /tʊk/ Vergangenheitsform von „take"

tool /tuːl/ Werkzeug 1/5

tooth (pl teeth) /tuːθ, tiːθ/ Zahn I

toothbrush /ˈtuːθˌbrʌʃ/ Zahnbürste III

top /tɒp/ oberes Ende, Spitze; Gipfel II; Top-, Spitzen- III

at the top (of) /æt ðə ˈtɒp/ oben, am oberen Ende (von), an der Spitze (von) III

topic /ˈtɒpɪk/ Thema 1/7

topping /ˈtɒpɪŋ/ Belag; Garnierung 2/10

tortoise /ˈtɔːtəs/ (Land)schildkröte II

total /ˈtəʊtl/ Gesamt- 4/1

totem pole /ˈtəʊtəm ˌpəʊl/ Totempfahl 4/12

touch /tʌtʃ/ berühren I

take a tour /ˌteɪk_ə ˈtʊə/ an einer Führung/Tour teilnehmen, eine Tour/Führung machen 6/10

tour guide /ˈtʊə gaɪd/ Reiseführer/in, Reiseleiter/in 3/P7

towel /ˈtaʊəl/ Handtuch I

tower /ˈtaʊə/ Turm II

town /taʊn/ Stadt 3/13

in town /ɪn ˈtaʊn/ in der Stadt 2/P4

toxin /ˈtɒksɪn/ Gift 1/M7

toy /tɔɪ/ Spielzeug III

track /træk/ Weg, Pfad; Nummer 1/2

tractor /ˈtræktə/ Traktor I

trade /treɪd/ Handel 3/2

traditional /trəˈdɪʃnəl/ traditionell 2/14

traffic light /ˈtræfɪk laɪt/ Ampel II

trail /treɪl/ Weg, Pfad 6/P6

train /treɪn/ Zug, Eisenbahn II

train /treɪn/ trainieren III

trap /træp/ Falle II

trash (AE) = rubbish (BE) /træʃ/ Müll, Abfall 1/12

travel /ˈtrævl/ reisen II

traveller /ˈtrævlə/ Reisende/r III

travelling (no pl) /ˈtrævlɪŋ/ Reisen 3/7

treat oneself to sth /ˈtriːt wʌnself tə ˌsʌmθɪŋ/ sich etw gönnen 5/12

tree /triː/ Baum I

tribe /traɪb/ Stamm 4/12

trifle /ˈtraɪfl/ Trifle (englisches Schicht-Dessert) 2/10

trip /trɪp/ Ausflug; Reise, Fahrt II

trophy /ˈtrəʊfi/ Trophäe, Preis 5/M7

trouble (no pl) /ˈtrʌbl/ Schwierigkeiten III

get into trouble /getˌɪntə ˈtrʌbl/ Schwierigkeiten bekommen II

trousers (only pl) /ˈtraʊzəz/ Hose I

true /truː/ wahr; richtig II

try /traɪ/ (aus)probieren; versuchen II

try hard to do sth /ˌtraɪ ˈhɑːd̬tə duː sʌmθɪŋ/ sich sehr bemühen, etw zu tun II

try on /traɪˈɒn/ anprobieren 5/3

tube (no pl) /tjuːb/ Londoner U-Bahn II

Tuesday /ˈtjuːzdeɪ/ Dienstag I

tug-of-war /ˌtʌɡ‿əv ˈwɔː/ Tauziehen 1/M1

Turkey /ˈtɜːki/ Türkei I

turkey /ˈtɜːki/ Truthahn/-henne, Pute/r 2/14

Turkish /ˈtɜːkɪʃ/ Türkisch; türkisch II

turn /tɜːn/ sich drehen; abbiegen II

(it's) your turn /ˈjɔː tɜːn/ du bist dran I

miss a turn /ˈmɪs‿ə ˌtɜːn/ eine Runde aussetzen Intro

turn into /ˌtɜːn‿ˈɪntʊ/ umwandeln

in, verändern in 5/P8

turn off /ˌtɜːn‿ˈɒf/ ausmachen, ausschalten III

turn on /ˌtɜːn‿ˈɒn/ einschalten III

turn round /tɜːn ˈraʊnd/ (sich) umdrehen III

take turns /ˌteɪk ˈtɜːnz/ sich abwechseln 1/1

turtle /ˈtɜːtl/ Schildkröte I

TV (= television) /ˌtiːˈviː, ˈtelɪˌvɪʒn/ Fernseher; Fernsehen I

watch TV /ˌwɒtʃ ˌtiːˈviː/ fernsehen I

TV series (only pl) /ˌtiːˈviː ˌsɪəriːz/ Fernsehserie II

twice /twaɪs/ zweimal III

twin /twɪn/ Zwilling, Zwillings- II

two-minute /tuːˈmɪnɪt/ zweiminütig 1/7

two-week /tuːˈwiːk/ zweiwöchig 6/8

type /taɪp/ Art; Typ, Sorte III

typical /ˈtɪpɪkl/ typisch 2/2

tyre /ˈtaɪə/ Reifen 0p7

U

ugly /ˈʌɡli/ hässlich I

UK (= United Kingdom) /ˌjuːˈkeɪ, juːˌnaɪtɪd ˈkɪŋdəm/ Vereinigtes Königreich II

uncle /ˈʌŋkl/ Onkel I

under /ˈʌndə/ unter I

underground /ˈʌndəˌɡraʊnd/ U-Bahn II

underline /ˌʌndəˈlaɪn/ unterstreichen 2/P9

understand (irr) /ˌʌndəˈstænd/ verstehen II

understood /ˌʌndəˈstʊd/ Vergangenheitsform von „understand"

unfortunately /ʌnˈfɔːtʃnətli/ leider, unglücklicherweise II

unfriendly /ʌnˈfrendli/ unfreundlich II

unhappy /ʌnˈhæpi/ unglücklich III

unhealthy /ʌnˈhelθi/ ungesund III

unimportant /ˌʌnɪmˈpɔːtnt/ unwichtig 4/P1

unique /juːˈniːk/ einzigartig 3/P2

(the) United States /juːˌnaɪtɪd ˈsteɪts/ Vereinigte Staaten 6/13

universe /ˈjuːnɪˌvɜːs/ Universum II

university /ˌjuːnɪˈvɜːsəti/

Universität 4/P9

until /ənˈtɪl/ bis II

up /ʌp/ (nach) oben; hinauf Intro

up and down /ˌʌp‿ən ˈdaʊn/ auf und ab III

up to /ˈʌp tuː/ bis (zu) III

be up to sth /biˌʌp tə ˌsʌmθɪŋ/ etw machen; etw vorhaben 5/M1

be up to sb /biˌʌp tʊ ˈsʌmbədi/ von jdm abhängen 3/M1

get up /getˌˈʌp/ aufstehen I

What's up? (informal) /wɒtsˌˈʌp/ Wie gehts?; Was geht?; Was gibts? 5/I

upgrade /ʌpˈɡreɪd/ Aufrüsten; neueste Version 1/P11

upstairs /ʌpˈsteəz/ (nach) oben II

us /ʌs/ uns I

the US (= United States) /ðə juː ˈes, ðə juːˌnaɪtɪd ˈsteɪts/ die Vereinigten Staaten 4/1

usage (no pl) /ˈjuːsɪdʒ/ Verbrauch 1/M5

use /juːs/ Verwendung, Gebrauch 5/10

use /juːz/ benutzen II

get used to sth /get ˈjuːstˌtu ˌsʌmθɪŋ/ sich an etw gewöhnen 4/6

used to do sth /ˈjuːstˌtu ˈduː ˌsʌmθɪŋ/ früher etw getan haben 4/4

useful /ˈjuːsfl/ nützlich, hilfreich 1/P9

usually /ˈjuːʒʊəli/ gewöhnlich, normalerweise I

Ute /juːt/ Ute-Indianer/in; Ute-; Ute (Sprache) 4/M5

V

vacation (AE) = holiday (BE) /vəˈkeɪʃn/ Ferien, Urlaub 1/3

valley /ˈvæli/ Tal III

vandalism (no pl) /ˈvændəˌlɪzm/ Vandalismus, Sachbeschädigung 3/M1

vegetable /ˈvedʒtəbl/ Gemüse I

vegetarian /ˌvedʒəˈteəriən/ Vegetarier/in III

vegetarian /ˌvedʒəˈteəriən/ vegetarisch III

verse /vɜːs/ Strophe 2/10

vertical /ˈvɜːtɪkl/ senkrecht,

vertikal 1/M5

very /'veri/ sehr I

vet (= veterinarian) /vet, ˌvetrɪ'neəriən/ Tierarzt/-ärztin II

vet's assistant /'vets ə,sɪstnt/ Tierarzthelfer/in 0p2

victory /'vɪktri/ Sieg 2/12

view /vjuː/ Sicht; (Aus)blick, Aussicht II

village /'vɪlɪdʒ/ Dorf II

VIP (= very important person) /ˌviː aɪ 'piː/ VIP, Promi 6/9

visit /'vɪzɪt/ Besuch 2/9

visit /'vɪzɪt/ besuchen I

visitor /'vɪzɪtə/ Besucher/in 6/2

voice /vɔɪs/ Stimme 4/9

volcano (pl -oes or -os) /vɒl'keɪnəʊ, vɒl'keɪnəʊz/ Vulkan 6/11

volunteer /ˌvɒlən'tɪə/ Freiwillige/r I

vote (for sb) /vəʊt/ (jdn) wählen, (für jdn) abstimmen 1/M1

vowel /'vaʊəl/ Vokal 1/P1

W

wait (for) /weɪt/ warten (auf) II

sb cannot wait (to do sth) /ˌsʌmbədi ˌkænɒt 'weɪt (ˌtə duː ˌsʌmθɪŋ)/ jmd kann es kaum erwarten (, etw zu tun) III

waiter/waitress /'weɪtə, 'weɪtrəs/ Bedienung, Kellner/in II

wake up /weɪk ˌ'ʌp/ aufwecken; aufwachen 3/13

walk /wɔːk/ Spaziergang II

walk /wɔːk/ (zu Fuß) gehen, laufen I

go for a walk /ˌgəʊ fər ə 'wɔːk/ spazieren gehen I

gallery walk /'gæləri wɔːk/ Galerierundgang 6/5

wall /wɔːl/ Wand I

wall climbing /'wɔːl ˌklaɪmɪŋ/ Klettern an der Kletterwand II

wallet /'wɒlɪt/ Portemonnaie, Brieftasche III

want /wɒnt/ wollen I

want to do sth /'wɒnt ˌtə 'duː ˌsʌmθɪŋ/ etw tun wollen I

war /wɔː/ Krieg 4/3

civil war /ˌsɪvl 'wɔː/ Bürgerkrieg 4/1

wardrobe /'wɔːdrəʊb/ Kleiderschrank I

warning /'wɔːnɪŋ/ Warnung II

was /wɒz/ Vergangenheitsform von „be"

wash /wɒʃ/ (sich) waschen I

wash the dishes /wɒʃ ðə 'dɪʃɪz/ abspülen, Geschirr spülen 3/13

waste material /'weɪst mə,tɪəriəl/ Abfall 1/CC

watch /wɒtʃ/ (Armband)uhr III

watch /wɒtʃ/ beobachten; anschauen; zusehen I

watch out (for) /wɒtʃ ˌ'aʊt/ aufpassen (auf), sich in Acht nehmen (vor) III

watch sth /'wɒtʃ ˌsʌmθɪŋ/ etw beobachten; auf etw achten 5/12

watch TV /ˌwɒtʃ ˌtiː 'viː/ fernsehen I

water /'wɔːtə/ Gewässer 4/9

water (no pl) /'wɔːtə/ Wasser I

water /'wɔːtə/ gießen II

water /'wɔːtə/ tränen III

waterfall /'wɔːtəˌfɔːl/ Wasserfall 6/7

watermelon /'wɔːtəˌmelən/ Wassermelone 2/2

wave /weɪv/ Welle III

wave /weɪv/ winken III

wave /weɪv/ wogen 4/9

way /weɪ/ Weg II

that way /'ðæt weɪ/ so, auf diese Weise 2/M2

the ... way /ðə 'weɪ/ auf die ... Art 1/CC

this way /'ðɪs weɪ/ so, auf diese Art und Weise 2/2

we /wiː/ wir I

weapon /'wepən/ Waffe II

wear (irr) /weə/ tragen I

weather /'weðə/ Wetter I

web designer /'web dɪ,zaɪnə/ Webdesigner/in 0p3

wedding /'wedɪŋ/ Hochzeit II

Wednesday /'wenzdeɪ/ Mittwoch I

week /wiːk/ Woche I

a week /ə 'wiːk/ pro/in der Woche III

weekend /ˌwiːk'end/ Wochenende II

at the weekend /æt ðə 'wiːk,end/ am Wochenende I

weight /weɪt/ Gewicht 5/12

welcome /'welkəm/ willkommen heißen, begrüßen 4/M1

welcome (to) /'welkəm/ willkommen (in) II

You're welcome. /jɔː 'welkəm/ Gern geschehen., Bitte. III

well /wel/ gut II; nun (ja), tja 1/3

well-paid /ˌwel'peɪd/ gut bezahlt 4/4

Welsh /welʃ/ Walisisch; walisisch III

went /went/ Vergangenheitsform von „go"

were /wɜː/ Vergangenheitsform von „be"

west /west/ Westen III

wet /wet/ nass II

blue whale /'bluː ˌweɪl/ Blauwal 6/7

what /wɒt/ was; welche(r, s) I

What about ...? (informal) /'wɒt ə,baʊt/ Was ist mit ...?, Wie wäre es mit ...? I

what else /wɒt ˌ'els/ was noch, was sonst 2/13

what if /wɒt ˌɪf/ was ist/wäre, wenn 4/M6

What time is it? /wɒt ˌ'taɪm ˌɪz ˌɪt/ Wie viel Uhr ist es? I

What's ... like? /wɒts 'laɪk/ Wie ist ...? II

What's the matter? /ˌwɒts ðə 'mætə/ Was ist (denn) los? II

What's up? (informal) /wɒts ˌ'ʌp/ Wie gehts?; Was geht?; Was gibts? 5/I

What's wrong? /wɒts 'rɒŋ/ Was ist los? III

What's your name? /ˌwɒts jə 'neɪm/ Wie heißt du?, Wie heißen Sie? I

wheat (no pl) /wiːt/ Weizen 4/9

wheel /wiːl/ Rad II

wheelchair /'wiːl,tʃeə/ Rollstuhl II

when /wen/ wann; wenn I; als II

where /weə/ wo(hin) I

Where are you from? /ˌweər ˌɑː jə 'frɒm/ Wo kommst du her? I

whether /'weðə/ ob 5/12

which /wɪtʃ/ welche(r, s); der/die/das III

which one /'wɪtʃ wʌn/ welche(r, s) 2/6

while *(no pl)* / waɪl / Weile 3/M2

while / waɪl / während III

whisper / ˈwɪspə / flüstern II

whistle / wɪsl / pfeifen 6/M1

white / waɪt / weiß I

who / huː / wer I; der/die/das III

whole / həʊl / ganz, gesamt 1/3

whom / huːm / wen; wem 2/12

whose / huːz / wessen 2/P10

whose is/are ... / ˈhuːz ɪz/ɑː / wem gehört/gehören ... 1/P10

why / waɪ / warum I

that's why / ˈðæts waɪ / deshalb; das ist der Grund, warum I

wide / waɪd / breit 5/15

wife *(pl wives)* / waɪf, waɪvz / Ehefrau I

the Wild West / ðə ˌwaɪld ˈwest / der Wilde Westen Intro

wildfire / ˈwaɪldˌfaɪə / Lauffeuer, nicht zu kontrollierender (Groß)flächen)brand 6/4

will / wɪl / werden II

win *(irr)* / wɪn / gewinnen II

window / ˈwɪndəʊ / Fenster I

windy / ˈwɪndi / windig I

wine / waɪn / Wein 6/P3

winner / ˈwɪnə / Gewinner/in, Sieger/in II

wipe out / ˌwaɪp ˈaʊt / auswischen; auslöschen 6/M1

wire / ˈwaɪə / Draht; Leitung, Kabel II

wish / wɪʃ / Wunsch 2/10

wish / wɪʃ / (sich) wünschen II

wishbone / ˈwɪʃˌbəʊn / Gabelbein *(zusammengewachsene Schlüssel- beinknochen der Vögel)* 2/10

best wishes / ˌbest ˈwɪʃɪz / viele Grüße II

with / wɪð / mit I

without / wɪðˈaʊt / ohne III

woman *(pl women)* / ˈwʊmən, ˈwɪmɪn / Frau I

won / wʌn / *Vergangenheitsform von „win"*

wonder / ˈwʌndə / sich fragen 4/M1

wonderful / ˈwʌndəfl / wunderbar, wundervoll II

wood / wʊd / Holz 1/5

wood/metal working class / ˈwʊd, ˈmetl ˌwɜːkɪŋ klɑːs /

Werkunterricht, Werken 1/5

word / wɜːd / Wort I

word web / ˈwɜːd web / Wortnetz 4/11

wordbank / ˈwɜːdbæŋk / Wortfeld 1/7

wordsearch / ˈwɜːdsɜːtʃ / Wortsuchrätsel 5/18

wore / wɔː / *Vergangenheitsform von „wear"*

work / wɜːk / Arbeit III

work / wɜːk / arbeiten I; funktionieren III

work experience *(no pl)* / ˈwɜːk ɪkˌspɪəriəns / Praktikum; Berufserfahrung 0p3

work long hours / wɜːk ˌlɒŋ ˈaʊəz / lange arbeiten; Überstunden machen 6/5

out of work / aʊt_əv ˈwɜːk / arbeitslos III

working hours *(only pl)* / ˈwɜːkɪŋ ˌaʊəz / Arbeitszeit 6/5

world / wɜːld / Welt, Erde II

all over the world / ˌɔːl_ˌəʊvə ðə ˈwɜːld / auf der ganzen Welt 3/17

World Series / ˌwɜːld ˈsɪəriːz / *Ausscheidungsspiele/Finale der US-amerikanischen Baseball- Profiligen* 5/LL

worried / ˈwʌrid / beunruhigt, besorgt III

worry / ˈwʌri / Sorge 4/M7

worry / ˈwʌri / sich Sorgen machen II

worse / wɜːs / schlimmer, schlechter II

worst / wɜːst / schlechteste(r, s), schlimmste(r, s) 5/11

be worth sth / bi: ˈwɜːθ ˌsʌmθɪŋ / etw wert sein 2/9

would / wʊd / würde(st, n, t) I

sb would like (to) / wʊd ˈlaɪk / jmd möchte (gern) I

sb would love (to) / ˌsʌmbədi wʊd ˈlʌv / jmd möchte sehr gern III

wrist guard / ˈrɪst gɑːd / Hand- gelenkschoner/-schützer 5/18

write *(irr)* / raɪt / schreiben I

write down / raɪt ˈdaʊn / aufschreiben 1/P7

writer / ˈraɪtə / Schriftsteller/in, Autor/in II

written / ˈrɪtn / *siehe „write"*

wrong / rɒŋ / falsch I

be wrong / bi ˈrɒŋ / nicht stimmen 5/8

go wrong / gəʊ ˈrɒŋ / schief gehen 1/M2

get sth wrong / get ˌsʌmθɪŋ ˈrɒŋ / etw falsch verstehen 2/8

What's wrong? / wɒts ˈrɒŋ / Was ist los? III

wrote / rəʊt / *Vergangenheitsform von „write"*

Y

yard / jɑːd / Yard (= 0,91 Meter) 5/15

yeah *(informal)* / jeə / ja 1/3

year / jɪə / Jahr I

year / jɪə / Jahrgang(sstufe) 3/P13

a year / ə ˈjɪə / pro/im Jahr II

yell / jel / laut schreien 6/P6

yellow / ˈjeləʊ / gelb I

yes / jes / ja I

yesterday / ˈjestədeɪ / gestern I

not yet / nɒt ˈjet / noch nicht II

yet / jet / schon; bis jetzt; trotzdem 4/M1

yoghurt *(no pl)* / ˈjɒgət / Joghurt III

you / juː / du, dich, dir, Sie, Ihnen; ihr, euch I

You're welcome. / ˌjɔː ˈwelkəm / Gern geschehen., Bitte. III

young / jʌŋ / jung I

your / jɔː / dein(e); euer/eure; Ihr(e) I

yours / jɔːz / deine(r, s); eure(r, s); Ihre(r, s) 1/3

yourself *(pl yourselves)* / jəˈself, jəˈselvz / dich, dir; selbst/ihr, euch; selbst 5/12

youth club / ˈjuːθ ˌklʌb / Jugendzentrum II

yuck *(informal)* / jʌk / igitt 5/7

yucky *(informal)* / ˈjʌki / eklig, widerlich 2/4

yummy *(informal)* / ˈjʌmi / lecker II

Z

zero-emission / ˌzɪərəʊ_ɪˈmɪʃn / abgasfrei, Nullemissions- 1/M5

zip / zɪp / Reißverschluss III

A

auf und ab up and down
abbiegen turn
Abend evening; night
am Abend in the evening
heute Abend tonight
Abendessen dinner
abends in the evening; pm (= post meridiem) *(nur hinter Uhrzeit)*
Abenteuer adventure
aber but
abfahren leave *(irr)*
abhängen hang out *(informal)*
abholen pick up
Abneigungen dislikes *(only pl)*
abschreiben copy
Absolvent/in graduate
abspülen wash the dishes
(für jdn) abstimmen vote (for sb)
Abzeichen logo
sich in Acht nehmen (vor) watch out (for)
Achtung respect *(no pl)*
Adler eagle
Adresse address
Affe monkey
Afrika Africa
Afrikaner/in African
afrikanisch African
Afroamerikaner/in African American
afroamerikanisch African American
aktiv active
Aktivität activity
albern silly
(Musik)album album
alle everybody; everyone
alle(s) all
allein alone
allein(e) on one's own
alles everything
Alles Gute zum Geburtstag! Happy birthday!
alles in allem all in all

als as; than; when
also so
alt old
Wie alt bist du? How old are you?
Alter age
ältere(r, s) elderly
am on
Amerika America
Amerikaner/in American
Amerikaner/in asiatischer Herkunft Asian American
amerikanisch American
amerikanischer Ureinwohner/ amerikanische Ureinwohnerin Native American
Ampel traffic light
sich amüsieren have a good time; enjoy oneself
an on; at; to
anbauen grow *(irr)*
(an)bieten offer
andere(r, s) other; different
ein(e) andere(r, s) another
andererseits on the other hand
(sich) (ver)ändern change
(Ver)änderung change
anders different
Anfang beginning
am Anfang in the beginning
anfangen start; begin *(irr)*
anfangs at first; first
anfeuern cheer on
(an)führen lead *(irr)*
Angebot offer
im Angebot sein be on sale
Angehörige(r) relative
angeln fish
angenehm nice
angreifen attack
jdn angreifen tackle sb
Angst haben (vor) be frightened (of sth); be scared (of sb/sth); be afraid (of sb/sth)
Angst machen scare
anhalten stop

sich anhören sound
(an)klicken click
ankommen arrive
(Stereo)anlage stereo
(an)malen paint
Anprobe fitting room
anprobieren try on
(Telefon)anruf (phone) call
anrufen phone; call
Anrufer/in caller
anrühren mix
anschauen watch; look at
sich anschließen join
anschließend after that; afterwards
Ansicht opinion
meiner Ansicht nach in my opinion
(an)statt instead (of)
anstrengend stressful
Antwort answer
(be)antworten answer
Anzeige ad, advert (= advertisement)
anziehen put on
anzünden light *(irr)*
Apfel apple
gedeckter Apfelkuchen apple pie
Apfelsine orange
April April
Aquarium fish tank
Ära age
Arbeit work
arbeiten work
lange arbeiten work long hours
arbeitslos out of work
arbeitsreich busy
Arbeitszeit working hours *(only pl)*
Argument argument
arm poor
(Armband)uhr watch
du Arme(r) poor you
Aroma flavour
Art sort; kind; type
Arzt/Ärztin doctor

asiatisch-amerikanisch Asian American

Amerikaner/in asiatischer Herkunft Asian American

Astronaut/in astronaut

Athlet/in athlete

der Atlantische Ozean the Atlantic (Ocean)

attraktiv attractive

auch also; too

auf on; at

auf einmal suddenly

Auf geht's! Come on!; Let's go!

auf und ab up and down

aufbewahren keep *(irr)*

aufbleiben stay up

aufgeben give up

aufgeregt excited; nervous

sich aufhalten hang out *(informal)*

aufhängen put up

(auf)hängen hang *(irr)*

aufheben pick up

aufhören stop; finish

aufpassen (auf) watch out (for)

aufräumen tidy up

aufregend exciting

aufstehen get up; stand up

auftragen put on

aufwachen wake up

aufwachsen grow up

aufwecken wake up

Aufzug lift

Auge eye

Augenblick moment

einen Augenblick bitte just a minute

im Augenblick right now

August August

aus from

(her)aus out of

(Aus)bildung education *(no pl)*

(Aus)blick view

ausbrechen escape

(aus)drucken print (out)

Auseinandersetzung argument

ausflippen go crazy *(informal)*

Ausflug trip

ausfüllen fill in

Ausgang exit

ausgeben *(Geld)* spend *(irr)*

ausgehen go out

aushalten stand *(irr)*

im Ausland abroad

etw ausmachen put out sth; turn off sth

(aus)probieren try

ausräumen empty

Ausrede excuse

ausreichend enough

Ausrüstung equipment *(no pl)*

ausschalten turn off

aussehen look

außerhalb outside

Außerirdische(r) alien

Aussicht view

Ausstattung equipment *(no pl)*

ausstehen stand *(irr)*

nicht ausstehen können hate

Ausstellung exhibition

Australien Australia

auswählen choose *(irr)*

auswandern emigrate

Auto car

Autogramm autograph

Autor/in author; writer

B

backen bake

Bad(ezimmer) bathroom

(Eisen)bahn railroad *(AE)*, railway *(BE)*

Bahnhof station

Bahnsteig platform

bald soon

bis bald bye for now; see you

Ball dance

Ballon balloon

Banane banana

Bargeld cash *(no pl)*

Bart beard

Bauarbeiter/in builder

Bauchschmerzen stomach ache

bauen build *(irr)*

Bauer/Bäuerin farmer

Bauernhof farm

Baum tree

(be)antworten answer

sich bedanken give thanks

bedeckt cloudy

bedeuten mean *(irr)*

bedeutend major

Bedienung waiter/waitress; service

sich beeilen hurry (up)

beenden finish; stop

jdn befragen question sb

begabt talented

begeistert excited

zu Beginn in the beginning

beginnen start; begin *(irr)*

begrüßen welcome

(be)grüßen greet

(be)halten keep *(irr)*

behindert disabled

bei at; by

beibringen teach *(irr)*

beide(s) both

Bein leg

beinahe nearly; almost

Beispiel example

zum Beispiel for example

wie (zum Beispiel) such as

beißen bite *(irr)*

beitreten join

(be)kämpfen fight *(irr)*

bekannt geben announce

bekommen get *(irr)*

belebt busy

Beleg receipt

beliebt popular

bellen bark

bemerken notice

Bemerkung comment

sich sehr bemühen, etw zu tun try hard to do sth

benachbart nearby

benutzen use

beobachten watch

bequem comfortable
Bereich field
bereit ready
Berg mountain
Bergsteigen climbing
Bericht report
berichten report
Beruf job; career
sich beruhigen cool down
berühmt famous
berühren touch
(be)schädigen damage
(Be)schädigung damage
 (no pl)
beschäftigt busy
beschließen decide
den Weg beschreiben give
 directions
(be)schützen protect
besondere(r, s) special
besonders especially
besorgt worried
besprechen discuss
(be)sprühen spray
besser better
(ein Schiff) besteigen
 board (a ship)
bestellen order
beste(r, s) best
am besten best
besuchen visit
Besucher/in visitor
stark besucht busy
betrachten look at
betreten enter
Bett bed
beunruhigt worried
Bevölkerung population
bevor before
bevorzugen prefer
sich bewegen move
Bewegung exercise
beweisen prove
bewölkt cloudy
sich einer Sache bewusst
 werden realize sth
(be)zahlen pay *(irr)*
bezaubernd charming

Bibliothek library
(an)bieten offer
Bild picture; painting
bilden form
Bilder machen take photos
(Aus)bildung education
 (no pl)
billig cheap
Biologie biology
bis to; until
(spätestens) bis (acht Uhr)
 by (eight o'clock)
bis (zu) up to
bis bald bye for now; see you
bis dann see you
ein bisschen a bit; a little
bitte please
Hier, bitte! Here you are.
Bitte schön! Here you are.
Wie bitte? sorry
bitten ask
Blase bubble
blasen blow *(irr)*
Blatt leaf *(pl leaves)*
blau blue
bleiben stay
Bleistift pencil
(Bleistift)spitzer pencil
 sharpener
(Aus)blick view
blockieren block
blöd stupid
Blume flower
Bluse shirt
Boden floor
Bohne bean
Boot boat
Botschaft message
Boxen boxing *(no pl)*
Branche industry
in Brand geraten catch fire
Brathähnchen fried chicken
brauchen need; take *(irr)*
braun brown
(zer)brechen break *(irr)*
breit wide
(ver)brennen burn *(irr)*
Brett board

Brettspiel board game
Brief letter
Briefmarke stamp
Brieftasche wallet
Briefumschlag envelope
Brille glasses *(only pl)*
bringen take *(irr)*
die Briten the British
 (only pl)
britische(r, s) British
Bronze bronze
Brot bread *(no pl)*
Brötchen bread roll
Brücke bridge
Bruder brother
brüllen roar
Buch book
Bücherei library
Bücherregal bookcase
Bücherschrank bookcase
Buchstabe letter
buchstabieren spell *(irr)*
Büffel buffalo *(pl - or -es)*
bügeln iron
Bühne stage
Bundesstraße highway
Burg castle
Büro office
bürsten brush
Bushaltestelle bus stop

C

Campingplatz campsite
Center centre
charmant charming
chatten chat
Chef/in boss
Chemie chemistry
Chinesisch Chinese
chinesisch Chinese
Chips chips *(AE)*, crisps *(BE)*
Cousin/e cousin
Creme cream
Curry(gericht) curry

D

da there
da ist/sind there is/are

Dame lady

danach afterwards; after that; then

vielen Dank thanks a lot

danke thanks; thank you

danken thank; give thanks

dann then

bis dann see you

das the; that; this; who; which

dass that

dasselbe the same

Datum date

dauern take *(irr)*

dauernd all the time

(Zimmer)decke ceiling

den Tisch decken set the table

dein(e) your

deine(r, s) yours

dekorieren decorate

denken think *(irr)*

(an etw) denken remember

deprimiert depressed

der the; that; who; which

derselbe the same

deshalb so; that's (the reason) why

Dessert dessert

Detail detail

(Privat)detektiv/in detective

Deutsch German

deutsch German

auf Deutsch in German

Deutschland Germany

Dezember December

dich you; yourself

die the; that; who; which

Dienstag Tuesday

diese these *(pl of* this*)*; those *(pl of* that*)*

diese(r, s) this

dieselbe the same

Ding thing

Dinosaurier dinosaur

dir you; yourself

Direktor/in director

Diskussion discussion

diskutieren discuss

Donnerstag Thursday

Dorf village

dort there

dort (drüben) over there

Dose can

downloaden download

Drache dragon

Draht wire

draußen outside; outdoors

nach draußen outside

dreckig dirty

sich drehen turn

drinnen inside; indoors

Drittel third

(aus)drucken print (out)

drücken push; click

Dschungel jungle

du you

Duft smell

dumm stupid; silly

dunkel dark

Dunkelheit darkness *(no pl)*

dünn thin; slim

durch through; by

durchdrehen go crazy *(informal)*

durcheinander confused

durchqueren cross

(durch)suchen search

dürfen may

etw tun dürfen be allowed to do sth

nicht dürfen must not; may not

Dusche shower

duschen take a shower

E

Echse lizard

echt real

Ecke corner

Ehefrau wife *(pl* wives*)*

Ehemann husband

ehrlich honest

Ei egg

Eidechse lizard

eifersüchtig jealous

eigene(r, s) own

eigentlich actually

ein(e) a/an; one

ein bisschen a bit; a little

einander each other

eindeutig clear

einerseits on the one hand

eines Tages one day

einfach easy; just

einige a few; some

einkaufen (gehen) do the shopping

einkaufen gehen go shopping

Einkaufsliste shopping list

Einkaufszentrum mall

Einkaufszettel shopping list

einladen invite

Einladung invitation

einmal once

noch (ein)mal again

einsam lonely

einschalten turn on

Einwanderer/in immigrant

einwandern immigrate

Einwanderung immigration *(no pl)*

Einzelfahrkarte single (ticket)

Einzelheit detail

einzige(r, s) only

Eis ice *(no pl)*

Eisenbahn train

(Eisen)bahn railroad *(AE)*, railway *(BE)*

Eishockey ice hockey

Eiskrem ice cream

Elefant elephant

elektrisch electric

Elektrizität electricity *(no pl)*

Elfmeter penalty

Ellbogen elbow

Eltern parents *(only pl)*

emigrieren emigrate

empfangen receive

Ende end

am oberen Ende (von) at the top (of)

am unteren Ende (von) at the bottom (of)

oberes Ende top
enden end; end up
endlich finally
Energie energy
eng narrow
Engel angel
Englisch English
englisch English
auf Englisch in English
entdecken discover
Ente duck
entfernen remove
(ent)fliehen escape
enthalten contain
entkommen escape
(ent)leeren empty
(sich) entscheiden decide
sich entschuldigen apologize
Entschuldigen Sie bitte!
  Excuse me!
Entschuldigung excuse
Entschuldigung! Excuse me!;
  Sorry!
**Entschuldigung, das tut mir
  leid.** (I'm) sorry.
entsetzt shocked
sich entspannen relax
entspannt relaxed
enttäuscht disappointed;
  frustrated
(sich) entwickeln develop
Entwicklungsland developing
  country
entzündet sore
er he
Erbse pea
Erdbeben earthquake
Erdbeere strawberry
Erde world
die Erde the earth
Erdkunde geography
Erdnuss peanut
erfahren von/über learn
  about
Erfahrung experience
erfinden invent
Erfindung invention
Erfolg success (no pl)

erfolgreich successful
erforschen explore
Ergebnis result
erhalten get (irr); receive
erhellen light (irr)
erhitzen heat
sich erinnern (an) remember
Erkältung cold
erklären explain
erlaubt allowed
Erlebnis experience;
  adventure
ernähren feed (irr)
Ernte harvest; crop
ernten harvest
(er)raten guess
erreichen reach
erschaffen create
erscheinen appear
erschöpft exhausted
erschrecken scare
erst only
erste(r, s) first
erstens firstly; first of all
in erster Linie mainly
als Erstes first; first of all
ertragen stand
erwachsen werden grow up
**jmd kann es kaum erwarten
  (, etw zu tun)** sb cannot
  wait (to do sth)
erzählen tell (irr)
Erzählung story
erzeugen produce
Erzeuger producer
Erzeugnis product
es it
es gibt there is; there are
es schaffen manage
Essen food (no pl); meal
zu Essen geben feed (irr)
essen eat (irr); have (irr)
etwas something; some; any
(irgend)(et)was anything
euch you; yourselves
euer your
eure your
eure(r, s) yours

Eule owl
Europa Europe
Europäer/in European
europäisch European
exklusiv exclusive
Experte/Expertin expert
extrem extreme

F

Fabrik factory
(Schul)fach subject
Fahne flag
Fähre ferry
fahren drive (irr); go (irr);
  ride (irr)
Fahrer/in driver
Fahrkartenschalter ticket
  counter
Fahrplan timetable
(Fahr)rad bike
(Fahr)rad fahren ride a bike
Fahrt trip
Fakt fact
Falle trap
fallen fall (irr)
fallen lassen drop
falls if
falsch wrong
Familie family
Familienname surname
fangen catch (irr)
Fantasie fantasy
fantastisch fantastic
  (informal)
Farbe colour
farbenfroh colourful
farbenprächtig colourful
fast nearly; almost
Februar February
Feder feather
(Feder)mäppchen pencil case
Fehler fault
Feier celebration
feiern celebrate
Feld field
Fell fur
Fels(en) rock
Fenster window

Ferien holiday
Ferienlager summer camp
Fernsehen TV (= television)
fernsehen watch TV
Fernseher TV (= television)
Fernsehserie TV series
  (only pl)
fertig ready
Fest celebration; festival
(feste) Freundin girlfriend
(fester) Freund boyfriend
fest(gesetzt) fixed
(Fest)land land
festnehmen catch *(irr)*
Feuer fire
Feuer fangen catch fire
Feuerwehr fire department
  (AE), fire brigade *(BE)*
Feuerwehrmann/-frau
  firefighter
fies mean
(Kino)film movie *(AE)*,
  film *(BE)*
(Spiel)film movie *(AE)*,
  film *(BE)*
filtern filter
Filzstift felt tip
finden find *(irr)*
Finsternis darkness *(no pl)*
Firma company
Fisch fish *(pl - or -es)*
fischen fish
flach flat
Flagge flag
Flamme flame
Flasche bottle
Fleisch meat *(no pl)*
fleißig hard-working
fliegen fly *(irr)*
(ent)fliehen escape
Flucht escape
Flughafen airport
Flugzeug plane
Flur hall
Fluss river
flüstern whisper
Folge result
folgen follow

Form form
formen form
Formular form
Foto photo; picture
fotografieren take photos
Frage question
fragen ask
sich fragen wonder
Frankreich France
Französisch French
französisch French
Frau woman *(pl women)*; lady
Frau *(Anrede)* Mrs
Frau *(Anrede für verheiratete
  und unverheiratete Frauen)*
  Ms
frech naughty
frei free
im Freien outside; outdoors
Freiheit freedom *(no pl)*
die Freiheitsstatue the Statue
  of Liberty
Freitag Friday
Freiwillige/r volunteer
sich auf etw freuen look
  forward to sth
Freund/in friend
(fester) Freund boyfriend
(feste) Freundin girlfriend
freundlich friendly; nice
jdn in Frieden lassen leave
  sb in peace
friedlich peaceful
frisch fresh
Friseur/in hairdresser
frisieren style
froh glad
fröhlich happy
Frucht fruit
früh early
Frühling spring
Frühstück breakfast
Frühstückspause morning
  break
frustriert frustrated
Fuchs fox
(sich) fühlen feel *(irr)*
(an)führen lead *(irr)*

funktionieren work
für for
furchtbar terrible
Furcht erregend scary
sich fürchten (vor) be
  frightened (of)
Fuß foot *(pl feet)*
zu Fuß on foot
(zu Fuß) gehen walk
Fußball soccer *(AE)*,
  football *(BE)*
füttern feed *(irr)*

G

Gabel fork
Galerie gallery
ganz whole; completely;
  altogether
Garten garden
Gärtner/in gardener
Gast guest
Gaststätte pub
Gebäude building
geben give *(irr)*
Gebiet area
geboren born
gebrochen broken
Geburtsdatum date of birth
Geburtstag birthday
Gedicht poem
Gefahr danger; risk
gefährlich dangerous
Gefangene/r prisoner
Gefängnis prison
Gefühl feeling
gegen against
Gegend area
Gegenstand thing
gegenüber(liegend) opposite
geheim secret
gehen go *(irr)*
(hinaus)gehen go out
(zu Fuß) gehen walk
gehören zu go with
jdm/zu etw gehören belong
  to sb/sth
Wie geht es dir? How are
  you?

Es geht mir gut. I'm fine.
Auf geht's! Come on!
Geist ghost
gelangweilt bored
gelassen relaxed
gelb yellow
Geld money *(no pl)*
Geld verdienen make money;
earn money
Geldautomat cash machine
Geldstück coin
Gelee jelly
Gemälde painting
gemein mean
gemeinsam together
Gemüse vegetable
(genau)so ... wie ... as ... as
Genesungskarte get well card
genießen enjoy
genug enough
genügend enough
geöffnet open
Geografie geography
gerade right now; just
gerade(aus) straight (on)
Geräusch sound; noise
Gericht dish *(pl -es)*
Gern geschehen. You're
welcome.
Geruch smell
gesamt whole
Gesamt- total
Gesamtschule comprehensive
school
Geschäft shop
geschehen happen
gescheit clever
Geschenk present, gift
Geschichte history; story
geschieden divorced
Geschirr spülen wash the
dishes
Geschirrspülmaschine
dishwasher
Geschmack taste *(no pl)*;
flavour
Geschwister brothers and
sisters

Gesicht face
Gespenst ghost
gestalten create
Gestank smell
gestern yesterday
gestresst stressed
gesund healthy
gesund werden get well
Gesundheit health *(no pl)*
Getränk drink
Gewächshaus greenhouse
Gewerbe industry
Gewicht weight
Gewinn prize
gewinnen win *(irr)*
Gewinner/in winner
sich an etw gewöhnen get
used to sth
gewöhnlich usually
Gewürz spice
es gibt there is; there are
gießen water
Gipfel top
Gitarre guitar
Glas glass
glauben think *(irr)*
glauben (an) believe (in)
gleich in a minute; just
gleichmäßig regular
Gleis platform
Gleise railroad *(AE)*, railway
(BE)
Glück luck *(no pl)*
Viel Glück! Good luck!
Glück haben be lucky
glücklich happy; lucky; glad
Glücks- lucky
glücksbringend lucky
Glühbirne light bulb
Goldfisch goldfish *(pl -)*
Gott god
Gras grass *(no pl)*
gratis for free; free
grau grey
Grenze border
Griechenland Greece
grillen have a barbecue
groß big; large; tall; great;

major
großartig great
Großbritannien Great Britain
Größe size
Großeltern grandparents
(only pl)
Großmutter grandmother
(Groß)stadt city
ein Großteil most (of)
Großvater grandfather
grün green
Grund reason
das ist der Grund, warum
that's (the reason) why
Grundschule primary school
Gruppe group
herzliche Grüße love
viele Grüße best wishes
(be)grüßen greet
(Salat)gurke cucumber
gut good; well; fine
Es geht mir gut. I'm fine.
gut aussehend good-looking
gut in etw sein be good
at sth
etw gut können be good at
sth
Alles Gute zum Geburtstag!
Happy birthday!
Gute Besserung! Get well
soon.

H

Haar(e) hair *(no pl)*
haben have got; have *(irr)*
Hafen harbour
Hähnchen chicken
Hai(fisch) shark
halb half
halb (neun) half past (eight)
Halbzeit half time
Hälfte half *(pl halves)*
Halle hall
hallo hello; hi
halten hold *(irr)*
(be)halten keep *(irr)*
Handschuh glove
Handtuch towel

Handy mobile (= mobile phone)

(auf)hängen hang *(irr)*

hart hard

Hass hate

hassen hate

hässlich ugly

häufig often

Haupt- main

Hauptgericht main dish

hauptsächlich mainly

Hauptspeise main dish

Haus house; home

Hausaufgaben homework *(no pl)*

nach Hause home

zu Hause (at) home

Haustier pet

Haut skin

Heft exercise book

heftig powerful

Heiligabend Christmas Eve

Heim home

Heimat(land) homeland

Heimatort home town

heiraten get married; marry

heiß hot

heißen be called

Wie heißt du? What's your name?

Held/in hero *(pl -es)*

helfen help

hell bright

Helm helmet

Hemd shirt

(her)aus out of

herausfinden find out

Herausforderung challenge

herausnehmen take out

Herbst autumn

hereinkommen come in

Herr *(Anrede)* Mr

(vornehmer) Herr gentleman

herstellen produce

Hersteller producer

herum around

herunterladen download

herunterspringen jump off

hervorragend brilliant *(informal)*

Herz heart

heute today

heute Abend tonight

heute Morgen this morning

heute Nachmittag this afternoon

heute Nacht tonight

Hier, bitte! Here you are.

hier(her) here

Hilfe help

hilfreich helpful

hilfsbereit helpful

Hin- und Rückfahrkarte return (ticket)

hinab down

(hinauf)klettern climb

(hinauf)steigen climb

hinausbringen take out

(hinaus)gehen go out

hinfallen fall down

hinter behind

hinüber over

hinunter down

hinzufügen add

hoch high; tall

Hochzeit wedding

hoffen hope

Hoffnung hope

höflich polite

Höhepunkt highlight

Höhle cave

holen get *(irr)*; collect

Holz wood

Honig honey *(no pl)*

hören hear *(irr)*

(zu)hören listen (to)

Horoskop horoscope

Hose trousers *(only pl)*

hübsch pretty; lovely

Hubschrauber helicopter

Hügel hill

Huhn chicken

Hund dog

Hungersnot famine

hungrig hungry

Hut hat

I

ich I

ich heiße my name is

Idee idea

ignorieren ignore

ihm him

ihn him

ihnen them

Ihnen you

ihr you

Ihr(e) your

ihr(e, n) her; its; their

ihre(r, s) hers

Ihre(r, s) yours

illegal illegal

im on

immer always

(immer) noch still

Immigration immigration *(no pl)*

in in; into; at; on; to

Indien India

indisch Indian

Industrie industry

Informatik ICT (= information and communication technology); computer science *(no pl)*

Information information *(no pl)*

innen inside

im Inneren inside

Insekt insect

Insel island

Inserat advert (= advertisement)

insgesamt altogether

interessant interesting

interessiert (an etw) interested (in sth)

Internat boarding school

etw ins Internet stellen post sth

im Internet surfen surf the Internet

irgendein(e) any

(irgend)(et)was anything

(irgend)jemand anybody

irgendwelche any
irgendwo somewhere
Irisch Irish
irisch Irish
Irland Ireland
Italien Italy
Italienisch Italian
italienisch Italian

J

ja yes
Jacke jacket
jagen hunt
Jäger/in hunter
Jahr year
pro/im Jahr a year
Jahrhundert century
Januar January
jede(r) everybody; everyone
jede(r, s) every; each
jedenfalls anyway
jemals ever
jemand somebody; someone
(irgend)jemand anybody
jene those (pl of that)
jetzt now; right now
Joghurt yoghurt (no pl)
Jongleur/in juggler
jubeln cheer
Jugendzentrum youth club
Juli July
jung young
Junge boy
Juni June

K

Kabel wire
Käfig cage
Kaffee coffee
Kalender calendar
Kalifornien California
kalt cold
Kälte cold
Kamin chimney
Kampf battle; fight
(be)kämpfen fight (irr)
Kämpfer(in) fighter
Känguru kangaroo

Kaninchen rabbit
Kapitän/in captain
Kappe cap
kaputt broken
die Karibik the Caribbean
die Karibischen Inseln
  the Caribbean
Karikatur cartoon
Karneval carnival
Karriere career
Karotte carrot
Karte card
(Land)karte map
Kartoffel potato (pl -es)
Kartoffelbrei mashed potatoes
Karton card
Käse cheese (no pl)
Kassenbon receipt
Katholik/in Catholic
katholisch Catholic
Katze cat
kauen chew
kaufen buy (irr)
Kaufhaus department store
Kaugummi (chewing) gum
  (no pl)
kein(e) no; not any
keiner no one
Keks cookie (AE), biscuit (BE)
Kellner/in waiter/waitress
kennen know (irr)
(sich) kennenlernen
  meet (irr)
Es freut mich, Sie/dich
  kennen zu lernen. Nice to
  meet you.
Kerl guy (informal)
Kerze candle
kicken kick
Kilometer kilometre
Kind child (pl children)
Kinn chin
Kino cinema
(Kino)film movie (AE),
  film (BE)
Kirche church
Kissen cushion
Klang sound

klar clear
Klassenarbeit test
Klassenkamerad/in classmate
Klassenzimmer classroom
klauen steal (irr)
Klavier piano
Kleid dress
Kleider clothes (only pl)
Kleiderschrank wardrobe
Kleidung clothes (only pl)
klein small; little
Kletter- climbing
Klettern climbing
(hinauf)klettern climb
(an)klicken click
klingeln ring (irr)
klingen sound
Klo toilet
Kloß dumpling
Klub club
klug clever
Kneipe pub
Knie knee
Knochen bone
Knödel dumpling
Koch/Köchin cook
kochen do the cooking; cook
Koffer suitcase
Kollege/Kollegin colleague
komisch strange; funny
kommen come (irr)
Kommentar comment
Komödie comedy
König king
Königin queen
königlich royal
können can; may
etw tun können be able to
  do sth
könnte(st, n, t) could; might
kontrollieren check
sich konzentrieren
  concentrate
Konzert concert
Kopf head
Kopfschmerzen headache
Korb basket
Körper body

korrekt correct; proper
kosten cost *(irr)*
Kosten cost
Was kostet/kosten ...?
  How much is/are ... ?
köstlich delicious
Kostüm costume
krabbeln crawl
Krach noise
Kraft energy
krank ill
Krankenhaus hospital
(Kranken)pfleger nurse
(Kranken)schwester nurse
Krankenwagen ambulance
Krawatte tie
kreativ creative
Kreide chalk *(no pl)*
Kreis circle
kreischen scream
kriechen crawl
Krieg war
Krimi thriller
Kriminelle/r criminal
Krokodil crocodile
Krone crown
Küche kitchen
Kuchen cake; pie
Kuh cow
Kühlschrank fridge *(informal)*
Kultur culture
sich kümmern um look after;
  take care of
Kunde/Kundin customer
Kunst art
Künstler/in artist
künstlich artificial
Kunststoff plastic
Kürbis pumpkin
Kurs course
kurz short
Kuss kiss
küssen kiss
Küste coast
Kuvert envelope

L

lächeln smile

lachen laugh
Laden shop
Lamm lamb
Lampe lamp
Land country
(Fest)land land
landen land
(Land)karte map
(Land)schildkröte tortoise
lang long
lange arbeiten work long
  hours
langsam slow
langweilig boring
Lärm noise
Lass (doch) den Kopf nicht
  hängen! Cheer up!
lassen let *(irr)*; leave *(irr)*
jdn in Frieden/Ruhe lassen
  leave sb in peace
lass(t) uns let's (= let us)
laufen run *(irr)*; walk
Laufen running
Läufer/in runner
Laune mood
laut loud; noisy
läuten ring *(irr)*
Leben life *(pl lives)*
leben live
lebend living
lecker delicious; tasty;
  yummy *(informal)*
leer empty
(ent)leeren empty
legal legal
legen put *(irr)*
Lehnstuhl armchair
Lehrbuch textbook
Lehrer/in teacher
leicht easy
Entschuldigung, das tut
  mir leid. (I'm) sorry.
leider unfortunately
leise quiet
leiten lead *(irr)*
Leiter/in director
Leitung wire
lernen learn *(irr)*; study

lesen read *(irr)*
Leser/in reader
letzte(r, s) last
Leute people *(no pl)*
Licht light
Liebe love
liebe(r) *(Anrede)* dear
lieben love
lieber better
lieber mögen prefer
Liebesfilm romance
Lieblings- favourite
am liebsten best
(Lied)text lyrics *(only pl)*
liefern deliver
lila(farben) purple
Limonade lemonade
Lineal ruler
in erster Linie mainly
auf der linken Seite
  on the/your left
links on the/your left
(nach) links left
Liste list
Loch hole
Löffel spoon
etw löschen put out sth
Löwe lion
Luft air *(no pl)*
lustig funny; fun
sich über jdn lustig machen
  make fun of sb

M

machen make *(irr)*; do *(irr)*
mächtig powerful
Mädchen girl
Magazin magazine
Magenschmerzen stomach
  ache
Magie magic *(no pl)*
mähen mow *(irr)*
Mahlzeit meal
Mai May
Mal time
(an)malen paint
manchmal sometimes
Mann man *(pl men)*

männlich male
(Feder)mäppchen pencil case
Mappe folder
Markt market
Marmelade jam; jelly
März March
Maschine machine
Mathe maths
Maus mouse *(pl mice)*
Medaille medal
Medikament(e) medicine
  (no pl)
Medizin medicine *(no pl)*
Meer ocean
das Meer the sea *(no pl)*
Meerschweinchen guinea pig
Mehl flour *(no pl)*
mehr more; better
nicht mehr not anymore
(noch) mehr more
Meile mile
mein(e) my
meine(r, s) mine
meinen mean *(irr)*; think *(irr)*
meiner Ansicht/Meinung
  nach in my opinion
Meinung opinion
das meiste (von) most (of)
am meisten most; best
die meisten most
Meisterschaft championship
Melodie melody
jede Menge lots of
(Menschen)menge crowd
Mensch person
Menschen people *(no pl)*
etw merken realize sth
Messer knife *(pl knives)*
Metall metal
Meter metre
Mexikaner/in Mexican
mexikanisch Mexican
mich me; myself
Mikrowelle(nherd) microwave
Milch milk *(no pl)*
Milchshake milkshake
mindestens at least
Minirock miniskirt

Minute minute
mir me; myself; mine
(ver)mischen mix
mit with; by
Mitarbeiter/in colleague
(mit)bringen bring *(irr)*
Mitglied member
Mitleid mit jdm haben
  feel sorry for sb
mitmachen bei join
(mit)nehmen take *(irr)*
Mitschüler/in classmate
Mittagessen lunch; dinner
Mittagspause lunchtime
Mittagszeit lunchtime
Mitte middle
in der Mitte in the middle
Mitternacht midnight *(no pl)*
Mittwoch Wednesday
mobben bully
Mobbing bullying *(no pl)*
Mobiltelefon mobile (= mobile
  phone)
jmd möchte (gern)
  sb would like (to)
jmd möchte sehr gern
  sb would love (to)
mögen like; enjoy
sehr gern mögen love
möglich possible
möglicherweise maybe
Möhre carrot
Mohrrübe carrot
Moment moment
einen Moment bitte just a
  minute
im Moment at the moment
Monat month
Mond moon
Mondlicht moonlight
Montag Monday
morgen tomorrow
Morgen morning
am Morgen in the morning
heute Morgen this morning
morgens in the morning; am
  (= ante meridiem) *(nur hinter
  Uhrzeit)*

Motorrad motorbike
müde tired
Müll rubbish *(no pl)*
Mülleimer bin
Mülltonne bin
München Munich
Mund mouth
Münze coin
Musik music
(Musik)album album
Muskel muscle
Müsli muesli *(no pl)*
müssen have to; must;
  need to
müsste should
mutig brave
Mutter mother
Muttersprache first language
Mütze hat

N

nach after; to
(nach) links left
(nach) oben upstairs
(nach) rechts right
(nach) unten down
Nachbar/in neighbour
Nachbarschaft neighbourhood
nachdem after
Nachmittag afternoon
am Nachmittag in the
  afternoon
heute Nachmittag this
  afternoon
nachmittags in the afternoon;
  pm (= post meridiem) *(nur
  hinter Uhrzeit)*
Nachname surname
Nachricht message
Nachrichten news
nächste(r, s) next
Nacht night
heute Nacht tonight
über Nacht bleiben sleep over
Nachtisch dessert
nachts at night
nah(e) near; nearby
in der Nähe gelegen nearby

der Nahe Osten the Middle East
Name name
Nase nose
nass wet
Nationalpark national park
Natur nature
natürlich of course; natural
(Natur)wissenschaft science
Nebel fog
neben next to
neblig foggy
negativ negative
(mit)nehmen take *(irr)*
nein no
nennen call
nervös nervous
nett nice
Netz net
neu new
Neuigkeit news
Neujahr New Year
neulich the other day
Neuseeland New Zealand
nicht not
nicht dürfen must not; may not
nicht mehr not anymore
nicht stimmen be wrong
nichts nothing; not anything
die Niederlande the Netherlands
sich niederlassen settle
niedlich cute
niedrig low
nie(mals) never
niemand no one
Nilpferd hippo (= hippopotamus)
(immer) noch, noch immer still
noch ein(e, r, s) another
noch (ein)mal again
(noch) mehr more
noch nicht not yet
Nord- north
Nordamerika North America
Norden north

Nordirland Northern Ireland
nördlich north
Nordwesten north-west
normalerweise normally; usually
(Schul)note mark
Notfall emergency
(sich) Notizen machen take notes; make notes
November November
Nudeln pasta *(no pl)*
Nummer number
nun (ja) well
nur only; just
nützlich helpful

O

ob whether
oben at the top (of)
(nach) oben upstairs
oberes Ende top
Obst fruit
obgleich although
obwohl although
oder or
offen open
öffentlich public
(sich) öffnen open
Öffnungszeiten opening times
oft often
ohne without
ohnmächtig werden faint
Ohr ear
Ohrring earring
ökologisch environmental
Oktober October
Öl oil
Olympische Spiele Olympic Games
Oma grandma *(informal)*
Omi grandma *(informal)*
Onkel uncle
optimistisch optimistic
Orange orange
orange(farben) orange
in Ordnung fine
Organisation organization
organisieren organize *(AE),*

organise *(BE)*
Ort place
Osten east
der Nahe Osten the Middle East
Osterfest Easter
Ostern Easter
Österreich Austria
Ozean ocean
der Atlantische Ozean the Atlantic (Ocean)
der Pazifische Ozean the Pacific (Ocean)

P

Paar pair; couple
packen pack
Paket package
Palast palace
Panik panic
Papa dad *(informal)*
Papagei parrot
Papier paper *(no pl)*
Pappe card
Parade parade
Parfüm perfume
passen zu go with
passieren happen
Pastete pie
Patient/in patient
Pause break
der Pazifische Ozean the Pacific (Ocean)
peinlich berührt embarrassed
Pelz fur
Penny p (= penny, pence)
perfekt perfect
Person person
Pfeffer pepper
pfeifen whistle
Pferd horse
Pflanze plant
pflanzen plant
(Kranken)pfleger/in nurse
Pfote paw
Pfund *(brit. Währung)* pound
Pilot/in pilot

Pilz mushroom
Pinguin penguin
Pirat pirate
Plastik plastic
platt flat
Plattform platform
Platz place; space; square
Plätzchen cookie *(AE)*,
  biscuit *(BE)*
plötzlich suddenly
Polen Poland
Polizei police
Polizeibeamter/-beamtin
  police officer
Polizeirevier police station
Polizeiwache police station
polnisch Polish
Pommes frites French fries
  (AE), chips *(BE)*
Portemonnaie wallet
etw posten post sth
Postkarte postcard
eine Schachtel Pralinen
  a box of chocolates
Preis price; cost; prize
preiswert cheap
Prinzessin princess
(Privat)detektiv/in detective
pro/im Jahr a year
pro/am Tag a day
pro/in der Woche a week
(aus)probieren try
Produkt product
Produzent/in producer
produzieren produce
Programm programme
programmieren program
Programmierer/in programmer
Projekt project
Prozent per cent
prüfen test
Prüfung test
Punkt point
einen Punkt machen score
punkten score
pünktlich on time
Pute/r turkey
putzen clean; brush

Q

Quadrat square
Qualität quality

R

Rabauke bully
Rad wheel
(Fahr)rad bike
(Fahr)rad fahren ride a bike,
  cycle
Radfahren cycling
Radfahrer/in cyclist
Radiergummi rubber *(BE)*
Radiosender radio station
Rasen lawn; grass *(no pl)*
(er)raten guess
Rat(schlag) advice *(no pl)*
Ratte rat
Rauch smoke
rauchen smoke
Raum space
Raumschiff spaceship
raus outside
(Taschen)rechner calculator
Rechnung bill
Recht right
Recht haben be right
auf der rechten Seite
  on the/your right
rechts on the/your right
(nach) rechts right
rechtzeitig on time
recyceln recycle
reden speak *(irr)*
reden (mit) talk (to)
reduziert sein be on sale
Regal shelf *(pl shelves)*
Regel rule
regelmäßig regular
Regen rain
Regenbogen rainbow
Regenwald rainforest
regieren rule
Region area
regnen rain
regnerisch rainy
reich rich

Reichtum fortune
Reihe row; queue
reinigen clean
Reis rice
Reise trip
reisen travel
Reisende/r traveller
Reißverschluss zip
Reiten riding
reiten ride *(irr)*
Rektor/in headteacher
Religion(sunterricht)
  RE (= religious education)
Rennen race; running
rennen run *(irr)*
reparieren repair
Reservat *(= ein den Indianern
  vorbehaltenes Gebiet)*
  reservation
Reservierung reservation
Respekt respect
retten save; rescue
Rettungswagen ambulance
Rezept recipe
Rhythmus rhythm
richtig right; correct; true;
  proper
Richtung direction
riechen (nach) smell (of)
Riese giant
riesengroß huge; great
riesig huge; great
Risiko risk
Robbe seal
Roboter robot
Rock skirt
rollen roll
Rollstuhl wheelchair
Rolltreppe escalator
Romanze romance
rosa pink
rot red
Rücken back
Rückenschmerzen backache
Hin- und Rückfahrkarte
  return (ticket)
Rückseite back
rufen shout

jdn in Ruhe lassen leave sb in peace

ruhig quiet; peaceful

Ruhm fame *(no pl)*

ruinieren ruin

Rüpel bully

Russisch Russian

russisch Russian

Russland Russia

S

Saal hall

Sachbeschädigung vandalism *(no pl)*

Sache thing

Saft juice

sagen say *(irr)*; tell *(irr)*

Sahne cream *(no pl)*

Salat salad

(Salat)gurke cucumber

Salbe cream

Salz salt

sammeln collect

Samstag Saturday

sandig sandy

Sänger/in singer

Sarg coffin

Satz sentence

sauber clean

sauber machen clean

Schach(spiel) chess

Schaden damage *(no pl)*

schaden damage

(be)schädigen damage

(Be)schädigung damage *(no pl)*

Schaf sheep *(pl -)*

es schaffen manage

Schal scarf *(pl -s or scarves)*

scharf hot

Schatten shadow

schätzen guess

schauen look

schaurig spooky *(informal)*

Schauspieler/in actor/actress

Schauspielerei drama

scheinen *(Sonne)* shine *(irr)*

Schere (pair of) scissors *(only pl)*

Scheune barn

Schichtarbeit shift work *(no pl)*

Schichtdienst shift work *(no pl)*

etw schicken post sth

(zu)schicken send *(irr)*

schieben push

Schiedsrichter/in referee

schief gehen go wrong

Schienen railroad *(AE)*, railway *(BE)*

schießen kick

ein Tor schießen score a goal

Schiff ship; boat

(Straßen)schild sign

(Verkehrs)schild sign

Schildkröte turtle

(Land)schildkröte tortoise

Schinken ham

Schlacht battle

schlafen sleep *(irr)*

Schlafzimmer bedroom

schlagen hit *(irr)*

Schlange snake; queue

schlank slim

schlau clever

schlecht bad

schlechter worse

schlechteste(r, s) worst

schließen close

Schließfach locker

schließlich finally

schlimm bad

schlimmer worse

schlimmste(r, s) worst

Schloss castle

zum Schluss finally

Schlüssel key

schmackhaft tasty

schmal narrow; slim

schmecken taste

schmerzen hurt *(irr)*

sich schminken put on make-up

Schmuck jewellery

schmücken decorate

schmutzig dirty

Schnee snow

schneereich snowy

schneiden cut *(irr)*

schnell fast; quick

Schnellhefter folder

Schnupfen cold

Schock shock

schockiert shocked

Schokolade chocolate *(no pl)*

schon already

schön beautiful; nice; lovely

Schornstein chimney

schottisch Scottish

Schottland Scotland

Schrank cupboard

schrecklich horrible; terrible

schreiben write *(irr)*

Schreibtisch desk

schreien shout; scream; cry

Schriftsteller/in writer; author

Schritt footstep

schüchtern shy

Schuh shoe

Schulabgänger/in graduate

Schulbuch textbook

Schuld fault

Schule school

Schüler/in student

(Schul)fach subject

(Schul)klasse class

Schulleiter/in headteacher

(Schul)note mark

Schultasche schoolbag

Schulter shoulder

(be)schützen protect

schwanger pregnant

Schwanz tail

schwarz black

Schwein pig

schwer heavy; hard; difficult

Schwester sister

(Kranken)schwester nurse

schwierig difficult

Schwierigkeiten trouble *(no pl)*

Schwierigkeiten bekommen

get into trouble

Schwimmbad swimming pool

Schwimmbecken swimming pool

Schwimmen swimming

schwimmen swim *(irr)*

Schwimmer/in swimmer

schwitzen sweat

See lake

die See the sea *(no pl)*

Seehund seal

seekrank seasick

Seeräuber pirate

Segel sail

segeln sail

sehen see *(irr)*; look (at)

Sehenswürdigkeit sight

sehr very; a lot; much

Seife soap *(no pl)*

Seifenoper soap (opera)

Seil rope

sein be *(irr)*

sein(e, r) his; its

seit since; for

Seite side; page

Sekretär/in secretary

Sekunde second

selbst myself; yourself *(pl yourselves)*; himself; herself; itself; ourselves; themselves; even

selbstbewusst self-confident

selbstsicher self-confident

Sendung programme

senkrecht vertical

September September

Sessel armchair

setzen put *(irr)*

sich (selbst) himself; herself; itself; themselves

sicher sure; safe

sichern save

Sicht view

sie she; her; they; them

Sie you

Siedler/in settler

Sieg victory

Sieger/in winner

silbern silver

Silvester New Year's Eve

singen sing *(irr)*

sitzen sit *(irr)*

Skifahren skiing

Skilaufen skiing

Sklave/Sklavin slave

SMS text message

so so

(genau)so ... wie ... as ... as

sobald as soon as

Socke sock

Sofa couch

sofort in a minute

sogar even

Sohn son

solche(r, s) such

sollen shall

sollte should

Sommer summer

Sonderangebot special offer

sonderbar strange

Sonne sun

Sonnenaufgang sunrise

Sonnenbrille sunglasses *(only pl)*

Sonnenschein sunshine

sonnig sunny

Sonntag Sunday

Sorge worry

sich Sorgen machen worry

sorgfältig careful

Sorte sort; kind; type

Soße sauce

sowieso anyway

Spanien Spain

Spanisch Spanish

spanisch Spanish

spannend exciting

sparen save

Spaß fun *(no pl)*

Spaß haben have a good time; enjoy oneself

(viel) Spaß machen be (great) fun

spaßig fun

(zu) spät late

(zu) spät kommen be late

später afterwards; after that; later

(spätestens) bis (acht Uhr) by (eight o'clock)

spazieren gehen go for a walk

Spaziergang walk

speichern save

Speisekarte menu

speziell special

Spiegel mirror

Spiegelei fried egg

Spiel game; match; play

spielen play; act out

Spieler/in player

Spielfeld sports field

(Spiel)film movie *(AE)*, film *(BE)*

Spielplatz playground

Spielzeug toy

Spind locker

Spinne spider

Spitze top

Spitzen- top

(Bleistift)spitzer pencil sharpener

Sport sports

Sportart sports

Sporthalle sports hall

Sportler/in sportsperson

Sportplatz sports ground; sports field

Sport(unterricht) PE (= physical education)

Sprache language

sprechen speak *(irr)*; talk (to)

Sprichwort saying

springen jump

(be)sprühen spray

spucken spit *(irr)*

Geschirr spülen wash the dishes

Stadion stadium

Stadt town

(Groß)stadt city

(Vieh)stall barn

Stamm tribe

(Verkaufs)stand stall

ständig all the time

stark strong; powerful
Station station
(an)statt instead (of)
stattdessen instead (of)
stattfinden take place
Statue statue
staubsaugen hoover
stehen stand *(irr)*
stehlen steal *(irr)*
steigen get *(irr)*
(hinauf)steigen climb
Stein stone; rock
stellen put *(irr)*
sterben die
(Stereo)anlage stereo
Stern star
Sternzeichen star sign
Stift pen
Stimme voice
Stimmung mood
Stock stick
Stockwerk floor
stöhnen moan
Stolz pride
stolz (auf jmd) proud (of sb)
stoßen (gegen) hit *(irr)*
jdn stoßen knock sb
Strafe penalty
Strafstoß penalty
Strand beach
Straße street; road
(Straßen)schild sign
streicheln pet
Streichholz match
Streit argument; fight
streng strict
stressig stressful
Strom electricity
Stück piece
(Theater)stück play
Student/in student
studieren study
Stufe step
Stuhl chair
Stunde lesson; hour
Stundenplan timetable
Sturm storm
stürzen crash

(unter)stützen support
suchen (nach) look for
(durch)suchen search
Südafrika South Africa
Südamerika South America
Süden south
Südosten south-east
Supermarkt supermarket
Suppe soup
im Internet surfen surf the
 Internet
süß sweet; cute
Süßigkeiten candy *(AE)*,
 sweets *(BE)*
Symbol symbol
symbolisieren symbolize
Szene scene

T

Tafel board
Tag day
pro/am Tag a day
Tagebuch diary
vor einigen Tagen the other day
eines Tages one day
Takt rhythm
Tal valley
talentiert talented
Tante aunt
Tanz dance
Tanzen dancing
tanzen dance
Tänzer/in dancer
Tasche bag; pocket
Taschendieb/in pickpocket
Taschengeld pocket money
 (no pl)
(Taschen)rechner calculator
Tasse cup
Tatze paw
Techniker/in technician
Tee tea
Teelöffel teaspoon
Teigtasche dumpling
Teil part
teilen share
sich teilen split up
teilnehmen (an) take part (in)

Telefon (tele)phone
(Telefon)anruf (phone) call
Telefonist/in operator
Telefonzelle telephone box
Teller plate
Tempel temple
Teppich carpet
testen test
teuer expensive
Teufel devil
Theater theater *(AE)*,
 theatre *(BE)*; drama
(Theater)stück play
Thema subject
die Themse the (River) Thames
Tier animal
Tierarzt/-ärztin
 vet (= veterinarian)
Tierpfleger/in keeper
Tipp tip
Tisch table
den Tisch decken set the table
Tischtennis table tennis
Titel title
tja well
Tochter daughter
Toilette toilet
toll brilliant *(informal)*; amazing
 (informal)
Tomate tomato *(pl -es)*
Ton sound
Tor goal
ein Tor schießen score a goal
Tormann/Torfrau goalkeeper
Tortendiagramm pie chart
tot dead
töten kill
Tracht costume
traditionell traditional
tragen wear *(irr) (Kleidung)*;
 carry
Tragödie drama
Trainer(in) coach
trainieren train
Traktor tractor
Träne tear
tränen water
Traum dream

traurig sad
treffen hit *(irr)*
(sich) treffen meet *(irr)*; get together
Treibhaus greenhouse
(sich) trennen separate; split up
Treppe stairs *(only pl)*
treten kick
trinken drink *(irr)*
etwas trinken gehen have a drink
trocken dry
Trommel drum
Truthahn/-henne turkey
tschüss bye *(informal)*
tun do *(irr)*
Tür door
Türkei Turkey
Türkisch Turkish
türkisch Turkish
Türklingel doorbell
Turm tower
Turnen gymnastics
Turnhalle gym (= gymnasium)
Typ sort; kind; type
typisch typical
tyrannisieren bully

U

U-Bahn underground
üben practise
über about; over; across
überall everywhere
überfüllt crowded
überhaupt nicht not at all
überleben survive
übernachten sleep over
überprüfen check
überqueren cross
überraschend surprising
überrascht surprised
Überraschung surprise
Überstunden machen work long hours
übrig left
Übung exercise
Uhr clock

(sieben) Uhr (seven) o'clock
Wie viel Uhr ist es? What time is it?
(Uhr)zeit time
(Armband)uhr watch
um at; around
(sich) umdrehen turn round
Umgebung environment
umher around
Umkleide fitting room
umsonst for free; free
Umwelt environment
umweltfreundlich environmentally friendly
umziehen move
Umzug parade
und and
unerschrocken brave
Unfall accident
unfreundlich unfriendly
ungefähr about
ungesund unhealthy
ungezogen naughty
unglaublich incredible; amazing *(informal)*
unglücklich unhappy
unglücklicherweise unfortunately
unheimlich scary; spooky *(informal)*
Universum universe
uns us; ourselves
unser(e) our
unsere(r, s) ours
unten at the bottom (of)
(nach) unten down
unter under
untergebracht sein stay
sich unterhalten chat
sich unterhalten (mit) talk (to)
unterrichten teach *(irr)*
Unterschied difference
unterschiedlich different
Unterschrift signature
(unter)stützen support
untersuchen explore
Urlaub holiday

Urlaub machen go on holiday
in den Urlaub fahren go on holiday
Urwald jungle

V

Vandalismus vandalism
Vater father
Vegetarier/in vegetarian
vegetarisch vegetarian
Verabredung date
(sich) (ver)ändern change
(Ver)änderung change
verärgert angry
Verband bandage
Verbrauch usage
Verbrecher/in criminal
(ver)brennen burn *(irr)*
verbringen (Zeit) spend *(irr)*
verdienen earn
Geld verdienen make money; earn money
Verein club
Vereinigte Staaten US (= United States)
Vereinigtes Königreich UK (= United Kingdom)
vergessen forget *(irr)*
sich vergnügen enjoy oneself
jdn verhaften arrest sb
zum Verkauf stehen be on sale
verkaufen sell *(irr)*
Verkäufer/in shop assistant; seller
(Verkaufs)stand stall
verkehrsreich busy
(Verkehrs)schild sign
sich verkleiden (als) dress up (as)
verkünden announce
verlassen leave *(irr)*
verlegen embarrassed
jdn verletzen hurt sb
verletzt injured; hurt
Verletzung injury
verlieren lose *(irr)*
verlockend attractive
verloren lost

(ver)mischen mix
vermissen miss
Vermittlung operator
Vermögen fortune
vermuten guess
verpassen miss
verrückt crazy
verschieden different
verschmutzen pollute
verschneit snowy
versorgen take care of
sich verspäten be late
den Weg versperren block
versprechen promise
(sich) verstecken hide *(irr)*
verstehen understand *(irr)*
sich (mit jdm) verstehen
  get along (with sb)
versuchen try
vertikal vertical
Verwandte(r) relative
verwechseln mix up
verwirrt confused
verwundet hurt
Verzeihung! sorry
(Vieh)stall barn
viel lots of; much
viel(e) a lot (of); lots (of)
viele many
Viel Glück! Good luck!
viele Grüße best wishes
vielen Dank thanks a lot
vielleicht perhaps; maybe
Viertel neighbourhood; area
Viertel (vor/nach)
  quarter (to/past)
violett purple
Vogel bird
voll full; packed
völlig completely; altogether
von of; from; by
vor before; in front of
vor (drei Tagen) (three days)
  ago
vorbei over
vorbei (an) past
vorbeifahren pass by
vorbeigehen pass by

(sich) vorbereiten prepare
Vorfahr(e)/Vorfahrin ancestor
vorführen demonstrate
Vorhang curtain
vorher before
Vorlieben likes *(only pl)*
vormittags in the morning;
  am (= ante meridiem) *(nur
  hinter Uhrzeit)*
Vorname first name
vorsichtig careful
Vorsingen audition
Vorspeise starter
Vorspielen audition
Vorsprechen audition
vorstellen introduce
Vortanzen audition
vorüber (an) past
Vorurteil prejudice *(no pl)*
vorziehen prefer
Vulkan volcano *(pl -oes
  or -os)*

W

wach bleiben stay up
wachsen grow *(irr)*
Waffe weapon
wählen dial
(jdn) wählen vote (for sb)
wahr true
während during; while
wahrscheinlich probably
Wald forest
Waldbrand forest fire
Walisisch Welsh
walisisch Welsh
Wand wall
Wandern hiking
wann when
Warnung warning
warten (auf) wait (for)
warum why
was what
(irgend)(et)was anything
(sich) waschen wash
Wasser water
Wasserfall waterfall
Wasserhahn tap

Wasserkocher kettle
Wechselgeld change
wechseln change
Wecker alarm clock
Weg way
den Weg beschreiben
  give directions
nach dem Weg fragen ask for
  directions
weg away
wehen blow *(irr)*
wehtun hurt *(irr)*
jdm wehtun hurt sb
weiblich female
weich soft
Weide field
Weihnachten Christmas
erster Weihnachtsfeiertag
  Christmas Day
Weihnachtsmann Father
  Christmas
weil because
Weile while
weinen cry
weiß white
weit far
welche(r, s) what; which
Welle wave
Wellensittich budgie
  (= budgerigar)
Welt world
auf der ganzen Welt
  all over the world
wenige few
weniger less
am wenigsten least
wenigstens at least
wenn when; if
wer who
Werbung ad, advert
  (= advertisement)
werden become *(irr)*; get *(irr)*;
  will; going to
werfen throw *(irr)*
Werk factory
Werkzeug tool
Westen west
Wettbewerb competition

Wetter weather
wichtig important; major
widerlich disgusting
wie how; like
(genau)so ... wie ... as ... as
wie (zum Beispiel) such as
wieder again
wiederholen repeat
wiederverwerten recycle
Wiese grass *(no pl)*; field
willkommen (in) welcome (to)
willkommen heißen welcome
windig windy
Windpocken chickenpox *(no pl)*
winken wave
wir we
wirklich really; real
wissen know *(irr)*
(Natur)wissenschaft science
witzig funny; fun
Woche week
pro/in der Woche a week
Wochenende weekend
am Wochenende at the weekend
wo(hin) where
Wohltätigkeitsorganisation
  charity
wohnen live; stay
Wohnung flat; apartment
Wohnwagen caravan
Wohnzimmer living room
Wolke cloud
Wolkenkratzer skyscraper
wollen want
etw tun wollen want to do sth
Wort word
Wörterbuch dictionary
wund sore
wunderbar wonderful; great;

fantastic *(informal)*
wundervoll wonderful
Wunsch wish
(sich) wünschen wish
würde(st, n, t) would
Wurst sausage
Würstchen sausage
Wüste desert
wütend angry

Z

Zahl number
(be)zahlen pay *(irr)*
Zahn tooth *(pl* teeth*)*
Zahnbürste toothbrush
Zauber magic
Zauberer/Zauberin magician
Zeichen sign; symbol
Zeichentrickfilm cartoon
zeichnen draw *(irr)*
Zeichnung drawing
zeigen show *(irr)*; demonstrate
(Uhr)zeit time
Zeitalter age
zeitig early
Zeitschrift magazine
Zeitung newspaper
Zeltplatz campsite
Zentrum centre
(zer)brechen break *(irr)*
zerbrochen broken
zerstören destroy; ruin
Ziege goat
ziehen pull
ziemlich quite
Ziffer number
Zigarette cigarette
Zimmer room
(Zimmer)decke ceiling

zornig angry
zu to; too
zu Fuß on foot
(zu Fuß) gehen walk
zu Hause (at) home
(zu) spät late
(zu) spät kommen be late
zubereiten prepare
Zucker sugar
zuerst (at) first
zufrieden happy
Zug train
Zuhause home
(zu)hören listen (to)
Zukunft future
zum Beispiel for example
zumachen close
Zündholz match
zurück back
zurückkehren return
zusammen together
zusammenfügen join
zusätzlich extra
Zuschauermenge crowd
(zu)schicken send *(irr)*
zusehen watch
(jdm) zustimmen agree
  (with sb)
Zutat ingredient
zuversichtlich optimistic
zuvor before
zweimal twice
zweitens secondly
zweite(r, s) second
Zwiebel onion
Zwilling twin
Zwillings- twin
zwischen between

Girls/Women

Akina / əˈkiːnə /
Alisha / əˈlɪʃə /
Allimar / ælɪˈmaː /
Amy / ˈeɪmi /
Angel / ˈeɪndʒl /
Antonia / ænˈtəʊniə /
Ashley / ˈæʃli /
Bridget / ˈbrɪdʒɪt /
Caroline / ˈkærəlaɪn /
Casey / ˈkeɪsi /
Cheryl / ˈtʃerəl /
Chloe / ˈkləʊi /
Donna / ˈdɒnə /
Elisha / iˈlaɪʃə /
Ellie / ˈeli /
Gillian / ˈdʒɪliən /
Helen / ˈhelən /
Hermione / hɜːˈmaɪəni /
Jane / dʒeɪn /
Jennifer / ˈdʒenɪfə /
Jessica / ˈdʒesɪkə /
Jessie / ˈdʒesi /
Kathy / ˈkæθi /
Katie / ˈkeɪti /
Kim / kɪm /
Lea / liːə /
Leotie / liˈəʊti /
Leya / ˈleɪə /
Lindsay / ˈlɪndzi /
Lisa / ˈliːsə /
Margaret / ˈmaːɡrət /
Marian / ˈmæriən /
Mary / ˈmeəri /
Meg / meɡ /
Melanie / ˈmeləni /
Miriam / ˈmɪriəm /
Nicki / ˈnɪki /
Rebecca / rɪˈbekə /
Sam / sæm /
Samantha / səˈmæntθə /
Sheena / ˈʃiːnə /
Sonya / ˈsɒnjə /
Stacy / ˈsteɪsi /
Susan / ˈsuːzn /
Tawny / ˈtɔːni /

Boys/Men

Aaron / ˈeərən /
Adam / ˈædəm /
Aidan / ˈeɪdən /
Alan / ˈælən /
Alek / ˈælɪk /
Alex / ˈælɪks /
Andy / ˈændi /
Ben / ben /
Bilal / biˈlaːl /
Bobby / ˈbɒbi /
Brad / bræd /
Brandon / ˈbrændən /
Brian / ˈbraɪən /
Caleb / ˈkeɪleb /
Carl / kaːl /
Carlos / ˈkaːlɒs /
Carlton / ˈkaːltən /
Chad / tʃæd /
Charlie / ˈtʃaːli /
Chris / krɪs /
Dan / dæn /
Dave / deɪv /
Derek / ˈderɪk /
DJ / ˈdiːˌdʒeɪ /
Don / dɒn /
Edgar / ˈedɡə /
Frank / fræŋk /
Fred / fred /
Gary / ˈɡæri /
Harry / ˈhæri /
Jake / dʒeɪk /
Jeremiah / ˌdʒerɪˈmaɪə /
Joel / ˈdʒəʊəl /
John / dʒɒn /
Johnny / ˈdʒɒni /
Josh / dʒɒʃ /
Joshua / ˈdʒɒʃjuə /
Kenan / ˈkenən /
Lee-Lee / ˈliːliː /
Lenno / ˈlenəʊ /
Marc / maːk /
Mark / maːk /
Miah / ˈmaɪə /
Michael / ˈmaɪkəl /
Mohamed / məʊˈhæmɪd /
Nicholas / ˈnɪkələs /
Nick / nɪk /

Oliver / ˈɒlɪvə /
Patrick / ˈpætrɪk /
Paul / pɔːl /
Pete / piːt /
Philip / ˈfɪlɪp /
Pierre / piˈeə /
Rajiv / raːˈdʒiːv /
Raúl / raʊˈuːl /
Rick / rɪk /
Sam / sæm /
Sammy / ˈsæmi /
Samoset / ˈsaːməzet /
Sebastian / səˈbæstiən /
Sergio / ˈsɜːdʒiəʊ /
Simon / ˈsaɪmən /
Squanto / ˈskwɒntəʊ /
Steffen / ˈstefən /
Steve / stiːv /
Thomas / ˈtɒməs /
Tom / tɒm /
Walter / ˈwɔːltə /
William / ˈwɪljəm /
Zack / zæk /

Families

Angell / ˈeɪndʒəl /
Beliard / ˌbeliˈaː /
Bradley / ˈbrædli /
Bradshaw / ˈbrædʃɔː /
Coley / ˈkəʊli /
Collins / ˈkɒlɪnz /
Cook / kʊk /
Diemer / ˈdiːmə /
Epperson / ˈepəsən /
Fleer / flɪə /
Graves / ɡreɪvz /
Gritt / ɡrɪt /
Hale / heɪl /
Hall / hɔːl /
Hansen / ˈhæntsən /
Henry / ˈhenri /
Hill / hɪl /
Hinawy / hiˈnaːwi /
Jones / dʒəʊnz /
Miller / ˈmɪlə /
Morrison / ˈmɒrɪsən /
Myers / ˈmaɪəz /

Nicholson / ˈnɪkəlsən /
Perez / ˈperəz /
Petrakis / peˈtrɑːkɪs /
Phillips / ˈfɪlɪps /
Rodriguez / rɒˈdriːgez /
Root / ruːt /
Siempre / ˌsiːˈempre /
Simsion / ˈsɪmsiən /
Watts / wɒts /
Webster / ˈwebstə /

Other Names

Abraham Lincoln / ˌeɪbrəhæm ˈlɪŋkən /
Adobe / əˈdəʊbi /
Annie Moore / ˌæni ˈmʊə /
Apple / ˈæpl /
the Big Apple / ðə ˌbɪg ˈæpl /
Blibber-Blubber / ˈblɪbəˌblʌbə /
the Bling Ring / ðə ˈblɪŋ rɪŋ /
Broadway / ˈbrɔːdweɪ /
Brooklyn Bridge / ˌbrʊklɪn ˈbrɪdʒ /
Brown University / ˌbraʊn juːnɪˈvɜːsəti /
Bureau of Labor Statistics / ˌbjʊərəʊˌəv ˈleɪbə stəˌtɪstɪks /
the Camden Chronicle / ðə ˌkæmdən ˈkrɒnɪkl /
Camden Market / ˌkæmdən ˈmɑːkɪt /
Cats / kæts /
Central Park / ˌsentrəl ˈpɑːk /
Channel Islands National Park / ˌtʃænlˌaɪləndz ˌnæʃnl ˈpɑːk /
Chief Massasoit / ˌtʃiːf ˈmæsəswɑː /
Chinatown / ˈtʃaɪnəˌtaʊn /
Christopher Columbus / ˌkrɪstəfə kəˈlʌmbəs /
Cisco / ˈsɪskəʊ /
City and Colour / ˌsɪtiˌən ˈkʌlə /
Claire Julien / ˌkleə ˈdʒuːliən /
Coney Island / ˌkəʊni ˈaɪlənd /
Crusher / ˈkrʌʃə /

Death Valley National Park / ˌdeθ ˌvæli ˌnæʃnl ˈpɑːk /
the Detroit Times / ðə diˌtrɔɪtˌˈtaɪmz /
Disneyland / ˈdɪznilænd /
Earth Day / ˈɜːθ deɪ /
eBay / ˈiːbeɪ /
Electronic Arts / ˌelekˌtrɒnɪkˌˈɑːts /
Emma Watson / ˌemə ˈwɒtsən /
the Empire State Building / ðiˌempaɪə ˈsteɪt ˌbɪldɪŋ /
Evans High School / ˌevənz ˈhaɪ ˌskuːl /
Evernote / ˈevənəʊt /
F. Scott Fitzgerald / ˌef ˌskɒt fɪtsˈdʒerəld /
Facebook / ˈfeɪsbʊk /
Fairtrade / ˌfeəˈtreɪd /
Fifth Avenue / ˌfɪfθˌˈævəˌnjuː /
Flatiron Building / ˈflætˌaɪən ˌbɪldɪŋ /
Fleet Primary School / ˌfliːt ˈpraɪməri skuːl /
George Washington / ˌdʒɔːdʒ ˈwɒʃɪŋtən /
Golden Gate Bridge / ˌgəʊldn geɪt ˈbrɪdʒ /
the Golden Globe / ðə ˌgəʊldn ˈgləʊb /
the Golden State / ðə ˌgəʊldn ˈsteɪt /
Google / ˈguːgəl /
Governor Bradford / ˌgʌvənə ˈbrædfəd /
the Grammy / ðə ˈgræmi /
the Grand Canyon Skywalk / ðə ˌgrænd ˌkænjən ˈskaɪˌwɔːk /
Grand Central Terminal / ˌgrænd ˌsentrəl ˈtɜːmɪnl /
Ground Zero / ˌgraʊnd ˈzɪərəʊ /
Halloween / ˌhæləʊˈiːn /
Harry Potter / ˌhæri ˈpɒtə /
Haverstock School / ˈhævəstɒk skuːl /
Hewlett-Packard / ˌhjuːlɪt ˈpækɑːd /

High Line Park / ˌhaɪ ˌlaɪn ˈpɑːk /
Hollywood / ˈhɒliˌwʊd /
Hollywood Film Studios / ˌhɒliˌwʊd ˈfɪlm ˌstjuːdiəʊz /
Intel / ˈɪntel /
the Isle of Tears / ðiˌaɪlˌəv tɪəz /
Israel Broussard / ˌɪzreɪəl bruˈsɑː /
Jacqueline Woodson / ˌdʒækəliːn ˈwʊdsən /
James Marshall / ˌdʒeɪmz ˈmɑːʃəl /
Jennifer Aniston / ˌdʒenɪfərˌˈænɪstən /
John Billington / ˌdʒɒn ˈbɪlɪŋtən /
John F. Kennedy / ˌdʒɒnˌef ˈkenədi /
John Wrangler / ˌdʒɒn ˈræŋglə /
Joshua Tree National Park / ˌdʒɒʃjuə triː ˌnæʃnl ˈpɑːk /
Katie Chang / ˌkeɪti ˈtʃæŋ /
Katy Perry / ˌkeɪti ˈperi /
Keith Haring / ˌkiːθ ˈheərɪŋ /
Kings Canyon National Park / ˌkɪŋz ˌkænjən ˌnæʃnl ˈpɑːk /
LA Lakers / ˌelˌeɪ ˈleɪkəz /
Lady Liberty / ˌleɪdi ˈlɪbəti /
Lake Park High School / ˌleɪk ˌpɑːk ˈhaɪ skuːl /
the Land of Milk and Honey / ðə ˌlændˌəv ˌmɪlkˌən ˈhʌni /
Langston Hughes / ˌlæŋstən ˈhjuːz /
Lassen Volcanic National Park / ˌlæsən vɒlˌkænɪk ˌnæʃnl ˈpɑːk /
Lassie / ˈlæsi /
Leonardo DiCaprio / ˌliːəʊˌnɑːdəʊ diˈkæpriəʊ /
Levi Strauss / ˌliːvaɪ ˈstrɔːs /
the Lion King / ðə ˈlaɪən kɪŋ /
Lucky Motors / ˌlʌki ˈməʊtəz /
MacDonald / məkˈdɒnəld /
Malcolm X / ˌmælkəmˌˈeks /

Mardi Gras / ˌmɑːdi ˈgrɑː /
Martin Luther King
   / ˌmɑːtɪn ˌluːθə ˈkɪŋ /
Max Havelaar
   / ˌmæks ˈhævəlɑː /
Max Lee / ˌmæks ˈliː /
Mayflower / ˈmeɪˌflaʊə /
Megan Fox / ˌmegən ˈfɒks /
Mickey Mouse / ˌmɪki ˈmaʊs /
Microsoft / ˈmaɪkrəʊsɒft /
the MoMA (= Museum of
   Modern Art) / ðə ˈməʊmə (=
   mjuːˌziːəm ˌəv ˌmɒdən ˈɑːt) /
Mozilla / mɒdˈzɪlə /
NBA (= National Basketball
   Association) / ˌen biː ˈeɪ /
Netflix / ˈnetflɪks /
NYPD (= New York City Police
   Department) / ˌen waɪ piː ˈdiː /
the One World Trade Center
   / ðə ˌwʌn ˌwɜːld ˈtreɪd ˌsentə /
Orlando Bloom / ɔːˌlændəʊ
   ˈbluːm /
the Oscar / ðiˌ ˈɒskə /
Paris Hilton / ˌpærɪs ˈhɪltən /
Paypal / ˈpeɪpæl /
the Perks of Being a Wallflower
   / ðə ˌpɜːks ˌəv ˌbiːɪŋ ˌə
   ˈwɔːlˌflaʊə /
Pinnacles National Park
   / ˌpɪnəkəlz ˌnæʃnl ˈpɑːk /
Pocahontas / ˌpɒkəˈhɒntəs /
Popeye / ˈpɒpaɪ /
the Redwood Forest
   / ðə ˌredˌwʊd ˈfɒrɪst /
Redwood National Park
   / ˌredˌwʊd ˌnæʃnl ˈpɑːk /
Rockefeller Center
   / ˈrɒkəfelə ˌsentə /
Roselle Special / rəʊˌzel ˈspeʃl /
Salazar High School
   / ˈsæləˌzɑː ˈhaɪ skuːl /
SanDisk / ˈsændɪsk /
Sequoia National Park / sɪˌkwɔɪə
   ˌnæʃnl ˈpɑːk /
Silicon Valley / ˌsɪlɪkən ˈvæli /
the Smiths / ðə ˈsmɪθs /
Sofia Coppola / ˌsəʊfiə ˈkɒpələ /

Spencer High School
   / ˌspentsə ˈhaɪ ˌskuːl /
the SS Nevada
   / ðiˌˌeses nɪˈvɑːdə /
St Patrick's Day
   / sənt ˈpætrɪks deɪ /
the Statue of Liberty
   / ðə ˌstætʃu ˌəv ˈlɪbəti /
Stephen Chbosky
   / ˌstiːvn tʃəˈbɒski /
Super Burger / ˈsuːpə ˌbɜːgə /
Super Hamburger
   / ˈsuːpə ˌhæmˌbɜːgə /
T-Rex (= tyrannosaurus rex)
   / tiː ˈreks, tɪˌrænəˌsɔːrəs ˈreks /
Taissa Farmiga / ˌtaɪsə fəˈmiːgə /
They Might Be Giants
   / ðeɪ ˌmaɪt bi ˈdʒaɪənts /
Times Square / ˌtaɪmz ˈskweə /
Titanic / taɪˈtænɪk /
Tom Cruise / ˌtɒm ˈkruːz /
the Twin Towers / ðə ˌtwɪn ˈtaʊəz /
Twitter / ˈtwɪtə /
Uintah River High School
   / ˌjuːntə ˌrɪvə ˈhaɪ skuːl /
Universal Studios
   / ˌjuːnɪˌvɜːsl ˈstjuːdiəʊz /
Venice Beach / ˌvenɪs ˈbiːtʃ /
Vince Lombardi
   / ˌvɪnts lɒmˈbɑːdi /
Walk of Fame / ˌwɔːk ˌəv ˈfeɪm /
Warner Brothers
   / ˈwɔːnə ˌbrʌðəz /
Woody Guthrie / ˌwʊdi ˈgʌθri /
the World Trade Center
   / ðə ˌwɜːld ˈtreɪd ˌsentə /
Yahoo! / jaˈhuː /
Yankee Stadium
   / ˌjæŋki ˈsteɪdiəm /
Yosemite National Park
   / jəʊˌseməti ˌnæʃnl ˈpɑːk /

Geographical names
Alabama / ˌæləˈbæmə /
Alaska / əˈlæskə /
America / əˈmerɪkə /
Arizona / ˌærɪˈzəʊnə /
Asia / ˈeɪʒə /
Austria / ˈɒstriə /
Badwater / ˈbædˌwɔːtə /

Bakersfield / ˈbeɪkəzfiːəld /
Beijing / ˌbeɪˈdʒɪŋ /
Belgium / ˈbeldʒəm /
Berlin / bɜːˈlɪn /
Birmingham / ˈbɜːmɪŋəm /
Boston / ˈbɒstən /
Brazil / brəˈzɪl /
Bremerhaven / ˈbreɪməhɑːvən /
Brent Street / ˈbrent ˌstriːt /
the Bronx / ðə ˈbrɒŋks /
Brooklyn / ˈbrʊklɪn /
California / ˌkæləˈfɔːniə /
Camden / ˈkæmdən /
Canada / ˈkænədə /
Cape Cod / ˌkeɪp ˈkɒd /
the Caribbean / ðə ˌkærɪˈbiːən /
Central America
   / ˌsentrəl əˈmerɪkə /
Chico / ˈtʃiːkəʊ /
Chile / ˈtʃɪli /
Coast Ranges
   / ˈkəʊst ˌreɪndʒɪz /
Cobh / ˈkəʊv /
Colorado / ˌkɒləˈrɑːdəʊ /
Detroit / dɪˈtrɔɪt /
Ellis Island / ˈelɪs ˌaɪlənd /
England / ˈɪŋglənd /
Europe / ˈjʊərəp /
France / frɑːnts /
Frankfort / ˈfræŋkfət /
Fresno / ˈfreznəʊ /
Georgia / ˈdʒɔːdʒə /
Germany / ˈdʒɜːməni /
Ghana / ˈgɑːnə /
Greece / griːs /
Harlem / ˈhɑːləm /
Haverstock Hill
   / ˈhævəstɒk hɪl /
Hawaii / həˈwaɪi /
Hollywood Hills
   / ˌhɒliˌwʊd ˈhɪlz /
Illinois / ˌɪləˈnɔɪ /
Iowa / ˈaɪəʊə /
Ireland / ˈaɪələnd /
Italy / ˈɪtəli /
Kandy / ˈkændi /
Kumasi / kʊˈmɑːsi /
London / ˈlʌndən /

Los Angeles / lɒsˈændʒəliːz /
Lower Manhattan
  / ˌləʊə mænˈhætn /
Madrid / məˈdrɪd /
Malibu / ˈmælɪbuː /
Manhattan / mænˈhætən /
Maryland / ˈmeərɪlənd /
Massachusetts / ˌmæsəˈtʃuːsɪts /
Mexico / ˈmeksɪˌkəʊ /
Mexico City / ˌmeksɪkəʊ ˈsɪti /
Michigan / ˈmɪʃɪgən /
the Middle East / ðə ˌmɪdl ˈiːst /
Minnesota / ˌmɪnɪˈsəʊtə /
Missouri / mɪˈzʊəri /
Mount Shasta / ˌmaʊnt ˈʃæstə /
Mount Whitney / ˌmaʊnt ˈwɪtni /
Nebraska / nəˈbræskə /
the Netherlands / ðə ˈneðlənz /
Nevada / nɪˈvɑːdə /
New Orleans / ˌnjuː ˈɔːliənz /
New Ulm / ˌnjuː ˈʊlm /
New York / ˌnjuː ˈjɔːk /
New York City / ˌnjuː ˌjɔːk ˈsɪti /
the New York Island
  / ðə ˌnjuˌjɔːk ˈaɪlənd /
North America / ˌnɔːθˌəˈmerɪkə /
North Dakota / ˌnɔːθ dəˈkəʊtə /
NYC (= New York City)
  / ˌen waɪ ˈsiː /
Oakland / ˈəʊklənd /

Oregon / ˈɒrɪgən /
Oxford / ˈɒksfəd /
Paris / ˈpærɪs /
Pennsylvania / ˌpentsəlˈveɪniə /
Philadelphia / ˌfɪləˈdelfiə /
Pico Rivera / ˌpiːkəʊ rɪˈveərə /
Plymouth Bay / ˌplɪməθ ˈbeɪ /
Pratt Street / ˈpræt ˌstriːt /
Puerto Rico / ˌpwɜːtəʊ ˈriːkəʊ /
Queens / kwiːnz /
Reading / ˈredɪŋ /
Redding / ˈredɪŋ /
Richmond / ˈrɪtʃmənd /
Rocky Mountains
  / ˌrɒki ˈmaʊntɪnz /
Roosevelt Avenue
  / ˌrəʊzəveltˌˈævəˌnjuː /
Roselle / rəʊˈzel /
Russia / ˈrʌʃə /
Sacramento / ˌsækrəˈmentəʊ /
San Diego / ˌsæn diˈeɪgəʊ /
San Francisco
  / ˌsæn frənˈsɪskəʊ /
San Joaquin (River)
  / ˌsæn wɑːˈkiːn /
San Jose / ˌsæn həʊˈzeɪ /
Santa Barbara / ˌsæntə ˈbɑːbərə /
Santa Monica / ˌsæntə ˈmɒnɪkə /
Saudi Arabia / ˌsaʊdi əˈreɪbiə /
Scandinavia / ˌskændɪˈneɪviə /

Siberia / saɪˈbɪəriə /
Sierra Nevada / siˌerə nɪˈvɑːdə /
Somalia / səˈmɑːliə /
South America / ˌsaʊθˌəˈmerɪkə /
Sri Lanka / srɪ ˈlæŋkə /
Staten Island / ˌstætnˌˈaɪlənd /
Telescope Peak
  / ˌtelɪˌskəʊp ˈpiːk /
Texas / ˈteksəs /
Toledo Street / təˈliːdəʊ ˌstriːt /
UK (= United Kingdom)
  / ˌjuːˈkeɪ, juːˌnaɪtɪd ˈkɪŋdəm /
the US (= United States)
  / ðə juːˌnaɪtɪd ˈsteɪts /
USA (= United States of
  America) / ˌjuːesˈeɪ, juːˌnaɪtɪd
  ˌsteɪtsˌəvˌəˈmerɪkə /
Vermont / vəˈmɒnt /
Vietnam / ˌviːetˈnæm /
Virginia / vəˈdʒɪniə /
Washington D.C.
  / ˌwɒʃɪŋtən ˌdiːˈsiː /
West Virginia
  / ˌwest vəˈdʒɪniə /
Western Avenue
  / ˌwestənˌˈævənjuː /
the Windward Islands
  / ðə ˈwɪndwədˌˈaɪləndz /
Wisconsin / wɪˈskɒntsɪn /
Yuba River / ˌjuːbə ˈrɪvə /

Numbers

Cardinal numbers

0	zero /ˈzɪərəʊ/	12	twelve /twelv/	30	thirty /ˈθɜːti/
1	one /wʌn/	13	thirteen /ˌθɜːˈtiːn/	40	forty /ˈfɔːti/
2	two /tuː/	14	fourteen /ˌfɔːˈtiːn/	50	fifty /ˈfɪfti/
3	three /θriː/	15	fifteen /ˌfɪfˈtiːn/	...	
4	four /fɔː/	16	sixteen /ˌsɪksˈtiːn/	90	ninety /ˈnaɪnti/
5	five /faɪv/	17	seventeen /ˌsevnˈtiːn/	100	one hundred
6	six /sɪks/	18	eighteen /ˌeɪˈtiːn/		/ˈwʌn ˌhʌndrəd/
7	seven /ˈsevn/	19	nineteen /ˌnaɪnˈtiːn/	...	
8	eight /eɪt/	20	twenty /ˈtwenti/	900	nine hundred
9	nine /naɪn/	21	twenty-one		/ˈnaɪn ˌhʌndrəd/
10	ten /ten/		/ˌtwentiˈwʌn/	1,000	one thousand
11	eleven /ɪˈlevn/	...			/ˈwʌn ˌθaʊznd/

Ordinal numbers

1st	first /fɜːst/	14th	fourteenth /ˌfɔːˈtiːnθ/	30th	thirtieth /ˈθɜːtiəθ/
2nd	second /ˈsekənd/	15th	fifteenth /ˌfɪfˈtiːnθ/	31st	thirty-first
3rd	third /θɜːd/	...			/ˌθɜːtiˈfɜːst/
4th	fourth /fɔːθ/	20th	twentieth /ˈtwentiəθ/	...	
5th	fifth /fɪfθ/	21st	twenty-first	40th	fortieth /ˈfɔːtiəθ/
6th	sixth /sɪksθ/		/ˌtwentiˈfɜːst/	50th	fiftieth /ˈfɪftiəθ/
7th	seventh /ˈsevnθ/	22nd	twenty-second	60th	sixtieth /ˈsɪkstiəθ/
8th	eighth /eɪtθ/		/ˌtwentiˈsekənd/	70th	seventieth
9th	ninth /naɪnθ/	23rd	twenty-third		/ˈsevntiəθ/
10th	tenth /tenθ/		/ˌtwentiˈθɜːd/	80th	eightieth /ˈeɪtiəθ/
11th	eleventh /ɪˈlevnθ/	24th	twenty-fourth	90th	ninetieth /ˈnaɪntiəθ/
12th	twelfth /twelfθ/		/ˌtwentiˈfɔːθ/	100th	one hundredth
13th	thirteenth /ˌθɜːˈtiːnθ/	...			/ˈhʌndrədθ/

infinitive	simple past	past participle	German
be /biː/	was/were /wɒz/wɜː/	been /biːn/	sein
become /bɪˈkʌm/	became /bɪˈkeɪm/	become /bɪˈkʌm/	werden
begin /bɪˈgɪn/	began /bɪˈgæn/	begun /bɪˈgʌn/	anfangen, beginnen
bet /bet/	bet /bet/	bet /bet/	wetten
bite /baɪt/	bit /bɪt/	bitten /ˈbɪtn/	beißen
blow /bləʊ/	blew /bluː/	blown /bləʊn/	blasen, wehen
break /breɪk/	broke /brəʊk/	broken /ˈbrəʊkən/	(zer)brechen
breed /briːd/	bred /bred/	bred /bred/	züchten
bring /brɪŋ/	brought /brɔːt/	brought /brɔːt/	(mit)bringen
build /bɪld/	built /bɪlt/	built /bɪlt/	bauen
burn /bɜːn/	burnt/burned /bɜːnt/bɜːnd/	burnt/burned /bɜːnt/bɜːnd/	(ver)brennen
buy /baɪ/	bought /bɔːt/	bought /bɔːt/	kaufen
catch /kætʃ/	caught /kɔːt/	caught /kɔːt/	fangen; festnehmen
choose /tʃuːz/	chose /tʃəʊz/	chosen /ˈtʃəʊzn/	auswählen
come /kʌm/	came /keɪm/	come /kʌm/	kommen
cost /kɒst/	cost /kɒst/	cost /kɒst/	kosten
cut /kʌt/	cut /kʌt/	cut /kʌt/	schneiden
do /duː/	did /dɪd/	done /dʌn/	machen, tun
draw /drɔː/	drew /druː/	drawn /drɔːn/	zeichnen
drink /drɪŋk/	drank /dræŋk/	drunk /drʌŋk/	trinken
drive /draɪv/	drove /drəʊv/	driven /ˈdrɪvn/	fahren
eat /iːt/	ate /eɪt/	eaten /ˈiːtn/	essen
fall /fɔːl/	fell /fel/	fallen /ˈfɔːlən/	fallen
feed /fiːd/	fed /fed/	fed /fed/	füttern, zu Essen geben; ernähren
feel /fiːl/	felt /felt/	felt /felt/	(sich) fühlen
fight /faɪt/	fought /fɔːt/	fought /fɔːt/	(be)kämpfen
find /faɪnd/	found /faʊnd/	found /faʊnd/	finden
fit /fɪt/	fit/fitted /fɪt/ˈfɪtɪd/	fit/fitted /fɪt/ˈfɪtɪd/	passen (zu)
fly /flaɪ/	flew /fluː/	flown /fləʊn/	fliegen
forget /fəˈget/	forgot /fəˈgɒt/	forgotten /fəˈgɒtn/	vergessen
get /get/	got /gɒt/	got/gotten /gɒt/ˈgɒtn/	erhalten, bekommen; (an)kommen; verstehen; holen; werden
give /gɪv/	gave /geɪv/	given /ˈgɪvn/	geben
go /gəʊ/	went /went/	gone /gɒn/	gehen; fahren
grow /grəʊ/	grew /gruː/	grown /grəʊn/	wachsen; anbauen
hang /hæŋ/	hung /hʌŋ/	hung /hʌŋ/	(auf)hängen
have /hæv/	had /hæd/	had /hæd/	haben; essen
hear /hɪə/	heard /hɜːd/	heard /hɜːd/	hören
hide /haɪd/	hid /hɪd/	hidden /ˈhɪdn/	(sich) verstecken
hit /hɪt/	hit /hɪt/	hit /hɪt/	schlagen; treffen; stoßen (gegen)
hold /həʊld/	held /held/	held /held/	halten
keep /kiːp/	kept /kept/	kept /kept/	(be)halten; aufbewahren
know /nəʊ/	knew /njuː/	known /nəʊn/	wissen; kennen
lead /liːd/	led /led/	led /led/	(an)führen, leiten

learn /lɜːn/	learnt/learned /lɜːnt/lɜːnd/	learnt/learned /lɜːnt/lɜːnd/	lernen
leave /liːv/	left /left/	left /left/	verlassen; abfahren; lassen
let /let/	let /let/	let /let/	lassen
light /laɪt/	lit /lɪt/	lit /lɪt/	erhellen; anzünden
lose /luːz/	lost /lɒst/	lost /lɒst/	verlieren
make /meɪk/	made /meɪd/	made /meɪd/	machen
mean /miːn/	meant /ment/	meant /ment/	bedeuten; meinen
meet /miːt/	met /met/	met /met/	(sich) treffen; kennenlernen
mow /məʊ/	mowed /məʊd/	mowed/mown /məʊd/məʊn/	mähen
pay /peɪ/	paid /peɪd/	paid /peɪd/	(be)zahlen
put /pʊt/	put /pʊt/	put /pʊt/	setzen, legen, stellen
quit /kwɪt/	quit /kwɪt/	quit /kwɪt/	aufhören (mit)
read /riːd/	read /red/	read /red/	lesen
ride /raɪd/	rode /rəʊd/	ridden /ˈrɪdn/	fahren; reiten
ring /rɪŋ/	rang /ræŋ/	rung /rʌŋ/	klingeln, läuten
run /rʌn/	ran /ræn/	run /rʌn/	laufen, rennen; betreiben, führen
say /seɪ/	said /sed/	said /sed/	sagen
see /siː/	saw /sɔː/	seen /siːn/	sehen
sell /sel/	sold /səʊld/	sold /səʊld/	verkaufen
send /send/	sent /sent/	sent /sent/	(zu)schicken
set /set/	set /set/	set /set/	(ein)stellen; (fest)setzen
sew /səʊ/	sewed /səʊd/	sewn /səʊn/	nähen
shine /ʃaɪn/	shone /ʃɒn/	shone /ʃɒn/	scheinen (Sonne)
show /ʃəʊ/	showed /ʃəʊd/	shown /ʃəʊn/	zeigen
sing /sɪŋ/	sang /sæŋ/	sung /sʌŋ/	singen
sit /sɪt/	sat /sæt/	sat /sæt/	sitzen
sleep /sliːp/	slept /slept/	slept /slept/	schlafen
speak /spiːk/	spoke /spəʊk/	spoken /ˈspəʊkən/	sprechen, reden
spell /spel/	spelt/spelled /spelt/speld/	spelt/spelled /spelt/speld/	buchstabieren
spend /spend/	spent /spent/	spent /spent/	ausgeben (Geld); verbringen (Zeit)
spit /spɪt/	spit/spat /spɪt/spæt/	spit/spat /spɪt/spæt/	spucken
stand /stænd/	stood /stʊd/	stood /stʊd/	stehen; ertragen, aushalten
steal /stiːl/	stole /stəʊl/	stolen /ˈstəʊlən/	stehlen, klauen
strike /straɪk/	struck /strʌk/	struck /strʌk/	(zu)schlagen
swim /swɪm/	swam /swæm/	swum /swʌm/	schwimmen
take /teɪk/	took /tʊk/	taken /ˈteɪkən/	(mit)nehmen; bringen; brauchen, dauern
teach /tiːtʃ/	taught /tɔːt/	taught /tɔːt/	unterrichten; beibringen
tell /tel/	told /təʊld/	told /təʊld/	erzählen; sagen
think /θɪŋk/	thought /θɔːt/	thought /θɔːt/	denken, glauben, meinen
throw /θrəʊ/	threw /θruː/	thrown /θrəʊn/	werfen
understand /ˌʌndəˈstænd/	understood /ˌʌndəˈstʊd/	understood /ˌʌndəˈstʊd/	verstehen
wear /weə/	wore /wɔː/	worn /wɔːn/	tragen (Kleidung)
win /wɪn/	won /wʌn/	won /wʌn/	gewinnen
write /raɪt/	wrote /rəʊt/	written /ˈrɪtn/	schreiben

Seite 18   1 American school life

b) I think it's surprising that students look at the American flag with their hands on their hearts.
It's interesting that the students dress up as king and queen.
I didn't know that students at American schools wear purple uniforms.
I think it's surprising that students can decorate their lockers.

c) In the photo some students are playing American football. – Oh, that's easy! It's photo H!
In the photo there is a girl with blonde hair and a boy. They are wearing crowns. – It's photo F!

Seite 19   2 Sounds like school

track	photo
1	E
2	A
3	G
4	B
5	H
6	D
7	F
8	C

Seite 20   3 Gillian's first day at Lake Park High School

a) I think Gillian is spending the day at Cheryl's high school./is going to school in America.

d) part A: **schedule:** American students have the same lessons every day.
part B: **lockers:** American students have to keep their things in their lockers. They aren't allowed to take bags or food into the classrooms.
part C: **Pledge of Allegiance:** American students look at the American flag when they say the pledge. Everyone puts their right hand on their heart. They say the Pledge every morning.
part D: **cafeteria:** Students eat lunch with their friends in the school cafeteria.
part E: **clubs:** There are more than 40 school clubs at Lake Park High School. For example, there is a dance club and a basketball club.

Seite 22   4 School facts

Gillian is allowed to spend a day at Cheryl's school.
The students can choose an elective.
The students have to put their bags into lockers.
The students aren't allowed to take food into the classroom.
The students have to wait to go to the toilet.
The students have to stand up during the Pledge of Allegiance.
The students are allowed to eat lunch at school.
Gillian can't go to the homecoming dance.

Seite 22   5 Electives

a) I would choose Spanish because I like learning languages.
I would choose video game design because I'm good at programming computers.

b) If you want to work as a secretary, you can choose office skills.
If you are interested in building a table, you can choose the wood/metal working class.

c) At my school there are no electives. But there is a handball club and a football club.

I would like to have a drama club because I like acting.

I'm interested in cooking, so I would also like a home economics elective.

Seite 23   L&L Schulen in den USA

the Pledge of Allegiance: "I pledge allegiance to the Flag of the United States of America, and to the Republic for which it stands, one Nation under God, indivisible, with liberty and justice for all."

Seite 23   6 What to do?

a) Andy cannot decide which elective to choose.

b) 1. Andy is interested in the wood and metal working class, Spanish and video game design.

2. He can choose a different elective during the first three weeks of the semester.

3. He could talk to his best friend Ricardo, who is half-Mexican, in Spanish and his parents would not know what they were saying.

c) There is no guidance counsellor at our school. If I were in Andy's situation, I would talk to one of my other teachers, for example my German teacher, because I really like her.

There is a careers officer at our school, and her job is to help us decide which job to learn after we leave school. She discusses and explains which subjects we should choose so that they can help us later in life. When you go and see her, she will ask you about your hobbies and the things you like and are good at. She always has good ideas and she knows a lot about different jobs.

There is also a teacher who can help you if you don't get along with some of the other teachers.

Seite 23   7 YOUR talk – School life in the USA

a) I think I'd like to talk about electives.

b) – students can choose different electives

– you should choose something you really want to learn

– some examples of electives: wood and metal working class, office skills, home economics (food technology), driver's education, child development, languages (e.g. Spanish)

– At our school, we don't have electives in year 8. But in class 9 we can choose Spanish if we want to. And of course, if we decide to go on to our Abitur, we can choose some of our main subjects.

c) Hello everybody. Today I am going to talk about electives at high schools in the USA.

Students in the USA can, or have to, choose some of their subjects. (But not all of them. Some subjects, like math and English, are a must for everyone, that means that everyone has to take them.) It's not always easy to choose your elective. The important thing is that you should choose something that you really want to learn. You shouldn't choose an elective just because your best friend chooses it.

Let me give you a few examples of electives.

Some electives are very practical, for example the wood and metal working class.

Others are life skills, such as driver's education, where you learn to drive a car, or home economics, where you learn how to cook and prepare food.

As you all know, we don't have the chance to do this at our school in year 8. Some students will choose their subjects for their Abitur, but we can't do that now, we have to wait a few more years before we can do that.

I like the idea of electives. I think it's a good idea to choose subjects that you're interested in because your marks will be better and they can help you get a job later.

Thank you very much for listening. Are there any questions?

Seite 24 8 Acting green at school

a) The students and teachers should walk to school or go to school by bike. Asking the cafeteria staff to buy local foods is a good idea. It would be good to plant a school garden. The students and teachers should recycle rubbish and close windows and doors to save energy.

b) At our school we recycle our rubbish and separate plastic and paper.
   We turn off the lights when we leave a classroom.
   Most of the students come to school by bike or by bus.
   We have planted a school garden.

Seite 25 10 A school project

major (l. 2): bedeutend, wichtig; there's a German word, Major, that's someone important, I think
go green (l. 11): umweltbewusst werden; from the context; I know the words 'go' and 'green'
solar panel (l. 22): Sonnenkollektor; German word solar; from the context (environment, power)
funding (l. 26): Finanzierung; from the context (sponsors, $185,000)

Seite 26 11 Lots of questions

a) 1. Joel Miller is a student at Evans High School who has helped the school to go green.
   2. Evans High School is in Detroit, Michigan.
   3. They have built a living wall, planted trees and installed rain collectors. They have also built a greenhouse where they will grow their own vegetables. The school also has solar panels and an electric school bus.
   4. The school got a $185,000 grant.
   5. Margaret Hall is a biology teacher and she helped to get funding for the project.
   6. She is very proud of the app that she and the students developed. It helps you to save energy in your everyday activities.

c) I like the living wall the most. Fresh air is very important and I think the wall looks nice, too.
   I think the electric school bus is the best because it is one of the first in the country. It is very impressive that they have one.
   I think that the living wall is the most important change that the students have made at Evans High. Having fresh air, especially in a school, where it can sometimes be stuffy and smelly, is a great positive change. Growing their own vegetables will also be a very important change because it will improve the quality of the school dinners. Both of these things will also introduce new wildlife to the school grounds.

Seite 26 12 Cleaning up

a) They found some of Gary's old baseball magazines, some empty milk bottles and a girl's jacket.

b) your baseball magazines: **yours**
   my baseball magazines: **mine**
   his job: **his**
   my jacket: **mine**
   her jacket: **hers**

Seite 27 13 Take action!

a) The clip is about the environment and what we can do to save the planet.

b) **B** (Reuse your carrier bags/shopping bags. Don't throw them away.) Recyle your cans.
   E (Plant a tree in your garden and watch it grow.)
   F (Don't throw bottles away but reuse them. You can use them as flower vases.)

c) Erdbeben: earthquake; Dürre – drought; Hochwasser – flood; Klimawandel – climate change

Seite 28   P1 School words

a) class, schedule, timetable, elective, semester, locker, pass, flag, cafeteria, homecoming
b) prd (period)   D crd (ID card)   Pldg f llgnc (Pledge of Allegiance)

Seite 29   P3 During the break

a) In the middle of the picture two boys are playing football.
   On the left there is a boy. He is wearing a red baseball cap and he is eating a sandwich.
   In the bottom right-hand corner a boy and a girl are holding hands.
   At the top I can see a teacher. He is talking to a girl with a rucksack.
   A boy is sitting on a green bench. He is reading a magazine.
   A boy next to the door is sitting on the stairs.
   The girl with red hair is talking to her friend. She is wearing a pink skirt.
   The girl with the orange schoolbag is waving at the girl in the green trousers.
   A black bird is sitting in the tree.

b) In picture A the two boys are playing football. In picture B they are talking.
   In picture A the teacher is talking to a girl. In picture B he isn't talking to anyone. He is watching all the children.
   In picture A a boy and a girl are holding hands. In picture B they are not looking at each other.
   In picture A the boy on the bench is reading a magazine. In picture B he is reading a book.
   In picture A there is a black bird in the tree. In picture B there is a cat in the tree.
   In picture A the boy on the left, in the blue shirt, is smiling. In picture B he looks very sad.
   In picture A the boy with the red baseball cap is eating a sandwich. In picture B he is drinking lemonade.
   In picture A the girl in the middle of the picture is wearing a red/pink skirt, and her friend has long hair. In picture B the girl is wearing a brown/orange/yellow skirt, and her friend has short hair.
   In picture A there is no bike. In picture B there is a yellow bike.

Seite 29   P4 Lake Park rules

a) 1. Students are allowed to wear jeans to school.
   2. They don't have to wear a school uniform.
   3. They have to do their homework every day.
   4. They aren't allowed to eat during class.
   5. They have to put their bags into their lockers.
   6. They have to carry their ID card at all times.
   7. They aren't allowed to use their cellphones during class.
   8. But they are allowed to use them in the cafeteria.
b) can: are allowed to / can't: aren't allowed to
c) We don't have to put our bags into lockers and we don't have to carry an ID card at all times.
   We aren't allowed to use our mobile phones/cellphones in the cafeteria.

Seite 29   P5 Special interests?

1–D If you are interested in books, you **should** go to the school library.
2–A If you like to invent things, you **should** join the science club.
3–F If you are under 16, you **won't** be allowed to join the driving club.
4–E If you join the basketball club, you **will** learn how to dribble well.
5–B You **should** be good at writing if you want to work for the school newspaper.
6–C You **will** learn how to draw if you join the art club.

Seite 29   P6 A school club

Der Spielmannszug nimmt an vielen spannenden Veranstaltungen teil.

Man kann sich den Fahnenschwingern im Spielmannszug anschließen, wenn man kein Instrument spielt.

Geübt wird das ganze Jahr über montags in der Mittagspause und donnerstags nachmittags.

Seite 30   P7 A "green" word snake

recycle, rubbish, save energy, turn off lights, separate paper

Seite 30   P9 Useful tips

Don't leave the computer on.

Turn off the water.

Close the window if the heating is on.

Recycle your wine bottles and your paper.

Separate your rubbish into paper, plastic and glass.

Don't leave the TV and the radio on.

Close the fridge.

Turn off the heating.

Seite 31   P10 Whose is it?

a) 1. At school Joel has got a locker, it's **his.**
   2. Katie has got a jacket, it's **his.**
   3. Our school has got a greenhouse, it's **ours.**
   4. They have got rain collectors, they're **theirs.**
   5. You have got a job to do, it's **yours.**
   6. I've got a new bike, it's **mine.**

b) 1. In der Schule hat Joel ein Schließfach, er ist seins. / Er hat einen Spind, er ist seiner.
   2. Katie hat eine Jacke, sie ist ihre.
   3. Unsere Schule hat ein Gewächshaus, es ist unseres.
   4. Sie haben Regensammelbehälter, sie sind ihre.
   5. Du hast einen Job zu tun, es ist deiner.
   6. Ich habe ein neues Fahrrad, es ist meins.

c) 1. yours   2. hers   4. his   5. mine   6. ours   7. ours

Seite 31   P11 An advert

Man sollte sein altes Handy nicht wegwerfen, sondern recyceln.

Man kann es z. B. einem Freund/einer Freundin schenken, sodass er/sie es weiter benutzen kann.

Oder man kann es für einen guten Zweck spenden.

Vielleicht kann man es auch verkaufen oder der Handyfirma zum Recyceln geben.

Man sollte allerdings daran denken, die SIM-Karte und alle persönliche Daten zu entfernen, bevor man das Handy weitergibt.

Seite 32 M1 Homecoming week

a) picture 1: the tug-of-war   picture 2: the homecoming dance
picture 3: Pajama Day   picture 4: the pie-eating contest

b) I've read an article about homecoming.
Homecoming is one week at the end of September or beginning of October. It is a very special week for the students in the USA, and I must say that it sounds like a lot of fun.
There are lots of activities, like karaoke and the homecoming dance, sports events and special fun days like Pajama Day, which means that they all come to school in their pajamas.
Students also vote for two students from their school to become homecoming king and queen.

Seite 32 M2 A homecoming week to remember

a) football game – tug-of-war – karaoke – decorating the school – homecoming dance

b) 2. The teams were having a tug-of-war when a dog ate all the pies for the pie-eating contest.
3. The seniors were singing karaoke when the lights went out.
4. The teachers were decorating the school for the homecoming dance when Mrs Cook fell and broke her foot.
5. The students and teachers were dancing at the homecoming dance when someone stole the equipment.
... Then, on Tuesday, the teams were having a tug-of-war when a dog ate all the pies for the pie-eating contest. On Wednesday, the seniors were singing karaoke when the lights went out. But that's not everything. On Thursday, the teachers were decorating the school for the homecoming dance when Mrs Cook fell and broke her foot. And finally, on Friday, the students and teachers were dancing at the homecoming dance when someone stole the equipment! It was the worst homecoming week ever!

Seite 33 M3 School facts

Gillian is allowed to spend a day at Cheryl's school.
The students can/have to choose an elective.
Gillian/Cheryl must/has to remember/The students have to remember a new schedule every day.
The students must/have to put their bags into lockers.
The students are not allowed to/mustn't take food into the classroom.
Cheryl has to wait/The students have to wait to go to the toilet.
The students must/have to stand up during the Pledge of Allegiance.
The students are able to eat lunch at school.
Gillian can't go/isn't able to go to the homecoming dance.

Seite 33 M4 What's different, what's the same?

a)

American high school students ...	Students at our school ...
put their jackets and bags into lockers.	take their jackets and bags into the classroom.
change classrooms after every lesson.	stay in the same classroom the whole day.
can wear jeans to school. → **same!**	can wear jeans to school. → **same!**
have to say the Pledge of Allegiance every day.	don't have to say a Pledge of Allegiance.
can choose an elective.	can't choose electives.
have lunch at school.	usually go home for lunch.
stay at school until 2:40 pm.	stay at school until 1:10 pm.

b) **S1:** I think it's easier to have a locker, because then there is more space in the classroom.

S2: But it also means that you have to go to your locker between classes. That doesn't make life very easy. The thing I like about our school is that we have all our classes in the same room.

S1: Yes, that's true. It means that we don't have to look at our timetable all the time and we don't have to move around so much. But what about lunch? I'm glad I can go home for lunch.

S2: No, I think it would be better to have lunch at school.

Seite 34   M5 A school project

major (l. 2): bedeutend, wichtig; there's a German word, Major, that's someone important, I think

solar panel (l. 5): Sonnenkollektor; German word solar; from the context (environment, power)

greenhouse (l. 11): Treibhaus; from the context; and I know the words 'green' and 'house'

vertical (l. 13): senkrecht, vertikal; similar to German word

row (l. 13): Reihe; from the context and the photo on page 34 in our book

fund/have been funded (l. 15): finanzieren; from the context ($185,000)

organize (l. 24): organisieren; similar to German word

environment (l. 27): Umwelt; similar to French word 'environnement'

is thrilled (l. 32): sich wahnsinnig freuen; from the context

Seite 34   M6 Lots of questions

a) 1. Joel Miller is a 16-year-old student at Evans High School.

   2. Evans High School is in Detroit, Michigan.

   3. They have planted trees and have installed rain collectors. They have their own greenhouse, solar panels that power 20 classrooms and a living wall. The school bus runs on electricity. The school has also developed an app to help people be more environmentally friendly.

   4. The school got a $185,000 grant for the project.

   5. Margaret Hall is a biology teacher and she helped to get funding for the project.

   6. Ms Hall likes the greenhouse because she would like to teach classes there and plant a vegetable garden. A greenhouse will make lessons more exciting.

   7. She is proud of the "Bloom" app, which was developed by the school's computer science class. It helps you to be more environmentally friendly.

   8. Fred Myers is an Earth Day activist.

c) I like the greenhouse the most because I think biology lessons there would be very interesting.

Seite 35   M7 A living wall

a) He is talking to the students at Evans High School.

b) 1. right   2. wrong   3. wrong   4. right   5. right   6. wrong

   2. Living walls are also called **green** walls.

   3. Living walls **can be inside or outside.**

   6. Especially in **winter,** an outside wall can reduce energy costs. It acts as insulation.

c) I have learned a lot about living walls. For example, you can make a living wall inside or outside your house, and it helps to make your house more eco-friendly. Having a living wall outside can help to reduce the amount of money people spend in heating. Having one inside can make the room fresher, because plants produce oxygen. It can help people to focus.

Seite 35   M8 Earth Day

Earth Day is on 22nd April every year.

Gaylord Nelson, an American politician, started Earth Day in 1970, after a large oil spill in California. He wanted to make people think more about the environment.

More than 20 million people took part in that first Earth Day in 1970. Since then, more and more people have taken part in Earth Day each year.

Today, Earth Day is celebrated in more than 190 countries and more than one billion people take part. There are events in many cities in the US, but also in Rwanda, China and Moscow, and Frankfurt am Main and Stuttgart!

The organizers try to do something different every year. In 2014 Earth Day was all about how to make cities greener. The organizers wanted governments to use more wind and solar energy and to stop polluting the water and the air in cities.

In 2015 the motto was "Cradle to Cradle". Earth Day activists wanted companies to produce greener products, products that last longer and that can be recycled again and again. They also showed people how to recycle things.

There is something for everyone on Earth Day. You can go to one of the large events, or you can organize something locally, in your own town, school or village.

I found some of the information at http://www.earthday.org/earth-day-history-movement

Seite 35   M9 An environment cartoon

On the left there are lots of people. They are pushing the planet Earth towards a cliff/over the edge. There is a rope around the Earth. One single person is pulling at the rope to try and save Earth.

I think the cartoonist wants to say that not enough people are trying to save our planet. Most of them are destroying it instead. The cartoon also says that it's almost too late to save our planet. Possible title: Whose side are you on?

Seite 36   Did you get it all?

What do students in the USA do and wear when they get their diploma? **They wear special clothes and hats. They throw their hats in the air because they are so happy that school is over.** (→ Land & Leute, TB Seite 23)

What is an elective? **a subject which you can choose** (→ TB 3, TB Seite 20)

Where does Gillian first meet Brian and Andy? **in the school cafeteria** (→ TB 3, TB Seite 21)

Why did Andy think of choosing the video game design course? **because his best friend Ricardo wanted to choose the video game design course and Andy thought it would be fun to do the same course** (→ TB 6, TB Seite 23)

What does a green wall do? **it filters air** (→ TB 10, TB Seite 25)

What will the cafeteria at Evans High School offer soon? **vegetables from their own greenhouse** (→ TB 10, TB Seite 25)

What subject does Ms Hall teach? **biology** (→ TB 10, TB Seite 25)

What sport does Gary like? **baseball** (→ TB 12, TB Seite 26)

Seite 38   1 Are you hungry?

b) First I'd like vegetable soup, then I'd like pasta with tomato sauce, and for dessert I'd like chocolate cake with vanilla ice cream. (What about you?)

Seite 38   2 Typical American food?

1. People in Alaska eat a lot of fish.
2. A PB&J sandwich is made with peanut butter and jelly.
3. Typical American fast food is a burger and French fries.
4. The lady with the sunglasses doesn't think that there is one typical American dish.
5. In Maryland a lot of people like to put sauerkraut on hot dogs.
6. Some people in New York like bagels.
7. Typical Southern food is fried chicken, green vegetables and mashed potatoes, and a lot of watermelon in the summer.
8. People in Texas eat a lot of meat and love to barbecue.
9. The lady with the grey hair thinks that apple pie is America's favourite dessert.
10. The Asian American girl is a vegetarian.
11. Tex-Mex is Mexican-style food.
12. Loco moco is a Hawaiian dish.

Seite 39   3 Have you ever tried ...?

S1: Have you ever tried peanut butter?
S2: Yes, I have. It was delicious. How about you? Have you ever tried a bagel?
S1: No, I haven't but I'd like to try it. My favourite food is pancakes, have you ever tried them?
S2: Yes, I have. But I didn't like them very much.

Seite 40   4 Yummy or yucky?

a)

delicious	OK	disgusting
– burger and French fries – Sauerkraut on a hot dog – apple pie with ice cream – Tex-Mex – fried chicken with vegetables	– peanut butter and jelly sandwich – chop suey with tofu – pasta with sauce – steak – mashed potatoes	– fish (salmon) – loco moco – bagel – watermelon

b) I'd like to try Tex-Mex because it sounds yummy and very different from anything I've tried before. I like spicy food and I think I would enjoy it.
I wouldn't like to try loco moco because I'm vegetarian, so I think it sounds yucky.

Seite 40   5 Fast food

For me fast food is food that is full of different ingredients./too many ingredients.
For me fast is anything that has been prepared in a factory, not at home.

Seite 41   6 Super Burger

a) **More than 7000** hamburgers are sold most Saturdays.
The most popular burger is **the Roselle Special.**

b) No, I would not allow my kids to eat at a fast food restaurant every day because I don't think it is healthy to eat burgers and other fast food every day.

Seite 41　7 Cheryl's thoughts

1. You really can sit more **comfortably** here than in other burger places.
2. The customers eat more **quickly** here than the guests in normal restaurants.
3. It's better to eat more **slowly** and take your time.
4. You can eat more **healthily** in normal restaurants.
5. I guess my mom can cook more **deliciously** than Super Burger.

Seite 42　8 Customer interviews

a) Cheryl spoke to one man and two women.

b) **customer 1:**
   – eats at Super Burger
     <u>five or six</u> times a week
   – likes the price of the food

customer 2:
   – eats at Super Burger
     twice a month
   – likes <u>their Super Salad</u>

customer 3:
   – <u>two</u> kids
   – eats at Super Burger once
     or twice a week
   – son Sam likes Super Hamburger
     with <u>French fries</u>

Seite 42　9 A restaurant review

a) **Name:** Pizza World
   Address: Karl-Marx-Straße, Hildesheim
   Food: pizza, chicken, desserts
   My favourite meal: farmhouse pizza (€6.50)
   Takeaway: yes
   Delivery: yes
   Music: local radio station
   Service: average
   Your opinion: pretty cool

c) The name of the restaurant I tested is "Pizza World".
   It's in Karl-Marx-Straße in Hildesheim.
   You can get lots of different pizzas, different chicken meals and yummy desserts there.
   My favourite is their farmhouse pizza with mushrooms and ham. That's 6.50€.
   They do takeaway but they don't bring food to your house.
   They play music from the local radio station.
   The service is great. They all know that the farmhouse pizza is my favourite.
   I think the restaurant is pretty cool. I can't wait to go again.

Seite 43　10 A food poem

b) pizza, pizza toppings, baked beans, toast, fish fingers, Sunday roast, burger, ketchup, milkshake, steak and kidney pie, spinach, sauerkraut, bread, butter, cauliflower, fish and chips, hamburger, trifle, (sherry), lamb, mint sauce, (gin and tonic), cheese, biscuits, strawberries, cream, chicken nuggets
   The message of the poem is that the boy is lonely and incomplete without his girlfriend and that he loves her and thinks they belong together.

Seite 43　11 Choose an activity

Your own food poem:　　I like beans, they taste so good.
　　　　　　　　　　　　　They really are my favourite food.
　　　　　　　　　　　　　They're better than fish, they're better than horse ...
　　　　　　　　　　　　　They're even better than chocolate sauce!

Seite 44   12 Time to celebrate

a) – I celebrate Christmas and Halloween.
    – I have never celebrated Thanksgiving, Mardi Gras, St Patrick's Day, Diwali or Eid.
    – I celebrate Halloween on 31st October, and Christmas in December. Sometimes we do some-
      thing fun for St Patrick's Day, but my family aren't Irish, so it isn't really important to us.
    – I've never celebrated Eid, or Diwali, but some of my friends do.
    – Because I don't live in America, I've never celebrated Thanksgiving or Independence Day.
    – Cinco de Mayo is new to me. I have been to Mardi Gras celebrations, but not in New Orleans.

b) **1–E** On Thanksgiving people give thanks for what they have.
    2–D During Eid Muslims celebrate the end of Ramadan.
    3–H On Cinco de Mayo Mexicans in the USA celebrate their culture.
    4–A During Diwali Hindus celebrate the victory of light over darkness.
    5–B On Mardi Gras people wear costumes and dance in the streets.
    6–C On Independence Day there are big parades and lots of people wear red, white and ...
    7–F On St Patrick's Day people celebrate Irish culture and usually wear green.
    8–G For Halloween people decorate pumpkins and wear scary costumes.

c) A special day for me and my family is Easter, when we celebrate new life. We celebrate Easter
    Sunday together, and invite the whole family. We cook a special meal, lamb, beans and potatoes,
    and celebrate by giving each other small presents, like chocolates. We invite my grandparents
    and my mum's sister and her two kids. We sometimes invite my dad's brothers and their families,
    too, but if we do that, we're more than twenty people!

Seite 45   13 Sounds like celebrating

dialogue	special day	words/phrases
1	Halloween	Trick or treat!, scary faces, jack-o'-lantern, salt and vinegar
2	Thanksgiving	the biggest turkey, delicious, stuffing, Stop fighting!, celebration
3	Mardi Gras	parade, carnival, New Orleans
4	Christmas	presents under the tree, I'm so excited., Oh, that's too bad.
5	St. Patrick's Day	a regular bagel with cream cheese, For here or to go?, green

Seite 46   14 Festivals in the USA

a)

festival	food	activities
Chinese New Year	dumplings	have dinner with family and friends, hope to find a coin in one of the dumplings after midnight
Thanksgiving	turkey, mashed potatoes, cranberry sauce, corn on the cob, apple pie	the whole family gets together, go shopping on Black Friday, go to the mall

b) Mondkalender – lunar calendar
    Mitternacht – midnight
    Münze – coin
    Maiskolben – corn on the cob

c) 1. After dinner Lee-Lee and his cousin **always play on Lee-Lee's computer.**
   2. If you find a coin in your dumpling, you **will have a lot of money in your life.**
   3. This year's Thanksgiving Sammy's **uncle from England will be there.**
   4. On Black Friday **Sammy and his parents go shopping.**

Seite 47   15 The first Thanksgiving

a) Christopher Columbus was the first European to find America in 1492. He thought he was in India, so he called the people Indians.

When more groups from Britain and other European countries arrived, they did not know how to look after themselves.

When the Pilgrims had a difficult time in the winter of 1620/1621, two Native Americans who could speak English showed them what they could eat, how to build houses, and how to hunt. To say thank you, the Pilgrims invited everyone to a meal to celebrate their first successful harvest.

b) **P** Over time explorers from all over Europe came to the New World and settled in different parts of North America.

E In 1620 the Pilgrims, a religious group from England, landed at Plymouth Bay in Massachusetts.

O Many of the Pilgrims died from cold and disease because they didn't know how to hunt or what plants to eat.

P Samoset and Squanto, two Native Americans who lived in the area, decided to help the new settlers.

L The Native Americans taught the settlers how to hunt and build houses. They also showed them new animals and plants.

E In October 1621 the Pilgrims invited the Native Americans in the area to celebrate their first harvest.

Seite 48   P2 Sound check

b)

/ e /	/ iː /	/ æ /
bread	peanut	add
jelly	meat	sandwich
healthy	cheap	hamburger
Mexican	people	café
watermelon	Chinese	
menu		

Seite 48   P3 The girl who ...

a) 1. Cheryl is the girl **who** wants to write a report on fast food for the school magazine.
   2. Kathy, **who** works at Super Burger in Roselle, has been the manager for two years.
   3. Her restaurant, **which** is open 24 hours a day, has thousands of customers every day.
   4. A lot of people **who** go to Super Burger order the Roselle Special.
   5. Hamburgers and chicken nuggets are dishes **which** are very popular with kids.
   6. Fresh salads are one kind of fast food **which** is healthy.
   7. The people **who** work at Super Burger have to wear special uniforms.
   8. The uniforms, **which** are red and yellow, look really nice.

b) You use **who** for people, and **which** for things.

Seite 49 P4 The best food in town

a)

busy	busier	(the) busiest
popular	more popular	(the) most popular
hot	hotter	(the) hottest
good	better	(the) best
healthy	healthier	(the) healthiest
nice	nicer	(the) nicest
fresh	fresher	(the) freshest

b) Come and have the **best** burgers at Super Burger.
They're the **healthiest, freshest** and **most popular** in town.
Also try our Super Burger Hot and Spicy Special – the **hottest** burger ever!

Seite 49 P5 Family dinner

My **busy** mum works all day, so my dad has to cook for the family. That's great
because he's a **brilliant** cook. He cooks his meals as **well** as the famous
cooks on TV! I often have to do the shopping for the family. After school I **quickly**
run to the supermarket. Then I sometimes help my dad in the kitchen. Our kitchen
is a very **noisy** place because my dad loves to sing **loudly.** It's horrible, believe
me ... My sister is often **late** for dinner, so my dad looks at her **angrily.**

Seite 49 P6 Think more carefully

1. On Sundays we decorate the breakfast table **more beautifully** than on other days.
2. I use salt **more often** than my brother.
3. My mum can cook **better** than my grandma.
4. I think we eat **more healthily** than my friend's family.
5. I can cut a cucumber **more quickly/faster** than my mum.
6. My sister can eat pizza **faster/more quickly** than I can.

Seite 49 P7 Food signs

Essen gibt es (täglich) bis 23 Uhr.   Das Restaurant ist vollklimatisiert.

Seite 50 P8 Word groups

a) 1. family   4. time
   2. food / Thanksgiving   5. colours
   3. festivals   6. people / cultures / ethnic groups / groups of people
b) **clothes:** pullover – trousers – skirt – T-shirt
   places: school – home – supermarket – restaurant
   sports: hockey – football – tennis – running
   jobs: nurse – teacher – manager – doctor

Seite 50 P10 On special days

a) 1. What does Lee-Lee do after the meal?
   2. When does the family eat Lee-Lee's favourite food?
   3. What is inside one of the dumplings?
   4. What is Sammy's favourite food?
   5. Whose uncle is visiting from England this year?
   6. Why does Sammy like Black Friday best?

b) 1. He plays on his computer with his cousin.
   2. They eat his favourite food (at Chinese New Year) just after midnight.
   3. There's a coin in one of the dumplings.
   4. Sammy's favourite food is their traditional Thanksgiving dinner.
   5. Sammy's uncle is visiting from England this year.
   6. He likes Black Friday because he goes shopping with his parents. He loves going to the mall.

Seite 50   P11 I never eat tomatoes

I sometimes eat peas and potatoes. I often eat toast with jam. And I often eat chocolate. I always eat lots of chips! I never eat meat or fish – I'm vegetarian.

Seite 51   P12 Gillian likes celebrating

1. I like Christmas, especially **when** we put up a Christmas tree and decorate it.
2. We always write Christmas cards **and** send them to friends and family.
3. I also enjoy Halloween **because** I love wearing costumes.
4. There is a great St Patrick's Day Parade in London **but** I've never taken part in it.
5. I'm sure that Rajiv's favourite festival is Diwali **because** he really enjoys the lights and fireworks.
6. What I love most is my birthday **when** friends and family come and give me presents.
7. I don't know much about American festivals **so** I should ask Cheryl about them.

Seite 51   P13 Cinco de Mayo

Was wird denn über das Essen gesagt? Es sollte eine richtige mexikanische Mahlzeit mit selbstgemachter Salsa und Guacamole sein. (Also kein Fast Food.)
„Decorations" heißt Dekoration, richtig? Was wird dazu geschrieben? Man soll mexikanische Dekorationen wir Papierblumen oder Ballons aufhängen und Sachen in den Farben der mexikanischen Flagge (grün, weiß und rot) benutzen.
Und wie soll man sich kleiden? Man soll traditionelle mexikanische Kleidung tragen. Frauen können bunte lange Röcke tragen, Männer einen Sombrero und ein weißes Shirt oder einen Poncho.
Was ist denn eine „piñata"? eine dekorierte Schachtel, mit Süßigkeiten und Spielzeug gefüllt; man hängt sie an die Decke und dann dürfen alle der Reihe nach mit verbundenen Augen und mit Stock dagegen schlagen, damit sie sich öffnet
Dort steht „maracas". Was soll das sein? Das sind Rumba-Rasseln, mit denen man die mexikanische Musik begleitet.

Seite 52   M1 Interviewing Kathy

a) They are talking about special offers at Super Burger.
b) **Cheryl:** Sorry, Kathy, we're back up and running now. Do you have any special offers for kids?
   Kathy: Yes! We sometimes have special offers at the weekend, where children can eat for half price, or sometimes they will get their French fries for free. And of course, we have special meals for kids. The portions are smaller – and cheaper, of course.
   Cheryl: That sounds great! I must come here with my little brother. Thank you Kathy, I've enjoyed speaking to you today.
   Kathy: Thank you. And see you soon!

Seite 52   M2 Why is fast food so popular?

a) To me, it is most interesting that American teenagers eat so much sugar every year. I wonder how much sugar German teenagers eat. It must be a lot, we love fizzy drinks!

b) a small metal container: **can**   the taste that food or drink has: **flavour**

   sweet with bubbles: **fizzy**   not natural: **artificial**

   make something stronger: **strengthen**

c) There is lots of sugar in the drinks that you normally have with your fast food.

   The fast food companies artificially change the colour and flavour of the food and drink.

   The companies also advertise on TV and on the Internet.

   When you buy the meals, kids get free toys.

Seite 53   M3 Customer interviews

a) one man and two women

b) **What do the customers like about fast food?** customer 1: it's cheap / customer 2: it's quick / customer 3: doesn't really like it, but her children love it

   How often do they eat at places like Super Burger? c1: five or six times a week / c2: about twice a month / c3: once or twice a week

   What do they like best? c1: the Roselle Special with French fries and a large coke / c2: the Super Salad / c3: doesn't like the food but her son loves the Super Hamburger with French fries

Seite 53   M4 Fast food: good or bad?

a)

good	bad
– you can eat it quickly	– can be unhealthy
– sometimes it can be healthy; for example, you can order salads	– there is often lots of sugar in the drinks that you have with fast food
– very cheap	– fast food companies try to get kids hooked on fast food by giving away free toys
– can be very tasty	
– fast food every now and again is OK	– sometimes it is better to eat slowly than quickly

b) **S1:** I think that fast food is great because you can eat it so quickly.

   S3: But there is so much sugar in it!

   S2: Not always. You can order lots of different things. Some things, like salads, are healthy.

   S4: That's true, but eating quickly isn't healthy.

   S1: No, I guess you're right. But sometimes it's very important to get somewhere quickly.
      And I think we all agree that fast food often tastes good.

   S4: Maybe, but think about how it affects children. It's such a bad idea.

c) Is fast food good or bad? This is not an easy question.

   Firstly, I think that there is nothing wrong with eating fast food every now and then. It's a fact that fast food is cheap, tasty and quick.

   On the other hand fast food is often unhealthy. In my opinion, people should only have fast food once a month and kids should not eat it at all.

   If you ask me, it is unfair and wrong that fast food companies make kids like fast food by giving them toys and by putting lots of sugar in the food. That's why I think fast food companies sometimes lie about how healthy their food is. They just want more customers.

   All in all, I would say that fast food is quite bad for you and that it is much better not to eat it.

Seite 54   M5 Festivals in the USA

a)

festival	food	activities
Chinese New Year	dumplings	– dinner with family and friends – hope to find coin in one of the dumplings after midnight
Thanksgiving	turkey, mashed potatoes, cranberry sauce, corn on the cob, apple pie	– whole family gets together – go shopping on Black Friday, go to the mall
Kwanzaa	sweet potatoes, peas, chicken and a seafood soup (called gumbo)	– decorate home in black, red and green – wear traditional African clothes – light candles in candle holder kinara – give each other home-made presents

b) Mondkalender – lunar calendar
   Mitternacht – midnight
   Münze – coin
   Maiskolben – corn on the cob
   Meeresfrüchte – seafood
   Mütze – hat

c) 1. After dinner Lee-Lee and his cousin **always play on Lee-Lee's computer.**
   2. If you find a coin in your dumpling, you **will have a lot of money in your life.**
   3. This year's Thanksgiving Sammy's **uncle from England will be there.**
   4. On Black Friday **Sammy and his parents go shopping.**
   5. People celebrate Kwanzaa **from 26th December until New Year's Day.**
   6. A kinara is **a candle holder.**

d) Kwanzaa is all about African traditions and celebrated from 26th December until New Year's Day.
   People eat sweet potatoes, peas and chicken, and a special seafood soup called gumbo.
   People's homes are decorated in the colours of Kwanzaa, that's black, red and green.
   People wear colourful clothes, usually traditional African clothes.
   The number seven is very special during Kwanzaa, which is why the festival is seven days long
   and the word 'Kwanzaa' has seven letters. (An extra 'a' was added to the word to make sure
   it has seven letters.) People have a special candle holder, called a kinara, which holds seven
   candles: three green ones, three red ones and a black one. Every day a candle is lit. The black
   candle is lit first.
   On the last day of Kwanzaa, people give each other presents. You shouldn't buy a Kwanzaa
   present, you should make it yourself.

Seite 55   M6 American English or British English?

a) chips and crisps

b)

British English	American English
sweets	candy
biscuits	cookies
crisps	chips
chips	French fries
tin	can

Seite 55   M7 Different Thanksgiving dinners

a) 1. I think the children in the first picture are saying that they don't like vegetables. Or maybe they are vegetarian and don't like turkey. / I think the children's mum is asking her son and daughter about vegetables for Thanksgiving dinner. I'm sure the boy and the girl don't like vegetables (broccoli and carrots). They think vegetables are disgusting. / "I'm tired already. This is such a lot of work. And it's always me who spends all day in the kitchen." (mum)

2. In the second picture, everyone is shouting at the cat because it has jumped on the table and is hoping to eat some turkey. / I think picture number 2 looks like a happy Thanksgiving dinner that has gone wrong because a cat wants to have some yummy Thanksgiving food, too. / "Oh no, who forgot to close the door to the garden?" (any of the people in the picture)

3. In the third picture, a brother and sister are fighting and shouting at each other, and their parents are telling them to calm down and stop. / It looks like a huge family fight, where the parents are trying to control their children. / "Will you two stop?! You are getting on everybody's nerves." (mother) / "I hate you. I will never talk to you again." (sister to brother) / "The football starts in ten minutes. Ten more minutes, and I'm out of here." (father)

4. In the last picture, everyone seems quite happy. Maybe they are talking about the yummy food on the table. Maybe they are telling each other how happy they are to see each other. / The picture shows a big, happy family who are celebrating Thanksgiving together. They all seem to be very happy. / "Next year there will one more of us at the table." (pregnant woman) / "Here's to all of you. So lovely to see you all again. Thanks for coming, I hope you'll enjoy the food. Dig in." (dark-haired woman with glass of red wine) / "I'm full already." (grey-haired man)

b) picture number 1
   Mum: Look how much food we have for our Thanksgiving dinner!
   Karen: Eww, gross! I hate turkey. It's disgusting. Why is there a dead bird on our table?
   Mum: ... because it's delicious. Now, be quiet or I'll forget that we agreed you didn't have to eat it. I've bought lots of lovely vegetables for you, and I'm going to roast them in the oven.
   Alex: Urgh, vegetables. I hate vegetables. Can I just have turkey and potatoes?
   Mum: *sigh* Why is everyone in this family so picky with their food?!

Seite 56   Did you get it all?

What is a PB&J sandwich? **peanut butter & jelly sandwich** (→ TB 2, TB Seite 38f.)

Where does Loco Moco come from? **Hawaii** (→ TB 2, TB Seite 38f.)

What is the busiest day in Super Burger? **Saturday** (→ TB 6, TB Seite 41)

Why do Sam and his mother sometimes eat at Super Burger? **the Super Hamburger with French fries** (→ TB 8, TB Seite 42, Hörtext)

What do Americans celebrate on 4th July? **Independence Day** (→ TB 12, TB Seite 45)

When can you buy green bagels? **on St Patrick's Day** (→ TB 13, TB Seite 45, Hörtext)

What do Americans eat on Thanksgiving? **turkey** (→ TB 14, TB Seite 46)

When was the first Thanksgiving? **October 1621** (→ TB 15, TB Seite 47)

Seite 58   1 New York City

a) In New York you can go to Central Park. In New York there are people from all over the world.
In New York life must be very busy and hectic.

b) We find it really interesting that there are so many people from different countries in New York.
We all agreed that New York must be a great place not only for sightseeing but for shopping, too.

Seite 58   2 Things to see in New York

I would like to see **Ground Zero** because it sounds interesting and it is very important.
I would like to go to **Fifth Avenue** because I love shopping!
I would like to see **the Statue of Liberty** because it is very famous.
I would like to visit **Broadway** because I enjoy musicals.
I would like to visit **Central Park** because it sounds fun.
I would like to see **Ellis Island** because it would be interesting to learn about immigration to the
US and because I like learning about history.
I'd like to see **the Empire State Building** because it is one of the most famous buildings in the
world.

Seite 59   3 What you can do

If you want to see animals, you can go to Central Park.
If you want to go shopping at 11 pm, you can go to Times Square
If you want to see some modern paintings, you can go to the MoMA/the Museum of Modern Art.
If you want to climb 1,860 steps, you can go to the Empire State Building.
If you want to visit a symbol of freedom, you can go to the Statue of Liberty.
If you want to go to a very expensive street, you can go to Fifth Avenue.

Seite 60   4 A song about New York

a) It's a love song. The singer's girlfriend lives in New York City. The singer lives three hours away.
Their first kiss was on the New York subway, in the middle of the night.
It's late winter in the song ("It's snowing, it's snowing!") but the singer remembers spring,
when he and his girlfriend met for the first time.

b) The singer is happy because he is going to see someone he loves in New York City. He has lots
of happy memories of the city.

c) The singer mentions: the Statue of Liberty, Staten Island Ferry, Central Park, Brooklyn Bridge,
the Empire State Building, Coney Island, Times Square, Rockefeller Center

Seite 60   5 Sights in the city

The clip shows lots of different sights from around New York City, including lots of very famous
buildings, and some important museums.
I'd heard of some of the sights, like the Statue of Liberty and the Empire State Building.
I'd not heard of the High Line Park or the Rockefeller Center.

Seite 62   6 Tourists in New York

a)

	Pierre	Lindsay	Steffen
where from?	France	UK	Germany
first things that come to mind	– lots of skyscrapers – great restaurants	– taxis – multicultural people	– culture – museums like MoMA – Broadway musicals

b)

	Pierre	Lindsay	Steffen
info from reporter	– over 100 skyscrapers in Manhattan – tallest building: One World Trade Center (1,776 feet) – over 20,000 restaurants: different kinds of food because people from all over the world live in NY	– New York is largest city in US, more than 8 million people – 100,000 new immigrants arrive in NY every year, that's why you hear so many different languages	– 40 theatres in and around Broadway – lots of world-class museums

Seite 62   7 Visiting New York

a) Central Park, Chinatown, Times Square

b) My favourite New York sight is Central Park because it is the perfect place to relax. You should go there because it is the ideal place to watch real New Yorkers.
Chinatown is a 'must-see' because the food there is amazing.
The most exciting place in New York is Times Square because there is always something going on 24 hours a day.

Seite 63   8 From Manhattan to the Bronx

a) Bilal Hinawy lives in Manhattan.
Joshua Rodriguez lives in the Bronx.
Paul Beliard lives in Queens.
Marian Jones lives in Brooklyn.
Antonia Siempre lives on Staten Island.

b) Bilal has lived there for eight years./Bilal and Paul have lived there for eight years.
Antonia has been a doctor for many years.
Joshua has never visited his family in Puerto Rico.
Joshua has already watched games in the Yankee Stadium.
Marian has been to many shops for clothes and shoes.
Paul has always been proud to live in Queens.
Bilal and Paul have lived there for eight years.
Antonia, Joshua and Marian have lived in New York all their lives.

Seite 64   10 Quiz time

a) **Who** lives in Harlem? (Bilal)
What does Bilal sell? (hot dogs)
Where can you find lots of little shops? (Brooklyn)
Where does Paul live? (in Queens)
Where did hip hop start in the 1970s? (in the Bronx) / **When** did hip hop start? (in the 1970s)
When did Bilal move to New York? (seven years ago)
When did Antonia's grandparents come to America? (in 1912)
Why is Marian glad to get back to Brooklyn in the evening? (Because there are lots of trees and parks in Brooklyn and it's not so loud and busy.)
Why does Antonia think of her grandparents when she sees the Statue of Liberty? (Because they came from Italy in 1912 and the Statue of Liberty was the first thing they saw when they arrived at Ellis Island.)

b) **S1:** Who speaks Spanish at home?

S2: Joshua, right? OK, my turn. Where can you find lots of little shops?

S1: Umm, that's Brooklyn, isn't it? OK, my turn again. Where does Paul live?

S2: That's Queens, right? Do I get to ask a question now? OK! When did Bilal move to New York?

S1: Seven years ago. OK, last question! Where does Antonia work?

S2: Well, she lives on Staten Island, but she works in Manhattan.

Seite 66   12 YOUR life

I live in Düsseldorf with my mum and my brother, Andreas.

I get up at 6:30 am and I have breakfast at 6:45. I leave the house at 7:00.

In my free time I watch TV or play with my friends. On Tuesdays I go swimming.

I have to clean my room and walk the dog. I don't have a room of my own, I share with my brother.

I have my own mobile phone, but I don't have my own computer or TV.

Seite 66   13 Different lives

a) Allimar and Raúl both have to work to help their families.

They are growing up without their mums. They both have brothers and sisters.

They have no water in their homes. Their homes don't have any electricity.

They both go to school.

Their families are quite poor. Life isn't easy for them.

b) 2. wrong / Allimar's mother works in Saudi Arabia.

3. wrong / Allimar washes the dishes in the river.

4. wrong / She has a radio.

6. wrong / Raúl hangs on to the back of the bus because he has no money.

7. wrong / He does not have a TV at home.

8. wrong / He does not earn a lot of money.

c) The little one is five and the other is seven years old. → The little brother is five.

It's only a small one with rice and vegetables. → It's only a small meal with rice and vegetables.

I clean shoes all morning, mostly expensive ones from business people. → I clean shoes all morning, mostly expensive shoes from business people.

My sisters share a bed – it's the one that belonged to our parents. → My sisters share a bed – it's the bed that belonged to our parents.

Seite 67   14 Sebastian's life

a) I think Sebastian is from somewhere is South America, maybe Argentina.

b) His life doesn't look very comfortable. I think he lives on the street. I'm sure he doesn't go to school.

c) **Where does he live?** in Rio, Brazil

Who earns the money for the family? Sebastian

What does Sebastian do to earn some money? watches cars to make sure nobody steals them, helps old ladies with their shopping, sells things that he finds

What else can you understand? Sebastian and his younger brother sleep under a bridge. If Sebastian doesn't have to work on a Saturday, he and his brother watch football games on TVs in shop windows. They play football, too, but sometimes a policeman tells them to leave. Sebastian looks for food that other people have thrown away. He sometimes finds it difficult to look after his brother, Paulo, who is just six years old. He has to look after him because their mother died and their father left. Sebastian doesn't go to school and he can't read.

d) If I could give Sebastian a present, it would be somewhere to live because if he and his brother had a house, they wouldn't have to fight other boys, and they wouldn't have as many worries.
If I could give Sebastian a present, it would be books, so that he could learn to read and maybe get a better job in the future.
I think that having a proper house or somewhere to live would make Sebastian's life better.
I also think he would like to have an education and more food.

Seite 67 15 A letter

Dear Mum,

How are you? We all miss you so much.

Let me tell you what has happened in the last four weeks.

Dad is still working hard. That means that I do all the jobs you usually do! In the mornings, I get up early and make a fire and collect water for tea. Then I make bread and wake everyone up for school.

School is OK. I found Saudi Arabia on a map.

After school, we all come home and eat lunch. After that I wash the dishes and collect wood. Then we eat a small meal in the evening. Yesterday we had extra some rice that Dad brought home!

I did all my homework last night before I went to bed. I then listened to the radio you sent. It's cool!

When are you coming home? I miss you.

Love, Allimar xxxx

Seite 68 16 Fairtrade

a) Yes, I've seen the logo before. They put it on bananas at the supermarket.
It's a logo that tells you that the food is better. I think they pay people more to grow it.
b) The website is about Fairtrade in general and about the Fairtrade Mark.
c) **Fairtrade wants to** make sure that farmers and producers are paid fairly for their work. That way they can look after and feed their families, and save money for the future.
The Fairtrade Mark helps to show people that a product has been produced fairly and that the farmers and producers have been paid fairly.
d) A Fairtrade School teaches students about Fairtrade. A school has to meet five criteria in order to become a Fairtrade School: → WB 16.
A Fairtrade Town is a town which supports Fairtrade. The town's shops and restaurants must sell/ offer Fairtrade products. There are many in Germany, e.g. Saarbrücken, Eberswalde, Dortmund.
Buying Fairtrade products is a way to support Fairtrade. You can ask your local supermarket to offer more Fairtrade products.

Seite 69 17 Helping small farmers

a) The banana farmers now get enough money for their work and products. They can support themselves and their families. They have also some extra money, which they use for special projects, like building better roads. They now also use fewer chemicals on their farms.
b) 1. Fairtrade organizations give banana farmers in the Windward Islands a **fair** price.
2. Now the farmers have enough money for themselves and their **families.**
3. They also get extra **money** for special **projects.**
4. Now the farmers also use **fewer** chemicals.
5. Today **85%** of the banana farmers in the Windward Islands are Fairtrade **producers.**

Seite 70   P1 City life

a) cars, lots to see, sights, lots of people, lots of cultures, tourists, theatres, shops, busy, roads, streets, parks, restaurants, cafes, cinemas, subway/Underground, airport, department store, factory, sightseeing, dirty, skyscrapers, dangerous, traffic, people everywhere

b)

positive	negative
– lots to see	– expensive flats
– lots of different cultures	– people can be more unfriendly
– lots to do	– often more crime than in the country
– easy to travel with public transport	– lots of traffic
– lots of choice of where to eat or go shopping	– not enough green spaces
– life is more exciting	– can be more stressful

Seite 70   P4 Working with a map

1. Times Square is on **Broadway.**
2. Brooklyn Bridge goes across the **East River.**
3. Chinatown is part of **Manhattan.**
4. Coney Island is part of **Brooklyn.**
5. The Rockefeller Center is on **Fifth Avenue.**
6. Manhattan is between **the Hudson River and the East River.**

Seite 71   P5 Facts about yourself

a) I have already visited New York.
   I have never gone up a skyscraper.
   I have never painted a picture.
   I have never drawn graffiti.
   I have already eaten a bagel.
   I have never met an American.
   I have already visited a museum.
   I have already been on a ferry.

Seite 71   P6 Definitions

A **park** is a place where it is quiet and where there are trees.
A **shop** is a place where you can buy things.
A **mother** is a person who loves you./who has brought a child into the world.
A **doctor** is a person who helps ill people.
A **stadium** is a place where you watch live sport.
An **aunt** is a person who is a sister of your mother or father.

Seite 71   P7 "Oh no, it's all in German ..."

The tour guide's name is Kai Müller.
The tour will take about two and a half hours.
We can eat lunch at one o'clock.
He will show us some important sights of Berlin and will explain the history of the places.
We can just ask him if we have any questions.

Seite 72   P8   Odd one out

a) 1. brother   4. oil lamp
    2. village   5. shoeshine boy
    3. Mexico City   6. meal

b) 1. "Brother" is the odd one out because it is not a job.
    2. "Village" is the odd one out because you can't travel in it.
    3. "Mexico City" is the odd one out because it is not a country.
    4. "Oil lamp" is the odd one out because it does not need electricity.
    5. "Shoeshine boy" is the odd one out because it is not a word for a person in your family.
    6. "Meal" is the odd one out because it is not a time of day.

c) sister · daughter · aunt · grandad (grandad is the odd one out because it is not a woman.)
    cucumber · banana · Fairtrade · chocolate (Fairtrade – because you can't eat it.)

Seite 72   P9   Sound check

a) 1. Allimar has a sister and two brothers.
    2. Her father doesn't earn enough money.
    3. Raúl cleans shoes in Mexico City.

Seite 72   P10   Raúl from Mexico City

In the morning Raúl's sisters go to the market place and collect **some** water for the family. Raúl doesn't have **any** breakfast. He leaves the house and gets on a bus to town. He doesn't have **any** money so he hangs on to the back of the bus. In the city Raúl earns **some** money because he cleans shoes all morning. Before he goes to school, he has **some** rice and beans at home. They don't have **any** electricity in their house so when it's too dark to read, Raúl goes to bed.

Seite 72   P11   Don't repeat it, please

1. Have you seen my sneakers? They are the red **ones** with the white label.
2. This bus is more comfortable than the **one** we usually take.
3. Most students at my school take the bus from the city centre. The others take the **one** from …
4. Our new kitchen is bigger than the **one** in our old house – and I have to clean it!
5. Our flat has three bedrooms and my sister and I sleep in the two smallest **ones.**
6. This computer is much faster than the **one** we use at school.

Seite 73   P12   Which ones?

a) 1. Every morning Allimar makes a fire. It's only a small **one** to heat the water.
    2. The country where Allimar's mother lives is much bigger than the **one** where her children live.
    3. Allimar wants to become a teacher. She loves children, especially the little **ones.**
    4. Every morning Raúl gets on a bus. It's the **one** that goes to the city centre.
    5. The shoes Raúl cleans are much more expensive than the **ones** his parents owned.
    6. Raúl loves books, especially exciting **ones.**

b) 1. Every morning Allimar makes a fire. It's only a small **one** to heat the water.
    2. The country where Allimar's mother lives is much bigger than the **one** where her children live.
    3. Allimar wants to become a teacher. She loves children, especially the little **ones.**
    4. Every morning Raúl gets on a bus. It's the **one** that goes to the city centre.
    5. The shoes Raúl cleans are much more expensive than the **ones** his parents owned.
    6. Raúl loves books, especially exciting **ones.**

Seite 73   P13 A bake sale party

a) Die Klasse 10E veranstaltet einen Kuchenverkauf für die Schüler- und Lehrerschaft, Eltern und Freundinnen und Freunde. Es gibt leckere Muffins, Kuchen und Kekse, alle mit Fairtrade-Produkten gebacken.

Der Verkauf findet statt am 21. Januar von 15.30 Uhr bis 17.30 Uhr in der Haverstock Schule. Ziel der Aktion ist es, Geld für Fairtrade zu sammeln.

b) Die Klasse hat die Fairtrade-Produkte in einem Fairtrade-Supermarkt gekauft und die Kuchen in ihrer Freizeit gebacken. In Erdkunde führte die Klasse ein Projekt über Fairtrade-Lebensmittel durch und hat dabei viel gelernt.

Das Geld geht an eine Wohltätigkeitsorganisation, die afrikanische Bauern unterstützt.

Die Organisation hilft den Bauern auch dabei, die Fairtrade-Produkte hier zu vertreiben.

Der Kundin kauft fünf Kekse und ein Exemplar der Backrezepte der Klasse.

Seite 74   M1 A graffiti artist

a) There aren't any graffiti paintings in my area, I don't remember ever seeing any. That's probably because I live in a small village where everybody knows each other.

I think that most graffiti is messy and makes a town look dirty. Sometimes graffiti is more like art, and people can make very clever pictures, but normally it's just teenagers who can't draw.

c) 1. The first graffiti / The history of graffiti
2. Keith Haring's beginnings / Who is Keith Haring? / Keith Haring – chalk, not spray
3. Doing things differently / Haring's works / From street artist to famous star
4. Making a change / Making the world a better place / Haring managed to change the world

d) Keith Haring was a graffiti artist who changed people's opinions on graffiti.

He was born in 1958 and died in 1990, at the age of 31.

Haring was one of the first graffiti artists in New York. The special and unusual thing about Haring's pictures was that he didn't spray his pictures, he used chalk instead.

People often watched Haring drawing his pictures. They often asked him what they meant, but the only answer Haring gave them was: "That's up to you."

Haring's pictures became famous and were sold to museums all over the world.

Seite 75   M2 Graffiti in New York

a) 1. People asked Keith Haring questions about his graffiti.
2. Haring would usually give them an answer like "That's up to you."
3. Graffiti vandalism was costing the people of New York thousands of dollars.
4. After a while the city authorities started to give graffiti artists more space.
5. They also offered artists special graffiti workshops.
6. Museums paid Haring lots of money for his paintings.

b) 1. People asked Keith Haring questions about his graffiti.
2. Haring would usually give them an answer like "That's up to you."
3. Graffiti vandalism was costing the people of New York thousands of dollars.
4. After a while the city authorities started to give graffiti artists more space.
5. They also offered artists special graffiti workshops.
6. Museums paid Haring lots of money for his paintings.

Seite 75   M3 A visit to New York

Dear Leila,

How are you? I haven't heard from you in ages!

I'm just writing to tell you about my trip to New York last week. It was really amazing!

I went with my mum and dad and we tried to visit as many sights as possible.

We saw the Statue of Liberty (because you have to in New York!) and we visited Ellis Island, because I love all that American history. We also visited Chinatown, because my dad and I love Chinese food!

We did most of our travelling on the subway, but we had to get the ferry to the Statue of Liberty and Ellis Island, because they're islands!

We ate so much food! There are lots of bagel shops and people selling food on the streets. I kept stopping to buy pretzels and ice creams!

It wasn't all fun though! We went to see the Empire State Building while we were there, but it was so busy! I absolutely hated it!

I hope you're enjoying your holiday in Turkey, but I guess you'll already be home when you read this!

See you soon, Dan

Seite 75   M4 From Manhattan to the Bronx

Bilal and Paul have lived there/in New York for eight years.

Joshua has already watched games in the Yankee Stadium.

Antonia has been a doctor for many years.

Paul has always been proud to live in Queens.

Joshua has never visited his family in Puerto Rico.

Marian has lived in New York all her life.

Seite 75   M5 The princess of Queens

a) The "princess of Queens" is Helen.

b) 1. Helen's whole family is from **Greece.**

   2. Queens is famous because **there are many restaurants there that serve food from all over the world.**

   3. Most guests come from **the local neighbourhood.**

   4. Helen really enjoys **the cool mix of people in Queens.**

   5. Her parents love **to speak Greek with their guests.**

   6. Although Queens is such a big place, **Helen likes living there./it feels good to live there.**

Seite 76   M6 Different lives

a) All three families find it difficult to make enough money.

   Allimar, Raúl and Miriam have to work to help their families.

   All three of them have brothers and sisters.

   They have no water in their homes.

   They all go to school.

   Their families are quite poor.

   Life isn't easy for them.

   Miriam and Allimar both live in villages and their families have farms.

b) 1. Allimar's mother went to Saudi Arabia because her husband/Allimar's father (is a farmer and) doesn't earn enough money to feed the whole family.

2. Allimar has to work so much in the house because her mother is away, in Saudi Arabia.

3. Raúl has to hang on to the back of the bus because he doesn't have enough money to pay for the bus./doesn't have enough money for a bus ticket.

4. Raúl tries to earn more than 100 pesos a day because 100 pesos isn't really enough money to feed six people.

5. Miriam only has two more years of school because she will then be 14 and her parents say that she will then be old enough to look after the house and her brothers and sisters.

6. Miriam wants to go to school for longer because she doesn't want to work on her family's farm. She would prefer a job that would make her happy.

c) The little one is five and the other is seven years old. → The little **brother** is five.

It's only a small one with rice and vegetables. → It's only a small **meal** with rice and …

I clean shoes all morning, mostly expensive ones from business people. → I clean shoes all morning, mostly expensive **shoes** from business people.

My sisters share a bed – it's the one that belonged to our parents. → My sisters share a bed – it's the **bed** that belonged to our parents.

The village we live in is a very small one without a market or a school. → The village we live in is a very small **village** without a market or a school.

I want to have a different job, one that would make me happy. → I want to have a different job, **a job** that would make me happy.

Seite 77   M7 Think about it!

a) If I had to sleep on the floor, I would be shocked.

If I had to do the cooking at home, I would feel angry.

If I had to live without electricity, I would be bored very quickly, I think.

If I had to collect water every morning, I would soon be very tired.

If I couldn't go to school, I would be angry and disappointed.

If I couldn't live with my mum, I would feel sad and frightened.

If I couldn't meet my friends in the afternoon, I would feel sad and frustrated.

If I couldn't choose my job, I would be angry.

b) If I lived in a developing country, I would be very happy to go to school.

If there was no Internet, there would be a library in every village.

If dogs ruled the world, my cat would be sad.

Seite 77   M8 A diary entry

(Allimar) It's nine o'clock and I'm really tired. It was a long day again today with lots of work.
In the morning, I woke up at half past five and started the fire.
Then I went and collected water for tea and made bread for everyone. While I was making the bread, the fire went out, so I had to start again. I tried to wake everyone up for school, but Ganesh took ages to wake up. Finally, after breakfast, we all went to school.
At school we learnt about geography, and the other countries in the world. I found Saudi Arabia on a map. Mum, I miss you. – After school, we all came home and had lunch. It wasn't very good. After lunch I washed the dishes in the river. Meera helped me. We then all collected wood for the fire. When we got back, it was time for our evening meal. It was only a small one, but we enjoyed it: rice and vegetables. It tasted a lot better than lunch.
I've just finished my homework. All ready for tomorrow. I'm listening to the radio.
I'll go to bed in a minute, because it is very dark and I'm tired. Good night.

Seite 77   M9 The Fairtrade Mark

The logo might show the balance between people growing things and people eating the things.
The blue field could symbolize blue skies, meaning happiness in the future for the people working with Fairtrade. It could also symbolize water, because water is very important in farming.
If you look at the black bit in the middle, it could be a person with their arm in the air, waving at you. It could symbolize that people are at the centre of everything that Fairtrade does.
People's lives are more important than money and profits.
The green bit on the left looks like a leaf, so it might symbolize nature and farming.
I think it is important that the logo is a circle. The circle could symbolize our planet. We're all in this together. What goes around, comes around.

Seite 77   M10 Raising money

a) They are talking about raising money for Fairtrade./a project to raise money for Fairtrade.
b) **What ideas have the students got?**
   – friendly football match with Fairtrade football
   – Fairtrade breakfast for students and teachers in the school cafeteria
   – a bake sale

What is Oliver's problem? doesn't understand what a bake sale has to do with Fairtrade
What is the answer to Oliver's problem? use Fairtrade products for the cakes and cookies: Fairtrade chocolate, cocoa, sugar, nuts, bananas; the tea and coffee should be Fairtrade, too
What else can you understand? will decorate their stall with flags and balloons; will put up posters about Fairtrade to inform their guests

Seite 78   Did you get it all?

What is the tallest skyscraper in NYC? **the new One World Trade Center** (→ TB 2, TB Seite 59)
Where can you find a zoo in Manhattan? **in Central Park** (→ TB 2, TB Seite 58)
What does the Empire State Building look like on St Patrick's Day? **It is green./It is lit up with green lights.** (→ TB Seite 60)
How can you get to Staten Island? **with the Staten Island Ferry** (→ TB Seite 61)
What is Bilal's job? **He has a hot dog stall.** (→ TB 8, TB Seite 63)
What does Raúl do to earn money? **He cleans shoes.** (→ TB 13, TB Seite 66)
Why does Allimar miss her mother? **She lives and works in Saudi Arabia.** (→ TB 13, TB Seite 66)
Where do Sebastian and his brother sometimes watch football matches? **on TVs in shop windows** (→ TB 14, TB Seite 67, Hörtext)

Seite 80   1 Many people, one nation

a) As far as I know, people from all over the world live in the US.

    I believe the US is very popular with immigrants from all over the world.

b) I think the number of illegal immigrants is the most interesting thing.

    I didn't know that so many Americans spoke Spanish.

c) 1. You need a green card to live and work in America.

    2. About 318 million people live in the US.

    3. Most illegal immigrants are from Mexico or other countries in South and Central America.

    4. Malcolm X and Martin Luther King fought for the rights of black Americans in the 1960s.

    5. A lot of Chinese people came to the US in the 1880s to work on the railroads.

    6. Most of the first settlers came from England.

    7. Some signs are in English and Spanish because in some places more than one third of the population only speaks Spanish.

    8. There are about 2.5 million Native Americans in the US today.

Seite 82   2 All kinds of people

13 per cent of the population in the US are Black and African Americans.

In the US there are fewer Asian Americans than Black and African Americans, but more White Americans (including Hispanics and Latinos) than any other group.

I find it surprising that there are more Asian people in the US than Native Americans.

Seite 82   3 Leaving home

a) **Photo number one** shows a line of children and men who are holding pots and pans. They are wearing loose clothes and some of the girls are wearing headscarves. I think they are waiting for something, maybe food or water. They look sad, scared and maybe a bit bored.

    Picture 2 shows a man with his two dogs. I think he is somewhere in the mountains. He is wearing shorts and a hooded sweater. He is carrying a backpack. He looks very happy.

    Picture number 3 shows two scientists in a lab. They are looking at something on a piece of glass, maybe results from an experiment. They are wearing colourful rubber gloves. They look excited because they've done something interesting.

    In **photo four** two people, a man and a woman, are hugging. You can see the woman's face but not the man's face, only his back. There is an American flag in the background, so it might be at an airport or at a train station. The woman seems very happy. I would say that the man and the woman haven't seen each other for a very long time.

b) war in home country; go and live with a partner; live in a nicer/warmer country; start a new job

    People move to another country to be with their families, or because their families back home won't talk to them anymore and they want to get as far away from their families as possible.

    People move because they have found a new and better job in another country, or because they think it might be easier to find a job there.

    Some people just like the adventure of being somewhere new.

    Sometimes people want to get away from something, e.g. a war or a dangerous government.

    People leave their home country because they are hoping for a better life somewhere else.

c) war, love, work, food, money

Seite 83   4 Family histories

a)

name	family from	why they left	experiences
Mohamed	Somalia	civil war	– misses farm in Somalia – father has to work very hard
Kim	Vietnam	to join family in USA	– found it hard learning English – missed friends from home
Sergio	Chile	so that his dad could work as a doctor	– misses his mother – was very shy at first

b) **Mohamed**'s family is from Somalia. They left Somalia because of a civil war. Mohamed misses Somalia, especially the farm where they lived. In America, his father has to work very hard so that there is enough money for all of them.

Kim's family is from Vietnam. They left Vietnam because their relatives in the USA said they should come and join them. At the beginning, Kim had a lot of problems at school.

Sergio's family is from Chile. Sergio came to the USA to be with his father, who is a doctor and couldn't find a job in Chile. Sergio's mum is still in Chile, and Sergio often misses her.

Seite 84   5 Learning English

a) Kim, Sergio, Mohamed
b) A: Sergio
   B: Mohamed
   C: Kim

Seite 84   6 A new beginning

I think I would miss my old friends.
I think I would have to learn a new language.
I think I would have to find a new home.
I think I would have to get used to life in another country.

Seite 84   7 What are they like?

a) The first picture shows the stereotype that all Americans drive big, expensive cars.
   The second picture shows the stereotype that Americans eat fast food and burgers all the time.
   I think I've heard a stereotype that Americans watch a lot of TV. I've also heard that Americans are really patriotic. At school they have to say the Pledge of Allegiance every day.
b) Lots of people think that Germans drink beer and eat sausages all the time.
   And they think that all Germans wear Lederhosen all the time.
   Some people think that Germans are always on time and really logical.
   Germans are very direct. They will tell you what they think, about you and the things you do.
   German people often stare at strangers.
   Germans don't like to be late. It is very important for Germans to be on time.
   Germans don't like it if you wash your car or hang out your washing on a Sunday.
   Germans sort their rubbish, they separate paper, glass, cans, plastic and compost.
   The environment is very important to Germans. – Rules are very important for Germans, too.
c) I don't think it's true that Germans don't have a sense of humour. I just think that different nationalities find different things funny.
   I think it's funny that people think Germans are always on time. I'm always late!
   I believe it's true that Americans drive bigger cars than Germans. I've seen it on TV.

Seite 85 8 Do as the Americans do …

a) I find it surprising that Americans say sorry if someone bumps into them. In Germany we never do that! But in Germany it is also rude to stare and bad to cheat.

b)

DOs	DON'Ts
Do say good morning to people you know.	Don't cycle on the pavement or on the wrong side of the road.
Do give tips to waiters and waitresses.	Don't be late.
Say your name when you answer the phone.	Don't expect a queue at the bus stop.
Say Sie to people in shops.	Don't wish anybody a happy birthday before the actual day of their birthday.
Do respect a red traffic light and wait for a green light even if there isn't a car anywhere.	Don't be surprised if people get straight to the point, which others might find rude.

Seite 85 9 This land is your land

b) The music sounds happy. I think the song is about America and all the different parts of it.
The song is about how America is a good home.
I don't like the melody but I like the lyrics.
The singer seems happy and proud to be American and to live in the United States.
The fact that "This land was made for you and me" is repeated again and again shows that the singer feels that the land belongs to all of us, not just to some of us.

c) The USA is described as a beautiful country. The singer talks about large fields, the desert and the very long roads. He mentions Redwood Forest, New York, the Gulf Stream and California.

Seite 85 10 Choose an activity

What would you take with you if you were going to live in another country?

– clothes for any weather (clothes might be a lot more expensive in my new country, so I think it's a good idea to take clothes with me; also, I don't know the weather conditions in my new country yet)

– a cosmetics bag, full of things to wash with (it will be important to look good and clean on my first day of school in my new country; I might want to go for a job interview so I would want to look and smell clean; it is very important to make a good impression when you arrive somewhere new)

– a torch, to help me see in the dark (I don't know where I will stay when I arrive in my new country; maybe there will be many other people, too, so I won't be able to switch on the light if I need to go to the toilet in the middle of the night, so a torch will be very useful; also, I will be able to read my book when everybody else is sleeping)

– maps, for when I don't know where a particular place or street is (I might want to look at a place to work, so it will be useful to have a map so I can check where it is before I call or email them)

– a picture of my family, because I would miss them (photos are really important for me; I'm afraid I wouldn't remember what my grandparents look like if I haven't seen them for a few months; I hope that my mum and dad and my sister would be with me so I don't think I would need photos of them)

– a smartphone, because then I could call my friends back home (or send them texts or emails; I think I would sometimes be homesick, so it would be great if I could get in touch with people back home)

Seite 86   11 Native Americans

tribes, pow-wows, tepees, reservations, buffalo, hunting, ceremonies and traditions, wigwam, tomahawk, totem pole, squaw, Apache, Sioux, Karl May, Winnetou

Seite 86   12 Then and now

a) 1–E 2–G 3–F 4–H 5–A 6–B 7–C 8–D

b) Native Americans who lived in cold regions hunted seals.

Some tribes built totem poles which showed pictures and told stories.

The Grand Canyon Skywalk is a bridge that you can see through.

The Lakota wear headdresses that are made of feathers.

Pow-wows are festivals which are celebrated by Native Americans today.

A teepee is a house which Native Americans built when they went hunting.

Many Native Americans who live in the North are Inuit.

Seite 87   13 A bus trip to ...

a) the Grand Canyon Skywalk (= picture number 1)

b) **name:** the Grand Canyon Skywalk

how long to build: almost four years

how many people: can hold 800 people but only 120 people allowed on at a time

how high: 4000 feet

other information: – glass made by German company

– money goes to Hualapai tribe and will help them improve their lives

– tourists must wear special shoes to protect the glass

Seite 88   L&L Die ersten Amerikaner

vermutlich zu Fuß über die Beringstraße, eine damals noch trockene Landbrücke zwischen Sibirien und Alaska; später wurde daraus eine Meerenge, also Überquerung mit Booten

Seite 88   14 The history of the Native Americans

a) – No one knows when, but the first Native Americans walked to America from Siberia in Asia.

– There were/are lots of different tribes and cultures. Some hunted buffalo by making them run over cliffs, others caught fish and used red cedar trees to build houses, boats and totem poles.

– When the white settlers arrived, about a million Native Americans were living north of Mexico.

– Lots of Native Americans died from European diseases. They had to fight for their land but in the late 1800s the government made them live on reservations.

– Over the next 100 years, they tried to fight for their rights. Now there are more than 550 Native American tribes. These tribes are recognized by the US government.

– They still live on reservations but try to keep their languages, traditions and cultures alive. They also try to make living conditions better. They celebrate old religious ceremonies, make sand paintings and try to use traditional art forms.

b) 1. wrong / The first people in America were hunters from Siberia.

2. right

3. right

4. wrong / In the late 1800s the US government forced Native Americans to live on reservations.

5. wrong / Today there are more than 550 tribes in the US.

6. right

Seite 89   15 A Native American

b) Meet Tawny
Keeping up traditions
Tawny's hopes and dreams for the future

c) **Name:** Tawny Hale
Age: 16
Family: lives with sister (Leya), father (Ben) and grandparents
Home: Pico Riviera, California
School: – Salazar High School
– favourite subjects: math, English, health and US history
– most students are Mexican Americans
Hobbies: – alternative rock and hip hop
– going to the mall with friends after school
– taking part in traditional dances and ceremonies
– making her own outfits
Plans for future: – wants to go to college after school but isn't sure what she wants to study
– wants to be a spokesperson for her people

d) Marc is 13 years old. He lives in Kassel and goes to the Süd-Kassel-Gesamtschule.
He lives with his mum, his dad and his two sisters Anna and Maria.
His hobbies are football, swimming and drawing. He plays football with his friends all the time.
He would like to be a car technician because he likes cars and finds electronics really interesting.

Seite 89   16 YOUR talk – Native Americans

a) I think I'd like to talk about reservations.

b) – in the late 1800s, the US government forced Native Americans to live on reservations
– were/still are controlled by the government; even today, Native Americans live on reservations
– many people without jobs, alcohol problems
– some reservations have schools, factories, shops etc.
– their goals/plans for the future: upkeep of traditions, improving life, representation

c) Hello everybody. My talk is about Native American reservations.
In the late 1800s, the US government forced Native Americans to leave their land and move onto reservations. Reservations are specific areas for Native Americans. Reservations were originally introduced so the government could watch the Native Americans and control what was going on.
Nowadays, lots of Native Americans still live on reservations all over the US.
There are many problems. Many people don't have jobs, and lots of them turn to alcoholism. But things are getting better. Lots of young Native Americans are learning how to make their communities better for everyone. People are learning and more jobs are being created. Lots of Native Americans now work in the tourist trade, showing people how they live. They keep their old traditions and crafts alive for the next generation.
Thank you for listening. Do you have any questions?

Seite 90   P1 Opposites

a) legal–**illegal**   difficult–**easy**   interesting–**boring**   large–**small**
poor–**rich**   unimportant–**important**   friendly–**unfriendly**   fast–**slow**
safe–**dangerous**   cheap–**expensive**   modern–**old**   quiet–**loud**

b) illegal immigrants, easy homework, boring film, small town, rich family, important person, unfriendly man, slow car, dangerous road, expensive dress, old house, loud music

Seite 90 P2 A word game

a) ill, alien, leg, grant gram, game tame, get mill, mile, train, team, maim, stem, steam, grime, strain, rain, range, rail, grime, grin, gel, gale, till, time, mate

Seite 90 P3 Rhyming pairs

year – here	two – shoe
came – same	find – kind
win – bin	they – pay
four – door	and – stand
free – three	read – need
fought – taught	group – soup

Seite 90 P4 Nouns from verbs

a)

verbs	nouns
inform	information
invent	invention
organize	organization
invite	invitation
decorate	decoration
present	presentation
product	production
celebrate	celebration

b) The "e" goes away/is dropped when the verb turns into a noun.

Seite 91 P6 Hopes and dreams

I hope I will live in an exciting city! Perhaps I will work as a tour guide. I'm sure I won't have children but I think I will be married.

Seite 91 P7 Special signs

Das erste Schild zeigt an, in welcher Richtung der Strand zeigt.
Das Schild darunter besagt, dass Hunde an der Leine geführt werden müssen.
Das dritte Schild informiert darüber, dass der Bahnhof wegen eines Notfalls geschlossen ist.
Das letzte Schild warnt vor dünnem Eis bzw. Einsturzgefahr.

Seite 92 P8 Letter detective

a)

-ea	-ee	-oo
seals	meeting	school
area	teepee	igloo
headdress		
wear		

b)

-ea	-ee	-oo
meal, lead, eat, teach, bear, year	bee, teenager, see, wheel, feel, feet	pool, look, took, book, cool, boot

c) When I was much younger, I was afraid of bees.

We see our English teacher every Monday, Wednesday and Friday.

The bear looked at the tourists, but then it ran away quickly.

I can see a swimming pool from my window.

I took the book from the shelf and put it into my bag.

Seite 92   P10 Different spelling

maths, favourite, colour, theatre, neighbour, programme, centre, mum

Seite 92   P11 Sound check

a)

/θ/	/ð/
math	another
birthday	with
north	together
think	feather
both	their
thing	that
	they
	brother

Seite 93   P12 Some facts

1. Native Americans **lived** in tepees when they went hunting.
2. Some tribes **made** totem poles which showed pictures and **told** stories.
3. The Inuit **built** igloos out of snow and ice and they **hunted** seals.
4. The Grand Canyon Skywalk **opened** in 2007.
5. Before they had horses, Native Americans **travelled/traveled** on foot.
6. Pocahontas **was** the daughter of a Native American chief. She **married** an English settler.

Seite 93   P13 Interviewing Tawny

a) 1. What's your name?

2. How old are you?

3. Where do you live?

4. Who do you live with?

5. What are your favourite subjects at school?

6. What do you do in your free time?

7. What are your plans for the future?

b) 1. My name is Tawny Hale.

2. I am sixteen years old.

3. I live in Poco Riviera, in California.

4. I live with my sister, Leya, my dad, Ben, and my grandparents.

5. My favorite subjects are math, English, health and US history.

6. Sometimes I go to the mall with my friends. I take part in Native American traditions and ceremonies and I make my own outfits for them.

7. I hope to go to college, although I am not sure what I will study. I definitely want to be a spokesperson for our people.

Seite 93   P14 Native American reservations

Die Mehrheit der vier Millionen Ureinwohner in Kanada und in den USA wohnt in Reservaten. Es gibt heutzutage mehr als 300 Reservate und das größte davon gehört dem Navajo-Stamm. Es ist zweimal so groß wie Belgien oder Maryland. Einige Reservate sind beliebt bei Touristen, die Büffel, Rothirsch oder Truthahn jagen wollen. Andere Stämme verdienen Geld, indem sie Pferde züchten und verkaufen oder Bodenschätze erschließen. Aber viele Stämme verdienen ihr Geld mit Casinos. In jedem zweiten Reservat gibt es ein Casino, in dem man Bingo und Poker spielen kann.

Seite 94   M1 Annie Moore's story

a) Annie was the first immigrant to land on Ellis Island after it was opened.
   (the first immigrant to arrive in the US through the new immigration station at Ellis Island in 1892)

b) **1845** great potato famine in Ireland → causes many people to emigrate
             (one million Irish people die from starvation)

   1889 Annie's parents leave Ireland with Annie's older brother to go to America

   December 1891 14-year-old Annie leaves Ireland to travel to New York with her two younger brothers; on the ship for twelve days; difficult journey

   January 1st, 1892 ship reaches New York; Annie is given a $10 gold piece because she is the first immigrant to leave the ship at Ellis Island; it is her fifteenth birthday

   Today: Ellis Island is a museum and there is a statue of Annie there.

c) The story is about Annie Moore, the first immigrant to arrive at Ellis Island after it was opened. In 1891 Annie and her two younger brothers leave their home country of Ireland and board a ship for New York. Their parents and older brother left Ireland two years earlier for a better life in the US. It is time that Annie and her brothers join them.
   After twelve difficult days on the ship they reach New York, on 1st January 1892.
   Annie is the first person to leave the ship, which makes her the first immigrant to arrive in the US through the newly opened immigration station at Ellis Island. An official welcomes her and gives her a $10 gold piece. Annie is very surprised and happy. It is also her fifteenth birthday! There is now a statue of Annie on Ellis Island.

Seite 95   M2 Changes

a)+b) **1–B** Before Annie went to America, <u>she had lived in Ireland for 15 years</u>.

      2–E When Annie arrived in America, <u>her parents had already lived there for two years</u>.

      3–A A statue was built on Ellis Island <u>after Annie had died</u>.

      4–C <u>After they had greeted each other</u>, Annie and her family went home.

      5–D <u>After she had received the $10 gold piece</u>, Annie could meet her parents.

c) line 14: They <u>had gone</u> to America two years earlier with her older brother.
   line 16: Life was better than it <u>had been</u> in Ireland.
   lines 27–28: She <u>had</u> never <u>seen</u> so much money and did not know why he <u>had given</u> it to her.

Seite 95   M3 Ancestors

This pie chart shows the ancestry of the US population in 2011.
17.1% of the population in the US have German ancestors. They are the biggest group.
In the US there are more people with Mexican ancestors than people with English ancestors.
There are fewer people with Native American ancestors than there are with Polish ancestors.

Seite 95   M4 Learning English

a) They are talking about learning English after they arrived in the United States.

order in which you hear them talk: Kim, Sergio, Mohamed

b) 1. Sergio was not very good at English in his school in Chile.

2. Mohamed came to America when he was very little; he was only five years old.

3. Mohamed can also speak Somali.

4. everyone at school was helpful; extra English lessons during first year; watched a lot of TV

Seite 96   M5 A Native American

a) Lenno is from the Ute tribe.

b) What Lenno likes about living on the reservation / Life on the reservation

Family troubles / Family life / Life at home / Lenno's family

Lenno's school / Life at school / School life

America's dark past

Proud to be Ute

c) **Name:** Lenno

Age: 16

Family: – lives with mum, dad, older sister, Leotie, and four younger brothers and sisters

– his dad doesn't do very much (doesn't have a job and stays out late with friends)

– his mum works in the mornings, so Lenno helps his younger brothers and sisters get ready for school

Home: Ute reservation, Utah

School: – Uintah River High School

– learns the Ute language and has classes in beadwork, dancing and drumming

– likes history and learning about the Ute tribe

Hobbies: usually does something with his friends after school

Plans for the future: studies hard because wants to get a good job when he is older

d) Marc is 13 years old. He lives in Kassel and goes to the Süd-Kassel-Gesamtschule.

He lives with his mum, his dad and his two sisters Anna and Maria.

His hobbies are football, swimming and drawing. He plays football with his friends all the time.

He would like to be a car technician one day because he likes cars and finds electronics really interesting.

Seite 97   M6 What if ...?

a) If I lived on a reservation, I would worry about some of the problems there.

If I went to a boarding school, I would really miss my family.

If I were Native American, I would try to learn my tribe's language.

If I had classes in drumming and dancing, I would be able to take part in the ceremonies.

If I weren't allowed to speak my own language, I would feel very angry.

b) You need the simple past in the if-clause (If I **lived** ...,) and would/could + infinitive in the main clause (I **would worry** ...).

You can start your sentences either with the if-clause or the main clause.

If you start your sentence with the if-clause, there must be a comma between if-clause and main clause. (If I were Native American, I would be worried about my chances in life.)

But there mustn't be a comma between main clause and if-clause if you start your sentence with the main clause. (I would be worried about my chances in life if I were Native American.)

Seite 97   M7 Native American teenagers

a) Jessie is from the Lakota tribe.

DJ is from the Navajo tribe.

b)

	Jessie	**DJ**
age	14	16
likes	– living with family on reservation – the traditions – being able to drive	– being in a gang – that the gang is his family
dislikes	the word "reservation"	there is nothing to do on the reservation
hopes	leave reservation and find a job	start a car repair shop in the reservation
worries	might forget Lakota traditions	that his gang will hurt him if he tries to leave

c) I enjoy ...ing ...

This is great because ...

I don't like ...

They are afraid to ...

One day I hope to ...

I love ...

The only thing I'm worried about is that ...

I hate that ...

At first I thought that ... were very cool but after ... I'm not sure any more.

I'm worried that ...

I'd love to ...

d) I enjoy living in my village because we live near some hills. It looks beautiful on a nice day.

But I hate that there is not much to do apart from going for walks.

On the one hand I think leaving home would be great, on the other hand I'm not sure. I love living with my family. Maybe when I'm older, it'll be easier to leave. I'd love to work abroad one day.

I like spending time with my family and our dog Woody.

I also like talking to my grandparents about what life was like when they were younger.

I don't like vegetables very much, and sometimes I hate it when it rains. I also don't like maths.

I hope I will one day visit the United States. It must be really cool there.

I'm worried about what happens in the world at the moment. Nothing seems safe any more.

I'm also worried about our next French test. I have no idea why I chose French as a subject.

At first I thought it would be really cool but now I'm not so sure any more. It's quite difficult.

Seite 97   M8 An interview

S1: Hi. My name is Ben. Is it OK if I ask you a few questions about your life?

S2: Sure. What would you like to know?

S1: Where do you live?

S2: I live on the Pyramid Lake reservation in Nevada.

S1: What do you like about living there?

S2: There are only about 1700 people there, so people are quite friendly. My tribe – the Paiute tribe – makes a lot of money from letting people fish in the lake but we can do it for free. I really like fishing.

S1: What do you find difficult about life on the reservation?

S2: Well, there are lots of problems. The lake is polluted. Nobody knows if people will be able to live here 50 years from now. I hope to leave the reservation when I am older but I also want to come back. But if all the young people left, life would be too hard for everyone else.

S1: Who do you live with?

S2: I live with my parents, my two sisters and my grandfather. My sisters are younger than me.

S1: Why does your family stay on the reservation?

S2: It's home! My parents are interested in our tribe's history and are trying to make life better here.

S1: What do you do in your free time?

S2: We live far away from any big cities, so I hang out with my friends. I love sitting by the lake in summer. In winter we cook together or watch TV.

S1: What do you learn at school?

S2: I learn our tribal language and in history we learn about what happened to the tribe, but otherwise school is quite normal.

S1: What are your hopes for the future?

S2: I'd love to live in a big city, but I also want to help improve life here. The one thing I worry about is that people often think all Native Americans drink and smoke too much. I want people to like or dislike me for who I am, not for my tribe.

S1: Why do people think that about Native Americans?

S2: People don't like it when people are different, and we are different. Some reservations are quite dangerous and parents pass on their own problems to their children.

S1: What would you say to anyone who thinks that?

S2: I would say that our people have made mistakes but that the government has done terrible things to us. It takes a long time for things to get better but we are working on it.

S1: That was very interesting. Thank you very much.

S2: You're welcome.

Seite 98 Did you get it all?

Where did the immigrants after the first settlers come from? **most of them came from Germany, Ireland and Italy** (→ TB 1, TB Seite 81, text F)

What are people called who came to the USA from Mexico and Central or South America? **Hispanics or Latinos** (→ TB 1, TB Seite 81, text H)

When were the black slaves freed? **in 1865, after the Civil War** (→ TB 1, TB Seite 81, text I)

What percentage of the American population is Native American? **1.1 per cent** (→ TB 2, Seite 82)

What do Native Americans do at a pow-wow? **dance, sing and meet friends; remember and share old traditions** (→ TB 12, TB Seite 86, text D)

Who wears headdresses with feathers? **only some tribes, like the Lakota** (→ TB 12, text G)

Where does the glass used for the Grand Canyon Skywalk come from? **from Germany** (→ TB 13, TB Seite 87, Hörtext)

Who wants to become a spokesperson for Native Americans? **Tawny Hale** (→ TB 15, TB Seite 89)

Seite 100 1 When school's out

a) meet friends, go shopping, surf the Internet, listen to music, computer games, football, baking or cooking, watch TV or films, read a book or magazine, go to the cinema, go for a bike ride, go for a walk, chat with friends, phone a friend, walk the dog, take photos, swimming, hockey, tennis

Seite 100 2 A typical day

a) **Lisa:** 1. On a typical day Lisa goes to school by car. 2. After school she does sports. 3. In the afternoon she sometimes goes shopping with her best friend . 4. In the evening she phones her friends.

Josh: 5. On a typical day Josh goes to school by bus. 6. After school he meets his friend Mike at the mall. 7. In the afternoon Mike and he surf the Internet. 8. In the evening he watches TV.

Tom: 9. On a typical day Tom drives to school. 10. After school he goes to a fast food restaurant. 11. In the afternoon he does his homework. 12. In the evening he listens to music.

b) "And then he said that he liked me! Do you think I should text him? Or wait until tomorrow?" (4)

"Hey Mike, what's up, dude?" (picture 6)

"Yuk. Look at him stuffing his face. There's food everywhere. It makes me sick." (girl in picture 10)

c) In the morning I have breakfast with my sister and then we cycle to school.

After school I cycle home and have lunch.

In the afternoon I do my homework.

In the evening I watch TV and text my best friend. I usually go to bed at 10 pm.

Seite 101 3 Shop till you drop

a) + c)

customer	shop assistant
How much is it?	Can I help you with anything?
Is it on sale?	I'll get you the dress in a smaller size.
Yes, please, I'm looking for …	Let me show you to the fitting rooms.
Where can I try it on?	That's $…, please.
It's too big. Does it come in a smaller size?	How would you like to pay for that? By card or with cash?
How do you think it looks?	You're welcome.
	I'll put your receipt in the bag.

d) **S1:** Hi, how are you today? Can I help you with anything?

S2: Hi! Yes, please! I'm looking for a present for my dad.

S1: What style does he like?

S2: He really likes the blue shirt in the window, but I can't find it anywhere.

S1: I know exactly which shirt you mean. Great quality! Let me show you. … Here it is.

S2: That's great! How much is it?

S1: It's $30. Unfortunately, it's not on sale.

S2: That's OK.

S1: Do you know what size your dad is?

S2: Yes, he's a medium.

S1: Oh, that's good. Because we've run out of the large. Medium … here it is.

S2: Perfect! I'll take it. Thank you very much.

S1: Would you like to look for anything else, or was that everything?

S2: Actually, I would like to have a look at some shoes. But I know where to find them.

S1: Great! Please do let me know if I can help you with anything else.

S2: Well, I have one more question. If my dad doesn't like the shirt, can he bring it back?

S1: Yes, of course. He can return it within 30 days and he will get his money back. But please make sure he brings the receipt with him. If there's no receipt, I'm afraid we can't take the shirt back.

S2: That sounds fair. Thank you! Thanks for your help.

Seite 102   4 A mall
a) A mall is a large building with lots of different shops and restaurants.
b) There isn't a mall in our area, but I have been to a mall in Ludwigshafen.
   I don't like going to the mall. The shops are all quite expensive and there isn't that much to do. Looking at clothes and spending money gets boring after a while.

Seite 102   5 Lisa and Amy
Going wild!
… "What do you think we should do?", asked Lisa.
"Let's go to the zoo!" said Amy.
Lisa wasn't sure. "How will we get there?"
"It's easy," said Amy. "We can get on the bus. There's a bus stop outside the mall."
The girls found the bus stop, jumped on the bus and made their way to the zoo.
It was so exciting! They saw lions, tigers, monkeys, zebras and penguins!
But then the zoo-keeper said it was time to go home. It took Lisa and Amy a long time because they had to get the bus back to the mall, and then another bus home. But they were so happy that they didn't notice how long it took. Their parents were pleased that they had done something different!

Seite 102   6 On the phone
a) They are going to hang out at the mall.
b) 1. at three o'clock
   2. Their moms are going to drive them./Their moms are going to give them a ride.
   3. to tell him that Ben is going to come, too
   4. at Cosmo's Pizza

Seite 103   7 A picture story
a) Hero for one day / An exciting time at the mall / A real Crusher fan!

Seite 104   8 A day at the mall
1–B Josh and Ben are at the mall and they are waiting for Alex.
2–E When Alex arrives at 3:15 pm, the friends join a crowd of girls.
3–G They hear that the singer Crusher is presenting his new album.
4–C When a girl suddenly faints, Josh catches her and gets the paramedics.
5–D Crusher notices that something is wrong.
6–A One of his bodyguards tells him that a girl has fainted and that Josh helped her.
7–F The singer thanks Josh for his help and gives him a ticket to his next concert.

Seite 104   9 You won't believe it!

... There was a crowd of girls in the mall and we found out that Crusher – can't stand him! – was presenting his new album. The girls were going crazy – and suddenly one of them fainted! I saw it happen, caught her and got the paramedics. No big deal. But Crusher noticed that something was wrong. One of his bodyguards told him that a girl had fainted and that I had helped her. Guess what, Crusher came over, thanked me for my help – and gave me a ticket to his next concert!!! He called me "a real Crusher fan"!!! Can you believe it?! I felt so embarrassed. Alex and Ben couldn't stop laughing. – Well, Ben's sister is a big Crusher fan, so I've given her the ticket. She'll love me forever, she says.

Speak soon. Josh

Seite 104   10 YOUR free time statistics

a) American teenagers use computers or play computer games for about 54 minutes on an average day. They spend six minutes on relaxing and thinking on an average day. The least popular activities are reading and relaxing and thinking. The most popular activity is watching TV.

b)

	sport	computers	TV	friends	reading	relaxing
Lana	70	10	0	150	25	30
Sean	60	120	60	180	0	10
Thomas	0	0	90	60	90	45
Helena	30	120	30	50	60	0
Sylvia	15	20	60	100	15	90
Max	30	60	5	90	75	30

Seite 105   11 American sports

a) 1. basketball   2. soccer   3. ice hockey
   4. cheerleading   5. American football   6. baseball

b) **basketball:** throw, net, foul, half time, penalty, jump, basket, pass, dribble / slam dunk, guarding

   soccer: goalkeeper, net, foul, half time, linesman, penalty, kick, pass, kickoff, dribble / offside, offside trap, injury time, extra time, defender, booking, equaliser, draw, corner, free-kick, header

   ice hockey: goalkeeper, puck, net, foul, half time, linesman, penalty, helmet, pass, hit / stick, pad

   cheerleading: throw, pompom, jump / chant, pyramid-building, stunt, show

   American football: foul, linesman, penalty, helmet, kick, pass, kickoff / touchtown, tackle

   baseball: throw, foul, hit / pitch/pitcher, bat/batter, fielder, strike, curve ball, home run, umpire

c) **What pieces of equipment does he need?** helmet with a visor, protective gloves, a stick, pants (to cover top of legs), pads, skates, shoulder pads

   How did he become interested in ice hockey? His best friend played hockey, and his best friend's dad was a coach.

   What has been his worst injury? The puck hit his face very quickly. He got eight stitches on his head, five above his eye and three under his eye.

   What else can you understand? He loves his job because he is paid to do something he would do anyway. He used to play for a Swedish team and so he can speak Swedish. He is from Minneapolis. The most exciting part of his career was when he became professional.

Seite 106   12 Come and join us!

a) "We go to all the football games and cheer our school teams on."

"we support all of our school teams"

"We write our own chants. We also practice singing and dancing"

b) Ashley has to be in really good shape.

She has to be good at writing chants, at singing and at dancing.

Ashley has to be good at gymnastics.

She has to watch her weight. / She has to stay slim.

She has to be careful because some of the stunts are a little big dangerous.

She has to practice a lot./two or three times a week.

Seite 107   14 At the game with Dad

a) Aaron and his dad took the subway to a football game in New York. Aaron felt excited and couldn't believe how big the stadium was. They watched the game, which was very exciting, and cheered their team on. After the game, Aaron bought a poster and met one of the players.

Seite 108   15 All about American football

b) **defensive:** Verteidigungs-

goal line: Torlinie

goalpost: Torpfosten

offensive: Angriffs-

opponent: Gegner

quarter: Viertel

tackle: jdn angreifen

d) **team:** a group of people who play together

quarter: one of four parts in a game of American football

high school: type of school in the US, teenagers usually start there at the age of 14

opponent: a player on the other team / the other team

Seite 109   16 American football rules

In American football you need **two** teams. Each team has **eleven** players.

The teams score points when they get the **ball** over the opponents' goal line.

Players can also **kick** the ball through the goalposts. There are **four** quarters in

a high school game. Each **quarter** is **twelve** minutes long.

Seite 109   17 Sports, sports, sports

a) I'm good at cycling. And I guess I'm OK at badminton. But I'm terrible at swimming.

We do lots of sports at school, like running and netball. We sometimes play tennis in the summer.

In my free time I like going everywhere on my bike. I also like playing football with my friends. I watch lots of football on TV.

I would like to try horse riding. I think it looks fun. But I think it's quite expensive.

c) Katarina is good at cycling and badminton but she says she's terrible at swimming.

They do lots of sports at school, she tells me, like running and netball. And they sometimes play tennis in the summer.

In her free time Katarina likes going everywhere on her bike. She also likes playing football with her friends. Katarina watch lots of football on TV.

She would like to try horse riding. She thinks it looks fun. But she thinks it's quite expensive.

Seite 109   18 Choose an activity

A quiz about the rules of American football

1. How can you score?

   You bring your mother with you.

   You jump up and down and shout as loud as you can.

   You get the ball across the goal line. (✓)
2. Can defensive players tackle the ball carrier?   yes (✓)   no
3. How many points do you get for a touchdown?   2   5   6 (✓)
4. How many quarters are there in a game?   2   4 (✓)   6
5. How long is a national game?   10 minutes   60 minutes (✓)   15 minutes

Seite 110   P1 Pairs

sports – **do**

surf – **the Internet**

evening – **dinner**

house – **rooms**

homework – **do**

shop assistant – **sell**

Seite 110   P2 Sound check

a) 1. Lots of students go to school **by bus.**

   2. Another word for shopping centre is **mall.**

   3. A person who sells things in a shop is a **shop assistant.**

   4. When you buy something, you usually get a **receipt.**

   5. Someone who guards famous people is a **bodyguard.**

   6. A large number of people in the same place is a **crowd.**

Seite 110   P3 What they like and don't like doing

a) Lisa likes phoning her friends./sitting on her bed and chatting with her best friend.

   Josh loves watching basketball on TV.

   Alex doesn't like doing his homework.

   Tom hates shopping for clothes./going shopping with his mum.

b) I love going to the mall and I love buying clothes.

   I like reading and watching films.

   But I don't like running or cycling.

   And I hate playing football at school.

Seite 111   P4 Tom

1. Tom is 16 years old **and** is allowed to drive a car.
2. He usually goes to school by car **because** he doesn't like the school bus.
3. Tom enjoys listening to music **when** he comes home from school.
4. Homework is something he can't stand **but** he has to do it.
5. Tom loves eating tacos **so** he often goes to fast food restaurants.
6. Yesterday he had a date with Stacy **but** she didn't enjoy it.

Seite 111   P5 Pictures

(picture 10 on page 100) In my favourite picture you can see a boy and a girl in a restaurant.

The boy is eating a hamburger, the bits of the hamburger are everywhere, it doesn't look very nice.

The boy is thinking only about his food, he pays no attention to the girl next to him. The girl doesn't look very happy. I think she thinks the boy is disgusting.

Seite 111   P6 Say it in English
a) 1–E 2–F 3–D 4–G 5–A 6–C 7–B
b) **S1:** Hi Lea! It's Casey. What's up?
   S2: Not much. Just watching a film.
   S1: Do you feel like going to the mall?
   S2: Sure, why not. When do you want to meet? Would 3:30 be OK?
   S1: Yes, 3:30 sounds good.
   S2: OK, see you then.
   S1: Bye!

Seite 111   P7 A phone call
Rick und seine Freundin Lucy gehen um halb vier ins Einkaufszentrum, weil Rick neue Turnschuhe braucht und Lucy neue Klamotten kaufen will. Sie schlagen vor, sich um halb sechs mit Mark bei Jo's Diner zu treffen, um etwas zu trinken. Mark kann Jenny mitbringen, wenn er möchte.

Seite 112   P8 Missing letters
a) 1. coach   3. risk   5. stunt
   2. soccer   4. hurt   6. introduce
b) c _ _ _ _ _ _ _ _ _ g (cheerleading)
   m _ _ _ _ r (member)
   d _ _ _ _ _ _ _ s (dangerous)

Seite 112   P9 Finding words

people	things they do	things they need
players	play	rules
opponents	get the ball across the goal line	ball
team	kick	goal line
offensive players	tackle	field
defensive players	keep out of the way	touchdown
ball carrier	block	goalposts
	carry the ball	field goal

Seite 112   P10 Sound check
b)

Ooo	oOo
national	gymnastics
pyramid	equipment
championships	defensive
strategies	opponent
dangerous	offensive

Seite 112   P11 Different pronouns

personal pronouns	reflexive pronouns
I	myself
you	yourself
he	himself
she	herself
it	itself
we	ourselves
you	yourselves
they	themselves

Seite 113   P12 You can do it by yourself!

1. Before the match Kenan looked at **himself** in the mirror.
2. Yesterday I introduced **myself** to the new coach.
3. Our coach says we just need to believe in **ourselves.**
4. They have to prepare **themselves** for an important competition.
5. You play better if you all enjoy **yourselves** at training.
6. Sonya hurt **herself** badly when she fell off her bike.
7. My friend's dog taught **itself** how to ride a skateboard.
8. Remember Johnny, you can treat **yourself** to a big meal after the game!

Seite 113   P14 At a German football stadium

Excuse me, how long are the tours? 90 minutes
Are there tours every day? Tuesday to Sunday; but no tours on days when there are matches
Where do the tours start? at the bus stop outside the stadium
How much are the tours for teenagers? three euros

Seite 114   M1 After Tom and Stacy's date

a) Stacy, the girl from the diary entry, thinks that the date went really badly. Tom picked her up late and said he'd almost forgotten their date. They went to a restaurant which Stacy didn't like. She was unhappy that she had to pay for her own food. Tom spent half an hour talking to a friend at the restaurant and ignored Stacy. When they got home, Tom tried to kiss Stacy. Stacy didn't enjoy their date at all.
Tom thinks that their date went OK and that everything is great. He arrived late for their date because he didn't want to look excited, he wanted to look cool. He thinks that Stacy liked the food at the Mexican restaurant and that it was OK that he spoke to his friend. He says he didn't kiss her, because he wants to make her wait. He's going to wait a few days before he calls her.

b) Tom arrived late and said he had almost forgotten about their date. Stacy was angry because she believed him that this was why he was late.
Tom didn't listen to Stacy when she said that she preferred Italian food to Mexican food. Stacy didn't like the food at the Mexican restaurant.
Tom ignored Stacy when he saw his friend at the restaurant. He thinks he only spoke to Chad for a few minutes, but Stacy says it was about half an hour.
Tom tried to kiss Stacy but she was so angry that she turned away.

c) I think Tom will ask Stacy out again but Stacy will say no.
   Stacy's diary entry from a few days later
   Friday, 7th April
   I can't believe it! Today Tom asked me out again in front of all my friends. I said I was sorry but that I had plans. His face went really red. He said he didn't understand why I didn't like him anymore! I told him he had been rude on our last date. I thought he would say sorry. But instead he said I was stupid and that there must be another reason. I just walked away. There was nothing to say! But a few hours later he texted to say he was sorry. He wants to take me to an Italian restaurant on Saturday. I'm not sure what to do. Must think about it for a bit.

Seite 114 M2 What did they say?

a) Sorry, I almost <u>forgot</u> about our date. → He said <u>he</u> <u>had</u> almost <u>forgotten</u>!
   <u>I've</u> never <u>eaten</u> Mexican food before. → She said <u>she</u> <u>had</u> never <u>eaten</u> it before.
   Don't worry. <u>You'll like</u> Mexican food. → He said <u>I</u> <u>would like</u> it.
   You know, I really <u>prefer</u> Italian food. → I told him I <u>preferred</u> Italian ...

b) When you turn direct speech into reported speech, the tenses change and go back one tense.
   If the tense is simple present in direct speech, it changes to simple past in reported speech.
   If it is simple past in direct speech, it changes to past perfect in reported speech.
   The pronouns sometimes change, too. When you are reporting what someone said, 'I' becomes 'he' or 'she'. When you are reporting what you said, 'I' does not change. When you are reporting what someone told you, 'you' becomes 'I'.

Seite 115 M3 If only they had a second chance ...

1–D If Tom had been on time, Stacy would have been in a better mood.
2–A If Stacy had said more clearly that she preferred Italian food, perhaps Tom would have ...
3–T If Tom had taken Stacy to a good Mexican restaurant, she might have found something ...
4–I Stacy wouldn't have felt so ignored if Tom hadn't talked to Chad for so long.
5–N If Stacy had walked home, Tom might have realized Stacy was not having a good time.
6–G Maybe the date would have gone better if Tom had asked Chris for advice before.
You get the word **DATING**.

Seite 115 M4 If things had gone differently ...

1. If Tom **had taken** the bus, he would have arrived on time.
2. If Tom **had taken** Stacy to an Italian restaurant, she would have enjoyed the food.
3. If Tom **had ignored** Stacy a little longer while he was talking to Chad, she would have ...
4. If Tom **had been** more of a gentleman, maybe Stacy would have kissed him.
5. If Stacy **hadn't gone** on the date with Tom, she would have watched a film.

Seite 115 M5 A radio report

b) **Why does each city need its own mall?** because cities are very far apart in America
   What is a plaza? an area where you can sit and eat food from all the different mall restaurants
   What do large malls offer? different entertainment options, like cinemas, ice rinks and bowling alleys; hundreds of shops; some very big malls even have hotels and amusement parks
   What do malls have to have? have huge car parks
c) Cities aren't as far apart in Germany as they are in America, so not every city has its own mall.
   I don't think malls in Germany have ice rinks, bowling alleys or hotels. But I think some have cinemas. I've been to a mall with a plaza: Rheingalerie in Ludwigshafen.
   German malls have car parks, too, but I don't think they're so big.

Seite 115   M6 You won't believe it!

Hi Julie,

You won't believe what happened to me at the mall yesterday! I was so excited because Crusher was there. He was presenting his new album and you know how much I love him. But I hadn't eaten very much, I was so excited!, and there were so many people there … everyone was pushing and shouting. Suddenly my eyes went all funny and I fainted! I don't remember much. But a boy caught me and called for help so Crusher gave him a ticket to his next concert. I wish he had given me a ticket!

My mom picked me up later. Now she doesn't want me to go to any more Crusher concerts … I'm going to talk to her about it tonight. Wish me luck!

How are you? What's up with you?

Love, Sarah

Seite 116   M7 Where is everyone?

a) I think a very big and important sports event takes place once a year. Everyone wants to watch it on TV, so the streets are empty. / The Super Bowl takes place once a year in the US.
b) The streets are empty because everyone is at home. They are watching the Super Bowl on TV. (It's Sunday, Super Bowl Sunday.)
c) **What time does the game start?** at 6:30 pm
   What can you watch before the game? live show where singers perform
Why is the trophy named after Vince Lombardi? the coach of the Green Bay Packers, the team that won the first Super Bowl in 1967

Seite 116   M8 American football rules

1. right
2. wrong / There are eleven players in each team. (There are a few extra players, too.)
3. right
4. right
5. wrong / A team gets six points for a touchdown.
6. wrong / A field goal happens without a touchdown. It is when a player has kicked the ball through the goalposts, from the field.
7. right

Seite 116   M9 Sport kills?

a) No, I don't agree with the author because not all sports are dangerous and exhausting. Let's take skiing and surfing, for example. People who enjoy skiing and surfing know that these sports are more dangerous than other sports, like football or jogging. But that doesn't mean that they all have accidents. You can have an accident at home, from falling down the stairs.
b) Yes, I think Antonia's arguments are convincing. She explains that doing sport makes you healthier and makes you feel better. She argues that people who don't do sports often eat too much or smoke. She also says that sport itself isn't dangerous – it's about whether you know what you are doing when you do a particular sport. I agree with all of Antonia's arguments.
c) **Comment on the article in a):** In my opinion, some parts of the article are true, but some of them are not. It is true that doing too much sport, doing dangerous sports or doing sports wrongly is bad for you. For example, top athletes often have health problems because they train too much. But for the average person, doing sport is a great idea and will make or keep him/her healthier.

Female football players should earn as much as male football players

Football is one of the most popular sports in Europe. But should female football players earn as much as male football players?

In my opinion, there are two main problems here. Firstly, I believe that women and men who do the same jobs should be paid the same. It is a fact that female football players work as hard as male football players. In other areas, men and women who do the same work are paid the same. Why should there be different rules for professional sportspeople?

Secondly, I believe that football players earn too much money for the work they do. What I am saying is that I am not so sure that paying female football players the same is such a good idea. Here is what I suggest: I think it would be best if male football players earned less and female players earned more, i.e. if they met half way and then all earned the same.

All in all, I would say that male and female football players should earn the same, but it should not be as much as male football players are earning at the moment.

Seite 117   M10 Donna's biggest challenge

a) I think the report is about a person called Donna who is trying to give up smoking.

c) put out, quit, butt out, start, peer pressure, feel stressed, smell of smoke, nicotine gum, cigarettes, patches, ruin your life, stop

d) – When did Donna start smoking? (at the age of 13)
   – Why did she start smoking? (she wanted to fit in, peer pressure, it seemed cool)
   – How did smoking change her life? (she felt stressed when she couldn't smoke, had no energy)
   – Why did she stop smoking? (had not energy, her parents were angry and wanted her to stop)
   – How did she give up smoking? (started smoking less and less; finally she was able to stop altogether / before that she tried nicotine gum but it didn't work for her)
   – How did she find giving up smoking? (the first weeks were the hardest, she kept thinking of cigarettes; had headaches and even less energy than before; she put on weight, so it wasn't easy; but after a few weeks things got easier: she lost weight again and started feeling better; her skin and her hair look so much better now than when she was still smoking)
   – What does she think about smoking now? (smoking can ruin your life)
   – What does she say about giving up smoking? (It's hard but you can do it. You just need to find out what works for you.)

Seite 118   Did you get it all?

Where can customers try on clothes in a shop? **the fitting rooms** (→ TB 3, TB Seite 101)

What time are Josh, Alex and Ben going to meet at the mall? **at three o'clock** (→ TB 6, Seite 102, Hörtext)

Why are the girls at the mall screaming? **because the singer Crusher is there, he is presenting his new album** (→ TB 7, TB Seite 103)

Why does Josh get a ticket to Crusher's concert? **he catches a girl, a big Crusher fan, when she faints and gets the paramedics; Crusher thanks him for helping** (→ TB 7, TB Seite 103)

What do cheerleaders do? **they cheer their school teams on at games** (→ TB 12, TB Seite 106)

What does Ashley's team want to win? **the state championships** (→ TB 12, TB Seite 106)

What is a touchdown in American football? **when a team gets the ball across their opponents' goal line** (→ TB 15, TB Seite 108)

How long is an American football field? **120 yards** (→ TB 15, TB Seite 108)

Seite 120   1 California – here we come!

a) When I think of California, I think of movie stars and celebrities. It can be very hot in California, and there are many beaches. Beaches come up in Katy Perry's song, too.

b) beaches, celebrities, warm/hot, sunny, sunshine, deserts, Baywatch, Hollywood, national parks, Los Angeles, San Francisco, Golden Gate Bridge, Venice Beach, street artists, inline skating, skateboarding

Seite 120   2 Lots to see and do in California

a)

places you can go to	activities you can do	people you can meet	problems in California
– deserts, forests, mountains, hills, the ocean – national parks – Los Angeles – Santa Monica and Venice Beach – Silicon Valley – Disneyland – Hollywood – San Francisco	– go cycling and inline skating in Santa Monica – see many different landscapes – visit film studios – visit Disneyland – watch the LA Lakers – go to the beach	– park rangers – stunt performers – border patrol guards – lifeguards – actors/actresses – the LA Lakers and their fans	– hot and dry weather – forest fires – earthquakes – illegal immigration

b) I would like to visit **Disneyland,** it must be amazing! I'm sure it's even better than Disneyland Paris because the weather in California is much nicer and warmer and the people are friendlier. I would like to see **Hollywood** because it is really famous and there are lots of celebrities there. And if you're lucky, you might see people like stunt performers, and they sound really cool. And it would be so cool to see someone really famous, someone I know from a movie or from TV. I would love to go to **San Francisco** because it's such a cool city and full of interesting people and things to see. I think San Francisco is a lot more relaxing than Los Angeles. And I would love to see the Golden Gate Bridge in real life, after I've seen it on TV so many times.

Seite 121   3 Working in California

Person 1 is a lifeguard.   Person 3 is a park ranger (in Yosemite).
Person 2 is a stunt performer.   Person 4 is a tour guide (in Disneyland).

Seite 122   4 A newspaper article

a) forest fires / I think the article is about some big fire in California that people can't control.

b) After the wildfires

   or: Mexico helps to put out wildfires

   or: Wildfires make California dangerous place to live

c) 1. After three weeks the fires were **put out.**

   2. Nine people were killed, 85 people were injured and **thousands of homes were destroyed.**

   3. Luckily, none of the state's national parks were **damaged.**

   4. In schools, churches and sports stadiums people were **given food, drink, medicine, and somewhere to stay.**

   5. A young boy was **rescued by a firefighter from a burning forest.**

   6. 61 firefighters were **injured by the flames.**

Seite 123 5 Jobs in California

a) If you want to be a make-up artist, you should be good with your hands.

If you want to be a firefighter, you should be very fit and brave.

You should be creative if you want to work as a cameraman.

If you want to be a programmer, you have to be good at working with computers.

You should like to work outdoors if you want to be a park ranger.

You must know how to swim if you want to be a lifeguard.

If you want to be a tour guide, you should get along well with other people.

If you want to be a stunt performer, you should know martial arts and be very fit.

b)

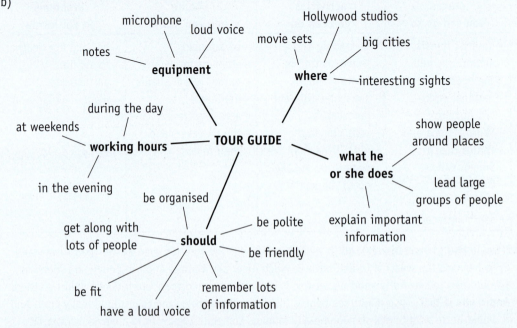

Seite 123 6 A job for YOU?

I wouldn't like to be a cameraman because you have to work indoors all day. And everything you do is on camera, because that's your job. So everybody knows when you've done something wrong. **I would like to be** a lifeguard because they are very important in California. I would like to work outdoors on the beach, and work with lots of different people. I also love swimming, so it would be the right/perfect job for me.

Seite 124 7 California's national parks

a) Redwood National Park is in the north-west of California.

Lassen Volcanic National Park is in the north-east of California.

Yosemite, Kings Canyon and Death Valley are in the east of California.

Sequoia National Park is in central California. Joshua Tree is in the south of California.

The Channel Islands National Park are in the west of California.

b) I would like to visit all of these national parks! But if I had to choose, I would visit Channel Islands National Park because I would love to see blue whales and sea lions in the wild.

I would like to visit Redwood National Park because of the huge trees. They must be beautiful.

I would like to visit Yosemite National Park because it is such a famous national park. I would love to see a bear.

I would like to visit Death Valley National Park. The desert scenery sounds fascinating.

Seite 125   8 Choose an activity

Fact files about the other five national parks in California

Joshua Tree National Park
Size: 1,017,748 acres
Founded: 1936
Attractions: two types of desert: the lower, drier Colorado Desert in the east, and the higher, wetter and cooler Mojave Desert in the west, with its Joshua tree forests
Animals: 204 types of bird

Lassen Volcanic National Park
Size: 106,000 acres
Founded: 1907
Attractions: one of the few places in the world where you can see all types of volcanoes; main attraction: volcano called Lassen Peak
Animals: amphibians, birds, fish, reptiles

Kings Canyon National Park
Size: 461,901 acres
Founded: 1940
Attractions: In the canyon of the Kings River there are wild rivers, waterfalls and glaciers.
Animals: mountain yellow-legged frog, bighorn sheep

Sequoia National Park
Size: 402,510 acres
Founded: 1890
Attractions: high mountains (for example, Mount Whitney at 14,494 feet), deep canyons, home to the largest tree in the world, a sequoia called General Shermann
Animals: There are many black bears in the park.

Pinnacles National Park
Size: 26,000 acres
Founded: 2013
Attractions: hiking, bird watching, climbing, exploring caves (bring your flashlight!)
Animals: American badger, big-eared kangaroo rat, colonies of bats (in the caves), e.g. Townsend's big-eared bat, Western mastiff bat

A two-week trip to California
Day 1: Arrive in Los Angeles, check into hotel
Day 2: Visit Hollywood sign (Hollywood Hills) and Walk of Fame
Day 3: Tour of a Hollywood studio
Day 4: A day at the beach
Days 5–7: Visit Yosemite National Park (there is so much to do!)
Days 8–10: San Francisco, see the Golden Gate Bridge, go shopping, see all the sights
Day 11: A day at the beach
Days 12 and 13: Visit Channel Islands National Park
Day 14: Pack everything up and leave
I would love to spend time at the different national parks because there is so much to see, and I love animals and nature! I'd also like to go to San Francisco because it's such a famous city. I've read that there are lots of really cool and interesting things going on all the time.

Seite 126   9 Visit Hollywood Film Studios!

1. No, you can't. The studios aren't open on Christmas Day.
2. at 7 pm
3. in English, Spanish and Chinese
4. The Front of Line Pass is good if you don't want to wait.
5. You have to phone them. The phone number is (818) 4708351.
6. $168 (The 5-year-old and the mother must pay $84 each. Entrance for the 2-year-old is free.)

Seite 126   L&L Hollywood

Mickey Mouse, Lassie, Shrek, Neil Armstrong, The Beatles, Walt Disney, Johnny Depp, Godzilla, Nicole Kidman, Winnie the Pooh, Queen, Arnold Schwarzenegger, The Simpsons, Rob Lowe, Matt Damon, Bradley Cooper, Quentin Tarantino, Stan Laurel, Emma Thompson, Cate Blanchett, Tom Cruise, Daniel Radcliffe, Muhammad Ali

In Las Vegas gibt es noch einen Walk of Fame (Walk of Stars), ebenso in Hongkong.

Seite 127   10 Take a tour!

a) On tour A you can see dinosaurs that lived 65 million years ago.

On tour B you can see a battle between machines and humans.

On tour C you can see how earthquakes are made in films.

On tour D you can see a big heavy monster.

c) I would like to go on tour A because I love dinosaurs and they always look so real in films.

Seite 127   11 Enjoying a movie

a) In the cartoon you can sees sharks at the cinema.

They are eating popcorn and are watching the movie "Titanic".

On the screen there is the Titanic. It is sinking.

The shark on the left says it/he loves happy endings. All the sharks are happy and are smiling.

b) The cartoon is funny because we people think that the film about the Titanic is very sad and with no happy ending, but the sharks think it is a happy ending because they like eating people.

Seite 128   12 What type of film?

b) A: drama

B: science fiction

C: romance

D: comedy

E: animation

F: horror

G: fantasy

H: action

c) **drama:** Titanic, Forrest Gump, To Kill a Mockingbird, Braveheart, Slumdog Millionaire, Amadeus, When Harry met Sally, Brokeback Mountain, Groundhog Day, Good Will Hunting, Gone With the Wind, Hawking, Rocky, Casablanca

science fiction: Star Wars, Men in Black, Gattaca, Alien, The Empire Strikes Back, 2001: A Space Odyssey, E.T. The Extra-Terrestrial

action: Spiderman, Superman, King Kong, Die Hard, Gladiator, Apocalypse Now

romance: Love Actually, Sleepless in Seattle, High School Musical

comedy: Back to the Future, Kung Fu Panda, Ghostbusters, Monty Python and The Holy Grail

horror: Jaws, Pulp Fiction, Frankenstein, Psycho, The Shining, Seven, The Silence of the Lambs

animation: Beauty and the Beast, Wall-E, Frozen, The Lion King, Toy Story, The Jungle Book

fantasy: The Lord of the Rings, Avatar, The Hobbit

Seite 128   13 A review

a) Yes, I'd like to see the film because the story sounds really interesting. I like the fact that it's a true story. And I must admit I love stories about celebrities. Another reason why I'd like to see the film is that I like Emma Watson, so I'm quite happy to see any film with her in it.

b) things you wear as decoration, for example rings: **jewellery**
a place where criminals are kept: **prison**
take something that isn't yours: **steal**
famous people: **celebrities**
the actors and actresses in a film: **cast**

c) – Guardians of the Galaxy
   – United States: 2014
   – **Running time:** 121 minutes
   – **Cast:** Chris Pratt, Zoe Saldana, Dave Bautista, Vin Diesel, Bradley Cooper
   – **Director:** James Gunn
   – **Genre:** Marvel superhero movie
   – **Story/Plot:** Peter Quill, also known as Star Lord, is a thief from Earth. He has stolen a power-ful object and now tries to sell it before the evil Ronan finds him. Unfortunately, Ronan's soldier, Gamora, and two bounty hunters, Groot and Rocket, are after him.
   The four of them are arrested and end up in prison, where they meet Drax, who is very strong. The five of them escape and try to sell the stolen object and split the money. But when they find out that the object is very powerful, they decide that they must give it to the right person.
   – **Why I didn't like it:** I found it a bit boring and the story was sometimes difficult to follow. I also didn't think it was funny, but my friends loved it.
   But I liked one thing: I liked the music.
   – two stars

Seite 129   14 Choose an activity

If you had the chance to look around your favourite celebrity's home: If I could look around my favourite celebrity's home, I would choose Jennifer Lawrence. I'm sure she has a big house, with lots of interesting things, like paintings and art. I think she also has lots of pretty clothes, because she always wears cool dresses to red carpet events. I would love to see what else she has in her home.

Seite 130   P1 Nature words

a) landscapes, desert, forests, mountains, hills, ocean, hot, dry, forest fires, beaches, earthquake
b) sea, lake, river, countryside, trees, flowers, trail, wildfires, valleys, cliffs, waterfalls, beaches, caves

Seite 130   P2 Sound check

speakers	AE	BE	words that helped you to decide
speaker 1		✓	timetable
speaker 2	✓		schedule, locker
speaker 3	✓		vacation
speaker 4		✓	holiday
speaker 5		✓	football match, fish and chips
speaker 6	✓		soccer
speaker 7	✓		movie
speaker 8		✓	film

Seite 130   P3 Some facts about California

1. California is **known** by many names such as "The Land of Milk and Honey" and …
2. In 1973, an 11 kilogram gold nugget was **found** by an amateur gold digger in the Yuba River.
3. Blue jeans and skateboards were **invented** in California.
4. The first cinema in the US was **opened** in Los Angeles on 2 April 1902.
5. Over 64 million litres of wine are **produced** in California each year.
6. The first Californian flag was **made** by a group of American settlers.

Seite 131   P4 Some research

1. Oregon, Arizona, Nevada
2. Los Angeles, Mount Whitney, the Sacramento River
3. (time difference between Germany and California: Germany is nine hours ahead of California)
4. grizzly bear

Seite 131   P5 National park quiz

a) Where can you find blue whales (the world's largest animals)? – Channel Islands National Park
   What is the name of the highest point in Death Valley National Park? – Telescope Peak
   When was Death Valley National Park founded? – in 1933

b) **S1:** OK, I'll start! Where can you find the world's largest animals, blue whales?
   S2: That must be Channel Islands National Park. My turn: what is the name of the highest point in Death Valley National Park?
   S1: Oh, that's a difficult one. Is it Telescope Peak? … Yes? Am I right? Excellent. I'll ask a question next. When was Death Valley National Park founded?
   S2: Was it 1933? / I think that was in 1933.

Seite 131   P6 Park rules

Man soll immer genug Wasser dabei haben.
Man muss immer auf einen plötzlichen Wetterumschwung vorbereitet sein.
Man darf nicht alleine wandern gehen.
Man soll immer auf dem Weg bleiben, um die Pflanzen zu schützen.
Beim Fahren muss man aufpassen, falls wilde Tiere die Straße überqueren.
Man darf die Tiere nicht füttern. Müll soll man in die Mülleimer werfen.
Man soll sich bei einem Ranger melden, wenn man einen Bären sieht.
Man soll sein Essen in einem der bärensicheren Schließfächer aufbewahren.
Man soll sich Bären nie nähern oder ihnen was zu fressen geben. Wenn ein Bär sich nähert,
sollte man so viel Lärm wie möglich machen, indem man sehr laut ruft, sodass der Bär abhaut.

Seite 132   P7 An acrostic

C ome and visit
A lways sunny
L os Angeles
I nteresting people
F antastic national parks
O rdinary? No!
R eal action heroes
N ew technologies
I nteresting stunt performers
A ctors and actresses

Seite 132   P9 At the cinema

a) In the first picture I can see a boy and a girl. They are at a cinema. They have already bought their tickets. Now they are buying some popcorn and some soft drinks.

In the second picture the boy and the girl are watching a horror film. On the screen a green monster is running towards them.

In the third picture the green monster has come alive and has jumped out of the screen.

It is in the cinema. People are shouting and screaming. Some of them are running to get out.

b) Last Saturday Mary and James went to the cinema. First they bought tickets. Then they bought some popcorn and some soft drinks.

After that they went to see a horror film. For the first twenty minutes everything was OK. Suddenly the green monster from the film came alive, jumped out of the screen and was in the room! Most of the people started shouting and screaming, but not Mary and James. Mary asked the monster, "Are you hungry? Would you like some of my popcorn?" The monster answered, "I love popcorn!"

In the end, the monster ate all the popcorn and then said, "I want to see America. Maybe one of the national parks will give me a new home." The monster left, and Mary and James went home.

Seite 133   P11 Being a star in Hollywood

a) regularly, quickly, politely, healthily, beautifully

b) A movie star has to travel **regularly.** He or she always has to answer reporters' questions **politely.**

At home and in a restaurant a movie star has to eat **healthily.** He or she has to learn lines for film parts really **quickly.** A movie star also has to smile for photos **beautifully.**

Seite 133   P12 At a German film studio

1. Don't take large rucksacks or bags with you.
2. The tours take about two hours. They can be exhausting, so don't bring young children with you.
3. Weekends are busy, so best to come early, around 9 am, if you don't want to have to wait too long.

Seite 134   M1 The Golden State

a) The song is about California.

The singer doesn't really understand what people like about California.

The singer seems critical of California. He doesn't really like California.

b) The song makes me feel quite sad and thoughtful.

The music sounds beautiful and I like the melody.

I like the lyrics because they are so simple and at the same time original.

c) The singer doesn't understand what people like about California.

No, he certainly does not want to live there. It's OK for him to visit but he wouldn't want to stay there for longer, i.e. live there ("from time to time I pass on by, but I will never stay").

He doesn't seem to like the fact that California is all about "fortune and fame", i.e. becoming rich and famous. And he doesn't like the fact that life can be dangerous in California, because of the constant risk of wildfires and earthquakes.

d) No, I wouldn't like to live in California. I would miss Germany and I think it would feel strange to live somewhere so famous. I prefer smaller places.

Also, I agree with what the singer says when he sings "I need to see the leaves change and the snowflakes falling". I like it when the weather changes, from summer to autum to winter to spring. I think I would be bored if it were hot and sunny all the time.

Seite 134   M2   A newspaper article

Thousands of homes were destroyed.

People had to leave their homes.

Nine people were killed and 85 were injured.

None of the state's national parks were damaged.

People had to stay in schools, churches and stadiums. They were given food, drink and medicine.

Almost 9,000 men and women worked to put out the fires.

Some firefighters came from Mexico to help.

A young boy was rescued by a firefighter who landed his helicopter in a burning forest.

61 firefighters were injured.

Seite 135   M3   Calling the emergency services

a) The caller's toaster caught fire and there's a huge fire in their kitchen.

b) Which service do you need – ambulance, fire or police?

    What has happened?

    What's your name and your phone number?

    (Where are you?) What's your address?

    Is anybody hurt?

c) **Operator:** 911 emergencies.

    Caller: Hello, you have to help my friend!

    Operator: Which service do you need – ambulance, fire or police?

    Caller: Ambulance, please!

    Operator: What has happened?

    Caller: My friend was doing a jump with his skateboard and fell off his board. He landed badly and now there's blood everywhere on his head and knees. He's saying strange things.

    Operator: OK. What's your name and your phone number, please?

    Caller: My name is Julie Lee, and my phone number is 657 395 4828. My friend's name is Ryan.

    Operator: OK. And where are you, Julie? Is Ryan with you?

    Caller: Yes. We are at Albany Skate Park, Kennedy Avenue, Los Angeles.

    Operator: Thank you, Julie. An ambulance is on its way. The paramedics will be with you in a few minutes. Ryan might have broken something, so don't move him. Stay where you are.

    Caller: OK, thanks. I will.

Seite 135   M4   National Park Hotline

b) 1. Yosemite National Park (He wants to visit Yosemite National Park.)

    2. www.nps.gov (He should look at www.nps.gov)

    3. He should plan his trip very carefully and book camping sites very early.

    4. (almost) 6 pm in Germany and 9 am in California

Seite 136   M5   Visit Hollywood Film Studios!

1. Thanksgiving (= fourth Thursday in November) and Christmas (= Christmas Day, 25th December)

2. at 7 pm

3. tours in Spanish and Chinese

4. A Front of Line Pass is good if you don't want to have to wait.

5. You can buy a VIP Experience ticket, which costs 299 dollars per person.

6. You have to phone them at (818) 4708351. You can call at any time.

7. $336 (The 5-year-old, the 9-year-old and the couple must pay $84 each. The 2-year-old is free.)

8. at the box office

Seite 136   M6 Jessica goes to Hollywood

a) If Jessica is lucky, she'll find a job to earn some money and will go to auditions in her free time.
I think she's going to find life in Hollywood much harder than she thinks because auditions are hard and she looks very young.
Maybe she'll understand that it was all a big mistake and go back to live with her mother.
I think Jessica is going to be very successful.
If she's lucky, she'll get a big film role and become a famous movie star. She will be rich and have a big house. Maybe she'll then give some money to her mother.
I think she's going to end up living on the streets of Los Angeles.

c) 1. She found an apartment where the rent was cheap and started going to auditions.
2. She worked as a waitress.
3. She was sometimes late for work because she went to auditions.
4. He told her that she couldn't work at the restaurant any longer. He asked her to leave.
5. She went to see her new friend Samantha.
6. She is worried because she is afraid she will not have enough money to pay her rent.

d) **Samantha:** First, you need to find yourself another job. I know a restaurant that is looking for a waitress. You would only work nights, so you could still go to auditions during the day.
Jessica: That would be good! Then I can pay my rent.
Samantha: Yes. I think you should go to more auditions but you need to find out how to do better. Here's a phone number. My friend Annie. She is an actress and she has been in films.
Jessica: Will she help me?
Samantha: She won't get you a job but if you audition in front of her, she will give you feedback. She will honestly tell you what she thinks of you and what you can do better.
Jessica: What if she says I can't act?!
Samantha: Jessica, you know you need to get better. You have got to try your best. And besides, it will save you a lot of trouble if Annie tells you the truth if she thinks you're wasting your time.
Jessica: You're right. Thanks, Samantha! What would I do without you?!

Seite 137   M7 At the audition

2. After she had gone to the film studio, she filled in a form.
3. After she had filled in a form, she read a text.
4. After she had read a text, she had lunch.
5. After she had had lunch, she acted out the scene.
6. After she had acted out the scene, she waited for the answer.
7. After she had waited for the answer, she called her mother.

Seite 137   M8 YOU at an audition

a) I'd like to watch a singing audition because I like watching talent shows.
I'd like to watch a modelling audition because I'd love to work in fashion./because I'd love to see what models look like in real life.
I'd like to go to a dancing audition because I love dancing and I think I am a good dancer.

b) I would wear smart clothes and a bit of make-up. I'd ask a friend to come with me, not my family.
I would prepare a song and a speech.
I would tell the judges a bit about myself but not too much. I would tell them that I've always wanted to act. I would make sure I know my lines really well and I would practise for hours.
I would choose the right clothes the week before.

For a dance audition, you should wear comfortable clothes, but for a modelling audition you should wear fashionable clothes. I would want my mum to come with me because she is really important to me. I would make sure I know my act perfectly. I would learn it all for weeks before and would make sure I can do everything. Then, if I have a bad day, I can still do my best. I'd learn to say a few sentences about myself and my hobbies and make myself sound really interesting.

Seite 138 Did you get it all?

What is the job of a park ranger? **looks after and helps visitors in a national park**
   (→ TB 2, TB Seite 120, text C)
Where can you find California's high tech industry? **Silicon Valley** (→ TB 2, TB Seite 120, text F)
Why did so many people in California have to leave their homes? **wildfires** (→ TB 4, TB Seite 122)
In which national park can you find some of the world's tallest trees? **Redwood**
   (→ TB 7, TB Seite 124)
When are the Hollywood Film Studios closed? **Thanksgiving and Christmas** (→ TB 9, TB Seite 126)
On which tour do Alan, Brandon and Meg go first? **the Earthquake tour** (→ TB 10, TB Seite 127, Hörtext)
What is the film "The Bling Ring" about? **group of five teenagers who steal from rich celebrities**
   (→ TB 13, TB Seite 128)

Seite 138 American licence plates

IML84AD8: I'm late for a date.
URAQT: You're a cutie.
CUL8R: See you later.
XQZME: Excuse me.
IMB4U: I'm before you.

Seite 139   1 Jobs, jobs, jobs

a) actor/actress, architect, banker, builder, bus driver, car technician, cameraman/camerawoman, cook, cleaner, dentist, designer, doctor, editor, electrician, farmer, firefighter, gardener, guidance counsellor, hairdresser, journalist, lifeguard, make-up artist, musician, nanny, nurse/male nurse, PA (personal assistant), painter, park ranger, pilot, police officer, plumber, programmer, receptionist, reporter, secretary, security guard, shop assistant, singer, social worker, stunt performer, taxi driver, teacher, tour guide, waiter/waitress, writer/author, vet, vet's assistant

Seite 139   2 Different jobs

a) A painter paints walls, doors or the outside of houses.
A hairdresser cuts and styles people's hair.
A secretary makes phone calls and prepares letters.
A nurse takes care of ill people.
An electrician repairs or installs electrical equipment.
A vet's assistant takes care of ill animals.
A security guard protects buildings and shops.
A gardener works with flowers and plants.

b)

interesting	boring	important	dangerous	just OK
vet's assistant	secretary	nurse	electrician	painter
security guard	gardener	police officer	stunt performer	hairdresser
doctor	teacher	doctor	firefighter	cook
farmer	banker	teacher	police officer	shop assistant

c) I'd like to be a gardener because I like working outdoors and with my hands.
I'd like to be a vet's assistant because it's an interesting job.
I'd like to be a doctor because I'll earn enough money to buy a house.
I'd like to be a nurse because it's an interesting job and I like working with people. I also like working in a team. But I won't earn enough money to buy nice things.
I'd like to be an actor/actress because I'll earn enough money to buy a house. You get to see the world and it's an exciting job. I also like working with other people.
I'd like to be a secretary because it's an interesting job. I think it's an easy job and I like working with computers. I love working in a team, too.

Seite 140   3 A new experience

a) I think Gillian is in a factory or maybe a big shop. I think Cheryl is in somebody's home.
Maybe Gillian and Cheryl are doing work experience, or maybe they have part-time jobs.
Gillian is cleaning something. A man is showing Cheryl something on a computer.
Gillian looks tired, dirty and bored! I don't think she likes it. But Cheryl looks happy and interested.

b) Cheryl spent a day "shadowing" a web designer. He showed her how to make really cool websites by adding sound and videos. Cheryl really enjoyed it, and Steve, the web designer, was cute.
Gillian is doing her work experience at a building centre, she is there for two weeks. It's OK.
The days are long and Gillian has to be on her feet all day. The work is quite hard.

c) 1. Gillian   4. Gillian
   2. Cheryl   5. Cheryl
   3. Gillian   6. Cheryl

Vorschlag:
... learned how to add sound and video to a website. (Cheryl)
... started work at 9. (Gillian)
... had to write a CV. (Gillian)
... worked for only one day. (Cheryl)
... knows a lot about DIY. (Gillian)

Seite 141   4 Gillian's interview

a)

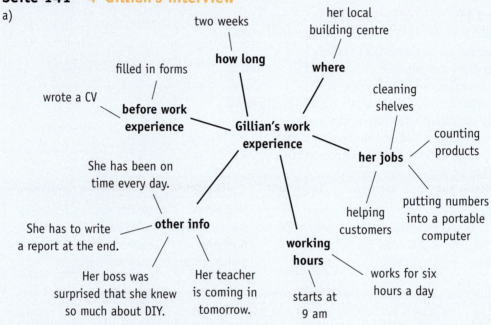

b) **Reporter:** Hi Gillian, thanks for your time. So, first question, where do you work?
Gillian: I work at the local building centre.
Reporter: How many hours do you work every day?
Gillian: I work six hours every day.
Reporter: That is a lot! When do you start?
Gillian: I start at 9 every morning. And I've been on time every day so far.
Reporter: And what are your jobs?
Gillian: On my first day I cleaned shelves all days. Not a very nice job. On day two I counted many different products and put the numbers into a portable computer. On my third day I was allowed to help customers. I was able to help a man who had a question about a drill.
Reporter: How long is your work experience?
Gillian: Two weeks.
Reporter: How did you prepare for your work experience?
Gillian: I had to fill in a lot of forms and I had to send them my CV.
Reporter: Is there anything you will have to do when you're back at school?
Gillian: I'll have to write a report. And my teacher is coming in tomorrow to see me at work.
Reporter: What has been the best part of your work experience so far?
Gillian: I like helping customers! And I was happy that my boss was quite surprised that I know a lot about DIY.
Reporter: Well, thanks for talking to us, Gillian. And good luck with the rest of your time there!
Gillian: Thank you!

Seite 141 5 Talking about work experience

a)

name	where	working hours	liked	didn't like	other info
Aidan	garage	7 am–2 pm	checking cars for problems	– washing cars – cleaning the garage	– used a computer to check car engines – boss was unfriendly – all in all was OK
Caroline	fitness club	8 am–2 pm	the people she worked with	– too much cleaning – too young to work at fitness bar	– every day she had to clean the equipment, water the plants and take the rubbish out – even had to clean shower floors – glad that her work experience is over
Nick	garden centre	9 am–3 pm	– working outside – practical work	working indoors	– a bit difficult as some plants need more water than others – learned about plants, trees and gardening – planted trees and flowers in a customer's garden with his boss

b) Caroline did her work experience at a fitness club. She had to work from 9 am until 2 pm.
She liked the people she worked with, but she didn't like the fact that she had to do so much cleaning.
She also didn't like the fact that she couldn't work at the fitness bar because she was too young.
Every day she had to water the plants, take the rubbish out and clean the equipment.
She even had to clean shower floors. She is glad that her work experience is over.
(false information: working hours; she started work at 8 am, not 9 am!)

Seite 142 6 Aidan's CV

a) His surname is Bradley.
He lives in London.
He was born in Birmingham.
He goes to Haverstock School in London.
He went to Fleet Primary School in London.
He speaks English and Spanish.
He likes basketball, music and cars.
He has had a summer job with Lucky Motors, a garage in London.

Seite 142   7 Aidan's report

b) 1. **I worked** at the garage ... **I worked** there ...
        I wore blue overalls and **I wore** shoes. / all the sentences starting with 'I'
    2. **Normally** I wore ... / I had to wash the cars and clean the floors, **too.** /
        Then I **often** ..., I am **really** interested in ..., That is why I didn't **really** ...
    3. The car technicians had a morning break at 9 o'clock **and** a lunch break ...
        Then I often ...
        I am really interested in cars **and** enjoy working ...
        I can even change a tyre **but** the boss ...
        I don't like the boss **because** he was ...
        That is why I didn't ...
    4. strong, unfriendly, new, really interested
    5. Bent Street → Brent Street

Seite 143   8 Choose an activity

A report about a job or work experience you did
Last summer I did one week of work experience in a kindergarten in Mannheim.
I had to wear sensible clothes for my work experience. It couldn't be too smart or stylish,
and I needed to be comfortable at all times.
My job was to play with the children and help them put their coats on when they went outside.
Sometimes I also had to read stories to them.
I had a break at 12 o'clock and then finished work at 2:30 pm.
I enjoyed my work experience because the people I worked with were really friendly.
I loved playing games with the children and just spending time with them.

A job poster
Here is a picture of a nurse.
I would like to be a nurse.
Nurses take care of ill people and help doctors to make people healthy again.
They take X-rays and give people medicine.
If you want to be a nurse, you should enjoy working with people and working in a team.

An interview about a job
We talked to Mrs Meyer.
She is the secretary at our school.
She works in a special office in the school. Her office is next to the headteacher's office.
She works for eight hours every day. She starts work at 7 am and finishes at 3 pm.
She likes working with people and helping people.
She started working at our school seven years ago.

Seite 145   A School Dance

Which motto fits Adam's story best? I think the motto "No risk, no fun!" fits Adam's story best because that's really what Adam says at the end. He enjoyed himself when he took a risk and asked the girl to dance.

On the other hand, if he hadn't been worried about dancing with girls, he would have had fun with his friends.

But if he hadn't asked the girl to dance, he would have felt as if he was missing out.

What was the girl thinking before Adam asked her? "I hope somebody asks me to dance. I want to have fun, too!"; "Eww, I hope Ben doesn't ask me, he smells funny."; "That guy Adam is nice, maybe he will ask me. He's always so friendly and polite to everyone."; "Oh look, he's coming over. I bet he's going to ask Alice instead of me."

Write Adam's email.

Hi Megan,

I really enjoyed dancing with you at the school dance last Friday.

I was wondering if you would like to meet up next weekend to go and see a movie? Is there a movie out at the moment that you would like to see?

Or, if you don't want to go to the cinema, we could meet up for ice cream somewhere.

I'd really like to see you again.

See you soon,

Adam

Seite 146   B The story of the first Thanksgiving

1–B   2–A   3–C   4–B

Seite 148   C Hannah and Zach

A. **Describe Hannah and Zach.** Zach has dark brown, curly hair. He is tall and he has dark eyes. He is also strong, because he catches Hannah when she falls over.
Hannah is excited because she thinks Zach is very attractive and she wants to talk to him. She feels surprised when she sees that Zach is staring at her. She feels shy when she talks to Zach, but when he replies, it makes her very happy.

B. **What is Zach's problem?** Zach is worried because he is in love with a white girl, and he is black. His friends think it's weird, and they don't like or accept Hannah because she is white. He doesn't know what to do because he really likes Hannah.
   What could or should he do? Zach could go on a date with Hannah./should see Hannah again./should stop thinking about Hannah./should talk to Hannah./could think about the problem a bit longer./should stop worrying, everything will be OK.

C. **What would YOU do?** If I had a black boyfriend, I would hope that my friends don't care about the colour of his skin. If I were with a white girl, I would want my friends to accept her. If I had a boyfriend that my friends don't like, I would talk to them about it.

D. **Write down what Hannah and Zach may think.**
   Zach: We've seen each other for four months.
   I want to spend time with Hannah and also with my friends. And I want Hannah to get to know them. Why won't they talk to me? Why can't they see that the colour of her skin doesn't matter?
   Hannah: I love him so much. But I'm afraid his friends will never like me. I don't want Zach to lose his friends because of me. But I don't want to lose Zach. Why is this so complicated?
   What could Hannah and Zach do? Hannah could talk to Zach's friends. She should ask them to talk to him again. Zach must ask his friends to accept that he loves Hannah. They could meet up with Zach's friends and hang out together. Then they could see that Hannah is a nice girl.

Seite 151   D How the raven got its black feathers

Do you know any other stories like this one?

The legend of the dream catcher

Long ago when the world was still young, an old Lakota Native American chief was on a high mountain and had a vision.

In this vision, Iktomi, the great teacher, appeared in the form of a spider. Iktomi, the spider, started to make a web with the branches and feathers on the ground.

He spoke to the Lakota chief about the Circle of Life: How we begin our lives as babies, become children, and then adults. Finally, we get to old age, where we must be taken care of as babies, completing the circle.

"But", said the spider, "in each time of life there are many forces: some good and some bad. If you listen to the good forces, they will push you in the right direction. But, if you listen to the bad forces, they'll push you in the wrong direction, and may hurt you."

While the spider was speaking, he kept making his web. When he had finished, he gave the chief the web and said, "The web is a perfect circle with a hole in the centre. Use the web to help your people reach their goals, make good use of their ideas, dreams and visions. If you believe in the Creator, the web will catch your good ideas and the bad ones will go through the hole."

The chief passed his vision on to his people, and today many Native Americans, and many other people, too, have a dream catcher hanging above their beds.

Seite 152   E The USA – a land of immigrants

"The Isle of Tears" vs "The Port of Hope". When people left Hamburg, they were hoping for a new life in America. This meant that they were full of hope for something better than what they had in Germany. However, when people arrived at Ellis Island, many of them were told that they could not stay in America and were sent back to their home countries. That made them very sad, and lots of people cried, especially if the other members of their family were allowed to stay but they weren't.

BallinStadt is a museum in Hamburg which tells the story of the over five million people who went from Hamburg to the US between 1850 and 1934. It is a place where visitors can experience how the emigrants felt and what they had to go through. When you enter the exhibition, there are nine different characters in historical costumes who tell you about their lives and why they emigrated. There are also interactive stations, which allow people to make up their own stories about emigration. In a historical pavilion, which visitors can enter after they 'register', just as the emigrants had to, there is a dormitory where things like letters, passports and other historical documents are shown. A special highlight of the exhibition is the collection of original passenger lists – they are the longest lists of emigrants in the world.

Seite 154   F The Perks of Being a Wallflower

Note down what you find out about Charlie, Sam and Patrick.

Charlie: a little awkward, and he writes exactly the way he thinks. He takes "shop class", which is the same as woodworking. He doesn't know a lot about American football. He is fifteen years old (l. 56). His favourite band might be the Smiths, but he isn't sure (ll. 60–63). He likes F. Scott Fitzgerald's "This Side of Paradise" because it is the last book he has read (ll. 68–70). He thinks that movies are all the same. He thinks Sam is attractive. He doesn't have a lot of friends, and having friends again is important to him.

Patrick: Charlie calls him "Nothing" for some reason. He is in the same shop class as Charlie. He is Sam's stepbrother. He really likes American football and understands the game well (l. 39). He is very friendly and Charlie feels that it's OK to approach him and Sam, even though he doesn't know them very well. He smokes all the time (l. 49).

Sam: She is friendly and smiles at Charlie. She has green eyes and brown hair, and Charlie describes her as "a very pretty girl" (l. 31). She smokes a lot (l. 49). She is very kind to Charlie and makes him feel welcome. Her mom got married again, to Patrick's dad, so Patrick is her stepbrother (ll. 90–92).

Say how Sam and Patrick are different from the other students. Charlie has so far found it difficult to speak to people at his high school. Sam and Patrick seem different and very approachable and Charlie doesn't feel nervous about going up to them and talking to them.

Would you like to read the whole book? Yes, I would like to read the whole book because it sounds like an interesting story. I find the style of writing very clever, and you don't always see books about love with a main character who is a boy. I would like to know whether Charlie and Sam start going out at some point. / No, I think I would prefer to see the film rather than read the book. I believe Emma Watson plays Sam in the film. And as I really like Emma Watson, I would really like to see the film.

Seite 156   G Going west

Choose the best headline for the text. I think number 2, "Going west: the challenges", is the best headline for the text, because the main point of the text is to explain the problems the people had to face when they travelled west.

Find a good heading for each paragraph. Leaving home – Spreading religion – The routes – Early challenges – To sell or not to sell – Life on the trail – Accidental deaths – Gold fever! – Levi Strauss's great invention

Seite 158   H Child labour?

Which stars do you recognize? What do you know about them?
1. Kristen Stewart (actress, "Twilight" series)
2. Christian Bale (actor, most recently in the Batman series)
3. Scarlett Johansson (actress, "Captain America: The Winter Soldier")
4. Miley Cyrus (singer and actress; album: "Bangerz"; TV: "Hannah Montana")
5. Neil Patrick Harris (actor; "How I Met Your Mother")
6. Leonardo DiCaprio (actor; "The Wolf of Wall Street", "Titanic")
7. Ryan Gosling (actor, directed his first movie in 2014)
8. Britney Spears (singer and actress; "Britney Jean" (her eighth studio album, 2013))
9. Jodie Foster (actress (The Silence of the Lambs), producer, director; "Carnage" (2011))

How is Adam's life different from yours? Adam has to work as well as go to school. That is very different to my life. He also has all his lessons at home instead of in a classroom. I think Adam is also under a lot more pressure than I am. He is always worried that he can't do everything right. Unlike me, Adam also knows what he wants to do when he grows up!

Are the rights of a child violated when they are child stars? I think that the rights of a child star are violated a little bit because they don't always have time to relax and play. I don't think it stops them from learning, because Adam said that he still has lessons. Plus, being an actor isn't dangerous. / Whether or not the rights of a child are violated depends almost entirely on the parents, I think.

What kind of problems do child stars often have? Many child actors find it difficult to live in the real world when they grow up. They don't know how to deal with problems because their parents have always done everything for them. Sometimes child actors have really bad childhoods because they cannot be normal and have fun. Their parents don't notice because they are busy. Sometimes their parents fight over their money, and that is always horrible for children.

Seite 160   I Silicon Valley

What does the term "Silicon Valley" stand for? I've heard of the term "Silicon Valley". Isn't it something to do with computers? / Silicon Valley is the area in California that is known for its high tech industry.

How many of these companies have you heard of?

high-tech development (computers, software and computer-related devices like printers and switches): Adobe, Apple, Cisco, Electronic Arts (computer games), Hewlett-Packard, Mozilla, SanDisk

Internet: eBay, Google, Yahoo!, Evernote (app), Netflix, Paypal

social media: Facebook, Twitter

Information about a company in Silicon Valley: Google was originally a research project of Stanford PhD students Larry Page and Sergey Brin. They were trying to develop an Internet search engine that did not simply rank the sites found by the number of times the search word(s) was/ were found on the website but gave more importance to the relevance of the sites and their inter-connections.

In 1998 the company was founded. Google makes most of its money through online advertising. Other important products include the Android operating system for smartphones, the web browser Chrome and the video portal YouTube.

Google is very successful. In the last quarter of 2014, they earned a total of 14.5 billion dollars.

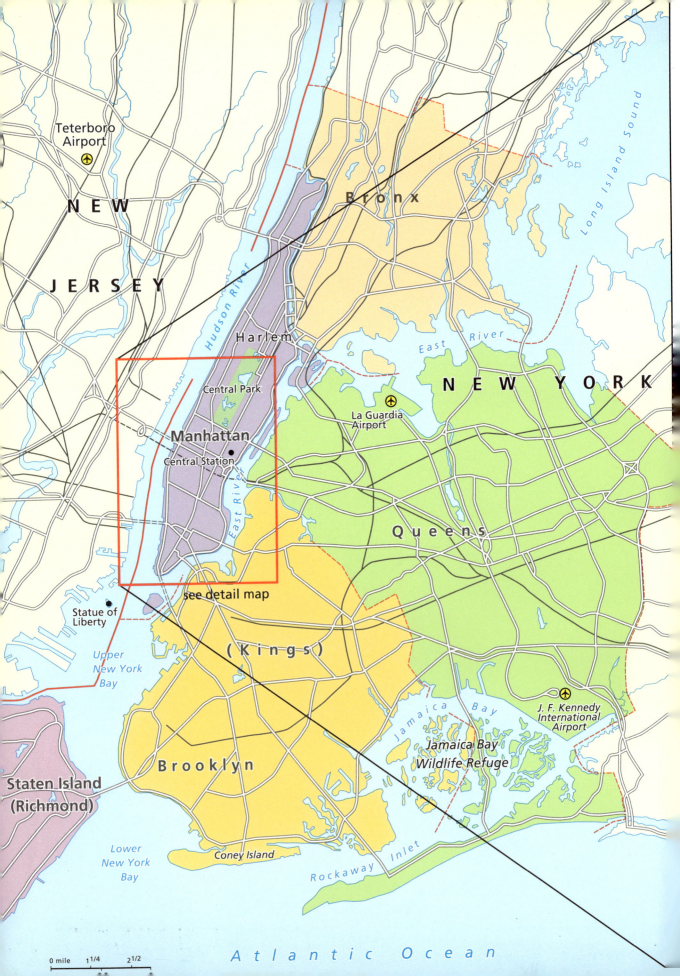

2. Bei deinem Vortrag

- Sprich langsam und deutlich.

- Sieh deine Zuhörer an, wenn du sprichst.

- Versuche, frei zu sprechen. Du kannst die wichtigsten Punkte von deinen Notizen, deinen Karteikarten oder deinem Poster/deiner Folie ablesen.

- Zeige deinen Zuhörern auf deinem Poster oder deiner Folie, worüber du gerade sprichst. So wird dein Vortrag für die Klasse noch interessanter.

3. Nützliche Redewendungen

Zu Beginn deines Vortrags:
Hello, everybody. My talk is about ...
I'd like to talk about ...
First of all, I'm going to ... Then I'll talk about ...
Finally I'll ...

Im Hauptteil:
My first/second/next/last point is ...
The next point I would like to make is ...
Let's now talk about ...
Another thing/important point I want to tell you about is ...
This is the reason why ...
On my poster you can see ...
Look at this picture. It shows ...

Wenn du über eine Statistik sprechen möchtest: *Look at the statistics. ...*
The pie chart shows/the statistics/the figures show ...
There are more/fewer than ... per cent ...
... per cent of the ... are/have ...
The smallest/biggest group are ...

Wenn du über ein Bild sprechen möchtest: *The picture shows ...*
As you can (all) see in the middle/on the left/on the right ...
At the top/bottom there is/there are ...
Let me show you on the picture how .../where ...

Wenn du mal den Faden verlierst: *Just a moment, please./Wait a second.*

Zum Schluss: *Thank you for listening. Have you got any questions?*

You can talk!

937.716 aus **Camden Market 4** (ISBN 978-3-425-73804-8)

... give a talk

Wenn du etwas vor der Klasse präsentierst

1. Bevor du etwas vorträgst

- Überlege: Was ist dein Thema? Was möchtest du sagen?
  Wie viel Zeit hast du für deinen Vortrag?

- Sammle deine Gedanken und schreibe sie in Stichpunkten auf,
  z. B. in einem *word web* oder auf Karteikarten.

- Entscheide, in welcher Reihenfolge du die Dinge sagen und
  wie du anfangen möchtest.

- Fertige ein Poster oder eine Folie an, um deinen Vortrag anschaulich zu machen.
  Du kannst aber auch eine PowerPoint-Präsentation gestalten.

- Überlege dir kleine Aufgaben für deine Zuhörer, damit sie aufmerksam bleiben.
  Erstelle z. B. einen Lückentext oder ein Quiz.
  Du kannst sie auch bitten, einen Feedback-Bogen als Rückmeldung zu deinem Vortrag
  auszufüllen. So erfährst du, was du demnächst noch besser machen kannst.

- Übe deinen Vortrag vor dem Spiegel, vor Mitschülern, Freunden oder deiner
  Familie – oder nimm deinen Vortrag zur Probe auf, z. B. mit einem Handy
  oder einem Easi-Speak-Mikrofon.
  Überprüfe, wie lange dein Vortrag dauert. Hast du flüssig gesprochen?
  Kannst du alle Wörter korrekt aussprechen?

> High schools in the USA
> - same lessons every day
> - electives
> - school clubs

TIPP

So sieht ein gelungenes Vortrags-Poster aus:

- ansprechende Überschrift
- interessante Informationen
- verständliche Sätze, aber: nicht zu viel Text
- große Bilder und Schrift:
  → Jeder im Raum muss sie sehen und lesen können.
- saubere Schrift
- Bilder mit Bildunterschriften

US high schools

A normal day
- Students go to school by bus.
- Every morning students say
  the Pledge of Allegiance.
- They have the same lessons every day.
- They can choose different electives like
  web design or drama.
- There are lots of school clubs after school.
- Students need a pass to go to the toilet.

a school bus

The school building
- There are lockers for the
  students.
- Students go to teachers'
  rooms for lessons.

a locker

Diesterweg
You can talk!

937.716 aus **Camden Market 4** (ISBN 978-3-425-73804-8)